Yanomamo Region

Pampa Grande

Chan Chan

Viru Valley

Machu Picchu

Nazca

Cuzco

Inca Empire

Tiahuanaco

TIERRA DEL FUEGO

OUT OF THE PAST

OUT OF THE PAST

An Introduction to Archaeology

DAVID L. WEBSTER

SUSAN TOBY EVANS

WILLIAM T. SANDERS

The Pennsylvania State University

MAYFIELD PUBLISHING COMPANY

Mountain View, California

London • Toronto

Library of Congress Cataloging-in-Publication Data

Webster, David L.
    Out of the past: an introduction to archaeology/David L. Webster, Susan Toby
Evans, William T. Sanders.
        p. cm.
    Includes bibliographical references and index.
    ISBN 1-55934-153-X
    1. Archaeology.   I. Evans, Susan Toby.   II. Sanders, William T.
III. Title.
CC165.W42   1992   92-15099
930.1—dc20   CIP

Manufactured in the United States of America
10 9 8 7 6 5 4 3

Mayfield Publishing Company
1240 Villa Street
Mountain View, CA 94041

Sponsoring editor, Janet M. Beatty; managing editor, Linda Toy; production editor, April Wells-Hayes; copyeditor, Lauren Root; text and cover designer, Donna Davis; art director, Jeanne M. Schreiber; illustrators, Mark Schultz and Joan Carol; manufacturing manager, Martha Branch. The text was set in 10/12 Galliard and printed on 45# Penntech Penn Plus by R. R. Donnelley.

ILLUSTRATION CREDITS
Cover image: Stone mosaic sculpture from Group 8N-11, Structure 66S, Copán, Honduras. Reconstruction and photograph by Barbara W. Fash.

To Thomas Malthus and Gordon Willey,
pioneers in understanding the relationship
between people and their environments.

PREFACE

Out of the Past is designed as an introductory textbook for students experiencing their first, and perhaps only, exposure to archaeology. Accompanying the rapid maturation of archaeology as a discipline has been the proliferation of many different "schools" of research and interpretation. No single textbook can possibly cover these rich, diverse perspectives in depth; one approach to this problem would be not to champion any particular one of them. While this book offers a survey of the methods and interpretations current in the field, it also emphasizes ideas essential to anthropological archaeology, namely, that adaptation is a fundamental function of cultural behavior, that the concept of evolution can be productively applied to culture change, and that the ecological interactions between cultures and their environments provide powerful clues to understanding the past.

FEATURES

Out of the Past has several distinctive features. We use many ethnographic and archaeological examples to reinforce the continuity between past and present, but because it is always easier to illustrate methods and concepts by using concrete examples and personal experience, we highlight in particular recent research on the Classic Maya kingdom of Copán, in western Honduras, including surveys, excavations, and analyses directed by two of us (Webster and Sanders). By featuring this site and region we are able to show how a battery of methods and techniques have produced a coherent picture of life in ancient Copán and to interpret the rich archaeological evidence produced by a long series of ambitious research efforts. But while this book features Copán, it uses ethnographic and archaeological examples from all over the world, as well, and instructors using it can easily add their own examples.

Most important, we have tried to make this a book that *uses ideas* and teaches critical thinking skills. Some introductory textbooks confine themselves to the basic methods of archaeology and assume that students will be exposed to the issues and concepts in more advanced courses. We believe that archaeology is made understandable through interpretive ideas and the history of their development.

These ideas cover two broad topics. One topic is how archaeologists identify important research problems and design research to investigate them. The other topic is theory and explanation—the interpretive framework archaeologists use to understand why things happened in the past. Because we believe that much of the vigor of anthropological archaeology lies in its dedication to cross-cultural comparison, many of these ideas are pursued in two chapters outlining the culture history of emerging civilizations in the Old and New Worlds. These chapters may be read both as sequences of culture history and as comparative reviews of culture process.

Developing a coherent framework of explanation for cultural evolution requires an informed and critical mind. Critical thinking skills, like any other skills, can be learned through research and writing. In a special appendix of this book, "Guidelines for Critiquing and Guidelines for Writing," we present instruction on developing critical thinking skills. These guidelines include basic formats for reviewing articles and books and for researching and writing a paper. The formats are simple and sound and can be applied to many other courses.

Doing background work to prepare for tests and papers is facilitated by the lists of suggested readings that appear at the end of every chapter and also by the bibliography, which includes classic works of lasting value as well as the most recent research in the many interest areas of modern archaeology. Each bibliographic entry is keyed to relevant chapters, so the bibliography can be scanned for articles and books related to particular topics.

The essential points made in each chapter are summarized at the end of the chapter as "Points to Remember." In many chapters an additional level of example is provided by special boxes that present case studies of living and archaeological cultures. The illustrations in the book are graphic as well as narrative and include a section of color photographs. Key concepts are defined in a running glossary in the page margins as well as in a full alphabetized glossary at the end of the book.

STRUCTURE OF THE BOOK

The book is divided into five parts. Part One, the first two chapters, introduces basic archaeological concepts and terms and explains how archaeology emerged as a professional field.

Part Two comprises the next four chapters. Chapter 3 shows how archaeologists conduct research, using the Copán Maya as a case example. Chapter 4 provides a general overview of the methods and techniques employed by archaeologists. Anthropological archaeology, like all sciences, is based on theoretical perspectives; these are reviewed in Chapter 5. Chapter 6 examines the ways in which humans have adapted to major world environments by using distinctive technological and food procurement systems.

Part Three systematically explores how archaeologists investigate particular aspects of culture and develop explanations about how cultures are structured and why they change and evolve in specific ways. The topics are family and household organization (Chapter 7), economic specialization and trade (Chapter 8), the functions of signs and symbols (Chapter 9), the evolution and function of political systems (Chapters 10 and 11), and religion (Chapter 12).

Chapters 13 and 14 (Part Four) are basic overviews of the emergence of civilization in the Old World and New World, respectively. These chapters not only describe what happened in particular cultural sequences, but also link changes perceived in the archaeological record to the evolutionary processes discussed in preceding sections of the book.

Part Five takes a closer look at the role of explanation in archaeology. The collapse of civilizations is the focus of Chapter 15, which presents a case study example: the collapse of the Classic Maya, as revealed by research at Copán. Finally, in Chapter 16, we discuss the nature of explanation in archaeology, using as examples explanatory theories or models that have been suggested for the evolution of complex societies. At the end of the chapter we reflect on the development of archaeology, its importance as an intellectual endeavor, and what we may expect from archaeology in the future.

TELECOURSE AND SUPPLEMENTS

A special feature of this book is its companion video series. The textbook, video series, Faculty Guide, and Study Guide together form the *Out of the Past* telecourse. Although the book can stand alone, eight one-hour video programs have been produced to accompany the textbook. Like the book, they weave together ethnographic and archaeological case examples from the Old and New worlds to illustrate anthropological and archaeological principles.

The first video, "New Worlds," presents some of the major ideas fundamental to the cultural evolutionary perspective and introduces some of the techniques and locales that are covered in the first six chapters of the book. Video segments 2–7, which are linked to Chapters 7–12, show how archaeologists design research to reconstruct basic cultural behaviors, culture history, and institutions. Linked to Chapter 15, the last video shows the dynamics of cultural collapse, focusing on the Maya and also on other ancient — and some modern — situations of falling civilizations.

The videos are explicitly connected to the textbook through the Faculty Guide and the Study Guide. These are effective learning aids for users of the textbook either with or without the video series. They include brief overviews, test questions, and ideas for further research and activities.

ACKNOWLEDGMENTS

The *Out of the Past* telecourse was developed as part of the Annenberg/ Corporation for Public Broadcasting Project, which provided major funding. Additional funding for development of the telecourse was provided by the National Endowment for the Humanities, the National Science Foundation, and The Pennsylvania State University. The video component was produced by WQED Pittsburgh and Cambridge Studios, of Boston. Producers of specific videos were Sam Low, Werner Bundschuh, Lance Wizniewski, Kate Raiz, and Sheila Bernard. We warmly thank our many colleagues who graciously consented to give their time to this effort by providing vital background information and by being filmed for the video segments of the telecourse. Our fieldwork at Copán was carried out with the permission and generous support of the Instituto Hondureño de Antropología e História, and we are also indebted to the collaboration and participation of our many colleagues whose own research at Copán has enriched our understanding of that great Maya center.

The book and videos have greatly benefited from the advice and criticism of an advisory panel of distinguished archaeologists, anthropologists, and historians: Lewis Binford, Southern Methodist University; Elizabeth Boone, Dumbarton Oaks; Charles Ellenbaum, College of DuPage; William Haviland, University of Vermont; Kenneth Hirth, University of Kentucky; Stephen Houston, Vanderbilt University; Michael Jameson, Stanford University; William Longacre, University of Arizona; Craig Morris, American Museum of Natural History; Robert Sharer, University of Pennsylvania; George Stuart, National Geographic; and Barbara Voorhies, University of California, Santa Barbara.

Development of the textbook was challenging, and we appreciate the work done by graduate students at The Pennsylvania State University; Nancy Gonlin, Glenn Storey, Ted Gragson, Scott Zeleznik, David Reed, Ann Stone, Richard Paine, and Stephen Taxman all worked on various phases of the project. Patricia Neff, Wendy Deibler, and Patricia McClure were essential to its administration, as were the full-time administrative staff of the Department of Anthropology. We received generous support and encouragement from many administrative units of The Pennsylvania State University, in particular, the Office of the Provost and the Office of Sponsored Programs. Ken Weiss, head of the Department of Anthropology, was unfailingly enthusiastic and provided essential advice and guidance. We thank Elisa Adams, Anne Buchanan, Brian Fagan, Lin Foa, Patricia Lyons Johnson, Jeremiah Lyons, John K. Mallory, Clare McHale Milner, George Milner, and James W. Wood for encouragement during the book production process. The textbook took shape as we applied the suggestions of colleagues who reviewed earlier drafts of the manuscript. Our thanks to Thomas Amorosi, Hunter College–City University of New York; Kenneth Hirth, University of Kentucky; Kenneth E. Lewis, Michigan State University; K. Anne Pyburn, Indiana University at Indianapolis, and to several anonymous reviewers for their help.

Finally, this book was brought to life by Mayfield Publishing. We extend our thanks to Boyce Nute, Tom Broadbent, April Wells-Hayes, Linda Toy, Jeanne Schreiber, Debby Horowitz, and Lauren Root. Most of all, we appreciate Jan Beatty's enthusiasm for the project and guidance of its development.

CONTENTS

PART TWO   DOING ARCHAEOLOGY   67

GOALS OF ARCHAEOLOGY

1) TO FIND, RECOVER & PRESERVE the past

2) TO RECONSTRUCT past lifeways

3) TO ESTABLISH cultural chronologies

4) TO interpret and EXPLAIN sequences of events

OUT OF THE PAST

PART ONE

WHAT IS ARCHAEOLOGY?

What is archaeology? Is it digging up the past? We hear about archaeologists looking for Columbus's original landing place in the New World, and archaeologists finding tombs of Maya kings beneath great temples in the forests of Mexico and Central America. How do archaeologists know where to look for these things? Is digging the only method they use? How do they decide what's important to find out and what's not? And, aside from being exotic relics, do archaeological finds mean anything?

The first two chapters of this book start to answer these questions. Chapter 1 defines archaeology and shows how it is related to the larger field of anthropology. We will see how science, as a way of learning about the world, is firmly rooted in the great voyages of discovery that began over 500 years ago. We will also see how science has revealed that human cultures existed in tremendous variety and over surprising lengths of time—knowledge that was fundamental to the development of scientific anthropology and archaeology.

We will also see that archaeologists pursue many goals, ranging from finding and preserving ancient things to explaining why past cultures changed and evolved in distinctive ways. Basic concepts and terms that archaeologists use in their work are presented in Chapters 1 and 2, and these will be used throughout the rest of this book.

To understand any field of study we must know something about how it developed through time. The origins of archaeology are traced in Chapter 2. First, we will see how the early explorers speculated about the remains of ancient cultures they encountered. Their accounts in turn stimulated the first professional archaeologists to develop systematic ways of recovering, describing, and classifying the material remains of the past. Finally, we will learn that there are different kinds of archaeologists, that archaeology has borrowed ideas and methods from other fields, and that collaboration of scholars of many kinds is fundamental to the ultimate goal of modern, scientific archaeology: to explain *why* things happened in the past.

CHAPTER ONE

INTRODUCTION
TO ANTHROPOLOGY
AND ARCHAEOLOGY

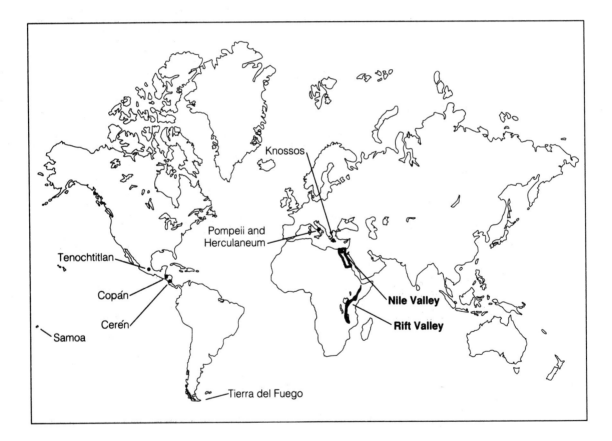

After a long search through the tropical forest of Central America, an American explorer reached the ruins of the lost Maya city of Copán in 1839. He wrote:

> All was mystery, dark, impenetrable mystery, and every circumstance increased it. Here an immense forest shrouded the ruins, hiding them from sight. . . .
> *(John Lloyd Stephens 1969[1841]:105)*

Copán (coh-PAHN) was nestled in a forested mountain valley, where the wild beauty of its surroundings enhanced its desolate splendor. Guided by references of a handful of earlier travelers, Stephens and the artist Frederick Catherwood located Copán and documented its buildings, monuments, and sculptures (Fig. 1.1). Many questions sprang into their minds: Who lived here? What caused the abandonment of the city? Did the people die out? Did they move somewhere else?

Today Copán is still shaded by tropical forest, but the ruined buildings have been uncovered and partly reconstructed, and the fallen images of the kings who ruled there over a thousand years ago have been set upright again. The drama and wonder of the place are even greater than in Stephens's day. What has been partly dispelled, however, is the mystery surrounding the temples, ballcourts, and palaces. We now have at least partial answers to the questions that intrigued Stephens, and to many more questions as well. We even know the names and titles of some of the faces who peer at us from the carved monuments.

FIGURE 1.1 At the Maya site of Copán in 1839, Stephens and Catherwood found ruined buildings and monuments, overgrown by tropical forest. This engraving by Catherwood shows Stela C, a sculpted portrait of Copán ruler 18 Jog. It dates from the late eighth century A.D., possibly A.D. 782.

archaeology The study
of past cultures, based on
their material remains.

Age of Discovery A
time of European explora-
tion, discovery, and en-
lightenment about the
world which occurred
from about the 15th
through the 18th
centuries.

Old World The conti-
nents of Europe, Asia,
Africa, and Australia and
all associated smaller land
masses.

New World The conti-
nents of North and South
America, and associated
smaller land masses.

societies Groups of people who share the same
culture, usually reside in
the same locality, and are
politically autonomous.

hunter-gatherers People
or societies dependent on
wild food resources. Such
societies are usually technologically simple, small
in size, and highly mobile.
Hunter-gatherers are
also sometimes called
"foragers."

This knowledge is largely a product of **archaeology,** the study of past cultures, based on their material remains — a field of study that did not formally exist in Stephens's time. Archaeology helps us to understand specific issues about the past, such as what happened to the people of Copán, a recurrent theme of this book. More important, we will see how archaeology can inform our thinking about how ancient cultures developed, functioned, and then sometimes failed. But archaeology is far more than the study of curious relics or even the reconstruction of past events and customs. Modern scientific archaeology has as its ultimate goal the explanation of why cultures functioned and changed in particular ways and of the means by which humans have adapted to the natural world around them and to each other. Modern archaeology has its roots in Europe about **500** years ago, in the era of exploration and discovery, when scientific methods of study were developed. Let us begin the story of archaeology's development by going back to that period.

HOW WE KNOW ABOUT THE PAST

The Age of Discovery

Before the **Age of Discovery** (roughly the 15th through 18th centuries), the **Old World** and **New World** knew virtually nothing of each other (Boorstin 1983, Morison 1974). In fact, most people knew little about what lay more than a few days' journey from their homes. Those who did speculate on the wider world tended to think of distant peoples either as like themselves or as strange, barbarous, exotic, and probably dangerous. There existed no comparative study of human cultures, such as anthropology or archaeology as we know them today, that would allow for a systematic appreciation of human diversity.

The Age of Discovery changed all this. The world turned out to be larger than Europeans had dreamed, but perhaps the biggest intellectual shock was the discovery of the Americas: two continents inhabited by people who did not figure in European geographical or historical knowledge. New World people were not only physically similar to Old World people but exhibited a remarkable variety of cultural and social forms, ranging from small **societies** of **hunter-gatherers** to immense empires like those of the Aztecs and Incas.

The comments of explorers capture this variety. In 1519 the Spanish soldier Bernal Diaz accompanied Hernan Cortés on the campaign resulting in the conquest of Tenochtitlan (TAY-nohsh-TEET-lahn), the capital of the Aztec empire in central Mexico (Fig. 1.2). This was one of the most dramatic encounters in all of human history — a true meeting of two different worlds. The drama is reflected in Diaz's words:

When we saw all those cities and villages built in the water, and other great towns on dry land, and that straight and level causeway leading to Mexico [City], we were astounded. These great towns and temples rising from the

Tenochtitlan.

FIGURE 1.2 Hernan Cortés met the Aztec king Motecuhzoma in the Aztec capital, Tenochtitlan (now called Mexico City) in A.D. 1519. This illustration from a 16th-century native account of the conquest of Mexico shows the two in conversation. Behind Cortés is a translator; Motecuhzoma is backed by three of his nobles. Various gifts for the Spanish are depicted in the foreground.

water, all made of stone, seemed like an enchanted vision. . . . Indeed, some of our soldiers asked whether it was not all a dream. . . . It was all so wonderful that I do not know how to describe this first glimpse of things never heard of, seen, or dreamed before.

(Diaz 1963:214)

In striking contrast to the rich complexity of Aztec culture, some New World societies were small and simple. After rounding the southern tip of South America by ship in the 1830s, Charles Darwin (Moorehead 1978) caught a glimpse of the inhabitants of this harsh region, who lived in some of the smallest and simplest human societies known (Fig. 1.3). Darwin describes his impressions this way:

Of individual objects, perhaps no one is more sure to create astonishment, than the first sight in his native haunt, of a real barbarian, — of man in his . . . most savage state. One's mind hurries back over past centuries, & then asks, could our progenitors be such as these?

(Darwin 1980:171)

Both Darwin and Diaz express astonishment, although of different kinds. Darwin is struck by the simplicity of Fuegian society (judged by 19th-century European standards), especially its lack of complex social and political institutions. He also makes the revealing evolutionary assumption

FIGURE 1.3 In the early 19th century there were still many groups of Native Americans living as they did before contact with European cultures. Among the least technologically and organizationally complex were the Fuegians, who inhabited the harsh region at the southern tip of South America. The exploration ship *Beagle,* on which Darwin served as a natural scientist, visited this area in the early 1830s. The ship's artist depicted the Fuegians in their homeland.

that such were the ancestors of modern people. Diaz, by contrast, expresses awe at the brilliance and complexity of Aztec culture and interprets it favorably in comparison with the complex European culture that he knows. Whatever their reactions, to both Darwin and Diaz the New World was precisely that — a new world of experience.

Apart from the historical drama they depict, these accounts and countless others like them are fascinating because they show that although New World and Old World cultures developed independently for thousands of years, they were essentially similar. Old World hunter-gatherers had much in common with the Fuegians, and Diaz intuitively understood the basic institutions of Aztec society, with its kings, nobles, state religion, and armies, because of their close resemblance to the institutions of his own. Yet there were differences as well. Aztec deities were not like the Christian god, and the people of Mexico lacked metal tools and many other technological innovations of the Old World.

Although these similarities and differences were recognized early on, no systematic fields of study emerged to investigate them until very recently. When Stephens and Catherwood wondered at the ruins of Copán in 1839, anthropology and archaeology were still almost as undeveloped as they were when the city was inhabited, a millennium earlier. Both anthropology and archaeology developed in conjunction with the maturation of the scientific perspective during the 19th century.

The Rise of Science

The Age of Discovery is one of the pivotal epochs in world history. Discovery and colonization are parts of a larger set of processes signaling the end of the European Middle Ages and the beginning of modern times. Not only were the Americas explored and exploited, but a new realm of ideas and questions was explored in Europe. This intellectual exploration heralded the **Renaissance,** the rebirth of European intellectual curiosity about the natural world and the role of humans in it (Mayr 1988).

During the Middle Ages, religious dogma supplied all explanations. Interpreting the natural world by observing it directly was seen as a threat to the authority of religion, since questions revealed doubt, and doubt precluded faith and brought about damnation. In such an atmosphere, the growth of the healthy skepticism so crucial to science was stunted.

Great voyages of discovery helped to shatter the narrow preconceptions of European thought in two ways. First, they produced a flood of information about new places, new plants and animals, and new peoples — a vast unsuspected world of experience. Second, they promised endless opportunities for those bold and informed enough to exploit them (Boorstin 1983). Exploration and colonization were risky and expensive. Those who understood the natural world best — how large it was, how to map it, how to navigate effectively — stood to gain the most. New tools were invented to ensure success, and many of these tools further expanded intellectual horizons. Telescopes, developed for the practical purpose of mapping and exploration, were directed at the stars, resulting in a whole new perspective on the place of the earth in the universe, and the place of humankind as well.

The New World of the Americas and the new world of ideas penetrated European consciousness during the same epoch, the existence of one sharpening the image of the other. Observations made during the Age of Discovery contributed to the fields of study we now call sciences (Bronowski 1978). **Science** is the systematic study of the physical or material world, seeking to discover and formalize general laws through testing of hypotheses and careful observation of results. Scientific methods of studying various phenomena have been developed over the last five hundred years, the earliest sciences deriving from nonscientific studies of natural phenomena during the Middle Ages. Thus the science of chemistry is rooted in alchemy, astronomy developed out of astrology, and so forth.

Far younger than the physical sciences, the social sciences focus on the systematic study of human behavior. They emerged in the mid- to late 19th century, when economics, psychology, sociology, and anthropology became established. They share the premise that human behavior can be scientifically studied in spite of the complexity of human experience and the many unique features of each person's life and each **culture** — patterned, learned, shared behavior based on symbolic communication. Social scientists believe that there are many regularities and recurrent patterns in the behavior of humans as members of organized societies, and in the ways human societies develop and function. The diversity of these patterns, and their similarities, are phenomena like those of the natural world and can be subjected to tests based on theories about why they occur.

Renaissance The rebirth of European intellectual curiosity about the natural world and the role of humans in it, originating in the 14th century in Italy and spreading throughout Europe. Changing social, political, and economic conditions, as well as rediscovery of Classical texts, were fundamental to this rebirth.

science The systematic study of the physical or material world, seeking to discover and formalize general laws through testing hypotheses and careful observation of results.

culture Patterned, learned, shared behavior based on symbolic communication.

FIGURE 1.4 Ethnographers live among the people they study, participating in cultural activities to a certain extent while they observe customs and practices. Margaret Mead, a pioneer in the field of ethnography, is shown here (left) in Samoa in the 1920s with a Samoan woman who was one of her informants.

anthropology The study of human physical and cultural diversity and similarity, throughout the world, for the whole history of our species.

ethnography The careful and accurate description of a particular group of living people based on direct observation, sometimes supplemented by written or other records.

Table 1.1 Subfields of Anthropological Study: Focus of Study

	Physical Diversity and Similarity (Physical anthropology)	Cultural Diversity and Similarity (Cultural anthropology: Ethnology)
Past:	Primate paleontology, fossil hominid studies Paleodemography	Archaeology, ethnohistory, epigraphy, iconography
Modern:	Human biology, primatology, genetics, demography	Ethnography, linguistics

Anthropology and Archaeology

Anthropology is the study of human physical and cultural diversity and similarity, throughout the world, for the whole history of our species. Today anthropology tries to provide an objective view of human physical evolution and cultural history, based on scientific observation documenting a wide range of behavior patterns, past and present (Haviland 1985). Our biological diversity includes the range of human physiological variation in the world around us today, plus the variability characterized by our ancestors. Cultural diversity covers the range of learned behavior practiced by people all over the world, plus the ways of life, now extinct, that were once practiced by our ancestors. This last topic is the focus of archaeology, the anthropology of past cultures.

Although all anthropologists study human diversity and similarities, anthropology has two major subdivisions. Anthropologists who study what we *are*, that is, humans as organisms, are called "physical anthropologists." "Cultural anthropologists," by contrast, study what we *do*, our culturally learned behavior, such as language, social organization, or religious and economic institutions. Another distinction is whether these things are studied in modern or past settings. Table 1.1 shows how these distinctions define major areas of specialization within anthropology.

"Anthropology" is often loosely used to mean **ethnography,** the careful and accurate description of a particular group of people. Margaret Mead was an ethnographer who lived among and described such groups as the Samoans (Fig. 1.4). Louis and Mary Leakey, who discovered important fossil ancestors of modern humans in the Rift Valley of eastern Africa, also were anthropologists, but not ethnographers (Fig. 1.5). Their field is "paleoanthropology," since they studied the ancestors of modern humans (Leakey 1977). "Human biology" is the study of the modern range of physical diversity and tendencies toward similarity among humans.

Note that in Table 1.1 archaeology as a subfield of anthropology occurs at the intersection of "cultural anthropology" and "past." **Ethnology** is the proper term for the systematic and comparative study of culture, and this includes both modern and past cultures (ethnography and archaeology are examples of these respective subfields). The root of the words *ethnology* and *ethnography* (and also *ethnic*) is *ethnos*, a Greek word meaning "race, culture or people." In the United States we use this in everyday language in the term *ethnic group* to denote a group of people sharing a distinctive set of customs, common history, origin, and possibly also a language. Polish-Americans and Italian-Americans are distinctive ethnic groups; the study of the cultural characteristics of either of these would be an **ethnographic study**.

Archaeology is the most common term in use for the study of past cultures, but it usually implies a more general research focus on the study of culture through its **material remains**. **Historical archaeologists,** for example, sometimes study quite recent remains. **Ethnoarchaeologists** study modern cultures for insights into archaeological materials. **Ethnohistory** focuses on original documents describing past cultures, and **epigraphy** and **iconography** on the interpretation of writing and symbol systems.

Table 1.1 is a useful device for understanding how anthropologists define

ethnology The proper term for the systematic and comparative study of culture, including both modern and past cultures.

ethnographic study The study of cultural characteristics of a particular ethnic or social group.

material remains The physical remnants of a past society, including ecofacts, artifacts, features, architecture, and the ways these are distributed and patterned.

historical archaeology The study of the remains of cultures for which historic documents are available.

ethnoarchaeology The study of the observable, dynamic behavior of living people in order to develop models to interpret archaeological remains.

ethnohistory The study of original documents describing the past, such as those written by travelers, explorers, and missionaries.

epigraphy The study and interpretation of ancient inscriptions.

iconography Illustrations based on stylized symbolic forms, or icons; also the study and interpretation of such images.

FIGURE 1.5 The Rift Valley of East Africa is the cradle of human origins, the area where remains of some of our earliest ancestors have been found. Geological processes have exposed strata dating back several million years, and the Leakey family and their colleagues have spent decades tracing fossil-bearing strata and recovering important finds. Here Mary and Louis Leakey are excavating a stratum.

ethnographic analogy
Use of both material and nonmaterial aspects of a living culture to form models to test interpretations of archaeological remains.

anthropological archaeology The tradition of archaeology that is derived from, and most strongly oriented toward, the larger field of anthropology. Many historical archaeologists do not share this tradition. Classical archaeology is another distinctive tradition.

lifeways Everyday cultural customs and practices, that is, ways of living.

themselves as specialists, but it is important to note that there is a great deal of overlap in what most anthropologists do. For example, physical anthropologists who study human reproduction must take into account many cultural practices, such as courting behavior, marriage, and child rearing. Similarly, archaeologists need to understand how living cultures function before they can interpret the material remains of extinct ones. Case studies by ethnographers provide evidence of cross-cultural regularities, and these help archaeologists to reconstruct ancient cultures, a practice called **ethnographic analogy.** Archaeologists also use many of the tools of physical anthropologists to study ancient human physical remains. Finally, anthropologists of all kinds — and especially archaeologists — borrow concepts, tools, and methods from other sciences. The important thing to remember is that although archaeologists work with the material remains of the past, their goals are to reconstruct and explain human behavior, and this is the essence of **anthropological archaeology** (Binford 1962). Overtly scientific and comparative, anthropological archaeology is the dominant perspective in American archaeology today.

As an introduction to anthropological archaeology, this book studies how people in past cultures lived, examining their patterns of social organization, economics, politics, and religion and their everyday cultural customs and practices, or **lifeways,** and how and why these lifeways changed through time. To the anthropological archaeologist, material remains are not merely collections of relics but are resources to reconstruct patterns of past behavior. To study the past in this way, we need to know about living cultures as well as about the issues, methods, and materials of modern archaeology, and throughout the book these two fields, ethnography and archaeology, provide the materials and methods of interpretation.

Many nonanthropological archaeologists, particularly those educated in art history and the classics, do not share this scientific attitude, preferring to regard archaeology as more closely related to history or the humanities (Daniel 1981). From this perspective, common among archaeologists trained in Europe and Britain, each culture is seen as unique, and it is inappropriate to make comparisons and generalizations, as does the scientific approach. We will review some alternative perspectives in later sections but wish to emphasize that a scientific understanding of human culture is not dehumanizing. Rather, it makes particular cultural patterns more universally understandable, which is a humanistic effect.

GOALS OF ARCHAEOLOGY

Broadly speaking, anthropological archaeology has four goals:

1. To recover and preserve material remains of the past and to document the patterned relationships among these. This includes the careful description of the physical context of each find.

2. To reconstruct lifeways at a particular place during a particular period of time.

3. To establish cultural chronologies to determine when archaeological materials were in use and to arrange reconstructed cultures into regional culture sequences, thus establishing what archaeologists call "culture history."

4. To interpret and explain sequences of events documenting cultural processes over the course of a culture's history.

These goals begin at the most concrete level of archaeology with the physical process of gathering information. Archaeologists dig, but they also collect **artifacts** and map remains on the ground surface; test samples of soil, rocks, plants, and bones; decipher texts; and study much else besides (goal 1). Then they begin the long process of fitting together the bits of evidence into a coherent picture of *what* happened to create the site, *how* the culture functioned on a day-to-day basis (goal 2), *when* major events transpired (goal 3), and *why* lifeways and chronologies are patterned in particular ways (goal 4). Thus the scientific procedures of observing and interpreting go through successive stages of building greater knowledge about an ancient culture until enough is known to explain broad patterns of change. The goals roughly restate, in more formal terms, the general questions given above. As we shall see, the "what," "where," "when," and "how" questions are the easiest to answer, but the "why" questions are ultimately the most important, because explanation lies at the heart of scientific archaeology, as it does of all science (Binford 1983a).

Theories are answers to "why" questions posed by scientists. Theory building in archaeology is complicated, because the archaeologist must first properly interpret how archaeological remains came into being — what "behavior" resulted in the particular site or artifact — before asking why the behavior took place. This intermediate step, reconstructing behavior based on the archaeological record, involves what archaeologists call **middle-range theory**. For example, suppose that we wanted to explain why an ancient society collapsed (as we attempt to do for the Copán Maya in Chapter 15). Before we could make a general theoretical explanation, we would have to make an accurate reconstruction of how the society functioned in social, political, economic, and religious terms, as well as reconstruct its history. The ideas, concepts, and methods used in this reconstruction, and the reconstruction itself, would constitute middle-range theory.

Spatial, Temporal, and Formal Context

Much of the information archaeologists use comes not from ancient objects in themselves but from the relationships among them. Such relationships are called **context**. Context is an object's setting in *time* and *place,* its affinity

artifact Anything that has been made, modified, or transported by humans and that can provide information about human behavior in the past.

middle-range theory The ideas and concepts archaeologists use to reconstruct the behaviors that have resulted in the material culture record.

context An object's setting in time and place, its affinity to other things of similar form, and its general relationship to other objects in the archaeological record.

FIGURE 1.6a Interior of the so-called House of the Wooden Partition in Herculaneum. The wooden partition screen slides on bronze tracks. The marble table in the foreground is in its original position.

to other things of similar *form*, and its general relationship to other objects. Context is important because it relates to one of the underlying assumptions of archaeology — that much of human cultural behavior is patterned in highly predictable ways. This assumption has been amply demonstrated in studies of historically well-known people. We cannot observe past human behavior directly, but we can assume that there is patterning in the material remains that ancient humans left behind and that it to some degree reflects their original behavior. The search for context is thus a search for "fossilized" behavioral patterns in material things.

spatial context The location of an object and its spatial relation to other objects as found in the archaeological record.

Spatial context refers to location, that is, to where something is found in relation to other things. **Temporal context** refers to the relationship of things in time, distinguishing when something was used compared to earlier or later things. **Formal context** refers, more abstractly, to classes of objects as we group them mentally, for example, according to their "form" as tools, weapons, buildings.

temporal context The age or date of an object and its temporal relation to other objects in the archaeological record.

Spatial and temporal contexts are crucial to document during the process of recovering archaeological materials, because archaeologists reconstruct lifeways on the basis of *all* the recovered material remains that were used in a particular place at a particular time. If materials are taken from context, or if materials from different places or times become mixed, interpretations concerning past behavior are very difficult. This is why looting archaeological sites is such an odious crime. Not only are the looted materials devalued scientifically because their contexts are unknown, but those contexts have been disturbed or destroyed in the search for relics.

formal context The affinity of an object to a general class of objects sharing general characteristics of form.

Very occasionally, spatial and temporal contexts are marvelously preserved. Pompeii and Herculaneum (southern Italy) were thriving Roman

FIGURE 1.6b The preservation of Herculaneum and Pompeii by the very volcano that destroyed them in A.D. 79 has permitted us a clear view of Roman lifeways. Shown here is a cook stove with the cooking pots that were in use when the catastrophe occurred.

towns abruptly overwhelmed by volcanic ash from Mt. Vesuvius in A.D. 79 (Conticello 1990; Deiss 1985). Buildings, tools, personal possessions, animals, and even some of the people themselves were trapped in their original spatial contexts by the enveloping ash (Figs. 1.6a and 1.6b). Temporal context was fixed as well, since earlier or later objects could not contaminate the sealed ruins (and of course we know the actual date of the eruption from ethnohistorical accounts). The superb preservation of houses and shops, furniture and food, and many other remains in their original contexts have allowed us to reconstruct the lifeways of these communities in great detail. In this regard Pompeii and Herculaneum are virtually unique. At most other archaeological sites contexts have been greatly altered, and much of the evidence needed to guide reconstruction is gone.

In most cases, when the material goods of life cease to be of use, they become subject to the same destructive processes that act on other materials on the surface of the earth: they weather and decay, and sooner or later break down, depending on what they are made of and on local environmental conditions. Pots break, buildings collapse, organic matter decomposes. Winds blow away light materials and bring dust to settle over the abandoned remains. Plants grow in the accumulated soil and penetrate the ruins with their roots. In time, the once-useful products of human enterprise will, if they survive at all, become cultural "fossils" embedded in the accumulated strata (Fig. 1.7).

As if all of this natural disruption of the archaeological record is not enough, human activity contributes as well. Instead of dropping tools where they were used, people dispose of them in garbage heaps. They tear

FIGURE 1.7 Volcanic eruptions in Central America sometime after A.D. 600 preserved this small house at Cerén (El Salvador). The sign rests on the house floor, and the stratigraphic undulations conform to the two house walls crushed under the deposits. "The eruption was not only violent, but judging from the archaeological evidence, occurred suddenly, perhaps with little warning. Possessions had not been removed . . . pots containing beans were excavated in one room. People may actually have been trapped in the structure." *(Zier 1983:122–123)*

site formation process
The natural and cultural processes or transformations that have, in combination with each other, produced archaeological sites.

down a house and use some of the materials to build a new one, or partially level an old temple to erect a bigger one, sometimes throwing the trash from the garbage heap into the fill of the structure. They save certain things from generation to generation as heirlooms. In short, archaeologists rarely find nice, neat, Pompeii-like situations, with almost everything in its correct behavioral context. Instead, what we find is an incomplete record of past behavior, one that has experienced continuous destruction and disturbance in undergoing a **site formation process** (Schiffer 1987), which the archaeologist interrupts at some point in the attempt to make sense out of what is left. In so doing, the archaeologist may destroy all or part of a site, even while investigating it.

Spatial Context The spatial context of each bit of evidence of human behavior that we find must be fully described so that we can interpret not just the act that produced the object but also the circumstances that brought it to its present location. In the course of gathering information, locations of all artifacts are noted in order to understand the combination of cultural activities and natural processes that caused the formation of the archaeological site. Pompeii and Herculaneum provide wonderful examples of preservation of the context of activities, but much can be learned from more general spatial contexts. An arrowhead found in a farmer's field indicates that at some time in the past, that locale was the scene of hunting, hostility, or residence. Years of plowing have so mixed the soil that the original context of the arrowhead cannot be reconstructed, but its general area of use can be noted. If someone picks up the arrowhead as a curiosity and then throws it into a junk drawer, the arrowhead is archaeologically useless, because even its general context is lost. Collecting arrowheads is a relatively minor example of removing archaeological materials from context. Far more destructive is looting archaeological sites for relics — statues, pottery, and so forth — that can be sold as art objects (Chase et al. 1988). As we noted above, looting destroys archaeological sites and the evidence they can provide. It is a form of cultural genocide (Fig. 1.8).

Temporal Context   Temporal context is also critical to archaeological interpretation. The temporal context of cultural materials has two dimensions, relative age and absolute age. **Relative age** means how old things are *relative to each other,* and the **absolute age** of cultures or artifacts is the *number of years elapsed* since the things were made or used. Our ability to measure accurately the time that has passed since materials were used is comparatively recent. For example, **radiocarbon dating** was only developed in the middle of this century, and other methods of absolute dating are still being refined.

Formal Context   The form of any item is similar to the form of a whole set of other items. If we find a piece of broken fired clay, we may recognize it as a **potsherd** (a piece of a broken pottery vessel) on the basis of its shape, thickness, and composition, and what we know about pots. Similarly, we label pointed, notched pieces of flint "projectile points" because

relative age   The chronological relationships among relatively younger and older things, even though no actual dates are available.

absolute age   The amount of time elapsed, with reference to a specific time scale, since an object was made or used.

radiocarbon dating   Absolute dating method developed by physicist Willard Libby which determines the absolute age of an organic object (wood, charcoal, bone) by measuring the amount of decay of radioactive carbon (^{14}C).

potsherd   A piece of a broken pottery vessel.

FIGURE 1.8   Much like vandals stealing stereos out of parked cars, these people are breaking into the undisturbed context of an archaeological site, destroying its potential to reveal the archaeological culture. The stereos are replaceable; the archaeological site is not.

of their shapes, and because they resemble those used by ethnographically known peoples. When we make such judgments, whether consciously or intuitively, we are defining formal contexts. Sometimes our interpretations are wrong (the "projectile point" may have been used as a knife), but some formal sorting into convenient categories has been accomplished and can be used as the basis for further analysis.

Much of the nuts-and-bolts work of the archaeologist involves determining and adequately recording spatial, temporal, and formal context. Such information forms the foundation for more detailed analysis and for comparisons with models of human behavior drawn from living cultures. All these sources of information are essential to reconstructing patterns of human cultural behavior, or lifeways, at particular times and places in the past.

Reconstructing Culture History

Once we have reasonable reconstructions of how people lived in particular places at particular times, we are in a position to construct regional cultural sequences (Willey 1966, 1971). This is done by arranging the initial reconstructions in chronological order. Suppose, for example, that we have several specific reconstructions of ancient lifeways for a region like the Nile Valley in Egypt at different periods of time—one at 6500 B.C., one at 2500 B.C., and another at 2000 B.C. If we arranged these reconstructions properly in chronological order, the sequence would reveal important changes in culture, the outline of **culture history**. We would see only small, simple foraging societies at 6500 B.C., a region unified under powerful kings at 2500 B.C., and some sort of political fragmentation evident by 2000 B.C.

culture history The chronological arrangement of the time phases and events of a particular culture.

Understanding Cultural Processes

Such regional sequences provide the basis for the analysis of cultural processes (Flannery 1967). By **cultural processes** we mean sets of interrelated changes occurring through time, operating very broadly in geographical, social, and temporal terms. In the Egyptian case the processes would include the origins and spread of agriculture, population growth, and warfare that contributed to the emergence of a politically centralized ancient state, and the internal strife that undermined royal power.

cultural processes Sets of interrelated changes occurring through time, operating very broadly in geographical, social, and temporal terms over the course of a culture's history.

The broad concept of process should not be confused with specific instances of historical cause-and-effect relationships through time. To illustrate this point, let us consider a process with which we are all familiar—industrialization, the emergence of economic systems based on industrial forms of production. Industrialization has been going on for several centuries in many parts of the world in many social contexts. As a general process, it involves such things as the use of machinery running on fossil fuels, mass production, a high degree of economic specialization, and the adoption of all-purpose currencies (money). This process began in Europe and spread virtually everywhere, altering patterns of culture. But industrialization does not characterize any single culture, society, or historical tradition. Exactly how these things emerged in any particular society is a more restricted historical question.

Although processes of cultural change are among the most important things archaeologists investigate, they are difficult to talk about without using labels. But the labels themselves present problems. For example, no one would disagree that the United States at the time of George Washington had a primarily agricultural economy or that the United States today has a predominantly industrial economy. These labels usefully characterize different situations two centuries apart on the historical continuum. Yet determining exactly when the changeover from an agricultural to an industrial economy occurred is an arbitrary matter, because the process of change is relatively continuous and unbroken and the economy is complex. Labels are handy tools, but they necessarily simplify the cultural processes we are trying to explain.

Obviously, the more that is known about a culture from interpretation of its material remains, use of living cultural examples, and ethnohistoric documentation of events and lifeways, the more accurate will be the interpretation and explanation of large-scale processes (Taylor 1967). As we mentioned above, the development of cultural sequences in many areas of the ancient world is a recent scientific achievement, and one that not only enhances the subject matter of archaeology but also lends considerable substance to the field of anthropology as a whole. Now that we have a relative wealth of information about cultural variation through time in the Old and New worlds, we can look for broad cultural processes that occur independently, and this is an exciting prospect.

Knowing the broad outlines of world culture history is far more important than any number of glittering prizes taken from royal tombs, though the latter get more news coverage. We agree with the point of view expressed in a recent book on how science in general is practiced, in which present-day archaeology was described as follows:

· Sometimes it seems that the heroic age of the discipline was the excavation of palaces and the opening of royal tombs, as when Arthur Evans excavated the Minoan palace at Knossos and Howard Carter opened the tomb of Tutankhamen. In a way this was a mere extension of the traditional picture of human history: a succession of civilizations and dynasties. It also gave rise to a public image of archaeology characterized by such films as *Indiana Jones and the Temple of Doom*.

. . . The true heroic period of archaeology is now, when archaeologists take a few burnt kernels of grain or a discoloration in the soil where once a post had been implanted and from such clues derive a picture of how ordinary people lived before history was preserved by writing. The greatest achievement of modern archaeology has been the working out of how nomadic hunters and gatherers across the world took up agriculture and settled life and then civilization. What we take for granted about it was scarcely known fifty years ago.

(Flanagan 1989:21)

BOX 1.1

THINGS ARCHAEOLOGISTS STUDY

What most archaeologists wish to understand and explain is past cultural behavior. What they actually study is material things, such as tools, weapons, fragments of dwellings, human burials, soil discolorations, and garbage. "Material remains" has been often used in the last few pages, and it stands as a general term for any physical marker of human use or alteration. Archaeologists have a set of specific terms for various kinds of material remains and particular kinds of collections of them. From the most particular to the most general, these are:

Attribute   A minor characteristic or recognizable quality of an artifact that is useful for describing, analyzing, or categorizing it. For example, among the attributes of a potsherd are those related to its "surface treatment," such as whether it is painted or unpainted.

Artifact   Anything that has been made, modified, or transported by humans and that can provide information about human behavior in the past. Most artifacts are portable objects such as arrowheads (more properly called projectile points) or potsherds (fragments of ceramic vessels), but they might also be such nonportable things as old structures or the remains of ancient fields. Such nonportable artifacts are often called **facilities**.

Ecofact   Floral, faunal, or geophysical material not used, altered, or transported by humans but of value in interpreting archaeological cultures — for example, a pollen sample that provides valuable information about past climates.

Assemblage   The whole set of artifacts representing the material culture inventory or repertoire used in a given cultural setting over a short period of time. For example, the range of things in a modern Sears or Spiegel catalogue is a fairly complete assemblage of durable household goods for middle-class Americans. (A **subassemblage** is a set of artifacts representing the tools used for a particular task, such as food-preparation vessels and tools).

Industry   The set of artifacts made out of the same material, using the same kind of techniques of production, such as all the ceramic artifacts at a site: pottery vessels, ritual figurines, and roof tiles.

Feature   Any highly localized area of human use or modification, sometimes part of a work area (e.g., a hearth that is part of a cooking area) or the location of activities (e.g., a built-in bench that serves as work area and sleep area). Features often consist of many artifacts and facilities associated within a particular context, and the term is often used temporarily during an excavation to denote particular sets of remains before they are completely understood.

Activity area   Localized zone of intensive, generally repeated use, as evidenced by artifacts, assemblages, and special-purpose features. Sometimes the activity area coincides with a particular room in a building, as it does in the kitchen (the food-preparation activity area) of a modern house, but often this is simply an area, indoors or out, exhibiting a particular kind of use. There may be several features associated with a single activity area.

Site   A spatially isolated area of concentrated archaeological remains. Note that this is a vague definition, reflecting the fact that places ranging from one-event activity areas (such as a scatter of stone fragments left when someone sharpened a stone tool, or a small campsite) to cities inhabited for centuries are called "sites." There is no strict rule for the use of this term. Archaeologists delineate sites situationally, according to their research concerns.

(continued on page 20)

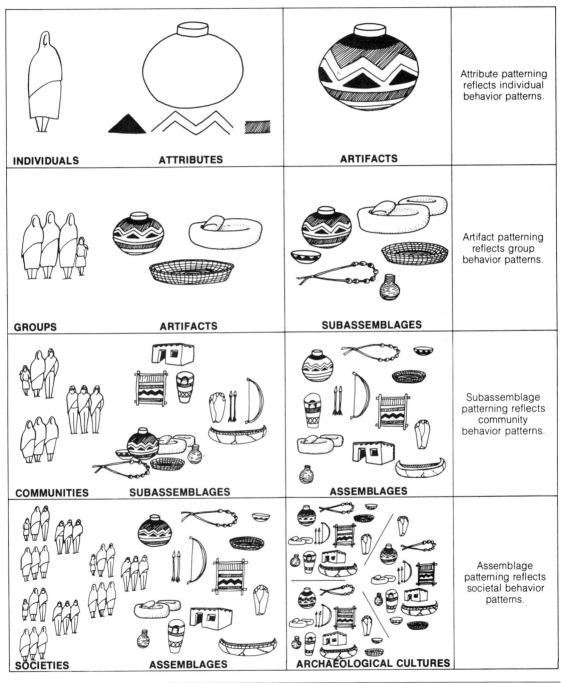

INDIVIDUALS   ATTRIBUTES   ARTIFACTS

Attribute patterning reflects individual behavior patterns.

GROUPS   ARTIFACTS   SUBASSEMBLAGES

Artifact patterning reflects group behavior patterns.

COMMUNITIES   SUBASSEMBLAGES   ASSEMBLAGES

Subassemblage patterning reflects community behavior patterns.

SOCIETIES   ASSEMBLAGES   ARCHAEOLOGICAL CULTURES

Assemblage patterning reflects societal behavior patterns.

[Deetz]

(continued from page 18)

Site layout The locations and spatial interrelations of artifacts, features, activity areas, and remains of structures at a site.

Environmental setting The physical and biotic surroundings—plants, animals, climate, inorganic resources—that influence social groups and their associated cultures including other human groups.

Settlement pattern The distribution of archaeological sites over the landscape of a defined region.

Settlement system The sites in a particular region during a particular period of time, and their social, economic, and political interrelations.

Region A geographically defined area containing a series of interrelated human communities that usually share similar cultural patterns and relationships with the environment.

Culture area The area inhabited by societies sharing cultural traits such as language, belief systems, sociopolitical organization, food-getting practices, and basic technology. Culture areas are most usefully defined on the basis of broadly shared stylistic or ideological features.

Archaeologists define material remains in time as well as space, for example:

Component Materials representing activities during a particular period of occupation at an archaeological site.

Sequence A series of periods of time in the history of a particular culture, each characterized by recognizably different material remains. Also, the arrangement of material culture into a time framework.

Horizon Period of time during which a distinctive set of archaeological remains (e.g., religious symbols, ritual objects, art styles, etc.) spreads over a very large region. When these distinctive remains are found at different sites, the sites may be assumed to be roughly contemporaneous.

Period, or phase Particular time interval within a sequence; characterized by similar behavior patterns, resulting in similar patterns of distribution of material remains.

We will use these terms throughout the book.

Although the public imagination is often captured by beautiful objects from ancient cultures, these objects out of their contexts can tell us little about how and when the culture operated and what processes marked its development. These larger issues are fundamental to modern anthropological archaeology, and all depend on the documentation of material remains in context.

CULTURE IN ITS ENVIRONMENTAL SETTING

Culture is the central concept of anthropology. One of the earliest anthropologists, Edward Tylor (1871), defined culture as "that complex whole which includes knowledge, belief, art, law, morals, custom, and other capabilities and habits acquired by . . . member[s] of society." We will explore the concept further in Chapter 5, but we should note something about the definition at this point. Tylor was defining culture in its most general, universal sense, as a complex set of things characterizing all humans. But we can also use the word in a more specific sense, as in "Aztec culture," "Eskimo culture," or "French culture." This usage refers to a particular set of beliefs, arts, laws, morals, customs, and so forth, that characterizes a particular society. One of the most productive ways of thinking about culture in this specific sense is that it is the principal means of adaptation of humans as social animals.

Archaeology, compared to other fields of anthropology, is particularly good at describing and explaining culture change over long periods of time. The most general theme of this book is the evolution of culture, its patterns and principles. The concept of evolution, as we shall also see in Chapter 5, is the most useful general scientific concept we possess for making sense of the changes we perceive in the archaeological record.

Cultural Ecology and Major Dimensions of Culture

Human cultures develop and decline in particular environmental settings. Each environment presents a specific set of challenges and problems to the people exploiting it. In fact, culture and environment interact, such that a significant change in one provokes or promotes a responsive change in the other. The study of these interactions is called **cultural ecology** (Steward 1955) and it is fundamental to reconstructing and analyzing past cultures. Cultural ecology is fully discussed in Chapter 5; here we should note that it is a *theory* about how cultures are structured and how they evolve, and a *method* for investigating culture change and evolution. Cultural ecology emphasizes the interaction between culture and its environmental setting in influencing culture process. Thus it helps us to understand what features of culture are more or less important in provoking change or ensuring stability. For example, we can isolate several major dimensions of each culture:

Technoeconomic organization   the way energy and materials (including food and other necessities) are produced, distributed, and consumed; the way labor is organized; and how technology is used

Social organization   the way relationships among members of a culture are structured, and how much differentiation in status or wealth exists in the society

Political organization   the way decisions are made and enforced to resolve conflict within the social setting and between societies

Ideology   the values and ethics of a particular society, the way the human role in the natural world is explained, and the way the existing social and political order is justified

Changes in any of these organizational subsystems of culture may influence the system as a whole, but some kinds of influences operate more powerfully than others. To cultural ecologists, technoeconomic factors are generally the most significant causal elements and social, political, and ideological factors are less often the ultimate causes of change, though they

cultural ecology   The theoretical perspective that culture and environment interact dynamically; a methodological program for analyzing cultures, based on understanding adaptation to the environment as well as technoeconomic, sociopolitical, and ideological organization.

technoeconomic organization   The way energy and materials (including food and other necessities) are produced, distributed, and consumed, the way labor is organized, and how technology is used.

social organization   The way relationships among members of a culture are structured, and how much differentiation (in terms of status or wealth, for example) exists.

political organization   The way in which a society is organized to make and enforce political decisions and to resolve conflict within the social setting and between societies.

ideology   The belief system of a particular society, including values and ethics, the place of humans in the natural world and their relationship with the supernatural, and the justification for the existing social and political order.

act as catalysts when changes are ongoing. Political propaganda, for example, is an ideological tool of great power and can mobilize people and inspire them to act in significant ways, but it operates when the economic and social conditions of everyday life cause people to seek or welcome change. A prosperous and satisfied population will ignore propaganda that promotes change, whereas a desperate and downtrodden people will be fired to action by it.

The events of the world around us play out the same themes that have always preoccupied humankind, and when we study cultural patterns and trends over the course of our human history, we see the present as firmly rooted in the past. The great value of learning anthropological archaeology is to understand better how cultural processes unfold and evolve, learn about the human cultural heritage, and thus perceive the significance of history as events happen, day by day (Deetz 1967).

PURPOSES OF THIS BOOK

This book will:

- Introduce archaeology and the archaeological record; describe the techniques, methods, and theories archaeologists use; and explain how they design research to investigate questions about the past
- Show how cultures operate, why they differ from each other, and how they change over time

To fulfill these purposes the book presents general concepts and discusses particular archaeological and ethnographic cases. Case examples from past and present cultures illustrate the same general principles, because human behavior has always functioned to meet basic needs, such as provisioning for material requirements, organizing a coherent set of relationships within each group, and accounting for the group's place in the larger natural world. Despite modern and ancient people's diverse solutions to these problems, enough similarities among cultures exist to demonstrate strong common trends; at the same time we can appreciate the richness of cultural diversity.

POINTS TO REMEMBER

- Archaeology helps us understand the present as well as the past by explaining how cultures develop and function, and why they succeed and sometimes fail.
- The Age of Discovery brought the New World and Old World into contact with each other. Each had a similar range of societies, from small groups of hunter-gatherers to huge empires.
- Science emerged during the Age of Discovery as a systematic, skeptical quest for the general laws governing the physical world.

- Anthropology and its subfields, including archaeology, emerged as professional disciplines in the 19th century.
- Archaeology aims to recover and preserve material remains, reconstruct lifeways, establish cultural chronologies, and explain cultural processes.
- *Context* is the setting or place of something, in terms of its time, space, and form.
- *Culture* is the human means of behavioral adaptation; it is a complex of customs and knowledge in a dynamic relation with the environment.

FOR FURTHER READING*

The Age of Discovery is documented by many eyewitness accounts. Cortés, *Letters from Mexico* and Diaz, *The Conquest of New Spain* provide the European perspective on Mexico, while the Aztec view of Europeans is presented in Anderson and Dibble's *War of Conquest*. Boorstin's *Discoverers* is an overview.

Useful general sources on anthropology and archaeology are Deetz's *Invitation to Archaeology*, Daniel and Renfrew's *Idea of Prehistory*, Wenke's *Patterns in Prehistory*, and Haviland's *Cultural Anthropology*.

*Full citations appear in the bibliography at the end of the book.

CHAPTER TWO

IN SEARCH OF OURSELVES: THE DEVELOPMENT OF ANTHROPOLOGY AND ARCHAEOLOGY

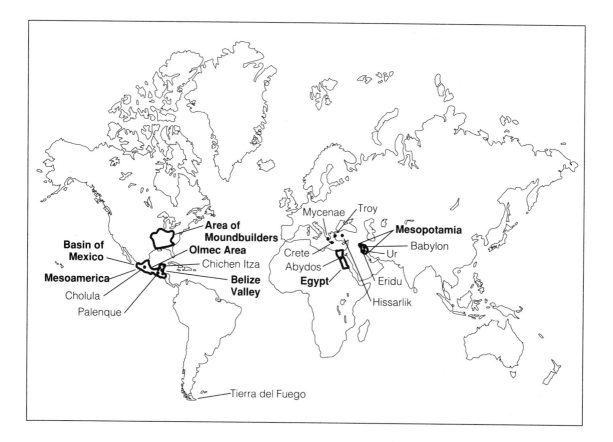

Anthropological archaeology emerged as a scientific field in the early 19th century, and from that time to about 50 years ago its major concerns were describing and classifying ancient cultures and establishing the chronological order of events. In the last few decades, the interpretation of lifeways and processes has emerged as a strong focus. In this chapter we first examine the roots of archaeology, before and during the Age of Discovery, and discuss the goals and methods of science; then we review the history of the discipline of archaeology to its practice in the present.

BACKGROUND AND ORIENTATION

Today, anthropological archaeology is a professional discipline and a scientific field of study, but it was not always so. In fact, historians of archaeology date its emergence as a profession (rather than a pastime) to only 150 years ago (see Willey and Sabloff 1980). Before that, a period of about 400 years (ca. 1450 to 1840) saw the development of the foundations of archaeology, and interpretation about the past was generally unsystematic and speculative. This speculative period begins with the European Age of Discovery and the Renaissance and continues through the early 19th century. During this time science emerged in European culture as the major means by which natural phenomena are interpreted. Archaeology developed within the context of older, more established scientific fields.

Science: Our Perspective on the World

The scientific perspective assumes that the world is real and knowable and that our basic experience of it is shared (Bronowski 1978). In commonsense terms, science looks at the world objectively, focusing on the nature of the world rather than on the subjective elements of an individual's perceptions of it. Strictly speaking, each of us perceives the world in a slightly different way. From person to person within a culture, or from culture to culture, none of us fully shares perceptions with everyone else. Our senses (the means by which we perceive) and the knowledge or emotions that color our perceptions are personal and subjective. Yet we share the world and interact with each other in ways that correctly assume a commonality of experience, and thus we operate as if the world were objectively knowable. In fact, tests of the extent to which humans share presumably "subjective" perceptions reveal that the common features of experience overwhelmingly outweigh the idiosyncrasies of individual senses and cultural conditioning.

The idea that the world around us is objectively knowable and operates according to certain larger laws of science has only been part of the European cultural tradition for the last few hundred years. We will trace the historical development of science in greater detail below, but let us now look more closely at the matter of how we see the world around us. In every culture explanations are made of natural phenomena, the place of humans in the world, and the world in the universe. Today in Western culture we explain our perception of natural phenomena through scientific interpretations, derived from systematic testing of ideas (theories) against observations made under controlled circumstances (i.e., experiments). In this continual search for better explanations of natural phenomena, **theories** are proposed to explain general patterns, and from these, **hypotheses** are made, predicting what will happen in particular circumstances. Then we set up these particular circumstances and carefully observe and describe the outcome. The results of experiments sometimes substantiate theory, strengthening it, or necessitate revisions. The scientific process is cyclical:

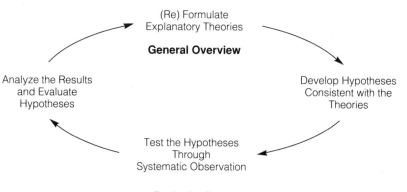

theory A scientific explanation of the world as we perceive it that has been widely tested and accepted as more useful than competing explanations.

hypothesis Tentative and testable premise that accounts for relationships between empirical observations.

The scientific process involves a continuous feedback, with constant readjustments of what we "know" because of new and more careful observations and the more accurate interpretations that these permit. On the theoretical side, science is a constant process of tinkering with **models** of reality (Clarke and Chapman 1978); these models can be sets of ideas explaining how things act under different circumstances, or they can be actual physical mockups, such as maps or scale models. Model building in intellectual terms proceeds in much the same way as does building and testing a physical model. If you wish to build a better paper airplane, you test your ideas by experimenting. So it is with science, but in scientific fields the hypotheses are carefully stated so that when the experiment takes place, its outcome will be clearly interpretable and will produce a worthwhile refinement of the model (Watson, LeBlanc, and Redman 1971).

model A representation of reality, often devised for the purpose of testing hypotheses.

deductive reasoning
Logical process of deducing the circumstances of particular cases from the conditions specified by general theories.

inductive reasoning The logical process of inducing the general conditions of a whole set of cases from the particular circumstances of one or a few.

Although the scientific process is cyclical, a constant interplay between theory and observation, a formal distinction may be made between deductive and inductive reasoning. **Deductive reasoning** begins with general theoretical statements and from these deduces the hypothetical circumstances of particular cases, which can then be tested by observation. **Inductive reasoning** starts with observation of particulars and from these builds general statements based on observation (Hempel 1965). Philosophers of science debate the relative merits of these approaches, but in reality they are well-integrated parts of the scientific process: No one deduces hypotheses from theories without some knowledge of actual cases, and no one proceeds with experimentation without some general idea of how the actual cases will behave. Good science depends on a thorough grounding in general theories and particular observations.

One of the most important tests of the scientific method is **replicability,** the ability of different scientists using the same methods of observation to achieve the same results. The test of replicability ensures the **intersubjectivity** of science — that the perceptions of different researchers correspond to each other — and that the results of experiments are robust and valid.

The theoretical model becomes more complete and accurate as new observations substantiate and thus strengthen certain features or, alternatively, fail to produce predicted results, causing the model to be revised or even abandoned. In any event, new hypotheses will be developed to test other parts of the theoretical model, and the scientific process continues to operate. For example, discoveries in astronomy are producing continued refinements of our theories about how the universe began.

Some scientific disciplines are called "historical" sciences, not in the sense that they depend on written records, but rather because they deal with unique sequences of events through time or with basic entities that change through time (Dunnell 1971). For example, many biologists study the evolutionary sequences of life forms. These forms have changed through time and are generally not the same today as ancestral forms that existed millions of years ago. On the other hand, the very basic things that physicists or chemists study do not change in these "historical" ways. Phenomena such as gravity or the recombination of atoms into molecules operated millions of years ago just as they do today. Archaeology, obviously, is a historical science; our subject matter — human organisms and their cultural behavior — changes markedly through time. It is much more difficult to develop fixed scientific laws in the historical sciences.

Science is not the exclusive preserve of white-coated laboratory workers. The scientific method of experimentation and refinement of theories is practiced by all of us in an almost reflexive way. In the most ordinary circumstances we find ourselves testing hypotheses and observing the results of these tests. If your desk lamp fails, you first check that the bulb is secure, then that the unit is plugged in, then perhaps try replacing the bulb. These are tests of hypotheses about why the lamp has failed, and in this and countless other mundane "experimental settings" the scientific method is operating.

Scientific Paradigms

Science can never hope to achieve ultimate "truth" and end its quest for more accurate explanation. Revision is a necessary part of the process, as all scientific disciplines engage in ongoing debates over what information is appropriate to each discipline and how to interpret it. Science, like

replicability The ability of different scientists using the same methods of observation or experimentation to achieve the same results.

intersubjectivity The validated correspondence of the subjective perceptions of different scientific observers.

religion, is a belief system. But whereas religion refers all questions back to a fixed body of dogma based on "revealed truth," science tests questions against observations. And although scholars may at times disagree over certain issues, at any point in time in a particular science, a general set of ideas and observations is accepted by most of the trained practitioners in that field. The precise word denoting this consensual framework is **paradigm** (Kuhn 1970).

We can think about science in terms of how its core ideas change over time, how knowledge and perceptions—the theoretical model of reality—are gradually altered. Sometimes the cumulative changes are so profound that we can identify the emergence of a new paradigm, replacing the old one. We will be applying this concept to the history of archaeology, but here we will illustrate the idea with a more familiar example, from astronomy.

We commonly hear that at the time of Columbus, many Europeans thought that the earth was flat and that everything in the universe revolved around it (Fig. 2.1). Actually, many others thought the world was round, and the earth's rotation around the sun had long been known, but in Columbus's time the size of the earth was just being explored, and the perception of the earth's place in the universe was undergoing drastic change. After Copernicus published his theory of the sun-centered solar system in 1543, the evidence kept piling up, indicating a smaller and smaller role for earth in the cosmos. Galileo built the first astronomical telescope in 1608, using the principle of the telescope discovered by Kepler in 1605. From 1609 to 1619, the latter developed laws of planetary motion. Newton presented his law of gravitation in 1666 and by 1669 had developed a reflecting telescope.

The advances made in observation of celestial events inspired a new sun-centered model of space. Today we know that the universe is neither sun- nor earth-centered, and we understand earth's position in the local territory of our own galaxy. When we look back over 500 years of changes in astronomical perspective, we see a good example of a paradigm change as well as an illustration of the cyclical process of science (as diagrammed above), since the changes in one phase of research and interpretation have provoked changes in another.

These changes show how science produced an objective perspective on the heavens. Let us now examine how anthropological archaeology developed and how it gave us a similarly improved perspective on humankind.

paradigm General set of ideas and observations accepted by most of the trained practitioners of a particular field of science at any point in time.

SPECULATION ABOUT THE PAST: 1400s TO 1840

Early in this century, excavations in Iraq at the ancient city of Babylon uncovered the palace of the last king of Babylon, Nabonidus, who lived about 2,500 years ago. In the private quarters of the king and his daughter, archaeologists found relics and texts from much more ancient times—the remains of archaeological "exhibits" set up millennia ago.

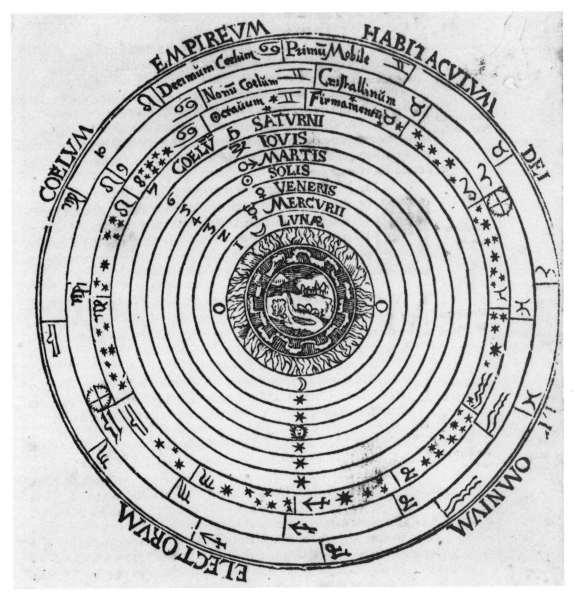

Curiosity about the past is an enduring preoccupation. We know that the Greeks and Romans, who speculated about the evolution of human technological sophistication, proposed successive ages of stone, bronze, and iron (as did the Chinese). But as the empires of Greeks and Romans passed into history, their intellectual traditions were largely abandoned, and during the Middle Ages, European intellectual curiosity narrowed to a focus on spirituality. The most important issue became the relationship of humans to the afterlife, not to the world they lived in, so the physical world was largely interpreted through a religious perspective.

FIGURE 2.1 A European medieval model of the structure of the universe shows the earth at the center, surrounded by the moon, Mercury, Venus, the sun, the other planets, and the stars.

During the Renaissance, the period of intellectual rebirth occurring in the 15th and 16th centuries, new interest arose in non-Biblical interpretations of time, inspired by the rediscovery of the ancient ideas of Greek and Roman cultures. Europeans developed an avid interest in classical cultures of the Mediterranean. The works of the ancient Romans and Greeks—their writings, sculptures, buildings—were held to represent the highest standards of their fields, and their intellectual traditions were rediscovered.

At the same time, the descriptions of cultures far beyond Europe and the Mediterranean began to reach Europeans. This evidence of cultural diversity fanned interest in the ancient past, as the presence of such a vast number of people in previously unknown continents could only be explained by great migrations, which were also required to validate the Biblical account of Adam and Eve. If the world was only 6,000 years old, as Biblical chronology indicated (Gould 1991), and humans were specially created at one time and place, then how did the New World and its peoples come about?

speculative period   The period in the history of archaeology in the New World between 1492–1840, characterized by unsystematic and speculative interpretations about the past.

Speculation about the past was so characteristic of its time that we call the period beginning about 1492 the **speculative period** of archaeology (Willey and Sabloff 1980). This was the preprofessional era of archaeology, before it matured as a field of study with scientific methods of observation and interpretation, a transition that would not occur until around 1840. Accurate measurement of the passage of time is an important issue in the development of archaeology. Objectively measured time is fundamental to a scientific understanding of any culture history, but not until the late 1800s did the general public accept the fact that the earth was much older than 6,000 years.

The roots of archaeology can be found in four fields that developed during the Renaissance and the Age of Reason that followed it: antiquarianism, social philosophy, the earth sciences, and the life sciences.

Antiquarianism

antiquarianism   The study of antiquity (the ancient past and its customs) and antiquities (the relics of the ancient past).

Antiquarianism is the study of antiquity (the ancient past and its customs) and antiquities (the relics of the ancient past). Relics were collected with great avidity and little discrimination from the ruins of Classical antiquity and also from European prehistoric sites. Interpretations of cultures of the past by antiquarians during the speculative period were based on available historical and religious documents, on a poor understanding of the age of the earth, and on a fairly limited knowledge of the range of human diversity.

Classical Antiquarianism   Interest in things Egyptian became something of a mania in Europe in the early 19th century, inspired by Napoleon's military campaign in Egypt (begun in 1798), which was accompanied by draftsmen and other specialists brought along to study and document antiquities. Perhaps the most famous discovery was an ethnohistoric document, the Rosetta Stone. The Rosetta Stone (Fig. 2.2) bears

FIGURE 2.2 The Rosetta Stone was found in Egypt by Napoleon's expeditionary force. Its text written in three different scripts, the stone provided the key to deciphering many other texts from ancient Egypt.

the same text written in three different languages (Egyptian hieroglyphics, Egyptian demotic script, and Greek) and when the hieroglyphic text was deciphered in 1822 by Champollion, it opened the door to translation of a wealth of ancient Egyptian texts (Hobson 1987). The public's interest in Egyptian and other antiquities had the unfortunate consequence of encouraging looting of archaeological sites, the most famous of such looters being Belzoni, a former circus strongman, who mined the ancient temples and tombs for interesting relics and then exhibited his finds in London in 1821 (Fagan 1975). Public fascination with antiquities increased, encouraging more looting.

Antiquarianism in the New World The same fascination with relics of the past that infected Europe also was felt in the Spanish colonies in **Mesoamerica,** the area that includes present-day Mexico, Guatemala,

Mesoamerica The archaeological culture area that includes present-day Mexico, Guatemala, Belize, Honduras, and parts of El Salvador.

Belize, and Honduras. In 1804 Charles IV of Spain sent an expedition to examine ancient ruins. Traveling through the central highlands and the Gulf Coast of Mexico, it visited the site of Palenque in southern Mexico and made a careful record of finds, including architectural monuments. Another European observer, Alexander von Humboldt, documented his travels through the New World in the early 19th century in his book *Views of the Mountains and Monuments of the Indigenous People of America,* published in 1810. This was the first time the general public in Europe had seen the New World's ancient treasures, and European antiquarian interest was captivated. The European publication of a report on excavations at Palenque in 1822, which also inspired interest in the Maya, stimulated Stephens and Catherwood to study Maya ruins (see Chapter 1).

North Americans of European descent shared with European scholars the general intellectual interests of the late 18th century, including natural history, social philosophy, and antiquarianism. But in the new setting, there existed different kinds of plants and animals—indeed whole new environments—for naturalists to study. More important, living native peoples could be studied and described, whose origins posed important questions. As colonization progressed westward, massive earthworks were discovered (Fig. 2.3). All had been unused for what was obviously a substantial period of time and old, large trees grew on some of them, but the big question was: Who had built these mounds? Could the remnants of Native American cultures living in these areas at the time of the American Revolution be the descendants of the moundbuilders? Many regarded this as unlikely, thinking it more probable that lost tribes of Israel, Vikings, or Phoenicians had been responsible.

excavation Systematic exploration of subsurface remains in the archaeological record by means of removing soil or other matrix and sometimes removing cultural materials as well.

While speculation raged, a ground-breaking event, literally and figuratively speaking, took place: the first scientific **excavation**. The excavation, in this case, into a burial mound, was conducted in Virginia in 1784 by America's most gifted citizen of the Age of Reason, Thomas Jefferson. Jefferson knew that the 4-m-high mound on his property was an ancient burial mound but wanted to investigate it carefully to learn the circumstances of its construction. This investigative approach toward remains was innovative, as was the excavational method of research that Jefferson used and the careful attention he paid to the soil layers he encountered (Fig. 2.4). Jefferson did not dig simply to loot a site of its relics, as Belzoni had done in Egypt.

surface survey and mapping The systematic location and recording of surface remains in the archaeological record; subsurface remains are also often mapped.

Excavation is an important research technique in archaeology, and we see in Jefferson's work the beginning of its systematic use. We should also note that another important research method, **surface survey and mapping,** was also used at this time to learn about the moundbuilders (Thomas 1885). As areas of Ohio (then the western frontier of the United States) were mapped to facilitate colonization, the maps included accurate plans of mound complexes. On top of one mound a large tree felled in 1787 had 438 rings, making the mound's date of construction at least A.D. 1300.

The identity of the moundbuilders was finally resolved by the combined force of different lines of evidence, revealing the moundbuilders to be ances-

FIGURE 2.3 Throughout the Midwest there are massive mounds that were built long before the Europeans arrived in the New World. This map of Ohio shows sites with mounds, clustered in the river valleys.

FIGURE 2.4 This 19th-century painting of a mound illustrates in a cutaway view the successive levels of construction holding human remains and grave goods.

tors of living Native Americans. In part, this sensible and straightforward explanation derived from a test devised by physical anthropologists, which compared the shape of the skulls of the modern and ancient local populations to see whether similarities justified the assumption of a biological link. The results published in 1839 showed that the moundbuilders were not a "lost race" but rather peoples related to modern Native Americans.

Social Philosophy

social philosophers
Scholars interested in explaining human social conditions and their moral implications, who were especially prominent in Europe in the 18th century.

At the end of the 18th century **social philosophers** were galvanized by political revolutions in the United States and France, as well as by rapid population growth and technological change in Europe. Their attempts to understand human social conditions were also stimulated by the accounts of explorers, soldiers, missionaries, colonists, and merchants, who told of cultures and lifeways that seemed beyond imagining. Explaining these different cultures — their origins and their moral implications — was an important concern of social philosophy, another field associated with the beginnings of archaeology. Social philosophers theorized about how best to study humans in systematic ways and why different cultures were differently organized, issues that still engage the attention of social scientists today.

Social philosophers promoted the view that because human behavior was malleable and could be perfected, social evils could be conquered. Inherent in their perspective was the idea that societies could progress toward social and economic equality, some societies achieving greater progress than others. But there was an enduring problem: How could humans achieve economic and social equality if our species's overwhelming power to reproduce created an ever-larger population needing resources? If conditions were right, populations could grow at prodigious rates. Benjamin Franklin observed that on the American frontier the population was doubling every 25 years, and at that rate any limited area would become impossibly crowded within a few generations. Franklin's observation inspired the Englishman Thomas Malthus to consider the consequences of human overpopulation and conclude that human reproductive potential was such that, unchecked, it would rapidly outstrip the food supply (Malthus [1798] 1970).

Decades later, in the mid-19th century, Malthus's ideas would strongly influence the development of biological evolutionism (we shall discuss these ideas further in Chapters 5 and 16). In the meantime, the influence of the earth sciences on evolutionary thinking was more direct.

Earth Sciences

earth sciences Sciences concerned with the study of formation processes that affect the earth's surface.

Natural sciences provided other sources of ideas and methods relevant to archaeology. The **earth sciences,** geology in particular, were instrumental in readjusting European perspectives about the age of the earth and in establishing the importance of the study of patterns of geological strata, essential to understanding archaeological deposits (Lyell 1850).

The Age of Discovery brought increasing interest in the natural landscape, and new interpretations of it. One of the most important 17th-century geological discoveries, for example, is still a foundation stone of modern archaeology. This is the **law of superposition,** which declares that under normal circumstances, what is oldest is on the bottom. In 1669 Nicholas Steno stated it thus:

> At any time when any given stratum was being formed, all matter resting upon it was fluid, and, therefore, at the time when the lowest stratum was being formed, none of the upper strata existed.
>
> *(Cited in Shelton 1966)*

When they are being laid down, geological deposits are usually in a fluid state (either molten or water-borne); deposits of soil over many archaeological sites are more often shifted and settled by wind, gravity, or erosion. In geology and archaeology, the study of strata and how they form is called **stratigraphy** (Wheeler 1954). In normal circumstances, newer layers (strata) form on top of older ones, but sometimes in geological and archaeological settings, the more newly formed layers are actually positioned under older formations, a situation called "reversed stratigraphy."

Deeply buried geological strata are sometimes visible. Stone tools that had long been collected as oddities in Europe were sometimes found in association with human and other animal bones in buried geological deposits in contexts indicating the very ancient presence of hunting populations. In 1797 John Frere made the daring interpretation of much greater antiquity for hand-axes found in England than the short 6,000-year span derived from the Bible would allow (Fig. 2.5).

law of superposition
The principle that the order of deposition in stratified material under normal circumstances is from bottom to top so that the older material is on the bottom.

stratigraphy   The deposition, distribution, and age of strata, or layers. Stratigraphy is used as a relative dating technique.

FIGURE 2.5   The engraving of these hand-axes found in England illustrated Frere's report in 1800. Clearly, they are carefully worked and could not have been natural rock formations. A basic part of archaeological work is distinguishing the handiwork of humans from natural effects — a first step toward interpreting the archaeological record.

uniformitarianism   The geological principle that the configuration of the earth's surface is the product of processes that may be observed to operate in the present; more generally, the principle that observations in the present are the key to understanding the past.

gradualism   The view that changes occur slowly and cumulatively rather than rapidly and disjunctively.

catastrophism   Theory that explains change through a succession of sudden catastrophes.

index fossil   An organism whose presence in various strata over a great distance links them to the same time period.

Accepting a much older earth demanded new concepts about geological processes. Two of the most important of these concepts, **uniformitarianism** and **gradualism,** which emerged in the early 1800s, are associated in particular with the work of geologists. What eventually became known as the principle of uniformitarianism states that the landforms visible in nature result from the action of processes that can be observed in the present, which processes were also ongoing in the past. These processes are "uniform" in the sense that their rates in the past were generally the same as those in the present, and they are "gradual" in the sense that their effects may be perceptible over centuries or millennia rather than in the course of one human lifespan. Given what we now know about such processes as erosion, earthquakes, and continental drift, uniformitarianism and gradualism seem self-evident, but these principles replaced the older idea of **catastrophism,** that a succession of sudden catastrophes had created the earth as we know it, the flood that Noah survived being the most recent.

The concept of gradualism has been refined in recent years, and a more accurate model of how change takes place is described by the phrase "punctuated equilibrium"; that is, periods of relatively little change are interspersed with periods or events of more rapid alteration (Eldredge and Gould 1972). Gradualism remains a valid approach to perceiving changes over very long periods of time. For example, southern California is gradually moving north because of shifts in the earth's crust along fault lines, though the incidents of movement, earthquakes, "punctuate" relatively stable periods of "equilibrium."

The idea that the landscapes around us are generally shaped by slow, gradual, familiar processes is extremely important for archaeologists. An essential key to understanding the past is understanding the way things work in the present. When we stop to consider the rate at which mountain chains rise, earthquake faults slip, and rivers cut through geological strata each year, it immediately becomes clear why gradualism and uniformitarianism cannot be accepted without postulating the earth's great antiquity. These interpretations are inevitably linked, and represent a profound change in thinking about the material world.

In 1815 William Smith produced a geological map of England and Wales showing that sequences of the same rock strata occurred in bedrock outcroppings in different parts of the country. Furthermore, Smith found "that each stratum is also possessed of properties peculiar to itself . . . and the same extraneous or organized fossils throughout its course" (cited in Shelton 1966). This consistency of strata and their characteristic fossils over a broad area stimulated the idea of the **index fossil,** an organism whose presence in various strata over a great distance linked them as belonging to the same time. The index fossil concept was extremely important for archaeology, since it could be readily applied to cultural materials in archaeological strata, linking different archaeological sites that have the same kinds of artifacts to the same period in time.

Charles Lyell's *Principles of Geology* (1830–1833) was an early compen-

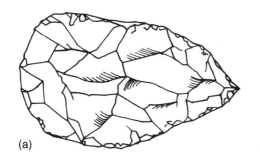

(a)

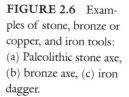

FIGURE 2.6 Examples of stone, bronze or copper, and iron tools: (a) Paleolithic stone axe, (b) bronze axe, (c) iron dagger.

(b)

(c)

dium of these new ideas and findings. Documenting major advances in geological interpretation, it spread ideas, such as uniformitarianism, about the formation of the earth and relations of strata and influenced biological evolutionists such as Charles Darwin, who took the newly published first volume with him as he embarked on the voyage of *The Beagle* in 1831 (Moorehead 1978).

Geological evolution was particularly important to the study of ancient Europe before the classical time of the Greeks and Romans, since there were few clues as to the age of preclassical remains. Nyerup, who became Denmark's first official archaeologist in 1806, commented that "everything which has come down to us from heathendom is wrapped in a thick fog: it belongs to a space of time which we cannot measure. We know that it is older than Christendom, but whether by a couple of years or a couple of centuries, or even by more than a millennium we can do no more than guess" (Daniel 1981:56). Nyerup, his successor Thomsen, and Thomsen's student Worsaae were pivotal in developing the **three-age sequence** as a model of human cultural development (Fig. 2.6).

Faced with the task of sorting a jumble of European archaeological materials into a coherent exhibition for the Danish National Museum, these archaeologists reasoned that the earliest tools used by humans were simple, made of stone and other natural materials. The period in which stone was the most important material used for tools is called the **Stone Age**. The Stone Age is followed by an advance in tool design based on the use of copper, which occurs in nature in a form workable with simple tools, and bronze, an alloy of copper and tin, and harder and more durable

three-age sequence A classification system developed by C. J. Thomsen which orders the cultural remains of the Old World into three major phases based on the raw material of such remains and technology—that is, the Stone Age, the Bronze Age, and the Iron Age. Inherent in this system is the idea that a chronological order could be achieved by placing things in this sequence.

Stone Age Term often used to characterize cultures that used stone for cutting and other primary tools, thus designating a stage of technological development.

metallurgy The knowledge of metals and their components and its application in metal working.

Bronze Age Period of time marked by the mastery of metallurgy and the predominance of tools of bronze; preceded by the Stone Age.

Iron Age Era during which humans mastered the complicated process of making tools and goods out of iron; preceded by the Stone and Bronze ages.

than either of them. Mastery of **metallurgy** (the knowledge and working of metals) was a great technological advance, with far-reaching economic and social consequences. The era of tool types this inaugurated is usually called the **Bronze Age**. Finally, humans mastered the more complicated process of making implements out of iron, which revolutionized technology and socioeconomic relations once more. The **Iron Age** is still with us, though in the last century it has come to be an age of steel (an alloy of iron and carbon) and most recently our information system could be said to have entered the age of the silicon chip (a "tool" made of a common constituent of rocks).

Note that the three-age sequence was a useful scheme for early archaeologists, since it implied a *relative* chronology, a sequence of tool materials and forms. For example, according to the model, sites having stone tools only would be viewed as probably originating from an earlier time than those in the same region having bronze tools, and so forth.

The three-age sequence has gained wide acceptance since the early 19th century, when it was just being developed and tested as a model of prehistory. By virtue of the broad workable relative chronology the model provided, by which cultural materials from all over Europe could be sorted, awareness grew that the styles of many kinds of artifacts within each age changed over time and that these stylistic changes were meaningful markers of different chronological periods. The three-age sequence also nicely corresponded with the ideas of cultural progress that were popular, and formed the basis for the concept of cultural evolution.

Life Sciences

The life sciences (e.g., biology, botany) contributed to archaeology the notion that species can be arranged and classified, which provided a model for the arrangement and classification of cultures and cultural materials. The life sciences also helped to explain how cultures changed over time. Whether species were created or whether they had evolved and how they related to the expanded time frame produced by geology had also become important issues. Archaeological interest in cultural evolution arose as a result of some of these early developments. We will come back to the topic of biological evolution and its influence on theories of cultural change in Chapter 5.

Summary: The Speculative Period

The amount of information gathered between the 1400s and the 1840s, plus changes in perceptions of physical and cultural diversity in the past and present, set the stage for the development of a science of anthropology and its subdiscipline archaeology. Finding reasonable explanations for the variation and similarities among living and extinct cultures was not easy, and some of the reasoning of the speculative period shows more imagination than critical thinking.

Table 2.1   Chronology of American Archaeology

Time Span	Focus	Major Research Goal
1492	Speculation	
1840	* * * * * Descriptive classification	* * * * * Documenting cultural materials and lifeways
1910	* * * * * Chronological classification	* * * * * * * * * * Establishing cultural sequences
1940	* * * * * Explanation	* * * * * * * * * * Explanation of cultural patterns and processes

THE PROFESSION OF ARCHAEOLOGY FROM THE 1840s TO THE PRESENT

As we have seen, professional archaeology as the systematic study of past cultures had its beginnings roughly 150 years ago. The goals of archaeology as described in Chapter 1, can be used to characterize three major periods of American archaeology and to delineate their respective focus: description, history, and explanation (Table 2.1). Dominating the profession each at a different time, the goals serve to define the professional archaeological paradigm in terms of research orientation and the interpretation of results. The two major shifts that have occurred since the beginning of the first paradigm correspond in fact to steps in the ongoing cycle of experimentation in archaeology.

The three major periods of archaeology can be integrated into the scientific cycle as follows:

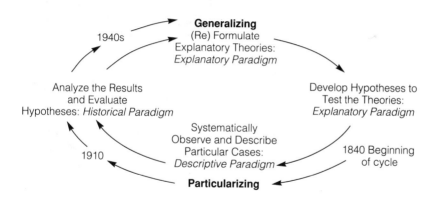

The first period was dominated by an interest in the documentation of the traits of different cultures—how each culture was distinguishable by its particular set of artifacts and styles, summarized in a "trait list." This provided a necessary basis—a "data base," in modern terms—for further analysis. As the focus shifted to developing culture histories, the traits could be analyzed and put into meaningful order. And once the historical frameworks were established, general trends and processes could be identified and explained and theories of cultural behavior refined. At present, archaeologists are involved in all stages of the cycle of science and archaeological research: We continue to describe, to analyze, and to theorize—and to test new theories by applying cycles of experimentation.

THE DESCRIPTIVE PERIOD: 1840s TO EARLY 1900s

Professional archaeology emerged in the United States somewhat later than it did in Europe. During the first 70 years (1840 to about 1910) archaeologists in the United States compiled cultural **trait lists,** cataloguing everything known about ancient Native American cultures and their living descendants. Meanwhile, in Europe, archaeologists and natural scientists focused heavily on the earliest phases of human settlement in Europe and how these related to the **Ice Ages** of the **Pleistocene.** We see the beginnings of interest in how the earliest Europeans lived in the cold, harsh conditions of these earlier times.

Questions about the earliest cultures of Europe reflect a major intellectual preoccupation of the 19th century: **evolution.** Geological studies had documented changes in life forms as well as rock formations. Now culture itself became grist for evolutionist ideas. The field of ethnography became dominated by the idea that cultures could be categorized in terms of their technological sophistication and their political and economic complexity. Arrangements of cultures according to hierarchies of stages of development became very popular in the 19th century.

During this time Lewis Henry Morgan, a New York lawyer, actively studied cultural diversity. Morgan's most important work was his description of cultural evolutionism; he saw all cultures as fitting into a **unilinear** sequence of stages. In 1877 Morgan published *Ancient Society,* in which he linked what he called "ethnic periods" in human cultural development with technological and subsistence features.

Morgan's evolutionary scheme is presented in Table 2.2. Note the emphasis on basic tools and food procurement as a basis for describing and classifying cultures. Morgan's work had a strong influence on Karl Marx. Marx tried to explain cultural variation in terms of economic patterns: the ways in which different societies produced the goods they used, and the extent to which particular people (or groups) within each society held greater access to the society's key resources, a situation we call **differential access to key resources.** Fundamental to Marx's ideas was the presence of

trait list   A list of characteristics describing an archaeological culture.

Ice Ages   The successive periods of glaciation that occurred during the Pleistocene.

Pleistocene   Geological period lasting from 1.8 million years ago to about 12,000 years ago.

evolution   Modification through a process of natural selection, resulting in adaptive change.

unilinear evolution   The idea, especially associated with 19th-century evolutionists such as L. H. Morgan, that all cultures pass through the same sequence of evolutionary changes, or stages.

differential access to key resources   Situation in which different individuals or groups within a society do not share equal access to necessary resources.

Table 2.2 Morgan's Evolutionary Scheme

Period: Most complex to most simple	Subsistence and Technology
Civilization	phonetic alphabet and writing
Upper Barbarism	iron tools
Middle Barbarism	domestication of animals (Old World) cultivation of maize; irrigation; adobe and stone architecture (New World)
Lower Barbarism	pottery
Upper Savagery	bow and arrow
Middle Savagery	fish subsistence and fire
Lower Savagery	fruit and nut subsistence

competition among groups, particularly of different social rank. As we discuss later, the process of development of social strata, called **stratification,** is a hallmark of the most complex kind of society, the state. But competition for limited key resources can also be found in simpler societies and is an essential part of the process of evolution.

Biological evolutionism also developed in the mid-19th century. Finds of human fossils, like those of the Neanderthals in Europe, and tools associated with them provided 19th-century European archaeologists with evidence of human cultural and biological evolution and antiquity. To establish and document earth's "long history" in a systematic fashion required a better understanding of the archaeological remains found in Europe and of the evidence of drastic climate change during the Ice Ages. The antiquity of humans was scientifically demonstrated by the association of chipped stone tools and bones of extinct animals, found together in France by Jacques Boucher de Perthes in 1841.

European Archaeology

The gathering evidence of geological and cultural changes over time in Europe showed that the Stone Age could be divided into two parts, **Paleolithic** and **Neolithic,** defined by the kinds of tools in use and the animals living in Europe at that time (the names are, respectively, from the Greek for "old stone" and "new stone"). Paleolithic flaked tools (Fig. 2.7) were contemporaneous with now-extinct cave bears and mammoths, while Neolithic technology included more refined ground stone tools, and **flora** and **fauna** (plant and animal species) like those of today. The Neolithic marked a transition in the pattern of **subsistence**—from getting food by hunting and gathering, to agriculture, and from using stone tools to using metal tools.

stratification The process of development of social strata (layers) or subdivisions within a society; the differential ranking of social groups with regard to prestige, power, and wealth.

Paleolithic Earliest part of the Stone Age, commonly known as the "Old Stone Age" in Europe, defined by flaked tools and many now-extinct mammals, such as mammoths, before the end of the last Ice Age.

Neolithic Latter part of the Stone Age commonly known as the "New Stone Age," characterized by refined polished stone tools and modern flora and fauna; term now generally synonymous with the period during which food production originated in the Old World.

flora Plants or vegetation.

fauna Animals.

subsistence Means of supporting life, in particular by obtaining food.

FIGURE 2.7 Paleolithic and Neolithic chipped and ground stone tools: (a)–(d) and (f) tools of the Paleolithic and their uses; (e) and (g) tools of the Neolithic, which include a sickle and a set of grinding stones.

This classification of archaeological materials by their associations with floral and faunal evidence was an important methodological breakthrough because it put materials in their larger context and because it encouraged a broader, more environmentally oriented perspective. But most typologies of cultural materials continued to be based on features intrinsic to the artifact itself: its shape and material. These typologies often had little value in elucidating the actual function of the artifacts, or the ancient patterns of behavior involving their use.

Overall, the evidence from Europe indicated a long period of cultural development, from hunting and gathering, through early efforts to raise plants and animals, to farming villages and then into the historically known past, the rise of the Roman Empire and its conflicts with the Celts and other European ethnic groups. European archaeologists of the 19th century began to fill in the gaps in their own ancient history and that of the Mediterranean and Near East.

Perhaps the most famous of these pursuits was Heinrich Schliemann's effort to find the ancient cities mentioned in Homeric legends. In the 1870s and 1880s Schliemann searched for the site of the Trojan War described in Homer's *Iliad*. He excavated a mound at Hissarlik, Turkey, that he thought was ancient Troy. He also excavated at Mycenae in Greece, and achieved some general success in linking epic stories, such as those of Homer, with archaeological sites (Fig. 2.8). By today's professional standards, Schliemann's work was of mixed value. On the positive side, he tried to separate the strata of successive occupations at Troy into a sequence of city rebuildings, but at the same time, because he was preoccupied with relics and with a particular time period, he failed to record his findings properly or save "irrelevant" material. He did, however, discover the actual material remains of an epoch of the ancient past previously known only from books.

Schliemann's unsystematic methods stand in contrast to those of his contemporary, Augustus Pitt Rivers, who pioneered strict practices of careful excavation, documentation, and preservation of archaeological evidence. Pitt Rivers possessed the disciplined attitudes of a professional soldier, the intellectual curiosity of a scholar, and a large personal fortune to subsidize his research and publication of results. Active during the last half of the century, Pitt Rivers emphasized the importance of ethnographic cases in understanding archaeological materials. He assumed that different types of

FIGURE 2.8 Excavations at the Acropolis of Mycenae, as depicted in the *Illustrated London News,* were extensive and revealed many rebuildings at this site (engraving from 1893).

FIGURE 2.9a   Petrie (at right) and Amy Urlin at work at Abydos, Egypt, in 1900.

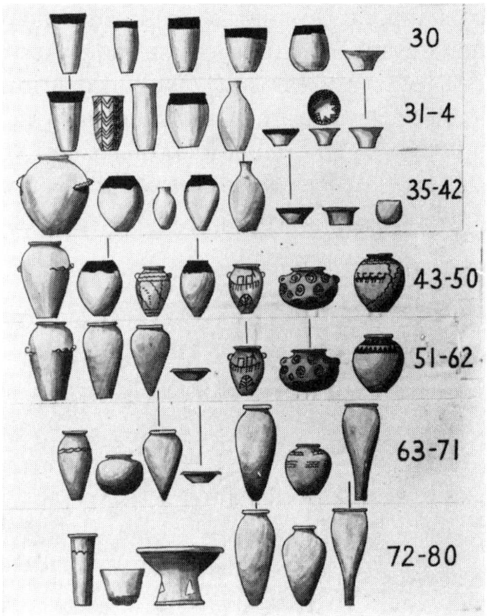

FIGURE 2.9b   Petrie's original sequence chart for dating pre-Dynastic Egyptian pottery.

artifacts could be associated with different stages in technological sophistication and cultural evolution. Pitt Rivers's careful methods of data gathering and interpretation brought professional archaeology to a new level of maturity.

In the 1880s, William Flinders Petrie began many years of research in Egypt, work that was characterized by exceptional care in the recovery of information, by broad scope in the range of issues addressed by his research, and by the development of useful methods of plotting change over time. His technique of **seriation** (literally, putting into a series) of utilitarian pottery on the basis of how the form of the vessels gradually changed over time demonstrated that archaeological remains did not have to be fascinating or unique relics to tell us important things about ancient cultures (Figs. 2.9a and 2.9b). Seriation was an important development in **relative dating,** establishing how sites (or artifact types) are ordered in time: The age of one site is determined, relative to other sites, based on similarities and differences among their respective artifact assemblages.

Petrie also discovered that cultural remains from different parts of the eastern Mediterranean region could be linked. He found Egyptian goods at Mycenae and knew their age from Egyptian historical records; from this he inferred the age of the Mycenaean remains. This method is known as **cross-dating,** which establishes the age of one find by its similarity to or association with a find of known age.

Mycenae was an impressive site, imparting useful knowledge about cultures at the time of the Trojan War. However, earlier Mediterranean culture was unknown until remains were discovered on the island of Crete, at the site of Knossos, by Arthur Evans at the turn of the century. Excavations there revealed the previously unknown Minoan culture (Fig. 2.10) and also that Knossos had been inhabited for a long time even before the Minoans. This pre-Minoan period covered a poorly understood time in European and Mediterranean history, the Neolithic. Evans knew the dates of Minoan civilization (about 2400 to 1400 B.C.), based on cross-dating with Egypt, but did not know how far into the past the Neolithic extended. So he attempted to calculate the time elapsed since the beginning of the formation of the Neolithic deposits, by calibrating a deposition rate for the deposits, which had accumulated to a depth of 6.5 m.

It is logical to assume that these two factors—elapsed time and depth of deposit—are linked, but the overall rate of deposit of soil over any archaeological site is highly variable. Evans devised an experiment to test the rate of deposition, based on a living ethnographic context (observations he made in Egypt in 1906 and 1907) to derive an estimate of the rate of soil buildup. Extrapolating from these observations, he calculated that the Neolithic at Knossos began as far back as 12,000–10,000 B.C., values far greater than those later indicated by more reliable methods, whereby 6000 B.C. was the earliest date. However, this marks a pioneering effort at **experimental archaeology,** the controlled testing of hypotheses about what happened in the past by observing analogous processes or behavior in the present.

seriation Placement of items in their proper order in a series.

relative dating The use of methods developed to establish the age of sites or artifacts, relative to other sites and artifacts.

cross-dating Establishing the age of one find by its similarity to or association with a find of known age.

experimental archaeology The controlled testing of hypotheses about what happened in the past by observing and manipulating processes or behavior in the present. Also known as "action archaeology."

FIGURE 2.10 The discovery of Minoan culture created tremendous excitement in Europe, in part because the Minoans seemed glamorous, hedonistic, athletic, and stylish. This painted statuette depicts a Minoan woman handling snakes.

American Archaeology: Describing and Classifying

Archaeology in the United States during the 19th century focused on documenting existing Native American cultures and the visible ancient monuments of their ancestors. Human biological evolution, so interesting to Europeans, did not seem to apply to the Americas. In Europe, it was clear from remains of Neanderthals that premodern human forms had lived there, but the Americas offered no evidence of premodern ancestors to modern humans (Dillehay 1988). Today, we know that human occupation of Europe extends back at least 700,000 years, but the peopling of the New World probably less than 30,000 years ago, after fully modern humans, *Homo sapiens sapiens,* had evolved.

To an American archaeologist of a century ago, however, the comparative lack of New World evidence of human evolution meant that determining the age of archaeological remains seemed a less attainable goal than that of reconstructing Native American cultures at the time of contact with Europeans (for a Native American's view of Euro-American culture, see Box 2.1). Archaeology in the United States in the 19th century had a general, anthropological perspective. Reconstructions were based in part on studies of existing Native American cultures (and also on ethnohistoric documents describing the cultures at the time of first contact; see Fig. 2.11). Archaeological methods were used to learn more about visible monumental remains but not to investigate issues of **cultural chronology** (the sequence of developmental stages particular to a culture's history).

Professional archaeology in the United States began with the establishment of the first American research institutions for ethnography and archaeology. Foremost among them was the Smithsonian Institution,

cultural chronology
Cultural things, events, or processes arranged in chronological order.

FIGURE 2.11 This 16th-century illustration of Native American farmers planting maize was made by European observer Theodore de Bry.

BOX 2.1

SITTING BULL COMMENTS
ON EURO-AMERICAN LIFEWAYS

The famous Sioux leader Sitting Bull was born into a small egalitarian hunting society on the northern plains of North America. During his lifetime, his society and its lands suffered continuous encroachment by European-Americans from the east — a wave of frontier colonization by the rapidly expanding United States. How did Native Americans perceive Europeans during the colonization of North America?

In 1876 a large encampment of Sioux, Cheyenne, and Arapaho on the Little Big Horn River in Montana was attacked by U.S. cavalry. The Native Americans retaliated, led by Sitting Bull and other leaders, and ultimately defeated General George Armstrong Custer and his troops. Afterward Sitting Bull neatly captured the essence of the expanding American state in a speech to his people in 1877:

We now have to deal with another race — small and feeble when our fathers first met them, but now great and overbearing. Strangely enough they have a mind to till the soil and the love of possession is a disease with them. These people have many rules that the rich may break but the poor may not. They take tithes from the poor and weak to support the rich who rule.

(cited in Thompson 1986)

Although Sitting Bull's comments may seem cynical (as he had every right to be) he identified several of the main defining characteristics of the American state: dependence on effective agriculture, division into socioeconomic classes based on wealth, laws and taxes that powerful people can manipulate to their advantage. All of these were in marked contrast to the social and economic institutions of his own society.

---

founded in 1846 and today known as "our nation's attic" because its museums in Washington, D.C., store and display our prized cultural artifacts. Equally important has been the Smithsonian's tradition of sponsoring systematic research. Founding the Smithsonian indicates the new spirit of systematic investigation of Native American cultures during the descriptive period, through the Smithsonian's Bureau of American Ethnology.

The Peabody Museum of Archaeology and Ethnology at Harvard University was founded in 1866. Of its projects, none have been more impressive than the investigation of the pyramids, temples, and palaces of the Maya and other peoples of Mesoamerica (Fig. 2.12), primarily undertaken to document artistic and architectural styles and to decipher the ancient native writing systems, including calendars (Maudslay 1889–1902).

European methods of observing archaeological strata were gradually adopted into American archaeology but had little impact before the 20th century. After decades of work on describing and classifying the materials of culture, developing cultural chronologies became an important facet of research. The need to establish sequences of cultural materials

FIGURE 2.12 Alfred P. Maudslay was one of the most important archaeologists working in Mesoamerica. He is shown here in the 1890s at Chichén Itzá, a Maya site, and he has set up his workroom in one of the rooms of the "Nunnery," a Maya building. The Nunnery was so named because it contained many small rooms (like the one Maudslay is using), not because it had any kind of religious function.

that reflected changing culture history would be a primary focus of American archaeology for the first half of the early 20th century.

Unfortunately, this orientation toward chronology was not enlightened by a coherent model of *how* cultures changed over time. The unilinear evolutionism of Morgan and others had eventually been rejected as repugnant by American archaeologists because it had come to represent a justification for Western social and economic domination of the rest of the world. Shifting their attention from generalization and comparison of cultures to **particularism,** ethnographers documented individual cultures without comparative reference to others.

A leading exponent of particularism was Franz Boas, a professor at Columbia University who trained many American ethnographers in the early decades of this century. While Boas and his followers accepted that there were patterns in the growth of culture (Benedict 1934), they rejected cultural evolutionists' attempts to explain change and to categorize cultures on the basis of their technological sophistication. They believed that it was inappropriate to make critical judgments about any cultural practice, since culture could only be assessed in terms relative to itself—the principle on which **cultural relativism** is based. That is, culture should be studied in terms of how well it functioned to meet the needs of its people rather than how its organizational or technological sophistication compares to that of another culture.

But note that these two cultural features downplayed by ethnogra-

particularism An interpretative framework that characterized American archaeology in the early 1900s, whereby individual cultures were documented without comparative reference to others.

cultural relativism The belief that all cultures are unique and thus can only be evaluated in their own terms, and that cross-cultural comparisons and generalizations are invalid or inappropriate.

phers — change through time, and tool types — are among archaeology's principal emphases. When early 20th-century ethnographers redefined anthropology's focus, archaeologists were stranded within their own parent field of anthropology. Fortunately, from the late 1930s onward renewed concern arose within ethnography for generalization about culture and about broad change over time, inspiring a new and more theoretically sophisticated goal for archaeology: to explain broad cultural processes as these occur in various settings.

THE HISTORICAL PERIOD: 1910 TO 1945

In the first half of this century, American archaeology focused on developing chronologies of culture history. One of the earliest projects to address this issue was undertaken by Manuel Gamio, working in the Basin of Mexico (the valley surrounding Mexico City in the central highlands of Mexico). Trained in research methods by Franz Boas and strongly influenced by Petrie, Gamio used excavation to reveal the sequence of strata associated with artifacts from a sequence of three different cultures (Fig. 2.13) (Gamio 1928).

When a chronological sequence of changing pottery styles is established, certain styles are associated with certain periods and can serve as index fossils. It is then possible to determine that other sites with the same kinds of artifacts were occupied at about the same time. But the big question remains: How *much* time has passed since they were in use?

Note that putting things into a relative chronological series is different from establishing the **absolute date** of each phase. Absolute dates are sometimes called **chronometric** (time-measure) **dates,** indicating a measured value of time (years, centuries) has elapsed since the culture was active, or the particular artifact was in use. If you have the absolute dates of all these features of ancient culture, then you know how the artifacts relate to each other along a time series. If you only have absolute dates for one phase of the cultural sequence, you can at least fix the overall sequence in time, even though you may not know the duration of the other phases of the sequence or when the sequence began or ended. We must note that in certain areas of Mesoamerica during certain cultural phases, absolute dates were inscribed on monuments and written in texts. The Maya left many such dates, mostly inscribed in the Classic period, from about A.D. 300–900.

But in the early 20th century, there were few keys to unlocking the puzzle of the age of artifacts. One chronometric method being developed at that time involved counting tree rings and, from this, dating associated artifacts. This method, **dendrochronology,** would develop into an enormously useful absolute dating method (see further discussion in Chapter 4) but at this stage simply aided in understanding relative chronology, using the changes in artifact styles recovered from stratigraphic deposits. Ceramic potsherds were popular artifacts for this purpose, pottery styles

absolute dating The use of methods developed to establish the number of years elapsed since an object was made or used.

chronometric date Date indicating that a measured value of time (years, centuries) has elapsed since a past event occurred.

dendrochronology Establishing dates through tree-ring patterns (also known as tree-ring dating).

FIGURE 2.13 This stratigraphic profile shows the superimposed strata uncovered by Gamio's excavations in the Basin of Mexico. Note the materials from three distinct archaeological cultures, the uppermost being Aztec remains, with earlier Teotihuacán materials underlying them.

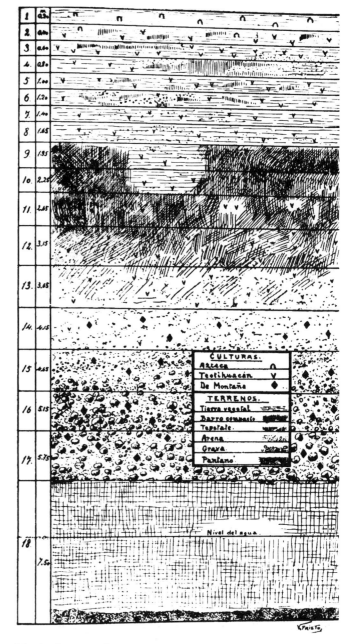

direct historical approach A research method which assumes that if there is continuity in culture through time in a given region, it is possible to interpret prehistoric archaeological remains by direct comparison with the historically known part of the culture sequence.

serving as sensitive indicators of cultural change and spatial variation. Once ceramic styles were linked to absolute dates, such as those obtained by dendrochronology, then the styles themselves could serve as markers of absolute dates.

The mid-1930s saw the development of a method of understanding ancient culture called the **direct historical approach,** which was applied to Nebraskan archaeology by W. D. Strong. This research method assumed that in a given region, if continuity of cultural patterns existed, then it was possible to work back into prehistoric times from the documented historical period and identify particular cultures in the past. This method was also applied to the U.S. Southeast and Southwest.

In addition to advances in understanding culture history, a major breakthrough occurred in understanding how cultures operated. In the late 1930s, the concept of cultural ecology was introduced. As noted in Chapter 1, *cultural ecology* assumes that culture and the environment interact, changes in one promoting or provoking changes in the other. This provides the means for explaining why cultures evolve and a way of measuring cultural adaptation to particular environmental settings. Julian Steward (1939) pioneered cultural ecology with an ethnographic study of the Shoshone Indians, foraging peoples of the western United States. Applicable to both living and ancient cultures, his method came to be used by both ethnographers and archaeologists. Cultural ecology integrated all cultural organization (social, economic, political, and ideological) into a coherent model of behavior, based on the subsistence method in use and on the environment serving as the resource base. Cultural ecology is one of the basic strategies archaeologists use today, but its impact on archaeology in the 1930s was not immediate.

In Mesoamerican archaeology in the early 20th century there was still a strong emphasis on **monumental architecture** (temples, palaces, and pyramids) and other elite features of ancient cultures, in contrast to those that reflected the lives of the mass of people. Emphasis was also placed on the study of ancient art and decipherment of the native writing systems (Morley 1920). Forstemann, called "the father of Maya hieroglyphic research," partially deciphered a pre-Colombian Maya manuscript (the Dresden Codex) in 1906. His interpretations of the numerical and calendrical data enabled archaeologists to determine absolute dates for inscribed Maya monuments. Other research efforts were aimed at deciphering Maya arithmetic, chronology, astronomy, and art (Spinden 1913) and at establishing chronological sequences based on the study of archaeological and ethnohistoric sources. Despite many further refinements in deciphering and interpreting script and calendars, these early studies were highly influential on subsequent research.

monumental architecture Large buildings such as temples, palaces, and pyramids, readily identifiable in the archaeological record and assumed to have been built by means of the collective labor of many people.

20th Century European Archaeology

Improvements in methods continued, as archaeologists investigated the cultures of Europe, the Mediterranean, and the Middle East. Archaeological documentation of the ancient places mentioned in the Bible became an important focus, and in 1918 excavations at the Mesopotamian sites of Ur and Eridu established Sumerian culture as a fact of prehistory. At Ur in 1926 the royal tombs were discovered by Leonard Woolley (1934). They included those of a king and queen plus dozens of servants and retainers

(a)

FIGURE 2.14 A lyre from the Great Death Pit of the Royal Graves at Ur, excavated by Leonard Woolley. The lyre itself, being made of wood, had long ago disintegrated, leaving an empty space. Woolley recovered the instrument's shape by pouring liquid plaster into the space (a). On the right (b) is the reconstructed lyre.

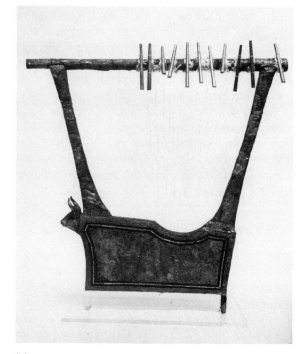

(b)

sacrificed for the funerals. The **grave goods** included musical instruments and games, fragile artifacts that were recovered because of Woolley's skill in excavation. He reconstructed partially disintegrating objects by pouring plaster of Paris into the cavities left in the soil by the decay of such artifacts as a wooden harp (Fig. 2.14). He trained workers to pay attention to subtle changes in color and composition of the soil—a paper-thin wavy lens of white powder was all that remained of the woven reed matting that lined the burial shaft.

Ancient Egyptian culture was also very much in the public eye in the 1920s, with the discovery and opening of Tut-ankh-amun's tomb by Howard Carter in 1922–1923 (Carter 1954), called the richest archaeological find ever made (Fig. 2.15). The treasures of the king were indeed impressive, but what made this find so valuable was that the tomb had not been seriously looted. Its original context was intact.

During the early decades of this century, the culture history of Europe and the Middle East was interpreted according to a **diffusionist** model. European developments such as farming, metallurgy, and stone architecture were seen as originating in the Middle East and being diffused from there to Europe much later. This diffusionist perspective was adopted by V. Gordon Childe (1925), who explained European prehistory both by the diffusion of people and ideas from the Near East and the East Mediterranean and by the adoption of these traits and their adaptation to the European setting. Several decades later, absolute dating of archaeological sites in Europe and the Middle East would show that the chronology of these features was more complex than Childe had suspected. Farming clearly occurs earlier in the Middle East, but metallurgy and massive stone architecture occur sufficiently early in Europe to indicate that the simple diffusionist explanation was untenable (Renfrew 1971, 1979).

grave goods Items and offerings interred with the deceased.

diffusionism Explanatory model of culture change that focuses on the spread of traits from one culture to another rather than on independent development of traits.

FIGURE 2.15 This is part of Tut-ankh-amun's tomb, showing its grave goods intact. This is the only unlooted Egyptian royal tomb ever found.

archaeological culture
Culture identified by a set of recurring material remains of features, house types, pottery forms, and burial styles.

Childe's enduring contribution to archaeology, however, was his focus on the larger culture that produced the artifacts (rather than just on the artifacts) and on larger issues of general cultural evolution. Childe saw **archaeological culture** as identified by a set of recurring features—house types, pottery forms, burial styles—that provided the material manifestation of a particular society or ethnic group. Therefore, when a trait associated with one group is found in another, the reason could be trade, or other interaction such as migration. When one archaeological culture is found to replace another, the reason might be migration or conquest. For European archaeologists, the identification of archaeological cultures became the chief aim of archaeology, and in areas where little material evidence had survived, cultures were identified on the basis of styles of a few artifacts.

THE EXPLANATORY PERIOD: 1945 TO TODAY

The period since the end of World War II has brought momentous changes of many kinds, not least in the field of archaeology. Several of the ideas central to modern anthropological archaeology—cultural evolution, cultural ecology, and cultural materialism—have emerged or been refined since World War II, and especially after 1960. The American educational establishment grew enormously; so too did the number of professional archaeologists on university faculties. Significant public funding for archaeology became available for the first time. Most important, American archaeology became much more theoretically and self-consciously scientifically oriented, and hence much more concerned with *explanation* (Watson, LeBlanc, and Redman 1971) in addition to description, classification, and construction of chronological sequences. One reason for this increased emphasis on explanation was that the information available to archaeologists had become very abundant—it was time to turn again to the exploration of theories that made sense of this wealth of information, rather than simply piling up more of it. Another reason was that new techniques and methods made the results of research much more comprehensive, reliable, and intelligible. In examining these postwar developments, we will focus on two periods: from 1945 to 1960 and from 1960 to the present.

Transition: 1945–1960

Critique of the Status Quo The period from 1945 to 1960 was one of rapid transition in archaeology. A major stimulus for change was a devastating attack on the state of American archaeology. Walter Taylor's book *A Study of Archaeology* (1967 [1948]) charged that archaeologists had become so preoccupied with classification and construction of chronological sequences that they had virtually ceased to be anthropologists—ignoring the reconstruction of ancient lifeways and behavior, they had lost the comparative perspective. Many, particularly those who studied the ancient Maya, were overly entranced with elite aesthetic and intellectual achievements at the expense of other parts of culture. Furthermore, archaeologists failed to capitalize on the many lines of evidence open to them in the vital task of reconstructing the past. Taylor's solutions were to reassert the identity of archaeology as anthropology and to advocate what he called the **conjunctive approach,** the integrated use of evidence from archaeology, ethnohistory, and ethnography to solve problems of reconstruction and interpretation.

Taylor's critique did not cause an immediate and comprehensive restructuring of archaeology but it was a beginning. Other trends contributing to the development of a revitalized profession of archaeology, which would emerge after 1960, included the multidisciplinary approach to research, settlement pattern studies, new techniques of determining age of materials, and focus on cultural processes.

Multidisciplinary Studies   In the 1950s the research designs of many archaeological projects were broadened by the inclusion of scholars from many disciplines, a trend that echoed Taylor's proposed conjunctive approach. For example, Robert Braidwood (1960), investigating the origins of agriculture in the Middle East, included as part of his research team not only archaeologists but specialists in such fields as ceramic analysis, botany, geology, and biology (Fig. 2.16).

Settlement Pattern Studies   Settlement pattern studies were an important development of the 1950s. Archaeologists recognized that the distribution of archaeological sites of all kinds, not just the most impressive ones, over the landscape was a powerful key to understanding how cultures operated as integrated **systems,** since adaptations of whole populations or societies to particular environments could be recognized and studied. Settlement pattern research is the method of recovering and recording site distributions in a particular region. Settlement distributions provide data for reconstructing the economic patterns, social and political structure, and population size, and how these change through time. Thus they help correct two deficiencies identified by Taylor: failure to reconstruct ancient lifeways and failure to investigate all segments of ancient cultures. Two of the earliest settlement pattern studies were carried out by Gordon Willey (1953) in the Virú Valley of Peru (Fig. 2.17) and the Belize Valley (Belize). Significantly, Willey's work was partly inspired by that of Steward, who advocated an ecological approach to the study of culture.

Chronometric Dating Techniques   Reconstructing prehistoric lifeways and cultural sequences is impossible unless temporal contexts of sites, artifacts, and features are known. Before World War II relative dating, for

conjunctive approach
The integrated use of evidence from archaeology, ethnohistory, and ethnography to solve problems of reconstruction and interpretation.

system   Group of interrelated and interdependent parts forming a whole.

FIGURE 2.16 Jarmo (Iraq) was one of the earliest farming villages known, dating to the sixth millennium B.C. Excavations there were notable for their interdisciplinary approach. Scientists from many fields, including archaeology, worked to reconstruct subsistence practices. The top photo (a) shows Robert Braidwood surveying with a transit. The bottom photo (b) shows the site being excavated. Note that the excavation trenches are set out on a rectilinear grid.

(a)

(b)

example, based on stratigraphy, was fairly well developed, but chronometric techniques for measuring elapsed absolute time were very few. A spin-off of the nuclear research of the war was *radiocarbon* (carbon-14) *dating*, developed by the physicist Willard Libby. This measured the age of organic materials (wood, charcoal, faunal material) by analyzing ratios of carbon isotopes in the material. Application of this technique immediately re-solved many important issues, for example, the vigorous and sometimes bitter debate among Mesoamerican archaeologists about whether Olmec culture was more ancient than Maya culture. Radiocarbon dates proved that Olmec culture was older, and as a consequence, archaeologists were able to reconstruct the relationships between the two cultures much more accurately. The success of radiocarbon dating stimulated the development of other techniques with chronometric applications. There is probably no other single set of innovations that has so fundamentally changed our perspective on the past.

Investigation of Cultural Processes   During the 1950s archaeologists increasingly identified important issues of broad cultural process and de-signed research to investigate them. These processes included the origins of food production, the emergence of civilization, and the appearance of the first cities in both the Old and New worlds. Archaeologists began to test general models developed by scholars in other fields. For example, the historian Karl Wittfogel (1957) set forth the theory that certain types of ancient states evolved particular despotic political institutions because of the importance of administering their irrigation systems, a suggestion that stimulated much archaeological research.

By the end of the 1950s, archaeology was much more rigorous and better integrated into anthropology than before. It was on the threshold of the most dynamic phase of its history as a scholarly field.

FIGURE 2.17   Gordon Willey during his survey of the Virú Valley, Peru.

Revolution and Maturation: 1960 to the Present

The trends of the early postwar period matured into what is commonly recognized as a revolution in American archaeology. Beginning in the 1960s, Lewis Binford and others convincingly reasserted that "archaeology is anthropology or it is nothing." Culture, increasingly defined in behav-ioral rather than mental terms, was seen as the primary adaptive system of humans as social beings. The "New Archaeology" proposed explicitly sci-entific procedures for archaeological research (Flannery 1973a), in partic-ular, the use of dynamic behavioral models drawn from observations of the present to help interpret the static remains of the past. Reconstruction of prehistoric behavior and institutions became a central goal, along with explanation of cultural process.

One result of this revolution was the application of some recently in-novated methods on a much larger scale than before. For example, settle-ment pattern research became much more frequently used and very ambitious in scope. Some projects developed into multiyear efforts to reconstruct the dynamics of settlement over thousands of years in very large regions. As we shall see later, two of the most important projects of this kind involved regions where two of the earliest civilizations appeared—the Basin of Mexico (Sanders, Parsons, and Santley 1979) and Lower Mesopotamia (Adams 1981). Such projects examined evolutionary processes on a grand scale and allowed powerful comparisons of the similarities and differences in evolutionary sequences.

Archaeologists began to look for new kinds of information in artifact patterns. For example potsherds, previously used for the most part to create typologies, were employed to investigate social organization (Deetz 1965; Hill 1968; Longacre 1964). The emphasis on scientific procedures promoted the use of statistical manipulation of data. Archaeologists increasingly incorporated ideas drawn from other sciences, such as biological ecology (Odum 1971), human geography, and human biology. Projects were designed to find out how the archaeological record had been formed and how it had been affected by natural and cultural forces (Schiffer 1972; Rathje 1974). One way to do this was through ethnoarchaeology, the study of living people to see how behavior directly affects the site formation process (Gould 1980; Schiffer 1987; Yellen 1977). Ethnoarchaeology also provided models for the functions of artifacts, facilities, and features (Box 2.2). The concepts of systems theory gave archaeologists new ways of thinking about change and stability in cultural systems (Flannery 1968a, 1972). In addition to the general emphasis on explanation and theory building, certain specific theoretical perspectives matured after 1960.

Cultural Evolution   As we have seen, cultural evolution was a major theme of early anthropology but was heavily criticized during the first half of the 20th century by all but a few scholars because the schemes of the early evolutionists were usually overly general, based on armchair theorizing, and lacking in sufficient ethnographic or archaeological support. Absent as well were any hypothesized generating mechanisms of cultural evolution, agents of change that would have caused evolution to occur. When, inevitably, ethnographers and archaeologists produced information that contradicted these schemes, an unfortunate reaction took place—the whole concept of cultural evolution was abandoned, not just specific flawed models of it.

Resurgence of interest in cultural evolution was largely due to the work of cultural anthropologists and ethnographers. Steward's early work on multilinear evolution became especially influential after 1960. Steward did not reject the goal of finding general trends or similarities in cultural evolution, but advocated a very different method from that of the 19th-century evolutionists. He felt that generalization could only take place after specific sequences of cultural evolution had been documented and then rigorously compared. For example, if one understood the specific evolutionary careers of several major civilizations, such as Egypt, China, the

BOX 2.2

ETHNOARCHAEOLOGY OF THE NUNAMIUT ESKIMOS

Ethnoarchaeology can help us to understand better the relationships among culture, behavior, and the archaeological record. While working with assemblages of animal bones from European sites of very ancient Paleolithic hunter-gatherers, Lewis Binford noticed that considerable variation marked the assemblages, especially in terms of which parts of the animals were included. Assuming that disturbance of the archaeological record can be ruled out, assemblages record ancient human behavior. But why did the collections of bones vary so much from one to another?

Two main alternate hypotheses presented themselves. One was that the variations reflected meaningful cultural differences, that people of different cultures with differing ways of killing and processing animals were responsible for different assemblages. The other hypothesis was that the assemblages were produced by people sharing the same culture but that people behaved very flexibly, adapting situationally to a wide variety of particular circumstances, such as the size and composition of the work groups, the season of the year, and the distances that hunters and other workers must travel. Each assemblage may thus have highly unique characteristics.

To test these ideas, Binford (1978) and his colleagues studied a small community of modern Nunamiut Eskimo in the arctic environment of northern Alaska. Nunamiut Eskimos still heavily depend on hunted food and consequently produce bone assemblages somewhat like those found in the archaeological record. They also share the same basic culture.

All aspects of Nunamiut animal use were recorded: what animals were hunted, and how; the butchering and transporting of the kills; the processing and use of meat, hides, and other animal parts; and discard patterns of the by-products of all of these activities, particularly the discard of bones. Observations made over the course of the year captured seasonal variations in these activities.

Binford found that even though the Nunamiut shared the same basic culture and did the same general kinds of things, they produced bone assemblages showing great variation. These data support the second hypothesis cited above.

The basic lesson here is that individuals and groups behave very flexibly, depending on a variety of immediate everyday circumstances, and not according to some preprogrammed set of cultural rules to which they must invariably conform. Much of the variation in the archaeological record is produced by the wide range of human behavioral patterns. This makes ascribing meaning to the archaeological record much more difficult than was previously thought. But a profoundly important lesson was learned by designing and carrying out appropriate ethnoarchaeological research. It did not matter that the Nunamiut were not doing exactly the same things as Paleolithic hunters. The present proved to be a rich guide for understanding the past.

Near East, Peru, and Mesoamerica, perhaps valid generalizations about evolutionary process could be derived from comparison of them. This perspective spurred Steward's interest in archaeological research.

During the 1960s, ethnographers using methods similar to Steward's developed typologies to categorize all known human societies, and these typologies also had evolutionary significance (Fried 1967; Service 1971). A

modes of sociopolitical integration Distinctive, recurring sets of political, social, economic, and religious behaviors and institutions that define societies in general adaptive or evolutionary terms (e.g., tribes, chiefdoms, states).

typology devised by Elman Service established four societal types based on degree of complexity of social organization: bands, tribes, chiefdoms, and states (see Chapter 5 for an extended discussion). Morton Fried later produced a more overtly evolutionary model of political types, based on three different modes of economic and political organization: egalitarian, ranked, and stratified (see discussion in Chapter 10). As we will discuss in Chapter 5, these two typological schemes have been synthesized into one workable model of **modes of sociopolitical integration,** which has been widely used (and occasionally refined) since then. Significantly, both Service's and Fried's typologies were based on firm ethnographic observations and emphasized organizational and institutional elements of culture, rather than technology or its more qualitative elements, such as religion. These and similar models provided testable hypotheses and ways of interpreting existing archaeological data and thus stimulated new interest in evolution among archaeologists.

Cultural Ecology Although Steward began to develop his concept of cultural ecology in the 1930s, its major impact came in the 1960s and later, when the idea that cultural behavior basically functioned to adapt human populations to their environments became a central assumption of the "New Archaeology." The adaptive significance of culture, studied through cultural-ecological relations, provides a motivating mechanism for the changes cultures undergo as they evolve. According to the theory of cultural ecology, the most important elements of culture with regard to evolution are those that provide the greatest interface with the environment; these may be technological, organizational, or ideological and are collectively called the "culture core." Although change may be caused by the interaction of any of these elements with the environment, it is most likely to be caused by the dynamic interaction between the technological/economic subsystems of culture and the environment. Such changes then affect patterns of social organization and ideology.

cultural materialism Approach which seeks to understand the structure and evolution of cultures through scientific investigation of the material conditions of life and which emphasizes culture as basically adaptive in function.

Cultural Materialism Building on the ideas of Steward and others, **cultural materialism** emerged in the 1960s as a synthesis of evolutionary, ecological, and scientific studies of culture. It is a broader approach than that of other evolutionary theories. Humans are seen as biological organisms sharing many basic needs and responding to stresses such as hunger in broadly similar ways. Culture is the principal means of adaptation, a strong distinction being made between the mental components of culture and actual human behavior. Cultural materialism seeks to understand the structure and evolution of cultures through scientific investigation of the material conditions of life. It uses the comparative, scientific approach to analyze how cultures function and how they change. Quantification is stressed, as is the use of universally applicable measures such as how much food energy a region can produce, compared with the caloric needs of its population (cf. Chapter 6) in the effort to formulate and validate theories of how cultures function and evolve. Cultural materialism is particularly identified with the work of Marvin Harris (1968, 1979), but as a general paradigm it has been broadly adopted by many archaeologists who may not share all of Harris's views. In this larger sense cultural materialism has been the dominant research strategy of anthropological archaeology since the 1960s.

The various trends in theoretical model building are essential to archaeology as it is practiced today. Scholars continue to argue about and refine elements of the modes of sociocultural integration and ways of measuring them, but the concepts have been internalized by the profession and provide a common parlance for theorizing about and observing cultures of the past and present. The term "New Archaeology" is seldom heard now, because the successful revolution in thinking that brought anthropological, explicitly scientific archaeology into maturity in the United States happened several decades ago and established professional practices that archaeologists now take for granted (Redman 1991).

Cultural Resource Management Further development of professional archaeology came in the 1970s, when legislation designed to monitor the effects of land development provided funding for archaeological research in areas slated for construction. Projects such as highways, dams, and buildings were required to assess the environmental impact of development, including locating and describing (and sometimes preserving) archaeological sites. Heightened sensitivity to destruction of sites in the course of development, backed by legal protection, led to the formation of a new and important branch of the profession: **cultural resource management** (CRM), also known as "contract archaeology" (McGimsey 1972, 1973). CRM has developed a strong corporate presence devoted to these projects, which complements the already existing professional base in academic departments. CRM work also provides experience and salaries for student archaeologists.

cultural resource management (CRM) The managing of the archaeological record through salvage operations and protective legislation.

Structuralism Another important trend in the 1970s was a new focus on mentalism—on how the participants in a culture perceive it—rather than on actions that create the archaeological record. For many years, a dominant school of cultural anthropology in Europe has been **structuralism,** whose most famous proponent is the French anthropologist Claude Levi-Strauss (1963). Structural anthropologists study such aspects of culture as kinship rules, myths, symbolism, rituals, and religion, in order to discover the basic mental structures that they believe all humans share. Structuralists assume that much of the content of culture can only be understood by recognizing the constraints on variability that are built into the human brain. Structuralism shares with more scientific approaches the search for regularities that crosscut specific cultural boundaries, but lacks a systematic program of research to reveal and explain such regularities (Gellner 1982).

structuralism Viewpoint which assumes that much of the content of culture can only be understood by recognizing the constraints on variability that are built into the human brain.

mentalist approach   Any approach to archaeology (including postprocessualism) which stresses the importance of symbolism, ideology, and meaning.

Partly as a reaction to cultural materialism, structuralist anthropology and a focus on mentalism became popular in the 1980s in American ethnography and archaeology, with a general objective of determining the meaning of cultural phenomena and behaviors and assessing how the mental dimensions of culture (whether universal or not) affect how cultures function and change. This perspective is in many respects the reverse of Steward's, in the sense that it attributes primary importance to the ideological components of culture as powerful determinants of particular sequences of cultural change and singles them out as the most essential subjects of research. Consequently, many archaeologists who advocate **mentalist approaches** stress the unique aspects of the cultures they study rather than search for broad comparative similarities. Mentalism is especially strong today among European archaeologists, who, as we have seen, often lack an anthropological perspective. Explicit in this noncomparative point of view is that the meaning of cultural phenomena, archaeological or otherwise, can only be determined within the context of particular traditions of culture, not the wider relationships of cultural systems and their environmental settings.

Historical Archaeology   Although we usually think of archaeologists unearthing ancient artifacts of distant and exotic cultures, some work much closer to home. Historical archaeologists investigate material remains from comparatively recent cultural contexts that are historically well documented (South 1977). For example, Plimoth Plantation in Massachusetts and colonial Williamsburg in Virginia are historical sites in the United States that are familiar to many tourists, and archaeologists have played an important role in reconstructing each of them. Industrial archaeology is a related field; it investigates the transformations in material culture brought about by the industrial revolution, particularly in the 19th century. Both historical and industrial archaeology have emerged as strong subfields since the mid-1950s.

There are two reasons why archaeologists are interested in such places and periods. First, although we may know a great deal about the general historical events of recent times, we may know little about the everyday lives of ordinary people. Historical archaeology helps to fill in these gaps. Sometimes it also serves to verify historical accounts or even change them. For example, historical archaeologists have recently been excavating Little Bighorn battlefield in Montana to sort out conflicting accounts of what happened to General Custer and his cavalry in their conflict with Sioux and Cheyenne warriors there in 1876. A second major concern for historical archaeology is to preserve or reconstruct the material cultural heritage of people in many parts of the world.

processual archaeology   School of scientific archaeology that emphasizes concern with the broad processes of change revealed in the evolutionary record, as opposed, for example, to description or classification of material remains.

Postprocessual Archaeology   The scientific, materialist, ecological approach to archaeology that emerged in the 1960s is often called **processual archaeology**, reflecting its concern with the broad processes revealed in the cultural evolutionary record. In the early 1980s an alternative movement, which has come to be known as **postprocessual archaeology** (Hodder 1985), began to develop. Partly rooted in the mentalist concerns of structuralism, postprocessual archaeology is also part of a larger intellectual movement that questions the objectivity of any utterance (from poems to scientific reports) and analyzes the subjectivity of text rather than focusing on the objective information the text might convey. In fields such as literary criticism, for example, emphasis is on the mental state of the writer, as studied through **deconstructionism,** which assumes that essential meaning is based in subjective attitudes. Translated into archaeological terms, the movement stresses the futility of objective science because of the hidden agenda of political motives guiding (perhaps subconsciously) the scientist. The political motivations of ancient peoples and modern archaeologists who interpret them are the particular concern of **Marxist archaeologists,** who see reconstructions of cultural relations as expressions of class struggles (Friedman 1974). Postprocessual archaeologists stress the importance of symbolism, ideology, and meaning in their reconstructions of the past. Such mentalist approaches to both anthropology and archaeology are not new: Boas advocated studying culture as shared mental concepts, attitudes, and values. There has, in fact, been a lengthy tradition of mentalist archaeology. For example, since the late 19th century much research has been designed to unlock the meaning of the spectacular Upper Paleolithic cave art of Europe.

The common themes of postprocessualism stress dissatisfaction with processual archaeology rather than a coherent program of reform. In a recent review of postprocessualism, Patty Jo Watson (Watson and Fotiadis 1990) summarized its major criticisms.

1. In their search for patterns in the material record of the past, processual archaeologists have largely neglected the study of how the archaeological record is formed.

2. The philosophy and method of science have been oversimplified, misunderstood, and misapplied.

3. All important causes of cultural change have been simplistically assigned to overly deterministic and mechanical environmental/cultural interactions.

4. Processual archaeology dehumanizes the study of the past. It pays little or no attention to the meanings inherent in material culture. It ignores the ways in which human symbolic behavior affects the archaeological record and dismisses ideology as unimportant. It ignores the role of particular individuals in shaping history.

5. Processual archaeologists are biased by their own cultural and political experiences, and such bias renders much of their research useless.

Space does not permit a full discussion of these criticisms, but some general comments are warranted. First, many of these points can be addressed within the anthropological, scientific framework of processual archaeology, for example, developing more accurate models of how the

postprocessual archaeology School of archaeology that emerged in the 1980s, partly in reaction to processual archaeology. A commonly shared assumption of postprocessual archaeologists is that it is impossible to study and write objective accounts of past cultures because archaeologists are always consciously or unconsciously biased.

deconstructionism School of literary criticism asserting that the meaning of texts is revealed by identifying the hidden or unconscious biases affecting the authors. This viewpoint assumes that essential meaning is based on subjective attitudes.

Marxist archaeologists Archaeologists who interpret and reconstruct cultural relations as expressions of class struggles.

archaeological record forms and how best to use scientific procedures. Many who are interested in postprocessual ideas are simply bored with scientific and materialist research, which they regard as insufficiently concerned with human values, and they find the investigation of the mental components of culture more satisfying. Revisions being part of the normal cycle of science, postprocessualists' critiques have provoked reform and augmentation in processual archaeology rather than wholesale abandonment of its principles.

It remains to be seen whether postprocessualism heralds another revolution in archaeology, but the current debate is very different from that of the 1960s. At that time the main issue was the adoption of an overtly scientific, behavioral approach to archaeology for which a paradigm already existed. An alternative, widely accepted postprocessual or mentalist perspective and attendant program of research have yet to emerge.

Feminist Archaeology   One of the strengths of the postprocessual movement has been to identify sources of bias in the archaeological record and to argue for correction of these biases. For example, anthropological research of living and past cultures has stressed the role of men in societies, at times altogether ignoring the roles and contributions of women (Gero and Conkey 1991; Spector 1983). This problem of biased perspective is related in part to pervasive sexism in our culture as a whole, which shapes our values and attitudes as researchers as well as our values regarding appropriate gender roles as participants. The bias in research is also related to the underrepresentation of women that has marked the profession until very recently. While anthropology as a profession is by no means an exclusive male preserve, there has been in the past, and is still, a disproportionate number of male researchers, and men dominate the most influential (and highly paid) ranks of the profession. A recent study of grants awarded in archaeology revealed that women apply for and receive research funding at disproportionately low levels, given the number of women who hold Ph.D.s in the field (Kramer and Stark 1988). The reasons for this are complex. Sexism exists in this profession, as it does in the larger culture, but other factors contribute to the different career histories of men and women, and some take us directly to that most basic component of the sexual division of labor in any culture, that women bear children, meaning that the choices of women who want children as well as careers will necessarily be more constrained and require more careful planning and scheduling than those of most men (Hochschild 1989).

Because we live in a society in which women are discriminated against and yet women's rights have not been constitutionally guaranteed, it is difficult to predict whether the bias affecting research goals, career choices, and hiring practices, will diminish, much less disappear. The scientific method itself cannot be held accountable. However, the ideal of continual refinement, hence improvement, of scientific models is built into the cycle of science. As biases in research goals and interpretations of finds are identified, our reconstructions of lifeways and explanations of processes will improve, and our working environment may as well.

Archaeology and Native Americans: The Reburial Issue In the 1980s and 1990s some Native Americans began to protest the scientific study of skeletal remains from archaeological sites (Goldstein and Kintigh 1990). Certain groups, feeling that the remains of their ancestors deserved veneration, considered analysis of the skeletons and grave goods as desecration and insisted that all remains should be reburied. The issue is extremely complex. Research by ethnographers and archaeologists has been essential for the preservation and reconstruction of Native American lifeways, so anthropological research has served to safeguard parts of the Native American cultural tradition that otherwise would have been lost or never brought to light. Skeletal remains are among the richest sources of information about the past. They tell us about a population's age and sex structure, about group conflict and individual development, stature, diseases, and diet. Grave goods, the items buried with individuals, reveal social status differences and highlight those items most valued within a particular society. These earthly remains speak to the present and tell us things about life in the past that otherwise cannot be revealed. If these "voices" are stilled because research along these lines is no longer permitted, the loss of cultural heritage will deprive all of us. Recently, understandings have been struck between Native Americans and archaeologists, permitting study of remains, which will be reburied.

Into the Future

Archaeology has been a highly dynamic field since World War II and continues to be so, with debates over future directions such as that between mentalists and materialists. But one thing is certain: Our knowledge about past cultures—what went on in the past and why—is immeasurably more comprehensive and accurate than it was a generation ago. In this sense the enterprise of archaeology has come of age. Presumably Walter Taylor would be pleased.

POINTS TO REMEMBER:

- Science is a continuing cycle of refinement of theoretical models through experimentation and observation.

- Sciences change according to accepted models of reality; these "paradigm changes" may be used to understand the history of archaeology, with its paradigms of speculation (1400s to 1840s), description (1840s to ca. 1910), history (ca. 1910 to 1940s), and explanation (1940s to the present).

- Archaeology has its intellectual roots in antiquarianism, social philosophy, the earth sciences, and the life sciences.

- The descriptive period in American archaeology focused on documenting Native American cultures and developing trait lists to characterize them.

- In the historical period, descriptive studies continued, made more meaningful by a concern with the chronological order of archaeological cultures. Also at this time, cultural ecology was introduced.

- The explanatory period has seen the maturation of anthropological archaeology as a science, with the establishment of workable models explaining cultural processes, tested by active research programs exploring a wide range of issues in archaeology.

FOR FURTHER READING*

Bronowski's *Common Sense of Science* is a general introduction to what science is, while Kuhn's *Structure of Scientific Revolutions* describes how changes in scientific paradigms take place. Changes in the larger paradigm of anthropology are encyclopedically documented in Harris's *The Rise of Anthropological Theory*. Willey and Sabloff's *History of American Archaeology* and Trigger's *A History of Archaeological Thought* are basic sources for the history of archaeology in the United States. Bernal's *A History of Mexican Archaeology* reviews developments in Mesoamerica. For a marvelous sense of how the past was "investigated" prior to modern methods and ethics, read Fagan's *The Rape of the Nile*. Two landmark publications of New Archaeology are Binford's "Archaeology as Anthropology" (1962) and Flannery's "Archaeology with a Capital S" (1973). Levi-Strauss's *Structural Anthropology* is the basic source on a complex topic; Hodder's *Symbolic and Structural Archaeology* presents the archaeological perspective. South's *Method and Theory in Historical Archaeology* and Gero and Conkey's *Engendering Archaeology* provide valuable introductions to their respective subjects.

*Full citations appear in the bibliography.

PART TWO

DOING ARCHAEOLOGY

How do archaeologists learn about the past? Most people know a few answers to this question. Archaeologists dig in the ground, recover ancient artifacts, and analyze them in laboratories. The first two chapters of Part 2 of this book will show that archaeologists do these things and many others as well. Chapter 3 introduces you to a set of research projects that have been carried out since 1975 at the great Classic Maya center of Copán, in western Honduras, and shows how these projects were designed and what their goals are. Most important, we will review methods used to assemble a picture of what the Copán Maya were like more than a thousand years ago, describing how their society grew and declined. Copán research is discussed in later chapters as well to illustrate specific issues about reconstruction of ancient cultures.

Chapter 4 provides a general overview of the methods archaeologists use. All modern archaeologists begin their research with particular questions or problems in mind. They develop a plan called a "research design." Central to research design are the tools at the archaeologist's disposal—the methods and techniques used to find ancient things, to understand what they were and how they were made and used, and to order them in space and time. Essentially the research design is a plan of hypothesis testing, using hypotheses drawn from ideas or theories about past cultures.

Chapter 5 introduces the conceptual framework on which we have based this book. It explains what culture is, how cultures operate as systems, the relationships of cultures to their larger environments, and how and why cultures evolve. Cultural evolution is both similar to and different from biological evolution, and issues directly or indirectly related to cultural evolution lie at the heart of most archaeological research.

Human cultures affect and are shaped by their larger environmental settings. In Chapter 6 we investigate cultural adaptations to different kinds of settings. We examine the concept of energy, and how, through cultural means, humans extract energy from their environments. We also survey the major environmental zones of the world and their potential as human habitats as reflected in both the ethnographic and archaeological record.

CHAPTER THREE

LEARNING ABOUT THE PAST: THE CASE OF MAYA COPÁN

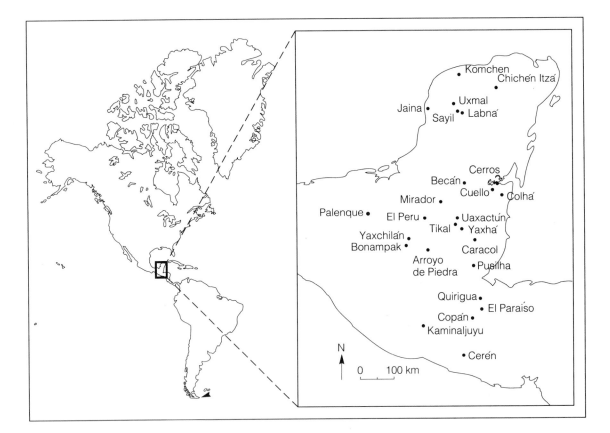

Recall the description given by John Lloyd Stephens at the beginning of this book about the mysterious ambience of the ruined city of Copán in Central America. Stephens further noted:

> In regard to the age of this desolate city I shall not at present offer any conjecture. . . . Nor . . . any in regard to the people who built it, or to the time when or the means by which it was depopulated, and became a desolation and ruin; whether it fell by the sword, or famine, or pestilence.
>
> *(Stephens 1969 [1839])*

As they stood in the forested ruins of Copán, Stephens and Catherwood were struck by one overwhelming question: What had happened to the people who had built these temples and monuments? Further exploration showed that Copán was not the only ancient abandoned city in Mesoamerica. All over this region explorers found a nearly deserted landscape, but one that clearly had once held thousands of people. A once-thriving civilization seemed to have collapsed, a mystery that has engrossed archaeologists since the profession began.

For the archaeologist, the growth and decline of Copán, and the larger Maya culture of which Copán was a part, are major research problems. From a scientific perspective, archaeological research is always carried out within a framework of testable theories and workable methods—we touched on some of these briefly during our survey of the history of archaeology in Chapter 2. Unfortunately, it is difficult to introduce, at the same time, actual research and the intellectual and methodological background to it, so at this point we must choose what to discuss first.

Leaving the general framework of methods and ideas until Chapters 4 and 5, here we will present an overview of archaeological research at Copán, a long-term venture involving interrelated projects and many scholars (Stuart 1989). We will refer to these projects throughout this book to illustrate how archaeologists design research to investigate particular aspects of culture. Many concepts and ideas that are briefly introduced here will be explained at greater length in later chapters.

COPÁN: THE BIOGRAPHY OF A RESEARCH PROJECT

Stephens and Catherwood's account of Copán in the mid-19th century eventually stimulated systematic, professional investigation of the site. Between 1881 and 1946, a series of expeditions at Copán focused attention on an impressive cluster of temples, palaces, monuments, and ballcourts known today as the **Main Group** (Figs. 3.1, 3.2). This early research spans the periods dominated by description and classification (see Chapter 2). Most work was devoted to recovering and deciphering monuments, uncovering and reconstructing large buildings, and developing ceramic sequences. A phase of intense archaeological research that began at Copán in 1975 continues to the present (Fash 1991). Copán thus presents us with

Main Group   At the Maya site of Copán (Honduras), the central core of monumental remains, including temples, palaces, and ballcourts, which served as the political, social, and economic center and the royal household during the Classic Period; it covers an area of approximately 0.15 km².

FIGURE 3.1 Reconstruction painting of the Main Group at Copán, by Tatiana Proskouriakoff. The area encompassed by the monumental architecture measures 0.15 km²; this view is toward the southeast.

a unique opportunity to study a long-term program of research that covers the complete history of American archaeology. Overtly scientific and aimed at a wide range of problems, research since 1975 has used many traditional methods and techniques as well as new ones unavailable to archaeologists even a generation ago. In the broadest sense, this research addresses a single evolutionary issue: how the population of the Copán region adapted to its tropical environment. This central issue encompasses a series of more specific questions:

1. How were the basic institutions of Copán society structured, and how did they change through time?

2. What was Copán society like during its period of greatest complexity, about A.D. 750–800?

FIGURE 3.2 (opposite) Plan of the Main Group at Copán (illustrated in Figure 3.1). This area was essentially the preserve of the royal dynasty and is a complex of temples, tombs, palaces, carved monuments, huge open courtyards, and ball courts. Although the architecture shown here was all built between A.D. 600 and 800, excavations in some buildings reveal construction sequences dating back to about A.D. 400.

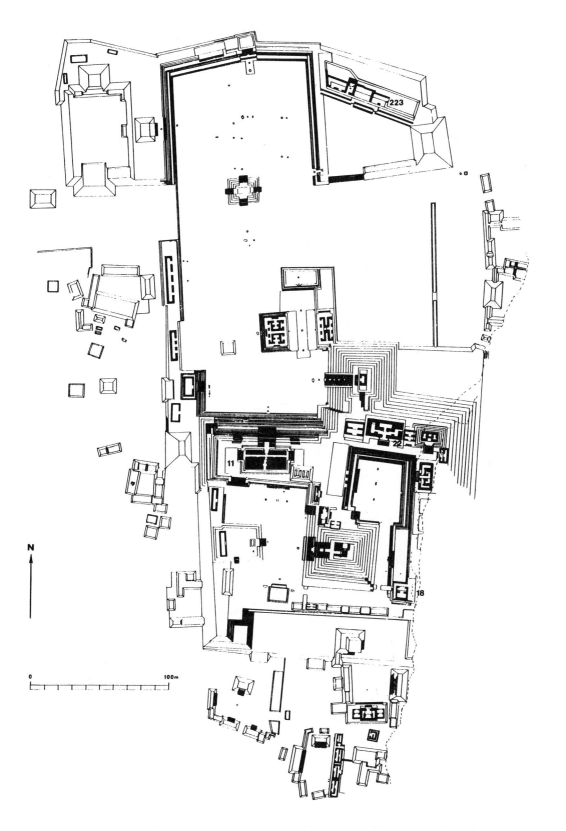

Table 3.1   Copán: History of Research

The history of research at Copán parallels the entire history of New World archaeology, as described in Chapter 2. The great burst of activity during the explanatory period in part reflects the appearance of generous institutional funding for archaeological projects in all parts of the world.

Speculative Period: Early Exploration of Copán

Diego Garcia de Palacio: 1576

Juan Galindo: 1834

John L. Stephens and Frederick Catherwood: 1839

Descriptive Period: The First Professional Archaeologists

Alfred P. Maudslay: 1881, 1885

Harvard University, Peabody Museum: 1891–1895

Historical Period

Carnegie Institution of Washington—Inscriptional studies by Sylvanus G. Morley: 1910–1919

Carnegie Institution of Washington—Excavation and restoration: 1935–1942, 1946.

Explanatory Period

Work sponsored by the Honduran Government: 1960–1975

Peabody Museum (Harvard University) Sustaining Area Project, directed by Gordon R. Willey and sponsored by the National Science Foundation: 1975–1977.

3. What was the pattern of specific events or processes through time at Copán (e.g., the sequence of its rulers or the stages of population growth)? In other words, what was the culture history of the region?

4. What happened to Copán and its vigorous culture, which left behind only the ruins that Stephens and Catherwood found so enthralling and mysterious?

5. Finally, can we usefully place what we know about Copán in a larger comparative perspective and produce generalizations about ancient cultures?

Because research began at Copán over a century ago, a great backlog of existing information has partly answered these questions. Since 1975, dozens of scholars from many universities and research centers have coopera-

Table 3.1   Continued

Explanatory Period (continued)

Copán Archaeological Project Phase I, directed by Claude F. Baudez and sponsored by the government of Honduras: 1977–1980.

Copán Archaeological Project Phase II, directed by William T. Sanders and David Webster and sponsored by the government of Honduras: 1980–1984.

Rural settlement Survey Project, directed by David Webster and William T. Sanders and sponsored by the National Science Foundation: 1983–1984.

Copán Rural Sites Project, directed by David Webster and sponsored by the National Science Foundation: 1985–1986.

Copán Pocket Test-Pitting Project, directed by David Webster and AnnCorinne Freter and sponsored by the National Science Foundation: 1988.

Copán Cosmological Project, directed by Wendy Ashmore: 1988–1989.

Excavations at Site 8N-11, directed by David Webster and sponsored by the Annenberg/CPB Project: 1990.

Copán Mosaics Project, Copán Hieroglyphic Stairway Project, Copán Acropolis Archaeological Project; directed by William Fash, with co-directors Barbara Fash, Ricardo Agurcia, Rudy Larios Villalta, Robert Sharer, and E. W. Andrews V; various sponsors, including the Honduran Government and the National Geographic Society: 1985–1991.

An essential characteristic of explanatory-period research at Copán has been the cooperation of many specialists, including not only archaeologists but epigraphers, iconographers, ceramists, photographers, artists, restorers, geologists, geographers, botanists, and geomorphologists. These are far too numerous to mention individually, but all have contributed to the data and interpretations in this book, as have the people of Copán, many of whom have had years of field experience and qualify as archaeologists in their own right.

---

ted to gather and interpret research data (see Table 3.1). Two of the authors of this book, Webster and Sanders have been part of this much larger research effort. The results, summarized below, are the product of work by many people, with funding from multiple sources. (In discussion of this work, "we" refers collectively to the numerous scholars who have advanced knowledge about Copán.)

Whenever archaeologists work outside their own countries, they do so only with the permission and support of the host country. The Honduran Institute of Anthropology and History (*Instituto Hondureño de Antropología e História*) oversees all archaeological work in Honduras; without its support, none of the work we describe here would have been possible. All artifacts recovered in Honduras remain the property of the Honduran government. Much of what has been excavated has been restored by the institute and may be seen in parks and museums under its administration. In addition, the institute maintains extensive collections of materials that scholars may study.

What We Knew in 1975

All problem-oriented archaeology begins with what is already known. The work undertaken at Copán provided a firm foundation of knowledge from which to start the new phase of research (Baudez 1983).

Maya Term referring to people who speak a set of related languages (Mayan) in southern Mesoamerica. It also refers to the general culture of Mayan speakers, especially those of the Classic and Postclassic periods of Mesoamerican culture history.

Classic period A.D. 300–900 in Mesoamerica, when Maya culture reached its highest level of sociopolitical complexity.

We knew that Copán was one of the major centers of **Maya** culture, which flourished during the **Classic Period** (A.D. 300–900) of Meso-american culture history. The Maya culture area and the location of its major centers are shown in the map at the beginning of the chapter. The Classic Maya and other Mesoamerican cultures will be discussed at greater length in other chapters, particularly Chapter 14. Here let us note that the Maya shared a distinct set of traits, such as social and political organization that featured ranking and perhaps stratification; a religion in which a wide range of deities and manifestations of natural phenomena (e.g., mountains, earthquakes, and rain) were revered; and the cultivation of maize (corn) and beans as staple crops. The Maya are known for their towering temples and multiroomed palaces; for their sophisticated art, expressed in sculpture, murals, and painted ceramic vessels; and for their intellectual achievements in astronomy, mathematics, writing, and chronology (Morley, Brainerd, and Sharer 1983.

Most of what we knew about Copán prior to 1975 concerned the Main Group, which covered an area of about 0.15 km². Long recognized as a major Maya royal center (Robicsek 1972), the Main Group is by far the largest aggregate of buildings in the Copán Valley, which has a length of about 30 km. We knew that there was no remotely comparable Maya center within about 70 km, so the Main Group was evidently the political capital for a region of several hundred square kilometers, the core of which was the fertile valley itself. Surveys had also shown that Copán was the southernmost large Maya center; thus it was located on a cultural frontier, hundreds of kilometers from the heartland of Maya civilization to the northwest.

We also knew that there had been people in the Copán region since about 1000 B.C. and were aware of a provisional sequence of changing ceramic types that had been established (Longyear 1952). Dated monuments indicated that recognizable Maya culture had appeared in the valley around A.D. 400 and that the Main Group had experienced rapid growth between 400 and 800, which had peaked at around 750–800. Finds of pottery and other artifacts imported from outside the Copán valley evidenced far-ranging economic and political contacts. Even though little systematic survey had been carried out, we knew that the landscape around the Main Group was covered with smaller sites. No royal monuments dated much later than 800, so we knew that some kind of crisis had overcome at least the leaders of Copán society. Since the valley was depopulated when Stephens and Catherwood visited it, clearly a general demographic decline had occurred as well. All this knowledge about Copán had been determined by the work of earlier archaeologists; without their efforts, the most recent phase of research could not have been planned and executed as effectively.

Research Design of Recent Projects

Yet previous research had not resulted in a broad understanding of Classic Copán society and its demise. This called for a new and different research program with a problem orientation derived from strong theoretical assumptions (such as those of cultural ecology); state-of-the-art methods to gather, organize, analyze, and interpret data; and scholars representing many diverse areas of expertise (Baudez 1983).

A basic proposition was that the *whole* of the Copán system had to be understood: the sociopolitical order from kings to commoners—for the entire Copán region (see Fig. 3.7) and for all time periods, but particularly the mature Late Classic polity. This is a **total system approach**. Another assumption shared by many (but not all) archaeologists working at Copán was that the best way to study the evolution of the whole Copán system was to use a cultural ecological perspective to interpret cultural patterns. Remember that this perspective emphasizes the interaction between human groups and their environments, in particular, the means by which humans exploit their landscapes to extract and use energy.

It is a basic postulate of science that a hypothesis is strongly substantiated when independent lines of research produce evidence supporting it; competing hypotheses may as a result be disregarded. Effective research design thus involves many different kinds of studies and must operate on a large enough scale so that the information collected is comprehensive and reliable. The high cost of such research is a practical limitation that affects scientific results and interpretations. Fortunately, archaeologists, epigraphers, art historians, and natural scientists have been able to work at Copán on a large and varied scale for many years. In the following section we review some components of this research, indicating the particular problem orientation, or *goal*, of each, *methods* used, and *results*.

total system approach
Research based on the assumption that in order to reconstruct an ancient culture, all parts of it must be examined.

ENVIRONMENTAL STUDIES

Goals The problem orientation of environmental studies was threefold: (1) to reconstruct the natural features of the Copán Valley environment as a setting for Maya culture; (2) to determine how the environment was used by the Maya, and (3) to detect how the Maya themselves transformed the environment through time.

Methods   For these goals, three different broad strategies were used. First, formal environmental surveys were made by specialists in geography, botany, geology, and geomorphology between 1977 and 1979 (Baudez 1983). Since many aspects of the modern landscape would have affected the ancient Maya, the results of these studies provided a background against which to assess settlement patterns and other archaeological information.

Second, an ethnographic study collected information on modern agricultural systems. Modern Honduran subsistence farmers grow many of the same crops as did the Maya, using very similar tools and subsistence strategies. Interviews with farmers provided important information about time spent in farming, crop yields under varying conditions of soil or rainfall, changing productivity of fields under intensification, and the potential of producing food surpluses in addition to the food needed by the farming family. This information gave us the necessary base for reconstructing the ancient Maya agricultural practices that provided food energy for the whole Copán polity.

Finally, survey and excavation recovered direct evidence for ancient environmental conditions, such as pollen and floral and faunal remains dating from the time of the Maya. Some of this information was routinely gathered during surface surveys (e.g., written comments on crops grown, slope of land, and soil type, in the areas being surveyed). Soil samples were taken from the same areas where surveys had located ancient sites. The object was to assess fertility, erodibility, and the potential for sustained cultivation.

Studies of floral and faunal remains help us to reconstruct diet, agricultural systems, and ancient environments. Much of what archaeologists recover is garbage: the remains of things used and discarded, accumulated around living places. Trash heaps, called **middens** by archaeologists, include utilitarian items made of inorganic material—potsherds or stone tools—as well as organic floral or faunal materials such as seeds, bone, shell, fish scales, or charred plant remains. Soil samples were routinely taken from middens at Copán, as well as from burials, house floors, and features of all kinds. Organic materials from these samples were analyzed to identify the species represented and their relative proportions (Fig. 3.3).

Results   This combination of environmental studies gave an excellent overview of the natural features of the modern valley, such as distributions of soil and bedrock types, vegetational communities, and drainage of streams and the river, features that would also have affected prehistoric Maya adaptation to the valley, particularly in terms of settlement location and land use.

Agricultural studies revealed that the productivity of maize in the Copán Valley varies greatly, with fields on the valley floor yielding two to three times as much as comparable areas on the hillsides. Clearly, the valley floor is the prime resource, both for subsistence and commercial crops. It is very stable in productivity, even if cropped annually, and this is particu-

midden   Trash heap at an archaeological site, accumulated during the occupation of the site.

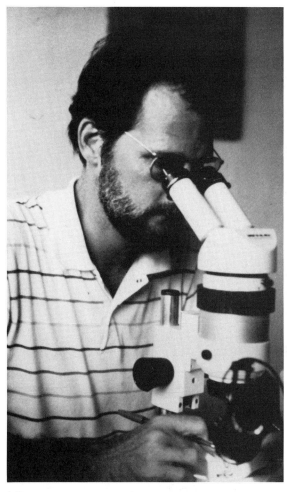

(a)

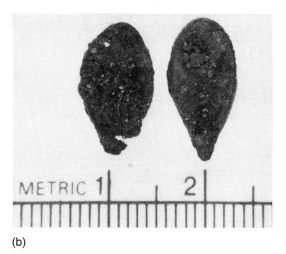

(b)

FIGURE 3.3 Below (b), seeds of the squash family (*Cucurbita moschata*), dating from Maya times, were among the floral materials recovered at Copán. Materials like these are identified visually and studied under a microscope, as David Lentz is using in the photo (a), at left.

larly true of the active floodplain. But the hillsides have thin soils and generally low soil fertility so that intensive cropping (with few or no seasons of rest from cultivation, called **fallow periods**) results in very rapid erosion and loss of soil fertility. We found that after a decade of intensive use, fields lose about three-quarters of their productive potential. Despite current overutilization of the landscape and declining yields, farmers almost never try to stop soil erosion by building terraces. Erosion must also have been a problem for the ancient Maya: Test excavations placed to detect hillside erosion in the past showed that in some locales, large Maya structures had been buried under two to three meters of soil eroded off nearby hillsides (see also Chapter 15).

   Palynology (pollen study) provides direct information about ancient environments, in particular through samples of organic materials that can

fallow period   The time allowed for a field to rest, when no crops are grown on it.

palynology   The study of ancient pollen with the objective of reconstructing the flora of a certain time period and the changes in flora through time. Such changes may reflect human activity or climatic change, for example.

(a)

(b)

PLATE III

20μm

FIGURE 3.4 Pollen grains (b) need even greater magnification to be visible than do remains such as seeds. They were taken from a soil core that was extracted from sediments of the Copán region by drilling with a hollow cylinder to extract a sample of sedimentary strata intact. In photo (a) David Rue is in the process of extracting the core.

be dated using radiocarbon analysis (see Chapter 4). Two pollen cores (samples of sediments containing ancient pollen, removed by drilling with a hollow tube) were taken from swamps at Copán (Fig. 3.4) to study the changes in pollen content in the soil, to determine whether plant communities have changed over time. Such changes reflect shifts in temperature or rainfall, as well as human-induced vegetational changes that occurred as the valley underwent heavy agricultural use.

The Copán Valley has a natural vegetation cover of tropical and pine forest. These plant communities produce a distinctive set of pollen "signatures." When forest is extensively cleared for crops, as it would have been when the Maya population expanded, new signatures appear, indicating fewer forest species and more pollen from domestic plants or from plants that invade disturbed forest environments. Sediments in the sample cores may also reveal such processes as erosion.

Only the shortest of the two pollen cores has been analyzed (generally the longer the core, the more time represented); its oldest pollen dates from about A.D. 900. Thus it does not record vegetational disturbances associated with the growth of Copán Maya society. Nonetheless, the core is very important because it reveals something unexpected about the period after the elite Maya collapse: Farming was practiced in the Copán Valley long after the last known date (probably A.D. 822) was inscribed on a

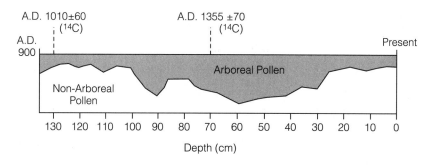

FIGURE 3.5 The changing ratios of non-arboreal to arboreal pollen in the Copán region from A.D. 900 to the present are shown in this simpli-fied pollen profile. The rel-atively high proportion of non-arboreal pollen early in this sequence is evi-dence of considerable dis-turbance of natural plant communities, consistent with agricultural activity. The proportions gradually shift to a preponderance of arboreal pollen, a pro-cess that begins at about A.D. 1200, long after the traditional date accepted for abandonment of the Copán Valley.

stelae (*sing.* **stela**) Standing monumental stone slabs, sometimes elaborately carved.

monument. According to the traditional reconstruction of the Maya col-lapse, when monuments such as **stelae** (*sing.* **stela**, standing monumental stones) commemorating events in the lives of the ruling elites, ceased to be erected, the Maya "mysteriously" disappeared. Rural farmers should have largely disappeared from the valley by 850, or at the latest by 900, and natural vegetation should have begun to reclaim the landscape. The core demonstrates that this process of natural reclamation did not begin until about 1200 (Fig. 3.5), indicating that until that time, there were still farmers in the valley.

Microscopic examination of floral and faunal remains from soil samples from the houses of elites and commoners support our expectations about the Maya diet. Meat was uncommon, and David Lentz has discovered that maize and beans (the two most important plants of Mesoamerica) were widely distributed, indicating their probable use as staple crops and allow-ing us to reconstruct the productivity of the prehistoric agricultural system.

Settlement System Studies

Goals The Main Group at Copán has not been a "lost city" since Stephens's time, but until recently little attention was paid to the countless small sites, mainly groups of mounds, that dot the landscape of the valley. By analogy with what was known about other Maya regions, such sites were assumed to be primarily residences of people of low rank, such as farmers — the bulk of the population of the Copán region. To understand the "total system," all visible sites of whatever kind had to be located and mapped.

Methods Settlement surveys were designed to do this. Wherever possible, collections of artifacts were picked up from the surface (Webster 1985; Webster and Freter 1990b). Distributions of sites of different kinds pro-vided a general overview of Copán region settlement. Such distributions provided preliminary information on density of population, on the parts of the landscape that were most heavily used, and on settlement trends through time. For the first time, considerable information on the lives of

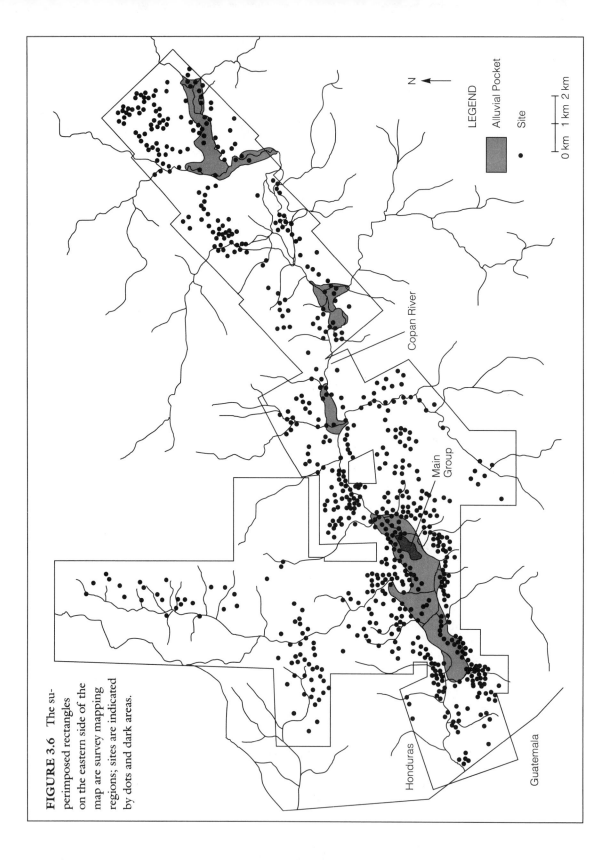

FIGURE 3.6 The superimposed rectangles on the eastern side of the map are survey mapping regions; sites are indicated by dots and dark areas.

N

LEGEND

Alluvial Pocket

Site

0 km 1 km 2 km

Copan River

Main Group

Honduras

Guatemala

common people was gathered, Maya research having traditionally focused on kings and lords.

In the Copán region, settlement surveys were conducted by teams of archaeologists, who walked over as much of the landscape as possible, locating and mapping each recognizable trace of ancient activity (Fig. 3.6). Until 1975, the structures of the Main Group had received almost all archaeological attention. In that year the first concerted effort to widen this focus on the settlement began, directed by Gordon Willey (Willey, Leventhal, and Fash 1978). Willey hypothesized that most of these sites were residences and that differences in scale and complexity among them were caused by differences in the social rank of their inhabitants. A typology of sites was devised, based on the number, size, and arrangement of grouped structures, the quality of construction, and the presence of sculpture (Fig. 3.7). Lowest on the scale were small single-mound and Type 1 (simple mound groups) sites, presumably the habitations of the lowest-ranking Maya. At the other end of the scale, large, impressive Type 4 sites, comprising many adjacent mounds, were hypothetically identified as the residences of the highest nonroyal Maya lords, members of Copán's elite. Types 2 and 3 fell in between.

Willey's project mapped the remains of hundreds of buildings in the dense residential zone called "Las Sepulturas" flanking the Main Group on the northeast, as well as many rural sites in the eastern end of the **Copán pocket** (the region of about 24 km² immediately surrounding the Main Group). Later, a project directed by Claude Baudez (1983) enlarged these surveys to include the "El Bosque" residential zone to the west of the Main Group and the rest of the Copán pocket (Fig. 3.8).

Between 1980 and 1983, William Sanders and David Webster directed surveys of about 110 km² of the landscape outside the Copán pocket, seeking to locate rural sites. These surveys extended up the drainage of the main Copán river and its major tributaries. Other information was gathered in the course of the surveys: topographic situations of sites, soil types, and modern land use around each site.

Information was also gathered about the region's present rural settlement pattern. Rural people live in houses (or groups of houses) built and arranged in much the same way as ancient houses; often modern residences are in exactly the same place as ancient sites. Copán houses today, like their prehistoric counterparts, are usually built on stone platforms. Although the houses themselves are perishable, the platforms are very durable, resembling stone platforms associated with archaeological sites. The ways activities are patterned in and around modern houses also provided clues about prehistoric behavior. In addition, data were assembled on the uses of structures, the numbers of people who live in them, and their relationships (Fig. 3.9).

Results These surveys and related work took about six field seasons to complete. Altogether 1,425 archaeological sites with 4,507 associated

Copán pocket In the Copán Valley (Honduras), a region of about 24 km² immediately surrounding the Main Group; contains dense alluvial soils that are excellent for agriculture.

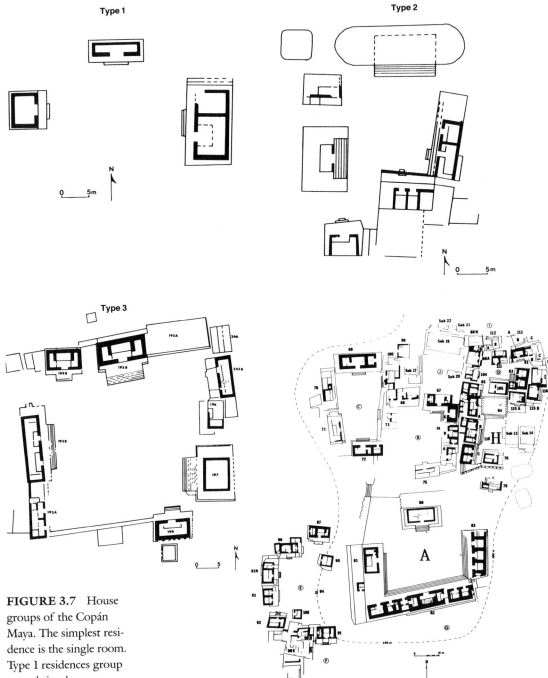

FIGURE 3.7 House groups of the Copán Maya. The simplest residence is the single room. Type 1 residences group several simple rooms around a plaza, a plan that becomes increasingly elaborate in Types 2, 3, and 4.

FIGURE 3.8 This map shows an area of 4 km² centered on the Main Group. "Sepulturas" and "El Bosque" are residential areas that, together with the Main Group, form the urban core of Copán, an area of about 1 km², where 10,000 people lived in about A.D. 800. Over 1,000 structures have been mapped in this urban core. There were originally many more buildings, but some on the north have been buried by soil eroding from hillsides, and on the south and east the river has washed others away.

FIGURE 3.9 Modern rural house, Copán region. These structures, the use of the space around them, and the number and relationships of the household members all provide clues helping archaeologists to interpret the remains of ancient houses.

structures were located and mapped (including the Main Group, which counted as a single site, and about 35 associated structures therein). At Copán, "site" usually means a single, discernably isolated concentration of the material remains of houses, typically a set of low rubble mounds. While it is clear that many sites have been destroyed or remain undetected, those recorded constitute an extremely large and reliable settlement sample. This sample provides preliminary information about how the Maya distributed themselves over the landscape, how they used resources, and how population changed through time.

About 80 percent of the land in the Copán Valley is very steep terrain with very poor soils. Brief surveys of this terrain show that it was largely unsettled. Most of the ancient sites were located in survey zones along the major streams and on or near the highest-quality agricultural land. Most of the modern population is distributed in the same way.

Settlement studies (Webster and Freter 1990a) reveal the heavy concentration of the population in the Copán pocket immediately around the Main Group; 64 percent of all known buildings fall within this 24 km² area. Even more striking is the concentration of large elite sites (those of Type 3 and 4 rank) in this area; 85 percent of all elite residence groups are in this zone. This distribution makes sense for two reasons. First, this zone is located in the best land in the whole valley. Also, for elites, an attraction lay in settling near the royal court, the center of sociopolitical decision making and the major ceremonial precincts where rites of the Maya religion took place.

An important step in analyzing settlement pattern is to establish chronology: arrange finds according to a sequence of stages in culture history. Information about time phases is gathered from a range of evidence collected during surveys and the test trenches dug concomitantly (see Test Excavations, below). Archaeologists on survey describe their finds so that the types of things useful in establishing chronology are identified. Potsherds are often used as phase markers. For example, in the Copán Valley a type of painted pottery called "Copador" does not appear widely until roughly A.D. 700, so sites bearing sherds of this type are assumed to have been occupied after that time. Chronological information about Copador and other ceramic types allows construction of a rough ceramic sequence (Fig. 3.10), which in turn can be used to date sites in a general way.

Even more valuable are absolute dates derived from radiocarbon analysis of organic samples and from hydration measurements on obsidian, or volcanic glass (see Chapter 4). With these dates, we can reconstruct the history of occupation of the Copán region, and estimate the population for the whole Copán polity at various points in time (Fig. 3.11). This method has been described by Freter and Webster (1990b) and by Webster, Sanders, and van Rossum (1992).

The population line on the graph peaks at about A.D. 750, then falls until abandonment of the region about 450 years later. The line, up to the peak, represents an impressive rate of growth. In A.D. 650, for example,

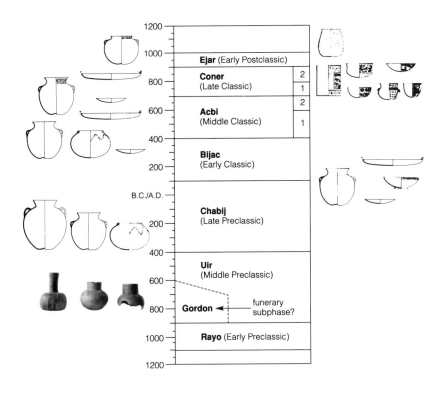

FIGURE 3.10 The Copán ceramic sequence. Each ceramic phase consists of distinctive mixes of ceramic types that can be identified and then used to establish approximate dates for associated materials. This sequence was constructed using data from stratigraphic excavations, comparisons with sequences from other regions, and associated radiocarbon and monument dates. The sequence is refined as new information becomes available; for example, obsidian hydration dates now indicate that the Coner Phase lasts until A.D. 1200.

the region's population was only about 8,000 people. By 800 it had shot up to about 27,500, doubling every 85 years. This rapid rate of increase suggests that not only were birth rates high but that people may have migrated into the valley.

We call the area of dense settlement that covers about one square kilometer around the Main Group the **urban core** of Copán. In A.D. 800, this zone had a population of about 10,000 people—currently the densest concentration of population known for any Classic Maya center. By 800 the Copán pocket had a population density of about 850 people per km²—extraordinarily high for a tropical environment.

Settlement patterns also tell us something about the structure of society. Of the 1,425 sites known from all phases, only about 47 sites (ca. 3 percent), all Types 3 and 4, are large or complex enough to have been occupied by elites. We estimate that about 25–30 percent of the population occupied these residential groups, most, as we already saw, near the Main Group. The other 70–75 percent resided in sites of Type 2 rank or lower.

Sometimes what is not found on survey is as revealing as what is found. Only in one small area did we come across any evidence for highly modified

urban core   At the Maya center of Copán (Honduras), an area of dense archaeological settlement, 1 km² in size, located around the Main Group; consists of the Main Group and the ancient residential neighborhoods known as Sepulturas and El Bosque.

FIGURE 3.11 The size of the population of the Copán region increased very rapidly between A.D. 600 and 750 and peaked between A.D. 750 and 800 at a size of about 27,500. This was the time of greatest political complexity in this region. This reconstruction of changes in population size is based on materials from surface survey, test-pitting, and large-scale excavations.

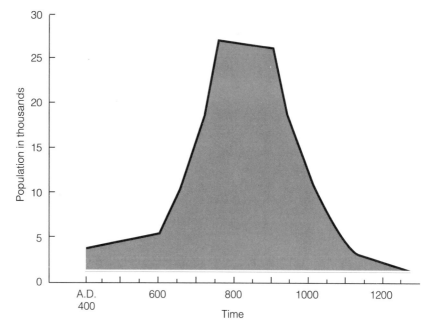

agricultural landscapes. This is important because many scholars believe that in some areas the Maya artificially transformed their landscapes to ensure high levels of productivity, for example by building terraces to halt erosion or creating drained fields in swamps; features indicating these practices have been found elsewhere in the Maya culture area. Interestingly, the modern population of the Copán region does not use terracing to any degree either, even though erosion is highly visible over much of the valley (Fig. 3.12). We also found no fortifications, which are common in some other parts of the Maya lowlands and which we expected we might find because of the warfare imagery in Copán art. While this absence cannot rule out the presence of warfare, it does suggest that it was not intensive at any time within the valley.

EXCAVATIONS

Digging is the activity many people immediately associate with archaeology. Though varied strategies of excavation are used by archaeologists, because excavation is expensive, they must try to make it as cost-effective as possible by selecting excavation targets that will be highly productive (in terms of information gained) as well as representative of the material culture repertoire as a whole. These are difficult courses to pursue simultaneously, and every choice of excavation targets involves practical compro-

FIGURE 3.12 This hillside was covered with tropical forest a few years ago. Intensive cultivation has caused erosion of the soil, leaving the bedrock exposed. This process can be observed today and serves as a model for similar processes in the past.

mises. Here we review four kinds of excavation projects undertaken in the Copán region: small test excavations at many sites over the region, large-scale excavations to uncover or probe whole buildings, excavation of burials (skeletons and associated grave goods), and studies of royal architecture.

Test Excavations

Goals Test excavations are small, cheap, probing operations that provide provisional information, in particular about the depth of deposits and the kinds of material remains present at a site. Usually used where many small samples are desirable or as preliminaries to larger excavations later on, test excavations have been used at Copán to determine whether the sites recorded by the surface survey were residences, as Willey had hypothesized. They would also recover potsherds or other artifacts that might help us order the sites in time. In dry environments with sparse vegetation, well-preserved artifacts may often be picked up off the surface without excavation, but this is usually not the case in the Copán Valley.

Method Small test trenches (most measuring 2 by 2 m) were a logical next step after the surface surveys were completed. Over the course of three field seasons, 700 test trenches were excavated, most in small rural sites outside the urban core. Testing typically consisted of excavating at least one trench adjacent to each mound at a chosen site, right down to bedrock in order to recover even the earliest materials. Of all known rural sites 17 percent (221) have been tested this way since 1981; this is an extremely large sample, chosen very carefully so that sites of all types in all parts of the valley are represented.

Results These excavations showed that most structures or plaza groups were residences, confirming Willey's hypothesis. Artifact collections from nearly all test excavations included a range of utilitarian household goods, such as potsherds from vessels for cooking, serving, and storing food and liquid, and stone tools for cutting and for processing food (especially maize). This repertoire of artifacts remained very similar no matter what level of affluence or social rank other site features (like architecture) indicated, suggesting that the largest groups had the same basic domestic functions as the smallest. On the basis of ceramics from test pits, it was evident that the vast majority of sites had been occupied after A.D. 650, confirming an earlier prediction made during surface surveys completed between 1975–1980.

"Negative evidence" was again revealing. Test pits showed very few obvious signs of specialized, nondomestic economic activities. Of the hundreds of sites excavated, only 13 exhibited any evidence of craft specialization (such as the manufacture of pottery, plaster, or grinding stones) beyond household needs. The only numerous artifacts imported from outside the valley were cutting tools made from obsidian. Recovered from test pits from virtually every site, this imported substance was thus widely available and provided the material for absolute dates for many locations in the valley.

Large-scale Excavations

The archaeological activity most familiar to the public is large-scale excavation. Such excavation may expose whole structures and many other kinds of features with behavioral significance. It also yields the largest possible samples of artifacts and features from well-understood contexts (Fig. 3.13). Besides the burst of excavation, consolidation, and reconstruction since 1975 at the Main Group at Copán, large-scale excavations have been carried out at sites of all sizes throughout the larger region as well (Baudez 1983; Fash 1991; Sanders 1986; Webster 1989; Webster and Gonlin 1988).

Goals Were the impressions about site functions and chronology gained from surface survey and test-pitting valid? Large-scale excavations would substantiate these impressions and also provide the artifacts, features, and patterns that could not be recovered on the basis of surface inspection or small excavations.

Method In all, 20 sites of all types have been completely or extensively excavated since 1975 (again, counting the Main Group as a single site).

FIGURE 3.13 A large-scale excavation at a rural site in the Copán region. When excavations extend over broad areas (this one covers several hundred square meters) they can provide information on many behavior contexts that were used at the same time.

The most complete excavations involved the horizontal stripping of 17 sites, ranging from the multiplaza compounds of Maya lords to the small house groups inhabited by Maya farmers. Approximately 165 structures, some as long as 50 m and some as small as 2 m long, are included in these sites.

By "horizontal stripping" we mean that areas ranging from a hundred to several thousand square meters are gridded and excavated, exposing not only buildings and other features, but also much of the peripheral space around them where the Maya carried out various activities. These buildings and spaces are then probed by deep trenches to recover information about older construction phases and such buried features as caches and burials.

Programs of large-scale excavation, carried out by several independent research teams, have so far required 15 field seasons (each four to six months of fieldwork), and researchers have had the good fortune to find the resources to work on this scale. But even with all the knowledge gained from large-scale excavation, 20 sites is a small sample of those known. It would have been disadvantageous to rely only on this kind of excavation, given our research goals to recover information about the whole system. This small sample would have provided a limited basis for generalizing findings to the whole Copán system.

Sampling is a crucial procedure in archaeology, because archaeologists always face the problem of validity: How do you know that what you have found is representative of all that once existed? How do you know that your sample is large enough to represent the whole? Logically, you don't — unless you can excavate everything, which is impossible, of course, and even undesirable because it precludes further excavation in the future. A reasonable solution to this difficulty is a mixed strategy, supplementing large excavations with test excavations. These two approaches reveal different dimensions of the archaeological record, and their combined results provide a more accurate reconstruction. If we consider all the different kinds of excavations carried out at the sites in the Copán region, then 17 percent of all known sites in the region have been tested by excavation. In most archaeological projects the percentage of sites sampled in this way is much lower; thus the Copán sample is relatively large and probably a reliable sample of the whole set of sites.

Results   Large-scale excavations have revealed architectural details for residence groups of all types, from palaces to rural houses. At the Main Group temples and other public buildings have been investigated as well (Fash and Fash 1990) (Fig. 3.14). Artifacts and other features, such as hearths and benches, demonstrate that groups of all sizes are primarily residences. The hypothesis of Willey's 1975 project that variation in size and quality of architecture in these groups was related to the status of the occupants has been strikingly confirmed (Table 3.2).

Elite residences are especially interesting in this regard. The largest of them, called Group 9N-8 (Fig. 3.15), is in the Sepulturas residential zone east of the Main Group. Group 9N-8 was probably the residential compound (a sort of palace) of a Maya lord ranking just below the king of Copán (Webster 1989). This lord's palace consisted of 50 buildings arranged around 12 adjacent patios. The lord's own personal patio and dwelling (Fig. 3.16) was the largest and most elaborate. The thronelike bench of the central room of his dwelling is richly sculpted with hieroglyphs displaying his name and title, and sculpture adorns the house's facade as well. His compound housed 200–300 people, including individuals of

FIGURE 3.14   The reconstructed community house, or "council house" on the Acropolis at Copán. Barbara and William Fash believe that the inscriptions and iconography on the building indicate that important political decisions were made here by major lords and the king of Copán.

Table 3.2   Excavation of Sites at Copán

	Nonmound	Single mound	Type 1	Type 2	Type 3	Type 4	Total
Total Sites Located*	148	445	643	136	30	19	1,421
Excavated							
test-pitting	28	48	114	23	8	5	226
large-scale	1	1	8	1	3	5	19
Total Excavated	29	49	122	24	11	10	245
% of Total Located	20%	11%	19%	18%	37%	53%	17%

*1,425 sites of all kinds were located. Here we disregard several special sites, such as quarries and the Main Group.

comparatively low status. Some inhabitants were artisans specializing in producing decorative items that served as status symbols for their lord (this is discussed further in Chapter 8). The first large Maya palace to be comprehensively excavated at Copán, Group 9N-8 has now been completely restored.

9N-8 and other similar sites were probably the establishments of sub-royal Maya lords who were heads of large kinship groups. The lords possessed their own substantial followings of kinsmen, loyal supporters who gave them political power independent of the royal lineage, thus making them potential competitors of Copán kings. Other recently excavated elite residential compounds are less complex, appearing to have had shorter occupations than 9N-8 (Sheehy 1991). Perhaps the elites who lived in them held power delegated by the king and thus did not weather the fall of the royal dynasty. The contrast between 9N-8 and other sites indicates that Copán society was not completely politically centralized and was less stratified than certain other ancient complex societies (see Chapter 10).

At the other end of the social and political scale were the rural farmers, whose house compounds proved to be very similar to modern examples. Ancient and modern houses were built on low stone platforms, and were made of perishable materials such as poles and thatch. Excavations have revealed the functions and sizes of buildings and their room layouts, information essential for reconstructing population size. Two of the rural sites that have been completely excavated were not permanent residences. One was a field hut where farmers temporarily lived during the agricultural season. The other was a place where great numbers of obsidian tools were used up in an as yet undetermined specialized economic activity, possibly the crafting of items out of wood.

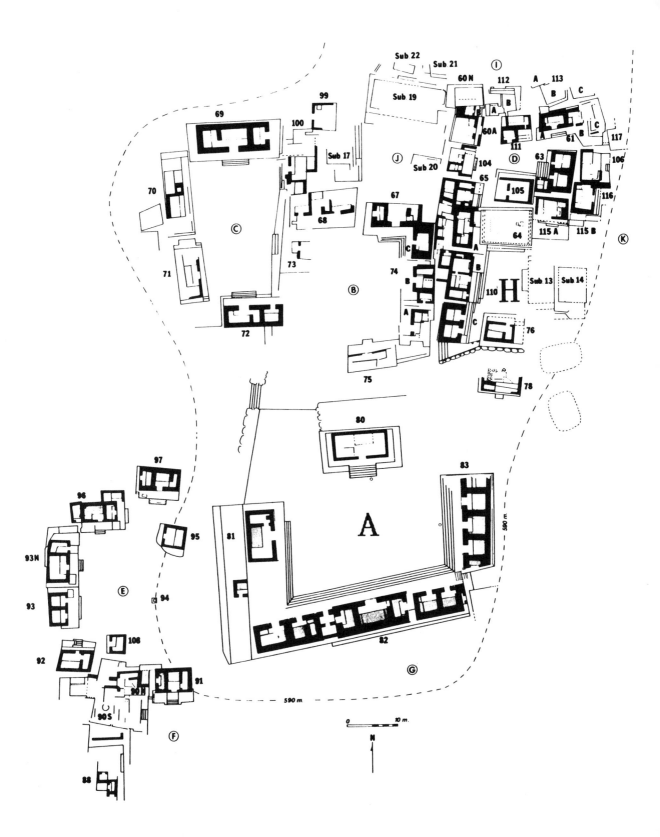

Artifacts and features have provided clues about variable functions of sites and buildings, for example, the rooms in 9N-8 that were used as workshops to produce jewelry and other ornaments from sea shells for use by elites (see Chapter 8). Full assemblages of ceramic vessels indicate the range of storage, cooking, processing, and serving functions common to residences (Hendon 1989). Ceramic collections are strikingly similar from sites on all status levels, indicating comparability in basic residential functions. This distribution also showed that decorated fine pottery was not an indicator of high status.

Burial Studies

Goals Burials are informative in three ways. First, ranking or stratification might be evidenced, since the method of disposing of the dead loosely reflects differences in status; for example, elite tombs may be differently placed, are more imposing and have more, and higher-quality, grave goods than those of commoners (Fig. 3.17). Second, burials can reveal the age and sex structure of a population for a given period of time (or through time), if enough skeletal remains are recovered, and this can tell us about rates of population growth or decline. Finally, the health and diet of the population can be assessed.

Methods Because burials are so informative, our test and large-scale excavations were designed to detect them. The remains of approximately 600 individuals have been recovered since 1975, primarily from in and around residences, but also from tombs in temples (Agurcia and Fash 1989). This is the largest sample for any Classic Maya polity. Most of these burials date to a time after A.D. 700, when the Copán polity was at its greatest extent, or when it was declining. Analysis by Rebecca Storey and Stephen Whittington has included determination of age and sex, physical health, diet,

FIGURE 3.15 (opposite) The largest nonroyal elite residential complex at Copán is Group 9N-8. This set of buildings and patios, which grew by accretion between about A.D. 700 and 950, overlies very early traces of occupation (dating back to ca. 900 B.C.). In about A.D. 800 this was the palace compound of a lord, who lived in the largest building in Patio A (lower right). The other buildings show great variation in quality, indicating a variety in status of people living in them. Besides houses, buildings include shrines, kitchens, a young men's house, and workshops used by artisans, for example, in Patio H.

FIGURE 3.16 This is the "House of the Bacabs," the central part of the largest building in Patio A of Group 9N-8, which was probably the residence of an important Maya lord. The building was constructed of fine-cut stone and was embellished on the outside by relief sculpture. Inside was a stone bench, its front panels decorated with Maya hieroglyphics.

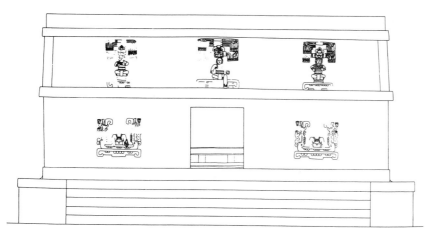

FIGURE 3.17 This individual was buried in the Type 4 group, 8N-11. The grave is simple, covered with rough stone slabs, and the burial was simple as well, lacking lavish grave goods. This indicates that in an elite residential complex like 8N-11 there were lower-ranking individuals as well.

and the social implications of burial mode (Storey 1992). Specific methods include the detailed examination of bones for physical signs of these features, using inferences drawn from modern human skeletons. Bone chemistry has also been studied to interpret diet.

Results   The Copán skeletal population lacks any significant number of injuries or mutilations associated with serious levels of warfare. But stresses of a different kind are clearly evidenced: The health and fertility of the Copán population deteriorated markedly between about A.D. 650 and 850. By the end of that period fertility was low and mortality high, especially for infants and children. Skeletons of elites and commoners alike show signs of recurrent and severe endemic diseases such as anemia, almost certainly related to poor nutrition. These signs include porosity of bone and patterns on teeth which document infections. Though all social ranks are affected, elites are better off than commoners. This is exactly what to expect from a population under severe stress in an environment with a rapidly deteriorating agricultural resource base.

The kind of carbon preserved in the structure of bone can shed light on certain aspects of diet, particularly whether people had high dependence on maize. Although studies of bone chemistry are not yet complete, David Reed has detected heavy reliance on maize by the Copán population (Fig. 3.18). This is consistent with the known importance of maize in the diets of modern Maya and with the recovery of maize fossils from many Copán sites. The hard data permit a more reliable assessment of the agricultural potential of the ancient landscape.

Burials vary in formality and in the elaboration of grave goods. Rich burials are rare; only a few (including one beneath a major temple) have

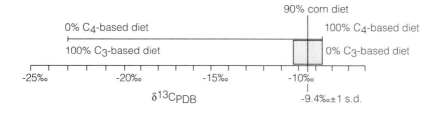

been recovered, which may reflect sampling bias rather than actual scarcity, since they are difficult to recover from deep within large structures. Most burials are fairly simple (Table 3.3). Of the small percentage composed of carefully prepared tombs of cut stone, even these have comparatively few grave goods. Most burials were placed beneath plazas or floors of residential sites, and many people were casually placed in construction fill or garbage middens. Many burials have no mortuary offerings at all. Apparently there was great flexibility in disposal of the dead among the Classic

FIGURE 3.18 The diet of ancient people can be directly studied by chemical analysis of human bone. Stable carbon isotope analysis reveals that the ancient Maya diet was perhaps as much as 90 percent maize.

Plants use three distinct photosynthetic processes, and each process results in a distinct stable isotope ratio, perceptible in the bone of the organism ingesting the plant. The top horizontal line in this graph shows the ratio resulting when the diet is maize-based. Maize uses the ^{4}C pathway; other staple plant foods in the ancient Maya diet did not. The grey area on the graph expresses the average values from 20 adults who lived in the Copán Valley between A.D. 700 and 1200 (the "Coner Phase").

Table 3.3   Comparison of Burials in Sites at Copán

	Most complex			Least complex		
	Dressed stone tomb	Rough stone tomb	Cist	Capstones	Cobbles	Pit
Type 4	4	14	15	10	20	121
Type 3	2	3	9	2	2	27
Type 1	0	0	0	0	2	13

SOURCE: Courtesy of Melissa Diamanti.

One measure of differences in status is the kinds of graves people are buried in. At Copán we commonly find grave types ranging from quite complex to very simple, considering both the skill and energy needed to construct the grave. Complex graves are far outnumbered by simple ones and are usually missing at low-rank sites. This can be seen by comparing the graves from elite Type 3 and 4 sites and lesser-ranked Type 1 sites, as shown above. Three different sites are used in this comparison, but many more have been excavated and tested. Notice that even in the elite sites there are many simple graves, indicating the burials of people of low status.

Dressed stone tomb = chamber constructed of well-cut stone; ceiling is vaulted or has heavy slab covering it.

Rough stone tomb = chamber with four clearly defined walls and possibly a floor, built of rough masonry.

Cist = two or more walls built of rough stone.

Capstones = simple pit covered with large slabs.

Cobbles = simple pit covered with river cobbles.

Pit = simple pit in the ground.

Copán Maya, and there was a gradation in burial types, rather than sharp distinctions signaling marked differences in social status. This gradation suggests a wide range of statuses and roles. Future statistical testing may reveal significant clusters of burial treatment that reflect subtle social variation among the Copán Maya.

Studies of Royal Architecture

Goals The entire Main Group at Copán is a massive architectural complex built under the patronage of the ruling dynasty over a period of at least 400 years. Studies of this architecture, together with the associated dates, inscriptions, and art, allow us to determine the functions of buildings, piece together the history of the royal dynasty, and reconstruct to some degree the institution of kingship (Fash 1991).

Methods Very sophisticated work in probing and reconstructing royal structures was done long before 1975, essentially to preserve them as aesthetic monuments. More recent research has been designed to understand the functions of buildings and determine the building sequences of the Main Group, through stratigraphic excavations in the plazas and by tunneling in buildings. By relating these sequences to dated monuments and inscriptions, archaeologists can identify the rulers who were politically powerful enough to engage in massive construction projects and can estimate the number of workers they could mobilize.

Results Elaborate royal structures have been found buried beneath more recent temples and plazas at Copán, showing that the tradition of royal architecture dates back to at least the time of Copán's third ruler (fifth century A.D.). It is clear that during some reigns, rulers could build on a large scale, and during others, building projects were few and shoddy. These phases of construction can be broadly correlated with important historical events, such as the violent death of the powerful 13th king, named 18 Jog, in A.D. 738 at the distant center of Quiriguá (Fig. 3.19). His successor, apparently politically weakened, was unable to build impressive monuments.

Continued archaeological research sometimes entails revision of previous reconstructions. As at other centers, royal architectural activity exhibits ebbs and flows that seem to reflect the varying political fortunes of particular rulers. For example, new studies of the stratigraphic relationships of buildings and associated monuments in the Main Group indicate that many buildings attributed to the 16th and last ruler, Yax Pac (reign A.D. 763–800), were actually built a generation or two earlier. If royal power is related to ability to marshal labor and build monumental structures and sculptures, then things might already have been going badly for the royal dynasty throughout Yax Pac's reign.

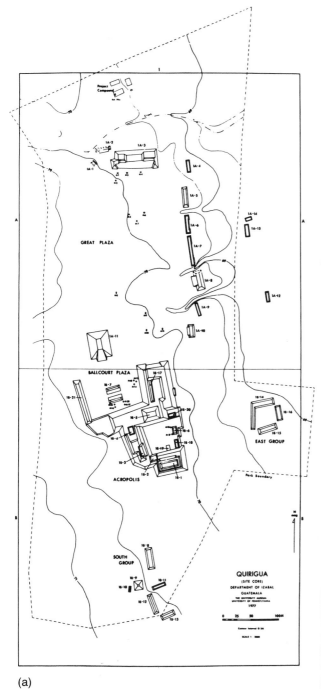

(a)

FIGURE 3.19 Quiriguá was the major Maya center closest to Copán. Note that the plan of Quiriguá (a) shows some remarkable similarities in layout to the plan of the Main Group at Copán. Archaeologist Wendy Ashmore has worked at both sites. In the photo (b) she is in a test trench at Quiriguá.

(b)

REPLICATION STUDIES: EXPERIMENTAL ARCHAEOLOGY

Experimental archaeology, or "action archaeology," is a research approach whereby the archaeologist tries to repeat an activity assumed to have been carried out in the past, and to learn things from the experiment that cannot be observed directly in the archaeological record. For example, if we want to measure the relative power of elites by the amount of construction labor they are able to command, how do we calculate the work required to build their palaces and sculpt their portraits? One method is to replicate the activity under controlled experimental conditions, and measure the labor involved (Abrams 1987, 1989).

Goals A basic goal was to measure, in quantitative terms, the ability of people of different statuses to summon labor for construction and monument carving. The striking difference in size and finishing between a royal building in the Main Group and the Type 3 or 4 residences of even the highest-ranking nonroyal nobility suggest well-developed stratification that separates members of the royal dynasty from other nobles. Was this difference perceptible when the actual labor required for construction projects was measured? Archaeologists also wanted to determine whether such projects required full-time artisans for this purpose, or part-time effort by farmers.

Methods Two kinds of experiments were conducted in 1981 at Copán. In one, workers were hired to quarry stone from the same quarries used by the ancient Maya and shape it into building blocks using both steel and stone tools. Workers also carved stones into some of the same design motifs found on ancient Maya monuments (Fig. 3.20). The amount of time required for these activities was carefully recorded.

The second experiment involved monitoring architectural reconstruction. Many of the buildings we excavated have been restored using human muscle and hand tools, in much the same way the ancient Maya built them. The time invested in modern reconstruction could thus be used as a model for ancient labor input. Both of these experiments provided quantifiable information on activities like those carried out by the ancient Maya.

Results Experiments with decorative stone carving showed that, contrary to some traditional views of Maya society, there were probably few professional full-time sculptors. An ornate royal stela, over 3 m tall, would have taken a master sculptor and two skilled helpers about six months to complete using stone tools. Experiments also revealed that sculpting skills could be quickly learned by workers with no previous experience.

Experiments to replicate construction labor provided important information that allowed comparisons between residences of people or groups

FIGURE 3.20 Experimental archaeology can clarify our understanding of ancient societies. One traditional view of the Maya hypothesized that sizeable groups of skilled artisans were needed to sculpt monuments and decorate buildings. Modern workers learned sculpting techniques quickly, and, even using stone tools, could duplicate motifs rapidly.

of different statuses. The last building episode of a royal structure in the Main Group, probably built by 18 Jog, required about 30,500 person-days to build (a person-day is one person working for six hours). By contrast, the central house of the subroyal elite person in Group 9N-8 required about 10,500 person-days. At the humble end of the status scale, the typical rural house of a farming family took only about 50–100 person-days to build (Fig. 3.21). Although lesser elites had sumptuous palaces far grander than houses of farmers, a fairly gradual continuum characterizes the residences between these two groups, suggesting that stratification below the royal level was not extreme (Abrams 1989).

The lesson here is that Copán buildings and other monuments, although visually very impressive, did not consume nearly as much skilled and unskilled labor as had been assumed before the experiments. This suggests that much of the Copán economic system was organized on a smaller and simpler basis than was previously thought, especially in terms of occupational specialization. It also indicates that earlier estimates of elite labor demands were too high.

CULTURE HISTORY: DATING, EPIGRAPHY, AND ICONOGRAPHY

To determine Copán's culture history, diverse methods were used. These included decipherment and interpretation of Maya glyphs and laboratory analyses to determine the age of materials.

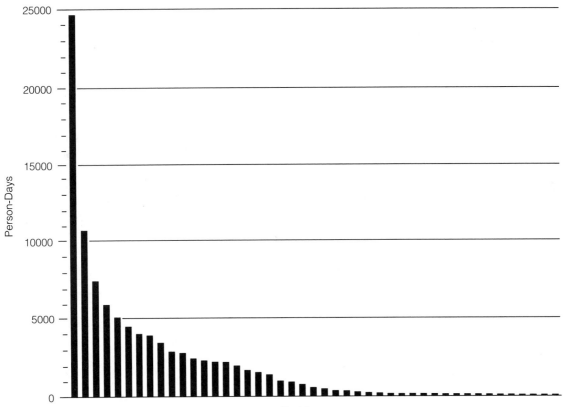

Person-Days

Residences

FIGURE 3.21   The effort that went into various buildings at Copán can be measured, which provides an excellent means of judging the amount of labor that any individual could mobilize. At the left is the effort required (measured in person-days of labor) to build a palace, and at the right, the effort for small rural houses.

Epigraphic Studies of Dates and Inscriptions

Goals   Recovery and decipherment of the records the Copán Maya left carved on monuments has been an important research objective since the 1880s (Morley 1920). Now that these records have been reasonably well-deciphered (Fig. 3.22), they provide a chronological sequence of monuments, rulers, and political events: a history (see Table 3.4). The inscriptions also provide direct information on political organization, functions of structures, and religious belief and ritual (Schele and Freidel 1990; Schele and Miller 1986).

Methods   Since 1975 many scholars, including professional epigraphers, have drawn together known ancient inscriptions, reassembled inscriptions from scattered fragments, and recovered new inscriptions. New inscriptions that could be securely dated were particularly important because they could be tied to the stratigraphic construction sequences of buildings and to the dynasties of Copán kings.

FIGURE 3.22 Decipherment of Copán monuments (a) has been the work of many scholars. Claude Baudez is shown here (b) in the Main Group, studying Stela 3.

(a)

(b)

Results Recent discoveries and interpretations of Copán Maya dates and inscriptions have firmly documented the known Copán dynastic sequence. The most dramatic reinterpretation involves Altar Q, featuring 16 seated figures. Several generations of archaeologists thought these represented a "congress of astronomers" (Fig. 3.23), since the Maya were famous for their astronomical skill. We now know (Marcus 1976) that this monument illustrates 16 rulers of Copán and that it was commissioned by the last of them, Yax Pac. He had his name and image portrayed on it as well as those of the previous 15 rulers. The political message is that Yax Pac is the legitimate heir of a long line of earlier kings. The carving asserts this lineage in a public and dramatic way. Newly discovered monuments refer to the first ruler in the early fifth century (who is also pictured as first in line on Altar Q). Only one later date (A.D. 822) on a monument has come to light; from this we believe that someone tried to assert royal authority but failed. The traditional notion that Yax Pac's royal dynasty collapsed at about A.D. 800 has not been changed.

Almost all dated and inscribed monuments at Maya centers depict royal

Table 3.4 Copán Dynastic History*

Ruler 1   K'inich Yax K'uk Mo'
Accession and death dates unknown, but inscriptions relating to this ruler fall between A.D. 426–435. K'inich Yax K'uk Mo' is presumably the founder of the Copán dynasty, and must have become king early in the 5th century.

Ruler 2   Name and dates of rule unknown.

Ruler 3   Mat Head
Accession and death dates unknown.

Ruler 4   Cu Ix
Accession and death dates unknown. Approximate dates of reign A.D. 485–495.

Ruler 5   Name and dates of rule unknown.

Ruler 6   Name and dates of rule unknown, but the fifth and sixth rulers probably span the period of approximately A.D. 495–500.

Ruler 7   Waterlily Jaguar
Dates of rule unknown, but inscriptions relating to this ruler have dates falling between A.D. 504–544.

Ruler 8   Name and dates of rule unknown.

Ruler 9   Name unknown; probably acceded to power in A.D. 551.

Ruler 10   Moon Jaguar
Accession A.D. 553, death A.D. 578.

Ruler 11   Butz' Chan
Birth A.D. 563, accession A.D. 578, death A.D. 628.

Ruler 12   Smoke Imix God K (Smoke Jaguar)
Accession A.D. 628, death A.D. 695.

Ruler 13   18 Jog (18 Rabbit)
Accession A.D. 695, death A.D. 738.

Ruler 14   Smoke Monkey
Accession A.D. 738, death A.D. 749.

Ruler 15   Smoke Shell
Accession A.D. 749, death date uncertain.

Ruler 16   Yax Pac (Rising Sun)
Accession A.D. 763, death A.D. 820.

Last pretender to throne — U Cit Tok'
Unfinished inscription A.D. 822.

*Information taken from Fash 1991 and Schele and Friedel 1991.

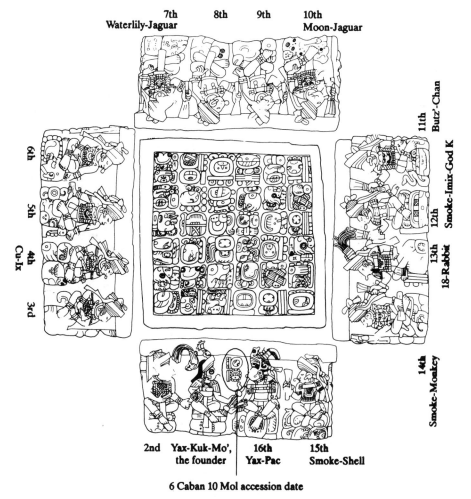

7th
Waterlily-Jaguar   **8th**   **9th**   **10th**
Moon-Jaguar

11th Butz'-Chan

12th Smoke-Imix-God K

13th 18-Rabbit

14th Smoke-Monkey

6th
5th
4th Cu-Ix
3rd

2nd   Yax-Kuk-Mo',
the founder   **16th**
Yax-Pac   **15th**
Smoke-Shell

6 Caban 10 Mol accession date

themes and personages. At Copán after about 750, other powerful sub-royal elites possessed their own inscribed monuments. This suggests that the political power was less centralized, or more segmented, than previously thought, since impressive inscriptions at Maya centers are usually restricted to royal contexts.

Studies of Maya Art and Iconography

Goals Maya dates and inscriptions are intimately related to Maya art. The conventions and symbols used in artistic embellishment of everything from small jade carvings and ceramic pots to stelae and entire buildings, often hold important meaning. These conventions and symbols can be conceived

FIGURE 3.23 Altar Q, located in the West Court of the Copán Acropolis, was commissioned by the 16th ruler, Yax Pac, and shows him accepting a sceptre from the long-dead first ruler, Yax Kuk Mo.

as texts, even though these express meaning more indirectly than do dates and inscriptions. Even when meaning eludes us, many status symbols can be identified and used to establish relationships between individuals and social groups.

Maya art strongly emphasizes elite perspectives and behavior. From a materialistic perspective, the primary reason for studying it is to reconstruct social and political institutions. Those interested in belief systems and the state of mind of the Maya try to reconstruct their world view and mental processes.

Methods Excavations since 1975, in particular, the work of the Copán Mosaic Project, have greatly enlarged the corpus of art available for research at Copán. The artistic compositions that once embellished the fronts of temples, palaces, and other elite buildings are being reassembled from scattered fragments. Old representations have been reexamined, and large-scale excavations have recovered new artistic compositions (Fig. 3.24). One set of excavations has deeply trenched major buildings to associate artistic themes and symbols with the sequence of constructions in the royal household. Another set has completely stripped the latest phases of subroyal elite groups to recover sculpture associated with buildings.

Results Manipulation of self-glorifying and legitimizing symbols is an important element of elite behavior. Work at Copán since 1975 has shown how individual rulers assumed new imagery in their attempts to express their authority. For example, Yax Pac used a distinctive set of military images portraying himself as a warrior; he also borrowed artistic motifs from the northern Maya lowlands. Many motifs have been identified that celebrate the ritual connections of Copán kings with the supernatural world, connections further augmenting their authority.

Perhaps the most interesting discovery is that subroyal elites enjoyed access to many of the same iconographic symbols used by royalty. Specific titles held by such elite individuals, and their relation to political authority, are beginning to be understood. Apparently the most recent kings of Copán had to share iconographic and epigraphic symbols with other nobles to an unusually high degree, suggesting that they were not extremely powerful rulers. The occurrence of these symbols on buildings at the largest residential compounds at Copán confirms the hypothesis that they were primarily residences for elites.

Non-historical Determinations of Chronology: Dating Techniques

Unfortunately, inscribed dates are very few, confined to elite contexts, and end shortly after A.D. 800, so they do not help sort out a wide range of chronological problems, and other dating methods must be used as well.

FIGURE 3.24 Archaeologist Will Andrews stands among piles of sculptural elements recovered from excavations in the Main Group. Note that many of the sculpted pieces have been tagged with their provenience numbers to aid in reconstructing whole designs.

We already saw that changes in ceramics through time can be used to make rough estimates of relative age. In addition, the absolute ages of some remains can be estimated by using various natural clocks, such as the rate of radiocarbon decay of organic materials; shifts in orientation of iron particles in the soil (investigated through **archaeomagnetism;** see Chapter 4); and the rate of absorption of ambient moisture into obsidian tools, measured by means of **obsidian hydration dating**.

Goals When, or how fast, did various events or activities or processes take place in the past? Chronology is important for understanding events of very short duration, such as the burial of an individual or the construction of a house, as well as for understanding much longer processes, such as changes in ceramics or population through time.

Methods Among the different dating strategies in use at Copán (apart from inscribed dates) are stratigraphy, archaeomagnetic readings, radiocarbon analysis, and obsidian hydration dating (dating methods are discussed in Chapter 4). A mixed strategy of dating methods helps to negate the errors associated with any particular one. Although many independent dating approaches are in use at Copán, by far the most important is that based on obsidian hydration. This laboratory technique involves the microscopic analysis of thin sections taken from obsidian tools, to measure the

archaeomagnetism A method of absolute dating that analyzes remnant patterns of magnetic orientations toward previous locations of magnetic north, which moves in an irregular path around the north pole.

obsidian hydration dating A dating technique that measures the depth of moisture absorbed by obsidian, that is, the hydration rim of the obsidian. Depending on whether the rate of hydration for a particular kind of obsidian has been established, the technique may establish relative or absolute dates.

FIGURE 3.25 Obsidian hydration dates from the entire Copán region have provided a new perspective on population and settlement history. Note that obsidian continues in active use long after Copán kings cease to rule, shortly after A.D. 800.

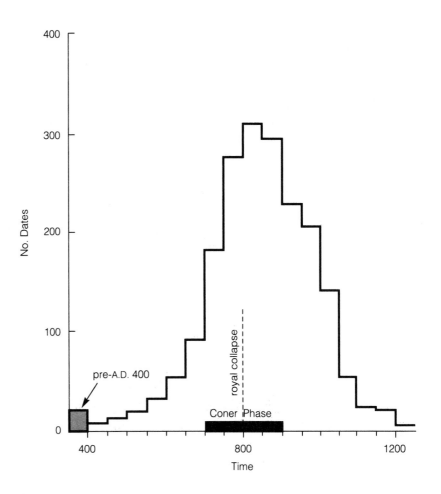

error factor The measurement error inherent in every chronometric dating technique, indicating the range of accuracy of the estimated date; usually expressed as plus or minus a certain number of years.

depth of absorbed moisture into obsidian. Once the absorption rate is known, obsidian tools from sites of all types in the Copán region can be dated with a fairly limited **error factor** of about ±70 years. Since 1984, 2,048 dates from every part of the region have been processed by AnnCorinne Freter (Webster and Freter 1990b). These dates relate not only to their immediate contexts (e.g., obsidian included with a burial provides its date) but, more importantly, to the periods of occupation of whole sites. One or more dates have now been derived from 240 sites, which can be chronologically arranged. This is a sample of almost 1 of every 7 sites known to be located in the valley (ca. 14 percent), providing the basis for a reasonable generalization from dated sites to those which remain undated.

Results The obsidian dates agree well with the established sequence of chronological phases for Classic Copán, particularly as reflected in carved dates on monuments. These dates also agree with relative dates derived from stratigraphy and with archaeomagnetic dates. But in one extremely significant way, obsidian dates have revolutionized our thinking about the collapse of Maya society. The royal crisis occurred in about A.D. 800; note that about half the obsidian tools date from a time after that point (Fig. 3.25) and are numerous even after 900. Dates continue to 1200–1250; those from some elite compounds indicate that these palaces continued to function, and even expand in size, long after the Copán kings were gone. The conclusion is obvious: However quickly the institution of kingship disappeared, other lords and much of the rural population persisted for hundreds of years longer. No catastrophic collapse occurred at Copán but rather a slow withering away of population and loss of political centralization over 400 years.

The population trends reconstructed from the combination of dates and settlement data (Webster, Sanders, and van Rossum 1992) show that Copán, unlike some other Maya centers, had only a single pulse of growth and decline. The enormous increase in population during A.D. 600–850 is mirrored by a more gradual decline until 1200 (see Fig. 3.11).

Dates reveal that larger sites tended to have longer occupations than smaller ones, as would be expected. Sites on hillsides with thin soils tend to be founded later than those on the valley floor, and to have shorter occupations—exactly what would be expected because of the variation in agricultural potential of the two zones. Similarly, sites far from the Main Group tend to be later than closer ones. The general picture is of early occupation of the valley floor of the Copán pocket, a later expansion into upland zones, and finally dispersal of occupation into the wider regional environment, especially as the core political system declined.

OVERVIEW

The research approaches taken at Copán are important for several reasons. First, they include many independent lines of evidence. Second, these lines of evidence may provide information on the same issue. For example, both burials and architectural studies can tell us about differences in social status. Third, these are long-term studies that have been carried out on a large scale, ensuring very reliable samples. Finally, specialists such as epigraphers, iconographers, geologists, and botanists have contributed their expertise. The lesson is that many varied approaches and a great deal of ingenuity are needed to make sense of the archaeological record. Even more important, scholars such as epigraphers and art historians may fruitfully cooperate with archaeologists and natural scientists even though they might not share the same theoretical perspectives. At Copán the conjunctive approach advocated by Taylor in his critique of American archaeology has worked extremely well.

Notice that to some degree there is a logical structure, or progression, to a complex research design. For example, surface survey precedes test-pitting (one must, after all, find something to test-pit), and decisions about where to do large-scale excavation can be better informed if test-pitting has been done. Constant feedback occurs among the various activities. Thus a basic ceramic chronology may be defined on the basis of a few test pits, then used during survey to assign dates to mapped sites, which provide materials to refine the ceramic chronology. Rarely do archaeologists have all the necessary information or resources to plan a complex research design in a highly structured manner. In particular, they must always be ready to adjust their research to the practicalities of field or laboratory, or to new insights or opportunities.

The structure of mature Copán society and its collapse are "big" research problems, requiring years of work and many methods. Other perfectly valid problems may be much less demanding of resources, such as determining what happened to refuse from houses being abandoned or what the functions are of a certain kind of ancient pottery. Here research design may be tighter and more limited in scope. But all research should proceed from a good grasp of the problem being addressed.

We presented the research design of recent projects at Copán to introduce you to some of the activities of archaeology. This has also given us the opportunity to summarize basic information that you will encounter again in later chapters, as we continue to use examples from research at Copán and other sites to illustrate the general conduct of anthropological archaeology and its reconstruction of particular institutions or behaviors in the past.

POINTS TO REMEMBER

- Research at Copán, which began with Stephens and Catherwood's accurate accounts and graphic renderings of the site and its monuments, has been carried out since the beginning of the descriptive period in archaeology.

- Copán's central cluster of monumental architecture, the Main Group, was the focus of excavations during the descriptive and historical periods.

- Since 1975 multidisciplinary research projects have conducted environmental studies, surveys of modern and ancient settlement systems, excavations of sites of all types, experiments in replicating ancient methods used in building and in the decorative arts, studies to determine absolute dates, and epigraphic and iconographic decipherment.

FOR FURTHER READING*

Agúrcia and Fash's "A Royal Maya Tomb Discovered," Fash and Fash's "Scribes, Warriors, and Kings," and George Stuart's "Copán: City of Kings and Commoners" are good introductions to the visual splendor of Copán. Morley, Brainerd, and Sharer's *The Ancient Maya* places Copán research in the larger perspective of archaeology of the Maya. Works produced in the course of recent research at Copán and in the Copán region include Willey, Leventhal, and Fash's "Maya Settlement in the Copán Valley"; Webster's *The House of the Bacabs*; Sanders's *Excavaciones en el area urbana de Copán*; Webster and Gonlin's "Household Remains of the Humblest Maya"; Webster and Freter's "The Demography of Late Classic Copán" and "Settlement History and the Classic Collapse at Copán"; Rue's "Early Agriculture and Early Postclassic Maya Occupation in Western Honduras"; Sheehy's "Structure and Change in a Late Classic Maya Domestic Group at Copán, Honduras"; Storey's "People of Copán"; and Freter's "Chronological Research at Copán."

*Full citations appear in the bibliography.

CHAPTER FOUR

ARCHAEOLOGICAL METHODS

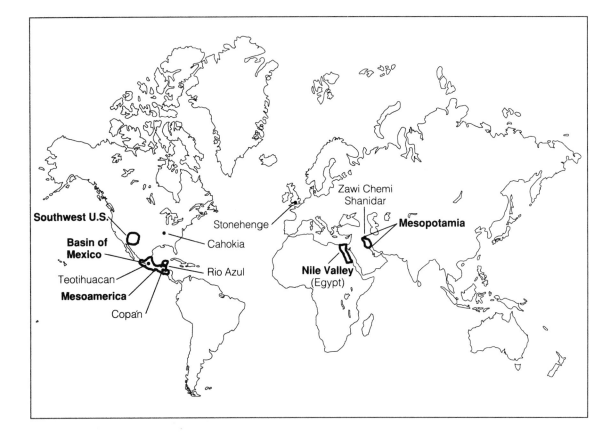

Southwest U.S.

Basin of
Mexico

Teotihuacan

Mesoamerica

Copán

Stonehenge

Cahokia

Rio Azul

Zawi Chemi
Shanidar

Mesopotamia

Nile Valley
(Egypt)

The research at Copán described in Chapter 3 is of exceptional scale, but archaeological projects of all sizes go through a similar general research process (Table 4.1). They also result from particular choices in research design—about how to gather information through fieldwork and materials analysis and how to interpret results—choices that correspond to stages in the scientific cycle (see Chapter 2.)

Theory testing begins with identifying a problem area, either in the theory itself or in the kind or amount of information substantiating it. The archaeologist must figure out not only what kinds of material remains and analysis of them will yield the necessary information but how to recover the remains. For example, theories about Maya society posit that the Maya rulers were powerful, but do not satisfy our curiosity about how the rulers compare with each other and with other royalty in general. We can measure their "power" by various means, hypothesizing that rulers could be ranked by the quality and amount of art produced during their reign, by the grandeur of architecture and size of the labor force they could command for construction projects, or by the extent of their territory. Research along all these lines took place in the Copán region.

The observational stage of the scientific cycle corresponds in the archaeological research process to fieldwork, materials analysis, and statistical analysis. The final phase, interpretation of data, brings the research project back to basic issues of cultural reconstruction and processes. The interpretive phase will be given little attention in this chapter, since interpretation is the focus of Chapter 5 and much of the rest of the book.

PHASE 1: RESEARCH DESIGN

Planning Fieldwork and Analyses

Phase 1 involves planning fieldwork and analyses that will provide necessary information needed to address a particular problem, given what is already known and the resources available for the project. **Research design** requires careful planning, because the tactics and tools available to archaeologists, though very numerous, are not all useful, suitable, or feasible in every circumstance (Binford 1964). **Problem orientation** focuses the research effort on a single issue or set of related issues. At Copán, for instance, a range of research projects was designed to explore the issue of Maya demographic and social changes. In our discussion of research design, we assume that the researcher has clearly defined the target problem, and (at least generally) the research location. The next step is to decide how to solve the problem.

research design The strategy of investigating a particular problem which combines appropriate methods and techniques.

problem orientation The question or issue that a particular research effort is designed to address.

Background Study
The first step in learning to recognize cultural patterning in an archaeological setting is to develop an idea of what you are looking for, based on what is known of the culture and past cultural

Table 4.1 Research Design Checklist*

Phase I: Design the Project (Prefieldwork)

A. Determine Objectives and Constraints
    1. Master areal, topical, and theoretical literatures
    2. Select specific topic
    3. Delimit research problems
    4. Formulate research questions
    5. Select field site
    6. Determine whether project is politically viable
    7. Identify appropriate granting agencies
    8. Determine probable limits of budget
    9. Identify critical points in schedule
    10. Outline thesis or final report

B. Select or Design Research Methods
    1. Establish basic characteristics of project design
    2. Identify relevant data sets
    3. Identify key variables in each data set
    4. Define nature and scope of methodology for data analysis
    5. Develop necessary analytical skills

C. Design Data Collection Procedures
    1. Set up data structures (forms, files, etc.)
    2. Set up data codes or recording language
    3. Operationally define all variables and values
    4. Formulate recording rules, sampling procedures, etc.
    5. Devise or select recording techniques
    6. Devise data quality control procedures
    7. Make sure that the methods and procedures are both valid and reliable

D. Finalize Research Design
    1. Plan logistics and living arrangements for fieldwork
    2. Prepare budget and schedule
    3. Finish writing proposal
    4. Prepare and submit proposal to funding agencies
    5. Submit proposal to cultural resources caretaker agencies

activity. Relevant background material includes this plus information on the environment, on ethnographic case studies that can serve as appropriate analogs, and on the range of methods appropriate to your needs and budget.

Understanding the Site Formation Process

Regardless of what archaeological materials are being sought, they are there because of human activity in the past plus the subsequent effects of natural and cultural processes. All of these are part of the *site formation*

Table 4.1   Continued

Phase II: Collect Data (Fieldwork)

A. Receive Funding and Permissions and Depart for the Field

B. Match Project Design with Reality
    1. Revise research problems and questions
    2. Revise methods
    3. Revise data collection and quality control procedures
    4. Revise schedule and budget

C. Do Fieldwork, Gather and Accession Materials, Record Field Data

D. Conclude Fieldwork and Close the Site

Phase III: Analyze Data (Postfieldwork)

A. Preprocess Data
    1. Edit data, detect, and correct errors
    2. Enter data into computer files
    3. Compile and document data base
B. Analyze Data
    1. Finalize analytical procedures; reformat files, if necessary
    2. Generate descriptive statistics on relevant data subsets
    3. Assess correlations and trends, refine test hypotheses, select analytic statistical methods
    4. Apply analytic statistical methods, assess results
C. Interpret Data
    1. Integrate results of various procedures
    2. Address research problems and questions (Phase I, A.3 and A.4)
    3. Write final report or thesis.

Source: Adapted from Denham 1979.

process, a dynamic set of cultural and natural transformations (Miksicek 1987; Schiffer 1987). A site begins with the perceptible traces of an ongoing cultural activity. At the beginning of the accumulation of the archaeological record at **habitation sites**, we might find a full repertoire of materials in active use: perishable things like food and textiles as well as durable stone tools. Yet in the course of daily life some things are used up or thrown away, whereas others are reused until they are worn out and then discarded. Discarded materials break down and decay, are moved around or buried by the actions of wind, water, and the gradual movements of the earth's crust, and by the actions of other people (Fig. 4.1).

habitation sites Archaeological sites where people lived.

FIGURE 4.1 Modern examples of deteriorating materials inform us about the site formation process. Here an adobe building in Arizona "melts" into its constituent parts.

matrix The material within which the archaeological evidence is embedded, such as soil, lava, and water.

Preservation and Deterioration Rates of deterioration and conditions of preservation vary greatly, depending on the nature of the material remains, the nature of the **matrix** in which the archaeological evidence is embedded, and the climate. Deterioration includes decomposition due to biological and chemical reactions, weathering due to abrasion, and expansion and contraction of the materials and their matrix (see Table 4.2). Some changes are slow and relatively nondestructive, as when obsidian gradually absorbs water into its surface. When these changes take place at very regular rates, and the rates are measurable, they may help archaeologists determine chronology.

Extreme conditions that do not vary preserve the widest range of materials. Examples include extreme dryness, as in deserts (which may be cold or hot), or the permanent cold wet of submerged areas or bogs. The bodies of long-extinct mammoths, for example, have been found in good condition preserved in a matrix of arctic ice. Egyptian pharaohs went to great lengths to have their corpses artificially preserved; ironically, the untreated corpses of commoners were often preserved just as effectively by the perpetually hot, dry desert sands of the Nile Valley.

Table 4.2 **Causes of Deterioration of Archaeological Materials**

Material	Destruction Caused By
ORGANIC: animal matter (including human bodies) and plant remains	biological decomposition, weathering, and chemical reactions
INORGANIC: earth/clay (ceramics, brick, etc.) stone (tools, artifacts), minerals	weathering, chemical reactions, hydration, patination

Understanding the Local Environment

The archaeologist must understand environmental conditions in the study area in order to account correctly for the site formation process and to plan an efficient and productive research program. Test excavations have supplemented surface surveys in the Copán region because of the heavy vegetation obscuring artifacts lying on the ground. In arid areas where vegetation is sparse (such as in much of the Puebloan culture area of the U.S. Southwest), surface surveys cull much more information because artifact scatters are visible.

Maps and Aerial Photographs Maps and aerial photographs tell us about terrain and vegetation in a region. The farthest meaningful view that archaeologists have of the regions they study is that from satellites at a distance of 700 km. This "remote sensing" imagery, which is based on visible and infrared wavelengths, documents broad areas of different kinds of vegetative cover and land use, certain mineral resources, and denser areas of present-day human settlement. Successive images of the same region show how rapidly processes like deforestation and erosion can occur (Ebert 1984; Ehrenberg 1987; Lyons and Avery 1984; Parrington 1983) (Fig. 4.2). The explanatory potential of environmental data drawn from many sources has been greatly enhanced by the development of Geographical Information Systems (GIS), a complex of software and mapped information that archaeologists are applying and developing (Allen, Green, and Zubrow 1990).

We know that settlement location depends on the proximity of necessary resources like water and food as well as access to other features, such as sources of raw materials for craft production. Landsat images are used to reveal the patterning of vegetation and modern land use. (Some archaeological sites are so large and cleared of vegetation that they are visible in Landsat images, but these photos aren't really useful in locating unknown

FIGURE 4.2 This Landsat image of the Copán region shows areas of modern communities (arrow points to the modern town of Copán), agricultural fields, forests.

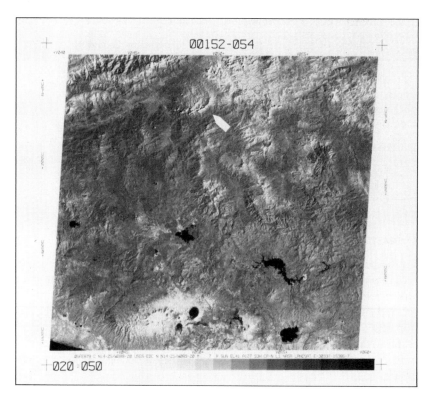

sites.) In studying patterns of resources to see how they relate to the distribution of known sites, we might map known sites onto the Landsat image, hypothesize about where other sites might be located, and then select a sample of areas to survey accordingly.

Air photos taken from planes, which include conventional photography and infrared (Nichols 1988) and radar imagery, are widely used by archaeologists. Some air photos reveal the locations of sites (Fig. 4.3) but the photos are also used to familiarize fieldworkers with setting and terrain, which they depict much more clearly than most maps. The photos also provide basic data for fieldwalking survey maps, which, when annotated with information about archaeological remains, document the pattern of settlements and other sites for a region.

Selecting Target Cases: Sampling

sample Any subset of a population.

population The whole set of things to be analyzed or on which observations are to be made.

Even though huge amounts of information are often collected in archaeological research, the question remains: How representative are the observations of all the cases that could have been observed, or that have ever existed? In other words, how good is our **sample** of remains, and how well does it represent the whole **population** of remains (Mueller 1975)? If we completely survey a region and find 20 different habitation sites, and then

FIGURE 4.3 Conventional air photos can reveal the extent of ancient buried structures. Concentric half-circles, seen from the air, are the remains of monumental architecture at Poverty Point (Louisiana), dating from 1500 to 700 B.C.

we excavate at one of them, this 5 percent sample of known sites is our window on the whole group. Note that there are two different kinds of "samples" here. The first is the sample made up of all known sites, which is part of a theoretical larger population of sites, including some that are imperceptible using our survey techniques and some that have disappeared altogether. The second kind of sample is our selected single example from the 20 different cases we know about; this is a subset of the first kind of sample.

Let us explore this sampling situation further. At the site we selected for further investigation, there are three surface concentrations of materials. We suspect these are **loci** of residential activity that, if excavated, would yield household remains. Our choices about where to excavate within the site and how many trenches to open up all depend on the time and money resources at hand, and on the problem orientation of the project. But in nearly every case, a sample would be selected: the entire site would not be excavated (Fig. 4.4).

Sampling is the process of choosing a limited number of cases out of a larger set. There are several ways to choose samples of archaeological materials. We could choose a **random sample,** as simple as a blindfold selection of 1 of the 20 sites. However, the random sample may not be the best choice for retrieving abundant and relevant information, since every site

loci   (*sing.* **locus**) Small concentrated areas.

random sample   Sampling technique in which each unit or sample has an equal chance of being selected.

FIGURE 4.4 The "site" (upper left) has been gridded into 20 equal units, and the density of artifacts on the surface is indicated by the relative number of dots (0–5). The random sample selects the units to be excavated from anywhere on the site; the representative sample ensures that the test units are located in an equal pattern over the site; and the stratified sample focuses excavation on the area with the most artifactual material on the surface.

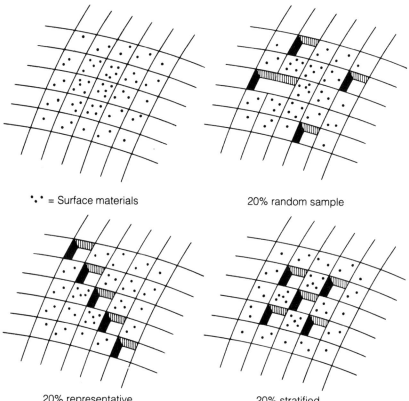

`∴∙˙` = Surface materials   20% random sample

20% representative sample   20% stratified sample

biased sample Sampling technique in which certain units have more chance of inclusion than others.

stratified sample A selection of cases which includes representatives from each of several important subgroups of the whole population.

systematic sample Sample that incorporates randomness and determinacy by specifying that the random selection of a case example has to occur within a certain group of cases.

has an equal chance of being selected, but some may be far more interesting and useful objects of research. Archaeologists often try to select case examples that are generally representative so that findings can be extrapolated to others in the region. To capture important patterns of variation in material remains a **biased sample** may be necessary. Say you make your selection from among the five largest sites. This would be a biased sample, because the cases would be ranked according to size, or, in other words a case example of a certain type would be deliberately selected. Creating subsets based on categories of interest "stratifies" the data set. The researcher can then select cases (randomly, if desired) from within these subsets, creating a **stratified sample** (Fig. 4.5). Finally, a **systematic sample** incorporates randomness and determinacy by specifying that the random selection of a case example has to occur within a certain group of cases; for example, one case is randomly selected from among all the cases in each of several different environmental zones.

Proposing Research

Once the researcher has mastered sufficient knowledge of the problem, and knows how to approach it, the plan of work is set out in a **research proposal,** which also includes a schedule of work, a budget, and plan for publication of research results. Proposals are submitted to funding agencies and to the authorities in charge of the cultural property proposed for investigation. Funders look for interesting, valuable, and reasonable research targets, thoroughly investigated and sensibly scheduled and budgeted. Guardians of cultural resources look for a responsible and respectful attitude toward the materials to be investigated — one seeking to minimize damage while maximizing our understanding of the culture.

PHASE 2: FIELDWORK

In the popular imagination, a typical archaeological field method is to find the slight air current indicating a secret chamber, reached by unlatching a concealed door. This method invariably yields wonderfully preserved artifacts. Real-world archaeology is painstaking, time-consuming, and the remains are often so fragmentary as to require an array of special techniques to observe and interpret them. In this section, we review fieldwork techniques, following a logical progression from mapping of surface remains to excavating beneath the surface to recover finds (Dillon 1989; Hester, Heizer, and Graham 1975; Joukowsky 1980).

Patterns on the Surface

Archaeologists are often asked, "How do you find sites?" The answer varies. Some sites are never lost — think of Stonehenge in England, the Pyramids of Teotihuacán in Mexico, the Great Pyramids of Egypt, or Cahokia's pyramid across from St. Louis, Missouri (Fig. 4.6). Other sites are less obviously visible, leaving little or no surface indications. Here the question of finding sites is also a question about how archaeologists see into the earth — how they can recognize the traces of human activity in the past from subtle indicators like a scatter of worn potsherds, or a low mound evidencing that a house stood there centuries earlier.

"Ground truth," the next step after remote sensing, is archaeological field research to map the visible sites in a region, which is fundamental to understanding cultural and demographic processes. Since air photos have limited potential to reveal unknown sites, fieldwalking surveys are used (Ammerman 1981; Lewarch and O'Brien 1991). In the last chapter we described the **systematic settlement survey** by fieldwalkers in the Copán region. Surveys of the same kind have been made in regions like the central highlands of Mexico and southern Iraq since the 1960s. In the course of

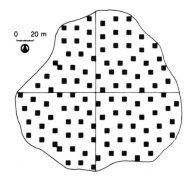

FIGURE 4.5 A stratified systematic sample used by Patty Jo Watson and Charles Redman at the site of Girik-i-Haciyan (Turkey). The site was gridded along its north-south and east-west axes into square units 15 m on a side, each containing 9 smaller units 5 m on a side. One smaller unit was selected at random from within each larger unit. Thus the sample units were fairly evenly distributed over the site but randomly covered a smaller unit within the larger unit.

research proposal A formally presented research strategy describing an intended project and its predicted results.

systematic settlement survey Reconnaissance of a region based on a sampling design ensuring that all types of areas within the region will be surveyed.

FIGURE 4.6 Stonehenge, in southern England, has never been a "lost" site, even though interpretations of age, manner of construction, and function have been frequently revised (Wainwright 1989).

datum point The reference point in an archaeological excavation used as the basis for all measurements on a site.

grid A rectilinear system of *X, Y* coordinates which is established over the area to be excavated so that spatial control can be maintained.

surveying, small subsurface samples may be taken by test-trenching (also called "test-pitting," or "shovel-testing"). Even more limited samples are drawn by augering, using a drill for earth, and coring, which extracts a cylindrical sample of earth (Stein 1986). These are, technically, intrusive methods, but they disturb little of the archaeological site and result in a more accurate site distribution map for the surveyed area. This map is the basis for describing and analyzing the settlement pattern and for locating areas of resource use (quarry sites or hunting kill sites, for example).

To determine the layout of a particular site, standard surveying methods are used. For every site, a permanent **datum point** is established, and the site's north-south, east-west **grid** is oriented from the datum using a compass and surveyor's telescope (called a "transit"; see Fig. 2.16), a stadia rod for vertical measurements, and measuring tapes of various lengths. Surface elevations and locations of features are noted with reference to this grid. The site itself may be physically gridded, using posts and twine, in those areas where surface and subsurface remains are going to be studied more closely. The grid marks out the units of surface collection of artifacts and excavation, which vary in size according to the research goals and sampling strategy.

Looking under the Surface

Maps and site plans are two-dimensional models of the distribution of archaeological remains. It is the three-dimensional distribution of remains in context that reveals the history of activity and the site formation process. Excavation is the best-known way of accomplishing this, but it is costly, and because it is an intrusive method, it destroys context, even as this "destruction" of parts of the site allows its cultural reconstruction.

Geophysical Surveying Nonintrusive survey methods also exist that permit seeing through the soil without disturbing context, for purposes of preexcavation reconnaissance as well as underground survey for its own sake; metal detectors are common examples of this kind of technology. Geophysical surveying procedures such as ground-penetrating radar (Kenyon and Bevan 1977), resistivity, magnetic, and electromagnetic surveying locate buried features and structures. Electric-current, radar, or electromagnetic impulses encounter varying resistance (from rock, bricks, change in soils) or changes in the magnetic field as they pass through a matrix (such as soil). The patterns of resistance are studied for similarities to cultural features.

These methods have successfully located buildings, empty spaces, hearths, and monuments. As it becomes more affordable and available the use of this promising technology at archaeological sites will become more common. At present, errors sometimes occur, arising from anomalies in resistance patterns produced by local geographic conditions, rainy weather, uneven terrain, and interference by electric power lines. Sometimes cultural features and structures are not detected, particularly if the relevant strata are deeply buried.

Intrusive Methods To recover archaeological materials from known contexts, develop chronological sequences, increase accuracy of information about spatial context of finds, and increase interpretive sensitivity to site formation processes, intrusive methods may be necessary.

Excavation cuts into the site, through its accumulated overburden and through the physical remains of human activity. How many trenches to excavate, and their size and placement, are dictated by the project's resources and its sampling strategy. The grid of the site provides orientation for excavation trenches, which are dug out in levels that may follow culturally or naturally occurring strata or that may be of an arbitrary depth (Drucker 1972; E. Harris 1979). Documenting the location of cultural materials according to stratum (vertical coordinates) and grid unit (horizontal coordinates) establishes **provenience,** the "address" of the remains in three-dimensional space. Without provenience, any artifact loses its value because it cannot be interpreted within the proper spatial and temporal contexts, and the behavior patterns that led to its deposition in that particular set of contexts cannot be reconstructed.

Archaeological record-keeping methods vary somewhat from project to project, but provenience of materials is often recorded in basic units called **lots.** A lot is any unit of collection in which artifacts are presumed to share the same particular context, typically a level of a trench. Each trench has an identification number (often its southwest coordinates relative to the datum), and each level within the trench its own lot number. Separate lot numbers may be assigned to features, samples (such as soil samples), and particular artifacts as necessary during excavation.

provenience The exact location in three-dimensional space of any material in its archaeological context.

lot Any unit of collection in which artifacts are presumed to share the same particular context, typically, a level of a trench.

FIGURE 4.7 Common forms of excavation are test trenches (top); lateral excavations (middle); and slot, or cross-sectional, trenches.

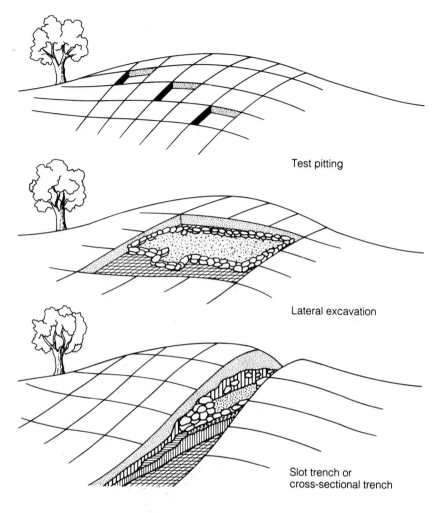

Test pitting

Lateral excavation

Slot trench or cross-sectional trench

lateral, or extensive, excavations The excavation or opening up of large areas so that subsurface features and architecture are broadly exposed.

cross-sectional, or slot, trenches An excavation technique in which a set of superimposed strata are cut across by deep trenches that expose the history of deposition.

baulk, or witness column The intentionally unexcavated portion of a trench, preserved to retain a stratigraphic profile for future reference and control.

stratigraphic profiles Drawings of natural and/or cultural deposits of strata of a trench which can be correlated with the collections recovered from that trench.

The grid on a site is rectilinear, and excavation trenches are usually square or rectangular to facilitate keeping track of provenience, though subunits of any shape or size may be excavated and analyzed in separate lots. There are several broad approaches to positioning trenches. Test trenches may be placed to get a representative sample of the site as a whole. **Lateral, or extensive, excavations** open up large areas so that subsurface features and architecture are broadly exposed. **Cross-sectional, or slot, trenches** are cut across a set of superimposed cultural (and natural) strata, exposing the history of deposition (Fig. 4.7).

Often, areas within each trench are left unexcavated. Unexcavated sidewalls of trenches, called **baulks,** and smaller unexcavated areas, called **witness columns,** maintain a record of strata. **Stratigraphic profiles** are drawings of these superimposed deposits, allowing correlation of the strata with the collections recovered when the trench was dug. The dirt from excavations is often screened through ¼-in. mesh so that small artifacts and ecofacts are recovered.

From different strata, soil samples can be taken for further processing. Materials contained in soil samples are often recovered by a kind of water screening, called **flotation**. The soil sample is dissolved in water, whereupon organic materials like seeds, roots, and bone will float, while inorganic material will settle. This is an easy way to segregate the floral-faunal materials from ceramics and stone (Fig. 4.8) and to recover fine remains that would otherwise be lost. Some soil samples are subjected to more sensitive screening to recover minute fragments of materials, and to chemical analysis for pH and other characteristics. Phosphate analysis of soils can show "hot spots" of phosphate concentration, which are places where food, garbage, and/or feces were deposited. Soil samples can also be examined for pollen and for **plant opal phytoliths,** the fossils of plant cellular structure, distinctive of particular species or genera (Dunn 1983; Pearsall 1978; Piperno 1988; Rovner 1983).

Excavating through a particular stratum is occasionally done by machine; a backhoe is sometimes used in salvage situations to scrape off upper strata and reveal extensive features. But far more often, strata are excavated by hand, with instruments varying in delicacy from dental tools to picks and shovels. The archaeologist often excavates cultural strata with a trowel, and American archaeologists favor a 6- or 7-in. Marshalltown pointing trowel, partly because of its strong construction (other, welded trowels

flotation Type of water screening which recovers small plant, animal, and artifactual remains from a soil sample.

plant opal phytoliths Fossils of plant cellular structures, distinctive of particular species or genera.

FIGURE 4.8 Soil flotation by Patty Jo Watson at a site in western Kentucky. The procedure is simple. Soil samples are dumped into water. Materials that sink to the bottom, the "heavy fraction," are generally inorganic remains. Materials that float, the "light fraction," are usually organic. Both provide valuable information that would otherwise be missed by simply screening the dirt.

break) and also because the brand has achieved a mystique within the profession (cf. Flannery, "The Golden Marshalltown," 1982). Finer excavating work is done with picks, grapefruit knives, dental tools, and brushes of various sizes. As excavation takes place, all visible relevant remains are mapped, drawn and photographed, then removed from their matrix and labeled with their lot number and catalogued (accessioned). Keeping track of all the materials that come out of excavation is like any other large bookkeeping job: tedious and exacting, but essential.

The results of excavation include a stratigraphic history of the site; the site's plan; artifacts and architecture, including such things as dwelling form, distribution, and orientation of dwellings and activity areas; and evidence of subsistency strategy and special features like drainage channels and farm terraces. In addition to recovering things made and used by people, we sometimes recover remains of the people themselves. Burials are a vitally important source of information about health and physiology, social status, and valued materials (if grave goods are included), and about demographic features of the population as a whole, which are inferred from individual cases.

What happens to sites after excavation is completed? Usually, they are "backfilled"—the trenches are filled in with the soil originally removed from them. Some sites may be left uncovered, and buildings and features are then consolidated and/or restored. Copán's architecture is an extreme case of care taken in consolidation and restoration (Fig. 4.9), the site being a world cultural treasure visited by many tourists.

Once a site has been backfilled, the landscape usually looks much as it did before excavation, except that fewer artifacts are visible on the surface. If you could see beneath the surface, though, you would see shafts of mixed materials (the excavation trenches, refilled) penetrating through the original strata of the site. Archaeologists make a point of not completely excavating sites, thus leaving unaltered contexts for further analysis—perhaps for the time when a new generation of methods and technologies of observation will have been developed. If further excavation is planned, the archaeologist can reestablish the grid over the site, based on the permanent datum point, and locate grid units that have already been excavated.

Note Taking

field notes A daily record and careful description of excavation activities.

Careful description is at no time more important than in the fieldwork phase (LeBlanc 1976). Fieldwork as scientific experimentation is difficult—when not impossible—to replicate, so the archaeologist describes the ongoing project and its findings in **field notes,** setting down firsthand observations and measurements that become raw data for further analysis. Artifacts and other materials that come out of the ground can, of course, be further described and measured in the lab, but permanent features of an excavated site, such as spatial contexts, usually cannot since in most cases they are removed or covered over in the course of excavation.

FIGURE 4.9 The Type 4 complex 9N-8 at Copán: before archaeological investigation (top), during excavation (middle), and after consolidation and reconstruction (bottom).

field operations journal
A running record of activities and finds during an archaeological excavation.

forms Standardized information sheets designed to record data in a programmatic way — that is, lot forms, trench forms, feature forms, and burial forms.

The **field operations journal** is a running record of activities and finds. Additionally, a series of **forms** permits findings to be recorded in a programmatic way: lot forms, trench forms, feature forms, and burial forms. A photographic record is kept of all operations, and drawings are produced

Potsherds

1. Morphological type:
   e.g. "high-necked jar"

2. Technological type:
   e.g. "coil-built"

3. Stylistic type:
   e.g. "linear incised"

4. Functional type:
   e.g. "storage vessel"

FIGURE 4.10 How any artifact is categorized depends on the problem orientation of the researcher. Potsherds can be classified according to their form, material, manner of manufacture, style, and function.

typology Process of establishing and selecting categories for data and for the systems of categories themselves.

incessantly, from quick sketches to highly accurate ink renderings to be included in reports. Finds are sorted into broad categories (usually based on their material), raw counts are made, and the finds are prepared for storage or further analysis (Dowman 1970). Once research has revealed basic spatial patterns and relations, materials in various numbered lots can be compared, and frequencies (counts of particular items) and distributions (patterns of varying frequency) can be calculated.

When fieldwork and field accessioning have been finished, the archaeologist makes sure that a complete extra set of field notes, photos, and drawings is stored separately from the originals.

PHASE 3: MATERIALS ANALYSIS

As finds are gathered from survey and excavation, they are sorted and cleaned at the field laboratory. They are usually sorted by material (lithics, ceramics, metal, wood, fiber, bone-antler-shell, and other faunal and floral substances), then arranged according to their most general "formal context." For example, within the broad category "ceramics," cultural materials might include pottery vessels (usually culinary), ceramic figurines, and clay roof tiles, all of which may be subject to the same sort of laboratory procedures to determine their physiochemical properties. However, the basic behavioral categories to which the finds are assumed to belong (cooking, rituals, house construction), and the testing of these behavioral assumptions or hypotheses, ultimately guide the selection of analytic techniques (Fig. 4.10).

Categorizing

Humans are pattern seekers: We cannot generalize from past experience unless we categorize. In science the study of categories is called **typology,** a word archaeologists also use to describe the process of establishing and selecting categories as well as the systems of categories themselves. For example, archaeologists have long depended on ceramic "typologies" to interpret the sherds they find. In many cases the archaeologist doesn't devise a typology but uses an established one for recording artifact counts. A major focus in the profession for a century (mid-19th to mid-20th century), typologies and trait lists have served as important orienting devices for learning about the culture to which finds belonged and recognizing and describing them. Walter Taylor criticized archaeologists for a preoccupation with typology at the expense of behavioral reconstruction; indeed typologies were sometimes badly organized, having been based on untested assumptions about function, for example. But we should not assume they are no longer essential. Without categories, objective description is impossible and results cannot be shared—science cannot be done.

Remember that in Chapter 2 we noted that anthropologists in general had to grapple with the problem of the difference between observational objectivity and the subjective view of a participant in a culture. Relevant categories may be very different from each of these perspectives. In the interests of the most accurate possible reconstructions, we must be aware of the biases embedded in any typology.

Typologies are hierarchically organized, with levels of observation that include all the variants at the next level of detail: for example, all the attributes of a particular artifact type, such as a potsherd or knife, or all the types of site comprised within the settlement pattern of a region. At each of these levels we divide the materials into more subtypes, based on the variety of cultural behavior that the materials reflect. If all ceramic vessels at a site were identical, then we could learn nothing about variation in function or affluence at that site from vessel size or surface decoration.

Typologies should be based on clearly defined features, including

1. **Morphology** (meaning "form study"): The shape, size, and superficial characteristics of artifacts, features, structures, sites, and so forth, are provided by measurements (including weight) that permit comparative statistical analysis of attributes and frequencies.

2. **Material:** What is an artifact made of? What materials are found in the site's assemblage, and where do they come from? Further lab study, using microscopic and physiochemical analyses, can be used to determine various properties like the source of minerals or the species of animals.

3. **Technology,** or **manufacturing process:** How a stone tool or ceramic pot or temple-pyramid was made tells us about its material and function and the society's level of technology, even the production sequence, specialization, and trade involved. Lab methods include optical microscopy of artifacts for manufacturing scars; ethnoarchaeological and replication studies can test hypotheses about the manufacturing process.

4. **Stylistic features**: Stylistic features include attributes that are also relevant to morphology, material, and technology, and others, such as design motifs on pottery, that may have little bearing on how a vessel functions but that may be extremely useful in typology because of associations with particular behaviors and time periods. Methods of study include describing and categorizing design elements and surface treatments, material composition analysis of physiochemical properties, and standardized color description. The Munsell charts (1954) provide color standards against which soils and artifacts can be compared and systematically described.

5. **Function**: It is crucial to know what purpose something served and how it was used to reconstruct behavior patterns from material culture remains. Unfortunately, function is not always apparent. Take the common "arrowhead." Many of these are actually spearpoints or hafted knives, so it is misleading to use the popular term with its implicit functional attribution. Archaeologists call such tools "unifaces" or "bifaces" (terms referring to stone tool morphology) until specific function can be determined, for example, by microscopic studies of edgewear.

morphology The shape, size, and superficial characteristics of artifacts, features, structures, sites, and so forth, provided by measurements (including weight) that permit comparative statistical analysis of attributes and frequencies.

material Substance of which an artifact is made, such as bone, obsidian, jade, and so forth.

technology, or **manufacturing process** The steps taken to produce an artifact.

This brief overview indicates the wide range of materials under investigation and the great variety of typologies that could be devised. Usually selected so that patterns in the data best reveal the solution to a particular problem (stated as a test hypothesis), most typologies permit several testing approaches.

Analyses

Laboratory analyses are used to study microscopic and physiochemical properties of materials. The goals of lab and statistical analyses of any substance are guided by three main questions: (1) how old is it, (2) what is it (function and composition), and (3) where is it from (source of material and place of use and deposition)?

How Old Is It? Before investigating any other issue of culture, the archaeologist must understand chronology. Without knowing the age of materials, little can be said about the activity that made them part of the site. Chronologies that archaeologists establish have categories: The *sequence* is divided into periods, phases, and subphases that represent times of relative cultural homogeneity as indicated by the material cultural record or by ethnohistoric documents, and each period is initiated by an episode of change. Note that because the archaeological record includes many kinds of evidence, defining the turning point of a period or subphase on the basis of one artifact category may ignore the stability of another category. At Copán, for example, ceramic styles changed while stone tool types did not.

Thus lengths of phases or periods vary. Indeed, chronological estimates are never fixed but are subject to revision through further research. Applications of new or refined dating methods can be used, for example, to revise chronology or to learn the actual age of remains.

Methods Dating methods are based on the fact that the world is full of natural "clocks" holding different records of the elapse of time (Michels 1973). A tree growing annual rings is a clock. Geological deposits are also clocks, in several senses: Strata accumulate during geological epochs, while the atomic structure of their constituent minerals decays at a measurable and predictable rate. Archaeologists, who are interested in clocks that keep track of culturally relevant time, use dating methods ranging from seriation of styles to measures of radioactive decay.

It is important here to recall the basic distinction between relative and absolute dating. An absolute date establishes the approximate actual age of artifacts and sites; from this the timing and relationship of different phases and their associated materials can be readily understood. Without absolute dates, the best understanding of chronology an archaeologist can achieve is through relative dating. By recognizing coexisting cultural traits that serve as the basis for phases and periods and by sorting these into a series that makes logical chronological sense, the archaeologist can establish a relative chronology. Most culture histories accepted by archaeologists are based on both kinds of dating methods. Used together, these allow scientists to reconstruct the most accurate and sensitive chronology possible.

For many different regions of the world, the first steps in reconstructing culture history and determining the timing of events were made long before absolute dating methods came into general use. *Relative dating* has been the basic means of putting materials in sequential order, according to their different artifact types. One approach to this problem is *seriation*, which is based on the assumption that in all cultures, styles change over time. We see this around us constantly, familiar examples being clothing and hair styles. But note that, at any point in time, you see a lot of variation in styles as modes change: a few articles of the very latest mode, lots of garments in still serviceable older styles, then a few outfits that are really outmoded. This pattern of change, whereby in each culture, each period exhibits different proportions of popular styles, is the key to the seriation method. As we noted in Chapter 2, seriation has made it possible to place different sites in a relative chronological series, based on what they had in common in terms of their artifact repertoires.

If you have a stratified deposit with several clear levels, each associated with different artifact types (or different proportions of the same types), the law of superposition tells you that their chronological sequence is from the lowest (oldest level) to the surface (most recent). This sequential order is based on principles of *stratigraphy*, and the order can then be applied to other sites, including single-occupation sites, to establish a relative chronology in a region. As absolute dates come to be known, they may substantiate the relative sequence, or cause it to be revised, providing control over events and materials.

Before about 1950, relative dating methods were virtually the only way to put things in chronological order in many regions, and seriation was the backbone of chronology. Seriation uses widely distributed artifacts exhibiting a range of stylistic types; if potsherds are present, they lend themselves especially well to this method, since they are common and stylistically varying. To seriate a set of artifact collections, for each sample collection, archaeologists tabulate the frequencies of the different styles, calculate their relative proportions, then arrange the samples in order, tracing the shifting proportions of styles as they change. This can be done in nanoseconds using a computer program to calculate a "coefficient of similarity" (Brainerd 1951; Robinson 1951). However, constructing a seriation histogram demonstrates the reasoning involved in the process (see Fig. 4.11).

Seriation can establish a relative chronology in cases where no other methods can be applied. Even after samples have been dated by absolute methods, the covariation revealed by seriation studies continues to identify periods and local components. But without some link to absolute chronology, it may be impossible to determine which end of a sequence is the

FIGURE 4.11 When all you know about a set of sites is that they share some (but not all) kinds of artifacts, it's a challenge to order them into a meaningful chronological series. If ten sites all have sherds from three ceramic types, your first step is to make a histogram of the ceramic types at each site, using relative percentages as the measures for the histogram. Then reorient the histogram values so that each site's relative proportions of types are on a strip (top). Arrange the strips so that the values at different sites form a continuous gradation (bottom). Note that the sites form a meaningful series, but without other evidence we cannot know if site 5 is earlier or later than site 9.

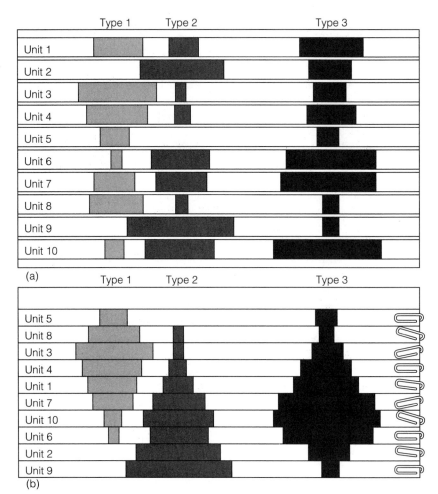

beginning. Nor is there any control over the duration of periods. Another confusing factor is the absence of a point of origin of any innovation in design, preventing proper assessment of the speed and direction of its spread over an area. Samples from different sites showing the same relative proportions of pottery types may not be contemporaneous, whereas other sites, lacking mutual types altogether, may have been occupied at the same time. In such cases, the absolute age of artifacts serving as "index fossils" allows relative chronologies to be made more accurate. Similar artifacts at other sites can be dated through cross-dating.

Until broadly applicable absolute dating methods were developed in the mid-20th century, accurate chronologies of ancient culture history were only found if there were written *historical accounts*, decipherable through *epigraphy*, the study of the meaning of scripts. Some ancient scripts still have not been deciphered (for example, that of ancient India's Harappan civilization; see Chapter 13), while others are slowly lending themselves to full study, such as ancient Maya glyph writing.

Historical accounts do not necessarily reveal absolute dates. They may simply describe sequences of events, or they may record time cyclically, so that dates are repeated regularly. If a culture used a calendar measuring elapsed time in a systematic way, we must be able to decipher it in order to link it with our own calendric system; it can then be used for absolute dating. This particular kind of epigraphy is called **calendrics**. Turn-of-the-century studies of the Maya calendar, for example, established the age of the Maya Long Count dates and translated the dates on monuments such as portrait stelae; however, correlation of the Maya and modern Western calendars has been revised since that time. (Fig. 4.12).

For the many archaeological cultures lacking written histories, archaeologists use *natural clocks* to calculate absolute and relative dates, through regular gradual changes in the composition of many materials. Certain methods study materials with annual marks, like growth rings on trees. This general principle—use of an annual accumulation of a distinctive layer to establish age—has long been employed in archaeology. Tree rings are the most widely studied annual markers, and *dendrochronology*, establishing dates through tree ring patterns, is perhaps the best known of these methods (Baillie 1982; Dean 1978).

Tree rings were used early in the profession of archaeology to estimate the age of trees growing atop ruined buildings, but the greater contribution of dendrochronology has been in determining the year that trees were felled. In regions where tree species produce distinctive tree ring patterns that demarcate different periods, a continuous master sequence can be pieced together. Where tree ring widths are dependably uniform from year to year, this method cannot be applied because no distinctive patterns are perceptible. But in some climates, the rings of certain tree species vary in width from year to year, usually depending on the amount of precipitation. A roof beam in an ancient pueblo in Arizona, for instance, may reveal its date of felling, if the outermost ring is there and the other rings provide a recognizable sequence, within the master sequence (see Fig. 4.13). Wood from house beams, logs in hearths, and wooden artifacts can be dated in this way, but the outside ring is needed to establish the year the tree was cut, and a sample should include at least 50 rings. The first major application of dendrochronology sequences was in the American Southwest, to sort out chronology of Puebloan cultures. Today, the master sequence for the Southwest goes back nearly 9,000 years, bristlecone pine samples having provided the earliest patterns; the European chronology goes back over 7,000 years, and that of Russia, 1,100 years.

In the 1950s, archaeologists began to use recently developed atomic physics technology such as radiocarbon analysis for dating. As noted in Chapter 1, *radiocarbon dating* is applied to organic materials and measures the time since an organism died. When organisms die, they stop accumulating the carbon-14 (^{14}C) isotope, and the amount of ^{14}C in their systems begins to decline. ^{14}C declines at a steady rate; it has a half-life of

calendrics The decipherment and study of calendars.

FIGURE 4.12 Calendric inscription from the Dresden Codex (page 29). Calendrics offers important means of establishing relative and absolute dates.

5730 ± 40 years, meaning that at the end of that time half the original ^{14}C remains in the sample. The range of the method is up to about 50,000 years, 70,000 if measured using "accelerator mass spectrometry," or AMS (Hedges and Gowlett 1986). Since being developed, radiocarbon dating has been applied to archaeological materials from all over the world, and represents a major advance in archaeology, providing the first reasonably priced, broadly applicable absolute dating method (Browman 1981; Klein et al. 1982; Taylor 1987). Radiocarbon dating furnished archaeologists with the technology to answer the basic question, "When?"—a milestone that made all other aspects of description and analysis more meaningful and interesting.

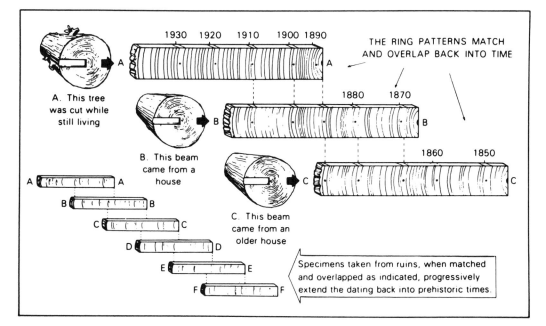

1930 1920 1910 1900 1890

THE RING PATTERNS MATCH
AND OVERLAP BACK INTO TIME

A. This tree
was cut while
still living

1880   1870

B. This beam
came from a
house

1860   1850

C. This beam
came from an
older house

Specimens taken from ruins, when matched
and overlapped as indicated, progressively
extend the dating back into prehistoric times.

FIGURE 4.13 Modern dendrochronology uses an immensely long master sequence developed from distinctive yearly growth patterns shared by the trees growing in a region. Problems with the use of this method generally arise when the sample is anomalous in its context, for example, a roof beam that is much younger than the other structural timbers because it replaced an older roof beam.

Another method that traces the transformation of one isotope into another (here, potassium [K] into argon [Ar]) analyzes the rock in geological formations (Miller 1969). **K-Ar dating,** with its range of 100,000 years to 1.3 billion years, has limited utility for most archaeological contexts but has established the age of early hominid remains in Olduvai Gorge (East Africa), where strata date to 1.75 million years ago (Leakey 1971).

In the wake of radiocarbon dating, other technologically sophisticated methods have taken advantage of the more subtle clocks embedded in various materials. **Thermoluminescence** (Aitken 1985), **fission track dating** (Fleischer 1975), and **electron spin resonance** all examine the natural radiation occurring in ceramics, minerals, glass, and bone, measuring changes in physiochemical structure of various materials. These methods are still being developed, in some cases moving from relative to absolute dating potential.

Obsidian hydration dating also uses a natural clock; in this case it does not count individual years but the continuous passage of time since a newly broken surface of obsidian began to absorb water from its matrix, which it does at a steady rate (Ambrose 1976). The longer the surface has been exposed, the deeper will be the hydration rim, which is visible in cross-section under a microscope and measured microscopically. The rate at

K-Ar dating Absolute dating technique that traces the transformation of one isotope into another (potassium [K] into argon [Ar]). Its range is 100,000 years to 1.3 billion years.

thermoluminescence, fission track dating, and **electron spin resonance** Relative dating techniques which examine the natural radiation occurring in ceramics, minerals, glass, and bone and which measure changes that have occurred in the physiochemical structure of the various materials.

which water is absorbed depends on two things: climate and the physio-chemical characteristics of the kind of obsidian. The hydration rate needs to be experimentally derived for every obsidian source and adjusted for the temperature at the archaeological site. If the hydration rate has not been established, measuring the hydration rims can establish the *relative* ages of obsidian tools from the same source, at a particular site: the older the tool, the deeper the rim. When the hydration rate is known, rim measurements reflect absolute dates.

Looking at the hard, glassy surface of obsidian, it is difficult to believe that it can absorb water. But processes like this are ongoing in many materials. Bone, for example, takes up fluorine from its matrix. This property of bone (and teeth) is why fluoridation of water supplies reduces the incidence of dental cavities by strengthening teeth. Bone also absorbs uranium but loses nitrogen. For bone specimens in any particular matrix, these processes will take place at a steady rate. The **F-U-N method** of establishing relative ages compares concentrations of fluorine, uranium, and nitrogen (whence the method's name) in various samples from the same matrix to determine contemporaneity, but these are relative dating techniques only. The most famous application of the method used fluorine concentration analysis to unveil the skull and jaw dubbed Piltdown Man as a fraudulent "fossil" hominid, a concoction of a modern human skull and an orangutan jaw.

Another natural clock in bone (and related materials, like hair) results from a shift in the form of amino acid molecules after an organism's death. **Amino acid racemization** refers to the change in left-to-right orientation that takes place at a regular rate. The method of determining dates by studying the ratio of left and right orientations is still experimental, inasmuch as the regular rate and its influences toward abnormality are not yet well understood. However, the method has a long dating range: between 1,000 and 1,000,000 years.

In addition to looking at clocks at the molecular level, archaeologists study the earth as a clock. Geologists have long understood that the location of the magnetic north pole moves around true north (the geographic North Pole) in an irregular path. At any time, magnetic north is a point of orientation for magnetized materials in the northern hemisphere, including iron particles in the soil of the earth's crust, and as magnetic north shifts, so does the orientation of the particles. But sometimes the position of the particles becomes fixed in the matrix, as when the clay soil beneath a hearth is heated by the high temperatures of a fire. Then, the iron particles record the position of magnetic north at that point in time, a situation called "thermoremnant magnetism." *Archaeomagnetic dating* is the method that analyzes the orientation, matches it to a master sequence of shifting orientations, and reconstructs the date (Wolfman 1984).

Error Factors   Virtually all chronological methods allow a range of error around an estimated date, expressed in archaeological reports as the date in

F-U-N method   Relative dating technique which compares concentrations of fluorine, uranium, or nitrogen in various samples from the same matrix to determine contemporaneity.

amino acid racemization Dating method based on the natural clock in bone which traces the shift in the form of amino acid molecules after an organism's death. The change from left- to right-orientation takes place at a regular rate and can be measured. This technique has a long dating range from 1,000 to 1,000,000 years.

years before the present date (B.P.), plus or minus an error factor in years, for example, in a 1990 report: "an obsidian hydration date of 700 years B.P. ±55 years." In this case, the error factor of 55 years on either side of the date brackets a range of 110 years, and the obsidian under analysis in 1990 was freshly broken sometime between A.D. 1235 and 1345. Note that when radiocarbon dates are expressed in years "B.P.," the "present" is 1950, not the date of the analysis.

In general, the greater the time depth of the method, the greater the error factor; some error factors can amount to hundreds (even thousands) of years. This can preclude precision in a result, if the date is recent. If you are investigating very early human history — say, 2,000,000 years ago — an error of a few thousand years is inconsequential. For cultures that were extant several hundred years ago, however, a dating method with an error factor of hundreds of years lacks the necessary precision. Selection of the appropriate method depends on dating range, error factors, convenience, and cost. Error factors can be minimized by testing as many samples as possible to derive clusters of dates; by using as many independent techniques as possible; and, more broadly; by continued refinement of established methods and development of new means of determining the temporal context of archaeological finds.

Developing Chronologies   In the course of research, developing a chronology is a feedback process, not a linear one. When some absolute dates are determined, they can be extrapolated to associated materials in the same immediate context and then to other sites by the use of artifacts serving as **diagnostics,** that is, artifactual index fossils, of a particular time period. Periods, phases, and sequences can be determined in this manner, and the associated changes can be interpreted and explained.

diagnostics Artifacts that can be used as index fossils in a cultural context.

What Is It and Where Is It From?

What do archaeologists find at the sites they study? An archaeologist might briefly answer, "At this site we found the remains of three small buildings, dwellings dating from the 11th century A.D. We found chipped stone tools, potsherds, plus some charred floral and faunal remains from what looks like a trash midden. We also came across burials, and from these we can learn about the physical characteristics of these people." What archaeologists find covers a huge range of materials and other kinds of evidence, but we can distinguish three broad categories: artifacts and architecture, floral and faunal remains, and human remains.

Artifacts and Architecture   In the section on typology we presented traits that are the bases for types: function, material, technology, style, and morphology. Since a typology is explicitly (or implicitly) based on what a researcher regards as the most important trait to investigate, typological concerns also can organize the different techniques we use to analyze archaeological materials. Ideally, the archaeologist wants to analyze materials as thoroughly as possible, but problem orientation and available analytic techniques may dictate a particular focus of interest (see also sampling, above).

Function is an essential feature: If you don't know what something was used for, it has only indirect archaeological value, such as its temporal and spatial association with more meaningful materials. We determine function from formal and spatial contexts and from ethnographic analogs of various kinds, including continued use of certain types of materials into the present. Archaeologists devise experimental or control settings to test hypotheses about function of materials in living societies; this is the realm of *ethnoarchaeology* (Gould 1980). Or archaeologists try to replicate ancient behavior using *experimental archaeology* (Coles 1979), an example of which is the stoneworking at Copán (Chapter 3). Observations of this kind document function, providing control artifacts that can be microscopically studied for their characteristic patterns of attributes. **Use-wear analysis** assumes that different activities leave characteristic microscars, polishes, edge-wear, rounding, and striations on tools and vessels (Anderson 1980; Hayden 1979; Keeley 1980; Vaughn 1985). Microscopic examination of marks on archaeological finds are compared to marks made in the course of controlled use-wear experiments in order to infer function. The method detects activities for which there may be no other evidence, but not all functions can be determined, and reworking of tools obliterates the original function. **Residue analysis** identifies the traces of materials left on tools or in vessels. Dramatic examples of this include identifying the species (or genus) of animals killed with projectile points by analyzing traces of blood, using crystallography to study the distinctive patterns of hemoglobin crystals, and immunoassay to study distinctive blood antigens (Loy 1983). Foods and other materials can be chemically analyzed; a Maya pot found in a burial context at Rio Azul (Guatemala) was found to have contained chocolate, used to make a beverage drunk by the elite (Hall et al. 1990).

Material and manufacturing analyses determine the composition of the raw material from which an item was made and how it was made. Such features indicate the technological base of a society, how its economy was organized, and patterns of trade. For example, the occurrence of a kind of stone or shell originating hundreds of miles from the site under study indicates contact with other cultures by some form of long-distance exchange.

Sorting finds according to material begins with visual inspection. Often composition and source are revealed through microscopy, and sometimes thin sections of rocks are examined, as in obsidian hydration analysis, to study the mineral crystals and composition. More sophisticated lab methods determine the elements present in the sample through physiochemical tests. The latter include **Mossbauer spectroscopy,** which measures gamma

use-wear analysis Technique for determining the use of an artifact which is based on the assumption that different activities leave characteristic microscars, polishes, edge wear, rounding, and striations on tools and vessels.

residue analysis Identification of the traces or residues of materials left on tools or in vessels.

Mossbauer spectroscopy Method of determining the elemental composition of an artifact by measuring gamma ray absorption.

ray absorption; **optical emission spectroscopy,** by which a sample is vaporized to release energy measurable as wavelengths of light distinctive of particular elements; **neutron activation analysis,** in which the sample is bombarded with neutrons in a nuclear reactor, the radiation released revealing the constituent elements; and **X-ray fluorescence analysis,** in which X-ray irradiation produces characteristic wavelengths and intensities.

Manufacturing details may show whether the artifact itself was produced far away and obtained through trade, or locally made of exotic materials. Or such analysis may reveal the manufacturing process, giving us a better understanding of an object's technological style, the expression of aesthetics and function within the constraints of the materials and technology. Experimental archaeology techniques, such as replication studies, can test hypotheses about how artifacts were made and used.

Style and *morphology* may be important in establishing chronology and for identifying ethnic group affiliation. Morphology is, of course, related to function. Style and morphology may be linked together in certain patterns (that is, certain shapes of pottery vessels may have associated designs) that are characteristic of social and ethnic groups, or even kin groups such as lineages, through interaction analysis (Rice 1987).

Analyzing Plant and Animal Remains There are several ways of determining the kinds of flora and fauna associated with archaeological remains, from visual inspection and sorting to chemical and molecular analyses. Identifying the species (or at least the genus) is a fundamental concern, followed by estimating the frequency of members (Fig. 4.14) and their special characteristics (Chaplin 1971; Grayson 1984). For example, at Zawi Chemi Shanidar, an early permanent settlement in the Near East dating from about 11,000 years ago, animal remains do not reflect the full age and sex range of the game populations in the wild but rather are biased in favor of young males. This is argued to be an indicator of domesticated rather than hunted beasts, since young males would be culled from the herds by farmers but might be the least likely to be captured by hunters.

Identifying culturally important species can be based on direct or indirect evidence (ethnohistoric or artistic documentation). The "typology" in use is the Linnaean species taxonomic nomenclature and standard anatomical terms. Subcategories would include the specimen's developmental level or age at death, the surviving parts, and taphonomy.

Taphonomy studies the natural and cultural processes affecting organic remains after death (Behrensmeyer and Hill 1980; Gifford 1981). For example, cut marks on faunal bone may have resulted from butchering or from animals' chewing on the bone. Experimental archaeology and microscopic analysis of the materials may reveal the patterns characteristic of these different activities.

Other relevant issues for the archaeologist are function and how the materials were produced. Whether the specimens are domesticated or wild,

optical emission spectroscopy Method of determining the composition of an artifact by vaporizing the sample to release energy measurable as wavelengths of light distinctive of particular elements.

neutron activation analysis Method of determining the composition of an artifact by bombarding the sample with neutrons in a nuclear reactor. The radiation released reveals the constituent elements.

X-ray fluorescence analysis Method of material-composition analysis in which X-ray irradiation reveals characteristic wavelengths of elements.

taphonomy The study of natural and cultural processes affecting organic remains after death, and their depositional characteristics.

FIGURE 4.14 Excavation at the Olsen-Chubbock Site (Colorado) (a) revealed the bones of bison that had been slaughtered and then butchered about 8,500 years ago. The lower photo (d) shows a complete skeleton of a bison, while the line drawings (b, c) show partial skeletons, the more desirable food parts having been removed. The number of individuals at the site is determined by counting the skeletal elements (e.g., the skull) that occur in greatest number.

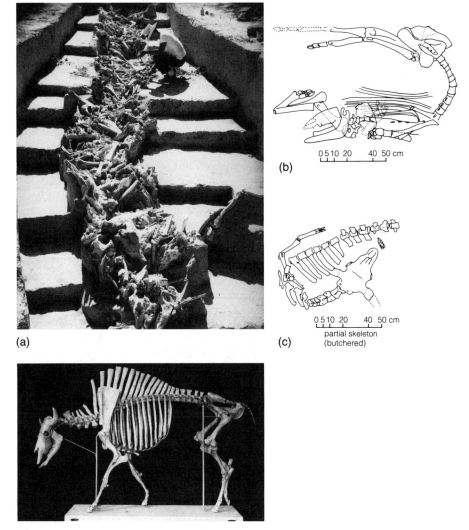

(a)

(b)

0 5 10 20   40 50 cm

0 5 10 20   40 50 cm
partial skeleton
(butchered)

(c)

(d)

we must know how they grew or were raised and how they were gathered. The implications of these productive activities enable accurate reconstruction of the culture. Of particular relevance here would be the material's value for subsistence, its other economic roles, social value, political importance, and ideological meaning. Analysis of these remains can also tell us during what time of year a site was used, and the resources that were exploited in different seasons.

Analyzing Human Remains In examining human remains, the focus is on the physical anthropology of the population. **Demography** (the age-sex structure in particular) and health are essential for reconstructing

demography The statistical study of human populations, particularly in terms of age-sex structure.

FIGURE 4.15 The bog-preserved Tollund Man (Denmark).

lifeways and culture history. Sometimes we can get information directly: Excavations in peat bogs in northern Europe have yielded the well-preserved remains of individuals who lived 2,000 years ago. For the Bog People, circumstances of their burial have ensured the preservation of the skin and organs of their bodies as well as their clothing; all can be thoroughly analyzed. Even the contents of their stomachs—their last meals—are well preserved: one individual had eaten a granola-like porridge (Brothwell 1986; Glob 1969). Similarly, bodies of Scythians dating from about 2,500 years ago were preserved by waterlogging and permafrost in northern Eurasia and reveal such details as tattoos. The diseases afflicting Egyptian pharaohs are known from their mummified bodies (Fig. 4.15). Preserved feces, called "coprolites," include dietary remains (Bryant and Williams-Dean 1975; Minnis 1989).

As the photo shows, these earthly remains of people recognizable to us dramatize the immediacy of the past—we feel a sense of common humanity that is not so readily conveyed by projectile points and settlement patterns. And the information obtainable from burials provides a level of detail that is extremely rare in archaeology. We can, for instance, extrapolate about the health of the general population from skeletal remains (Buikstra and Cook 1980; Huss-Ashmore, Goodman, and Armelagos 1982) and derive population size estimates based on site size, using a set of paleodemographic models based on modern demographic studies, and on osteology, diagnostic studies of bone to determine age, sex, health status, and diet (Gilbert 1985). Skeletal populations also directly reveal behavioral patterns such as violent conflict (see Box 11.2)

Preservability of Human Remains   Diagnostics for skeletal features are read from the different attributes of human bone, usually found in burial contexts. Sometimes individuals have been interred in tombs (e.g., Egyptian pharaohs, Maya kings, and other elites), but more often the dead have been simply buried in pits dug in the soil (exceptions include those cultures in which cremation is common, such as the Aztec, and those which expose corpses to the elements and then bury the bones, such as certain Plains Indian groups). Soil chemistry plays a major role in preserving remains. Mostly calcium, bone is dissolved by contact with acid; thus acid soils can reduce a skeleton to a whitish stain, while alkaline or neutral soils result in much slower deterioration. Animals also affect preservation of bone. Burrowing animals such as gophers can disrupt a burial context and destroy the bones, and so can insect activity.

Preservation of bone varies with the age and health status of the individual and with the size, density, and shape of various bones. The skull (cranium) preserves best because the ovoid or sphere shape is less likely to break under pressure than would the same mass of bone shaped into the long bones of the arms and legs. The cranium also reveals more about the individual than any other skeletal part. Teeth, which preserve even better than bone, reveal individual health, age, and diet.

If every individual who died at a site were buried there, and the remains were well preserved and could be dated, it would be easy to reconstruct the general health of the population, individual size and stature, as well as rates of maturation, sex ratio, and age. From these observations at various sites we could study population dynamics very readily. Unfortunately, the burials remaining for archaeologists to study represent a biased sample of the whole population, and sometimes it is difficult to understand the direction of the bias. If most of the burials recovered are young adults, for example, how do we explain this? Possibilities include: (1) The sample is not biased: Death only occurred in young adulthood (no infants or juveniles died, no one survived past young adulthood). (2) The sample is biased: The bodies of infants, juveniles, and older adults were disposed of in some other way (cremation, for example) or in some other place. If the sample is biased, then the archaeologist must try to reconstruct demographic features from other sources, including extrapolating population size from settlement pattern data such as the number of dwellings and the area of sites.

Skeletal analysis has provided important insights into human history. For example, the transition from foraging for food to farming generally led to population growth, but farming populations were by no means healthier than hunter-gatherers, as study of their skeletons has revealed. The farmers of the Copán Valley showed the effects of malnutrition, as we saw in the last chapter.

Laboratory analysis of bone is a dynamic field, with new and promising developments in DNA identification and solid results from trace-element analysis and stable isotope analysis to determine diet (Table 4.3). The last two methods use laboratory procedures such as **X-ray emission,** whereby bone is bombarded with electrons to produce a signature pattern of X-rays; **activation analysis,** which induces radioactive reactions to produce

X-ray emission Method to determine the elements of a bone by bombarding it with electrons to produce a signature pattern of X-rays.

activation analysis Method to determine the elements of a material by inducing radioactive reactions to produce radiation characteristic of material composition.

Table 4.3 Elements in the Diet

DIET	Manganese	Strontium	Vanadium	Copper	Zinc
vegetarian	high	high	high	low	low
meat-rich	low	low	low	high	high

radiation characteristic of material composition; and **mass spectrometry,** which converts the material to a gas, then disperses its components according to mass to identify the composition. Trace elements characteristic of particular diets can tell us about social status and changing subsistence practices, as well as nutrition.

Stable isotope analysis, which distinguishes between the different kinds of plant foods consumed, is based on the fact that plants have several distinct pathways for fixing carbon dioxide and nitrogen and these become characteristic of the bones of the organism eating the plants (DeNiro and Schoeniger 1983). For example, the ratios of two carbon isotopes (^{13}C and ^{12}C) may tell us if the diet featured maize (more ^{13}C) or nuts, fruits, and root crops (less ^{13}C).

PHASE 4: DATA ANALYSES

Using phases of research outlined in Table 4.1 to organize the subjects of this chapter may create the impression that the various activities succeed each other in a simple, linear, clear-cut fashion. Of course, this is not the case. As we have stated before, the scientific cycle encompasses myriad feedback processes. Of these, statistical analyses seek and examine many kinds of patterns in archaeological data. The data fit into statistical equations are drawn from tabulations of material remains that have been arranged according to various typologies, beginning in the fieldwork stage, and then tracked according to their spatial, temporal, and formal contexts.

Archaeological materials are not, by themselves, "data." An artifact, attribute, or site becomes a datum (a piece of data) when it is recorded as a case example of a particular type. Sound interpretations about data sets depend on careful observation of all pertinent features of archaeological materials, but the amount of data generated by research is huge (even for small, narrowly focused projects) and must be well organized and readily accessible. Computers have become essential for these purposes.

Computer Use

Computerized record keeping is now widely used to keep track of archaeological materials and their contexts, to provide spreadsheets summarizing frequencies of different types of materials, to calculate descriptive and

mass spectrometry
Method to determine the elements of a material by converting it to a gas and dispersing its components according to mass to identify the composition.

stable isotope analysis
Method used to distinguish between the different kinds of plant foods consumed; based on the fact that plants have several distinct pathways for fixing carbon dioxide and nitrogen, elements which become characteristic of the bones of the plant-eating organisms.

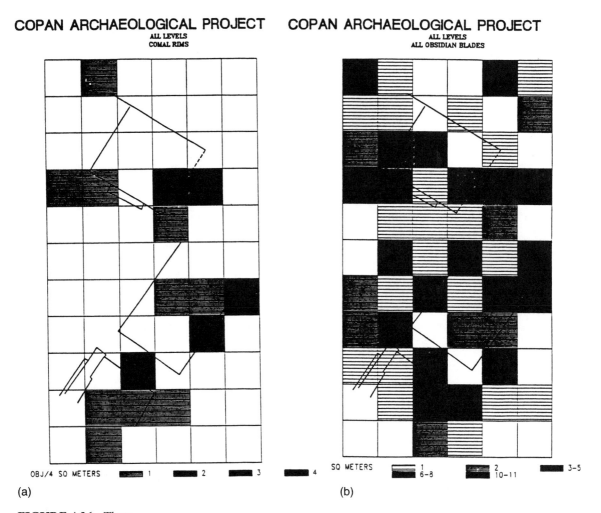

COPAN ARCHAEOLOGICAL PROJECT
ALL LEVELS
COMAL RIMS

COPAN ARCHAEOLOGICAL PROJECT
ALL LEVELS
ALL OBSIDIAN BLADES

OBJ/4 SQ METERS ▬ 1 ▬ 2 ▬ 3 ▬ 4

SQ METERS ▬ 1 ▬ 2 ▬ 3-5
6-8 10-11

(a)   (b)

FIGURE 4.16 These two drawings provide graphic displays of the density of different kinds of artifacts as they were found in the vicinity of three small buildings at a rural site in the Copán region. On the left (a), the density of potsherds from griddles, and on the right (b), the concentration of obsidian blades.

analytical statistics, and to produce graphic displays of site layout and artifact frequency (Fig. 4.16). Computer use was an innovation of the 1960s that made possible a more rigorous and scientific approach to observation, analysis, and interpretation because it became so much easier to keep records and generate statistical summaries and analyses. Now common in the remotest field situations, computers have made field research far more productive. Computer programs (like the humans who design them) are pattern seekers, and can reveal or assess the strength of culturally relevant patterns in the archaeological record.

Statistical Calculations

Statistical operations have two main functions: description and analysis. Descriptive statistics are summary statements such as averages, the number of cases in different categories, and ranges of variation. Analytical statistics take two or more sets of cases and compare them, providing a measure of their similarity and assessing the strength and direction of relationships among variables (Shennan 1988; Thomas 1986; Whallon 1973).

Spatial Analysis

Also known as "locational analysis," **spatial analysis** covers a range of operations to define and assess spatial patterns, and is applied to the artifacts in localized activity areas as well as to intrasite spatial patterns and settlement patterns in a region. The goal is to perceive and explain the causes for spatial patterns in material remains.

Clustering of points in a pattern can be measured using the **nearest-neighbor statistic**. This is calculated by observing the distance between each point and its nearest neighboring point, determining the sum of these distances, and deriving an average, the "mean nearest-neighbor distance" (d_0). This value can be compared to the "expected mean nearest-neighbor distance" (d_e), the value if the same number of points in the same area were randomly distributed. The nearest-neighbor statistic (R) equals d_0/d_e, and it varies from 0 (all points clustered together), to 1 (random spacing) to 2 (uniform rectilinear grid) to 2.149 (a uniform, equilateral triangular pattern) (Clark and Evans 1954; Stark and Young 1981).

This triangular spacing of points — the most efficient distribution of a set of points, enabling each point to maintain a maximum distance from all other points — is a common phenomenon in nature. The area around each point forms a hexagon, a shape taken naturally by clustered soap bubbles and the packed cells of beehives. Translating this to human behavior, geographers have found that when agrarian communities are distributed over a homogeneous plain they tend to space themselves so that each has as much farmland as possible — each community is a point with a hexagonal area around it. On this generalization is based **central place theory**, which predicts the relative spacing of central towns and outlying settlements, given different economic and political conditions (Fig. 4.17).

Another method of analyzing the relations among sites uses the **rank-size rule**. This states that in a politically integrated area, when sites are ranked as to size, each site's size is a fraction of the size of the largest site in the region, the denominator of the fraction being equal to the smaller site's rank. Thus the third largest site is one-third the size of the largest, and so on. In Chapter 11 we discuss archaeological applications of this rule.

PHASE 5: INTERPRETATION

The interpretive phase pulls results together and examines them through the perspective of behavioral models based on previous archaeological research and on ethnographic and ethnohistoric documentation. In fact, interpretation takes place throughout the research process and may alter the design of ongoing research.

---

spatial analysis General statistical approach used to recover geographical patterns inherent in the data on any level (i.e., within one site or within an entire region).

nearest-neighbor statistic Measure of the relationship between a cluster of points in a pattern based on the expected value (d_e) and the observed value (d_0). The statistic (R) equals d_0/d_e.

central place theory Theory of community location and arrangement that posits regular patterns of settlement distribution over the landscape, influenced by the constraints of the environment and the opportunities provided by economic and political interaction.

rank-size rule Principle stating that in a politically integrated area, for sites ranked according to size, each site's size is a fraction of that of the largest site in the region, the denominator of the fraction being equal to the smaller site's rank; thus the third-largest site is one-third the size of the largest, and so on.

FIGURE 4.17 Central place theory posits that a community distribution reflects the most important organizational imperative. If a landscape is settled by farmers who need to maximize their holdings while minimizing the distance to market, a maximal spacing pattern like that described in the top drawing will result (a). If transportation facility is the overriding influence, then the pattern is also equilateral and triangular (b). If administration of smaller sites around the larger sites is the main influence on community location, then the smaller sites will cluster around their capitals (c).

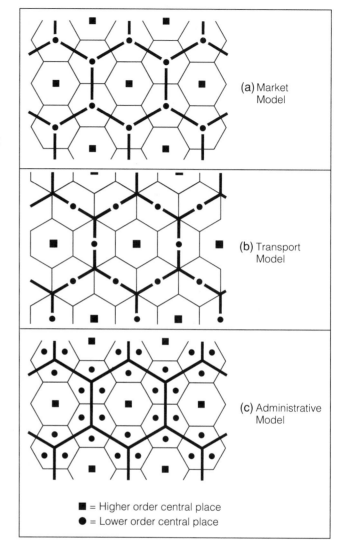

(a) Market Model

(b) Transport Model

(c) Administrative Model

■ = Higher order central place
● = Lower order central place

Interpretation of archaeological remains aims to study them according to theories of human cultural behavior and to refine these theories in the light of particular research results. Over time, archaeological research has led to the development of a well-integrated explanatory framework about cultural adaptation and process—the subject of the next chapter.

CONCLUSION

In projects large and small you will recognize the same general process of defining a research problem, selecting methods to investigate the problem, undertaking research in the field and in the lab, and analyzing the materials and the observations that come out of analyses, and reporting on results. The various data-gathering and analytical techniques are constantly being refined, and designing research demands that the archaeologist keep up-to-date about techniques as well as about materials and processes in a particular culture area. Having reviewed the general role of scientific techniques in research, in subsequent chapters of the book we will highlight their applicability to particular problems of cultural reconstruction.

POINTS TO REMEMBER

- Regardless of size, all archaeological research projects go through an established procedure: research design, fieldwork and lab work, materials analysis and statistical analysis, and reporting on the project.

- The site formation process is dynamic, beginning with the cultural behavior that creates the material record and continuing through the natural and cultural events that are revealed in the site as archaeologists investigate it.

- Fieldwork involves investigating patterns in the material culture record as these occur on the surface or within the matrix of the find.

- Archaeologists use many kinds of typologies to classify and organize their materials. All typologies are abstractions, perspectives on how to understand the range of variation encompassed by any set of materials.

- Problem orientation varies greatly, but analyses of archaeological materials address three basic questions: How old is it? What is it? Where is it from?

- Computers are widely used in archaeology to keep track of materials and to analyze patterns in the material culture record.

FOR FURTHER READING

Gowlett's *Ascent to Civilization* is an excellent overview of archaeological research over the world, combining descriptions of techniques with culture histories. Binford's *In Pursuit of the Past* describes the basic issues archaeologists address. Joukowsky's *A Complete Manual of Field Archaeology* is a good source on field methods. Schiffer's *Formation Processes of the Archaeological Record* describes how sites develop. Thomas's *Refiguring Anthropology* introduces statistics with actual anthropological and archaeological data sets. For more on analysis of human and other organic remains, we recommend Brothwell's *The Bog Man and the Archaeology of People*, and for interpretation of burials in their broader cultural context, see Tainter's "Mortuary Practices and the Study of Prehistoric Social Systems."

*Full citations appear in the bibliography.

CHAPTER FIVE

CONCEPTUAL
FRAMEWORK

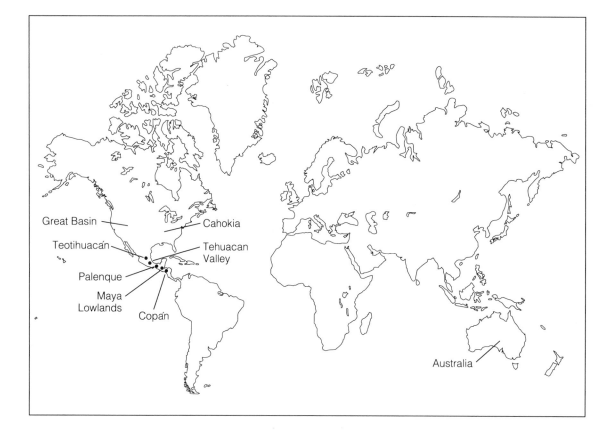

During our review of the historical development of anthropology and archaeology, we briefly introduced a number of interrelated theories, concepts, and terms that are central to modern archaeological interpretation and that will be often used in the chapters that follow. In this chapter we will explore

- The concept of *culture*
- The theory of biological evolution and its implications for *cultural evolution*
- The method and theory of *cultural ecology*
- *Modes of sociopolitical integration* and the concept of *civilization*
- Cultures as *systems*
- *Cultural materialism*.

We will illustrate these ideas with short examples, often drawn from our own culture. In later chapters the concepts are applied to archaeological cultures and issues.

THE CONCEPT OF CULTURE

Although the concept of culture is central to anthropology and archaeology, it is difficult to define; whole books have in fact been written about it (Kroeber and Kluckhohn 1952). We offered a traditional definition of culture in Chapter 1.

> Culture . . . is that complex whole which includes knowledge, belief, art, law, morals, custom, and any other capabilities and habits acquired by . . . member[s] of society.
>
> *(Tylor 1871)*

This definition articulates several important aspects of culture: Culture is *acquired* by people as members of *social groups*; culture is a "complex whole," an integrated collection of *beliefs* and *behaviors* that fit together well; finally, culture is both *information* (knowledge) and *behavior* (capabilities and habits).

Anthropologists commonly use the concept to refer both to the general human capacity for symbolically learned, patterned behavior and to the specific patterns of a particular society. Culture in the specific sense also implies a tradition of beliefs, customs, values, and behaviors shared by a social group through time, transcending the lifespans of any of its members. The two definitions of culture used in this book are based on this dual perspective:

1. Generally, culture is the human capacity to learn, share, and transmit behavior rapidly by using symbolic communication such as spoken and written language.

2. Specifically, culture is the particular set of symbolically learned, shared, transmitted behaviors used by members of a social group.

Humans are able to learn quickly, share what they know with others, and transmit information using complex forms of symbolic communication (see also Chapter 9). These behaviors define culture in its most general sense and, by this definition, other species besides humans may have rudimentary forms of it (Fig. 5.1). But only humans appear to have such a heavy dependence on culturally learned behavior that without it we could not survive. In this regard, as many anthropologists have pointed out, culture is the mode of adaptation peculiar to our species and must itself be subject to the process of evolution.

In very broad terms, all humans share equally the general capacity for culture; indeed this trait is rooted in our common biological evolution (Pfeiffer 1969). This does not mean in any sense that culture is genetically inherited, however. For example, all humans have inherited the physiological capability to use symbolic language — our basic cultural skill — which is made possible by the physical structures of the human brain, tongue, and larynx. Likewise, we humans can all effectively make and use tools because of our dextrous hands. No one, however, inherits the capacity for a particular language or a particular set of tools.

The human capacity for culture is also related to our species's reproductive patterns. Humans produce relatively few young, who require parental care for many more years than do the offspring of other mammals. This extended process of maturation allows a long period of learning. These basic human characteristics are clearly the products of biological evolution. Early humans who had these traits, or had them in more efficient forms than other humans, survived and reproduced most effectively.

Specific sets of cultural behavior, that is, specific cultures, are characteristic of particular groups, or societies. But no individual in any society internalizes all available cultural information or expresses all possible forms of cultural behavior. People of different ages, sexes, occupations, or classes do not understand or participate in their society's culture in precisely the same ways.

Culture as Mind or Culture as Behavior

Anthropologists and archaeologists have traditionally emphasized culture, in the specific sense, as information — as a consciously held mental blueprint consisting of learned knowledge, ideas, attitudes, and values that is broadly shared by people in social groups and that allows them to interact in highly patterned ways. Many early ethnographers felt that the goal of anthropology was to understand the mental blueprints of the people they studied. The best way to do this was to interview informants, thereby presumably gaining direct access to thoughts and attitudes. Similarly, archaeologists have sometimes sought to reconstruct the "minds" of ancient peoples (Leone 1982). In this sense, culture would mean a collective body

FIGURE 5.1 Chimpanzees use sticks to catch and eat termites and to scratch themselves. This behavior illustrates that many nonhuman primates have rudimentary forms of culture.

of information, values, and beliefs that was disembodied from individual humans and that could be analyzed on its own terms.

A broader approach is to emphasize culture as behavior—to define as the goal of anthropology and archaeology the investigation and explanation of not only what people think but what they *do* as culture-bearing social beings. In this behavioral sense the culture of a particular social group may be defined in terms of common behavioral patterns, or **norms**. If we watched large numbers of people in a particular cultural setting exhibit a certain behavior, we would usually see a range of variation in the behavior, but statistically one form of it would occur most frequently, which would constitute the norm. Normative behavior, at any given time, tends to reflect the cultural information people possess and what they regard as positive cultural values. Such norms are what anthropologists frequently refer to as "customs"; for example, it is a custom in the United States to eat three meals a day. Ranges of cultural behavior exist at any point in time because individuals do not participate in their cultures in precisely the same ways. Furthermore, modes of behavior shift through time as a result of innovations, new information that has entered the cultural system, or even mistakes.

norms Common behavioral patterns of particular social groups.

Emphasis on the collective, mental aspects of culture obscures an important point: Culture is used by individuals to cope with the circumstances of their everyday lives. Cultural behavior is continually tested by everyday problems, opportunities, and challenges; it is often modified or changed and thus is constantly "reinvented."

One advantage to regarding culture as learned behavior is that we can

operational model   A representation of reality that is based on observation of how the component parts of the real situation operate.

cognized model   A representation of reality that is based in part on idealized expectations about the real situation.

distinguish between an **operational model** of culture, consisting of what an observer would perceive as action and results, and a **cognized model** of culture, involving what the participant would describe as action and results. If we observe cultural behavior systematically, we find that many operationalized attitudes, values, and habits are not cognized—they may not be expressed by participants, but the behavior associated with them can be directly observed.

For example, ethnoarchaeologists investigating modern garbage disposal have discovered that people drink more alcohol than they say they do judging from the bottles and cans they discard (Rathje 1974; Rathje and Ritenbaugh 1984). People have a certain cognized model of appropriate behavior (low levels of alcohol consumption) and either knowingly or unconsciously behave contrarily to it, but are unwilling to acknowledge this. In this case the description of culture in behavioral, operational terms would be very different from the mental, cognized one.

Sometimes it is impossible to act according to highly valued cultural expectations. For example, certain traditional societies dictate that marriage partners must be chosen from specified categories of relatives. However, if there are no prospective mates in these categories, the spouse may be chosen from outside them. The latter such marriage may even be the most common, but it does not conform to the preferred cultural value.

The distinction between operational and cognized models of behavior is particularly important for archaeology, because archaeologists observe and interpret the results of what people did, not what they said they did or the rationalizations or justifications for their actions (Harris 1979). Because archaeologists have no direct access to informants, they must use the recovered material relics of behavior as a basis for their reconstructions and explanations. As we will see shortly, behavior is what is acted on during the process of cultural evolution.

Before we move on to a discussion of evolution, it should be noted that in common parlance culture is often alluded to in ways that imply it exists independently of people, as in descriptions of "cultures" contacting or interacting with each other or "cultures" in conflict. Remember that cultures do not perform actions, *people* do, as culture-bearing members of social groups.

BIOLOGICAL AND CULTURAL EVOLUTION

Evolution is a special kind of change, usually thought of as gradual, directional, and relatively predictable (Dawkins 1986; Mayr 1988). We apply this concept to biological and cultural change, but even inorganic things undergo such change, for example, radioactive elements, which eventually transform into nonradioactive ones according to highly predictable processes (this change is the basis for radiocarbon dating). We tend to use the word *evolution* generally for changes of this relatively gradual, predictable kind. In a strict sense, the term refers to biological or behavioral changes in living systems; we now understand, however, that evolutionary changes may not be gradual, directional, or highly predictable at all.

The material record of past cultures reveals patterns of change that resemble biological evolution and that are generated by the same sorts of mechanisms. For this reason, we begin our study of cultural evolution by examining how biological evolution operates.

Biological Evolution

As a highly developed concept, evolution is most closely identified with biology, where it refers to specific kinds of changes that eventually result in the appearance of new species (Darwin [1859] 1958). The idea of biological evolution is very old, but only in the 19th century did scientists such as Charles Darwin begin to understand how and why species change through time. Evidence of geological change influenced thinking about *both* biological and cultural change. That biological evolution occurred was obvious, but the question remained: What caused it? Why did some species become extinct and new ones develop out of the old?

From his observations of the variation among individuals in many animal species and from reading Malthus's ([1798] 1970) essay on the relation of human populations to their food supplies, Darwin hit upon the concept of **natural selection**. His theoretical formulations describe the effect of the constraints and possibilities presented by the natural environment on the patterns of survival and reproduction by individuals within species and of species competing against each other.

The general circumstances allowing evolution to occur are as follows:

1. Individuals within any species exhibit variation among themselves, and some of this variation is inheritable.

2. Organisms produce many more offspring than the environment can support, yet most species maintain relatively stable numbers from generation to generation because, for example, in each generation some individuals die before they mature and reproduce.

3. Some individuals have characteristics that enhance their chances of surviving and reproducing, given the conditions of the natural environment. In other words, when individuals are better adapted to their environments than others, they have a greater chance of producing offspring. This **differential reproduction** is, in fact, the measure of fitness. Natural selection is more popularly known as "survival of the fittest," the fittest individuals in biological evolution being those who bear the most offspring who themselves survive and reproduce.

4. Insofar as the traits that enhance adaptation to the environment (and thus ensure evolutionary fitness) are genetic (can be passed on from generation to generation), the species will change over time, toward better adaptation to the environment. Environmental conditions thus

natural selection The effect of the constraints and possibilities presented by the natural environment on the patterns of survival and reproduction by individuals within species, and species competing against each other.

differential reproduction The measure of fitness calculated by the relative rates at which different individuals produce live offspring.

exert a "selective" pressure on the genetic variation expressed in each generation.

mutation Random shifts of the genetic code.

The ultimate source of genetic variation is **mutation** of the genetic code; the causes of mutation are complex but mutation is a random occurrence—mutations do not arise in order to take advantage of opportunities that environmental changes set before them. Mutations may be deleterious, or neutral, but some result in characteristics that enhance adaptation, and such changes in the genetic code may then be passed on to future generations.

gene flow Sharing traits by mating between otherwise distinct populations of the same species.

genetic drift The branching off of a separate population that bears some but not all of the traits of the parent population; sometimes called "founder's effect."

Mutation provides the raw material for selection to operate, but selection also operates on genetic variation that results from **gene flow,** whereby traits are shared through mating between otherwise distinct populations of the same species, and from **genetic drift,** sometimes called "founder's effect," which is due to the branching off of a separate population bearing some but not all of the traits of the parent population. Whatever its source, variation must be present if selection is to work, causing populations to diverge from one another, which eventually results in the appearance of new species. Sometimes environmental conditions change very rapidly, much faster than genetic variation is introduced into the population for selection to act upon. In such cases the outcome is extinction. (For an extended discussion of genetics see Feder and Park 1989.)

This discussion of evolution by natural selection oversimplifies a complex set of processes, but their general operation is familiar to us today (Fig. 5.2). Consider, for example, the evolution of insects that attack our food crops. To eradicate these insects highly toxic pesticides such as DDT have been used. DDT was at first very effective, destroying large proportions of insect populations. There were always survivors, however. Because of variation due to random mutations, each generation included individuals whose genetic makeup enabled them to resist DDT better than others. The resistant individuals became the progenitors of whole new generations. Since insects with their short life spans are among the most prolific breeders of the animal world, insect populations were soon back up to normal levels, with a slightly different genetic makeup inherited from the pesticide-resistant progenitors. These insect species have evolved.

The process of biological evolution is both haphazard and determined. Random or accidental changes produce genetic variation on which selection acts, but reproduction and selection are highly patterned. Long-term evolutionary processes thus have a "historical" dimension in the sense that they depend on unique, unpredictable events that occur through time.

Although Darwin knew nothing about genetic inheritance and his theory has been refined many times, his basic conclusion still stands: All species share a common descent through evolution, which may be defined as *descent with modification through selection*. In scientific terms, evolution is the most successful paradigm we have for explaining major transformations in living systems over long periods of time.

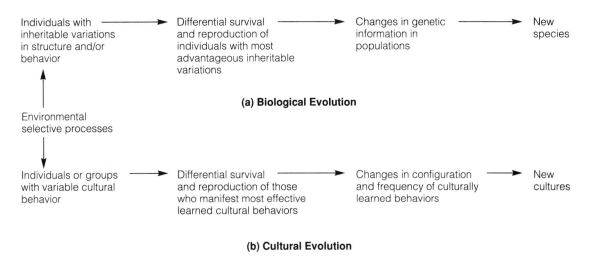

(a) Biological Evolution

(b) Cultural Evolution

Cultural Evolution

Culture is integral to human life. It consists, in large part, of information, which in turn motivates behavior. Like genetic information, cultural information is replicated and transmitted from individual to individual, especially from one generation to the next, so there are continuities in culture through time (Dawkins 1986). Unlike our biological heritage, culture is transmitted through learning—a phenomenon with enormous consequences. For example, new cultural information may be passed between any individuals, not just from parent to child as is the case with genetic information. Cultural information can be transmitted immediately and does not depend on the reproductive process. All people share a basic biological capacity for cultural behavior, including physiological structures necessary for symbolic language and for tool use, and all are equally capable of learning to use any particular language or tool.

As noted earlier, a basic proposition of modern archaeology is that culture is fundamental to human adaptation (Binford 1972). We can therefore usefully apply the concept of evolution to changes in culture, bearing in mind the essential differences between cultural and genetic transmission.

Selection For any kind of evolutionary process to work, there must be variety and there must be selection. Biological selection exploits the variety in genetic information. Essential to cultural selection is the variety of learned, shared information that is the basis for cultural behavior in human social groups. The principle of cultural evolution is thus, simply stated, that certain learned behaviors are more successful than others at allowing

FIGURE 5.2 While there is general similarity in the processes of biological and cultural evolution as diagrammed above, there are also important differences. In both cases information is selected for, but since cultural information is learned, it is transmitted in more rapid and flexible ways than genetic information. We call the result of both processes "adaptation."

people to adapt to particular environmental conditions. Adaptively successful behaviors displace less successful ones; metaphorically, they "reproduce" more effectively. They do so either because those who fail (or are unable) to adopt more successful behaviors die out or because less successful behaviors are discarded in favor of more successful ones.

As we will see at the end of this chapter, archaeologists have documented that over the last 12,000 years the practice of hunting and gathering food has been almost entirely replaced by "food producing" — that is, farming (Flannery 1973b) (see Box 5.3). Both strategies of food procurement involve learned information and behavior. Both are obviously capable of effectively supporting people. Yet in a comparatively short period of time (relative to the roughly 2 million-year-long period of the genus *Homo*) one has almost completely replaced the other, and today there are virtually no hunter-gatherer cultures left. As replacement occurred, hunter-gatherer populations were sometimes eradicated by food producers. More commonly, hunter-gatherers themselves adopted food production, rapidly learning this alternative subsistence strategy, and thus adapting to a new set of learned subsistence practices. What became "extinct" is not the people or their genes but rather a learned way of life. In either case, cultural selection favored farming as a food-getting strategy.

An example more familiar to us today would be the competition among businesses in a free-market economy for a scarce resource: customers. Companies that are more effective in attracting and satisfying customers prosper, and other companies have no choice but to emulate them or go out of business. This is why businesses are constantly experimenting with new products, new advertising campaigns, or new technologies. The selective pressures of the environment of consumers make the "culture" of business very dynamic.

Where does variation in cultural behavior originate? What in culture is analogous to, say, mutation? **Innovations,** or inventions, are new ideas and practices; if they are more effective or satisfying than old ways of doing things, they may be widely adopted. They may also be independently developed by different people at different times and places. Innovations may spread by a process of **diffusion** (not unlike gene flow) from one culture to another. Cultural evolution, unlike biological evolution, often involves intentional experimentation and change, reflecting the continuous search for new solutions that so distinguishes our species from others.

It should be clear now why the distinction we made earlier between operational and cognized behavior is so important. Selection only acts directly on what people do, not what they think. In biological and cultural terms, individuals or groups who have successfully adjusted to their environments are said to be well adapted. Thus farmers achieved a more successful adaptation than hunter-gatherers in most cases in which they both competed for the same environments. In modern times, if one bank installs automatic teller machines that become popular with customers, the rest must do so as well, or they will be at a selective disadvantage.

innovations New ideas, practices, or inventions which may lead to change.

diffusion Spread of a trait from one culture to another.

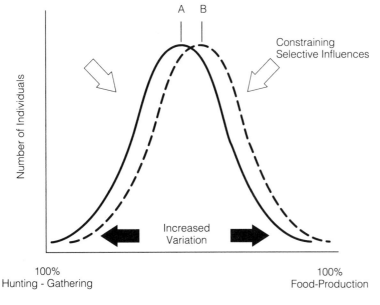

FIGURE 5.3 How do cultures change while maintaining "normal" behavior? Imagine that a society has begun the transition from hunting-gathering to agriculture. At this point, "A" represents the norm of behavior, while the large white arrows indicate selective environmental influences that constrain behavior to a narrow range. But note that variation exists, as indicated by the black arrows: A few people might still use wild foods, while a few others would depend on unusually high proportions of cultigens. Suppose that innovations made food production more attractive, that is, advantaged those who adopted them. Such innovations might spread quickly throughout the whole population, resulting in a shift of the whole system toward a new "norm" of behavior ("B").

Although our examples emphasize the changes that have been brought about by selection, stability can also be favored. Let us return to the idea of normative behavior for a moment. The reason normative behavior patterns exist (why large numbers of people do things the same way) is that such patterns are found over time to be successful, or at least not harmful. Once a behavior pattern becomes an integral part of culture, it is difficult to dislodge or change it without destabilizing the whole system of behaviors. In fact, pressure to change can result in modifications that are conservative in their effect on preserving existing behavioral patterns (see Romer's Rule below and Fig. 5.3). Individuals or groups who depart from the norm tend to be disadvantaged by selection. Normative behavior is thus reinforced, and selection acts to promote stability in cultural systems. When the relationship of the cultural system to its environment changes, however, selection may favor some of the nonnormative behaviors, thus promoting change. As long as a foraging population had plenty of wild food available, the experiments of a few of its members with food production were unimportant: Foraging remained the normative subsistence behavior. Under changed conditions, food production might become a more frequent, and eventually dominant, form of subsistence behavior.

Since the evolutionary perspective helps us understand cultural stability, it can help answer the questions "How does a culture work at any point in time?" and "How did a culture come to be this way?" Just as a biologist can study a species at any point in time as the product of an evolutionary process, so too can we study cultures at particular points in time (Johnson and Earle 1987), using an evolutionary point of view.

Important Characteristics of Cultural Evolution

1. Cultural evolution can occur as fast as an idea can be passed from one person to another — much more rapidly than genetic inheritance.

2. Cultural evolution may act on the technological, organizational, or ideological components of cultural behavior. When selection acts to change any one of these parts of culture, related changes will usually occur in the others as well.

3. Selection in cultural evolution, as in biological evolution, is opportunistic; it works on whatever is immediately available. This is why cultures exhibit so much variation in their solutions to similar adaptive problems.

4. Cultural evolution selects solutions to immediate, short-term problems or stresses, the long-term consequences of which may be unknown or ignored.

Since biological and cultural evolution are closely related, anthropologists have found certain concepts of biology to be useful:

law of biotic potential Rule stating that most organisms have the potential to produce far more offspring than can possibly be supported by their environments.

1. The **law of biotic potential** states that most organisms have the potential to produce far more offspring than can possibly be supported by their environments. Malthus ([1798] 1970), for example, recognized that this principle applied to humans. He noticed that population growth was very slow in many parts of Europe but that where resources were abundant, such as on the North American frontier colonized by European immigrants, population growth was extraordinarily rapid (as Franklin had documented). Thus the European populations were realizing a much slower rate of reproduction than their "biotic potential" would permit under circumstances of more abundant resources. Darwin was greatly influenced by this concept. The implications of it are important because cultural evolution emphasizes population changes.

Leibig's law Rule stating that the numbers of a population are regulated by the essential resource in shortest supply.

2. According to **Leibig's Law,** the numbers of a population are regulated by the essential resource in shortest supply. This rule highlights the relationship of humans to resources. For example, if farmers have plenty of fertile land, but there is a serious shortage of water every ten years, then water availability, not land, will primarily limit the amount of food grown and (in turn) the size of the populations supported by it. Essential resources other than food and water may be involved, such as materials for tools.

law of least effort Rule stating that organisms will generally accomplish necessary tasks with a minimal expenditure of time and effort.

3. The **law of least effort** posits that organisms will generally accomplish necessary tasks with the minimal expenditure of time and effort. Those that expend more time and energy than necessary are, in the long run, selected against. For example, iron or steel tools have invariably replaced utilitarian stone tools wherever the choice was available. This is because

iron or steel tools allow tasks to be accomplished with much less effort than stone tools.

4. **Romer's Rule** states that successful biological innovations are initially conservative, in the sense that they function to maintain traditional ways of life. (This rule relates to the fourth general characteristic of cultural evolution reviewed above.) A cultural illustration of the rule is provided by the ancestors of the modern Eskimo, who domesticated the dog so that they could pursue more efficiently their traditional hunting way of life.

Romer's Rule   Rule stating that successful biological or cultural innovations are initially conservative in the sense that they function to maintain traditional ways of life.

These four biological principles are not as fixed nor as generally applicable as those of physics or chemistry, but they may serve to elucidate the nature of evolutionary processes and to evaluate information about the events and trends detected in the archaeological record.

General and Specific Cultural Evolution

Borrowing another idea from biologists, anthropologists make a distinction between general and specific cultural evolution (Sahlins and Service 1960). The broadest trends characterizing human cultural evolution, such as the change from hunting and gathering to agriculture, provide us with examples of what is called **general evolution**. **Specific evolution** is another, equally important perspective that looks at the changes in particular societies and cultures whose specific evolutionary sequences may vary greatly. Not all foraging societies are exactly alike, nor did all of them become agricultural. Not all societies with simple organization evolved into complex states or empires, nor do all states have identical social and political structure. Some egalitarian foragers such as the Eskimo have survived into the present.

general evolution   Broad trends of human cultural change observed on a worldwide, comparative basis.

specific evolution   Changes in particular societies and cultures whose specific evolutionary sequences may vary greatly.

But comparison of many examples of adaptation to specific environments shows the following *general trends in cultural evolution* (Pfeiffer 1977):

1. Humans have become much more numerous through time. Our numbers have increased from approximately 10 to 20 million at the end of the last Ice Age (about 12,000 years ago) to a present world population of over 5 billion.

2. Human societies have become larger and geographically more widespread through time.

3. Cultural behavior has become more diverse and complex through time.

These trends are interrelated and are linked to several major *transformations in cultural adaptation* during the last 12,000 years:

1. *Means of subsistence.* The transition from foraging (hunting and gathering) to food production (planting and herding) transformed the way people acquired food energy (see Chapter 6).

2. *Sociopolitical organization.* The growth of small, egalitarian societies into

large, politically centralized, stratified societies transformed the ways people relate to each other (see below and Chapter 9).

3. *Technology and energy use.* From economies based on the muscle power of humans and animals emerged industrial economies based on machines and fossil fuel or nuclear energy.

The first two of these transformation was discovered through archaeological research. A major goal of archaeology is to see if, or how, these three transformations happened in specific sequence of culture change, and to explain why they occurred (Steward 1955). Only by looking at examples of specific cultures adapting to specific environments can we investigate how cultural evolution works in particular circumstances. And, of course, our ability to generalize about cultural evolution (as Julian Steward insisted) derives from our knowledge of how evolutionary processes have worked in many specific instances.

For example, the Spanish were impressed with the cultural accomplishments of the Aztecs (Cortés 1986), whose civilization had resembled their own in many respects (see Bernal Diaz's description, Chapter 1). In fact, comparisons between complex Old World and New World cultures are fascinating from the anthropological perspective because of their many similarities despite independent courses of development. We will come back to this topic in Chapter 14; now let us note that such similarities reveal that the general processes and trends listed above have produced important regularities in general cultural evolution.

Progress and Cultural Evolution

Nineteenth-century evolutionists made the mistake of equating the evolution of cultural complexity with "progress," an abstract notion of change toward improvement. They had some grasp of the transformations we just mentioned, especially the last, and believed that Western industrial societies were self-evidently more highly evolved and progressive than non-Western societies. A number of evolutionists even believed that the variation exhibited by living cultures was based on inherent biological capabilities, an idea that is patently false. Such false ideas were used in objectional ways to justify Western presumptions of moral and intellectual superiority and to assert political dominance over other peoples. This cultural imperialism was an important reason why 19th-century cultural evolutionism was rejected.

We cannot state too strongly that there is no implication of progress inherent in the evolutionary processes investigated in this book. We can, however, point to measures of evolutionary success. Farming has been a more successful strategy than hunting and gathering, as indicated by the spread of the former at the expense of the latter. But all evolutionary change is a process of gain and loss. Evidence suggests that farmers often have poorer diets than hunter-gatherers, are prey to a greater range of diseases, and work harder and longer for their food. On the other hand, farming generally provides a more stable food supply and can support a higher population density than can hunting and gathering. Whether the replacement of hunting and gathering by farming is "progressive" is impossible to know, however, and whether it is "good" or "bad" is not a scientific issue.

MODES OF POLITICAL INTEGRATION

Political evolution is the change in how a society is governed and how power is held. Focusing on political organization dramatizes important features of the society as a whole. As noted in Chapter 2, anthropologists have devised a model of political evolution and organization that has been widely used by archaeologists. This model describes several basic "modes of political integration" observed by ethnographers and is itself an example of cultural evolutionary thinking. This is the model that will be used, either directly or indirectly, throughout much of the rest of this book. It is explored in detail in Chapter 10; here we will consider only its most basic ideas.

In the 1960s, stimulated by Steward's work (1939, 1949, 1955) and by a general resurgence of interest in cultural evolution, ethnographers again began to generalize about broad cultural patterns. Two of these generalized models of cultural organization were particularly useful for archaeological interpretation; archaeologists have since altered and refined them in a number of ways.

The first model was developed by Elman Service (1971), who identified four basic *societal* types—"bands," "tribes," "chiefdoms," and "states"—based largely on economic and social organizational characteristics (see Box 5.1). Societies of each of these kinds were found in the ethnographic record; they represented cultural adaptations, in the cultural ecological sense. Arranged from simplest in organization to most complex, they also provided a model for cultural evolution.

The second, more overtly evolutionary scheme, derived in part from Service, was developed by Morton Fried (1967), who identified several basic kinds of *political* systems, which he called "egalitarian," "rank," "stratified," and "state." Though his information was primarily derived from the ethnographic record, Fried considered his typology to reflect an evolutionary sequence. The model of general evolution that he devised has been tested in fact by archaeologists for many years. Although the focus of Fried's scheme is political leadership, it also incorporates many aspects of social organization and economic behavior (Box 5.1).

In the discussion that follows, we combine Service's and Fried's models to describe three modes of political integration: egalitarian, ranked, and stratified.

BOX 5.1

MODES OF SOCIOPOLITICAL INTEGRATION

Egalitarian Societies (Bands and Tribes)

Population   Group size: several dozen to several thousand. Overall density is low, <1 per square kilometer.

Communities   Communities are self-sufficient and, although many of the larger regional social groups may comprise many communities, each is politically autonomous. Communities are similar in scale and range of functions, though there may be considerable seasonal variation. Hunter-gatherer communities are often unstable in terms of membership and location. Egalitarian agriculturalists' communities may be permanent, or moved periodically.

Territoriality   Well-known local territories and cultivated fields are habitually exploited and use rights respected.

Economy   Subsistence is based on hunting and gathering, simple nonintensive food production, or a combination of the two. There is little occupational specialization; people of the same age and sex perform similar tasks. The basic unit of production and consumption is the family. The most important mode of redistribution is sharing among kinspeople. There is some trade in utilitarian and exotic goods, but little or no differential access to limited necessary resources.

Society   Social integration is based on kinship and frequent face-to-face interaction, within a common ethnic and linguistic identity. Positions of prestige are defined by age, sex, and personal ability. In tribal societies, theoretical descent groups and sodalities promote cohesion.

Politics   There are few or no formal offices and titles. Leadership positions are highly situational and based on achievement, within the constraints of age and sex.

Leadership depends on authority, persuasion, and consensus, with little or no use of coercive force. Feuding is common, often leading to community fissioning. Raiding and warfare are common, particularly among tribes. Confrontations are often ritualized with few casualties, but highly lethal raids can occur. Warfare may stimulate short-term military alliances.

Religion   Specialists include shamans, and sodalities may perform religious functions. Sacred places are revered, and community rituals common.

Ranked Societies (Chiefdoms)

Population   Size: several hundred to several hundred thousand people. Density: sometimes very low (as for chiefdoms based on hunting-gathering or pastoralism) but settled agriculturalists can number several hundred per square kilometer.

Communities   Communities are usually permanent and most resemble each other in size and function. A single political system is made up of many communities with one, the residence of the chief, differentiated as a central place or capital and often having more elaborate architecture. Simple hierarchies of central places may exist.

Territoriality   Regional political system is mainly defined by allegiance to a chief. Territorial boundaries are more strongly defined than in egalitarian societies. Raiding and warfare are common and often lethal.

Economy   Occasionally the subsistence base is hunting and gathering, but usually it is food production, and intensive agriculture is common. Basic units of production and consumption are households and larger kin groups. Trade is common, particularly for exotic items used as chiefly status symbols. Occupational specialization is generally part-time and under the patronage of chiefs. Chiefs redistribute status symbols and may have greater access to other forms of wealth.

Society   Social integration within communities is based on kinship and face-to-face interaction. Kinship, including large theoretical descent groups, is the primary integrating mechanism among communities, and kin groups are ranked in terms of prestige.

Politics   The political hierarchy includes formal offices and titles, and may include several grades of dominant and subordinate chiefs. Access to offices and titles is ascribed, though achievement plays an important role. Leadership depends on prestige, authority, and consensus, with comparatively little use of coercive force. Fissioning of the polity is common, particularly under weak leaders.

Religion   There are specialized sacred and ritual specialists, places, buildings, and monuments. Rituals involving the chief are important, and the chief is typically sacrosanct, and chiefly ancestors may be revered as deities.

Stratified Societies (Nonindustrial States)

Population   Size ranges from a few thousand to many million. Densities may range into the hundreds, even thousands, per square kilometer.

Communities   A single polity includes many permanent communities, forming a hierarchy of size and function, with urban central places and clearly defined capitals.

Territoriality   States have well-defined boundaries. Warfare is common, often involving conscript armies and specialized elite warriors.

Economy   Food production is well-developed and often intensive. Particularly in urban settings, there is part-time and full-time occupational specialization. Production units may be, but are not necessarily kin-based. Widespread trade involves the exchange of utilitarian and luxury items. Exchange takes place in formal marketplaces and sometimes uses state currencies. The state receives taxes and tribute in goods and services from commoners and subject peoples. Basic resources are differentially distributed, with preferential access by the ruler and elites.

Society   Whole social groups are hierarchically ranked as social strata (classes or castes), with elites ranking highest. Kinship remains important for social integration within classes, but not for integrating the society as a whole. Ethnic diversity is common, particularly in large states and in urban centers.

Politics   States are generally dominated by hereditary elites. There are complex hierarchies of specialized administrative positions with formal offices and titles. The highest of these are usually ascribed; lesser offices may be awarded for achievement. Wealth and coercive force are mechanisms of power.

Religion   Commonly there is a state religion, with professional specialists organized into complex religious bureaucracies, sometimes holding their own lands and other resources. There are sacred and ritual places, buildings, and monuments, and the rulers may be sacrosanct or even deified.

FIGURE 5.4 Australian aborigines are among the few band-type societies that have persisted into the 20th century. The photo shows some of the material culture features of their life. Considering the site formation process, what archaeological traces would remain of the dwelling, for example?

bands Small, highly mobile egalitarian societies based on hunting and gathering and characterized by a lack of formal government institutions and economic specialization. Political dominance is gained through achieved leadership rather than ascribed leadership; as many leadership positions exist as circumstances require and there are qualified people to fill them.

tribal societies Egalitarian societies larger and more complex than bands, often sedentary; practice either hunting and gathering or food production, with politically autonomous communities. Political dominance is gained through achieved leadership rather than ascribed leadership, and sodalities are important in integrating the social system.

Egalitarian Societies: Bands and Tribes

In the late 20th century there are probably no people on earth who do not have contacts with the larger world of industrial societies — and who are not influenced by it in some way. However, the Eskimos, the !Kung Bushmen of South Africa, and Native Australians are egalitarian groups that have persisted into recent times.

The smallest known human societies are those we call **bands**. Bands are also, no doubt, the oldest societal form. The Fuegians who so startled Darwin (Chapter 1) and the Shoshone studied by Steward were band-type societies. Although different bands have adapted to different environments, all bands have had certain things in common. All have been small, highly mobile societies based on hunting and gathering, in which resources are available to all. Simple forms of kinship have linked nuclear families into loose groups (usually 50 people or less, but sometimes in the hundreds). Settlements are usually impermanent and technology generally simple and portable. Everyone of the same age and sex carries out most of the same economic tasks (Fig. 5.4).

Tribal societies are larger and more complex. Although many tribal peoples of the past, such as the Plains Indians, were hunter-gatherers, some were completely dependent on food production, and others practiced some combination of the two subsistence strategies (a *mixed economy* strategy). Tribal peoples tend to live in larger, more permanent communities, often made up of hundreds of people. Communities are politically autonomous, varying little from one another in size and composition. Although they share cultural practices and interact with each other, there is no all-encompassing political authority. Each community is a self-contained society in the strict sense of that word. Within and between communities, people are linked by kinship systems based on descent from distant ancestors, and associations, or **sodalities,** exist (such as the Plains Indian warrior societies) that link nonkinspeople as well. Warfare between groups has been common.

Even small-scale, **egalitarian societies** have political problems and require leaders. Egalitarian political leadership can be exercised when it is needed by anyone who has the necessary personal talents (within the limitations of age and sex). There are no limited, highly formal offices to which only a few have access. Individuals thus gain **achieved leadership** through their own abilities, rather than inheriting leadership, that is, gaining **ascribed leadership.** Leadership is often highly situational, in the sense that different people lead in different circumstances and cease to lead when conditions no longer require it. Finally, egalitarian leaders can be extremely effective, but they have virtually no ability to manipulate others through wealth or force. They lead, rather, by persuasion and personal example.

Ranked Societies: Chiefdoms

Ranked societies (sometimes called "middle-range hierarchical societies") have many of the same characteristics as bands and tribes, in particular, that of kinship as a means of integrating social groups. The principal difference is that individuals are ranked vis-à-vis one another in terms of kinship status and social prestige, which are largely ascribed. Thus, institutionalized social hierarchies exist that are absent in egalitarian societies. Only high-ranking people are able to assume those limited, formal offices of leadership; such people we call "chiefs" and their societies "chiefdoms." Leadership is thus largely ascribed by birth, though personal achievement may play a role as well. Permanent leaders with many political, ritual, military, and economic functions, chiefs may have subchiefs under them. The settlement with the chief's house is the political center.

With hierarchies of political statuses, chiefdoms have more elaborate government than bands or tribes. Chiefs may live in larger houses and have more possessions than people of lesser rank. But, as in egalitarian societies, chiefs generally are not wealthy in the sense that they control vast amounts of essential resources, and they must give generously to their people. Nor do they command much force. They too must lead largely by persuasion, though the prestige and authority derived from their high birth and supernatural importance predisposes others to accept their decisions.

Although there have been some very small **chiefdoms,** most have been larger than tribes, their population sometimes ranging in the thousands. Particularly strong chiefs have sometimes controlled 50,000 people or more, and dominated subchiefs. As such numbers imply, chiefdoms usually have had effective agricultural economies (although a few hunter-gatherer chiefdoms have existed). Population densities have been high, and often many communities have been ruled from the chief's capital—a politically

sodality   Social group organized around specific interests or goals, whose members are not necessarily kin.

egalitarian societies Collective term for bands and tribes, societies in which all members have equal access to basic resources. Leadership is situational and attainable by achievement within the confines of age and sex.

achieved leadership Leadership gained through one's own abilities rather than inheritance of a position.

ascribed leadership Leadership assigned by birthright, sex, or some other fixed criterion.

ranked societies   Societies in which individuals are ranked vis-à-vis one another in terms of kinship status and social prestige, which are largely ascribed. Fewer positions of authority or leadership exist than there are individuals capable of filling them, and access to these positions is generally ascribed.

chiefdom   The kind of political system characteristic of most ranked societies, politically dominated by chiefs.

specialized community usually distinguished by larger size and special features such as temples, tombs, or elaborate houses. A good archaeological example of a ranked society is that centered on Cahokia in the American Midwest (see Box 11.1).

Stratified Society and the State

In some societies whole groups of people are ranked vis-à-vis one another, with high-ranking groups having more access to political office, authority, and wealth than those of lower rank. Such ranked groups are called social strata, or classes; societies that have them are called **stratified societies**. There is a hierarchical structure based largely on wealth and power; that is, some people have more control of essential resources than others, and this inequality confers high status, prestige, and access to positions of political leadership. In nonindustrial stratified societies such wealth is usually inherited, so there is a kinship component to political structure. On the other hand, kinship does not serve effectively to integrate the society as a whole, and social interactions are not highly conditioned by the awareness of common kinship, as in ranked societies.

Though wealth can be used to manipulate others, thus constituting a source of power, stratified societies are fragile because of their built-in economic inequalities. When institutions such as armies, legal systems, police forces, and organized religions appeared that upheld and strengthened stratification, the **state** was born — this is the dominant political form today, and one in which we all live. States are strongly territorial, characterized by complex, well-defined political leadership and hierarchies of settlement, and often elaborate and highly specialized bureaucracies. These societies are very large, their populations ranging from a few thousand to hundreds of millions.

We intuitively understand the complexity of state-level societies, because we live in them. Box 5.2 describes the essence of hierarchical organization, using the example of a modern corporation.

Fried's is a general evolutionary model, but it is not universal or inevitable. Not all societies evolve according to the series of forms the model describes, and if change takes place, it is not necessarily in the order given. Nevertheless, over the last 10,000 years there has been a general tendency for more complex, hierarchical societies to replace smaller, simpler ones, and from an evolutionary perspective such a process is presumably the result of selection. In addition to being a provocative model for archaeological research (see Chapter 10), Fried's scheme incorporates some of the trends in cultural evolution we discussed earlier — especially changes in social scale and internal complexity. The real challenge, however, is to specify *why* such selection might have taken place, a topic we will return to later, especially in Chapter 16.

stratified society   Large society in which whole groups of people are ranked vis-à-vis one another, with high-ranking groups having more access to political office, authority, and wealth than lower-ranking ones.

state   Stratified society that has developed the institutions that effectively uphold an order of stratification. States are strongly territorial, with complex, well-defined political leadership, hierarchies of settlement, and often elaborate and highly specialized bureaucracies. Populations can range from the thousands to the millions.

BOX 5.2

THE MODERN CORPORATION: HIERARCHY AT WORK

Fried's political model has at its core the fundamental distinction between egalitarian and hierarchical systems. Some might characterize modern American society as "egalitarian" since equality of opportunity and equal treatment under the law are so important. But Fried's model deals with how society is structured, and there is no denying the striking differences between hunting-gathering bands and even the simplest state. One of the essential differences between these kinds of systems is that in egalitarian societies the number of leadership positions is only limited by the occurrence of circumstances requiring leadership and the number of people capable of serving, but in hierarchical societies strict limits are set on leadership.

To understand this difference, consider the structure of the modern large business corporation, one employing thousands of people. At the top of the organization there is a single person, usually called a "chief executive officer" (CEO). At the bottom of the organization are thousands of people doing basic work, such as assembling cars. Between the two extremes is a complex hierarchy of roles and statuses: factory foremen, office managers, accountants, vice-presidents, and so forth. Even if the CEO had to be recruited from the ranks of the corporation, many individuals would never qualify as applicants for the job; many employees would lack the experience, talent, and/or education, while others might be disqualified by built-in inequalities, resulting, for example, from discrimination against nonwhite and female employees. Still, in a really large corporation many employees would be qualified for the job. Unfortunately, there is only one CEO, and once the position is filled, all the other potential "leaders" are relegated to subordinate positions. This process is a fundamental feature of a hierarchical, nonegalitarian organization, whether it is a corporation or a whole society.

If we further specify that this corporation is not public but family held, then we have a situation wherein the office of CEO may be inherited in a family line by descent: ascribed rather than achieved. In most traditional hierarchical societies the highest leadership positions were assigned in this way, further eliminating eligible people. In egalitarian societies such restrictive structures of leadership are lacking.

The Concept of Civilization

Since at least the mid-19th century the concept of **civilization** has been closely identified with cultural evolution (Morgan 1877). At first the word was used interchangeably with that of *culture,* as defined at the beginning of this chapter. Later it came to mean, as well, a type of complex society presumed to be at the pinnacle of progressive evolution—for example, "civilization" as opposed to "savagery" (see Morgan's evolutionary scheme in Table 2.2). Anthropologists today reject these connotations of moral or social superiority or progress, but "civilization" is still often used by social scientists, sometimes in poorly defined ways. Since this book describes and

civilization Complex sociopolitical form defined by the institutions of the state and the existence of a distinctive Great Tradition.

explains the evolution of early civilizations, it is important to discuss this issue in some depth. The meaning used here is similar to that suggested by Charles Redman (1978) in his study of Near Eastern civilizations.

Redman, who, like many other archaeologists, builds on the work of V. Gorden Childe (1950), defines the essential features of urban civilizations as follows:

1. *Cities,* which are large, densely populated settlements with different and more complex functions than rural settlements.

2. *Occupational specialists,* who provide specialized goods and services rather than simply make their living as farmers. This category would include ritual and administrative specialists and artisans.

3. *Food surpluses* to support these specialists and members of the elite; the presence of administrative institutions to extract these surpluses from farmers, as taxes or offerings.

4. *Social classes,* especially a ruling class, which is economically and politically dominant.

5. *Increased importance of residence and economic function* as overall organizing principles in society, with reduced importance of kinship.

6. *Long-distance trade and commerce.*

7. The use of *writing,* as well as other intellectual achievements such as arithmetic, astronomy, and calendars.

8. *Monumental public architecture,* such as temples and palaces.

9. *Distinctive and sophisticated art styles.*

The first six characteristics are the most important, because they are fundamental features of the political form we call the state. As we already saw, states are large in scale, highly territorial, politically centralized around a capital, and economically stratified into classes (see also Chapter 10). Specialized institutions such as government bureaucracies, law courts, armies, a police force, and state religions help to uphold centralization and stratification. The last three items on Childe's list are not present in all civilizations, and some are found in nonstate societies as well.

Another important element in defining civilizations is less organizational, and more stylistic and qualitative. Childe realized that each of the world's great civilizations had its own distinctive expressions of architecture, art, and other intellectual achievements. He also realized that there were important symbolic and political as well as utilitarian dimensions to these achievements. For example, monumental public buildings may function as places of worship or administration, but they also symbolize the power of the rulers and elites who built them. In each civilization, such elites are not only politically and economically dominant but are identified with impressive sets of cultural values, ideology, rituals, and intellectual accomplishments that are expressed in manners, art, architecture, and writing. These cultural sets, which anthropologists often call "Great Tradi-

FIGURE 5.5 Elite monumental architecture is a distinctive component in many civilizations. Although such architecture has many of the same basic ritual, political, and residential functions from one civilization to another, the forms vary widely in terms of construction techniques, plan, and style.

tions," are highly unique from one civilization to another, giving to each a particular and distinctive "style" (Kroeber 1957). No one would ever mistake, for example, elite Egyptian architecture, art, or writing for that of China (Fig. 5.5). During the course of cultural evolution, Great Traditions develop out of earlier Folk Traditions (Redfield 1953), a process we should familiarize ourselves with, since we will return to it later. Ranked societies have Great Tradition elements, as well.

Folk Traditions, Great Traditions, and Little Traditions

All cultures, however small and politically simple, have sets of beliefs with distinctive elements of ideology, symbolism, and ritual. Such traditions are among the most sacred and hence the most conservative parts of any culture. Among egalitarian societies, or the simpler hierarchical societies, these are called **Folk Traditions**. They are essentially folk belief systems, usually not expressed in writing (though other symbols may be used) and are fairly localized (i.e., in a large region there may be many societies with many local folk traditions). Specialized religious roles are rare, often confined to spiritual practitioners, and in general all adults are knowledgeable about the beliefs, rituals, and symbols appropriate to their ages and sexes.

As **Great Traditions** of elite art and ritual emerge from Folk Traditions during the process of cultural evolution, several changes occur. Great Tradition elements come to be expressed in writing or other systems of highly codified symbols. They also become very widespread over large geographical regions. Specialized religious roles, offices, and institutions emerge. As we shall see in the case of the Maya (see Chapter 11), kings retain some of the functions of earlier egalitarian spiritual leaders.

Folk Tradition Local traditions and beliefs associated with small-scale egalitarian societies or the commoner levels of complex societies, usually expressed in media other than writing.

Great Tradition Sets of elite values and behaviors that emerge from Folk Traditions during the evolution of complex societies and that are expressed in distinctive rituals, art, writing, or other symbolic forms.

FIGURE 5.6 The sacred tree, shown as a cross on this panel from Palenque, was a conspicuous feature of the Classic Maya Great Tradition. Veneration of trees was probably part of a much earlier Maya Folk Tradition.

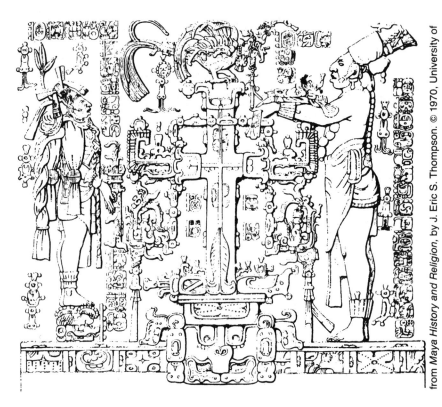

Individuals or groups of high rank have privileged access to information about the Great Tradition, some of which is exclusively for their own use. Elite custodians of the Great Tradition are able to consciously or unconsciously manipulate Great Tradition elements in self-serving ways. In their most extreme forms, Great Traditions become highly dogmatic state ideologies of religion and political power.

Many elements of Folk Traditions are incorporated into Great Traditions, both because of their sacred nature and because emergent elites must espouse belief systems that are to some degree inclusive—that is, are familiar to, and valued by, everyone. For example, very ancient ideas about sacred trees probably characterized folk religion in the Maya Lowlands. As chiefs and kings emerged and religion became institutionalized, the sacred tree was retained as an important religious concept in the Maya Great Tradition and was often the subject of elite art (Fig. 5.6). The stelae of the Classic Maya (for example, Fig. 1.1) were apparently conceptualized as stone trees (Schele and Freidel 1990).

Evolving Great Traditions often incorporate the elements of many localized Folk Traditions into a more coherent and uniform system found over large regions. As this amalgamation occurs, the political factions most successful in dominating the process of political evolution often *promote* distinctive elements of their own folk traditions to high status in the emerging Great Tradition. Thus the Aztecs promoted their own tribal god Huitzilipochtli to an exalted position in the pantheon of Central Mexican gods worshiped in the state religion (Berdan 1982). Sometimes transformations occur as such promotion takes place. For example, folk patterns of ancestor worship may be retained, but royal ancestors may come to have a great supernatural significance for the society as a whole, not just for a particular family.

Some folk elements survive alongside the Great Tradition, which are called **Little Traditions**. Linkage between Great and Little traditions helps to legitimize new, hierarchical social and political forms and stresses continuity between past and present and all social ranks. Something else often happens, however, signaling exclusivity and discontinuity: Great Traditions incorporate elements that are not part of its Folk Tradition foundation. For example, at some Classic Maya centers rulers borrowed symbols of authority from distant regions, such as Central Mexico. In Figure 3.23, Copán's Altar Q shows the sixteenth ruler facing the presumed first ruler, whose "goggles" are a feature associated with Teotihuacán, the most powerful city in all Mesoamerica during the Classic period (further discussion in Chapter 14). Such symbols and the meanings associated with them are monopolized by elites and manipulated by them for their own advantage. On one level, these function as status symbols identifying elites as special people. On another level, and insofar as people believed in supernatural manipulation of the world, they become instruments of ideological power and authority.

To the extent that Great Tradition elements become instruments of elite power and policy, surviving Folk Tradition elements that threaten elite dominance are eliminated or driven underground. But even when Great Traditions have matured, folk traditions may continue to survive and thrive on the local level. We should thus think of Great Traditions as something supplementing, rather than replacing, Folk Traditions, while transformed and surviving elements of the latter are Little Traditions. Influence between these levels is not one-way, but rather a feedback relationship exists.

In summary, civilizations exhibit the organizational characteristics of the state, coupled with distinctive Great Traditions. These two dimensions of culture evolve in tandem with each other.

> **Little Tradition** Folk elements which survive alongside the Great Tradition.

The Limits of Cultural Evolution as an Explanatory Perspective

Not all cultural behavior can be explained as the consequence of cultural evolution. In fact, much of the content of any culture may be of no immediate evolutionary significance, in the sense that it is not acted on by selection. In using an evolutionary approach, we must be very careful about stating our purpose. For example, archaeologists might want to explain why two adjacent communities had markedly different designs on their pottery. One possible explanation might be that these two communities were competing with each other over resources and that there was little social interaction between them, thus no opportunity to share ceramic designs. Their mutual isolation may have enhanced community social solidarity and competitive spirit. This would be an evolutionary explanation. But we could not use an evolutionary explanation to understand why particular motifs were selected over others to decorate the vessels, since any distinctive designs would be equally effective in expressing community identity.

Although a great deal of cultural variation cannot be explained by cultural evolution, the most important and fundamental transformations we see in the archaeological record can be explained by this most powerful model of cultural change. The perspective of cultural evolution emphasizes humans and their behavior as parts of nature, linking them to larger theories of biological evolution and uniformitarian ideas about how the world works.

CULTURAL ECOLOGY: THE RELATIONSHIP BETWEEN ENVIRONMENT AND CULTURE

The environment is central to the evolutionary process, as the agent of selection. The idea that culture and environment interact so that each sets limits and possibilities for the other, in a dynamic relationship, is the essence of *cultural ecology* (Steward 1955). The environment is seen as an interactive partner with culture, providing cultural evolution with its selective mechanism, while culture comprises those traits on which selective pressures act. An example familiar to all of us is global warming, which studies indicate is the result of industrial pollutants. The climate seems to be changing as the result of cultural practices, and these changes will in turn affect culture. How cultural practices will be altered to respond to these changes remains to be seen.

The word *environment* is used here in its broadest sense, to include the physical environment, the biotic environment, and the sociocultural environment—all the external influences on an individual or group.

How Cultures Operate: The Culture Core

The perspective of cultural ecology was developed by Julian Steward (1939) on the basis of his ethnographic research during the 1930s in a desert region of the United States, the Great Basin-Plateau (an area that includes Utah, Nevada, and portions of neighboring states). The vast, dry region was occupied in aboriginal times by small bands of Shoshone hunter-gatherers. Steward described 35–40 local Shoshone groups in his study (Box 5.3). He tried to show that cultural variations and similarities among them could best be explained by the interaction of Shoshone culture with particular environmental features. These descriptions were based on a rigorous, systematic method of data collection and presentation he

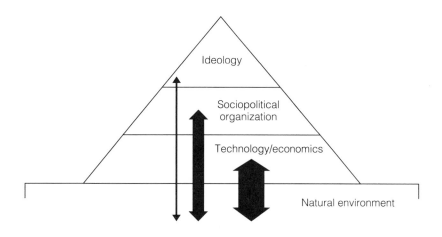

Ideology

Sociopolitical
organization

Technology/economics

Natural environment

FIGURE 5.7 Julian Steward defined the culture core concept as "the constellation of features which are most closely related to subsistence activities and economic arrangements. The core includes such activities and economic arrangements. The core includes such social, political and religious patterns as are empirically determined to be closely connected with these arrangements" (Steward 1955:37). Each level interacted with the environment, and changes in culture could result from any of those interactions, though it was more likely to be initiated on those levels with the strongest and most direct cultural environmental links.

culture core Technological, organizational, and ideological features most directly related to meeting the most important material needs of a society.

subsistence strategy Decisions and actions that affect the raw material procurement of a society.

called the *method* of cultural ecology. Cultural ecology thus is both a theory about why cultures vary and evolve and a method of investigation.

Steward coined the term **culture core** for elements of a culture which could be empirically shown to be interrelated to each other and to the natural environment. The culture core consists of the technological, organizational, and ideological features most directly related to meeting the essential material needs of the society (Fig. 5.7). These features provide a population with its means of adapting to the resource base. Although Steward recognized that the interaction of culture and environment could initiate change in any part of culture (technological, organizational, or ideological), he felt that changes were most likely to originate on the level of technology, but wherever change was initiated, it would, in turn, affect the other levels. Technological changes, for example, would influence social organization and, ultimately, ideology.

According to the culture core model, basic limits and possibilities for cultural change are set by the interaction between core aspects of culture and the local environment. The most essential component of cultural adaptation is **subsistence strategy,** which in turn strongly influences social organization. As selection operates, economic strategies, social relations, political organization, and ideology and ritual expression all influence each other.

Environmental Constraints and Possibilities

The culture core model encompasses all the subsystems (see below) of culture and grounds them in their environment. Within this relationship of culture and environment develop the dynamic cultural-ecological interactions that shape the direction of cultural processes. The culture core model ranks the subsystems singled out by Steward — technology, organization, and ideology — in terms of their impact on long-term change or stability. Basically Steward's argument is that environmental interactions

BOX 5.3

CULTURAL ECOLOGY OF THE SHOSHONE: METHOD AND THEORY

The environmental setting establishes the constraints and possibilities for cultural exploitation.

As a habitat for hunter-gatherers, the Great Basin-Plateau has the following features: *Rainfall* is low (250 mm average per year) and varies greatly, from year to year and from place to place. *Permanent water sources* are few and localized. There are marked seasonal extremes of *temperature*; during the winter, food plants become dormant. *Topography* is diverse, with valley floors as low as 925 meters above sea level and surrounding mountains as high as 4,600 m. Each valley includes a set of "microenvironments," localized zones with somewhat different ecosystems; valley floors have the least rainfall and lowest plant "biomass" (the total weight and volume of material in a given area); the richest zones are the middle and lower slopes of hills. Distribution of animal species follows that of plants. Everywhere, however, both plant and animal biomass are low.

Given the potential productivity of any setting, techniques of resource extraction set limits on how much food human populations can get from the
environment and on the size of the population that can be supported, determining whether they must migrate to meet their food needs.

Food available for hunter-gatherers in the Great Basin was largely edible seeds and pinyon nuts. Animals were less important in the diet, but three kinds were regularly hunted or collected: antelope, rabbits, and grasshoppers. The yearly round of Shoshone hunting and gathering followed the seasonality of resources, and was marked by flexibility in the size of the group of people living together, as people moved from one temporary encampment to another throughout the year. During the spring food was scarce, and small family groups scattered over the hillslopes foraging for what was available. In summer food became more abundant, and families began to congregate in locales where key resources could be found. By late summer and early fall, much of each valley's population would be concentrated near grassy areas and pinyon tree groves. This was also the time of the hunting season. Hunts were cooperative ventures involving many people. Animals were driven into prepared enclosures and trenches and dispatched. The collective effort of these animal drives

involve certain subsystems more directly and powerfully than others, in the order just listed. Alterations in the subsystems of culture will generally respect this order; for example, if related changes in technology and social organization occur, the stimulus for change most likely originated on the level of technology.

Steward's position is an extension of the basic materialist philosophy of general evolutionary schemes set out by White (1949, 1959) and Childe (1951a, 1951b). But unlike White, who held environment as a constant, Steward made culture part of a larger system—the ecosystem. On the one hand, he stressed the interface between cultures, and the particular environ-

contrasts with the far more solitary pursuit of plant food. In fact, too many plant collectors in one place would interfere with others' harvests. The tools required for gathering and for hunting were simple: digging sticks and carrying baskets for seeds and nuts, and nets, clubs, and bows and arrows for the animal drives.

There was a long period of scarcity from winter to early spring. People depended on seeds that had been ground into flour. During the winter, bands of a few families would congregate in sheltered locations around springs, surviving primarily on stored foods, but only in the seed-producing season were all the people in a valley living together, and nuclear families were along during much of the year. The movement of the nuclear family from season to season and year to year had to be highly flexible because of the variation in available resources.

Resources and their exploitation are the basis of sociopolitical organization.

Among the Shoshone, the nuclear family was the only stable social group. Larger groupings were situational aggregations. All aggregates were highly flexible in membership and size, which depended on food supply. Leadership positions only emerged situationally, functioning mainly during the hunt. There were virtually no notions of territorial ownership. Resources were available to everyone. Considering how unpredictable these resources were, insistence on territorial claims would have been dangerous to the survival of the group. In this area of highly localized and unpredictable food sources, group survival was enhanced by marriage ties between local aggregates.

Ideology and ritual have less direct relation to the resource base and technology than does sociopolitical organization.

Steward was able to find links between ideology and ritual, on the one hand, and the resource base and technology, on the other. The series of religious ceremonies the Shoshone held during the pinyon nut harvest served to lend cohesiveness to the aggregated group. Recreational gatherings also took place that were occasions for marriage negotiations. Given the importance of the nuclear family, these events were significant for group survival.

ments in which they are found. Environments, like cultures, may be described at various levels of specificity. On one level, every local environment is unique, just as every human society is unique. On the other hand, many localized environments over large regions share numerous characteristics. The valleys in the Great Basin where Steward worked can be grouped in terms of shared features. Climatic conditions were similar; all had the same species of plants and animals; all had relatively few species compared to other environments; permanent water sources were very restricted; and overall biomass (amount of living organisms per unit of area) was low. On the other hand, each valley also had unique local conditions.

The Method of Cultural Ecology

Steward's Shoshone study was designed to explain variation and similarities among the local groups in a broadly similar environment. Why did most of the groups share fundamental behavioral and organizational characteristics? On the other hand, why did the cultures of the 35–40 groups found in the area differ from one another in many details? Finally, how and why were these foragers, taken together, different from foragers in other parts of the world? Steward's *method* consisted of gathering systematic data on a series of issues that were related in a steplike fashion, with each level empirically linked with the next:

1. What *technological equipment* did the particular society have? What were the *resources available* to a group having only that technology? How abundant were these resources, how reliable were they, and what was their spatial and temporal availability over a year, or over many years?

2. How did resource availability affect population size, density, and distribution? What *subsistence strategies* (e.g., cooperative hunting vs. solitary hunting) would be necessary to acquire resources, and what sorts of human actions and interactions would they require?

3. What forms of *social organization* would allow people to carry out these actions and interactions?

4. What aspects of *ideology* (how people view themselves and the world) relate most closely to social organization, or, more directly, to the use of resources? How does this world view integrate and validate social organization? What group activities, particularly rituals, help to achieve social integration?

This method of data gathering can be applied to research about living *and* ancient societies. Implied in the method is the idea that cultural ecology is a theory of cultural evolution as well, since the adaptation of human groups through time follows much the same process. For example, suppose that hunter-gatherers like the Shoshone adopted agriculture. Old resources like game would be less important, and perhaps displaced. Forms of social organization appropriate to farming as opposed to hunting would be adopted. Eventually people would adopt world views more consistent with food production, and their beliefs, values, and rituals with regard to hunting would be replaced by those more appropriate to farming. This is a process of cultural evolution.

It is no surprise that foragers who, like the Shoshone, live in harsh environments, have cultures strongly affected by their environmental settings. But what about larger, more complex cultures? Steward (1949) also compared several of the major civilizations of the Old and New worlds in an attempt to show that similarities existed in their evolutionary sequences, in part because of similar economic adaptations.

Since Steward's time, ecological approaches to culture have become much more varied and sophisticated, especially in archaeology. Archaeologists now reconstruct the environmental settings of ancient societies, investigate how energy was used in prehistoric cultures, and study the biological remains of ancient human populations to determine population structure (demography), nutrition, and levels of health (Butzer 1982). Perhaps more than anything else, Steward reminded us that humans are organisms, caught like all other organisms in a web of ecological relationships that profoundly affects all aspects of our lives.

CULTURES AS SYSTEMS

System, a term frequently used in all sciences, including archaeology, has already been used in this book. The simplest definition of a system is: a set of interdependent parts that affect one another. In this simple sense, anthropologists and archaeologists have long recognized that cultures and societies are systems (Clarke and Chapman 1978; Salmon 1978). Cultures, like other living systems, exchange matter, energy, and information among their parts and between each other. They are **open systems** in the sense that they exchange all of these things (**closed systems** do not). Exchange of information from one culture to another is an important source of the variation on which evolutionary selection acts.

Sociocultural Systems

Cultures, seen as systems, are *integrated* in that their parts (**subsystems**) fit together and work together reasonably well. In fact, it is easier to understand how the whole cultural system works and changes if we break it down into subsystems, even though these subsystems cannot exist without one another and mutually affect each other. For example, we commonly refer to the economic system of the United States, as distinguished from the political system or the educational system. Within the economic system we might further identify systems of extraction of raw materials, systems of transportation of goods, or market systems with exchange commodities. These are also subsystems (Fig. 5.8). On a more inclusive level, particular societies or cultures are parts of larger systems, such as sets of other societies and the biosphere, the ecosystem of the planet (Campbell 1985; Little and Morren 1976). These more inclusive systems are our physical and sociocultural environments.

Whether consciously or not, most archaeologists design research which focuses on particular cultural subsystems and their relationships to other parts of the larger system. Many of the chapters of this book focus on particular cultural subsystems.

open system Type of system that exchanges matter, energy, or information with other systems.

closed system Type of system which does not exchange matter, energy, or information with other systems.

subsystems Parts of a system that have distinctive functions and that are arranged in hierarchical levels.

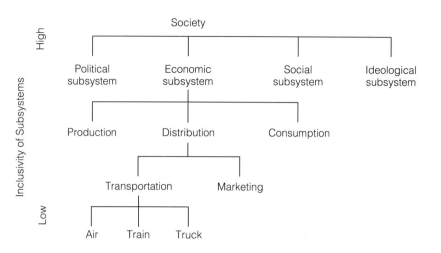

FIGURE 5.8 It is possible to break down any complex system into many levels of subsystems. In the most general sense, any society consists of political, economic, and social subsystems. The economic subsystem can in turn be broken down into production, distribution, and consumption subsystems; distribution includes transportation and marketing, and transportation includes still further different types.

Systems Terminology

Although the general idea of cultures as systems is an old one, only since the 1960s have archaeologists borrowed special terms and concepts developed in other sciences to express how systems evolve and function.

Integration   Systems are composed of interrelated parts, which affect one another. In complex systems, parts exhibit mutual cause-and-effect relationships; that is, they are **integrated**. Steward's culture core concept emphasizes that culture is a subsystem in a larger ecological system. Cultural behavior is influenced by the subsystem of the biological environment but may in turn alter that environment. We already saw an example of this — insect pests affect agricultural crops (part of the cultural system) and are themselves altered by the cultural response. In systems terminology this is a case of **feedback** — two parts of a larger system mutually affecting each other (Maruyama 1963).

How well systems are integrated depends in part on how they are formed. A car is an engineered system; all of its parts are purposefully designed to act together efficiently so that the major function of the car — transportation — is fulfilled. In contrast, sociocultural systems evolve, they are not engineered. That is, in part their structures are determined by their histories. Like all evolved systems, they have internal stresses and strains caused by parts that do not fit together well. One reason for this is that different subsystems evolve and change at different rates. For example, our economy has evolved rapidly to encourage and even require more women in the work force, but institutions that take care of children while both parents work have not yet become widely available. This creates stress.

Hierarchy   Systems have multiple levels of complexity and scale. The arrangement of subsystems into larger, more inclusive systems is called **hierarchy**. For example, the economic system as a whole has a subsystem

integration   Mutual cause-and-effect relationships of a system's interrelated parts.

feedback   The mutual effect of the interaction of two parts of a larger system.

hierarchy   Ranked, multiple levels of complexity and scale within a system.

that produces goods. This subsystem has smaller, specialized subsystems which produce industrial commodities on the one hand, and food on the other. In turn, the industrial subsystem is composed of still smaller subsystems, some of which produce raw materials while others produce finished products.

Regulation   Systems that are subject to change are called dynamic. To maintain stability, also known as **equilibrium,** dynamic systems require **regulation,** or they may damage or destroy themselves. In living systems, exchanges of matter, energy, and information are regulated. When there is a threat of recession in the economy, the government may set a lower rate on interest to stimulate buying, thus serving as a regulator to keep the economic system within desired limits.

Regulating mechanisms depend on feedback to maintain a dynamic system within acceptable limits of equilibrium (Fig. 5.9). Feedback exists in two forms. When **positive feedback** dominates a system, change is encouraged; the system becomes very dynamic and moves rapidly away from its original state. Looking at cultures as systems, we can readily see that rapid unhampered change in one subsystem will create stresses in other subsystems, because the whole system must maintain reasonable stability to function properly. In modern societies where the cost of living sometimes increases rapidly, pay raises (a compensating change in another subsystem) lag behind, causing stress as the standard of living declines. Although positive feedback is essential for change to take place, when it dominates a system too strongly, it can be very destructive. Consider the example of the arms race between the United States and the Soviet Union after World War II: It required a significant proportion of the economic resources of each nation. The motivating factor was fear, and as each side announced new military capabilities the other would devote even more resources toward this end, removing resources from such needs as education, urban renewal, and mass transportation, with resulting stresses on the larger society. **Negative feedback** relationships dampen or reduce impulses toward change, thus helping to keep systems in equilibrium (i.e., maintain them within acceptable limits). Lowering the interest rate to dampen recession by stimulating borrowing and spending is negative feedback. Since sociocultural systems cannot tolerate too much rapid change, they include many such negative feedback relationships.

equilibrium   State of relative stability within a system.

regulation   The force needed to maintain stability in a system.

positive feedback   Feedback that causes a system to change from a former state.

negative feedback   Feedback that dampens or reduces impulses toward change and thus helps keep systems in equilibrium or within tolerable limits.

Archaeological Significance of Systems Concepts

Systems concepts allow us to think more rigorously about how cultures operate and change. One of the first applications of systems concepts was an analysis of the transformation from hunting and gathering to agriculture as it began to occur 7–8,000 years ago in the Tehuacán Valley, Mexico (Flannery 1968a). Tehuacán hunter-gatherers lived in an arid envi-

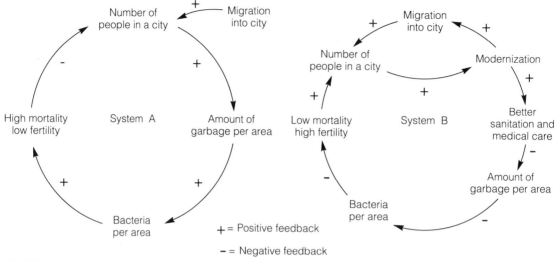

FIGURE 5.9 Feedback System A is typical of traditional, nonindustrial cities. Higher population results in greater potential for disease and death, a negative check on population size. Feedback System B exemplifies a city with modern health and sanitation facilities, circumstances reducing the effects of disease and permitting the population to grow. Both systems are dynamic, but B has an amplified tendency to deviate from the equilibrium of stable population size. In B, several factors operate mutually, for example, the population size both "causes" and is "caused by" modernization. These models do not express a hierarchy of importance for causes. (After Maruyama 1963)

maize The domesticated corn plant *Zea mays,* native to the New World.

ronment and had general cultural adaptations remarkably like those of the Shoshone studied by Steward.

Kent Flannery analyzed this cultural transformation using systems concepts. He broke down the general hunting-gathering subsistence system into several food-procurement subsystems, each focused on a major food resource such as deer, cactus, grass seeds, or maguey (a kind of tropical succulent plant). Although each of these subsystems contributed significantly to the overall diet, most provided food only in specific parts of the valley during particular times of the year (Fig. 5.10). The *seasonality* (timing of availability) of these resources and *scheduling* of harvests (the choices people made about what to exploit when) regulated the overall subsistence strategy. Regulation mainly operated to maintain a stable equilibrium, a very conservative set of relationships between people and their resources. Flannery also tried to show that if there were a series of sudden, unpredictable genetic changes in grasses (which included the wild ancestor of the domestic plant **maize**) that increased their productivity, people would reschedule their seasonal activities to take advantage of this. As the positive feedback reinforced the changes in the subsistence strategy, the whole system would undergo radical change, eventually reaching a new state dominated by food production rather than hunting and gathering.

Whether such a change actually occurred in the Tehuacán Valley in this manner is less important than this new way of thinking about what might have happened. Steward's analysis of the Great Basin Shoshone might have been much more sophisticated had systems concepts been in use a generation earlier. Since Flannery's work, archaeologists have increasingly applied systems perspectives to a wide variety of problems, including the rise of civilization and the state (see Chapter 16). Archaeological systems analysis

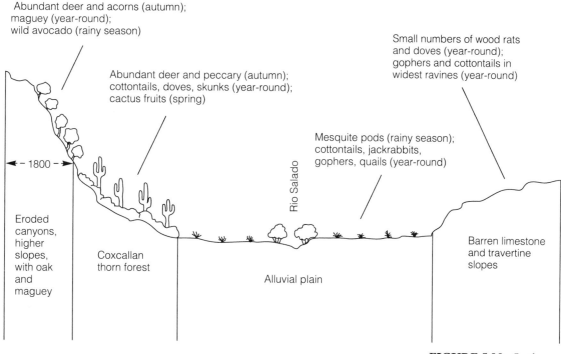

Abundant deer and acorns (autumn);
maguey (year-round);
wild avocado (rainy season)

Small numbers of wood rats
and doves (year-round);
gophers and cottontails in
widest ravines (year-round)

Abundant deer and peccary (autumn);
cottontails, doves, skunks (year-round);
cactus fruits (spring)

Mesquite pods (rainy season);
cottontails, jackrabbits,
gophers, quails (year-round)

– 1800 –

Rio Salado

Eroded
canyons,
higher
slopes,
with oak
and
maguey

Coxcallan
thorn forest

Alluvial plain

Barren limestone
and travertine
slopes

FIGURE 5.10 In the Tehuacán Valley in highland Mexico there are several distinct "micro-environments." Each produced resources important to early foragers, but the presence or abundance of these resources varied throughout the year. The system of exploitation devised by hunter-gatherers was regulated by seasonality (a biological factor) and scheduling (a cultural factor).

now commonly includes quantification of many aspects of cultural systems. Quantification helps to determine which parts of systems are most sensitive to change and under what conditions, and to measure the magnitude of change.

Systemic perspectives are important to archaeologists for a practical reason as well. Ethnographers working with living sociocultural systems can observe most forms of behavior (most subsystems) directly. Archaeologists not only lack such observations but are also limited by the fact that some parts of ancient cultures are more observable in the archaeological record than others. It is much simpler to reconstruct basic elements of the economic subsystem, for example, than it is to reconstruct the subsystem of social organization. But if we know how various subsystems are linked, we may be able to reasonably extrapolate from those we know about best to those we know about least.

CULTURAL MATERIALISM

Cultural materialism, broadly conceived, is the idea that the most fundamental function of culture is adaptation and that the structure and evolution of cultures are best understood through the scientific investigation of the material conditions of life. Leslie White, V. Gordon Childe, and Julian

Steward were all cultural materialists in this sense, although they did not apply that label to their work.

An explicit formulation of what has come to be called cultural materialism emerged in the 1960s, especially associated with the work of the ethnographer Marvin Harris (1968, 1979, 1988) and his colleagues. The central theme of cultural materialism is developing a science of culture — that is, applying overtly scientific principles and procedures to the explanation of cultural variation and behavior. Cultural materialists insist that cognized and operational models of culture be rigorously separated (for reasons we have already discussed).

Infrastructure, Structure, and Superstructure

Harris, building in part on older ideas of Steward, defined three major components of cultural systems, which he called "infrastructure," "structure," and "superstructure."

infrastructure Materialist term for "the interface between nature in the form of unalterable physical, chemical and biological constraints, and culture which is *Homo sapiens*' primary means of optimizing health and well-being" (Harris 1991:73).

Infrastructure is "the interface between nature in the form of unalterable physical, chemical, and biological constraints, and culture, which is *Homo sapiens*' primary means of optimizing health and well-being" (Harris 1991:73). In simpler terms, infrastructure encompasses the complex set of feedback relationships between cultural behavior and the environment. In this context, humans are emphasized as organisms that share a common biological inheritance and that are parts of larger, natural systems. The infrastructural components of culture are the ways in which we accommodate ourselves to these larger systems and in turn affect them, in order to survive, reproduce, and maintain well-being.

To better grasp this concept, remember that our colloquial use of the word *infrastructure* is closely related to its scholarly meaning. We often read in newspapers that the infrastructure of the United States is deteriorating, meaning that basic elements of our technological and economic systems — highways, railroads, bridges, and industrial plants — need renovation or replacement. All these things are essential to our culture's pattern of adaptation — it is "news" that they are deteriorating because of their importance to our survival and well-being.

structure Materialist term for the social and political organizational components of human cultures.

Structure is the social and political organizational components of human cultures. These would include domestic and kinship organization as well as larger organizational features of whole communities and societies, such as governmental institutions, labor unions, religious sects, universities, armies, and political parties. **Superstructure** refers to "the realm of values, beliefs, aesthetics, rules, symbols, rituals, religions, philosophies, and other forms of knowledge, including science itself" (Harris 1991:74). Notice that infrastructure and structure both refer to things that are directly observable (although they have their associated values, rules, symbols, etc.). On the superstructural level we move into the mental domain of culture, which is not directly observable.

superstructure Materialist term for "the realm of values, beliefs, aesthetics, rules, symbols, rituals, religions, philosophies, and other forms of knowledge, including science itself" (Harris 1991:74).

Because infrastructure, structure, and superstructure are subsystems of cultural systems, there are feedback relationships among them. As Harris puts it, "Structure and superstructure are not mere passive, epiphenomenal products; rather they actively contribute to the continuity and change in infrastructures" (Harris 1991:74). This gets us back to the idea of cultures as systems. One of the problems raised by the systemic perspective is that feedback muddles the notion of cause. When things mutually affect one another, how do we know what causes what? One way out of this dilemma is to recognize that certain parts of systems are much more important in terms of causation than others. This is essentially Harris's argument — infrastructural causes are generally, and over the long run, more important than causes that originate elsewhere. We are more likely to understand how cultures work and change by directing research to the infrastructural components than elsewhere.

Many anthropologists and archaeologists accept ideas such as cultural evolution, cultures as adaptive behavioral systems, and scientific approaches to the study of culture but would disagree with cultural materialism as espoused by Harris. Many believe that changes in superstructure (how people think) play dominant, independent roles in cultural evolution, affecting all other aspects of culture. Whether or not this is the case, archaeologists must base their interpretations on evidence of human action, not intention.

Whether or not one agrees with Harris's specific ideas, cultural materialism clearly outlines a procedure for doing archaeology as science. Incorporating many related perspectives, such as cultural evolution, cultural ecology, and cultures as adaptive systems, the methodology accords primacy in explanation and research to the material conditions of life. This broad cultural-materialist perspective is fundamental to the approach to archaeology presented in this book. We can apply it to the study of the general evolutionary transformation realized by agriculture. This transformation occurred primarily through the process of **domestication** (see Box 5.4).

domestication   Selection of particular plants and animals for breeding, which makes them more useful and productive for human purposes.

INTERPRETIVE FRAMEWORK

In this chapter we have reviewed a number of interrelated ideas. The idea of culture as a distinctive form of human behavior lies at the heart of anthropology and archaeology. Cultural evolution is intimately related to biological evolution; though different in important ways, both exhibit specific dimensions, general dimensions, and general trends through time. Cultural ecology is both a theory about how cultures evolve and a method for designing research, reminding us that humans are parts of larger systems. The idea that cultures are systems helps us to think rigorously both about how cultures work and how they evolve. Finally, cultural materialism incorporates all of these ideas, asserting that cultural behavior is fundamentally adaptive, that it can best be studied scientifically, and that the material conditions of life have the greatest causal significance. We will return to these ideas, implicitly and explicitly, throughout the rest of this book.

BOX 5.4

THE ORIGINS OF AGRICULTURE

For the first several million years of our species' existence, people met their subsistence needs by hunting and gathering. Beginning about 12,000 years ago, some hunter-gatherers began to manipulate the life cycles of the plants and animals they depended on for food in ways that eventually led to *food production,* or farming. The resulting "food-producing revolution" is the most far-reaching evolutionary transition that humans have experienced in the last 40,000 years. Its long-term effects have been profound: Hunting-gathering has been all but eliminated as a way of life; the human population has expanded enormously; and complex, hierarchical societies have come to dominate the globe.

In the following discussion this revolution serves to illustrate some of the ideas and perspectives presented in this chapter: culture as adaptation, general and specific cultural evolution, cultural ecology, cultural materialism, and cultures as systems.

Domestication

The origins of food production lie in the process of domestication, whereby people select particular plants and animals and breed them for traits that make them more useful and productive. Domestication is a form of *artificial* selection—Darwin's observations of selective breeding of domestic pigeons and other animals helped him to understand natural selection. Central to the process is the deliberate selection by humans of those individual plants and animals that will breed (in other words, that will be reproductively successful, a defining characteristic of fitness). People select individuals with the most desirable characteristics—animals with more meat, more abundant wool, more resistance to disease, more docile temperaments; plants that are

more palatable and productive, tolerant of greater extremes of temperature and soil quality.

Domestication in the larger sense is the establishment of new, mutually interdependent relationships between people and selected, modified plant and animal species. Because it concerns the linkage between people, their cultures, and important aspects of their environments, domestication is an excellent example of an adaptive, cultural-ecological, materialist process.

Domestication is still ongoing: it is the essential business of farmers and agricultural research laboratories today. Of course, today the genetic basis of reproduction and artificial selection is well understood, and breeding programs can be consciously designed to produce desired results. But knowledge of genetics is very recent; during the early stages of the food-producing revolution, people only knew that certain traits were inheritable. We do not know when people began deliberately to breed plants and animals for particular results. Many early transformations were probably completely unintended. Some plants, for example, grow better in the disturbed, organically enriched soils of human occupation sites. When people returned to these places year after year, they would find these plants growing more abundantly. If the plants were edible and palatable, they might become a more important part of the diet—not through a deliberate effort, but because the plant species and humans were mutually adapted.

Whether domestication occurred as a result of conscious or unconscious efforts, many species of plants and animals eventually have become so altered that they no longer resemble natural forms but depend on human manipulation to survive and reproduce. Maize is a good example. Large seed clusters ("ears") and juicy seeds ("kernels") are highly desirable, but today's maize plant is a genetic monstrosity; without deliberate manipulation of its life cycle, the species could rapidly become extinct. Dairy cattle and domestic turkeys would not fare well on their own, either. Certain hybrid varieties of plants and animals are, in fact, sterile. Archaeologists study the morphology of floral and faunal remains to detect domestication; the process usually requires that many generations be represented before recognizably modified forms emerge.

Archaeologists have long been interested in finding the "hearths of domestication"—those areas where the process began and from which it presumably spread. One indicator that this process originally involved massive diffusion away from relatively few centers of innovation is the existence of comparatively few **staples** (plants and animals widely used for food) that are widespread and of major economic importance in the world (cf. Chapter 6). For example, wheat has for thousands of years been widely grown in Europe, western Asia, and North Africa, and is associated with other staples in a characteristic "package" that includes barley, goats, sheep, pigs, and cattle. Presumably these staples originated in a particular region and then spread to others as an effective constellation of plants and animals. Also, consider how few major staple crops there are in the world today. Among grain and seeds, for example, wheat, rice, and maize account for most of what is consumed. Of the thousands of different plants and scores of animal species that have been domesticated during the last 12,000 years, only a few have become major staples, the most generally productive of these being wheat, goats, sheep, and cattle from the Near East; maize from Mesoamerica; rice from southeast Asia; and the potato from northern South America. These animals and plants have diffused very widely, some of them within the last 500 years.

We now know that the practice of food production evolved independently as an effective alternative to hunting and gathering in many places: in the Old World in the Near East, southeast Asia, and northern China; in the New World in Mesoamerica and northern South America. These are, in a sense, the major hearths of domestication, but these regions are very large and include many different local environments and cultures. It is impossible to identify one or two restricted places as central to the food-producing revolution, even within these major hearths. In many other regions, such as North America and sub-Saharan Africa, useful local domesticated plants, such as the sunflower and sorghum, were used as adjuncts to wild resources. The independent manipulation of plants and animals in new ways by many populations of hunter-gatherers demonstrates *general evolution*. Domestication followed many parallel evolutionary paths.

Where domesticated plants and animals were indigenously developed, the transition from hunting and gathering to fully effective food production was very long. It lasted for at least 2,000 years in the Near East, and 4–5,000 years in Mesoamerica. One reason for such slow change was that wild species required many generations of selective breeding before they became significantly more useful than wild foods. Another reason is the necessary feedback relationship between human diet and the makeup of the "package" of plants and animals that people exploit. Plants and animals must together supply adequate food energy and food nutrition, but not all components of the original package of wild species are equally domesticable. Even in the Near East, where domestication occurred early, it took many generations for specific domesticates to become widely available and for the complex of plants and animals to form.

(continued)

(Box 5.4 continued)

"Revolution" implies rapid change, but except where developed food production was introduced and quickly adopted, changes came about slowly. "Revolution" applies to the long-term, general evolutionary consequences of the adoption of efficient food production. These included greater **sedentism** (the practice of settling in one place for an extended period of time), larger communities and societies, dependence on smaller segments of regional environments (i.e., those most suited to crops), appearance of new tools and facilities (i.e., for manipulating, processing, and storing crops and animal products), and new patterns of social and economic relationships among people. Perhaps most important, food production is largely responsible for the enormous growth of the human population, from 10 to 20 million roughly 12,000 years ago, to 5.5 billion today, a phenomenon that demonstrates the *law of biotic potential*.

Although it is tempting to envision a sharp contrast between hunter-gatherers and farmers, during the transition periods of thousands of years it would have been impossible to categorize neatly many cultures as either, so mixed were their economies. The same people who hunted wild cattle and pigs during some seasons of the year would, at other times, plant wheat and herd goats. Food production was not a sudden innovation, recognized by its first adopters as a new way of life, but rather a long process of change largely unnoticed by the innovating peoples themselves. The systems perspective on this situation, introduced by Flannery (1968a), provides a plausible scenario for these changes.

Ethnographic studies have revealed that hunter-gatherers do not necessarily live the difficult precarious lives that some scholars envisioned, but have successful strategies for procuring wild foods, and actively manipulate their environments to increase the productivity of the foods they depend on. Nineteenth-century Shoshone of the western United States not only gathered wild grasses but sometimes dug small canals to irrigate them. Native Australians methodically burned huge swathes of vegetation they had no use for to encourage the growth of useful plants, which in turn attracted animals that could be hunted. Eskimos used a domestic animal, the sled dog, to be more effective hunter-gatherers. These are all good examples of *Romer's Rule*: Innovations were made so that traditional hunting and gathering practices were more productive and secure rather than to "progress" toward some foreseen food-producing way of life.

Hunter-gatherers everywhere no doubt experimented with the life cycles of plants and animals on which they depended and were receptive to new species and ways of manipulating them. That these experiments were probably taking place all over the world after the end of the Pleistocene contrasts with the traditional perspective that only a few peoples had the talent to domesticate plants and animals and that widespread adoption of food production depended on diffusion from one or two restricted regions.

However widespread these experiments were, some were obviously more successful than others, and changes occurred more rapidly in some places than in others. This variation says nothing about the inherent capacity of different people to innovate. Caused by particular conditions in different environments where experiments took place, variation shows how *specific evolution* operates. For example, wild wheats in the Near East resemble their domesticated descendants more closely than the wild ancestor of maize resembles modern maize, and the domestication of maize took much longer than that of wheat. In the Near East there were large mammal species amenable to domestication, while in Mesoamerica there were none. The combination of domestic animals and plants greatly accelerated the tempo of evolution of food producing in the Near East. The difference between the Near East and Mesoamerica is inherent in the plants and animals, however, not in the capabilities of the incipient farmers of the two regions.

Because the tempo of change was faster in some regions, domesticated plants and animals, and often populations of farmers themselves, tended to spread to adjacent areas of slower change. For example, between about 5600 and 3000 B.C. domesticates and human migrants spread from the Near East to much of the Mediterranean basin, and to central and northern Europe. From Mesoamerica, maize spread into North America, becoming an important staple crop in the east after A.D. 800. Local experiments in Europe and North America were swamped by the introduced plants and animals. We do not conclude that Europeans and Native North Americans were somehow less innovative than the people whose cultigens (domesticated plants and animals) they adopted, but rather that they sensibly used the most productive species to which they had access. This is a good example of *cultural adaptation*.

Roughly 2,000 years ago, domestic foods had replaced their wild counterparts as principal energy sources for most of the earth's peoples. But there was nothing inevitable in this process. Until 200 years ago many peoples were hunter-gatherers; even today a few still are. There are even isolated examples of farmers reverting to hunting and gathering. For example, the modern horse was introduced to the Americas from Europe. When it spread to the Great Plains and was adopted for use by Native Americans there, farming and mixed economies were abandoned in favor of bison hunting, since mounted hunters were far more efficient than those on foot. This is not some sort of evolutionary degeneration but rather a good example of adaptation and of the *law of least effort*: Hunting bison from horseback provided more food with less work than growing maize and squash.

What Caused the Food-Producing Revolution?

Because of the research into the problem in the decades since World War II, archaeologists are now able to provide plausible explanations for how the food-producing revolution occurred. We understand where and when food producing developed, and how and when it spread. We are still trying to understand *why* it occurred.

One of the explanations under consideration in the early 20th century was most closely identified with V. Gordon Childe (1951a). It posits that increasing dryness at the end of the Pleistocene forced populations of humans, plants, and animals into restricted "oasis" environments, thus stimulating domestication under conditions of scarcity. Robert Braidwood (1960) believes that once people had settled into particular environments and become culturally mature, agriculture was the logical result. Lewis Binford (1968b) and Kent Flannery (1968a) have both emphasized food production as adaptation to changing relationships between peoples and their resources. More recently, David Rindos (1984) has proposed a "co-evolutionary" model that sees food production as an unintentional by-product of the mutual interaction of plant and human populations over very long periods of time.

Each of these general explanations has its strengths and weaknesses. Archaeologists do not agree that any one of them is universally applicable, and it may be that more specific explanations are necessary to account for certain processes of change. Nevertheless, it is widely believed that the key to the origins of agriculture lies in the relationship between population size and food resources. It has been recognized that food production is not always demonstrably more efficient than hunting and gathering. Some farmers work very hard for a living, while some hunter-gatherers do not. The latter have generally better diets than farmers. But the one thing that any mature food-production system can do better than any hunting and gathering system is to support more people per unit area of the productive landscape — that is, sustain higher population densities.

As archaeologists continue to investigate the origins of food production, we can anticipate not only new data but new explanations as well. Whatever the reasons food production emerged, it has enormously transformed humankind, with evolutionary consequences that we still do not fully understand even today.

POINTS TO REMEMBER

- Culture is learned and shared behavior that is transmitted largely through symbolic communication.

- Culture has both mental and behavioral components, and because it is constantly tested against the everyday world, it is constantly changing.

- Biological evolution selects for genetic information.

- Selective processes work on cultural information as well, so culture evolves in both general and specific terms.

- Cultural ecology stresses the interactive relationship of culture and its larger environment.

- Cultures are systems that exchange information with other systems, that regulate themselves, and that are capable of both stability and rapid change.

- Cultural materialism stresses that the most fundamental function of culture is adaptive and that we can best understand adaptation through scientific study of the material conditions of life.

FOR FURTHER READING*

A good general introduction is found in *Scientific American's Evolution*. Darwin's *The Origin of Species* is the landmark work that changed the way we think about our world. Theoretical approaches to cultural evolution are treated in Steward's *The Theory of Culture Change*, Harris's *Cultural Materialism*, and Flannery's "Archaeological Systems Theory and Ancient Mesoamerica." Clarke and Chapman's *Analytical Archaeology* was an important step toward systematizing archaeology. The agricultural revolution is studied in Flannery's "The Origins of Agriculture," Struever's *Prehistoric Agriculture*, and Rindos's *The Origins of Agriculture*. Leonard and Jones's *Quantifying Diversity in Archaeology* applies ecological principles to various areas of archaeological inquiry.

*Full citations appear in the bibliography.

CHAPTER SIX

HUMAN HABITATS

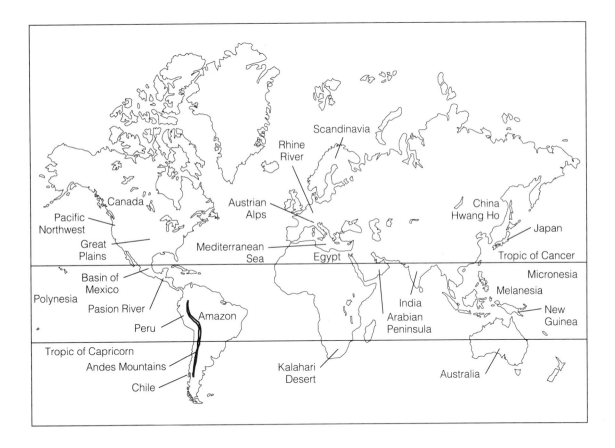

Hunting and gathering on the one hand and food producing on the other are our species's major means of adapting to the environment. Applied to the special features of the various "hearths" of food production, cultural ecology elucidates adaptive relationships in particular settings. From a materialist perspective subsistence strategies are the interface between culture and environment: They provide the essential flow of food energy (as well as other materials) that allows humans to survive, increase their numbers, and colonize new environments. By "environment" we mean all external conditions and objects to which the group and individuals in it must adjust. These include the basic features of the landscape (e.g., minerals, topography, hydrology) as well as climate, plants, and animals. The environment also includes other people. Although we sometimes distinguish "natural" from "cultural" environments, people and their creations are parts of nature, and few "natural" environments have been unaffected by human activity (Hardesty 1977).

This chapter looks at the earth's major terrestrial environments as settings for human cultural adaptation, given the variety of basic subsistence, technological, and transport systems that characterized nonindustrial cultures in the "ethnographic present." A central theme is how nonindustrial cultures differ from the industrial ones that most of us live in today, particularly with regard to basic tools, transport, and energy sources. We will examine some of the implications of these differences in later chapters.

Our focus will be what ethnographers call the **ethnographic present** — that point in time when **traditional** cultures came into contact with literate cultures (so we have some sort of written records of them) but before this contact significantly altered traditional lifeways, through colonization or industrialization, for example, or through radical changes in population or political structure (Trigger 1981). These points in time differ from culture to culture. For the Maya of the Yucatán Peninsula the ethnographic present would be about A.D. 1517. For the Shoshone of the Great Basin, it would be about 1850. Many of the models we use to evaluate the archaeological record are drawn from cultures in the ethnographic present, but a major problem is the assumption of cultural isolation. No traditional society, no matter how geographically isolated, was unaffected by contacts with other cultures. Nevertheless, the ethnographic present approach is a useful, commonsense way to describe traditional technological systems and their relationship to environment and food procurement. Cultures in the ethnographic present adapted to virtually all major terrestrial **biomes,** a process that is patterned in complex ways by technology, transport, and systems of food procurement. To begin our survey of the world's habitats and how people have exploited them, let us review the basics of energy flow, and the human place in ecosystems.

ethnographic present That point in time when traditional cultures came into contact with literate cultures and were recorded by them.

traditional Adjective applied to societies and economies strongly shaped by conservative adherence to long-established customs.

biomes Communities of plants and animals.

ecology Study of the relationships of plants and animals within their habitats.

ECOLOGY AND ENERGY

The word **ecology** was coined by 19th-century botanists. It refers to the study of the relationships of plants and animals within their habitats, and of course a fundamental assumption of cultural ecology is that humans are part of ecosystems (Colinvaux 1973; Odum 1971; see below).

Ecological Communities: Ecosystems

The **ecological community** consists of the biotic species of a specific region and the network of interrelationships that exists among them. Each species occupies a particular position or **niche** within the network. Biologists often compare the niche concept with status in human social systems and the division of labor in human economies. The various species in an **ecosystem** are interdependent, and elimination of any one species, or drastic alterations of its numbers, may have repercussions on the community as a whole. Humans all belong to the same species, but their varied cultural adaptations allow them to occupy strikingly different niches, much as different species of animals do.

The most important set of symbiotic relationships among species in an ecological community is the **food chain,** or more correctly the **food web** (Fig. 6.1). The basic producers in a food web are plants, which absorb sunlight and use it as a source of energy for growth, extracting nutrients from the air and soil. Herbivores consume plants to obtain energy and nutrients, and they in turn are eaten by carnivores, who may then become prey for other carnivores. Dead plant or animal material is broken down by microorganisms, thus becoming available for recycling by living plants. These various levels in a food chain are called **trophic levels** (Fig. 6.2). Food webs and trophic levels structure the exchange of food energy throughout ecosystems. Humans occupy the top trophic levels in their ecological communities. As we shall see, studies of energy flow are important in understanding many facets of cultural adaptation and evolutionary change.

Biologists define the **carrying capacity** of an ecosystem as the theoretical limit to which a population may grow and maintain itself without deleterious effects on its environment. The most crucial component of carrying capacity is usually food supply, although other resources such as water may be equally important in determining it. This concept is often applied to humans in an attempt to understand how increases or decreases in human numbers might promote evolutionary change. We should emphasize that carrying capacity is a dynamic, not a fixed, value. Humans, through cultural innovations in technology, transport, organization, or knowledge, can increase carrying capacity by increasing the productivity of the landscape (**intensification,** discussed below) and thus render it capable of supporting more people (e.g., through some forms of agricultural intensification). They may also degrade landscapes and thereby lower carrying capacity, as we shall see in Chapter 15.

Energy in Industrial and Nonindustrial Societies

In all societies work must get done, and **energy** (the ability to do work) must be produced, distributed, and consumed (Davis 1990). In both

---

ecological community The different biotic species of a specific region and the network of interrelationships that exists among them.

niche The particular position of a species within the environmental network.

ecosystem Ecological community of plants and animals together with the physical environment.

food chain or **food web** The set of relationships among plant and animal species in an ecosystem through which energy is channeled.

trophic levels Levels within the food chain characterized by similar energy consumption.

carrying capacity The theoretical limit to which a population may grow and maintain itself without deleterious effects on its environment.

intensification The use of a piece of agricultural land more frequently or with the input of increased labor or other resources.

energy The ability to do work.

FIGURE 6.1 The food chain, or food web, showing how food energy flows through an ecosystem.

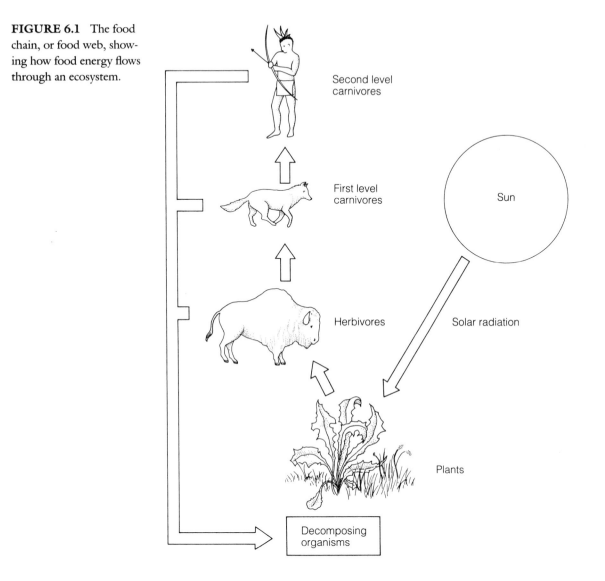

Second level carnivores

First level carnivores

Sun

Herbivores

Solar radiation

Plants

Decomposing organisms

industrial and nonindustrial societies, energy is extracted from the environment—this is the most fundamental task of the cultural infrastructure and one of the most important things to understand and measure using the cultural materialist perspective.

We saw in Chapter 5 that one of the major transformations in general cultural evolution—the Industrial Revolution—involved new sources of energy. Profound differences exist between industrial and nonindustrial societies in terms of energy use. These differences are significant, because most of us live in industrial societies, whereas most of the societies archaeologists study are nonindustrial. Although observations of present behav-

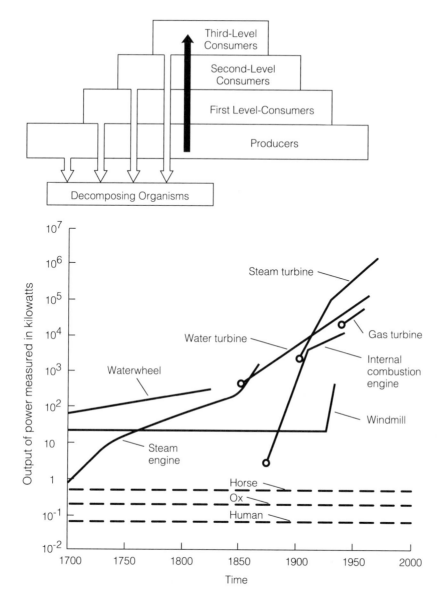

FIGURE 6.2 Energy and matter are transmitted through the trophic, or feeding, levels of ecosystems. Energy enters the system as solar radiation, for example, and is converted to usable food by plant "producers." First-level consumers are animals that ingest plant food. Humans operate as first-level consumers when they eat plants and as second-level consumers when they eat animals such as cattle. With each trophic level there is a loss of up to 90% of the energy already captured. For example, to produce 1,000 edible kcals of beef may require 10,000 kcals of plants as fodder. Eventually, members of all trophic levels contribute their remains to the decomposer level.

FIGURE 6.3 A comparison of the energetic output of muscular and nonmuscular power sources. Nonmuscular sources produce much more power and have increased their energetic potential because of technological innovations. Low-energy societies depend on muscular power sources. (After *Energy* 1971)

ior frequently provide useful models for investigating the past, our own use of energy and associated economic systems are so distinctive that they serve as poor guides to those of nonindustrial cultures.

In industrial societies, most of the energy consumed is derived from fossil fuels (e.g., oil, gas, or coal), and to a lesser extent, hydroelectric and nuclear power (Fig. 6.3). Most of this energy thus does not derive from the functioning ecosystem in a direct sense. For example, oil, gas and coal

Table 6.1 Protein and Daily Energy Requirements for Males and Females

Body Weight (kg)	Age (yr.)		Protein grams/day		Energy kcal/day	
	Males	Females	Males	Females	Males	Females
3		Birth	12	12	350	350
9		10 mos.	15	15	970	970
13		2 yrs.	16	16	1,300	1,300
20		5 yrs.	20	20	1,800	1,750
30	8.5	9.0	26	26	2,400	2,200
44	13.0	12.5	33	30	2,800	2,400
54	14.5	17.0	37	29–46*	2,900	2,100
58	15.5	adult	37	29–46*	3,000	2,000
70	adult	—	38		2,700	—

SOURCE: From Little and Morren 1976. Protein values are from Jelliffe and Jelliffe 1989.
*Higher values reflect greater protein needs during pregnancy and lactation

high-energy societies
Societies characterized by high per-capita consumption of energy, mostly through nonfood sources. Industrial societies, with their reliance on fossil fuels, are high-energy societies.

low-energy societies
Societies in which most energy comes from food and there is little dependence on nonhuman forms of energy.

kcal The kilocalorie is a measure of food energy, popularly known as the calorie. It is the amount of energy needed to raise the temperature of a kilogram of water one degree centigrade.

come from very ancient "fossilized" organic matter, sources that are not renewable; at present they are relatively cheap and accessible.

In industrial societies only a tiny percentage of the work that gets done involves human or animal muscle power, and this is where the essential difference lies. In nonindustrial societies *most* work must be done by human and animal muscles, which in turn get their energy from food (Table 6.1). In a real sense, food energy is to nonindustrial societies what fossil fuels are to industrial societies (although some nonindustrial cultures have other energy sources as well, as we shall see shortly). Food energy is not stored by nature for us as fossil fuels are, but rather must be continuously extracted from functioning ecosystems; it is thus a renewable resource as long as ecosystems remain productive.

Industrial societies are called **high-energy societies** because the per-capita amount of energy consumed or utilized in various forms is high compared to that used in nonindustrial, **low-energy societies,** where most energy comes from food. Consider several different consumption rates. A rough per-capita daily energy consumption value for hunter-gatherer adults would be approximately 2,000 to 3,000 **kcal,** an amount roughly equivalent to their daily intake of food energy. For tribal agriculturalists such as the people of highland New Guinea, the per-capita figures would be very similar. But in societies where most work is done by machines, human caloric intake is a negligible proportion of the daily per-capita consumption. In 1988 in the United States, the per-capita average was 162,000 kcal, both from food and nonfood energy sources. Such consumption rates would be impossible without cheap industrial energy sources. In the same year in India, a largely agrarian and partially industrialized nation, daily per-capita consumption averaged about 7,800 kcal, between these two extremes, but much closer to the nonindustrial rate.[1]

Great variation exists even within the category of low-energy societies. Some nonindustrial societies were well supplied with nonhuman sources of energy. The ancient Romans, for example, used animals for traction and as beasts of burden, and sails to harness the power of the wind. The Romans also possessed tools that made the application of energy more efficient, such as wheels (for vehicles, winches, or making pottery), and effective cutting tools of iron. In this respect the Romans resembled most other Old World complex cultures. New World complex societies were, by contrast, technologically less well developed. Andean complex societies were relatively more technologically complex than those of Mesoamerica, since in the Andes metallurgy was better developed and llamas served as pack animals (Hassig 1985). But in general in the New World, effective beasts of burden were scarce or absent in most places, as were traction, sails, wheeled vehicles, and other labor-saving devices, and bronze or iron tools. The New World effectively had a Stone Age technology. Since technology forms a fundamental cultural interface with the environment (see below), especially for resource extraction, these variations placed important constraints on some forms of cultural evolution.

FOOD PROCUREMENT AND TECHNOLOGY

Food Procurement Systems

At the end of Chapter 5 we discussed two kinds of basic food procurement systems, hunting-gathering and **food production**. We noted that wherever food production is possible in a particular biome it has tended to replace hunting-gathering, but this process is by no means universal or complete. Nevertheless, many societies are classifiable as hunter-gatherers or food producers in the sense that the bulk of their food supplies comes from one or the other of the two basic systems (Lee and Devore 1968).

food production The production of food using domestic plants and animals.

Wild foods tend to be more widely dispersed, more seasonally variable, more limited in quantity (per unit of area exploited) and less dependable than domestic foods. Hunter-gatherers thus tend to live in smaller, more dispersed, and more mobile groups than food producers (Steward 1939; Yellen 1976). With a few exceptions, political structure is egalitarian. Food production has several advantages over hunting and gathering. The food supply may be obtained from much smaller areas, it may be more dependable from year to year, and *generally* (but not always) there is a greater return in proportion to the per-capita time spent working.

---

[1]Figures for the United States and India were calculated using data from "Energy for Planet Earth" by G. R. Davis (*Scientific American* 263:3:57, 1990). To get the per-capita rate, total daily energy expenditure for each country is estimated, then divided by the total population.

These differences have had important consequences. With the exception of specialized herding peoples, food producers can live in permanent settlements and hence lead more sedentary lives than most hunter-gatherers, since food supplies are closer to habitations. Settlements can also be much larger in size, and the overall population density can be much higher (Hassan 1974). Substantial food surpluses can be produced and stored under these circumstances. Greater sedentism allows or encourages the elaboration of material culture, such as erecting larger, more permanent buildings or other facilities and accumulating substantial inventories of utilitarian items (such as pottery) that are not highly portable. It is partly because of such elaboration that the sites of food producers are generally easier to identify archaeologically than those of hunter-gatherers.

These contrasting situations generally pertain to hunter-gatherers and food producers but not to all of them. Under extremely favorable environmental conditions in which wild food resources are abundant and dependable, hunter-gatherers may live in nucleated, permanent communities with ranked political structure, the cost of procuring food and the potential for generating surpluses approximating productive performance in food-producing economies (Widmer 1988). On the other hand, some egalitarian farmers live in relatively poor habitats and are quite mobile, moving their villages frequently. They may have low potential for producing food surpluses, and the cost of their food production may be higher than that of hunter-gatherers. The limits and possibilities of particular habitats play an important role in productivity.

Hunter-gatherers generally cause only minor effects on their ecosystems since they are few in number and simply move around their environments to find nutrients, which are recycled (but there are exceptions, as when foragers deliberately burn up large areas; see Chapter 5). Food producers, however, can permanently alter the nutrient balance and supply in a region, sometimes with disastrous effects, as when misuse or overuse of the landscape causes soil erosion or **salinization,** the buildup of harmful chemicals that poison the soil; see Chapter 15.

salinization Buildup of chemical salts in soil.

Features of Food-Producing Economies

Food-producing economies vary considerably in specific features. In virtually all farming economies prior to the commercialization and industrialization of agriculture in the 19th and 20th centuries, the production unit was the household, and most food consumed by the household was also produced by it (Sahlins 1972). Little food was imported into the household from outside, and surplus production beyond its own needs was also generally quite limited. In many past and present egalitarian agricultural societies, virtually all families produce and consume their own food; the same was true of many chiefdoms.

In more complex nonindustrial civilizations, between 60 and 90 percent

Table 6.2 Food Energy and Nutrients of Staple Crops

Crop	% moisture	kcal of energy per kilogram (2.2 lbs)	Protein (gr. per 100 gr. edible portion)	Fat (gr. per 100 gr. edible portion)
Yellow maize	10.6	3610	9.4	4.3
Barley	10.5	3480	9.7	1.9
Wheat	13	3300	14.0	2.2
Brown rice	13	3570	7.2	1.5
Sweet potato	68.9	1160	1.3	.3
White potato	77.9	790	2.8	.2
Lettuce	95.8	130	1.0	.1

SOURCE OF DATA: Woot-Tsuen Wu Leng 1961.

of the population produced food for both themselves and for nonfarmers, who are political and religious leaders and artisans and traders, often living in cities. There are relatively few nonfarmers because comparatively limited surplus energy can be derived from nonindustrial farming; thus a high proportion of food producers must always be present. Compare this with our own society, in which a tiny number of farmers support the rest of the population (cf. Chapter 8).

The range of the diet is another strong contrast between nonindustrial and industrial societies. Especially where population density is high, most of the food energy consumed by the average person in traditional food-producing societies comes from one or a few staple crops, or, much less frequently, from domestic animals. With a few exceptions these are grain crops (such as wheat, rice, or maize) or root crops (such as sweet potatoes, taro, or manioc). Grains yield the highest values of energy (measured in calories) per weight (Table 6.2) as well as higher concentrations of protein, one reason they are such widespread staples today. Grains are more easily stored for long periods than are root crops. Although generally superior as foods, grains yield fewer calories per unit of cultivated land than do root crops.

So that we can compare the productivity of different areas and understand their carrying capacity under different circumstances, we need to establish some rough basic values of how much food people need. Let us assume (Table 6.2) that the average person needs about 2,000 kcal per day, and that a family of 6 thus would need about 12,000 kcal per day. We can further assume a largely vegetarian diet, and if perhaps 75 percent of the kcals come from grain (see Table 6.3) the family would need about 3 kg (6.6 lb.) of grain per day, or about one ton per year per family. This value is very rough, but we can use it to translate the known productivity of any region into the size of a population that could be supported.

Table 6.3   Distribution of Population among World Habitats

Habitat population	% of earth's land surface	% of human population
Drylands	17	4
Tropical forests	13	27
Mediterranean scrub forest	1	5
Midlatitude mixed forest	7	53
Grasslands	19	6
Marginal biomes (boreal forest, polar, and mountain lands)	43	5

SOURCE: Chapple and Coon 1942, pp. 74–95.

Intensification

Food production involves working the land rather than gathering its wild resources (Grigg 1975). Food production to meet subsistence needs thus involves an "intensification" of effort into a particular piece of land, beyond the hunting and gathering of wild foods, and effort intensifies as more labor is invested. There can be a marked contrast between the caloric harvest of hunter-gatherers and that of farmers from the same area of land. In the Basin of Mexico, for example, the total land area in pre-Columbian times was roughly 7,000 km². The carrying capacity of this area for hunter-gatherers was estimated at 16,500 people, or 2.7 per km² (Sanders, Parsons, and Santley 1979:289). At around 1500 B.C., farmers began to settle in the basin, and within 3,000 years, at the time of European contact, all cultivable land in the Basin was in use. Marginal areas like sloping hillsides had been terraced and planted in maize and edible cactus. These marginal areas, for example, produced between 30 and 80 tons of grain per km². Another intensified marginal zone was swampland, which was drained by digging a grid of canals and heaping the muck from the canals onto the "fields" created between the canals (Armillas 1971). These fields were the **chinampas** (sometimes incorrectly called "floating" gardens), the productivity of which was about 300 tons per km². At about A.D. 1500, the carrying capacity of the basin was nearly 1.5 million people (Sanders, Parsons, and Santley 1979:378), an increase of nearly 100 times the carrying capacity of the region for hunter-gatherers. This demonstrates the dynamic quality of the carrying capacity calculation; changes in the environment, whether natural or human-induced (intensification of cultivation practices, or soil degradation) result in changes in the productivity of that environment and in its ability to support human populations.

No matter how much the potential productivity of the land can be enhanced, farming isn't successful unless farmers expend less energy culti-

chinampas Extremely productive and fertile rectangular plots of land created from lake beds or swamps by piling up mud from the lake bottom. This agricultural technique was employed by the Aztecs and is in use today in Mexico.

vating crops than the crops yield. Food-producing economies vary considerably as to the ratio of labor inputs to crop yield returns. Relationships of input to output are adjusted by processes of intensification. Intensification occurs when a particular piece of land is cultivated more frequently (as opposed to lying fallow) and/or improved by such techniques as terracing, irrigation, or use of fertilizers. Another way of intensifying production is to switch to crops that yield more caloric energy per unit of land (e.g., from seed crops to root crops). As we shall see throughout this book, intensification is related to cultural evolution in many ways, even serving to explain for some scholars the emergence of civilization (Chapter 16).

Fallowing Generally speaking, the less often a piece of land is used, the higher its crop yield when it is cultivated, unless specialized intensification practices such as fertilization are used (Boserup 1965). During pioneering stages of agricultural colonization, when land is readily available, fields are left to rest between periods of cultivation, sometimes for many years—a practice called **fallowing**. This is a practical way of controlling weed growth that at the same time allows soil fertility to be restored, because an overgrown field can be burned to clear off weeds and other vegetation. Lengthy fallow periods enhance fertility and weed control, making farming easier for farmers, who, like other people, prefer to get the greatest possible return for the lowest input (law of least effort). **Swidden farming** is particularly widespread in tropical forest biomes. As population density rises and pressure on land becomes greater, fallow periods are shortened and other intensification strategies may come into use. Where soils are rich, fields may ultimately be cropped every year, but in areas of poor soil, annual cropping may be impossible or cause such soil degradation that fields are permanently abandoned. Some forms of intensification are triggered, not by changes in population density but rather by reduction of agricultural risk (as when irrigation provides water in dryland biomes).

In many parts of the Old World agriculture was made more productive and less risky by combining animal husbandry with the farming of plants. Some societies specialize in **pastoralism,** such as the camel-raising Bedouin of the Arabian desert, but the most common pattern is to raise goats, pigs, sheep, cattle, and fowl to supplement plant foods. In the New World, domestic animals played a far less important role in the economy (the exception is the Andes: see Chapter 14).

Frequently intensification entails a shift in technology. Swidden farmers use simple cutting tools like axes to clear land, and digging sticks to plant crops. Shortening the fallow periods means more work to control weed growth, using tools like hoes, shovels, or animal-drawn plows. Adoption of such more efficient tools helps keep human energetic input low in proportion to agricultural return. Before we review the kinds of tools nonindustrial peoples have developed and used, let us provide a broad spatial context for these discussions, and describe the major habitat zones of the world's people.

fallowing Practice of letting agricultural fields lie unused through one or more planting seasons in order to restore their fertility.

swidden farming Type of agriculture based on cutting and burning natural vegetation to provide nutrients to the crops. In this method, it is necessary to change fields every few years. Also known as "slash-and-burn agriculture."

pastoralism Mode of subsistence based primarily on herd animals.

HABITATS OF THE WORLD: SETTINGS FOR CULTURAL EVOLUTION

We made the point earlier that cultures are parts of ecosystems and that, in a very specific sense, each local ecological "community"—including its constituent human communities—has a unique mix of plant and animal species, rainfall and temperature, topography and bedrock. On a more general level, many local ecosystems share similar conditions over large regions. Here we will review major world biomes (communities of plants and animals) as habitats for human exploitation and evolution in the last 10,000 years (these descriptions are based on information presented in Campbell 1985 and Chapple and Coon 1942). We must bear in mind that there are often no sharp boundaries between them; that many have been heavily affected by human activity, particularly in the last 200 years; and that smaller subdivisions could be made of each. Human use of these biomes by nonindustrial cultures was quite varied, reflecting opportunities and constraints imposed in part by technology and transport.

The major (and marginal) biomes are mapped in Figure 6.4 and listed in Table 6.3, which also gives their relative proportions of land area, their proportions of population in the period just before World War II, and a relative measure of population density. By far, the most densely habited areas are the mixed and scrub forests, which together hold 58 percent of the population but represent only 8 percent of the land. Tropical forests also account for a considerable proportion of the population but are much less densely settled. Far less densely settled are the other biomes.

Tropical Forests

Because humans are tropical animals, let us begin our look at the different biomes with tropical forests. Our closest evolutionary relatives, such as monkeys and apes, are still largely restricted to tropical environments today, and until about a million years ago, the same was true of our human ancestors. Since then, we have expanded rapidly throughout virtually all of the world's environments, becoming much more numerous than any other form of **primate**. Common to successful species, such proliferation is called "adaptive radiation." Since we humans retained our essential tropical physiology throughout this process of geographical expansion, our success in nontropical environments largely reflects *cultural* adjustments to them.

Geographically speaking, the tropical regions of the world are close to the equator and fall between the latitudes of the Tropics of Cancer (north) and Capricorn (south). Although these regions are generally hot and often humid, both temperature and rainfall can be heavily affected by elevation above sea level.

Tropical forests are found in parts of the world where the average temperature exceeds 18°C during each month of the year and where there is abundant rainfall. Covering about 13 percent of the earth's land surface,

primate Order of mammals that includes monkeys, apes, and humans.

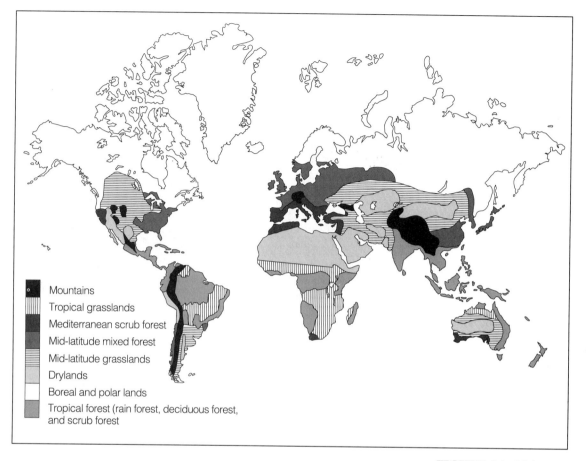

FIGURE 6.4 Major biomes of the world.

Legend:
- Mountains
- Tropical grasslands
- Mediterranean scrub forest
- Mid-latitude mixed forest
- Mid-latitude grasslands
- Drylands
- Boreal and polar lands
- Tropical forest (rain forest, deciduous forest, and scrub forest

they are restricted to a belt extending about 20° north and south of the equator. Heaviest concentrations of the forests are in northern South America, southern Mexico and Central America, West Africa, and Southeast Asia, including the archipelagos extending toward Australia (Fig. 6.5).

There is much variation among tropical forests, depending mainly upon the amount of rain and its seasonal distribution. Where rainfall is heaviest and occurs throughout all or most of the year, tropical rain forests form the most diverse plant biomes in the world—multiple canopy forests which can have more than 100 plant species packed in an area the size of a football field. Where rainfall is lower and there is a pronounced dry season, semi-deciduous or scrub forests prevail. In some regions with poor soils, coniferous forest may be found in the tropics.

Tropical forests present distinctive challenges for human exploitation. The overall biomass of large animals tends to be low, and members of particular plant species tend to be dispersed rather than concentrated. Both

FIGURE 6.5 High tropical forest along the Pasion River in northwestern Guatemala. Note that the trees and shrubs in the tropical forest create a number of distinct levels, called "canopies."

factors affect hunting-gathering strategies, presenting advantages and disadvantages for farmers. There is no risk from frost or drought, but lush natural vegetation must be laboriously cleared for fields and kept from reclaiming them. Rapid plant growth and equally rapid decay caused by the year-round action of microorganisms continually create rich soil nutrients, but these are quickly leached from the soil by high rainfall, and if the soil is thin, erosion quickly removes it. Most nutrients are stored in living plants rather than in the soil, so when forests are cleared, soils rapidly lose their fertility. For these reasons, tropical forests are fragile, especially where heavily used by farmers and ranchers, and they have been badly damaged by deforestation during the last century. Where rivers are present, silt from flooding may replenish the soil, producing fertile and stable alluvial areas. These, together with riverine resources such as fish, support fairly large and permanent populations (e.g., in the Brazilian forest along the Amazon).

Preservation of archaeological materials in tropical forests is poor, and so is site visibility, especially where tools, weapons, and buildings were often made from plant materials such as bamboo (e.g., in Southeast Asia). This is unfortunate, because some important early agricultural innovations appear to have occurred in Southeast Asia and the Orinoco/Amazon forests of South America. The Classic Maya created a complex civilization in the tropical forest zone of southern Mesoamerica, much of which is underlain by limestone bedrock that weathers into particularly rich soils.

Grasslands

In the tropics and in midlatitude regions large transitional areas run between forest and desert, where rainfall is sufficient to support lush vegetation but insufficient for heavy tree growth except along rivers or streams. Precipitation ranges from 250 to 1,250 mm per year, and grasses dominate the typically flat or rolling landscape. About 19 percent of the land surface of the world is grassland. We distinguish between two types of grassland; they differ in temperature and rainfall.

Midlatitude Grasslands Precipitation ranges from 250 to 750 mm per year in the midlatitude grasslands, and there is strong seasonal variation in temperature, frequently with hot, dry summers and extremely cold winters. At lower rainfall levels a dense mat of short vegetation called a "steppe" predominates (e.g., in eastern Russia and parts of central and northeastern Asia). Where rainfall is greater tall grasses ranging from 1 to 3 ms in height form prairies—great seas of grass such as those found on the high plains of the United States in the mid-19th century and still found in eastern Europe, southern Russia, and several parts of South America. Animal biomass—particularly of large herbivores such as American bison—may be very high. Grass roots produce thick sods that eventually decay into enormous amounts of organic matter, forming a deep layer of fertile humus, especially in prairies. Surface water is common; only the smallest streams dry up seasonally.

Tropical Grasslands Tropical grasslands or savannas exist in hot regions with rainfall of about 400–1,250 mm falling in a strongly seasonal pattern. The largest are found in Africa, South America, and northern Australia. Depending on annual rainfall, the grassland borders merge with scrub forest or desert. Where rainfall is high, scrub forest tree species occur interspersed with tall grasses, forming a parklike savanna. These grasses do not form thick sods. Surface water varies strikingly during the year, with many streams disappearing during the dry season. Animal biomass is variable, but some tropical savannas in East Africa support a diversity and density of herbivores and carnivores unparalleled anywhere else in the world.

Grasslands have limited value for hunter-gatherers in terms of edible plant species but may provide plentiful game. Because of heavy sod layers, midlatitude grasslands are very difficult to cultivate by people lacking metal tools and draft animals. Once such tools are available, these grasslands are among the most productive agricultural landscapes, especially for growing grains (Fig. 6.6). Tropical savanna soils lack sods and so are easier to cultivate, but they have fewer nutrient reserves and are subject to moisture deficiency. In Eurasia and East Africa grasslands of both kinds are ideal for pastoralists, particularly those who raise cattle.

FIGURE 6.6 Grasslands have tremendous potential food productivity, given effective technology. Their productivity is understandable, considering that grains, which are domesticated grasses, are the food plants with highest overall nutrition (calories and protein, see Table 6.2).

The Drylands

Dryland biomes, which include true deserts, cover about 17 percent of the earth's land surface: much of northern and southeastern Africa, the Arabian Peninsula and interior Asia, the central part of Australia, western North America, and the west coast of South America. Scarcity of water determines the vegetation of this biome. However, the seasonality of rainfall is as important as the total amount; likewise seasonality and degree of temperature are critical factors. Where temperature is high, the evaporation rate may exceed the rate of precipitation, and much of the sparse moisture that does fall is unavailable to plants. True deserts get less than 250 mm of rainfall annually; moister drylands in varous parts of the world receive from 250 to 500 mm. Wild plants must be well adapted to water deficits (**xerophytic**) in such settings, where total plant biomass is low, corresponding to the level of rainfall. Since animals directly or indirectly depend on plants, their biomass is low too, so energy sources for hunter-gatherers and farmers are limited. Only in the driest deserts, however, is the landscape devoid of vegetation. Dryland vegetation consists primarily of a combination of widely spaced low shrubs and grasses that have roots able to tap deep sources of moisture, structures that can store water through dry periods, or seeds that can survive drought.

xerophytic Adapted to grow in arid environments.

Patterns of human exploitation and settlement are strongly determined by access to sources of surface water—oases, and rivers that originate in wetter climates—which serve to overcome the stressful problem of the evaporation rate. Fertile soil may be widespread, but water is limited and limiting (cf. Leibig's law). In spite of this, or perhaps *because* of it, drylands

FIGURE 6.7 !Kung hunter-gatherers at an encampment in the Kalahari Desert of southern Africa.

have supported cultures of many kinds. These include some of the best-studied surviving foraging peoples, such as the !Kung Bushmen of the Kalahari Desert in southern Africa (Lee 1979; Fig. 6.7) and the native Australians. Several of the earliest civilizations of the Old and New worlds emerged in desert or dryland biomes watered by rivers with good irrigation potential (Chapters 13 and 14). Dryness facilitates archaeological preservation, and sites are comparatively easy to identify where vegetation cover is sparse.

Mediterranean Scrub Forest

As its name implies, this biome includes the Mediterranean Basin and adjacent parts of the Near East; it is also found in California and the northern coasts of the western United States, as well as parts of Chile, southwest Africa, and Australia (a total of about 1 percent of the earth's land surface). Its outstanding feature is low to moderate moisture (250–750 mm) that falls as rain during the coolest months of the year. There is thus an alteration of hot, dry summers and cool, moist winters (which may include light snow and frost). Most regions with Mediterranean biomes are mountainous, so rainfall patterns are complex and moisture is more abundant at higher elevations. Vegetation consists of broadleaf evergreen forest that often has a savannalike appearance, with trees such as evergreen oak interspersed with grasses and shrubs.

Mediterranean biomes everywhere from ancient times were heavily occupied by hunter-gatherers, who collected nuts, fruits, and grasses and preyed on the abundant game supported by this rich vegetation. The first

FIGURE 6.8 Excavated floor and foundations of an ancient house from Çayonu, an early settlement in eastern Turkey. When this house was occupied (ca. 7500–5000 B.C.), the people of Çayonu practiced a mixed economy of farming and hunting.

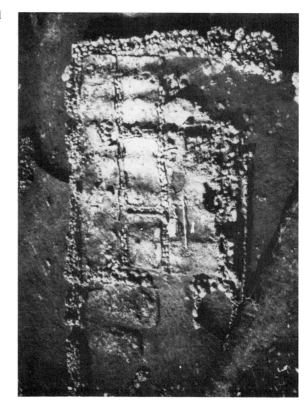

domesticated plants and animals were native to Mediterranean biomes of the eastern Mediterranean and the Near East, appearing about 12,000 years ago. Many of our staple foods, such as wheat, barley, cattle, pigs, goats, and sheep descend from Mediterranean biome ancestors. Much archaeological research has focused on the cultures that densely settled Mediterranean biomes, including the early food producers of the Near East (Redman 1978; Fig. 6.8), the classical urban civilizations of the Mediterranean Basin, and the Native American hunter-gatherers of California (Baumhoff 1963). Because of intense exploitation, Mediterranean biomes have been heavily altered by humans, with particular damage to their once-rich fauna and flora.

Midlatitude Mixed Forests

The midlatitude mixed-forest biome is concentrated in four major regions: the eastern United States and southeastern Canada; Eurasia north of the Mediterranean Basin; northeastern China; and Japan (about 7 percent of the earth's land mass). Smaller pockets of this biome are found in many other parts of the world. Mixed vegetation of coniferous and broadleaf (usually deciduous) trees is adapted to a strongly seasonal set of variations in rainfall and temperature, which includes cold winters; hot, moist summers; and transitional spring and autumn intervals. Precipitation includes both rain and snow. Such variation occurs less near the seacoast than it does in inner, continental land masses. Wild vegetation goes through a period of dormancy in winter, with rapid plant growth in the warmer months and fruiting in the late summer and early fall. Depending on local conditions, forests may be dense or sparse; this biome includes extensive plains as well. Rainfall is high (750–1,500 mm), but decay and leaching of soil nutrients is retarded by cold temperatures much of the year and topsoils are deeper and more fertile than in tropical forests. Rivers are abundant and include some of the largest systems in the world, such as the Mississippi/Ohio, the Rhine of Europe, and the Hwang Ho of North China.

Although both plant and animal resources are plentiful in the mixed-forest biome (O'Brien 1987), climate is a problem for hunter-gatherers; during the protracted cold season, plants are dormant and many animals migrate or hibernate. Snow and bad weather may also lessen mobility and create physical stress during winter (one response to this is storage of seeds and nuts). Once forests are cleared, this biome provides exceptionally good terrain for grain cultivators who also raise livestock such as sheep, cattle, and pigs. Many early agricultural colonists in this sort of biome, for example, practiced a mixed hunting-farming strategy; for example, the European colonists in the woodlands of the eastern United States.

Marginal Biomes

Boreal and Polar Lands

Regions where average temperatures do not rise above 10°C for at least four months of the year hold the least potential for human habitation. Here winters are very cold and prolonged, and summers are short, with very sharp transitions between these seasons. Boreal and polar lands together make up about 25 percent of the earth's surface but the greatest single expanse, Antarctica, has never been inhabited by humans without regular importation of resources from other biomes.

Depending on climate, two kinds of surface vegetation exist: taiga and tundra. **Taiga** (coniferous forest) covers the warmer zones. Further north, where all months of the year have temperatures below 10°C taiga shifts to tundra or polar environments. **Tundra** vegetation is a combination of grasses, lichens, sedges, mosses, and scattered dwarf trees (Fig. 6.9). Because of low temperature, low evaporation rates, and generally flat terrain, soils are waterlogged and there are extensive lakes and bogs. Taiga and tundra ecosystems are among the simplest in the world in terms of species diversity; often a single species dominates the ecological community. High-latitude polar environments lack plants altogether. Hunter-gatherers must depend almost entirely on animals since few plant foods are available. In

taiga Coniferous forest in the northern latitudes.

tundra Plant community comprised of grasses, lichens, sedges, mosses, and scattered dwarf trees.

FIGURE 6.9 The tundra environment is common in high latitude zones in all northern continents.

such regions human population densities are among the lowest in the world (Binford 1978). Large game animals, which occur in interior regions, occasionally concentrate in very large herds, especially during annual migrations, but overall biomass is still very low. Coastal fauna—both fish and sea mammals—are much richer subsistence resources. While there are many taiga and tundra peoples, only the Eskimo have successfully adapted to the truly polar northernmost climates of the Arctic. Farming is of course impossible in the cold lands, but some peoples in northern Eurasia (of these the Lapps are the best known) herd reindeer in much the same way as pastoralists herd their animals in more temperate climates. Because low temperatures retard decay, preservation is frequently excellent in cold lands, and the archaeological record correspondingly rich.

Mountain Lands In areas of the world dominated by large mountain masses, we find a complex mosaic of diverse environmental conditions; hence different ecosystems are closely juxtaposed because of the combined localized effects of elevation, slope, temperature, and precipitation. Though this kind of zoning is found in all mountain regions, it is particularly pronounced in the tropics. Mountain regions offer extraordinarily diverse habitats for human utilization, packed into very small zones. Such diversity offers a range of options for foragers, and for farmers and pastoralists as well.

Marine Ecosystems Seas and oceans are not habitable biomes for humans, such as those discussed above, but they offer a wide range of resources and are found adjacent to many terrestrial biomes. For example, one of the driest and most inhospitable deserts in the world is on the coast of Peru, but rich marine resources made the coast very attractive to both foragers and farmers. Among the few hunting-gathering societies that were reasonably sedentary in residence and had elements of ranked political organization, several were heavily dependent on marine resources (e.g., Northwest Coast societies in North America [Box 6.1], and the Calusa of southern Florida [Box 10.2]).

We have characterized major biomes in very general terms, but this perspective should not obscure the fact that humans adapt to particular features or zones (often called microenvironments) of their larger regional environments. For example, the Shoshone whom Steward studied lived in a general dryland environment with overall sparse plant and animal resources, but they exploited particular microenvironments that (at least situationally) were very lush and productive.

THE TECHNOLOGY OF RESOURCE PROCUREMENT

Having become familiar with the range of major habitats the world has offered as settings for human use, let us now consider the different kinds of technology (tools and techniques) devised to exploit them. According to Steward's concept of the culture core, technoeconomic aspects of culture are directly related to extracting food energy and other materials from the environment. The anthropologist Eric Wolf defines a similar concept (although for a different purpose), the **mode of production,** as "a specific, historically occurring set of social relations through which labor is deployed to wrest energy from nature by means of tools, skills, organization, and knowledge" (1982:75). In this section we will briefly review the technology of the mode of production (later chapters discuss how it is organized).

Technology has played a highly significant role in cultural evolution, accounting in fact for much of the evolutionary variation we seek to explain as archaeologists. Because tools, weapons, and facilities of all kinds make up a large portion of the archaeological record, they constitute an important window onto the past.

Chapple and Coon (1942) identified a nexus of cultural features — *transport, cutting tools,* and *food acquisition* (the latter including foraging, farming, and animal husbandry, as discussed already) — as essential to how traditional, nonindustrial cultures patterned themselves over the world's landscapes through long-term adaptational processes. Their concepts form the core of the following brief review.

mode of production "A specific, historically occurring set of social relations through which labor is deployed to wrest energy from nature by means of tools, skills, organization, and knowledge" (Wolf 1982:75).

Transport

Although the construction of transport tools or facilities is logically dependent on primary tools, we will discuss transport first, because transport

BOX 6.1

NATIVE AMERICANS
OF THE PACIFIC NORTHWEST

Given that marginal habitats do not support large-scale food production, do "marginal habitats" only support egalitarian societies? We tend to associate hunting-gathering with egalitarian social organization, with little or no ranking, or inheritance of property. But human ingenuity in exploiting the cold, mountainous boreal forest-marine ecosystems of the Pacific Northwest Coast resulted in sufficient food resources to support permanent year-round villages, ranked social organization, and strong development of territorial and ownership rights. Our information about the Northwest Coast culture area derives from ethnographic study of these groups at the time of contact and from archaeological investigation of sites in Washington State and in British Columbia, Canada.

The environment as a resource zone

The Northwest Coast area, which includes the Pacific Coast of North America from southern Alaska to Washington State, features steep, rocky topography; numerous bays; inlets; and offshore islands. High annual rainfall supports lush boreal forest with few but seasonally abundant food species (berries and roots, deer, elk, and bear), and the rivers and sea yield abundant fish, shellfish, and sea mammals. Northwest Coast peoples of the ancient past were hunter-gatherers, taking advantage of resources that were plentiful but extremely variable locally from year to year. These two characteristics had a significant impact on sociopolitical organization.

Settlement and food procurement

Northwest Coast tribes adapted to the seasonal rhythms of weather and food availability through their settlement pattern and the scheduling of their subsistence strategy. For example, the Kwakiutl, a linguistically distinct group of several thousand at the time of European contact, lived along the west coast of Canada and on Vancouver Island. There were 25 or so distinct local groups of Kwakiutl, each numbering several hundred people and each exploiting a small area of bays, islands, interior streams, and forests. The local group's yearly life centered on a large permanent village, located in a coastal cove sheltered from the stormy winter weather. During winter there was little subsistence activity; the Kwakiutl stayed indoors, preparing

capabilities have strongly influenced certain important evolutionary trends, such as economic specialization and urbanization (Chapter 8).

All humans face the same transport problems: how to move themselves and the things they need in order to exploit their environments and interact with one another. In nonindustrial cultures, the energy to move things comes from human or animal muscles, or from tapping environmental energy movements such as wind or flowing water. As organisms, humans obviously move themselves about by walking or running. In some environments simple, specialized devices have been developed to make walking or running more efficient, for example, skis or snowshoes in cold climates; similarly, watercraft propelled by paddles or oars (powered by the arms

for and engaged in ceremonial activities and feasting on stored food. From later winter to midsummer, ocean fishing became their principal subsistence activity. Highly favorable fishing sites were limited; people either lived at the village and traveled to the sites daily in large dugout canoes or moved to fishing site camps for weeks, even months at a time. During the summer and fall, forest resources were gathered and hunted, and temporary camps were established along salmon streams. Technology for fishing, hunting, and gathering and for storing food was specialized, including many heavy items of wood that would have been inappropriate for migratory hunter-gatherers.

Each of the large Kwakiutl villages formed a small chiefdom made up of several ranked kin groups called "Numayn." Each Numayn numbered 25–50 people, who proclaimed territorial rights over fishing sites, berry patches, hunting territories, and items such as buildings, canoes, and equipment. In principle, Numayn members were related by **patrilineal descent** (through the male line), and they lived together in a large and substantial wooden house in the winter village. In reality, the residents of these houses at any point in time were related through various kin ties. The core of each Numayn was a ranked group of related individuals, headed by a chief who owned titles, rituals, songs, and goods. The Numayn chief organized his people for subsistence, craft production, and feasting activities.

The **potlatch** was the most elaborate kind of feast; guests were laden with gifts of blankets, wooden and copper items, and gold. During potlatches titles and property were assigned to those who would inherit positions of high rank; these ceremonial feasts and gifts thus served to legitimize the ranking system. Feasting also had a competitive aspect: Numayn chiefs tried to enhance their own prestige through their generosity, and within the village competitive potlatching lead to a clear ranking of village chiefs. The highest-ranking chief of the village enhanced his prestige with his counterparts in other villages by holding potlatches for them.

Ecological perspective

The ecological perspective on Kwakiutl ranking and potlatching reveals a predictable pattern. Food resources were extraordinarily abundant but seasonal and localized, providing short-term, intermittent production of substantial surpluses. Their exploitation required relatively complex technology and considerable cooperation, hence leadership, organization, and a strong sense of territoriality. The function of precontact potlatching was to reduce the insecurity of food availability by redistributing food and gifts that could be traded for food. The small-scale chiefdom organization of the Kwakiutl was a highly effective response to their environmental conditions.

rather than the legs) allow people to move across bodies of water. In order to transport things, humans have developed a wide range of containers (e.g., bags, baskets, pots), some of which were probably among the oldest technological innovations, though they do not always survive in archaeological contexts.

The most important innovations in transport technology, apart from small watercraft, appeared only during the last 10,000 years. Some animals were domesticated to carry or pull humans and their goods (as well as to provide food), thus adding an important new source of energy to supplement human muscles not only in transport but also in plowing fields. Innovations such as the wheel made vehicles, whether drawn by humans or animals, more efficient in many types of terrain. Improved designs in watercraft, especially the innovation of the sail, allowed the utilization of other energy sources. We discuss below how these transport capabilities were linked to other forms of tools and to resource procurement systems in the ethnographic present.

Primary Tools

Most tools in nonindustrial societies do not make more energy available, but they do render the application of muscle energy more efficient. Primary tools are those necessary to produce the rest of the technology. The most important class of these is **cutting tools** (a general term for tools that cut, gouge, shave, pierce, scrape, and saw). Without these, it would be impossible to carve a dugout canoe, to cut poles to build a house or fiber to weave a basket. Anthropologists have traditionally identified three classes of cutting tools: chipped stone, ground stone, and metal. Remember that during the early stages of the growth of archaeology, tools of these classes were arranged into hypothetical evolutionary sequences.

cutting tools Tools used for cutting, gouging, shaving, piercing, scraping, and sawing.

Chipped Stone Tools The earliest recognizable cutting tools found in the archaeological record (from about 2.5 million years ago in East Africa) are made of hard stone that is chipped or flaked to form a sharp edge. Increasingly sophisticated **chipped stone tools** did most of the cutting work in all human cultures until about 5–6,000 years ago, and a few cultures still used them until the beginning of this century (see Fig. 2.7). An advantage of stone as a raw material is that it is found in most environments; flint and obsidian (volcanic glass) were favorite raw materials, but a wide variety of other minerals also served. In environments where suitable stone was unavailable, cutting tools were made from other materials such as hard wood and shell, and everywhere chipped stone tools were supplemented with those made of organic materials.

chipped stone tools Tools produced by flaking or chipping off pieces from a stone core to produce an implement.

There is a strong association between chipped stone tools and hunting and gathering societies. Hunter-gatherers equipped with stone tools and the technologies derived from them colonized virtually the entire world and adapted to an enormous range of environments 8–10,000 years ago. The only unoccupied places were the most extreme polar regions and the more geographically isolated island chains of Micronesia and Polynesia. During this expansion many varied tool kits evolved. Some hunter-gatherers, especially those like the Eskimo, who lived in harsh, cold climates, developed highly complex technologies, with many specialized tools made from skin, fiber, wood, bone, and ivory as well as stone. Eskimo and other northern hunters also developed sophisticated watercraft and used the domesticated dog to pull sleds, because effective transport was essential to exploiting cold environments.

In the ethnographic present hunter-gatherers equipped with stone tool–based technologies were found in many parts of the world, especially in those biomes where conditions were inhospitable for nonindustrial agriculture: the drylands, the boreal and polar lands, and many tropical forest and tropical savanna regions. Most such hunter-gatherers also possessed basin- or trough-shaped stones, shaped by grinding, that served as mortars for processing seeds, nuts, or other vegetable foods into edible paste or flour. Archaeological research documents the earlier presence of foragers in the Mediterranean, midlatitude mixed forest, and midlatitude grassland biomes as well, but hunting-gathering economies have generally been supplanted in these agriculturally productive environments by agriculturalists or pastoralists.

Ground Stone Tools Cutting tools made by grinding or pecking hard stone are called "polished stone tools." **Polished,** or **ground stone, tools** that perform the same tasks as primary cutting tools only become abundant in the archaeological record about 8–10,000 years ago; in many parts of the world they do not replace chipped stone tools but rather supplement them, adding a new dimension to stone tool technology (see Fig. 2.7). Although chipped stone tools can be made more rapidly, ground stone tools are more durable, can be resharpened more effectively, and can be hafted in sophisticated ways to make axes, adzes, hoes, chisels, and weapons. Although some hunter-gatherers used ground stone tools, there is a strong association between this technology and cultures that practiced food production or had mixed economies, because ground stone tools were especially effective for clearing natural vegetation from fields (axes), for cultivation (hoes), and for processing domestic grains (grinding stones) (Fig. 6.10).

In the ethnographic present hunter-gatherers using ground stone tools were found throughout many of the dryland and cold land regions of western and northern North America, the grasslands and temperate forests of southern South America, and the entire continent of Australia. Cultures with mixed or farming economies using ground stone tools inhabited the temperate woodland biome of the eastern United States, much of the tropical forest zone of South America, and virtually all of the tropical forest biomes of Melanesia, Micronesia, and Polynesia. There was great variation in transport capability. Small watercraft were found virtually everywhere, but some peoples of Oceania developed seagoing sailing canoes capable of long voyages. Domestic animals for transport were not found in most regions. Just how recent the ethnographic present is for some societies using stone tools is illustrated by the exploration of the interior of New Guinea. In the early 1930s the agricultural tribes of highland New Guinea were first contacted by outsiders, (Connolly and Anderson 1987) who counted approximately a million people who were using a basic ground stone and wood technology.

Metal Tools Although there was desultory use of readily worked metals such as copper as long ago as 7000 B.C., metal tools did not become

polished, or ground, stone tools Tools produced by the pecking or grinding of hard stones.

FIGURE 6.10 Some women in Central and Latin America still grind corn using stone tools, as has been done for millennia. Although tools of this kind may vary somewhat in form, they have been used all over the world for thousands of years to process plant foods and for other purposes, such as to grind minerals for dyes.

common anywhere in the world until after about 4000 B.C. Between 4000 and 500 B.C. the use of metal spread widely throughout the Old World: first copper, then copper alloyed with other metals to make bronze, and finally iron. In some parts of the Old World, such as Egypt in 4000–3000 B.C., tools of chipped stone, ground stone, and copper or bronze were all in use simultaneously (see also Box 6.2).

Metal tools had several advantages over stone ones. Metal could be hammered or cast into virtually any shape (unlike stone) and tools could be resharpened or recycled completely when they wore out. Most important, metal tools were vastly more efficient for cutting than stone tools, for most purposes; experiments have shown, for example, that iron or steel axes are at least four times as efficient as stone axes for felling trees (Saraydar and Shimada 1971). Metal plowshares enormously increased the efficiency of food energy production where animal traction was available. Prairie biomes in particular were of minimal use to farmers without metal plows to break up the heavy sod. Here is an excellent example of how technology alters carrying capacity. North America's prairies could not be farmed before European colonists introduced metal plows, and the carrying capacity of this vast region increased dramatically with this technological change.

Reliance on metal tools has disadvantages as well. Some chipped stone tools are sharper and thus more efficient for cutting plants, meat, and leather. Unlike stone, metal sources are restricted (especially copper), so complicated systems of exchange are necessary to obtain them, and they

BOX 6.2

THE TOOL KIT OF AN ALPINE TRAVELLER
OF 5,000 YEARS AGO

"Stone Age," "Bronze Age," "Iron Age": These familiar labels have been used for over a hundred years. It would be convenient for archaeologists if tools made of one material suddenly and universally replaced those made of another. If this occurred, it would be simple to sort out chronological differences on the basis of artifact assemblages. Unfortunately there is considerable overlap, as a recent and spectacular archaeological find demonstrated.

In July 1991 receding glaciers high in the Austrian Alps revealed the body of a man dressed in leather and fur clothing, believed to have died about 5,000 years ago. Apparently he died while crossing the Alps; he fell into a crevasse and his body was then frozen in a matrix of glacial ice. After millennia the ice retreated, uncovering this individual's well-preserved body. The man had tattoos on his legs and back and had stuffed hay into his shoes to protect himself against the cold. He carried an assortment of tools, including a copper axe; a knife with a chipped stone (flint) blade; and a quiver of arrows, some with chipped flint points. Although metal tools were in use, traditional stone tools obviously still played an important role.

SOURCE: Fowler 1991a, 1991b.

---

are therefore expensive. Iron, though widely available, must be smelted and wrought by specialists. Despite these disadvantages, copper, bronze, and iron were widely used by food producers throughout all the major biomes of Europe, Asia, and Africa by 500 B.C., and metal use vastly accelerated the expansion of farming populations, not only because of their effectiveness in clearing and cultivating land but also because metal weapons proved more lethal than those of stone and wood (Wenke 1980). So rapid was the diffusion of iron tools that some regions (e.g., northern Scandinavia) went directly from stone to iron tools—a distinctive example of specific evolution. Most of the complex societies of the Old World (chiefdoms and states) were firmly based on metal technology in the ethnographic present. Throughout Europe and Northern Asia metal technology was closely associated with the cultivation of wheat, barley, rice, and other grains (often using intensive forms of agriculture such as irrigation) and with animal husbandry. In sub-Saharan Africa grains, root crops, and livestock were staples. Also highly associated with metal technology were domestic animals for transport or plowing, and innovations such as sailing vessels and the wheel (though the latter was not used everywhere).

Some isolated foragers who did not produce metal themselves acquired small amounts of it by trade, but in certain large regions, including Melanesia, Micronesia, Polynesia, and Australia, metals were not used in the ethnographic present. Most of the New World used chipped and polished stone tools into the ethnographic present (the 15th–16th centuries). Although metals such as copper, gold, and silver, were commonly used to make elite goods, widespread use of effective cutting tools of hard metal (bronze) was confined to the Inca empire in western South America. Lack of metal tools is one reason why most of the tropical forest and prairie biomes of the New World had light populations.

We have mentioned that wheeled vehicles, sails, and domestic animals useful for transport were absent in the New World before Europeans arrived (the exceptions being dogs, and llamas used as pack animals in South America, as already noted), and in Chapter 8 we shall discuss this variation in tool technology and transport systems and its important evolutionary consequences. Transport, technology, energy extraction, and environment all influence the productivity of food-getting by any society in a particular region; thus the carrying capacity of the region is not a fixed value.

This dynamic dimension of carrying capacity is precisely what makes it useful. Let's go back to Wolf's definition of mode of production introduced earlier in this chapter. This definition is useful because it captures the basic elements that determine the cultural basis for carrying capacity: the organization and social relationships of people, their knowledge, and their tools at a particular point in time. Modes of production are important in defining carrying capacity for a particular region. If an element of the mode of production changes — say, technology (e.g., iron plows replace digging sticks) — then carrying capacity may suddenly shift, bringing about a new level of productivity. Innovations are sometimes devised or adopted because human populations have experienced stress (i.e., food shortages) using a less intensive mode of production. We often perceive such shifts in the archaeological record, and they are important evolutionary indicators. There is strong evidence that human populations sometimes exceed carrying capacity, thereby wreaking extremely deleterious effects on their environments and themselves (Chapter 15).

SUMMARY

People, like other organisms, are parts of ecosystems and must extract food energy from their environments. Their capacity to do so depends on many factors, including application of the technology of transport and tools within particular ecosystems or biomes. Although cultures in the ethnographic present demonstrate adaptation to virtually all major terrestrial biomes, this process is patterned in complex ways by technological factors. The most widespread and complex indigenous evolutionary transformations have occurred in Mediterranean and midlatitude mixed-forest biomes, which are especially durable, energy-rich environments, and to a somewhat lesser degree in tropical forest and grassland biomes. Needless to say, these different evolutionary histories have nothing to do with innate differences among the different peoples of the world but rather with the challenges of different sorts of environments.

The distribution of the world's population in various major biomes just prior to World War II is striking in that only a small percentage of the population is found in the largest category, the marginal biomes. In contrast, the midlatitude mixed-forest, and Mediterranean biomes, with only 8 percent of the land, hold dense and disproportionately large populations, in part reflecting their agricultural productivity and potential to support hunter-gatherers. These figures must be used with care. One reason for the extremely high population figure for tropical forest biomes is that a specialized and stable kind of farming—wet rice agriculture—is found throughout much of south and southeast Asia (Reischauer and Fairbank 1960). Where rice agriculture is lacking in tropical forests (e.g., in West Africa or the Amazon basin), populations were very small in the ethnographic present. Although the carrying capacity of the Mediterranean and midlatitude forest is high for foragers and farmers, the large populations in the recent past also reflect the success of industrial populations, who live in such environments in North America, Europe, and Japan. Nevertheless, the figures in Table 6.3 reflect to a high degree the varied capacity of major biomes to yield food energy and other essential materials to nonindustrial populations.

Unfortunately, no neat correlation exists between technology, food procurement systems, political organization, and environmental factors. Early states emerged in the Mediterranean biomes of Europe, but similar habitats in California supported egalitarian hunter-gatherers until the 19th century. Although most New World tropical forest zones supported egalitarian farmers or small-scale ranked societies, the Classic Maya created a brilliant tropical forest civilization. The Aztecs forged a huge empire based on simple stone tool technology in the complex but essentially drylands environment of the Basin of Mexico (Berdan 1982). The lesson is that while general evolutionary tendencies may exist, we must examine specific evolutionary sequences as highly individual cases. Although humans are parts of nature, cultural behavior is highly dynamic. Many highly distinctive adaptations have been made by hunter-gatherers and farmers to particular environments, and these have changed through time. Tracing when, where, and how such changes have occurred, and trying to explain them, is a major preoccupation of scientific archaeology.

POINTS TO REMEMBER

- What we know about cultures in the ethnographic present helps us understand human adaptation.

- Human cultures are parts of large ecosystems and, humans, like other organisms, are limited at any given time by their ability to extract resources from the environment.

- Societies vary enormously in the amounts and kinds of energy they use; most societies studied by archaeologists were low-energy societies.

- Two major kinds of food procurement systems are hunting-gathering and food production.

- Food production, as a strategy for acquiring energy from the environment, can be highly intensified, with important implications for cultural change.

- Major habitats of the world have provided varied settings for both hunter-gatherers and food producers, and each has a distinctive archaeological record of human adaptation.

- Adaptation to any environment is largely determined by tools and transport capabilities.

FOR FURTHER READING*

A comprehensive introduction to the field of energy is Scientific American's *Energy*. Odum's *Fundamentals of Ecology* outlines how ecosystems operate. Chapple and Coon's *Principles of Anthropology* is an invaluable look at the world's cultures and habitats. Three general works on cultural ecology are Campbell's *Human Ecology*, Butzer's *Archaeology as Human Ecology*, and Hardesty's *Ecological Anthropology*. Coale's "The History of the Human Population," Winterhalder and Smith's *Hunter-gatherer Foraging Strategies*, and Lee's *The !Kung San: Men, Women and Work in a Foraging Society* offer perspectives on the lives of hunter-gatherers during the agricultural revolution. Grigg's *Agricultural Systems of the World* summarizes crops and habitats.

*Full citations appear in the bibliography.

PLATE 1: Extensive stratigraphic excavations at the site of Koster, Illinois, have revealed fourteen superimposed occupation levels spanning the period from 7500 B.C. to A.D. 1200, providing a wealth of information about the development of food production among the peoples of North America. (Photography by D. Bastion, courtesy of the Center for American Archaeology, Kampsville, IL.)

PLATE 2: The Pueblo people of the American Southwest constructed huge, apartment-like residential compounds, such as Chetro Ketl in Chaco Canyon, New Mexico. This thriving center was abandoned in the twelfth century A.D., probably because drought and human-induced environmental degradation made the landscape unproductive for farming. (Courtesy Linda M. Nicholas.)

PLATE 3: Buildings in the Mexican city of Teotihuacán were decorated with wall murals. This mural from the residential compound of Tepantitla shows a deity iconographers call the Great Goddess, from whose hands spring fountains of water, a precious substance in Teotihuacán's semiarid valley. The scene illustrates elements of an ideological system otherwise unavailable for archaeological study. (Courtesy Mary Ellen Miller.)

PLATE 4: Town markets have been important economic institutions in many cultures for thousands of years. Traditional markets that can be observed today, such as this one in highland Guatemala, help archaeologists reconstruct ancient economic behavior. (Marion Patterson/Photo Researchers.)

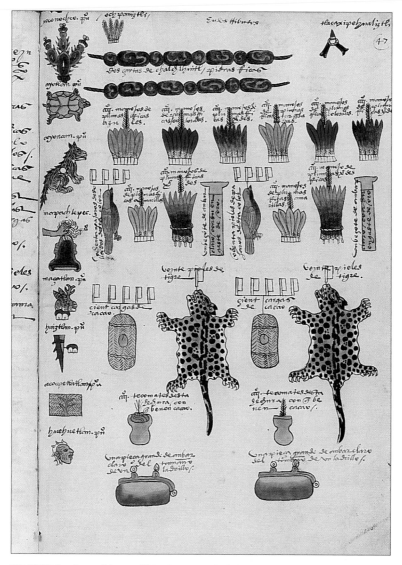

PLATE 5: Aztec kings of Mexico recorded the tribute they exacted from conquered peoples in books called codices. This page from the Codex Mendoza shows the name symbols of tributary towns and the kinds and amounts of tribute they owed. Such documentary evidence supplements data available from the archaeological record. (Bodleian Library, Oxford University.)

PLATE 6: This wall mural from the Classic Maya site of Bonampak, Mexico, depicts the ritual designation of a royal heir. Such representative art is enormously helpful in understanding ancient cultures. (Mural from reproduction of Room 1, Structure 1, Bonampak Chiapas, Mexico, for the Florida Museum of Natural History, Gainesville, Fla. Reproduction painted by Felipe Davalos and Kees Grootenboer, assisted by Janis Gore. Photo by Stan Blomeley.)

PLATE 7: This artist's conception of a sacrificial ritual at the Classic Maya center of Copán, Honduras, is based on the archaeological discovery of jaguar skeletons buried beneath this stone altar depicting a dynasty of sixteen successive kings. (H. Tom Hall, © 1989 National Geographic Society.)

PLATE 8: The superbly preserved Inka administrative center of Machu Picchu, high in the Peruvian Andes, was discovered by Hiram Bingham in 1911 during his attempt to find the final capital of the Inka empire. (Robert Frerck/Woodfin Camp & Associates.)

PLATE 9: The Rift Valley system of East Africa has revealed evidence of human activity that extends back several million years. The geological strata of Olduvai Gorge, Tanzania, shown here, provide the evidence that has allowed dating of the associated fossil remains of our early ancestors. (K. Cannon-Bonventre/Anthro-Photo.)

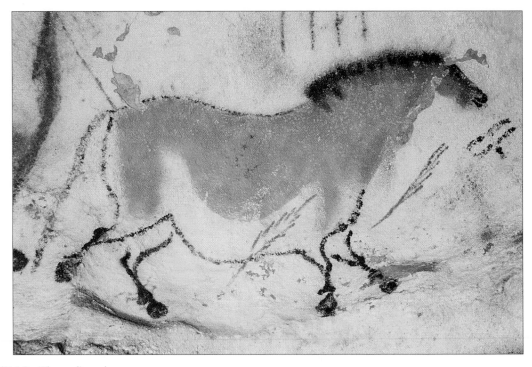

PLATE 10: The earliest clear examples of human symbolic behavior, dating to more than 15,000 years ago, are recorded in the elaborate cave art of Europe. Images of animals, such as this one from Lascaux in France, are not only aesthetically sophisticated but probably had complex and important meanings which may never be fully understood by modern scholars. (© Jean Vertut, Issy-les-Moulineaux, France.)

PLATE 11: Pharaohs of Old Kingdom Egypt (2600–2200 B.C.) built enormous pyramid complexes at Giza, near modern Cairo, to glorify themselves and provide for the survival of their souls. These elaborate complexes preserve much tangible information concerning ancient Egyptian belief and ritual. (PHOTRI, Inc.)

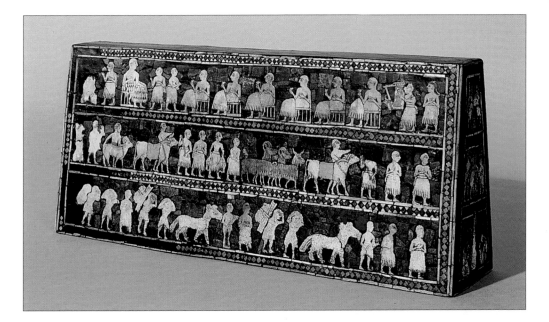

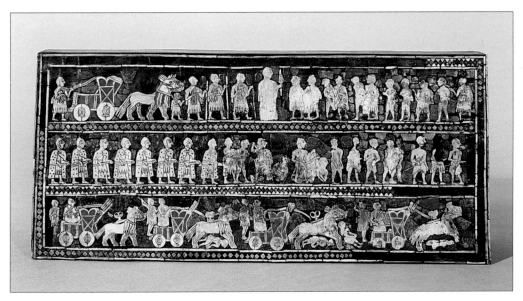

PLATE 12: The Royal Standard of Ur was recovered by Sir Leonard Woolley from a complex of royal graves at Ur, an ancient city in southern Mesopotamia. Presumably a symbol of political authority, it records scenes of peace and prosperity on one side (top) and war and discord on the other (bottom). (Courtesy of the Trustees of the British Museum.)

PLATE 13: One of the best-preserved early cities in the world is Mohenjo-Daro, in the Indus Valley of modern Pakistan. Abandoned in about 1500 B.C., its houses and public buildings, built of fired brick, have survived remarkably intact and provide insights into the social and economic organization within the ancient city. (© Dilip Mehta 1984. All rights reserved./Woodfin Camp and Associates.)

PLATE 14: The vast wealth and power of the first emperor to unify all China (221 B.C.) is reflected by his enormous mortuary complex just outside the modern city of Xian. Near the mountain-like tomb itself, huge pits hold life-sized ceramic replicas of soldiers, horses, and chariots representing the army he led during his life. (Wally McNamee/Woodfin Camp & Associates.)

PART THREE

RECONSTRUCTING

THE PAST

Anthropologists know that all societies, past or present, have many basic things in common. In all societies people are born into families and raised in households that provide care, education, and economic support. Everywhere food and other necessary things must be produced, redistributed, and consumed. All cultures are rich in symbolic language, art, and ritual. Everyday life requires that political decisions be made, so all societies have leaders and some form of government. Different societies must interact with one another, politically or otherwise. Finally, all cultures have what we can broadly call religion.

On the other hand, families and households are structured very differently the world over. Hunter-gatherers would find the economic behaviors of urban dwellers almost incomprehensible. Cultures are highly distinctive in their languages, their art, and their rituals. In certain societies there are no permanent leaders, while others have formal offices and bureaucracies. What is sacred in one culture is blasphemy in another.

One of the basic tasks of the archaeologist is to understand and explain patterns of similarity and the range of variation so that we can interpret the behavior that produced the archaeological record. In Chapters 7–12 we examine major kinds of cultural behaviors or institutions to see how to reconstruct them, using the theories, research designs, methods, and techniques reviewed earlier in the book. Our discussions focus on a wide range of comparative ethnographic and archaeological examples. We also return frequently to research at Copán to show how archaeologists design research to investigate particular behaviors or institutions. These examples demonstrate the problems archaeologists face in reconstructing the past and how they interpret their findings to investigate issues of cultural adaptation and evolution.

CHAPTER SEVEN

FAMILY AND HOUSEHOLD, COMMUNITY AND SOCIETY

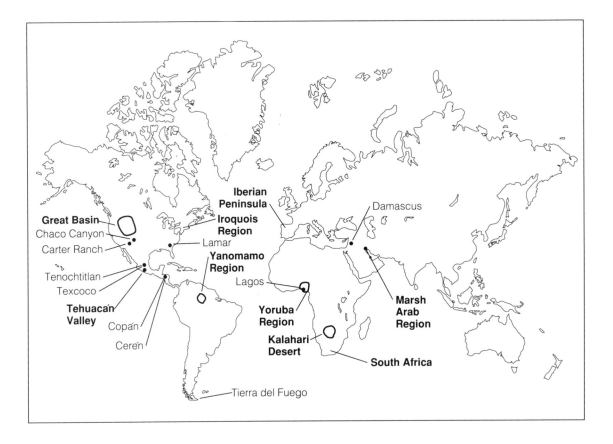

Great Basin
Chaco Canyon
Carter Ranch
Tenochtitlan
Texcoco
Tehuacán Valley
Copán
Cerén
Iberian Peninsula
Iroquois Region
Lamar
Yanomamo Region
Lagos
Yoruba Region
Kalahari Desert
South Africa
Tierra del Fuego
Damascus
Marsh Arab Region

Archaeologists study humans as members of social groups. In all societies, people live and interact in social groups that have clear spatial dimensions (Haviland 1985). Most commonly, people live as families in dwellings. The dwelling, or house, is the most basic level of the spatial context of life in archaeological societies. Other levels are the community as a whole and the regional settlement system (Fig. 7.1). The three levels are intermeshed and each level is not fully understood without the others. Here, we look at social groups and their spatial contexts: the household and dwelling, and the social community and physical settlement. Settlement system studies will be introduced in this chapter and discussed again in Chapters 10 and 11.

The goals of this chapter are to describe these most basic domestic patterns of human adaptation to social and natural environments, to discuss how household composition relates to social structure and economic organization, and to examine how archaeologists learn about the spatial aspects of social organization.

FAMILY AND HOUSEHOLD

Ethnographically known patterns of social relations reveal a wonderful variety in solutions to the basic problem of how people interact as social animals. The overwhelming majority of people in the past, and many in the present, have spent their lives within or near the homes and communities of their birth, as members of traditional societies whose strongest bonds were those of kinship. In virtually all societies, individuals are parts of families, and the **nuclear family** is the fundamental social **institution**. Families generally live together in dwellings, as **households** (Deetz 1982; Netting, Wilk, and Arnould 1984). But the traditional household also often served as an economic unit, producing most of what it needed and used plus sufficient surplus to support nonproducers, and consuming food and goods characteristic of the society.

The dwelling is sometimes a single structure, sometimes a cluster of structures. It is the archaeological remains of the household, so dwellings are basic units of archaeological study; they are the building blocks of communities, which form the component parts of settlement systems. In traditional societies dwellings of common people are the most abundant and important form of cultural evidence so household archaeology can reconstruct such features as craft activities and diet as well as household size and composition and larger patterns of social organization and social structure (Wilk 1989b; Wilk and Rathje 1982a).

Functions and Forms of the House and Household

The nuclear family (Haviland 1985; Keesing 1975; Murdock 1965) is a basic two-generation unit, consisting of one or both parents and unmarried children. It is a useful concept, but we must remember that the term covers a range in size and composition, the most fundamental version

nuclear family Two-generation family unit, consisting of one or both parents and unmarried children.

institution Organization with socially recognized functions, established by custom or charter whose life span extends beyond that of any of its individual constituent members.

household Group of co-residing individuals who share a set of facilities and act cooperatively on a day-to-day basis.

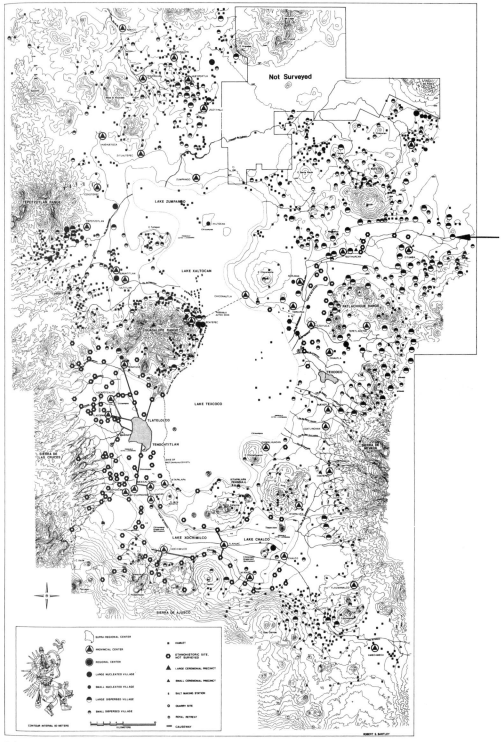

(a)

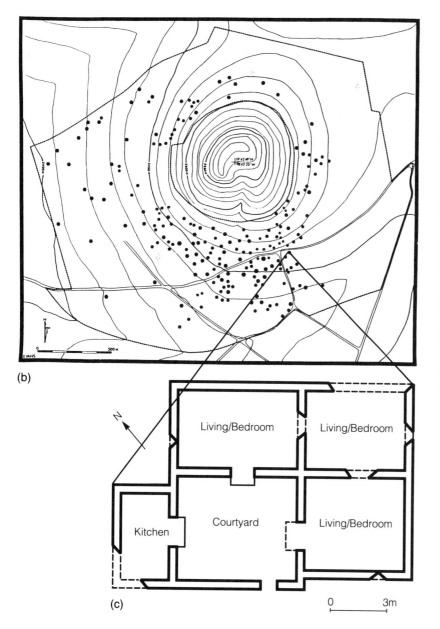

(b)

(c)

FIGURE 7.1 Three different levels of archaeological analysis for the Aztec period Basin of Mexico at the time of Spanish Conquest (A.D. 1521): (a) The entire basin is an area of about 7,000 km²; the symbols indicate the communities of various sizes that covered it (Tenochtitlan is just southwest of the center of the map). The Teotihuacán Region is in the northeast corner of the basin. An arrow points to the village of Cihuatecpan, shown in (b) with its 200 housemounds indicated, covering its slopes. One of the houses excavated at Cihuatecpan is illustrated in (c). Another appears in Figure 7.12.

being that of mother and children, yet even this is not universal. Keeping in mind the variety that can be encompassed by the term, we can still use it as a generalization of the basic unit for cohabiting, food sharing, sexual activity and reproduction, child rearing, socialization, and enculturation, no matter how many nuclear families co-reside as a household.

If each nuclear family forms its own household, the typical dwelling will be relatively small and located far enough from its neighbors to maintain considerable functional isolation. In our society the nuclear family often

joint family household
Household type that consists of two or more families, not necessarily related.

extended family Family type consisting of relatives by descent and marriage belonging to several generations: for example, grandparents, their offspring and spouses, and grandchildren.

polygamous family One individual and several spouses and their children.

polygamy General term for the practice of marrying more than one spouse.

polygyny The practice of multiple wives sharing a single husband.

polyandry The practice of multiple husbands sharing a single wife.

bride-price Compensation offered to the bride's family, usually by the groom's family, for the loss of her companionship and labor to another group upon marriage.

comprises the household, though this is far less true today than it was in the 1950s. The household of traditional societies is often larger and serves a wider range of functions. Households are frequently made up of several closely related nuclear families; anthropologists call these **joint family households.** The two most common joint family types are **extended families** (several related couples and their children) and **polygamous families** (one individual and several spouses and their children). These joint families often include more than two generations of relatives.

Polygamy, which means "many marriages," is a gender-neutral term; in practice, the overwhelming majority of societies permitting multiple marriages are **polygynous,** with one husband being shared by several wives. Very few are **polyandrous,** with one wife shared by several husbands. Typically, the polygynous joint household in such societies consists of a man, his wives, and their children, his adult married sons, and their wives and children.

Houses for joint family households are large, serving as loci of collective domestic enterprises. They require several private rooms or buildings for the different nuclear families, a communal work and social area, and perhaps special purpose areas and structures (granaries and other storerooms, kitchens, etc.)

The polygamous house involves a somewhat different pattern. In the case of polygyny, for example, the husband often has a room for himself, where he entertains friends, calls meetings, and enjoys his privacy, while in various smaller adjacent rooms or buildings his wives and their children have their living space. If there is one principal wife, her quarters may be larger than those of the co-wives. This pattern of one large and several smaller living rooms is an architectural signature for polygamy in archaeological cultures; ethnographic and ethnohistoric cases provide substantiating evidence. (Fig. 7.2) For example, ethnohistory documents polygyny among the 16th-century Maya of northern Yucatán; perhaps the 9th-century Maya were polygynous as well. We could use the layout of houses to test this hypothesis.

Where polygamy is permitted, it is usually a prerogative of the wealthy and/or powerful, who can afford **bride-price** and the cost of maintaining a large household, including not only a large family but also retainers, servants, and slaves. Frequently the added work done by the co-wives contributes further to the family's level of affluence.

FUNCTIONS OF THE DWELLING

It is convenient for the archaeologist that the household is a cultural universal with a cross-culturally limited range of patterns, because the physical remains of household life, the house and its associated artifacts, are rich, ubiquitous sources of information about cultural practices and patterns of behavior (Oliver 1987).

Much of a house's space is multifunctional, but first the house must provide *protected shelter* for numerous activities. In many traditional soci-

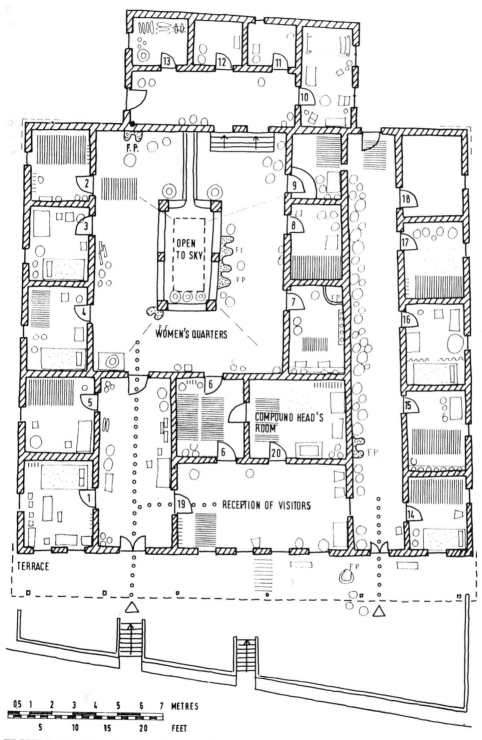

FIGURE 7.2 The plan of a polygynous house in Africa.

eties each nuclear family sleeps together in the same room, though in some societies young and adult men sleep in a separate dormitory of their own. In multifamily houses or compounds, component nuclear families have separate rooms. More affluent households in ranked and stratified societies may have retainers, servants, or slaves, the most valued sometimes even having their own living quarters, while the others bedded down in the kitchen, storeroom, or service yard.

Care of the sick can also take place in family quarters. Personal hygiene practices, which vary greatly, can take place outside the house, even outside the settlement, in settings lacking effective sanitation facilities. Sexual activity can also take place outside the house; in many societies couples seek privacy elsewhere because they share their sleeping quarters with other family members.

Child rearing requires an area where very young children can be easily watched while other tasks are being performed and where older children can play and begin to acquire adult skills. The family's sheltered space may suffice, or a common work or recreation area can be used for this purpose.

Food preparation and *craft activities* to produce items needed by the family (that possibly will be traded to others) require a lighted workspace with sufficient room for materials and the activity itself. In multifamily dwellings each nuclear family might have its own hearth for heating food, the area serving as a focus of food sharing and socializing.

Storage of prepared materials need not be immediately adjacent to the work area but must provide protection from weathering and destruction by vermin. Note that the range and complexity of these activities will vary, depending on the mode of sociocultural integration, and that a big difference between mobile societies (particularly those depending only on human muscles for transporting goods) and sedentary ones is that only in the latter can surpluses be stored in significant amounts. Storage permits the food supply to be extended past the harvest, permitting some individuals, through skill or luck, to store food or crafted items and build up surpluses that can advantage their families or that allow them to establish themselves as patrons to less-well-off kin or neighbors. Among mobile peoples, shelters also have storage areas, but since goods are limited to those that can be transported and food and water are brought in virtually every day, the material culture patterns of housework and storage are very simple.

Social interaction (including food sharing) may involve only the nuclear family, either in its separate dwelling or in its own quarters of the dwelling of a joint household, or the entire household, and even guests, thus requiring more space. If the house serves a "central place" function—that of a gathering place for members of other households, such as a village headman's house—then the reception area must be large enough for the biggest meeting.

There must be space in the dwelling for *ritual activities*: family or individual *rites of passage* (see Chapter 9) and caring for household shrines and deity effigies.

General *maintenance* of the house, including cleaning, gathering up trash and other wastes, rebuilding and adding on or abandoning rooms as needed, requires space for the materials used and for disposal of trash, generally at some distance from the house.

Activity Areas

Archaeologists look for evidence of the virtually universal activities described above when they investigate the remains of dwellings. Unfortunately the site formation process commonly includes an abandonment episode, in which the residents remove anything usable from the premises (Lange and Rydberg 1972; Longacre and Ayres 1968). Evidence for activities has to be sought at a more subtle level, such as close analysis of soil samples taken from room floors (Flannery 1976b; Kent 1984, 1987). But sometimes a wealth of activity area information is preserved when people and their houses abruptly become part of the archaeological record, as happened in Pompeii and other communities, which were buried suddenly by volcanic debris.

A Maya example of this kind of catastrophic site formation was unearthed recently at the site of Cerén (El Salvador), where a bulldozer cut revealed Classic period (ca. A.D. 600) houses and cornfields, all buried by volcanic debris up to 4 m deep (Sheets 1979, 1983a; Zier 1983). Figure 1.7 shows the volcanic overburden. Preservation of materials on the house floor evidenced such activities as food storage and preparation in Area 4 (Fig. 7.3), which seemed to be a pantry with storage jars, two of them containing beans. Other activity areas were for ceramic production, child's play, sleeping, textile manufacturing, obsidian tool use, and refuse dumping. Some of the materials in use by the Cerén Maya—obsidian, salt, painted ceramics—came from far away, so these people were linked through exchange networks to distant places, as well as to regional suppliers of minerals such as andesite, basalt, and hematite (Sheets 1983).

House Form

The people living in Cerén's Structure 1 used its rooms and surrounding platforms and surfaces for a range of activities. That so many of these took place outdoors is typical of Mesoamerica, where open patios and plazas were household work and leisure areas. In other climates and cultures, the arrangement of activities in the living space differs, but ethnographic cases show certain regularities.

The first regularity is the presence of enclosed or semienclosed *rooms,* which vary as to the privacy they provide. These include forms like the brush huts of the !Kung Bushmen (see Fig. 6.8), the section claimed by a Yanomamo family in their continuous circular house-village (Chagnon 1983), the family divisions of the Iroquois longhouse (Nabokov 1989), and enclosed rooms of a southwestern pueblo (Hill 1970). All give their

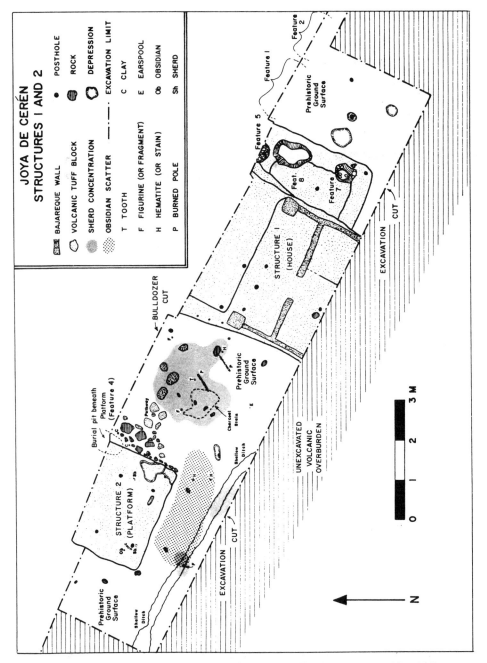

FIGURE 7.3 This house at Cerén was part of a larger area used by the household. Excavations uncovered a living surface extending well beyond Structure 1, and artifact distributions indicate that many activities took place outside the house.

component nuclear families shelter and privacy; they may also serve as loci of craft and other productive activity if there is sufficient space and light. Some rooms may also be used for communal activities, certain rituals, or storage. Large or complex houses may have special-purpose rooms, including those that serve as passageways from one wing of the house to another.

Second, where climate permits, many activities take place outdoors, typically in an open space near or within the house. This yard, or *courtyard*, which may be enclosed or semienclosed but not roofed over, is the locus of activities such as crafts and food preparation, food sharing and other social events, and certain rituals (Webster and Gonlin 1988).

The combination of these two types of living space, indoor and outdoor, forms the dwelling. House compounds for joint households involve more shared space within the dwelling, but these vary in size and density. Some consist of a set of contiguous enclosed rooms clustered around one or more open patios (see Fig. 7.2), while in others one-room houses may surround an open plaza (see Fig. 3.7) or share a bounded space (Fig. 7.4)

Finally, some household activities may take place in the area surrounding the house and yard. The space may be used for depositing trash, planting the house garden, tending to personal hygiene, performing sexual activities, and so forth.

House forms vary according to local building materials and conditions, climate, cultural norms of need and taste, and individual affluence and choice. "Vernacular architecture" is the name of the general topic of archi-

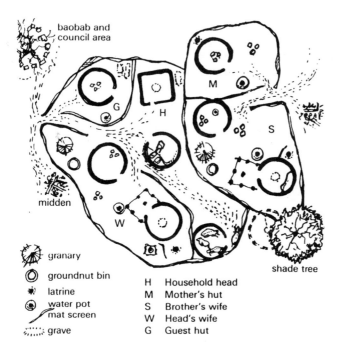

FIGURE 7.4 The plan shows the dwellings of a polygynous family of the Fulani (West Africa). Their dwellings are surrounded by fences of woven straw.

baobab and council area

M

G   H

S

midden

W

shade tree

granary
groundnut bin
latrine
water pot
mat screen
grave

H   Household head
M   Mother's hut
S   Brother's wife
W   Head's wife
G   Guest hut

tecture in traditional societies (Guidoni 1978; Oliver 1987; Rapoport 1969; Rudofsky 1977). The archaeologist should be aware of the building options available in an area, given a particular set of needs and level of technology.

Over the world, the most popular building materials are what is at hand that can be used to create a safe dwelling, from the huge grass houses of the Marsh Arabs (Fig. 7.5) to those made of wood, bark, animal bones and skins, earth, or stone (Table 7.1). Recalling the site formation process, we should note that preservability and visibility of these materials vary greatly, depending on local climate. There are many cases of dwelling designs evolving simultaneously. For example, the Spanish brought to the New World a courtyard-style dwelling plan that they had copied from the Moors who had lived for hundreds of years in the Iberian peninsula. They found that a similar courtyard house was the basic design in use in many parts of Mexico, for similar reasons: It was well adapted to the climate, provided privacy for the household, suited the household's social and work needs, and was made of local stone or adobe bricks, mud- or stucco-plastered to seal it against the weather (Margain 1971).

Structure 1 at Cerén revealed a great deal about house construction, in for example, the **in situ** evidence of the roof, which was built of perishable materials in much the same way that rural Maya today build thatched roofs. The walls, made of **wattle** and **daub,** and floor and platform areas divided up the space of the dwelling.

Estimating Household Size and Population Size

Population estimates of archaeological cultures are sometimes derived by multiplying the estimated number of persons per dwelling by the estimated number of dwellings per unit of area in a community by the combined area of known communities. Since the sample of actual dwellings excavated is tiny in proportion to the total that ever existed, archaeologists use standardized methods of extrapolation to derive population values. There are two basic methods of extrapolating population from dwelling size.

in situ   Latin for "in its original place." Refers to the location of archaeological finds that have been preserved in the same place in which they were originally used. Alternatively, something still in the position where it was originally found.

wattle   Framework of poles and other thin pieces of wood for the construction of a wall.

daub   Mud packed around the wattles, or framework, of a structure.

Table 7.1   Architectural Materials Characteristic of Certain Cultures

Building Material	Culture
Bone/antler	Eskimo (Siberian)
Grasses/vines/leaves	Yanomamo, Marsh Arabs
Framework of brush/skins	!Kung San
Wattle and daub	Maya, Southeast Asia
Wooden	Northern Europe, Mediterranean
Earthen/adobe	Aztec
Stone	Puebloans

(a)

FIGURE 7.5 Strong dwellings can be made from seemingly fragile materials. The houses of the Marsh Arabs of southern Mesopotamia are shown under construction (a) and in use (b). Dwellings like this are depicted in the art of ancient Mesopotamia, but it would be virtually impossible to perceive any archaeologial trace of these structures.

(b)

1. *Floor space method.* Based on a small sample of observations of ethnographically known dwellings, an estimate of 10 m² per person was derived (Naroll 1962), which has been widely applied as a rough conversion measure for estimating the number of residents who lived in a dwelling. Naroll's work was later criticized for insufficient consideration of cultural variability and for allowing too much area per person in small dwellings; nevertheless his ideas are often used.

2. *SRP Method*. The SRP (structure × rooms × persons) approach is a more sensitive method, since it uses the number of *habitation* rooms (not the total area of the structure) as a basis for determining household size. The number of habitation rooms in a structure is multiplied by the number of persons who share such rooms in ethnographically known societies that are appropriate analogues to the archaeological situation (Ammerman et al. 1976).

In either method of estimating household size, the characteristics of a small number of actual excavated dwellings are extrapolated to a whole community on the basis of the density of dwellings in a community, as identified in the archaeological survey. Sometimes there are no physical remains such as low mounds of earth that indicate ruined structures, so the size of the community is determined by the extent of artifact distribution, visible either on the surface or by subsurface testing.

The population of a region is then estimated by extrapolating from the number of communities and their estimated populations. Obviously, all along the estimation process there is considerable room for error: Are the known rooms/dwellings/communities fully contemporaneous? How much of the culture is represented by its archaeological record? How appropriate is the ethnographic model for household size? In spite of the problems associated with these estimates, it is critical to establish the general range of population size, consider changes over different periods, and study the relationship of population size to available resources.

Whether the floor area or the SRP method is used, the characteristics of a small number of actual excavated or mapped dwellings are extrapolated to a whole community or region. The reliability of such extrapolations obviously depends on the nature of the sample of household remains. At Cerén, preservation of individual houses is excellent, but they are so deeply buried that it would be practically impossible to recover information on a significant number of them. Extrapolation would be very difficult.

In many places, such as parts of eastern North America (see Box 7.1) very few traces of houses remain, but they are close to the surface. Farmers plow up artifacts which signal the presence of buried structures; subsequently shallow excavations can confirm their presence and reveal their forms. In the Copán region, even small, perishable buildings were built on stone and rubble platforms that survive indefinitely. Even very small, low platforms are visible on the surface, which can be reliably located and mapped during surface survey, providing a good basis for extrapolating population size. Our estimates of the Copán region population (Chapters 3 and 15) derive from surface survey, followed up by extensive test-pitting and large-scale excavation of some sites.

Where remains of whole communities are not only visible on the surface but are well preserved, such as some Puebloan sites of southwestern North America, extrapolation plays a less important role. Although one must still decide how many people lived in rooms or houses and determine the contemporaneity of occupation of rooms, dwellings, and communities, at

BOX 7.1

EXCAVATING HOUSES, RECONSTRUCTING HOUSEHOLDS

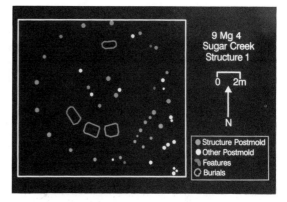

The photo and plan show a round house recently excavated in east central Georgia by James Hatch. In this temperate forest environment lived people of the Lamar culture, dating from the early 16th century A.D. Clusters of small houses similar to this one are scattered at invervals of several hundred meters over much of the region; most seem to have been occupied for only a generation or so. Each cluster represents a small farmstead. From European accounts made in the contact period we know that the residential pattern in this region included substantial round houses for winter use and summer houses that were rectangular and more lightly built.

The remains of all these houses lie close to the soil surface, and in this area, where modern farming takes place, they were within the "plowzone," the soil stratum disturbed by the action of plowing. Plowing destroys archaeological contexts and mixes materials; at this site it had obliterated the house living floor and its features. But plowing also brings artifacts to the surface, where they are visible indicators of the archaeological site. Surface collections here produced very abundant artifacts, particularly pottery, reflecting the habitation function of this site. On the basis of surface surveys, Hatch predicted the presence of buried residential structures, and initiated a large excavation.

Once the plow zone had been cleared away, the

house was visible. Its floor was gone, but its outline remained in the pattern of post holes made when the upright posts that formed the substantial walls rotted away, leaving regular conical areas of soil of different color. This particular house is about 10.5 m in diameter. Post-hole patterns nearby revealed a second round house, as well as at least four smaller, flimsier rectangular structures, presumably the summer houses.

Fourteen burials were recovered from within and around the structures. They included people of both sexes and a range of ages, children, and adults. Only one adult male was present; he and three other people were buried under the floor of the round house. Accompanying his burial was a faceted piece of galena (a mineral used for pigment) and a clay pipe in the shape of a stone axe. These items recall a centuries-old set of status symbols and ritual paraphernalia that has been found over much of southeastern North America (see Brose, Brown, and Penney 1985).

From the structures and burials it seems likely that this site represents an extended family residence, or possibly the residence of a polygynous family. Family organization, population density, political structure, and land use all can be reconstructed more fully from excavations like these. Current information indicates that thousands of dwellings like this one were probably integrated into a large regional chiefdom.

least the remains themselves are observable. Unfortunately for the archaeologist, this kind of situation is rare, and extrapolation is almost always necessary.

Nonresidential Architecture

So far, we have focused on dwellings, mentioning other architecture only in passing. This is because the house establishes the context of an overwhelming proportion of human social experience. Other kinds of structures serve to interpret other cultural patterns. The diversity of buildings within a community attests to the relative complexity of these.

In virtually all communities structures serve specialized purposes, such as ritual or storage. Sometimes these are part of dwellings, but in larger and more permanent communities they may be set apart. Temples and elaborate tombs are two cases in point. Looking back over the history of archaeology, we see that impressive specialized structures have attracted the lion's share of attention, at the expense of research in more modest but essential settings.

COMMUNITY CHARACTERISTICS

community A general term for different kinds of settlements, from clusters of a few households to huge urban aggregates.

We use the term **community** to cover a broad range of settlements, from clusters of a few households to huge urban aggregates (C. Smith 1976). Like families and households, communities are categorized according to their functions and form: whether habitation is year-round or temporary; the community size (area and population); spatial context (kind of terrain and its potential subsistence productivity); orientation; location relative to landscape features and resources; and spatial relation to other cultural features such as other communities. We also study how people in the community make a living, relate to each other in an organized fashion, and perceive the cosmos. Within any particular community, we study the range of variation in building types and sizes and their proximity to resources within and beyond the community as well as the degree of affluence displayed in different types of residence. We also look at functional complexity: What roles does the community play in the region, in terms of political administration, craft production, agriculture, and trade? Although each community would exemplify the ranges of variation in a different way, we would find a strong convergence of these toward a limited number of types.

Permanence

Most people today are more familiar with cities than they are with encampments, though throughout most of human history, people have lived in much smaller places than they do now. In the discussion of the Shoshone,

BOX 7.2

A PALEOLITHIC AGGREGATION SITE

The "Magdalenian" period, from about 17,000 years ago to about 10,000 years ago, was the last (most recent) subdivision of the European Paleolithic and is probably best known for the spectacular cave paintings that date from this time. Seen in terms of cultural processes, this is the European threshhold of the worldwide set of changes in subsistence practices, settlement patterns, and sociopolitical organization that would take place over the next 10,000 years, transforming human societies from the hunter-gatherer past of all our forebears to the industrialized present.

Although the best-known Magdalenian sites are caves with paintings, the "contexts of action" for this period — the places where the yearly round of social and subsistence activities took place — are less well known. Understanding these contexts has been the focus of work by Margaret Conkey (1980, 1991). The site of Cueto de la Mina (Spain) is a rockshelter and cave near the coast that may have served as an "aggregation" site, a place where the usually dispersed households of mobile hunter-gatherers came together at certain times during the year, in a group perhaps numbering 30–50 people. In reviewing some of the existing reconstructions of Paleolithic life, Conkey finds

them peopled by men: male hunters using the stone and bone implements that form most of our artifactual record for this era. Looking beyond the technologies for which we have existing evidence, Conkey notes that many other activities are implied by them. Harpoons, for example, are effective because they are attached to cords, permitting the hunters to haul in the catch. Cord and other fibers, being organic substances, would seldom be preserved in the archaeological record, thus rendering invisible the people who made them. From analogies with ethnographically known cultures, Conkey assumes that women were the fiber processers; they would have done most of the work in gathering materials, spinning them into thread and cord, making the spun fibers into woven and netted cloth, and probably making the assemblage of tools required to do these tasks. This perspective argues for cultural reconstructions that honor the balance of contributions by both men and women that characterize known societies. There are few real-life cases in which the sexual division of labor operates so severely that there is not considerable sharing of tasks; generally work parties, such as for butchering and processing a large animal, are made up of all able-bodied members of the group.

---

and the early people of the Tehuacán Valley, we saw examples of very *small temporary communities*. The houses might be like those shown in Figure 6.7: built for a week or a season, out of readily available materials, using simple, common tools. Some temporary communities are quite large, for example, annual gatherings (see Box 7.2), but the shifting pattern of seasonality of wild food resources limits community size.

A significant point on the continuum of permanence of residence is the *year-round community,* for which resources (food and water in particular) are sufficiently abundant to support a settlement throughout the year. Some groups shift their locations every several years. For example, people who practice shifting cultivation (swidden farming, or swiddening) may exhaust the fertility of local land in a few years and need to move their farm plots and village to a new location. Many settlements survive for generations, then are abandoned for any number of reasons, from plagues to politics. Some settlements have been in the same place for millennia: Damascus (Syria), often cited as the world's oldest continuously occupied city, was probably founded about 4,000 years ago.

Density

Density of habitation can be calculated for the community and for the region of the society as a whole by deriving the number of people per unit of area. This can be compared with the region's carrying capacity and thus provide a rough quantitative value for population pressure. This is often expressed as "persons per square mile" or "per square kilometer." But in some hunting-gathering societies, density is so low that it is expressed as "square kilometers (or miles) per person," because so much land is needed to support hunter-gatherers. Food-producing methods like farming and herding involve a marked increase in the productivity of the land and in predictability of the food supply.

Density of occupation within the community can vary in "nucleation." A continuum of intensity of land use runs from the heart of the city to wilderness. Areas that are densely settled are being intensively used.

Geographers have noted that the land nearest to settlements is generally the most intensively used, with use becoming more extensive as distance from the settlement increases. This "distance decay function" is familiar to us all, though in modern societies the ease of transporting even bulky foodstuffs great distances has reduced the need to use the land immediately around settlements for farms. However, the same principle is in operation: intensity of land use forms a bulls-eye pattern, with the densest population at the center of the settlement, then grades of less dense settlement (more extensive use of land, for example, in today's suburbs), and finally land which has not been "improved" (its value as a commodity has not been increased by its use or occupation). Such a pattern emerges from the combination of factors that draw people together in aggregates for economic, social, and political reasons and that keep them close to their place of work for economic and energetic reasons. The law of least effort states that, other things being equal, humans will try to minimize the effort involved in making a living, including minimizing the effort to get from home to work.

Farmers generally live near their fields, either in dispersed farmsteads surrounded by plantings or in settlements close to them. Particularly where farmers also produce crafts to trade, they and their families would live in settlements to maximize their closeness to supplies and to the consumers whose needs they meet.

Settlements with large populations are often more nucleated than smaller aggregates, since the higher value of land within communities encourages buildings that house many people. Some parts of modern Hong Kong, for example, have as many as 100,000 people per km².

Functional Diversity

The range of roles any community plays in the lives of its members depends on the overall mode of sociocultural integration and how it is locally expressed. In egalitarian societies, there are no political capitals, market towns, affluent neighborhoods, or temple complexes. In stratified societies, all these may exist, the functions expressed in various ways in communities of all sizes. Political functions of component communities in this kind of settlement system extend from small communities of tax- or tribute-paying farmers to the next largest town where these taxes are gathered (a **lower-order central place**) to the even larger towns (**higher-order central places**) overseeing several lower-order centers, up to the political and economic capital, the apex of the settlement hierarchy (Christaller 1966; Clarke 1977; Haggett 1966; Hodder and Orton 1976).

SETTLEMENT HIERARCHY AND THE MODE OF SOCIOCULTURAL INTEGRATION

"Settlement hierarchy" implies that there will be at least two different community types to rank and that one will somehow dominate the other. This differentiation of types is not always the case: Egalitarian societies show little variation among communities. These societies can have permanent, year-round settlements (as do the Yanomamo, for example) as well as patterns of temporary encampments (e.g., the Paiutes, or early inhabitants of the Tehuacán Valley), but in either case, there is only one level to the settlement hierarchy; no community in a region administers the others. A regional settlement survey of archaeological sites sharing egalitarian social organization would reveal communities of the same general size (relatively small) and complexity (relatively low). All communities would perform the same basic functions, and none would display central-place functions for the region. Social control would rest in the kin groups, with the village headman holding various leadership roles but wielding no real coercive power. In this mode of integration, the society as a whole (*society* defined as the largest politically autonomous unit) is coextensive with the community, since no higher authority is exercised over the region and its group of communities. Thus when tensions arise within a community, it may not be possible for kin-based mechanisms of social control to ease the situation. In spite of the headman's efforts to arbitrate disputes, the community may "fission," with some people going off to live in another established settlement or to form a new one (Chagnon 1983).

lower-order central place A small and functionally simple community in a regional hierarchy of communities differentiated by number, size, and function.

higher-order central place A large and functionally diverse community in a regional hierarchy of communities differentiated by number, size, and function.

Differentiation of Communities and Cultural Evolution

The situation just described illustrates an important principle of the cultural evolutionary process: The egalitarian mode can be maintained as long as each community replicates the others and as long as social control rests within the family or household. Where circumstances promote interdependence of communities, it may be because some have developed special features sought out by the others, perhaps specializing in the production of a local important resource like salt or stone for tools. Differentials of access to resources may emerge, as well as authority positions that administer social control beyond the family.

Another situation from which interdependence might emerge would involve resolving tensions arising within a village. We noted above that if land is available for dissidents to found a "daughter" community or relocate in an established one, then tension is relieved. But what if there is no place else to go? Then the village would either destroy itself through internal strife or reach social equilibrium as villagers accepted the authority of the headman. This would reduce the strength of family social control, for the village population would exceed the size that one family elder could advise and administer efficiently, and the new village headman would be less closely related to many residents than would be the headman of a smaller village.

With more complex forms of ranking, and with stratification, the settlement hierarchy assumes even greater complexity, reflected archaeologically in the emergence of new types of communities serving as central places. In the modern United States, the political central-place hierarchy encompasses our nation's capital, state capitals, and county seats. Our even more complex economic central-place hierarchy does not always correspond with the political hierarchy. Washington, D.C., is our political capital, but New York City is economically much more significant.

In traditional societies with complex ranking or simple stratification a simpler situation would prevail, with many functions of centrality overlapping in the same community. The capital of the political system would probably also be the central place of the highest order in other ways as well: the controlling center of the economy and usually the locus of cultural sophistication and spiritual authority. Second-order central places function as local centers of administration of various kinds, moving goods and services up from the lowest-order centers and providing goods and services to the population in the hinterlands. A complex settlement system is convincing evidence of cultural complexity in a region.

For traditional societies, the settlement system and its spatial layout are more important sources of information about resource exploitation, which is part of the infrastructure, and about disposition of surpluses, which is organized on the structural level. The range of community types, their sizes and number of examples of each, and their patterns of location, all will depend on the mode of sociocultural integration of the society.

FIGURE 7.6 Traditional Eskimo igloos are built of materials that are readily available, with tools possessed by all members of society.

Settlement systems reveal general social organization, which is further detailed by investigations into individual residences in various communities. Houses and households are the essential building blocks of society as a whole, and of cultural reconstruction of ancient societies. From house remains and associated artifacts we learn about household composition and size, social status and level of affluence, the productive work that the householders did, and even the spirits they worshipped.

HOUSE AND HOUSEHOLD IN EGALITARIAN SOCIETIES

Egalitarian societies are characterized by a lack of differential access to resources, reflected in a simple standard of living and limited material culture repertoire. There are no egalitarian societies today that are not affected by the industrial economy, but we know enough from ethnographies and ethnohistories to understand major aspects of lifeways. Figure 7.6 shows one of the best-known 20th-century examples of egalitarian societies with subsistence based on hunting and gathering, the Eskimo, illustrating the traditional dwellings. The Eskimo today have adopted customs and materials from modern industrial societies, but they reveal important clues to life in archaeologically known egalitarian societies.

Egalitarian Mobile Hunter-Gatherers: The !Kung of Southern Africa

The !Kung are changing their lifeways as pressure on the land of South Africa—from warfare as well as intensification—restricts their traditional foraging activities and pursuit of game animals; ethnographic accounts of their traditional patterns are the basis of the following discussion. Some ethnoarchaeological studies have also been made (Lee 1979; Yellen 1976).

Settlement System   The !Kung live in one of the world's harshest environments, the Kalahari (KAHlahHAHree) Desert, where the water supply is even more limited than the food supply. Camping groups, which number about 35–55 people, change their campsites frequently during the year— every 3–4 days in the rainy season (returning repeatedly to some sites) but during the dry season for as long as six months. The territory encompassed by a group's yearly migration measured about 320 km² and focused on a waterhole and its surrounding land. Important resources included groves of nut trees. The camping group included members of two to four extended families. The group's composition was flexible, with the nuclear family as the basic unit of inclusion.

Settlement and Dwellings   Figure 7.7 shows a dry season camp, with huts arranged in a rough circle facing inward. Wet season camps were smaller, presenting a more irregular pattern of huts. The short time of occupation precluded extensive clearing, each hut being located wherever there was already sufficient open space. The central open space of the dry season camps was the locus of social activities involving the whole group, such as sharing meat from the hunt or dancing and story telling.

Dwellings are huts up to 2 m across, built quickly (in an hour) of branches, grasses, and animal hides, with stones to secure the perimeter of the structure. Huts vary in size and sturdiness, depending on the weather and the number of people sheltered. (Each !Kung hut in Fig. 7.7 housed between one and five people; a few individuals lived alone, the others with their nuclear families.) Each nuclear family has its own hut, and huts are grouped according to extended family ties of the various nuclear families. In front of each hut is a hearth for cooking and warmth, and this is also a focus of social activity. It is also where trash (mostly vegetable and animal remains) is thrown. The trash would build up significantly during the dry season; occasionally it and ash from the hearths would be moved and dumped behind the huts (Yellen 1976).

Household Functions and Division of Labor   !Kung men and women hunt game, gather vegetable foods, and fetch water. To some extent there is a sexual division of labor, with men hunting and foraging for small game while women gather plant resources. Studies of !Kung food-getting patterns have proved that hunting-gathering populations could enjoy a rela-

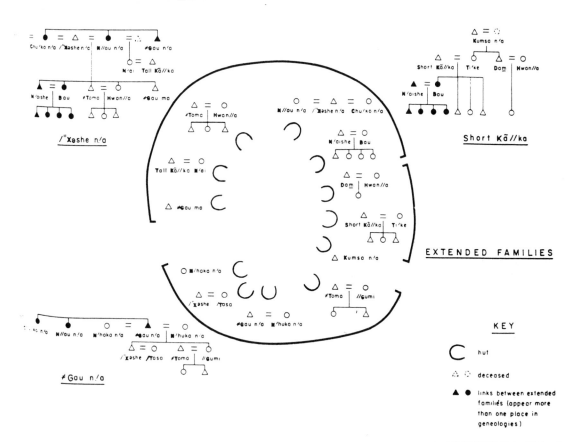

FIGURE 7.7 This plan of a !Kung encampment features circular arrangements of dwellings.

tively secure steady diet without working more than part time by modern standards. Despite the harshness of the environment and the lack of long-term food surpluses, food-getting activities take the women about 15 hours a week, the men about 20. For several hours a day, women cook and prepare food, tend children, collect firewood, do other jobs, then spend the rest of their time doing needlework, visiting friends, and entertaining. Similarly, when men are home from the hunt they make and repair tools, visit, entertain, and dance.

Ethnographers have noted that the !Kung, like other highly mobile peoples who lack beasts of burden, are limited in their personal possessions. They tend to keep and carry with them only those items that are particularly valuable, such as hunting and gathering tools. Since they retrace their steps through the same territory, they may leave behind heavy implements such as stones used for grinding food. This basic fact of foraging existence marked the lives of all our ancestors up to the last 10–12,000 years, when permanent communities began to be established and goods and food could be accumulated and stored. When no surpluses can be stockpiled, no one can control them and use them to control other people.

Ethnographic studies of groups like the !Kung illuminate the archaeological record of countless migratory foraging cultures, sensitizing us to the kinds of remains common to such situations: dwellings that are easily made and quick to decompose; traces of food remains and artifact debris around the huts; possibly a communal space among the huts for group activities. Archaeological remains of such cultures exist throughout the world but are sometimes extremely difficult to detect, since they may lack substantial features such as permanent structures and an artifact repertoire with lots of durable goods (such as ceramics that break into virtually indestructible potsherds). If the remains of foraging communities are deeply buried under layers of soil, it may be virtually impossible to detect them.

Egalitarian Sedentary Peoples: The Yanomamo of Brazil and Venezuela

In general, sedentary peoples leave a more visible mark on the landscape than nomads. The Yanomamo are among the egalitarian groups of the Amazon and adjacent rivers of South America, and, like the !Kung, their traditional homeland is being encroached upon by the modern world (Chagnon 1983; Oliver 1987).

The Yanomamo live in a tropical forest habitat, occupying their villages all year, and practice slash-and-burn agriculture as well as hunting and gathering. Their technology is based on simple tools made from local materials, so no village specializes in production of a particular good. As among the !Kung and other egalitarian peoples, the community is the highest autonomous political group; no village dominates over the others. The villages interact through marriage alliances, trading partnerships, and through demonstrations of hostility, mounting frequent raids to kidnap each other's women.

Usually no larger than several hundred people, villages are frequently much smaller. There is no authority beyond that of family elders to settle quarrels within and between villages, so villages tend to fission when kin ties can no longer maintain order, with one faction moving off to join another village or to form a new one elsewhere. The village will relocate entirely if relations with neighboring villages become hostile. Thus, though villages are permanent in the sense that they are occupied throughout the year, a site may become too dangerous; the villagers may be compelled to abandon it and build at another location after only a few years. These limits on village size result in a settlement pattern of only one type, with the villages spaced so as to maximize access to land for gardens and foraging and to avoid conflict.

The characteristic Yanomamo village is a roughly circular structure of poles, leaves, and vines that is built by the villagers, each nuclear family

FIGURE 7.8   The Yano-mamo community was one large "shabono" with each family's quarters forming a segment of the circle.

working on the section that will be its dwelling (Fig. 7.8). All share the central plaza for group activities. Ringing the village is a defensive palisade of logs about 3 m high. The palisade is well maintained when hostilities flare up, otherwise it is used as a handy source of firewood. The village must be replaced every several years because of infestations of vermin. The roof becomes home to countless spiders, scorpions, and cockroaches, which can only be discouraged by burning the village to the ground and rebuilding.

Division of Labor and Subsistence Sex and age are the determinants of the individual's work life. Men and women work together on family garden plots; men clear the forest for gardens, and women do most of the planting, cultivation, and harvesting. While no village produces special goods for trade, sometimes friendly relations will be established between two villages on the pretext that one cannot supply its own needs with regard to a common material good. Occupational specialization among Yanomamo is limited to the situational leadership role of the village headman, who is usually the senior male of one of the village families, and to individuals functioning as shamans and curers.

Yanomamo material culture and customs are typical of many agriculturalists in tropical forest areas, with low overall population densities that militate against the development of integrated political systems joining groups of villages together. Villages fission when social tensions rise; thus the trademark egalitarian pattern of homogeneity of settlement types is preserved.

SETTLEMENT PATTERNS IN NONEGALITARIAN SOCIETIES

In egalitarian societies there are built-in constraints to the development of centralized authority, such as the tendency to fission rather than grow more organizationally complex. This means that each community has a built-in size limit as well, preventing it from growing to a significantly larger size than the others. The settlement pattern in egalitarian societies consists of communities that are roughly the same size as each other. Thus the settlement pattern itself provides important general information about a culture's organizational complexity, in terms of site size and distribution over the landscape and the number of different **site types**. Small villages clustered around a larger "central place" community might indicate a situation of political dependency in which villages no longer held their own political autonomy but had moved away from the egalitarian mode of life toward ranking. Archaeologists identify greater cultural complexity in settlement patterns from the presence of a two-part settlement hierarchy, with one community assuming the role of central place for a particular region.

site types Kinds of sites, as distinguished by size and function. Examples would include habitation sites, quarrying sites, burial sites, and so forth.

Central Places and Settlement Systems

Archaeologists have adapted models used by cultural geographers to analyze the distribution of central places and the conditions and locations of their emergence. Cultural geographers posit three main functions of communities that serve as central places: administration, marketplace trade (so that marketplaces are available to as many consumers as possible, while limiting transport costs for the producers), and long-distance trade and transportation (secondary settlements develop at convenient stopping places between "higher order" central places (Fig. 4.17). Since the last two conditions seem to prevail where a relatively complex settlement system already exists, the first function, administration, provides the most useful guide to an archaeological settlement system characteristic of the development of ranked social organization. Under this administrative central-place pattern, we would expect at least two levels to the hierarchy, with lower-order centers grouped around the higher-order center to which they owe political allegiance. The two-level settlement hierarchy characterizes the Puebloan archaeological cultures of the U.S. Southwest.

Puebloan Indians

Communities and Settlement System Puebloan Indians are among the most distinctive ethnic groups in the United States today. Their traditional dwellings are multistoried stone or **adobe** pueblos, aggregates of rooms that can comprise the whole settlement. This pattern of community organization is very old, extending back at least 1,000 years. Prior to the development of the pueblo "apartment houses," typical dwellings consisted of a single round room, partially subsurface. As storage of corn over the winter became an important feature of the subsistence pattern, these semi-subterranean houses were less well suited to this purpose, and groups of rectangular rooms were built adjacent to the pithouses. As this architectural form matured, the round pithouses were retained in the community plan, serving as ritual rooms called **kivas** (KEEvahs), while the rectangular-room blocks were for habitation and storage; rooftops and plazas served as work and social areas.

By about A.D. 1000 the rectangular-room block form of the pueblo was widespread. Between A.D. 900 and 1150 there developed a two-tiered settlement system in the Chaco Canyon area of New Mexico (Cordell 1984; Lekson 1987). The two settlement types were as follows:

1. *Small pueblos,* which had a single story, to which rooms were added over time, averaged 16 rooms and several kivas each. There are between 200 and 400 of these, outnumbering the large pueblos by about 25:1.

2. *Large pueblos,* which seem to have been built as single units up to four stories high averaged over 200 rooms. There are 13 large pueblos. Each had several styles of kiva: small ones (one for each several dozen rooms), tower kivas, and "great kivas" (at least one for each large pueblo, semi-subterranean and measuring up to 20 m in diameter) (Fig. 7.9).

Other features of the Chacoan landscape were signal towers, water-control systems, and roads. The latter run in straight lines through and away from Chaco Canyon, linking the large pueblos with each other, with

adobe Building material comprised of earth and other materials such as straw or gravel to enhance structural solidity; commonly in the form of sun-dried bricks.

kiva Underground room in a pueblo, used for ceremonial purposes.

FIGURE 7.9 The Chaco Canyon (New Mexico) settlement system included small pueblos and much larger towns like Pueblo Bonito, which housed hundreds of families in the rectangular rooms lining its curving outer wall, facing in on a plaza inside this semicircle of habitation and storage rooms. Both settlement types have kivas: circular, partially subterranean ritual rooms.

descent reckoning The rules by which people in a particular culture determine membership in defined kin groups.

matrilocal postmarital residence Residential situation in which a newly married couple lives with or near the bride's mother's family.

distant pueblos, and with resource areas. Over 400 km of roads have been identified, one of them nearly 100 km long. The roads, irrigation systems, the pueblos themselves, and their great kivas were all massive projects requiring considerable planning and a large, well-administered labor pool—indications of sociopolitical ranking.

Social Structure The historical continuity of Puebloan culture has provided archaeologists with the opportunity to apply the direct historical approach, and use present-day Puebloan social structure as a model for that of their ancestors. **Descent reckoning** is matrilineal (traced through one's mother and her family), with **matrilocal postmarital residence** (a newly married couple lives with or near her mother's family). An extended family would consist of a married couple, their married daughters and sons-in-law, and offspring. Could we detect these patterns if they existed in the Puebloan archaeological culture (Hill 1968, 1970)?

To address this issue, archaeologists needed to find some pattern in the material culture record that would reflect the structural rules of kin reckoning and residence pattern. One innovative effort began with the assumption that stylistic similarities in artifacts reflect a high degree of social interaction, and chose ceramic styles to study this. Puebloan ceramics (Fig. 7.10) are famous for their quality of craftsmanship and distinctive design motifs, traditions that go back centuries.

Among present-day Puebloans, women make pottery and teach pottery making to their daughters and nieces in the context of the household.

Ceramic design elements are part of the repertoire of skills. Thus, specific design motifs should be found in highly localized areas, because the women who make the pottery live out their lives in the place they were born. If archaeological Puebloan populations were matrilineal and practiced matrilocality, design motif distribution would reflect this.

Recalling that seriation of pottery has been an important method for establishing chronology in the Southwest since long before the advent of absolute dating methods, this new application of stylistics, to reconstruct family and marriage patterns, would reveal social relations in even greater detail. In fact, analysis of design element distribution at Carter Ranch Pueblo in Arizona (ca. A.D. 1050–1200) shows clustering into two areas, suggesting that each represents a group much larger than any nuclear family. This pattern is consistent with matrilineal-matrilocal rules of social structure (Longacre (1964).

This approach, which has been used in a number of studies (cf. Deetz 1968), has been critiqued for the assumption that similar design elements reflect social relations and that the degree of similarity is positively correlated with the closeness of the social bond (see discussion of "interaction analysis" in Rice 1987). In fact, the ethnographic record shows that stylistic isolation can occur in situations of considerable social interaction and that, conversely, stylistic similarity can characterize separate groups. Furthermore, site formation processes are sufficiently unpredictable that the spatial patterning of potsherds may not reflect the patterns of behavior ascribed to them. Regardless of these problems, the development of testable models like these "interaction" models has been an important step in research.

Incipient Stratification: The Yoruba of West Africa

Let us turn now to an ethnographically known society, with more complex sociopolitical organization. The agrarian Yoruba of West Africa have state-level political organization with incipient stratification (Bascom 1955; Schwerdtfeger 1982). Yoruba social structure and household composition represent what were probably among the most common forms of social aggregate in agrarian situations, with **patrilocal** residence patterns and joint-family extended households. Yoruba dwellings and households reflect the combined features of balance in the sexual division of labor and land holding in the male line.

The Yoruba have long had a multilevel settlement system, focused on higher-order central places, cities such as Lagos (Nigeria), and lower-order central places, the less urbanized towns. Cities are large and densely settled (Lagos in 1900 had 10,000 people per km², a population density comparable to that of New York City in 1960). Older cities and towns are surrounded by areas of farmland and have resident populations of farming families. Some farmers live in field huts in the seasons when work requires it. Men are usually the farmers, though many women farm and keep livestock as well. Both sexes keep house and engage in craft activities.

FIGURE 7.10 The Puebloan ceramic tradition goes back hundreds of years. The distinctive styles permit archaeologists to trace cultural interactions.

patrilocal Residential situation in which a newly married couple lives with or near the groom's father's family.

The most common traditional household is a joint extended and poly-gynous family sharing a house compound that is a contiguous aggregate of rooms and courtyards, built on a rectangular or square plan, and added onto as was necessary and external space permitted. The courtyards served as work places and the surrounding rooms were private quarters for each nuclear family (see Fig. 7.2).

These nuclear families are usually related through the male line, and newly married couples move into quarters in the husband's father's com-pound. The joint household sharing a compound includes men and their wives (including co-wives, if the option for polygyny is exercised) and children, and married sons and their families. Household size may be as large as several hundred.

The Yoruba provide a good model for what may have been a fairly common house and household pattern in nonindustrial state-level societies. As we have indicated elsewhere in this book, archaeology of the house and household of commoners is a fairly recent area of interest in archaeology; our reconstructions of the social and economic relations among household-ers are enhanced by studying groups such as the Yoruba.

Stratified Societies: The Aztecs of Central Mexico

The Aztecs of Mexico had a state-level, stratified society, and we know from ethnohistoric sources that, like the Yoruba, Aztec city dwellers often lived in extended-family, joint households and that some Aztec men were polygynous. Figure 7.1 shows the settlement pattern of the Basin of Mex-ico; note that this immense region was thickly settled and had many types of communities, from single-family rural farms, to farming villages, small towns, and regional capitals, to the great city of Tenochtitlan, capital of the Mexica (maySHEEKah) Aztecs, rebuilt after the Spanish conquest as Mexico City.

The Mexica Aztecs ruled Mexico 500 years ago. We know about Aztec culture from archaeology and from ethnohistory, particularly the memoirs and reports of the conquistadores and colonizers (Berdan 1982; Sahagun 1950–1963). Aztec society was clearly stratified into noble, commoner, and slave classes, with considerable variation in status within each, and there were marked differences, by class, as to who had access to key resources such as land. A number of levels in the hierarchy drew surpluses from an agrarian peasantry of farmer artisans. No matter how elaborate the tribu-tary hierarchy became, its basic producers were still the households of the peasants, organized into territory-holding groups called **calpullis** (cal-POOLees) (Carrasco 1971b). Fulfilling social, political, and economic functions, calpullis occupied whole villages or neighborhoods of towns and cities. The village shown in Figure 7.1b was probably a calpulli. Cal-pulli members corporately held rights to farm plots as long as they contin-ued to use them, and these rights could be inherited on approval by the calpulli headman.

calpulli Corporate group in Aztec society which functioned above the level of the household. Calpullis had social, politi-cal, and economic func-tions. They occupied whole villages or neigh-borhoods of towns and cities; members corpo-rately held rights to farm plots as long as they con-tinued to use them.

Household and Calpulli In a layered hierarchy of relations, the household formed part of the calpulli, which in turn was a unit of the local city-state. Tribute came from households; individuals served in work and war parties, but all were organized by the calpulli. The calpulli headman, who was in charge of seeing that these tributes were duly presented to the local and regional capitals, also served as a magistrate for his people, arbitrating quarrels, performing marriages and marriage counseling (the calpulli was generally **endogamous;** that is, people sought marriage partners within their own calpulli), serving as a repository of wills and titles, leading important group rituals, and so forth.

endogamy Choosing a marriage partner from within one's own group.

The calpulli functioned as a lower-order administrative central place, whose administrative functions are archaeologically discernible in special-purpose buildings different from the houses of the commoners. In addition to the headman's house, there might also be a pyramid and temple (though these have often been found adjacent to and shared by several villages) and a young men's house forming a special, pan-calpulli household for teenage boys where they would learn basic military skills and work on village projects, such as tending the farm plots held in common for supporting the elite or the temple.

Residence Rule and Household Composition The traditional calpulli encompassed a certain amount of variation in social class, since it included a noble headman as well as peasant farmers (Carrasco 1971b). This diversity of households is revealed in the house sizes in Aztec communities, from small structures with 2 or 3 rooms to those with over 20 rooms (Evans 1989a, 1989b). Not all rooms were residential quarters — even small houses might have a storage room or kitchen — but large houses exhibit a greater diversity of types of rooms as well as more of them. Large houses were obviously for joint households, either the male-oriented extended family, or, far less commonly, the polygynous family and its retainers. Among Aztec commoners, a newly married couple typically moved in with relatives on either side in an extended-family household, most often with the husband's parents or brother(s) (Harvey 1985). A couple might establish a new home for themselves when their first child was born.

Since polygyny was a perquisite of the affluent, we would expect it to be uncommon among rural farmers. But each calpulli village may have had one or more polygynous households, such as that of the village headman (Evans 1991). In the larger towns and cities, there would have been numerous polygynous households as well as the other variants. More affluent households would have had servants, possibly even slaves. The palaces of Aztec rulers had rooms for a thousand or more people.

The archaeological evidence for these great noble houses is now buried beneath the modern cities of the Basin of Mexico, most of which were continuously occupied from long before the conquest and into the present (Calnek 1976). Motecuhzoma's palace, for example, is under the present National Palace of the Republic of Mexico, on the main square in Mexico

FIGURE 7.11 This royal palace in Texcoco (Basin of Mexico), dating from the 15th century, shows the king of Texcoco and his son and heir in the upper center room. Their noble vassals are in the courtyard. Around the courtyard are judicial chambers, an armory, hall of science, music room, guest quarters and storage rooms, and council chambers for financial and defense administration.

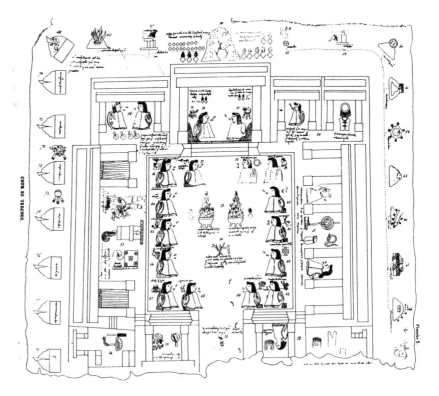

City (which was also the central plaza of Aztec Tenochtitlan). While it is possible that such royal residences may at some point be unearthed (as was the Templo Mayor, also in the main square area), our best evidence comes from the descriptions of the conquistadores and native chroniclers, and from a few floor plans of palaces (Fig. 7.11). The Mapa Quinatzin, dating from the 1540s, shows the royal palace at Texcoco in a plan view. Archaeological evidence of elite residences is limited to a palace excavated at a regional capital (Vaillant 1966) and a smaller, more countrified example (Fig. 7.12) excavated at a rural village (Evans 1989a, 1989b, 1991). Like the Mapa Quinatzin palace, the village example shows suites of rooms grouped around an open plaza or patio appropriate for councils and other gatherings. The village palace layout of suites of habitation rooms with one larger, more finely finished habitation room suggests a polygynous joint family household.

Household Functions Most Aztec householders were part-time farmers and craft workers, not unlike Yoruba householders. Men and women shared farm duties on their small plots, with men also performing extractive activities like mining and lumbering, and also doing as much hunting and fishing as opportunity allowed in this densely settled area. Women ground

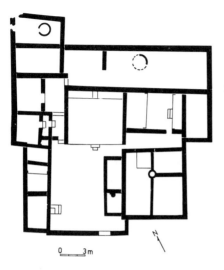

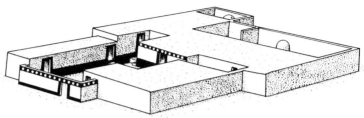

FIGURE 7.12 This building was excavated at Cihuatecpan, an Aztec village in the Basin of Mexico (see Figure 7.1). Consisting of suites of rooms grouped around a courtyard, it may have been the village headman's house. The central room might have served as a deliberation room, while the suites of rooms around the courtyard served habitation functions such as sleeping, cooking, and storage.

grain (generally corn) into flour for tortillas, cooked, spun thread out of cotton and other fibers, and wove cloth. These activities were performed in each household; in addition, many households specialized in the production of a particular item (e.g., pottery or obsidian blades) for marketplace trade.

Archaeological remains at commoner houses include a full range of artifacts—utility and decorated ceramics of all kinds for food preparation and storage, obsidian and other stone tools for processing raw materials into other tools or finished goods for local use or trade, ceramic **spindle whorls** (weights for the sticks onto which newly spun thread was wound), and ceramic figurines used in household rituals. The houses also have activity areas: hearths with concentrations of ash, low adobe brick platforms for sleeping and working, and trash middens.

spindle whorls Weights for the staffs used to spin yarn or other fibers.

The tributes that found their way to Tenochtitlan began as household contributions. The head of the household was responsible for seeing that its share of community and polity obligations of goods, labor on work parties, and military service was fulfilled. Men or women could be household heads and holders of rights to property, but typically the head was the eldest male, who also held the property rights.

At the highest elite level, the palaces served as government buildings. Looking at the Mapa Quinatzin plan of the royal palace at Texcoco (and the accompanying commentary in a native history written around 1600), we see that the functions of the various rooms—visitor's suites, deliberation rooms, music halls, and armories—encompass a variety comparable to that of palaces in many other stratified cultures. Abstract and schematic, this plan tells us little about the size of the palace.

In the regional capitals there were special schools for boys and a number of girls from elite families, where they would learn religious, literary, and historical traditions of the culture, and boys could receive military officer training. The capitals also had administrative offices forming part of the palace complex, as in the case of Texcoco—numerous temples, residences for priests of both sexes, and a marketplace and attached structures for its administration and storage of goods. There would also be distinct neighborhoods of the urban calpullis, where the household work revolved around craft production more heavily than agriculture, but even in the largest Aztec cities many people were part-time farmers.

Whereas the individual calpulli, rural or urban, largely represented one social level (commoners, ruled by a member of a noble lineage), more urbanized communities tended to have greater social complexity, with noble lineages, wealthy merchants and their families, other commoners ranging from affluent to destitute, and slaves. More urbanized communities also offered greater opportunity for women to achieve positions of power, very occasionally even rulership, and responsibilities beyond the household, such as administering the marketplace, but in this society success in war was the primary path to advancement, and women were excluded from this critical opportunity for political advancement.

The most urbanized Aztec community was Tenochtitlan, a diverse city with over 100,000 inhabitants, resplendent royal court, complex government bureaucracy, and busy craft workshops. Attended by thousands each day, its market sold an extensive range of goods. This indicates to us that numerous craft specialists supplied the market with these items and that urbanites pursued a wide variety of trades. The division of labor within the city was extremely complex, but still, the household comprised a basic economic unit.

Ethnohistoric sources on Aztec lifeways provide us with what could be called a "paleo-ethnography," since so many aspects of social organization and social structure have been documented. If the Aztecs were a completely archaeological culture, we would have to infer these relationships from material cultural information such as artifacts, architecture, and settlement patterns. Archaeologists reconstructing Aztec culture can draw on archaeological remains as well as descriptive documents—a particularly good research opportunity for the conjunctive approach.

PERCEIVING CULTURAL ORGANIZATION

Aztecs, Yoruba, Puebloans, Yanomamo, !Kung: All use space in patterns distinctive of their overall mode of sociocultural integration and of their rules of social structure. The mix of archaeological, ethnohistoric, and ethnographic documentation of these patterns shows the strengths of various approaches and the necessity of drawing on living cultures to interpret the remains of those of the past. The daily lives of people interacting in social groups form the foundation of any ongoing society. Fortunately for us, the archaeological record is rich in the remains of places where families lived and where people worshiped, socialized, and carried out countless other ordinary activities. These may not be the most exciting, glamorous, or obvious places to excavate, but they are among the most important.

POINTS TO REMEMBER

- As basic institutions in all societies, the family and household form the building blocks of larger communities.

- The archaeological record is made up largely of remains of household activities.

- Recovery and analysis of household remains can tell archaeologists what people did in everyday life and enable them to reconstruct population size.

- Distributions and densities of household remains provide clues about how people adapted to particular landscapes.

- The hierarchical structure and nature of settlements provide clues to social and political organization.

FOR FURTHER READING*

Nabokov's *Native American Architecture* and Oliver's *Dwellings: The House Across the World* give a sense of the range of dwellings and settlements. Netting, Wilk, and Arnould's *Households;* Wilk and Rathje's *Archaeology of the Household;* and MacEachern, Archer, and Garvin's *Households and Communities* include general summaries and in-depth studies. Flannery's *The Early Mesoamerican Village,* an important introduction to village archaeology in general, provides a reconstruction of life in a particular setting. Sheets's *Archaeology and Volcanism in Central America* offers studies of Cerén and its surroundings.

*Full citations appear in the bibliography.

CHAPTER EIGHT

ARTISANS AND TRADERS

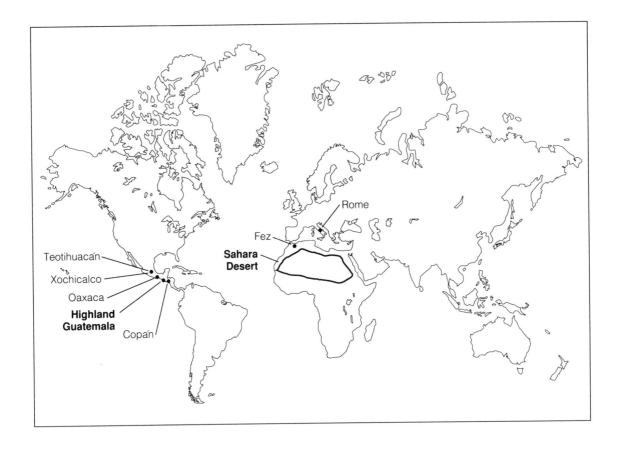

Economic systems form the principal link between human cultures and their natural environments. Economic behavior is our means of producing, distributing, and consuming things that are culturally and biologically useful or necessary. In Chapter 6 we discussed food procurement and subsistence. The principal subject of this chapter is another kind of economic behavior called **economic specialization,** whereby economic tasks become increasingly differentiated and the members of a society, as a consequence, increasingly interdependent. We will also examine the closely related topic of **distribution,** the transferal of goods, focusing in particular on exchange and trade.

ARCHAEOLOGICAL APPROACHES TO SPECIALIZATION AND DISTRIBUTION

Cultural evolution is marked by a general trend or process toward increased economic specialization and interdependence and toward less self-sufficiency (Heilbroner 1985; Sahlins 1972). In trying to detect various forms of specialization and exchange in specific evolutionary sequences and to evaluate their functions in ancient sociocultural settings, archaeologists still have not resolved the most important issue: *why* people have developed specialization so strongly in the last few thousand years, particularly in hierarchical, nonindustrial societies, after living in cultures with little specialization for hundreds of thousands of years.

Archaeologists trace and explain the origins of specialization and trade for their own sake. But studying economic patterns is also important because increased complexity in these behaviors and institutions is a good barometer for more general patterns of cultural evolution and because remains of economic activity are abundant in the archaeological record. Development of specialization is systemically linked to other changes toward greater societal size or complexity, such as population growth, competition, urbanization, stratification, and the emergence of the state (Plattner 1989).

Our own industrial economy exhibits highly developed specialization. The products we use or consume each day, including our food, are virtually all produced and distributed to us by economic specialists. The very names of our jobs or professions—taxi driver, college professor, lawyer, manager—indicate our diverse economic roles as well as the essential interdependence of our economic specialties and of the complex systems of distribution that interlock these specialties. Specialized products and services are produced and exchanged in complex ways. A little reflection reveals how impossible our lifeways—perhaps our survival—would be if this interdependence broke down. We take for granted this extremely specialized division-of-labor and exchange system, but it is a comparatively recent development in the evolution of human cultures.

Archaeologists face several thorny problems concerning specialization

economic specialization Situation in which necessary or useful economic tasks are not equally shared by all members of society, making individuals or groups economically interdependent.

distribution The means by which things are transferred from producers to consumers.

and distribution. First, are they present in a prehistoric culture? If so, on what scale? How were they organized? Finally, how did they function in their larger cultural contexts and contribute to evolutionary processes? Even the first and most basic of these questions may be hard to answer.

Inferences from Objects

Archaeologists have frequently tried to make inferences about specialization based on objects themselves. In some cases this works reasonably well. An elaborate bronze sword from a 3,000-year-old archaeological context in Greece reveals several things about the economy. Copper and tin are necessary to make the bronze; probably neither was locally available, so some kind of trade or exchange is indicated. Casting metal into an elaborate shape is a time-consuming task requiring considerable skill as well as special tools and facilities, so the artisan was almost certainly a full-time or part-time specialist. Because swords were costly, elite items, it is very likely that a client-patron relationship existed between the swordmaker and the elite warrior. Although all of these inferences might be wrong, they are at least highly probable, and all could be checked using additional archaeological evidence.

Ethnographic cases, which could also serve to substantiate the inferences, might even prove more useful in this respect. For example, archaeologists sometimes make assumptions about the existence of prehistoric specialization on the basis of workmanship. If an item is of very high technical and aesthetic quality, it is tempting to jump to the conclusion that it must have been made by a specialist. Unfortunately, we know from the ethnographic record that objects of superb quality are often created in societies that have no institutionalized specialization, such as the wood carvings of the Maori of New Zealand and pottery in the Pueblo societies of the American Southwest. In fact, sometimes the evolution of specialization has produced inferior quality in mass-produced goods. The lesson is that the ethnographic record (and evidence from ethnoarchaeology and experimental archaeology) can correct much archaeological wishful thinking.

It is somewhat easier to infer exchange and trade patterns from the archaeological record, since this involves information about distributions of things, not subjective judgments about quality. If abundant, widely used stone tools are found in a region, and the only source of stone is very distant, the existence of some sort of exchange or trade is almost certain, unless the tool users traveled to the source themselves. Archaeologists call such materials derived from distant sources "exotics." Imported objects are often highly conspicuous in archaeological contexts, providing some of the most direct evidence for economic relationships beyond the local household or community. Yet sometimes sweeping and erroneous conclusions are drawn on the basis of a few exotic artifacts, and even if some form of exchange or trade can be assumed, we still must be able to recover adequate samples of exotic artifacts to understand the scale and organization of exchange. Otherwise we know nothing beyond the fact that things traveled from one place to another.

Contextual Research

Contextual research involves the systemic relationships of specialization, exchange, and trade with other aspects of culture. Data on economic behavior may emerge out of general research designs or from research specifically aimed at economic issues, as we shall see later. Material by-products of economic specialization usually wind up where they were produced or where they were consumed. For example, the extraction and processing of obsidian leaves behind unmistakable debris at quarry sites and production sites, and when obsidian has been used up in a household at the other end of the system, it often winds up in the garbage middens. Residual or discarded obsidian can be analyzed to determine its source. Although we can learn a great deal from production and consumption sites, the question remains of *how* things were distributed — a much more difficult problem to resolve.

ECONOMIC SPECIALIZATION
AND DISTRIBUTION

As noted earlier, economic specialization means that necessary or useful economic tasks are not equally shared by all members of society and that individuals or groups thus are economically interdependent, not self-sufficient. According to this very broad definition, economic specialization is a feature of all societies, because all societies have **division of labor by age and sex** (Durkheim 1933). Adult men and women have different tasks, as do children of various ages and sexes. In hunting and gathering societies such as the !Kung, men commonly do most of the hunting and women most of the gathering. In many Middle Eastern pastoral societies young boys are shepherds.

Other kinds of specialization are found even in the simplest egalitarian societies. Although everyone of the appropriate age and sex may know how to make an arrow or a carrying bag, there will always be variations in skill; some people will make arrows that are straighter or bags that are stronger than those of others. Such people will be sought out, and their products acquired through some form of exchange. However, there is little interdependence in this kind of situation, because the absence of the skilled individual's products creates no serious economic hardships for anyone else. During certain kinds of cooperative enterprises, tasks may be divided up among participants to make work more efficient. For example, during a Plains Indian bison hunt, some people did the hunting itself, others the butchering, while a third group carried the meat. These divisions of labor

division of labor by age and sex   Task allocation based on the age and sex of individuals.

**institutionalized speciali-
zation**   Situation in
which people specialize to
make all or part of their
living; work on a perma-
nent, or at least frequently
recurring, basis; and are
dependent on exchanges
with others in social
groups beyond the family
for their survival and well-
being.

exchange   The transfer
of goods or services from
one party to another.

were situational; all people of the same age and sex were prepared to
undertake any of the tasks, if required.

Simple forms of specialization such as these are probably universal (for
an example of specialization and distribution in an egalitarian society, see
Box 8.1). **Institutionalized specialization** exists only when certain people
specialize to make all or part of their living, working on a permanent or at
least frequently recurring basis, and depend on exchanges with others in
social groups beyond the family for their survival and well-being.

Household Economy, Consumption, and Distribution

Households in nonindustrial societies tend to produce most of the things
they consume (Sahlins 1972). Between these households many kinds of
economic **exchange,** or transfers of products or services, occur: Guests are
provided with food during feasts, bride-price or a dowry is transferred
from one household to another, and one family may help another family
build a barn or harvest a crop. But in all of these cases, exchanges are made
between economic units that are essentially similar, most of the things
exchanged originate in the local system, and participants in the exchange
have highly personal relationships. No effective specialization is involved,
and little absolute interdependence. If for some reason patterns of exchange are interrupted, households can scrape by on their own, at least for
a while. Moreover, relationships are generally reciprocal in the sense that
exchanges balance out over the long run; more are undertaken as much for
social as for economic purposes; they lack the largely impersonal buyer-
seller dimension.

Types of Distribution

Anthropologists distinguish between three roughly overlapping modes of
distribution of goods and services: reciprocity, redistribution, and exchange (Haviland 1985).

reciprocity   Roughly
equivalent exchanges of
goods or services between
two parties.

Reciprocity   Reciprocity is perhaps the most universal form of distribution. It plays a major role in distribution in egalitarian societies and still
forms the basis for distribution within households in modern industrial
societies. "Generalized reciprocity" refers to exchanges of goods and services that are reciprocated over the course of the individual's lifetime or
within the household or family setting, whereas "balanced reciprocity"
involves more immediate reciprocation, the value of each side's contribution being roughly equivalent to the other. Today's practice of holiday gift
giving provides a useful example: The gifts we receive as children from our
parents are not reciprocated by things of equal value — we are beneficiaries
of generalized reciprocity and will become the givers of "unbalanced" gifts
when we have children of our own. Gift giving among friends is more
likely to express balanced reciprocity.

BOX 8.1

PRODUCTION AND DISTRIBUTION IN EARLY FORMATIVE OAXACA

In Mesoamerica, the Formative period saw the development of sedentary villages that practiced a mixed economy with increasing emphasis on cultivation. During the Early and Middle Formative period (1500–500 B.C.) in the Valley of Oaxaca, the villagers lived in one-room houses made of wattle and daub with hard earth floors. These floors are extremely important archaeological contexts, because they preserve the minute debris of everyday life, including evidence of economic activities. In analyzing household activities at 22 houses and household clusters in the Valley of Oaxaca, Flannery and Marcus (1976) determined four general categories of household activities:

1. *Universal:* Every house evidenced food procurement, preparation, and storage. Typically there were remains of grinding stones, storage pits dug into the floors, potsherds from large (5- to 10-gallon) jars and from ceramic braziers used as stoves, plus food remains like maize fragments and rabbit bones, and often bones of dog and turtle.

2. *Possible household specialization:* Although certain tools were universally distributed, these were not made by every household. Rather, in some houses and household clusters unusual amounts of debris occurred, indicating possible tool-manufacturing specialization at the household level. One house had many chert flakes, the by-products of making and retouching tools. At another house an unusual cache of deer bone was recovered—perhaps a store of raw

materials for making bone tools. Several houses contained tools and raw materials for making ground-and-polished celts.

3. *Possible regional specialization:* A number of activities were universal to the houses in a village but unique to particular villages or localities. Two villages seem to have specialized in the production of ornaments made of shell. In another village, debris in several pits included the remains of macaws, whose feathers were valued as decoration; perhaps villagers here specialized in the production of such ornaments. Small sites near saline springs may have been loci for salt production.

4. *Possible unique specializations:* In several villages archaeologists found fragments of mirrors made of highly polished magnetite. Rare artifacts, these were possibly used in rituals. At only one set of households in the region was evidence found of their manufacture. Furthermore, mirror-making activity areas were found in four superimposed strata, indicating that occupants of the household cluster may have specialized in this activity over the course of several generations.

These levels of household activity reveal the range of economic behavior typical of societies characterized by a high degree of local autonomy and by household self-sufficiency. In such societies, specialization may arise from the exploitation of regional resources.

Redistribution **Redistribution** takes place when goods or services are gathered into a central place and then redistributed, usually by a local, politically dominant individual or institution. Like reciprocity, redistribution is still very much part of the modern economy; a familiar example is

redistribution Acquisitions of goods by one individual or institution, often politically dominant, who then redistributes them to others.

federal taxes. Anthropologists commonly regard redistribution as a form of exchange that begins to develop in cultural evolution as social control mechanisms extend beyond the family; thus, as ranking emerges, so does the material basis for control over people: pooled resources and administrative control over the labor force. We must note that in the transition between egalitarian and ranked forms of sociopolitical organization, this control is as ephemeral as the charisma of a village elder hosting a feast. That is, villagers and guests from other villages may be impressed with the amount of goods accumulated and by the largesse of redistribution, but these features cannot be simply translated into a measure of the power of an individual. However, redistribution at this level encourages economic specialization and interdependence; it provides a basis for the concentration and centralization of material goods and services; and it represents a step toward more "rational" and fewer family-based forms of distribution.

barter A type of direct exchange of different goods, not using any sort of currency, in which each party tries to get an advantage, however slight.

Exchange Exchange involves transferring things of equal value. In our society exchanges largely involve transferring money for goods and services. Occasionally we **barter,** exchanging goods and services in the absence of money and trying to gain an advantage, however slight, in the process.

Trade is a special kind of exchange: raw resources or finished goods not locally available are obtained from somewhere else, often from distant sources, in exchange for something else. In our society, long-distance trade usually consists of straightforward commercial transactions, but in many nonstate, nonindustrial societies, where it is deeply embedded in social and political relationships, "down-the-line trade" from one person to another, from source to point of consumption, may bring goods over great distances. For example, many tribal people of highland New Guinea use marine shells traded in from distant coasts in their marriage ceremonies, but the shells are not really bought or sold (Fig. 8.1). For this reason, it is better to think of the shells as circulating through a kind of social or political exchange that also involves trade rather than in terms of commercial trade as we know it. In North America, the Hopewell traded extensively in this way 2,000 years ago (Box 8.2).

trade A special kind of exchange whereby raw resources or finished goods not locally available are obtained somewhere else, often from distant sources, in exchange for other goods.

Complex patterns of commercial trade are found in many nonindustrial societies. One example is the extensive salt trade that until recently took place in northern Africa. Salt, extracted from mines in the Sahara Desert by specialists, was transported by other specialists and sold in huge slabs throughout the tropical areas of Africa to the south, where it was in great demand.

part-time specialist A food producer who also specializes in nonfood goods or services.

Food, Specialization, and Distribution

full-time specialist A nonfood producer who earns a living by an occupation other than farming and who must exchange goods or services for food.

Part-time specialists produce some food (but often less than they need) in addition to special nonfood goods or services. **Full-time specialists** produce no food at all. (Here, we do not include people involved in specialized food production—for example, fishing—as specialists per se.) In

FIGURE 8.1 A New Guinea bride, bedecked with huge "kina" shells, displays the common form of wealth in the traditional societies of the New Guinea highlands. These shells are larger than the shells traded before European and Australian contact. Since then, shells as a form of currency have been "devalued" because many larger ones were brought in by foreign traders, who first arrived in the 1930s.

any particular cultural setting great variation in intensity of specialization may occur at any time. For example, some subsistence farmers in the Copán Valley today produce almost all the food or other commodities they need but exchange firewood or labor (i.e., specialized goods and services) for things such as medicine, coffee, tea, or metal tools. Other farmers, particularly those with insufficient landholdings, may exchange labor or specialized products for much or most of their food supply. Some families may give up farming entirely to run shops in the town or to engage in full-time crafts such as carpentry. This kind of continuum of specialization is found in many nonindustrial, hierarchical societies.

Specialists, whether full-time or part-time, may be of several kinds. They may provide products or services. Some of their tasks may require little skill; others, such as pottery or carpentry, may demand special skills, tools, and facilities. Certain artisans or specialists, such as goldsmiths, scribe-accountants, or physicians, may apply extremely specialized skills or knowledge in their work. As specialists of any kind become more numerous and varied in a particular culture, the economic system evolves toward greater complexity.

BOX 8.2

HOPEWELL TRADE

The Hopewell culture flourished in the woodlands of what is now Ohio between about 100 B.C. and A.D. 600. The Hopewell have captured the imagination of generations of archaeologists because of their impressive arrangements of mounds and earthworks and their use of exotic materials obtained through trade. Their earthworks and embankments include mounds of various geometric shapes and stylized representations of animals. Associated caches and burials have yielded superbly crafted objects, including stone effigy sculptures, copper axes, plaques (such as the one shown here) and headdresses, chipped stone tools, and necklaces of marine shell beads.

The raw materials used by the Hopewell evidence their extensive economic exchange networks. In addition to comparatively local resources such as mica, the Hopewell used copper from the Great Lakes region, chalcedony (a kind of quartz) from the area of the Dakotas, obsidian from what is now Yellowstone, grizzly bear teeth from the Rocky Mountains, shark teeth from the southern Atlantic coast, and marine shell and alligator teeth from the Gulf Coast. Not only did the Hopewell obtain materials from distant sources, but they passed them on both as raw and finished products to other peoples in eastern North America, particularly those to the southeast.

This kind of exchange is particularly intriguing because the Hopewell seem to have had egalitarian tribal political organization and a mixed subsistence economy based on small-scale farming, hunting, and gathering. Nevertheless, clearly there were leaders who enhanced their prestige by obtaining exotic materials, displaying them in rituals or as status symbols, and redistributing them to others. Archaeologists would like to know how this interregional exchange was managed. One possibility is that the Hopewell had a "Big-Man" pattern similar to that found in New Guinea. In this kind of system, charismatic individuals (Big-Men) acquire great influence over others, in part by manipulating and displaying shell, stone, feathers, and other exotic materials, which they exchange in trading-partner relationships with other Big-Men. The perspective this example provides on Hopewell exchange demonstrates how ethnography contributes models for archaeological research.

(Data from Brose 1985.)

SPECIALIZATION AND DISTRIBUTION AS EVOLUTIONARY PROCESSES IN NONINDUSTRIAL, COMPLEX SOCIETIES

A society can support specialists only if it can produce sufficient surplus food energy and realize effective transport for goods and services so that everyone gets what they need or want (Hassig 1985). This is what makes the issues of energy production and transport so important (see Chapter 6). There is no automatic relationship, however, between the ability to produce food surpluses and the emergence of economic specialists in general evolutionary terms. Anthropologists know that even many foragers could produce such surpluses but for the lack of institutionalized specialization.

A complex feedback relationship exists between specialization and production of surplus food energy. Specialists require support from farmers, who in turn must see some advantage in producing surpluses for exchange or trade or taxes or who must be coerced into doing so. What allows farmers to produce more food, in part, is that their dependence on specialists frees up labor within the household. This labor can be used to produce more food for exchange. Surpluses thus stimulate specialization, and specialization stimulates surpluses — a classic positive feedback relationship. Technology plays an important role here. Farmers who use only stone and wooden hand tools produce much less surplus, even if they want to produce surplus and land is available, than farmers with animal-drawn iron plows.

In effect, specialization emerges and grows because each party to the transaction offers an opportunity to the other. In Guatemala specialists supplement their food supplies in a social environment in which there is much competition over land, capitalizing on local resources that are not in short supply (e.g., clay for pottery). Farmers can obtain ceramic vessels more cheaply (in terms of time and labor) than they could if they made them themselves. Despite this mutual advantage, however, the food-producer part of the exchange system is the dominant one, at least at first, because it provides the more fundamental resource. If anything happens to disrupt the exchange, farmers suffer less than potters. But when specialization becomes well established, even some farmers who have sufficient land may turn to specialization because of the opportunities it offers.

Eventually, all parties to the transactions may become highly interdependent. Farming families gradually lose the skills to do many things for themselves. As specialists produce a wider variety of goods or services, these become more sophisticated, eventually perhaps surpassing in quality anything originally produced in the household economy. New products or services appear as a result of innovations or ideas introduced from elsewhere. People come to believe that they "need" these new things or services, encouraging farmers to further intensify their agricultural production. Localized exchange systems merge into regional ones. Specialists become more numerous, and new kinds of specialists appear (e.g., to transport ever-larger amounts of things). Particular crafts become internally specialized—for example, someone digs the clay, someone makes the pot, and someone else sells it. Competition among specialists and the advent of new technology, such as potter's wheels, may result in the production of cheaper and more abundant products or services. Specialists who once did handwork themselves become managers of lower-status employees. Formerly independent specialists band together to form associations such as guilds. Long-distance trade is stimulated as incomes and demand rise. Intermediaries begin to intervene between producers and consumers.

This is the evolutionary process of economic specialization. It results in a far larger web of economic interdependence than found in household economies and gives rise to whole new sets of economic institutions. It also encourages agricultural intensification, hence the growth of population and greater population densities as well.

Larger sets of feedback relationships also emerge. Increasing economic specialization, interdependence, and trade all stimulate new social and political behaviors and institutions. Political offices and roles appear, for example, that guarantee the security and freedom of marketplaces and transportation routes. Elites are enriched by new opportunities for taxation. New legal institutions arise to deal with disputes over ever-more complex economic transactions. New pretexts emerge for warfare (e.g., protection of trade routes). As specialization requires substantial facilities and capital, new ideologies emerge concerning property. All of these developments in turn encourage more specialization and trade. In other words, the process of economic specialization is intimately related to the more general evolutionary process of the growth of cultural complexity (Fig. 8.2).

Distribution in Nonegalitarian Settings

We have already seen that transport technology has important implications for specialization and trade. Let us now briefly look at some institutions of commercial distribution that are found in nonindustrial societies.

Markets and Marketplaces   One of the most widespread and ancient economic institutions in the nonindustrial world is the **market** (Berry 1967; Diskin 1976). This word has several definitions. It is a shortened term for **marketplace,** or locality where people come together to exchange goods. It also refers to the process of buyer-seller transactions (as in "doing the marketing") and to the number of available consumers for something (as in "there is a big market for this product"). Finally, we use the word to describe a particular kind of economic system whereby labor and goods are traded as commodities (as in a "free market" economy).

Marketplaces are common throughout the world. In Latin America, for example, larger communities often have a plaza, surrounded by stores and

market   Variable meanings: (1) a process of buyer-seller exchange (as in "doing the marketing"), (2) the demand (market) for something, or (3) a kind of economy (market economy).

marketplace   A designated place where goods and services are exchanged.

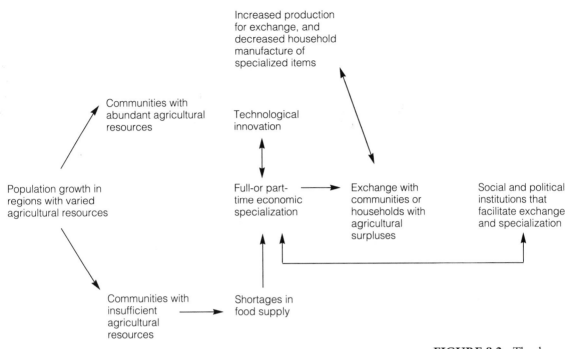

Increased production
for exchange, and
decreased household
manufacture of
specialized items

Communities with
abundant agricultural
resources

Technological
innovation

Population growth in
regions with varied
agricultural resources

Full-or part-
time economic
specialization

Exchange with
communities or
households with
agricultural
surpluses

Social and political
institutions that
facilitate exchange
and specialization

Communities with
insufficient
agricultural
resources

Shortages in
food supply

FIGURE 8.2 The development of economic specialization is part of a set of feedback relationships within the larger process of increasing cultural complexity.

warehouses, that is used as a marketplace. People bring goods to the marketplace and exchange them for agricultural and other products, many of which have been made by specialists. Some goods are local, whereas others might be traded in from great distances. In large communities daily markets may operate, but a typical pattern in many parts of the world is for small communities in a region to share a revolving sequence of market days, thereby using what is called a **periodic market** system. If a community is too small to support a periodic market, its commercial needs may be served by visits from **itinerant traders,** who travel from place to place selling their services or wares. An example is the blacksmith families that circulated among the camps of nomadic Bedouin Arabs until very recently.

These different systems provide markets convenient to almost everyone in a region. Urban populations, in particular, are heavily dependent on market exchange. In 1519 the main market in the Aztec capital attracted 40,000 to 50,000 buyers and sellers on its busiest days (Berdan 1982). Most goods in markets may be freely exchanged. We say "exchanged" here, rather than "bought and sold," because until quite recently most cultures lacked all-purpose money such as we use today. Goods would have been bartered, that is, exchanged directly after negotiation — so many pots for so much grain, for instance. In the barter situation the producer of specialized goods must get back a return that is at least the food equivalent

periodic market Locus of exchange that convenes on a regular but not a daily basis.

itinerant trader A person who travels from place to place selling services or wares rather than being stationed in one place, as in a market.

negative reciprocity   A type of exchange in which one person gains at the expense of another.

of the time and effort expended in making the specialized item (i.e., the amount of maize that could have been produced using the time and labor necessary to produce a cooking pot).

We are accustomed to thinking of market exchanges as being motivated by profit seeking, which amounts to **negative reciprocity,** in which one person's gain is another's loss of value. But many such exchanges in nonindustrial societies have as their main function simply the provisioning of households. Potters get grain, farmers get pots, and nobody makes much of a profit, though everyone barters for as much as possible. Although money is not used, barter is still a general form of buying and selling, being primarily an economic transaction in which each party seeks an advantage, however slight.

Specialists and traders are of course conspicuous at markets and heavily dependent on them. As a direct relationship exists between the number of specialists and the size of the consumer population, population density in a region strongly affects specialization. For example, a community of 1,000 people consumes only so many ceramic vessels each year. No one is going to pay very much for a household pot, for instance, exchange very much grain for it, so many pots must be sold if potters are to support themselves. With a market of only 1,000 customers, perhaps only one family of potters might be supported. If the population doubled, another family could be added, and so forth. Too many potters would create more goods than can be used; the "surplus" potters, unrecompensed for their efforts, could not support themselves as specialists.

Though it may be possible to identify markets as places in the archaeological record, it is much more difficult to document transactions. This requires sophisticated research design, as did for example, the testing for market interaction at Xochicalco, Mexico, described in Box 8.3.

Patron-Client Relationships   Another way of producing and distributing things is through patron-client relationships, as when a customer seeks out a specialist of some sort—a carpenter or a doctor—and purchases or commissions a special product or service, thus serving as a "patron" in the sense that a "patron of the arts" supports the services of painters and musicians, who are the "clients." The exchange of goods or services between the patron and the client may be very similar to a market transaction as described above, except that it often does not occur in a marketplace and the specialist may have highly developed skills and facilities. If, as in the case of carpenters or doctors, specialists offer their products or services widely to many patrons, they form part of a market system. In this kind of system the client (e.g., the doctor) may be more wealthy or powerful than the patron.

In many societies clients are not free to sell their services where they choose but rather are attached to wealthy, powerful patrons, in some cases as part of the patron's household. This was quite common in nonindustrial hierarchical societies, like those of dynastic China, feudal Japan, and Renaissance Europe. In some ranked societies, such as those of Polynesia,

BOX 8.3

DETECTING MARKET EXCHANGE
AT XOCHICALCO

Xochicalco, a hilltop city in central Mexico, prospered between A.D. 750 and 900 (Hirth and Guillen 1988). It is the kind of community where we would expect to find markets and market exchange, as well as specialization. After being imported into Xochicalco from several distant sources, obsidian was made into tools in several workshops in different parts of the city. Each workshop made basically the same set of tools, which were somehow redistributed throughout the city so that each household had a similar domestic obsidian tool kit. How was obsidian exchanged within Xochicalco; that is, how was it transferred from workshops to houses? Kenneth Hirth has developed two hypotheses about this exchange:

Hypothesis 1: Individual consuming families had social relationships with one or more of the workshops and went there to get their tools.

(a)

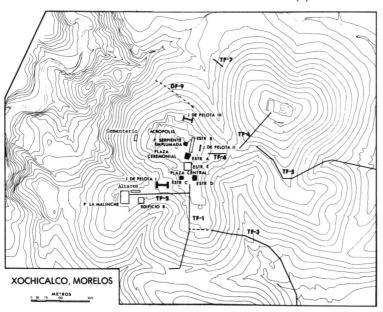

(b)

Aerial photo (a) and plan (b) of Xochicalco, Mexico. Market exchange is an important institution in Mesoamerica today. Indications of its past importance are found at prehistoric centers such as Xochicalco.

(continued)

(continued)

Hypothesis 2: Tools were brought from workshops to central marketplaces, where they were bought by people from all over the city.

An implication of the first hypothesis is that if people got obsidian from a particular workshop, it would be one near their homes—obsidian from a particular workshop would not travel far from where it was made. An implication of the second hypothesis is that obsidian from all workshops would be evenly distributed throughout all the houses at Xochicalco, since everyone would have access to products of all the workshops at the markets. Surface mapping, collection, and excavation provided the necessary samples of obsidian from houses and workshops to evaluate these suppositions.

Workshops made the same range of tools, using for the most part the same kind of raw material, but one had particularly high proportions of an easily recognizable green obsidian. According to the implication of the first hypothesis, such green obsidian should be most abundant in houses close to the workshop. The implication of the second hypothesis suggests that it should be found in roughly the same amounts (proportionate to other obsidian) in houses everywhere in the city. Statistical analysis of the known distribution confirmed the latter implication.

In scientific terms, tests supported the second hypothesis (market exchange) and were inconsistent with the first. As a result, the first hypothesis may be rejected and the second is strengthened. But we still do not know for sure that markets were present at Xochicalco. Some other means of distribution may have existed to produce the same patterns of obsidian consumption as market exchange. Only when several likely hypotheses are adequately tested can we reasonably infer the presence of market transactions involving obsidian tools. Science works as much by rejecting some explanations as by supporting others.

---

chiefs would be intermittent patrons of individual craftspeople. When a chief desired a particularly elaborate canoe, or a carved decoration for his house, he might commission a skilled artisan to execute the task (Fig. 8.3). But this sort of relationship was not permanent, and artisans typically did not make a living by doing such things over the long run.

Because the specialist produces only for the patron, not for a wider, open market, permanent patron-client relationships are expensive, and they have distinct political and social dimensions in addition to economic ones. The artisan's family might have to be supported, as well as the artisan. For this reason, full-time client artisans usually produce high-status goods or services (e.g., high-quality art or scribal documents) that demand a high rate. Generally only rich and powerful people can afford such clients, so the patron-client pattern is more characteristic of stratified societies.

Urbanization and Specialization

The development of economic specialization and that of urbanization are strongly interrelated because cities create specific needs for the population and thus encourage specialists to supply goods to meet those needs, further stimulating specialization (Fox 1977; Sanders and Webster 1988).

FIGURE 8.3 A Maori wood carver at work (New Zealand).

Since most urban dwellers are not full-time food producers (Childe 1950; Redman 1978), even the first cities, which appeared about 5,500 years ago in Mesopotamia (see Chapter 13), featured well-developed specialization. But in nonindustrial societies the potential for urban growth is more limited by local availability of food energy than in industrial societies. In 1990 the farm population of the United States was only about 5 million, or roughly 2 percent of the total population of around 250 million (1990 World Almanac). This tiny percentage of farmers produced not only enough food for themselves and the rest of the population but produced enough for export as well. This sort of extraordinary productivity, based on industrial technology and transport, enables most North Americans today to be urbanized, economic specialists. In 1990, 77 percent of all citizens of the United States lived in cities and suburbs and depended on food producers elsewhere.

As we noted in Chapter 6, the ratio of food producers to nonfood producers is very different in nonindustrial populations, a pattern that has important implications for urbanization. In 1800 in China, farmers constituted approximately 80 percent of the population (exact figures are not available), almost the reverse of the industrial-era ratio (Stover 1974). As a general rule of thumb, anywhere from 70 to 90 percent of the population

FIGURE 8.4 The Moroccan city of Fez (a) retains many preindustrial urban patterns, including very high population densities and a striking degree of urban economic specialization. Effective transport (b) allowed such urban densities to be maintained; here, hides are being delivered using pack animals. By studying surviving traditional cities such as Fez, we can make observations that help us reconstruct ancient urban economic institutions.

(a)

(b)

of nonindustrial states must be food producers. It has only been in the last 200 years that industrial productivity has permitted the existence of a society like our own, in which most people are nonfood producers and urban dwellers. However normal this seems to us, it is very odd indeed in evolutionary terms. Even today, some cities, such as Fez in Morocco, retain many of their traditional, nonindustrial economic patterns (Fig. 8.4).

Defining the City

Scholars differ over how to define the concept of "city" or "urban center" (see also Chapter 11 for a discussion of cities as central places). A useful definition combines elements of both form and function (Sanders and Webster 1988; Wirth 1938):

1. Cities have large populations in absolute terms (as a rule of thumb, more than 5,000 people).

2. They have high population densities (usualy in the thousands of people per km²), and population is highly nucleated (i.e., there is a sharp transition between dense "urban" and less dense "rural" zones). Many nonindustrial cities actually had a boundary wall encircling them.

3. City dwellers are relatively heterogeneous in terms of their ethnic identities, their social statuses, their standards of living, and, most important here, occupational specialization.

4. Social stratification and class structure are well developed.

5. Cities have many diverse functions (though these may vary from one city to another), including administration, economic production and exchange, long-distance trade, defense, religion, and education. These involve not only city dwellers themselves but also people in the wider society.

6. Cities are central places integrated with rural hinterlands and smaller communities but are differentiated from them. Providing a wide range of specialized goods and services to their hinterlands, cities may exercise political or administrative control over them.

Cities are, by this definition, found only in state-type societies, although central places that share some of these attributes are found in ranked societies too. Later we will explore some of the noneconomic functions and processes associated with the growth of cities (Chapter 11), but for now our concerns are primarily economic.

The presence of a large, dense urban population has important effects on specialization, since it creates a large market of potential consumers in a spatially restricted area. The large number of buyers of products and services means that many specialists can be supported. Because buyers live close to specialists, transport costs are low, so even cheap, bulk goods may be efficiently produced and exchanged. Wealthy or elite patrons can afford to support clients, and the diversity of urban institutions creates demand for many kinds of specialists: administrators need scribes, generals need soldiers, priests need artisans to decorate and maintain temples.

Such complexity attracts foreign trade and commerce as well, along with professional merchants who serve as intermediaries. Sometimes whole cities have a basically mercantile identity. A good example is Venice (Italy), which depended far less on its own rural hinterland for its prosperity than on foreign commerce, made possible largely by its merchant fleet and navy. Such cities may be called **mercantile cities** since their survival and prosperity depend primarily on the activities of merchants.

One of the principal differences between urban centers is how much they depend on their own rural hinterlands. Cities in low-energy societies find it difficult to supply themselves with cheap bulk goods like staple foods imported from far away (or to export such goods), so dependence on local production is high.

mercantile city Urban center whose primary function is the control of trade.

INVESTIGATING SPECIALIZATION, EXCHANGE, AND TRADE: THE ARCHAEOLOGICAL RECORD

Two contrasting archaeological cases illustrate the issues discussed thus far about specialization. First we examine archaeological evidence for specialization, exchange, and trade at the great pre-Colombian urban center of Teotihuacán (TAYohTEEwahKAHN) near modern Mexico City (Millon 1981). A huge city by anyone's definition, Teotihuacán was the capital of one of the earliest great native states of the New World. We then turn to Classic Maya Copán, a hierarchical society of smaller size and less complexity, where urban and political development took very different forms.

Teotihuacán

Teotihuacán (Fig. 8.5) was founded over 2,000 years ago. It grew into a huge metropolis between roughly 100 B.C. and A.D. 100, remaining the political, economic, and cultural capital of much of central Mexico until about A.D. 700. Thereafter it was eclipsed by other centers and lost much of its population, though it continued to be occupied by thousands of people. Teotihuacán's period of florescence began a bit before the Maya Classic period and ended a little earlier than it did. Teotihuacán influences can be found in the art and architecture of Maya centers, including Copán.

Archaeologists have been investigating Teotihuacán for over a century, particularly since the early 1960s. Fortunately, the site has never been buried or destroyed, its state of preservation due in part to its location in a semiarid region. Most of its remains are visible on the surface, including mounds (representing the remains of structures) and great quantities of artifacts. As a result, we have learned much about it on the basis of surface survey and surface sampling of artifacts.

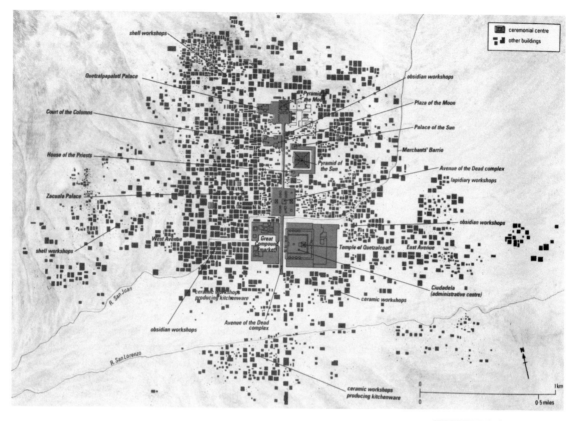

FIGURE 8.5 Map of Teotihuacán, showing all the sites located in Millon's survey. Important civic and ceremonial areas of the city are identified as well as the locations of many of the craft workshops. The "ceramic workshops producing kitchenware" marker at the bottom of the map points to Tlajinga 33.

The City At its height, at about A.D. 600–650, Teotihuacán was one of the great urban centers of the world; probably only a half-dozen contemporary cities (all in the Old World) exceeded it in size and complexity. Teotihuacán sprawls over an area of about 20 km², and has a well-defined core area (Millon, Drewitt, and Cowgill 1973). At its core lie the great ceremonial complexes of the Pyramids of the Sun, Moon, and the Ciudadela, arranged along the Street of the Dead (these names date from the Spanish colonial period). Excavations have revealed that most of the architecture consists of walled square or rectangular multiroomed compounds built of stone or adobe (mud bricks). The rooms are arranged as "apartments" around interior patios. Compounds housed 60–100 people, probably family groups of some kind. Residential housing varies from elaborate, highly decorated palaces near the site core to shabby, cramped, shoddily built houses; most fall between these extremes. The remains of the compounds are large, sprawling mounds of rock and soil. There were more than 2,000 of them, many of which were surveyed and surface-sampled during the Teotihuacán mapping project (Million, Drewitt, and

Cowgill 1973). Although we cannot know the exact population, Teotihuacán at its height probably had at least 125,000 inhabitants. There is no question that Teotihuacán was the urban capital of an extensive nonindustrial state, thus conforming to our definition of a city.

Food Supply   Teotihuacán's location and eventual massive size are explained in part by the permanent springs that watered this otherwise dry environment (Sanders, Parsons, and Santley 1979). These water sources were used for irrigation in the 16th century, as they are today; almost certainly they fed an extensive irrigation system in Teotihuacán times as well. Infrared photos show ancient canals, which were probably contemporaneous with the city, although this has yet to be confirmed (Fig. 8.6).

An estimated 9,500 ha of land within 16 km of Teotihuacán were irrigable and, if planted with maize, could have provided about 40–50 percent of the food energy required by the urban population at its peak. Other food could have been efficiently carried from greater distances by using canoes on the nearby lake. Thus most of the food energy to support the city did not have to be brought from a great distance, a circumstance permitting a dense urban concentration in a low-energy state. Also, during certain periods of Teotihuacán's history, almost everyone in the larger region lived in the city. This absence of rural population strengthens the argument that nearby irrigated land was the primary agricultural resource and indicates that many (perhaps most) of the urban dwellers were also farmers. Although this is not typical of many cultures, ethnographic analogs do exist, such as the Yoruba of Africa. An additional characteristic of the agricultural system was that a family of four or five people could support itself by cultivating about one ha of land and still produce a 40–60 percent surplus for market (or other) exchanges. In many parts of pre-Columbian Mesoamerica, particularly where there was no irrigation, surpluses of this size would have been impossible.

Specialization, Exchange, and Trade   Evidence for specialization, exchange, and trade at Teotihuacán is based on three research approaches: survey, excavation, and artifact studies.

Survey and artifact studies   During the mapping project of the 1960s, extremely accurate maps of surface features could be compiled because of the sparse vegetation in the dry environment. Since artifacts were well preserved and visible on the surface, assemblages and subassemblages of different kinds could also be recorded. Of the roughly 2,000 mapped mounds that represent remains of residential apartment complexes at Teotihuacán, more than 800 show distinctive signs of specialized craft production, and nearly half (398) exhibit unusual amounts of obsidian on the surface, about a quarter (213) produced evidence of pottery production, and others yielded evidence of working jade, other stones, and shell (Santley 1980). Not only do the surface data strongly suggest that different

FIGURE 8.6 Infrared aerial photo of the southern part of Teotihuacán. Modern roads are visible; beneath them, in the lower right quadrant, a wide white line indicates the location of a possible irrigation canal for the city.

compounds had different economic specialities in a general sense but that even within particular crafts further specialization occurred. For example, some compounds produced obsidian cores for blade manufacture, while others produced bifacially flaked scrapers and knives of the same material. Pottery workshops produced particular kinds of pottery, including highly specialized forms.

Obsidian specialization By far the most obvious indications of specialization involve obsidian (Clark 1989; Spence 1986). Raw material was procured from two quarries northeast of the city. Abundant remains of quarrying operations have been found, particularly at Pachuca (50 km distant), where approximately 500 deep shaft mines were dug in prehistoric times to acquire distinctive green obsidian (most obsidian in Mesoamerica is gray or black). Obsidian nodules were roughed into basic forms called "macro-cores" at the quarry sites. As no substantial Teotihuacán period habitation is indicated around the quarries, specialists from the city may have been involved in the initial stages of mining and transport. Once the obsidian reached the city, it was distributed to other specialists, who lived in apartment complexes. They further processed the obsidian into final form for exchange. Some artifacts were manufactured to be sold, either in an urban market or further abroad in Mesoamerica. These items included finished cores (from which blades are produced) and bifacially worked blades. Signs of intense tool production around a number of the major temple complexes at the city core suggest that a certain amount of this production was directly under control of the state (as, perhaps, was access to the mines). Interestingly, green obsidian is most abundant in the areas indicating state production.

Archaeologists used to think that most of the residential mounds exhibiting unusual concentrations of obsidian on the surface were workshops where obsidian was processed for exchange. But analysis of tool assemblages from about half of these house compounds show that the tools were not made in them but rather were used and discarded there in unusual quantities. This may mean these compounds were engaged in craft activities in which obsidian was part of the productive technology, but we still do not know what special items were being manufactured.

In summary, a number of Teotihuacán compounds produced many obsidian tools; others consumed them to produce other goods. In the great majority of compounds, relatively small amounts of obsidian were present in the form of normal household artifacts.

Excavation of a potter's compound   Whenever Teotihuacán apartment compounds have been tested by excavation, buried room floors and plazas have produced the same materials found on the surface. In 1980, half of a large apartment compound, Tlajinga (tlahHINgah) 33 (Fig. 8.7), located on the southern edge of the city, was excavated (Storey and Widmer 1989). A number of compounds in this area had been tentatively identified as specialized ceramic workshops producing one particular type of pottery, called San Martin Orange — cheap domestic storage jars and basins, widely used throughout the city.

One research objective of the Tlajinga excavations was to test whether indications of ceramic specialization on the surface could be substantiated by the exposure of artifacts and features. Horizontal control of the excavations was based both on a grid and on architectural features, such as room walls, and both natural and cultural stratigraphic levels were utilized. About 1,144 m² of the compound's final building phase were exposed, and about half of this area was excavated down to bedrock. Broad, shallow, lateral excavations of this type yield maximum information about the behavior that went on in different parts of the compound.

Excavations revealed that the compound had been occupied 450–500 years (about A.D. 250–700) and had been rebuilt frequently. In the excavated zone 104 rooms (not all contemporaneous) were identified. Domes-

FIGURE 8.7 The archaeological site of Tlajinga 33, a Teotihuacán apartment compound that specialized in pottery production.

tic refuse and burials (found under house floors or plazas at Teotihuacán) showed that the compound had been a residence. Occupational specialists who produce cheap utilitarian goods (such as San Martin Orange pottery) are usually not high-status people in their communities. The excavations showed that, throughout much of its history, Tlajinga 33 had been constructed largely of adobe, a cheaper and flimsier material than the stone used in more substantial compounds nearer the city core.

In the earliest levels, evidence for specialization came from soil samples that contained tiny fragments of nonlocal stone as well as partly finished artifacts of such material. Apparently the compound had originally been a lapidary workshop where stone ornaments were made. Eventually specialization had shifted to ceramic production, as indicated by several kinds of evidence. Broken, misfired pieces of pottery, the inevitable by-products of ceramic manufacture, were extremely abundant. Pits dug into the ground, which were filled with charcoal and burned potsherds, may have been used

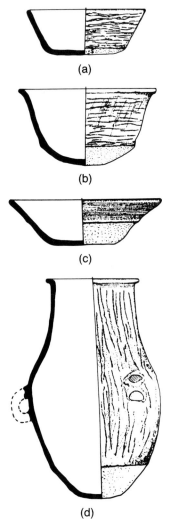

FIGURE 8.8 The most common vessel forms of San Martin Orange ware, pottery of the kind produced at Tlajinga 33 and used in house compounds all over the city of Teotihuacán: (a) basin; (b) crater; (c) bowl; (d) jar.

as kilns. Special rooms had been set aside for ceramic manufacture. Artifacts associated with ceramic production, such as stone shapers and scrapers, were also found. Tlajinga 33 was so specialized that only one type of pottery was produced (San Martin Orange), and only restricted shapes (large basins and jars) within that pottery type (Fig. 8.8). Such extreme specialization allows the efficient production of cheap goods, an important consideration in a competitive urban market. Other compounds in the vicinity made San Martin Orange pottery as well, so this district was probably a specialized enclave of the city. This pattern of neighborhood specialization is characteristic of many recent nonindustrial cities, particularly in the Middle East (Coon 1958).

Whether the people of Tlajinga 33 were full-time or part-time specialists is unknown. If specialization at Teotihuacán was as widespread as surface indications suggest, some people in most compounds must have spent at least part of their time farming, since the rural population around the city was comparatively small.

In addition to providing evidence on a particular residence-workshop, the Tlajinga excavations substantiated the conclusions drawn from surface inspection. This meant that reasonable inferences could be made on the basis of surface remains alone. When more excavations are carried out at other compounds, it should be possible to reconstruct the urban economy of Teotihuacán in considerable detail.

Distribution   Many goods produced by specialists were widely used throughout the city and beyond. Teotihuacán was such a huge community, and so internally specialized, that we would expect it to contain a marketplace to provide for distribution. Since much nonindustrial market exchange simply requires an open space, an exchange could have occurred wherever such space was conveniently available. What may have been the remains of a huge formal marketplace were in fact detected at the southern extreme of the Street of the Dead—the Great Compound (Fig. 8.5). Its scale approximately 400 m on a side) and lack of major civic or ceremonial buildings indicate that it may have served distinctive functions. Surface survey suggests that some rooms on the periphery of the Great Compound may have been storerooms where particular items were stockpiled, while other rooms may have housed administrative facilities. Unfortunately, parts of the Great Compound were heavily disturbed by modern construction before it could be adequately investigated through excavation. It is certain that specialized products were efficiently distributed throughout the city, however, and most archaeologists assume that a marketplace system of impressive scale was one of the mechanisms of distribution.

Teotihuacán certainly received many materials from distant parts of Mesoamerica (such as shells from both the Pacific and Atlantic), and its own exports traveled widely. Teotihuacán goods were common in the Mexican highlands within a few days' journey of the city; considerable exchange also took place with more distant regions, especially the Gulf Coast. Teotihuacán ceramics, obsidian, and other objects are commonly found as far away as the Maya lowlands and the highlands of Guatemala, though in small amounts. We do not know yet what the mechanisms of movement were, although some archaeologists believe that commercial trade may have been responsible.

Given these indicators of trade, it is possible that enclaves of foreigners resided at Teotihuacán. On the eastern edge of the city, a zone containing archaeological materials from the Gulf Coast and the Maya lowlands suggests the presence of Teotihuacán merchants who traded with these regions or with resident foreign traders from them. Another neighborhood on the west side was certainly inhabited by people from the Valley of Oaxaca (wahHAHkah) about 300 km to the south, judging from tombs reflecting Oaxacan religious customs and pottery in Oaxaca style (Spence n.d.). Current excavations are testing whether the foreigners had any hand in specialized production or trade.

By any measure, Teotihuacán was an urban state with highly developed institutions of both part-time and full-time specialization. Other contemporary Mesoamerican civilizations present a rather different picture.

Specialization and Trade among the Classic Maya of Copán

One of the basic propositions of this chapter is that the scale and complexity of specialization and trade are closely related to population size and density. We now turn to a hierarchical society of much smaller size and less institutional complexity than that of Teotihuacán: the Classic Maya of Copán. What can we say about specialization and trade there, given the research design and interpretations reviewed in Chapter 3?

Setting   We estimate the total population under the effective authority of the Copán kings in A.D. 750–800 at about 27,000 people, who were scattered over the Copán Valley, an area of about 450 km². This is a tiny system even when compared with the urban population of the Teotihuacán state, much less its larger political domains. Despite the dense core of population (11–12,000 people) around the royal compound at Copán, there was no urban development on the scale of that of Teotihuacán. We would predict that evidence of complex institutions of specialization and trade would accordingly be much less impressive. Do the results of research bear out this assumption?

Scale of Specialization   Of the 1,425 known sites, only 13 show any signs of specialized production of goods, either on the basis of surface materials or excavation. While many specialized sites undoubtedly remain unrecognized, the small number of those verified as such strongly suggests that specialization was not developed on anything like the same scale as at Teotihuacán. Not only are there few such sites, but most of them are small, rural places. All the data we have indicate that full- or part-time specialization at Copán was on a very limited scale.

Trade Many kinds of things were traded into the Copán Valley, including obsidian, pottery, jade and other minerals in raw or finished forms, marine shell, turtle shell, alligator teeth, and sting-ray spines. Doubtless many other perishable trade items have not been recovered. Except for obsidian, very few exotic items have been recovered from the small rural sites where most people lived. Pottery is about the only thing we can reasonably be sure was produced in the valley and exported elsewhere.

Although we know that certain sorts of exchange took place over long distances, we face two related problems: (1) What was the scale of these exchanges, and (2) how were they organized and carried out? Except in the case of obsidian (see below) we cannot even begin to answer these questions on the basis of the archaeological evidence itself. One could argue that there was well-developed trade or mercantile activity at Copán, as there was at Teotihuacán and Tenochtitlan. One could argue just as convincingly that many imported objects were the result of noncommercial exchanges, especially between elite people. One way to try to answer these questions is to investigate intensively one kind of trade or exchange; this we did in the case of obsidian (Mallory 1984).

Obsidian at Copán: Economic Implications

Sources Obsidian is not locally available as a raw material in the Maya lowlands, yet is found in most large sites, where it is used to make chipped stone cutting tools (usually in the form of blades) (Fig. 8.9). Because obsidian clearly had to be brought in from considerable distances, a number of archaeologists support the hypothesis that trade in this material was organized on a considerable scale by Maya rulers and operated by them for their own profit (Rathje 1971). The logic is that obsidian trade, extensive and complicated enough to require specialized management and institutions, was manipulated by rulers to augment their power and authority. Copán is one of the few sites at which this idea has been adequately tested.

Copán is closer to obsidian sources than most other Lowland Maya centers. Thus it is not surprising that obsidian is present there in large amounts; hundreds of thousands of pieces have in fact been recovered. Most of it seems to come from a single source, Ixtepeque in the mountains of Guatemala, about 90 km to the southwest. Outside Copán's political orbit, Ixtepeque (ISHtahPECKkay) was undoubtedly controlled by its own local lords.

Consumption and elite management Our excavated sample of Copán households (the loci of obsidian consumption) shows that obsidian was available to households everywhere in the valley regardless of social rank, in amounts roughly proportional to the number of residents. It did not function as a status symbol but rather as a common utilitarian tool (Webster and Gonlin 1988). Analysis of wear patterns on the edges of collections of obsidian tools from sites of all social ranks show that the same basic range of actions (sawing, slicing, scraping) was carried out almost everywhere; this is consistent with the idea that obsidian was part of the general residential tool kit of all households. Only at two known sites is there sufficient obsidian debris to indicate that it was being consumed at an unusual rate, doubtless in the manufacture of other objects (see below).

Calculations of the per-capita consumption of obsidian at Copán suggest that only a few pieces were necessary for each person per year—it was a "low turnover" item. If these calculations are correct, only about 18 to 20 porter-loads a year had to be brought into the Copán Valley to supply the needs of the entire population. The conclusion is that, however it was organized, the obsidian trade at Copán was on a scale sufficiently small to require little management. Obsidian was cheap enough so that everyone could afford it; there was little political advantage to be gained by controlling its flow. Consumers could certainly have done without it, since there was local flint available to make cutting tools.

An independent study of the chronology of sites reinforces this conclusion. There was plenty of obsidian when both rulers and nobles dominated the Copán political system. After the disappearance of the rulers, the obsidian supply remained plentiful and continued to be so even as the nobles gradually lost their power (this process of political collapse is examined in Chapter 15).

Distribution. As a result of all this research we know where obsidian came from, where it was consumed, and that its availability did not depend on the presence of kings or nobles. We still do not know how it was acquired or distributed. Since few people were necessary to bring it from its source, there was little scope for specialization in obsidian transport. In fact, a few Copán farmers could easily have acquired all that was necessary in the agricultural off-season by simply going to the quarries. Similarly, we do not know how the obsidian was distributed within the Copán valley system itself. It may have been bartered in market transactions, or carried from household to household by itinerant traders.

Other Evidence of Specialization At Teotihuacán the evidence of economic specialization is abundant, even from surface indications. At Copán, where excavation was in part designed to retrieve evidence on specialization, this evidence turns out to be very sparse. Of all the sites tested or excavated, only 13 show signs of any sort of specialized production (plaster making, obsidian consumption, ceramic production, stone and shell working, and possibly weaving). Of course, we have undoubtedly failed to detect specialization at many sites, either because obvious evidence of it is not preserved or because our excavations were not in the right places. Still, if the same proportion of sites in the Teotihuacán settlement system had been excavated as in the Copán sample, there is little doubt that the evidence of specialized production would have been overwhelming in comparison. Obviously a qualitatively greater institutionalized development of specialization existed at Teotihuacán than at Copán.

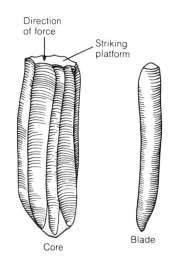

FIGURE 8.9 How blades are detached from a core. Once the core has been properly prepared, an artisan can manufacture hundreds of sharp prismatic blades very quickly (one movement detaches one blade, ready for use). The blades can be used as they are or further modified into other shapes.

Excavating Specialized Sites Evidence gained from test-pitting has been suggestive but not conclusive; larger excavations must follow to provide a larger sample of artifacts and features that might indicate specialization. This has been done at 4 of the 13 sites.

El Duende, an obsidian-use workshop Surface survey indicated an enormous amount of obsidian at the site of El Duende (DWENday), which was excavated by John Mallory. This little site, consisting only of three small, unimpressive structures, is in an unusual location — high on a hill in pine forest, not the sort of place we would expect farmers to live. In 1981 El Duende's extensive excavation produced unmistakable signs of specialization. Obsidian tools were recovered in densities hundreds of times greater than in other sites. The edges of these tools show patterns of use different from those at known residential sites. A large cache of unused obsidian blades was also found in one of the structures. But El Duende was not a place where obsidian tools were produced for exchange, as they were at some of the compounds at Teotichuacán. Tools were consumed, broken, and discarded at El Duende — they were used to manufacture other products. We do not know what these products were, but they were probably made of wood.

Two other lines of evidence, burials and nonobsidian artifacts, suggest specialization as well. In this part of the valley the Maya commonly buried their dead in and around their homes. El Duende, however, lacked burials. Although a normal range of different domestic artifacts (grinding stones, pottery in a variety of forms, etc.) were found, these were few in number. This is odd, because the site was used for several hundred years and should thus have had dense concentrations of domestic artifacts if people had lived there permanently. These lines of evidence, taken together, suggest that people who normally resided elsewhere came to El Duende intermittently, lived there for short periods of time while engaged in making special items using obsidian tools, and then returned to their homes.

Petapilla, a grinding-stone workshop One of the most durable and frequently encountered artifacts at archaeological sites in Mesoamerica is the grinding stone. Grinding stones are important for archaeologists not only because they are products of specialization with rather well-understood functions but also because they are very durable and usually are not transported very far from their original cultural contexts.

Two stones make up a set: a cylindrical stone held in the hands, called a **mano,** and a slablike stone, or **metate,** used as a grinding surface (see Fig. 6.10). This set of stones is used today, as it undoubtedly was in the past, for many grinding purposes, but by far the most important is grinding maize, the major staple in the diet, into a dough. Although several kinds of stone are used for manos and metates at Copán, hard stone is best, since it is more durable. Most manos and metates are made of a hard stone called "rhyolite," which is not found everywhere in the valley.

mano Cylindrical stone held in the hands, usually used in combination with a metate for grinding.

metate Slablike stone used as a grinding surface in combination with the mano.

Today, manos and metates of hard stone are low-turnover items. A woman typically has only one or two sets in her house (often the first set is a wedding present) and uses them until they are worn out (most of the ones we recover are broken). She may consume only a few sets in her entire life, and this was probably the prehistoric pattern as well. Making grinding stones before metal tools were available was a laborious, hence costly, task. However, people could afford to "pay" specialists well for them because so few were required by individual households. On general principles we could thus hypothesize that grinding stones were produced by specialists, given the demands of the task but that few such specialists were present at Copán at any given time, since the demand for manos and metates would have been low in a population of only 27,000 or 28,000.

Initial stages of research into prehistoric grinding stones at Copán focused on finding the source of rhyolite (Spink 1983). As many active streams in the Copán valley transport stone from its sources, pebbles in streams were carefully examined, and rhyolite pebbles "backtracked" to a source in the hills north of the valley floor. Here, in the upper channel of a stream, was a rhyolite outcrop, its surface scarred where people had split off large slabs.

Immediately adjacent to this area was a small mountain valley called Petapilla (PETahPEEyah), where archaeological remains of small rural households had been located as well as a larger, more impressive site. The general settlement area had long been known to the modern inhabitants of Copán as a place where whole or partly finished metates could be picked up off the surface. Two sites, including the large one, were partly excavated in this settlement zone. Both excavations turned up unusual numbers of rhyolite grinding stones, some broken, some partly finished, and some "blanks," the roughed-out slabs that were the initial products of the process of manufacture. One of the rooms in a building at the large site yielded about 20 metates; such a concentration has never been found elsewhere at Copán. Geochemical sourcing demonstrated that about 70 percent of the rhyolite metates found in houses all over the valley came from the Petapilla source.

The main implication of this research is clear. The inhabitants of at least some of the Petapilla sites were engaged in the specialized production of metates, using a local source of the raw material. Concentration of metates in a room in the largest residential site suggests that there was some sort of centralized coordination of this activity. Soils in the Petapilla valley are rich but thin and often poorly drained; it was not an optimal area for agriculture. Specialization at Petapilla no doubt supplemented an insufficient local agricultural resource base, and the Petapilla metate makers might have been only part-time specialists otherwise engaged in farming, as were most rural Maya. A second explanation is that well-organized, full-time specialists were opportunistically taking advantage of a special resource to find themselves a niche in the Copán economic system. At this point neither explanation can be fully substantiated; however, the bulk of the evidence supports the first.

Distribution: The Question of Marketplaces No matter how specialization and long-distance trade were organized, goods such as obsidian
tools, metates, the unknown products of El Duende, and a host of others
had to be distributed throughout the Copán system. This brings up the
question of marketplaces. If by marketplace we simply mean an area where
people gather periodically to exchange necessary or useful products, then
marketplaces undoubtedly existed at Copán. Huge open plazas in the royal
compound or at dozens of other sites provided the necessary facilities, as
did spaces between sites. To what extent did households depend on marketplace transactions to provision themselves? So far we have found no special
marketplace facilities such as those clearly present at Tenochtitlan and almost certainly present at Teotihuacán. On the basis of current evidence,
marketplace exchange was more informal and occurred on a much smaller
scale than in either of these two urban capitals. Unlike the Basin of Mexico,
the Copán valley, with its lack of environmental diversity, had less potential
for development of complex patterns of specialization and marketplace
exchange.

Although items such as obsidian and metates might have been exchanged in a marketplace, other possibilities exist. Itinerant traders might
have visited rural households a few times each year to supply obsidian
tools. On the very few occasions when a family needed a metate, it would
be no hardship for someone simply to go to Petapilla for one. However,
these suppositions must remain sheer conjecture. Reasonably convincing
evidence exists only for a single form of distribution, exchanges between
patrons and clients.

Client Artisans of the Copán Elite Between 1980 and 1984 Randolph
Widmer excavated virtually all of the extensive elite compound 9N-8 at
Copán. Occupied for centuries, this compound reached its peak about
750–850 A.D., when it was presided over by a line of important Maya
lords with their own titles and emblems (as reflected in inscriptions and
art), who surrounded themselves with several hundred followers, probably
kinspeople and retainers. Among these were artisans who made elite
objects.

The obvious place to look for remains of craft activities is in the buildings, usually sturdy constructions of stone, where such activities presumably took place. Such buildings are well preserved at Copán, but interiors
generally lack artifacts, having been periodically swept clean before being
abandoned. As part of our general excavation of dozens of buildings in
9N-8, we discovered three that had suddenly collapsed, probably during
an earthquake. Buried beneath the debris of walls and roofs that filled the
rooms were many items used to make specialized objects. Str. 110B was
especially informative (Fig. 8.10). Evidence of specialization here comes
from room layout, artifacts, soil analysis, burials, and art.

Room layout Str. 110B has many of the general construction features of
a high-status elite house but is distinctive in its floor plan. In addition to

its large central room (room 1), it has three other rooms with restricted access (rooms 2, 3, and 4). Even without artifact remains, we would suspect that something special took place in this structure.

Artifacts Many artifacts indicating specialized activities were recovered from the floors and benches of the rooms in Str. 110B, especially room 2 (Fig. 8.11). These include ceramic vessels, obsidian blades, ground stone bowls and palettes, polishing tools of horn and antler, stones used for cutting and polishing, and both unworked and partially finished objects of imported marine shell. All lay where abandoned by the inhabitants of the building when the roof collapsed. This collection of items constitutes a tool kit, or subassemblage, used in the specialized activity of cutting and polishing shell and stone. Many of the tools show signs of cutting and polishing; edgewear analysis of the edges of the obsidian blades indicates that they were used mainly for sawing.

Soil analysis Many kinds of processes, both natural and cultural, destroy archaeological contexts. If people simply allowed debris to pile up in their homes and workplaces where it was produced, archaeologists would be gratified, but unfortunately, people periodically clean up after themselves, and larger debris is often carried off and disposed of at some distance from its original context. The Maya today sweep their houses frequently, just as the ancient Copán Maya seem to have done. Although the larger debris may be missing from residential sites tiny particles of it can never be entirely eliminated.

Soil samples from surfaces of floors and benches in Str. 110B were carefully recovered, then processed by flotation. Tiny particles of minerals and shell of many kinds were found in this soil, particularly in the patio in front of all three buildings. Apparently this debris was swept into the patio when the rooms were cleaned. Such concentrations of raw materials, which were not found in soil samples taken elsewhere in the patio, reflect specialized activities that took place in the adjacent buildings. Even if the roofs had not collapsed, preserving the artifacts, we would still infer the presence of specialized activities from the soil samples alone.

Burials Beneath room 2 was an immense, well-constructed tomb. It contained the remains of five people—four adult men and a child. The mortuary goods included a marine shell of the same kind that was being worked in the room above. Presumably these are burials of some of the artisans associated with the craft activity. The quality of their tomb and the residential architecture of the buildings, suggest that these were persons of considerable status in Copán society.

Art It is clear that the artisans made several products of shell and stone. Since the finished products were put to use, none was left in the buildings.

FIGURE 8.10 This building had extensive remains of a workshop sealed under its collapsed roof, especially in room 2. These are marked as separate features on the drawing.

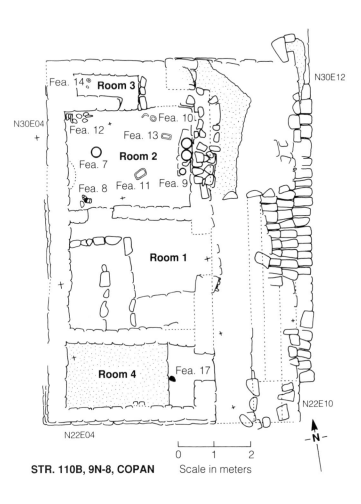

STR. 110B, 9N-8, COPAN

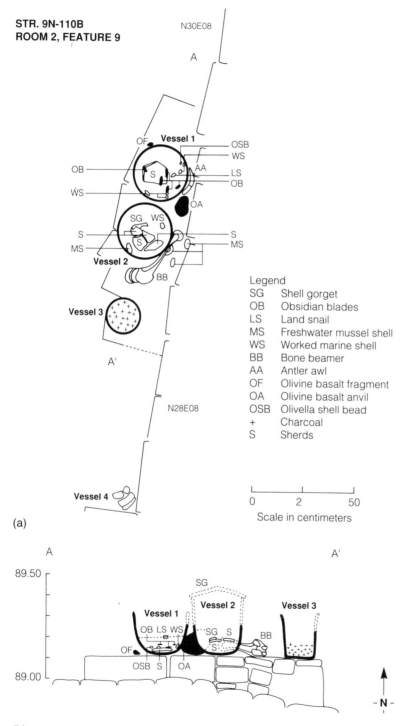

STR. 9N-110B
ROOM 2, FEATURE 9

N30E08

FIGURE 8.11 Workshop features associated with the bench in room 2, Structure 110B: (a) a plan; (b) a side view of the features.

Legend
SG   Shell gorget
OB   Obsidian blades
LS   Land snail
MS   Freshwater mussel shell
WS   Worked marine shell
BB   Bone beamer
AA   Antler awl
OF   Olivine basalt fragment
OA   Olivine basalt anvil
OSB Olivella shell bead
+   Charcoal
S   Sherds

0   2   50
Scale in centimeters

(a)

(b)   **STR. 9N-110B ROOM 2, FEATURE 9, Profile**

FIGURE 8.12 The inscribed front of a bench in a noble house in Plaza A, 9N-8, is rich with imagery suggesting that the noble may have been a scribe. The figures supporting the bench are "Pauah Tuns," associated with scribal functions, and are usually shown wearing flower-shaped shell pendants (see detail). Similar pendants were being crafted by artisans in Plaza H of the same compound; the drawing shows one of these (measuring about 7 cm across) recovered from that context. This was probably commissioned by the scribal lord to be worn by him.

But we did recover a broken, unfinished eight-pointed shell star from room 2 (Fig. 8.12). Shown as chest ornaments (gorgets) in Maya art, such stars are symbols of a class of minor Maya deities called "Pauah Tuns," who are in turn emblematic of the position of scribe in Classic Maya society.

Immediately to the north of the artisan buildings is a patio dominated by an elite building containing a hieroglyphic bench and covered with facade sculpture. This was the house of the principal lord of Compound 9N-8, who bore a scribal title and whose carved throne shows Pauah Tuns wearing star gorgets identical to the unfinished one from room 2.

The lines of evidence drawn thus far strongly suggest that the lord of 9N-8 had families of artisans attached to his household. These families were supplied with exotic raw materials, with which, at least in part, they produced objects associated with the elite symbolism of the lord's titles. We cannot know whether the artisans were full- or part-time specialists. On one hand, their houses and tombs suggest high status and probable independence of food-producing activities; possibly they were junior members of the lord's family. On the other hand, demand for their products would probably have been low. In any event, they were very likely clients of their elite patron — the lord of 9N-8.

This evidence of craft production and clientage was recovered during general room-clearing operations. As is so often the case in archaeology, luck played a large part in the find — the preservation of such unmistakable signs of specialized production could only be due to the fortuitous collapse of the buildings. Nonetheless, the archaeologist had to be able to recognize and capitalize on the opportunity at hand. Sometimes, as in the investigation of Tlajinga 33, El Duende, and Petapilla, research specifically designed to investigate specialization has paid off well. But opportune discovery of pertinent evidence can take place in the course of more generalized operations too, as at 9N-8, if the archaeologist is perceptive enough to take advantage of it. Both serendipity and conscious research design allowed us to recover enough information at Copán to show that it was less complex in terms of specialization and trade than Teotihuacán, and to suggest reasons for which this was so.

Comparing Teotihuacán and Copán

Our archaeological examples are at once encouraging and discouraging. On the plus side, we have been able to detect many basic patterns of trade and specialization both at Teotihuacán and Copán. Further work at these centers would lend the patterns even more detail and credibility.

Teotihuacán and Copán exhibit quite different patterns of specialization, trade, and exchange, as we predicted. On the basis of existing evidence, the domestic, highly self-sufficient, agriculturally based rural household seems to be the most important economic institution at Copán. Very few households show any obvious signs of specialization or appreciable access to items of long-distance trade, apart from obsidian. Specialized activities that we can investigate in some detail, such as obsidian trade and consumption, were organized on a smaller scale and more simply than we had originally expected. We are able to reject, at least for Copán, managerial hypotheses about the Maya obsidian trade. We can plausibly identify patterns of production and consumption of specialized goods but cannot make a clear case for full-time specialization.

All of this is in striking contrast to Teotihuacán, where most households in the city may have practiced at least part-time specialization and where the division of labor even within particular crafts was very highly developed. Teotihuacán trade was much more widespread and carried out on a larger scale than at Copán. An immense formal marketplace was probably present, and certainly mechanisms of distribution must have been better developed and more complex than at Copán, given the obviously greater economic independence of households. Our general evolutionary expectations are supported. Teotihuacán, with its enormous, largely urban population, had more complex economic institutions than Copán.

What is disappointing is our inability, at least on the basis of current evidence, to specify in detail what these institutions were like. This is especially true for institutions of distribution. Were there itinerant traders in the hills of Copán? Did the Petapilla metate makers take their goods to a Copán market and, if so, how did it differ from a huge urban market like that at Teotihuacán? Were professional merchants responsible for long-distance trade in Teotihuacán's manufactures? All of these questions and others remain unanswered. Future work may be able to resolve them, particularly if archaeologists bear in mind how useful the historic, ethno-historic, and ethnographic records are as sources of hypotheses and re-search design — and as constraints on fanciful or wishful interpretations of archaeological data.

POINTS TO REMEMBER

- A general evolutionary trend is toward more economic specialization and less self-sufficiency.

- Although data related to economic activity are commonly recovered from ar-chaeological contexts, specialization is often difficult to reconstruct.

- Specialization implies effective exchanges between individuals or groups.

- Specialization in nonindustrial societies evolves as a result of feedback between food producers and specialists, and stimulates the emergence of other institu-tions as well.

- Economic exchanges, involving production, distribution, and consumption, are conditioned by the available technology and transport facilities.

- Patterns of distribution are extremely difficult to reconstruct for the archaeologist.

- Urbanization is closely tied to the process of economic specialization.

- Great variation marks the economic specialization and urbanization of archaeo-logically known societies.

- Patterns of economic specialization, if reconstructed properly, provide effective barometers of cultural evolution.

FOR FURTHER READING*

For an excellent introduction to how economies work, read Heilbroner's *The Mak-ing of Economic Society*. Plattner's *Economic Anthropology* offers an overview. Texts applying economic principles to different modes of sociocultural integration are Sahlins's *Stone Age Economics*, Wolf's *Peasants*, and Polanyi, Arensberg, and Pearson's *Trade and Market in the Early Empires*. Fox's *Urban Anthropology* and Hassig's *Trade, Tribute, and Transportation* focus on complex societies.

*Full citations appear in the bibliography.

CHAPTER NINE

SIGNS AND SYMBOLS

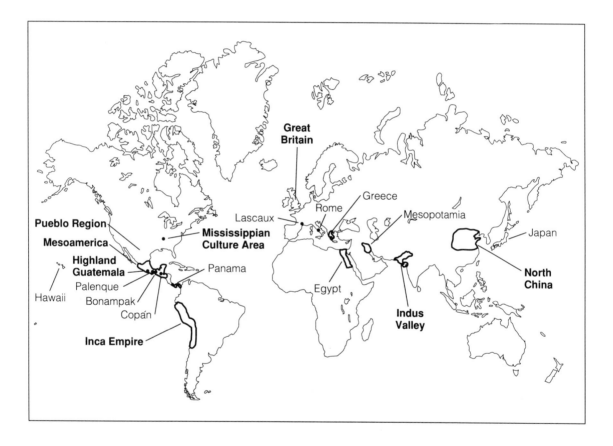

Symbolic communication is essential to culture; it is the basis for the most elemental cultural behavior — spoken language — as well as for writing. There are many other kinds of symbolic behavior as well, since symbols function on all of the levels of culture defined in Chapter 5: infrastructure, structure, and superstructure. In this chapter we will review the nature of symbols and symbolic systems, the evidence for them in the archaeological record, and how archaeologists approach the difficult problem of interpreting ancient symbols.

People are culturally conditioned to respond powerfully (and often unconsciously and irrationally) to symbols, even those that they do not fully understand. This is one of the reasons why archaeologists have traditionally been so fascinated with the symbols associated with ancient civilizations and their Great Traditions, which are aesthetically impressive and rich in meaning (Fig. 9.1). These symbols may contain very precise and condensed information invaluable for reconstructing the past. But many symbolic systems, though recoverable from the archaeological record and undoubtedly meaningful, are extremely difficult to interpret. Fortunately, as we will see, we can often make inferences about a society on the basis of its use of symbols even if we cannot determine their specific meanings.

SIGNS OR SYMBOLS?

Transmitting information is essential to all forms of life (Dawkins 1986). At the most basic level, genetic information is passed from one individual to another, but most organisms obviously transmit information in more immediate ways as well. The cry of a hungry baby, the snarl of a frightened dog, the mating song of a bird — each has a special meaning (fear, rage, sexual availability) and each may be conveyed in many ways, such as through visual cues, touch, posture, sound, or smell. The innately understood meanings of these **signs** form the basis for successful social behavior. All share one other distinguishing characteristic — the sign and what it means are linked for all members of the species. Because hungry babies and frightened dogs sound much the same the world over, recognizing the meaning of their verbal signs needs no enculturation.

People communicate on many levels with signs of all sorts, whether we are conscious of it or not. But more characteristic of human communication is the use of **symbols**. By symbols we mean expressions that are abstractions *arbitrarily* associated with what they convey (Fig. 9.2). Take, for example, the concept of numbers one through five. The numbers themselves are very simple concepts, shared by most or all humans, regardless of their cultures. Yet they are expressed linguistically in very different ways, as verbal symbols arbitrarily associated with meaning, and this is the essence of all symbolic language systems (spoken, written, mathematical, musical, ritual, etc.).

sign Innately understood signal to which meaning is attached in a nonarbitrary way.

symbol Expression which is arbitrarily associated with what it conveys.

(a)

(b)

(c)

(d)

(e)

(f)

FIGURE 9.1 Great Tradition symbols and their imagery are very distinctive from one civilization to another: (a) Mesopotamia, (b) Egypt, (c) Indus Valley, (d) China, (e) Peru, (f) Mesoamerica.

(a)

(b)

FIGURE 9.2 The difference between signs and symbols is demonstrated by these two road markers. At the top (a) is a *sign:* it expresses unambiguously and universally the idea that children are present. The bottom marker (b) functions as a "symbol," both in the linguistic abstraction "STOP" and in our learned association of red with danger.

Some symbols are purely personal; things and words take on special meanings from our experiences as individuals. However, in this discussion our focus is on symbols with shared cultural meaning. We learn spoken languages or other symbolic systems as part of the enculturation process, but very seldom, as individuals, do we invent symbols that become widely used. Symbolic systems change gradually. The words *laser* and *xerox* would have had no meaning for our great grandparents but are now part of the English vocabulary. In our lifetimes new countries have devised flags to symbolize their sovereignty, and new political parties create symbols to distinguish themselves from others. Like signs, symbols may be expressed in many forms—figures, sounds, colors, motions, smells, and so forth. But because they have in common the arbitrary association of form and meaning, all must be learned. We all may cry at birth, but we must learn to talk, to write, and to use many other systems of symbols as well.

Because symbols are so pervasive and so saturated with cultural meaning, they are a major concern of archaeologists (Hodder 1982a). As we shall see below, there are two main problems in dealing with ancient symbolic systems. First, many kinds of symbolic behavior leave no direct traces. They were not, nor were they meant to be, durable. Second, even if more or less complete sets of symbols can be recovered, it is often difficult to decode their meanings. One difficulty is precisely the arbitrary relationship of the symbol itself with what it means. Another is that the archaeologist is not a member of the culture in question and may have few informed insights into symbolic meaning. Understanding the overall archaeological context of recovered symbolic information can be essential in reconstructing meaning. When properly understood, ancient symbolic systems offer unparalleled information about ancient cultures. When their meanings elude us, symbols are the most baffling elements of the archaeological record.

FUNCTIONS OF SYMBOLS

Symbolic systems serve many functions in human cultures. The most general are to communicate, manipulate, and store information.

Infrastructural Functions of Symbols

Throughout our lives we constantly communicate, manipulate, and store symbols in mundane, utilitarian ways: in keeping records, sending messages, attempting to influence other people, and projecting images of ourselves. The evolutionary history of our species demonstrates selection for effective symbolic behavior, which is understandable since symbolic communication increases our chance for survival by letting us more successfully exploit our environments. Many anthropologists believe, for example, that language helped early humans cooperate effectively as hunters and foragers.

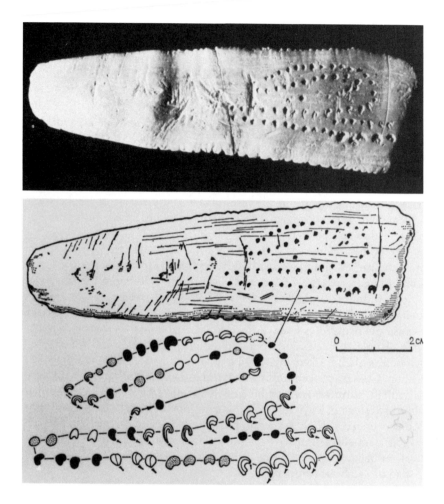

FIGURE 9.3 Alexander Marshack believes that sets of marks made on bones or other objects by people in Upper Paleolithic Europe may represent counting or tallying devices that keep track of elapsed days, months, or other numerical information.

Some of the earliest direct evidence of symbolic systems comes from European archaeological sites 15–30,000 years old (although humans clearly had language and other forms of symbolic behavior much earlier than that, we seldom find evidence of them). Alexander Marshack (1972a, 1972b) believes that marks on cave walls or bone objects represent tallies — devices to record counts of things, such as the passage of units of time. If Marshack is correct, this is a very early utilitarian use of symbols to store information (Fig. 9.3).

For over a century scholars have sought the meaning of Late Paleolithic "cave art," which depicts animals, humans, and sometimes abstract designs in the form of modeled, carved, or painted images on cave walls and portable objects (Leroi-Gourhan 1968a, 1968b). Early interpretations linked such images to rituals of hunting magic. More recently, they have been interpreted by structuralists as symbolizing fertility and death, male-ness and femaleness (Watson and Fotiadis 1990). Either or both of these interpretations (as well as others) remains plausible, showing how difficult it is to decipher the meaning of graphic images when the larger cultural context is poorly understood.

The earliest writing system known appears in Sumerian culture of the Mesopotamian region of the Middle East (in what is now Iraq and Iran) shortly before 3000 B.C. (Redman 1978). This early script, called Sumer-ian, seems to have functioned primarily to keep track of economic produc-tion and redistribution. This is a classic infrastructural use of symbols; they store, communicate, and manipulate information about how resources ex-tracted from the environment were produced, moved through the social system, and were consumed and written. Mathematical symbols are still used for these purposes today.

The Sumerians wrote by inscribing a tablet of wet clay with a stylus; even the earliest examples are highly developed, so its antecedents were sought in earlier forms of symbols. These were possibly in the small clay objects thought to serve as tokens (Fig. 9.4) found in Middle Eastern archaeological sites for about 4,000 years before the first writing appears. Denise Schmandt-Besserat (1978) hypothesizes that these objects, with their distinctive shapes and inscribed designs, were parts of a widely used symbolic system for keeping, storing, and communicating economic infor-mation. Classes of tokens represented things of economic importance, such as animals, garments, or ceramic vessels. By increasing or decreasing their numbers, storing, or transporting them (often in clay "envelopes"), ac-counts were kept. Early Sumerian pictographs incised on clay tablets often exhibit symbolism similar to that associated with the tokens. Schmandt-Besserat believes that the forms of the pictographs evolved from the earlier system of symbolic counters.

Structural Functions of Symbols

On the structural level of culture, one of the most powerful functions of symbols is to communicate social relationships, roles, and statuses. Cloth-ing is a clear example in many complex cultures. Uniforms serve both to symbolize a group, past and present (police, army, religious order, medical worker), and the express function of that group. In some cultures, many communities or even whole societies have distinctive modes of dress which identify their members. Women in Maya Indian communities in highland Guatemala, for example, are identifiable by their distinctive costumes, each characteristic of a particular town or region. Other uniforms serve to dis-tinguish members of different sexes, ages, or occupations, or to express a particular social role (e.g., bride, college graduate, Eagle Scout).

Symbols function differently in societies with different types of socio-cultural integration (Chapter 3). An important function of symbols in hierarchical societies, and one useful to the archaeologist, is to differentiate

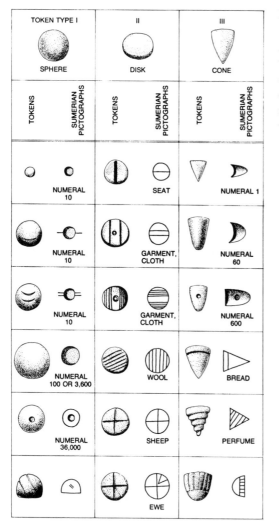

FIGURE 9.4 Denise Schmandt-Besserat believes that in Mesopotamia tokens on the left, used as simple recording devices, eventually evolved into the formal written symbols on the right.

individuals or groups in terms of power, authority, prestige, and wealth. These *status symbols* express rank and dominance. People in our own society go to great lengths to acquire and display houses, clothing, automobiles, college diplomas, or more intangible things such as proper speech or manners, in order to compete with others for recognition, and to signal their level of social position (or what they would like others to think it is). Significantly, status symbols need not have meaning in their own right — their distribution (who has them) confers their meaning — a characteristic with important implications for interpreting the archaeological record. Because tangible remains of status symbols often are preserved, they provide clues about the nature of social and political structures in past societies.

In our society status symbols primarily relate to differences in wealth, since power is derived from wealth, and most goods or services may be freely acquired by anyone who can afford to purchase them. The sociologist Thorstein Veblen (1953) called the use of such purchased symbols "conspicuous consumption." In many traditional societies, however, status symbols were confined by custom or law to particular subgroups. In India only members of the highest castes could wear a sacred string. Among the Incas, members of royal lineages were instantly identifiable by their immense earrings. Until the middle of the 19th century in Japan, only members of the dominant military class (samurai) were allowed to carry two swords. In Hawaii, only the ruler could be carried on a litter, a symbol of his political and supernatural authority and power.

Less tangible but equally effective are the patterns of speech and manners that further distinguish social classes from one another and signal relationships between people who are not equals, enhancing solidarity among those who share the same statuses.

Social or political symbols are not merely static reflections of human relationships; they may be manipulated very dynamically to reflect or promote changes in such relationships. For example, in the evolution of political systems in ancient Mesoamerica, rulers sometimes adopted new sets of symbols, or attached new meanings to old symbols, in order to enhance their political positions (see below). When the United States became independent of Great Britain, new political symbols emerged (for example, the flag) and old ones (crowns, judges in powdered wigs) were rejected. The new set of symbols reflects both independence itself and the change from a monarchical to a republican form of government. In fact, the conscious use of emotionally powerful new symbols is an important element in social and cultural changes of all sorts, as any politician knows.

Superstructural Functions of Symbols

Perhaps the most psychologically powerful symbols are those identified with *ideology*. As we saw in Chapter 1, a culture's ideology is its belief system, behavioral values, the place of people in the world, and their relationship with the supernatural. Ideology encompasses **sacred** beliefs, as opposed to **profane,** everyday matters; the former are so fundamental to our cultural behavior, and so ingrained and valued, that we seldom even reflect on them, much less question them. Symbols of ideology function to communicate shared sacred beliefs and values and thereby promote stability in cultural systems. Those who challenge sacred beliefs are rebels and iconoclasts, who threaten stability.

Rituals play important symbolic roles in all societies. Two important kinds of ritual are **rites of passage** and **rites of intensification** (Gennep 1960). Rites of passage symbolically communicate transitions in lives of individuals and their changed relationships to others (e.g., birth, marriage, and death) (Fig. 9.5). Rites of intensification communicate group concerns

sacred Pertaining to beliefs or propositions so valued that they are unquestioned.

profane Pertaining to everyday matters.

rite of passage Ritual symbolizing a transition in the life of an individual and his or her altered relationships to others.

rite of intensification Ritual that symbolizes group concerns and solidarity, especially at critical times.

FIGURE 9.5   Rituals themselves are not directly preservable, but their material residues often are. Sometimes they are recorded in durable form for the archaeologist to find. Carving on this Roman tombstone shows a funeral, a rite of passage.

and solidarity (e.g., communal religious or political rituals). We will discuss these in greater detail in Chapter 12.

Sacred religious symbols are expressed in many ways, particularly through art and ritual. Great changes in religious ideology, such as the spread of Christianity or of Islam, were accompanied by the emergence of new artistic symbols and rituals, which served to distinguish converts from heretics and to educate people about proper beliefs and behavior. So potent are religious symbols that they are sometimes thought to have supernatural power in their own right, quite apart from their meanings. Thus the cross is thought to ward off evil, and some Moslems who cannot read wear passages from the Koran — written symbols — in amulets for the same purpose. These symbols are magical objects to their users.

We automatically associate sacred things with religion; although this is part of ideology, social, political, and economic beliefs may also form part of a culture's ideology (Box 9.1). For example, in our society the rights to vote and to own private property are sacred, and for many, so is the right to own a gun. Because feelings about such sacred political, social, or economic postulates are often as intense as religious feelings, the symbols associated with them, such as the flag, are correspondingly powerful. Complex feedback relationships operate among infrastructural, structural, and superstructural functions of symbols. Thus the sacred symbol of the flag (superstructure) facilitates military organization (structure), which in turn is supposed to safeguard lives and resources (infrastructure).

BOX 9.1

SYMBOLS OF THE SOUTHEASTERN CEREMONIAL COMPLEX

How do we interpret the symbolic meaning of images in archaeological cultures lacking writing?

Strange and complex images appear on artifacts from major Mississippian culture sites, the capitals of chiefdoms in south-central and southeastern North America, dating from about A.D. 1000–1450. The images, which are part of what has come to be known as the Southeastern Ceremonial Complex, include an eye (probably of a falcon), an upraised human palm, snakes, panthers, a crosslike motif, human skulls and decapitated heads, and warriors in elaborate costumes. The figure at right shows a stone disk that combines several of these images.

It was once thought that this complex iconography was the product of a widespread religious cult, but more recent interpretations suggest that these artifacts symbolized the social and political status of prominent groups or individuals, and some may even have been insignia of office. This hypothesis is substantiated by

the contexts of some artifacts; objects recovered from impressive burials or large temple structures have the most elaborate symbolism. Another clue is that these objects are often made from costly exotic materials, such as mica, copper, or shell, and are of fine workmanship. But even in sites without temples or elaborate burials, some of the images appear on ceramic vessels or other common items in everyday use, so they seem to have broader mythological or ritual significance than serving only as political symbols.

Clearly, the symbols played important roles in the lives of the people who used them. But can we "decipher" them in the same sense that we can decipher Egyptian or Maya symbols? On a descriptive level their significance—as hands, eyes, snakes, skulls—is clear because they are rendered very realistically. Ethnohistory also provides some clues. A few Southeastern Ceremonial Complex traditions were preserved by Native Americans into the 16th and 17th centuries, and Eu-

---

Recreational Functions

Symbols also provide pleasure and recreation. One very well-developed symbolic system in our society—the system of musical notation—is used to compose music, which plays most directly on our emotions and feelings. Some systems of symbols are specific to games (chess, for example), whereas other games use writing and mathematical symbols. In addition to conveying useful information, the written word is a source of recreation, as every fan of fiction knows.

TYPES OF SYMBOLIC SYSTEMS

symbolic systems Sets of symbols that mutually reinforce each other and that are used in combination to convey meaning.

Symbols often occur in sets and mutually reinforce each other; such sets are known as **symbolic systems**. Symbolic systems can be broken down into types according to how they are expressed and their important functions.

ropeans wrote accounts documenting the social, political, and mythological significance of some of the symbols. It is generally agreed that the complex relates to beliefs and practices associated with rulership, ancestral cults of the elite, war, death, and fertility.

The archaeologist James Brown (1975) believes that one set of images associated with sacred ancestors was exclusive to the elite and manipulated by them for po-

litical purposes. War and military symbols were more widely available and displayed by individuals who acquired social prestige and advancement through prowess in battle. Finally, some images such as the serpent, the panther, and those connected with the fertility cults were widely used by common people. If this reconstruction is correct, the Mississippian chiefdoms of southeastern North America had Big Tradition and Little Tradition elements similar to those of ancient states.

Unfortunately, we may never have highly specific and detailed insights into their cognized meaning. Unlike Egyptian or Maya symbols, Southeastern Ceremonial Complex symbols were not accompanied by a well-developed and decipherable system of writing. Furthermore, between about A.D. 1500 and 1650 Native American peoples of the southeast experienced severe social, political, and demographic disruption, and as a consequence it is difficult to apply the direct historical approach, although some meanings are preserved in the ethnohistoric record. In spite of these difficulties, our understanding of Southeastern Ceremonial Complex objects and symbols should improve as more sites are carefully excavated, yielding larger samples of materials in their original context.

Spoken Language

Spoken language is the principal nonbiological means by which humans everywhere, and in all times, have communicated, manipulated, and stored information. Spoken language is not confined to the meanings of words but forms the basis for all other symbolic systems. Language is an important defining characteristic of social and ethnic identity. Patterns of language, including vocabulary and pronunciation, are status symbols, as we noted previously.

In nonliterate societies, spoken language is the principal mode of transmitting information from one generation to another, which maintains cultural continuity and reinforces cultural tradition (Murra and Morris 1976). Literate societies also maintain such practices; familiar examples include learning national anthems in school. But where maintaining the cultural heritage depends on memorization of spoken language, there may be highly specialized or institutionalized ways of transmitting such information to ensure accuracy over time. In the European preliterate tradition, poets and bards transmitted information from one generation to the next, using oral songs or recitations. This tradition survives in many parts of the world, such as Africa.

Unfortunately, spoken language as a symbolic system is not recoverable by the archaeologist; hence it is of limited use to us in reconstructing the past. But language is sometimes expressed in another symbolic system, writing, which may be of great value.

Writing

Writing is a set of graphic symbols, related directly or indirectly to a particular spoken language and "read"—transformed into actual speech. However, writing is a late innovation in human culture. Although effective writing systems were invented independently in several parts of the world, their appearance is so late, and the spread of literacy so slow, that most human societies that have ever existed are in effect prehistoric. Most archaeologists are thus faced with the task of reconstructing societies that lack anything we could properly call history; for this reason many call themselves "prehistorians."

The earliest known writing systems appeared in Mesopotamia and Egypt just over 5,000 years ago (Redman 1978). By 2000–1500 B.C., writing was also present in China, India, and the eastern Mediterranean, thereafter spreading to much of the rest of the Old World. In the New World, systems of writing emerged later and were confined to Mesoamerica prior to European contact (Benson 1971). Early forms may have been present in the southern highlands and on the Gulf Coast of Mexico by 500–600 B.C., and were elaborated to the highest degree by the Classic Maya of southern Mesoamerica about A.D. 300–900.

History, Prehistory, and the Written Record Reconstruction of the past on the basis of written documents or texts is what we call *history*. Such documents include anything that, set down in writing, can inform us about what happened in the past.

The word **prehistoric** literally means "before writing" but is not always used in that sense by archaeologists (Daniel and Renfrew 1988), who would apply it in the following situations. Some literate societies left behind writing we cannot yet decipher. Other ancient writing can be read, but very few texts have survived (the Maya). Sometimes abundant and decipherable texts are available, but these are very narrow in subject matter (e.g., early Sumerian texts, which are almost exclusively concerned with economic matters). Perhaps the best way to think about the word *prehistoric* is to ask the question "How much do we know about an ancient culture from written records?" If the answer is "Very little," that culture may be properly regarded as prehistoric, or perhaps more accurately, nonhistoric.

Writing is generally associated with complex, hierarchically structured societies, in particular, civilizations. V. Gordon Childe (1950) hypothesized that writing was an essential defining feature of civilizations, but many

prehistoric Generally refers to societies that lacked writing but also can refer to societies about which the written record is largely uninformative.

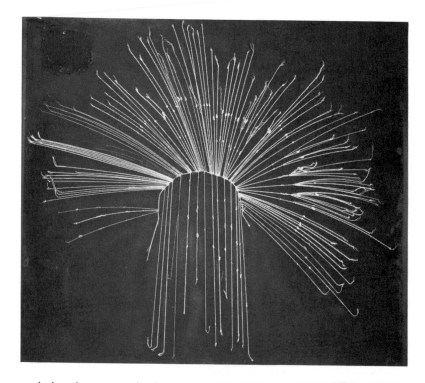

FIGURE 9.6 The Inca, as well as earlier cultures in Peru, used arrangements of colored and knotted cords called "quipus" to keep track of many kinds of information essential to political and economic administration. Unfortunately the last quipu "readers" died in the 16th century, so we are not sure how to decipher the many surviving quipus.

societies that were clearly states or civilizations in terms of social and political structure lacked writing altogether. For example, in the 15th and early 16th centuries the Incas of northwestern South America created the largest and most complex empire ever known in the New World (and one of the largest in the world at that time), but they lacked writing entirely, as did many of the great precolonial era kingdoms of Africa. This is not to say that these societies lacked the means to keep records. The Inca used elaborately knotted and colored cords called **quipus** (KEEpoohs) to record information essential to the administration of their empire (Fig. 9.6), and the Ashanti of west Africa kept track of such things as taxes by using boxes of stones. In other complex societies, such as the elaborate chiefdoms of Polynesia, oral traditions about religion, past events, and royal genealogies were maintained by professionals who committed information to memory, recited it, and passed it on with great accuracy. The point is that there is no necessary connection between complex sociopolitical organization and the presence of writing as a cultural feature, at least in nonindustrial societies.

Some societies lacking written records were documented by adjacent literate societies. The Japanese did not use writing until the sixth century A.D., but long before that they had been in contact with nearby China, one of the oldest literate civilizations (Reischauer and Fairbank 1960). The first records concerning Japan were compiled by Chinese officials and travelers. Similarly, the Greek historian Herodotus left accounts of nonliterate people such as the Scythians in the fifth century B.C.

quipu Record keeping device of the Incas, consisting of patterns of knots on a set of strings.

FIGURE 9.7   Like Figure 9.3a, the image here at the top realistically portrays its meaning and is thus a "sign" and a pictograph. Ancient Mesopotamians graphically represented water in much the same way, as a set of wavy lines. The person who designed the highway sign probably never saw Sumerian writing. Many pictographs have been independently invented, because they make such intuitive sense.

pictograph   Element of a type of writing in which symbols depict directly and in reasonably realistic form what they are meant to convey.

Literacy and Its Implications for History   In most modern societies great value is placed on literacy. General education aims to make literacy widespread, and illiteracy is seen as an unfortunate handicap limiting access to important information, thus adversely affecting ability to function in society. Our cultural belief system holds that everyone should be given the opportunity to learn to read and write, and the ability to do so should not be an elite status symbol.

In most literate nonindustrial societies, however, writing was used for very limited purposes, and literacy was confined to very small numbers of people. Sometimes, as in the case of China, this was because the writing system was so cumbersome and difficult to learn that only privileged people could afford the necessary education. Literate people were, almost by definition, members of an elite. As the avenue to the economic security and prestige of an official bureaucratic position, literacy became a potent and visible status symbol.

We do not know if the earliest kings or nobles of Sumer or Egypt could write, but certainly they surrounded themselves with professional scribes. In early medieval Europe kings and nobels often were illiterate, regarding literacy as a technical utilitarian skill best left to their lower-ranking officials. Often these scribes or officials were people of fairly humble origins, whose literacy made them essential to elites. Nonetheless reading and writing were essentially elite prerogatives, whether the elites were themselves literate or made use of literate retainers.

The limited extent of literacy has important implications for reconstructing the history of nonindustrial civilizations. Most of the stored and communicated information reflects elite perspectives and was often manipulated for elite purposes. In addition to inadvertent errors, sometimes ancient historical accounts include deliberate falsehoods — in short, they are propaganda. Nonindustrial rulers and nobles used writing as a tool to establish or enlarge their own power. Thus, ancient documents and inscriptions (even if we decipher them correctly) provide only a partial basis for reconstructing ancient societies.

Forms of Writing Systems   We saw earlier that writing systems are sets of symbols related directly or indirectly to spoken language. But there are many kinds of symbols for speech. Ideally, a writing system should be easy to learn, flexible, comprehensive in expression, and unambiguous in meaning. The forms reviewed below vary considerably in their ability to do these things (Houston 1988, 1989).

A **pictograph** is simply a realistic representation, often conventionalized, of the meaning of something, thus a visual "sign," according to the definition given at the beginning of this chapter. The picture of a dog represents a dog — it stimulates one to think of the concept "dog." Some of the earliest writing is pictographic; for example, in early Sumerian, water was symbolized by wavy lines which indicated waves (Fig. 9.7). There are two serious drawbacks to pictographic writing: (1) many symbols are

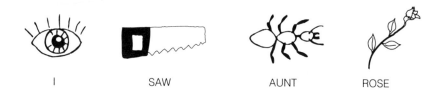

| | SAW | AUNT | ROSE |

FIGURE 9.8 We all toyed with rebus writing as children. In rebus writing a symbol indicates a part of speech that is visually suggested.

needed, and (2) abstract concepts cannot be easily expressed. Even if only "things" (nouns) were represented, there would be thousands of pictographs, but what about verbs or adjectives? And abstractions, like "love" or "peace"?

In **rebus writing** pictographs indicate another part of speech than what is visually suggested. As a pure pictograph, in English, an eye would refer to the bodily organ. But in rebus writing, the image might represent the first-person pronoun *I*, which has the same sound, or perhaps the verb *to see*, and the intended meaning would be gotten from the context of the image or by a determinative symbol. Some reasonably complex "sentences" may be constructed using rebus writing (Fig. 9.8).

An **ideograph** is another refinement of pictographic writing; it is simply a symbol conveying an idea, but the symbol does not necessarily resemble what it conveys. For example, in Aztec writing the feather indicated the number 400 (Fig. 9.9a). Since the association between an ideograph's structure and meaning is highly arbitrary, one can create ideographs for any concepts one might wish to express in speech, but (as with pictographs) one needs many ideographs to create a writing system; to read a Chinese newspaper requires knowledge of about 3,000 symbols. In pictographic or ideographic writing, the meaning of a symbol is not directly tied to how it is pronounced when read; in effect, one must "decode" pictographic or ideographic writing into speech.

Logographs are abstract written symbols tht correspond to actual spoken words (Fig. 9.10). The correspondence is not (as in pictographs) necessarily based on any resemblance between the symbol and what is meant. We can invent logographic symbols arbitrarily: We could say, for example, that a triangle would always mean the word *cat*, a square the word *fly*, and so on. Logographs are a considerable advance over pictographs, because all words or meaningful parts of speech, whether nouns, verbs, articles, adjectives, and so forth, can be unambiguously represented. Abstractions present no problem; one does not have to draw a picture of "love," but can directly signal the word, for example with a heart-shaped symbol, as in "I ♥ New York." Note that the heart as an *ideograph* could mean the internal organ itself or any arbitrary concept, but as a *logograph* in this sentence, it means "love." Still, anyone with a decent vocabulary would have to learn at least hundreds, and perhaps thousands, of logographs in order to read and write effectively.

rebus writing Drawings of objects which may indicate another part of speech than what is visually suggested.

ideograph Symbol conveying an idea without resembling what it conveys.

logograph Abstract written symbol that corresponds to actual spoken words.

(a)

20

400

8000

FIGURE 9.9 Above (a) are three Aztec ideographs for the numbers 20, 400, and 8,000. They can be seen in use in the tribute records shown in (b). This page from the Codex Mendoza lists various goods, among them, 1,200 woven blankets in three styles (top). The number symbols have no intuitively obvious connection with the concepts they convey.

(b)

Phonetic symbols represent sounds. These are efficient because the numbers of basic sounds in any language (unlike, say, the number of individual words) is very limited: No language uses more than about 50. English uses only 26 such symbols, which form an alphabet. Alphabetic symbols for phonemes are combined to make syllables and then words. Alphabets were

(a)

(b)

FIGURE 9.10 Maya logographs and alternative syllabic representations of the same word: (a) on the left is the logograph for the sound "ahaw," which means "lord"; on the right is the syllabic spelling; (b) the sound "pacal," which means "shield" is on the left, with its syllabic equivalent on the right.

first invented around 1500 B.C. in the eastern Mediterranean and have since become the basis for most written languages. Because they are easy to learn, they encourage widespread literacy.

In summary, most nonphonetic forms of writing combine pictographic, ideographic, and logographic symbols. Although the evolution of written language may have followed a rough progression in the order described above, a number of highly sophisticated modern scripts such as Chinese have remained nonalphabetic.

Deciphering Ancient Scripts The key to the decipherment of ancient Egyptian writing was the Rosetta Stone, which has the same text inscribed in three writing systems—Greek and two forms of ancient Egyptian (Hobson 1987). Because the Greek portion could be read, the Egyptian segments could be deciphered, even though they were written in a dead language using a nonalphabetic writing system.

The Rosetta Stone was recovered by Napoleon's troops in Egypt in 1799 and studied by many *epigraphers* (scholars specializing in decipherment of writing). Thomas Young showed that cartouches enclosed the names of rulers; he also realized that Egyptian hieroglyphic writing was in part

FIGURE 9.11 Two cartouches enclose the hieroglyphs spelling out the names of Ptolemy and Cleopatra in the Rosetta Stone. The location of hieroglyphs common to both names provided the clues to the phonetic expression of these elements.

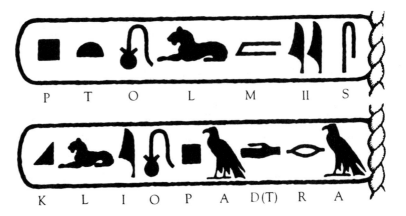

P   T   O   L   M   II   S

K   L   I   O   P   A   D(T)   R   A

alphabetic, not merely pictographic. Jean Francois Champollion demonstrated in 1822 the phonetic value of Egyptian written symbols, and through this work we are now able to read Egyptian texts (Fig. 9.11).

Unfortunately, some ancient writing systems still resist decipherment for many reasons. The ancient script of the Indus Valley (used in approximately 2400–1900 B.C.) is not deciphered, and the Indus texts themselves are few in number and very short, so linguists have little to work with (Allchin and Allchin 1982). The same is true of Linear A writing, used in the eastern Mediterranean between about 2000–1500 B.C. (Fig. 9.12a).

Even when we translate an ancient inscription into something comprehensible in our own language, much of the meaning escapes us. For example, the Classic Maya used the word *sahal* as a title to refer to people who occupied certain very important political offices below the rank of ruler. Yet neither the word itself, nor its context in inscriptions tells us exactly what the offices were, how *sahals* were recruited, or what they did.

Etiquette: Behavioral Symbols

All societies have systems of behavior expressing the proprieties of social conduct: etiquette. As we become enculturated we learn that there are "proper" ways to behave (or not to behave) in social circumstances. Although mannered behavior becomes so much a reflex that we seldom are conscious of it, it is highly arbitrary and symbolic, communicating to others that we are acceptable individuals in terms of culturally valued forms of interaction.

Imagery and Art

Another extremely important set of symbols is expressed graphically in painting, sculpture, and architecture (as distinguished from literary art

(a)

(b)

FIGURE 9.12 Some writing systems remain undeciphered. These include (a) Linear A, an eastern Mediterranean script, and (b) Harappan script from the Indus Valley.

such as poetry or literature or performing arts such as music or theater). For convenience, we will simply refer to these graphic representations as "art," recognizing that many graphic images have important sociopolitical and ideological functions and are not simply exercises in aesthetics. Analysis of the sets of patterns and images which characterize a particular artistic tradition is called *iconography* (Chapter 1). Most cultures produce many kinds of artistic representations. Some of them may be purely decorative and devoid of meaning, but others contain highly complex symbolism.

Understanding the meaning and function of images as symbols requires much familiarity with the general cultural background of the society. Take, for example, one of the most familiar pieces of public art (a real icon) in the United States, the Statue of Liberty. When most Americans (and many foreigners) see it, the symbolism and the associated emotions are more important than the aesthetic value of the statue. But the meanings of freedom, opportunity, equality, and security are indirectly connected with the physical image. To someone unfamiliar with Western culture and history, the statue conveys no symbolic meaning. The meanings inherent in a set of artistic images constitute a "language" in their own right, but one not expressed by writing—one difficult to decode by the unenculturated.

Archaeologists are outsiders to the systems they investigate, so we face two difficulties in interpreting graphic symbolic meaning. First, we must decide whether images are meaningful symbols at all; second, we must ascribe meaning to symbols and substantiate the interpretation.

Art may convey powerful status symbols even in egalitarian foraging societies. In Native Australian societies only adult men were initiated into the meanings of certain tribal symbols displayed on sacred objects, which

FIGURE 9.13 It was conventional in Egyptian art to show rulers larger than other people, to indicate their relative importance.

were jealously hidden from children and particularly from women. Such knowledge served to emphasize differences in status based on age and sex.

Artistic status symbols operate most powerfully in hierarchical societies. Chiefs or kings may wear on their persons the artistic products of elite craftspeople, such as jewelry and costumes, replete with political symbolism, which articles may be reserved to them by custom or law (anthropologists call such display of symbols "sumptuary behavior"). They may commission public art that glorifies them by means of important symbols. Egyptian rulers had themselves portrayed as physically larger than lesser folk in their paintings and carvings, thus asserting social dominance (Fig. 9.13). People of high rank may jealously guard access to the possession or meaning of artistic symbols, thus setting themselves off against lesser people. The various grades of the Aztec nobility were assigned symbolic forms of dress and bodily adornment which clearly signaled their respective ranks and were strictly forbidden to others. The chiefs of traditional societies in Panama owed much of their authority to the possession of secret languages, rituals, or more tangible symbols acquired from distant places (Helms 1979). Powerful people may commission palaces, religious buildings, or other public projects which symbolize their ability to mobilize labor and expend wealth. Many of these status symbols are fortunately preserved in the archaeological record.

FIGURE 9.14 This massive Aztec monument was commissioned by King Tizoc of Tenochtitlan to commemorate his purported victories. Here, the impressiveness of the monument bears no relation to reality, since we know from ethnohistoric sources that Tizoc was a weak military leader, assassinated after a few years in power by more militant Aztec nobles. But if we had only Tizoc's propagandistic monument for evidence, we might have misinterpreted his military prowess.

As with writing, art can be used as propaganda to deceive or mislead. One of the most important Aztec sculptures is the Tizoc stone, so-called because it was commissioned in the late 15th century A.D. by an Aztec ruler of that name. The iconography of the stone celebrates Tizoc's military prowess, something highly valued among Aztec rulers. We know from other sources that in fact Tizoc was a weak ruler with little military talent, who was probably assassinated for his ineptitude. He apparently hoped the monument would create the opposite impression among his subjects; if we lacked alternative sources of information, his deception might have fooled us as well (Fig. 9.14).

Ritual

Ritual behavior characterizes many animals and all human societies. In its broadest sense, ritual consists of "conventional acts of display through which one or more participants transmit information concerning their physiological, psychological, or sociological status" (Rappaport 1971c:25).

Rituals may be of many kinds—individual or collective, public or private, religious or secular—and serve numerous functions (Rappaport 1971b). Many rituals are linked directly to the infrastructure, such as ceremonies associated with the agricultural cycle. In the American Southwest, Puebloan community rituals are designed to propitiate the rain gods, essential for crops (Fig. 9.15). In foraging societies elaborate rituals symbolize the dependence of hunters on prey, to ensure that prey animals remain obtainable.

On the structural level rituals indicate who is part of the group and who is not, as well as the relationships of the respective participants; they thus

FIGURE 9.15 Costumed dancers at Hopi villages in the U.S. Southwest represent kachinas who are the bringers of the gentle rain. In this harsh arid climate, rituals to bring rain are deemed essential. Shown here is a carved figure representing a Kachina.

reinforce relationships and can be used as status symbols. Rituals indicate transitions in the lives of individuals or groups.

A great deal of ritual relates to ideology (superstructure), reaffirming sacred propositions and reinforcing values. Religious rituals are virtually universal in human societies. In fact, so obtrusive are they that archaeologists tend to overemphasize the religious importance of traces of ritual behavior they recover from the archaeological record, forgetting that ritual operates on many levels.

enculturation The process of learning whereby an individual acquires the beliefs, customs, values, and behaviors appropriate to a specific culture.

One of the most potent functions of ritual is **enculturation**—education about and indoctrination into belief systems. The role of ritual in fulfilling this function is especially important in nonliterate societies. Children who take part in rituals are enculturated to the meanings behind sounds, smells, colors, and motions. Rituals in a sense store up information about the cultural tradition, the nature of the world, and the place and proper behavior of people in it. This information is transmitted and periodically reinforced through the repetition of certain rituals.

Mathematics, Music, and Games

Notational systems also exist in many cultures to symbolize mathematical concepts, music, and games. Mathematical symbols, which serve the same functions as other symbolic systems, are particularly useful for such infrastructural utilitarian purposes as accounting and engineering. They may also be used to keep track of periods or cycles of time; such calendrical systems often have religious or mystical implications as well as practical ones, as we shall shortly see in the case of the Classic Maya. Calendrical symbols are of particular importance to the archaeologist, since they help sort out chronological context.

Decipherment of Symbolic Systems

There are many kinds of symbolic systems, each storing, conveying, and manipulating different kinds of information in different ways. From an archaeological perspective each is potentially useful in reconstructing the past, but unfortunately not all symbolic systems are well preserved in the archaeological record. Some, such as spoken language and ritual, are never preserved at all in a direct sense. Other symbolic systems are more durable, in part because people design them to be so. The **cuneiform** tablet of the Sumerian scribe was important in storing and transmitting information through time, and hence was made to last. The graven images of Maya lords were intended to be enduring monuments symbolizing the greatness of those portrayed for generations. Wall paintings or carvings in Egyptian tombs were literally intended to last throughout eternity (Malek 1986). The makers of all these things designed them in part to store information for considerable periods of time, though none of them ever envisioned their products as storage devices for archaeologists. Speech (in the form of writing) and ritual (in the form of graphic representations) may be indirectly preserved through such media. Even so, only a tiny fraction of the symbolic content of ancient cultures can be recovered.

cuneiform Earliest writing system, with wedge-shaped symbols inscribed on a wet clay tablet with a stylus.

Even when preservation is good, archaeologist face two additional problems: deciding which ancient patterns do in fact represent symbols and then decoding them in an effective way. Sometimes symbolic systems can be informative even if details of meaning elude us (as with the distribution of status symbols). In other cases, as with written or iconographic symbols, actual decipherment is most useful. When decoding is successful, symbolic information provides the richest and most detailed information we can recover from the past — information that is especially valuable because it records how ancient people saw themselves, or wanted to be seen, or what they found important and useful. But when inaccurately decoded or incorrectly interpreted, such symbols can seriously mislead us. This is why they must be tested against independent lines of evidence in their larger archaeological contexts.

INVESTIGATING SYMBOLIC SYSTEMS OF THE CLASSIC MAYA

The Classic Maya offer a particularly rich archaeological context for evaluating symbolic systems. Maya civilization was very complex, including all of the types of symbolic systems we have mentioned (Schele and Freidel 1990; Schele and Miller 1986). The Maya were literate; their inscriptions, insofar as we can read them, have immeasurably enhanced our reconstruction of Maya culture and society. They also had a sophisticated system of mathematics, which they used, among other things, to record calendrical information. Maya centers are also embellished by innumerable sophisticated artistic images, many of which related to rituals. All of these things are often combined to convey complex meanings.

Early explorers of Classic Maya ruins, such as Stephens and Catherwood, recognized that the designs carved on monuments were symbols. Although Stephens could not read these symbols, he assumed that sets of them represented hieroglyphic writing and that they recorded Maya history. The inscriptions presumably would include mathematical and calendrical information as well as narrative, and their decipherment seemed to hold an important key to the nature of Classic Maya society. Mathematical and calendrical components of the inscriptions were reasonably well understood by about 1910 (Morley 1920) and were of enormous archaeological significance; they provided the first absolute chronological framework not only for Maya archaeology but for all of Mesoamerica.

Mathematics and Calendrics

Ethnohistoric accounts by the first Spanish to arrive in northern Yucatan in the early sixteenth century describe the Maya using both arithmetic and calendrical systems. Earlier, during the Classic period (A.D. 300–900), even more sophisticated systems had been used.

Maya Arithmetic   The Maya used three important number symbols: the dot (1), the bar (5), and another symbol—sometimes taking the form of a stylized shell—signifying "completion" or "0." Whereas our system is 10-based; the Maya counted in units of 20 (Fig. 9.16). Instead of arranging their symbols horizontally, as we do, they arranged them vertically. Numbers below 20 were easily expressed; for example, the numbers 9 or 18 are simply combinations of the appropriate arrangements of bars and dots. To represent higher numbers the Maya developed the extremely sophisticated concept of "place," in which the value of a number depends on its position.

Thus the Maya, like us, could express whole numbers of any order of magnitude, though they did not use fractions or decimals. The notion of position and "0" is a great intellectual achievement, making Maya arithmetic more sophisticated than that of the Greeks and Romans, who lacked these concepts.

Calendars   Although the Maya undoubtedly put their arithmetic system to many utilitarian uses—keeping track of things and designing structures—they used it most conspicuously for reckoning time (Aveni 1989; Morley, Brainerd, and Sharer 1983). Time was measured both in terms of repeating cycles and in a linear direction from a starting point, using the day as the basic unit, just as in our modern calendars.

The oldest calendar used by the Maya, the *Tzolkin*, was shared with many other Mesoamerican peoples. Consisting of 260 days, each uniquely identified by one each of 13 numbers and 20 names, it seems not to be based on any known celestial cycle but on one closely corresponding to the length of time between conception and birth; one's Tzolkin birthday might be the same as the day of conception. The Tzolkin was probably used mainly for ritual purposes. The Maya also used the *Haab,* a solar calendar

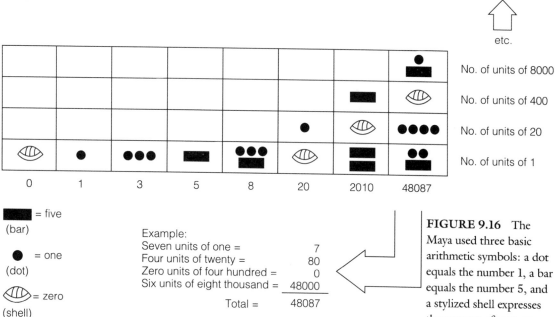

								●
							▬	
						●	𓂀	●●●●
𓂀	●	●●●	▬	●●●/▬	𓂀	▬/▬		●●
0	1	3	5	8	20	2010		48087

etc.

No. of units of 8000

No. of units of 400

No. of units of 20

No. of units of 1

▬ = five
(bar)

● = one
(dot)

𓂀 = zero
(shell)

Example:
Seven units of one =   7
Four units of twenty =   80
Zero units of four hundred =   0
Six units of eight thousand = 48000
                   Total = 48087

FIGURE 9.16 The Maya used three basic arithmetic symbols: a dot equals the number 1, a bar equals the number 5, and a stylized shell expresses the concept of zero or completion. They counted by units of 20 (rather than 10, as we do). Numerical place was expressed by bottom-to-top vertical position (rather than right-to-left horizontal position, as we do in our numerical system). By putting the three basic symbols in their proper positions, the Maya could express any positive whole number, as shown above.

Calendar Round The meshing of the two Maya calendars, the Tzolkin and the Haab, in a 52-year cycle.

Long Count Term for the Maya calendar that counts the number of elapsed days from an initial day in 3114 B.C.

consisting of 365 days—18 named months of 20 days each, plus a 5-day short month.

When the Tzolkin and Haab are joined, they result in a much longer cycle of nonrepeating named days—a cycle lasting 52 years (that is, the designation of a particular day would only recur once every 52 years). This **Calendar Round** cycle allowed the Maya to date historical events within a reasonably long period of time (Fig. 9.17).

To deal with even longer periods the Maya used a linear count of time called the **Long Count,** which simply measured the number of elapsed days from a beginning point in time (which has been calculated as a particular date over 5,000 years ago, occurring by our reckoning, in the year 3114 B.C.). Since we can correlate this calendar with our own Christian calendars, anything associated with a Long Count date can be expressed in absolute chronological terms.

Writing

Decipherment of Maya writing proved much more difficult than calendrics. No Maya Rosetta Stone existed, nor was it clear whether the inscriptions were pictographic, ideographic, logographic, phonetic, or some combination of these (Chippendale, Hammond, and Sabloff 1988; Houston 1989). Based primarily on knowledge of the mathematical and calendrical parts of the inscriptions, two schools of interpretation emerged. One school

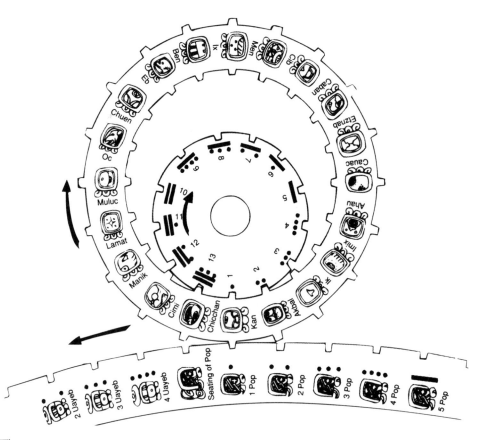

FIGURE 9.17 The Maya Calendar Round was a cyclical count of named and numbered days created by meshing the Haab (365 days) and the Tzolkin (260 days). In the longer cycle thus produced, it required 18,980 days (52 years) for a particular day to recur. In the drawing, the top two "gears" of day names and day numbers together make up the 260-day cycle, and are then meshed to the cycle of 365 uniquely named and numbered days.

emphasized Stephens's idea that inscriptions were mainly historical. The more influential scholars, however, thought that inscriptions were primarily concerned with astronomy, ritual, and religion.

Although there were many premature claims of decipherment, real breakthroughs did not occur until the late 1950s and early 1960s, when there appeared convincing evidence that the Maya used inscriptions for primarily political/historical purposes, as did elites in other early civilizations. Many scholars were involved, but Tatiana Proskouriakoff's (1960, 1961) work was particularly important. She showed that Maya sociopolitical organization was similar to that of other civilizations and thus opened up a new perspective on Maya writing that facilitated further decipherment.

Perhaps the most important lesson of Proskouriakoff's work is that archaeological context is essential to understanding ancient symbolic systems. She noticed that carved and inscribed monuments (especially stelae and altars) were set up in independent groups in front of particular buildings at some sites. Dates on these monuments could be read, and seemed

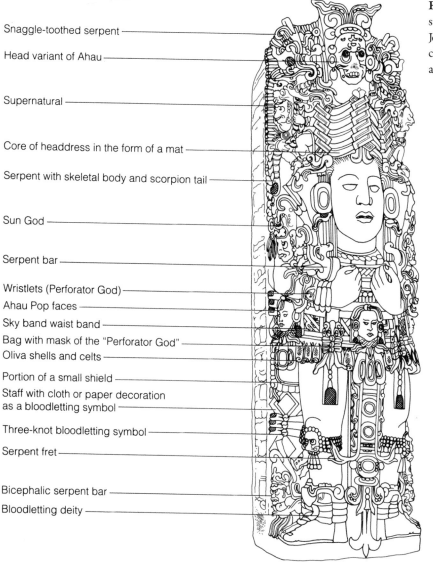

Snaggle-toothed serpent

Head variant of Ahau

Supernatural

Core of headdress in the form of a mat

Serpent with skeletal body and scorpion tail

Sun God

Serpent bar

Wristlets (Perforator God)

Ahau Pop faces

Sky band waist band

Bag with mask of the "Perforator God"

Oliva shells and celts

Portion of a small shield

Staff with cloth or paper decoration as a bloodletting symbol

Three-knot bloodletting symbol

Serpent fret

Bicephalic serpent bar

Bloodletting deity

FIGURE 9.18 This stela shows the ruler 18 Jog wearing symbols associated with royal status and royal rituals.

to fall into intervals consistent with human life spans. Proskouriakoff hypothesized that the succession of dated monuments in fact commemorated important events in the lives of successive rulers and that glyphs recorded important events such as royal births, enthronements, and deaths — in short, the monuments composed dynastic records (Fig. 9.18).

We now interpret Maya writing as a mixture of pictographic, ideographic, logographic, and syllabic elements (Coe 1991; Houston 1989).

Because it was so complex, probably few people were literate and these were of high social rank. By the eighth–ninth centuries A.D. Maya writing incorporated at least 100 syllabic signs, so it was becoming flexible and directly tied to the sounds of spoken speech. By A.D. 800 the Maya may have been able to render anything they could say verbally into writing.

Maya hieroglyphic writing conveys the following historical information: family relationships (father, mother, sibling, wife); events in the life cycle, particularly that of rulers (birth, adoption of titles or roles, accession to power, marriage, death); ritual events (sacrifice, burial, dedications of monuments, ball games); titles or social positions (king, subsidiary lord, royal wife, scribe); emblems (of place names, political territories, royal families, or some combinations of these); general events (warfare, conquest, capture, and sacrifice of captives); dynastic sequences at particular sites; personal names, ownership, and identity of craftspeople; functions (for example, the purpose of ceramic vessels); names of gods or supernatural beings; and directions (which had symbolic and cosmological significance to the Maya). Our interpretations of ancient Maya society are of course vastly richer since extraction of so many meanings from the inscriptions was made possible through detailed and accurate knowledge of general archaeological context.

Classic Maya Art

The elaborate artistic tradition of the Classic Maya was expressed in many media: monumental and portable sculpture, architecture, books, mural painting, ceramics, and even possibly the layouts of whole groups of buildings. Since art is so closely connected with inscriptions and ritual, we will consider these together in our analysis of research design at Copán.

RESEARCHING THE SIGNIFICANCE OF SYMBOLS AT COPÁN

Proskouriakoff's work integrated two methods of investigating symbols in archaeological contexts. The first was to determine the actual meaning of the symbols themselves; the second was to study carefully the archaeological distributions (contexts) of sets of symbols, since context alone can often tell us about how symbols (especially status symbols) functioned, even when their specific meanings remain unknown.

Distribution of Symbols

Since a major research issue at Copán is the structure of Classic Maya society, status symbols are of great interest. Two major categories of status symbols have been investigated: architectural features and nonarchitectural artifact assemblages. Information on context has been acquired through settlement survey and excavation.

Architecture Archaeologists have long known that the Maya had hierarchical sociopolitical organization in general evolutionary terms, but specific features of the sociopolitical structure have been poorly understood. Ethnographic analogs suggest that, in hierarchical societies, houses of high-status people were commonly larger and of higher quality than those of lower status people. High-status people commanded more labor (including more skilled labor) than low-status people, and large, high-quality residences were important symbols of status (Abrams 1989).

Surveys revealed distinct patterns of architectural symbols among the 1,425 archaeological sites (here, groups of mounds) in the Copán Valley (most dating from the Late Classic A.D. 700–900). A small subset of sites (49, or 3 percent) had extremely impressive architecture. Most of these sites contained many buildings, but, most important, the largest buildings were of extremely high quality. Maya who could afford the labor investment erected high platforms faced with cut stone, then built rooms on top of them, also of cut stone, frequently using specialized techniques such as **corbel vaulting** (see Fig. 2.12). These large buildings were often ornamented with carved symbols (including hieroglyphs), collapsed fragments of which were recorded on the surface during survey. Both architectural *scale* and *design* conveyed elite Maya status.

Artifacts Elaborate architecture is an obvious status symbol, but artifacts are more difficult to interpret. When we began our project, we hypothesized that certain kinds of artifacts functioned as status symbols: polychrome painted pottery, which often is decorated with symbols and is more costly to produce and rarer than other forms; precious stone inlays in the front teeth; and jewelry ear plugs (carved earringlike cylinders worn in the earlobe). But when we looked at the distribution of such artifacts found in excavation, they did not correlate neatly with elite and commoner sites. All were found in sites of every rank (although elite sites had more and higher-quality artifacts of these kinds). Therefore the mere presence of such artifacts did not indicate higher status; it was, instead, the quantity one possessed that distinguished social rank. In fact, very few artifacts of any kind were restricted only to elite sites.

Recovering Sets of Related Symbols: Insights into Meaning

The most durable and obvious symbol sets at Copán consist of images or texts carved in stone. Many were originally arranged on the facades of elite or royal buildings; symbols or other images were carved into individual stone blocks that were then assembled into larger compositions. The mere possession of decorated buildings was a status symbol, but the iconography conveyed more specific meaning. When buildings were abandoned and then collapsed, coherent sets of sculpture fell apart; individual pieces lost their relationships to one another. In effect, archaeologists are confronted with a huge jigsaw puzzle of jumbled pieces. Some early archaeologists

corbel vaulting Building technique which forms a false arch; corbel vaults do not effectively transfer the weight of the roof to the walls (as do true arches), and thus are weak.

(a)

(b)

FIGURE 9.19 Embellishments of Maya buildings serve in part as status symbols. It is essential to our understanding of Maya culture history to be able to reconstruct these graphic symbols: (a) fallen pieces of sculpture, labeled by the archaeologist to record context; (b) reassembled image as it may have once appeared on the front of a building.

simply picked up or excavated pieces of sculpture and removed them, thus destroying their contexts and making it difficult or impossible to reassemble the original composition.

Without information about what symbols go together in sets, it is difficult for epigraphers and iconographers to determine meaning. At Copán great care has been taken in recording exact contexts of fallen sculpture (Fig. 9.19). Compositions can then be reassembled (at least on paper) and meaning sought in related sets of symbols.

Symbol Sets and the Copán Nobility Outside the Main Group (the royal compound) all the elite residential sites we have tested have yielded impressive symbolic sculpture, sometimes featuring hieroglyphic inscriptions (Sheehy 1991; Webster 1989). Carved benches have also been unearthed, the most elaborate of which functioned as thrones in Maya society. This architectural sculpture celebrated the social and political statuses of the residents, who were clearly powerful people of subroyal rank. Each of the households so far investigated has a distinctive set of symbols, possibly indicating different court ranks. Our current interpretation is that the kings of Copán granted the use of titles, images, and inscriptions to lesser nobles in return for political support. The most exalted nobles had the right to use carved benches (usually restricted to Maya royalty). Each is very different; we do not know yet whether these differences symbolize variations in rank among the nobles themselves, or different titles or functions, or some combination of the two.

Symbols and the Copán Royal Dynasty   As noted in Chapter 3, the Main Group was the royal residence and ritual center of the Copán kings; there the research focus is on recovering inscribed monuments from successive architectural phases of temples, palaces, and other civic structures (Fash 1991). This is accomplished by deep trenching into buildings. Emphasis is on recording the exact archaeological context of anything of potential symbolic significance, preserving the integrity of symbolic sets, and interpreting them using the decipherment methods pioneered by Proskouriakoff and others. Because art and inscriptions (frequently with names of rulers and dates) are associated with stratigraphically known contexts, they reveal the following important information:

1. The Copán dynastic sequence—the names of kings, durations of their reigns, and events such as wars or marriages associated with them. "Emblem glyphs," identified in some way with particular Maya centers and used in royal titles, allow archaeologists to track elite interaction.

2. The particular buildings associated with each ruler: The number, scale, and quality of such buildings provide a measure of how kings mobilized and used labor and thus indicate how powerful they were.

3. How kings used traditional Maya symbols to express and legitimize their rule, creating symbols to add new dimensions to their political authority—an example of elite manipulation of the Great Tradition. For example, the ruler Smoke Jaguar adopted a distinctive set of warfare symbols, some from far away in Central Mexico. The final powerful king, Rising Sun, emphasized a similar set of warfare images 200 years later. In both these cases, rulers manipulated political and religious symbols in new ways, to make their reigns distinctive from those of their predecessors.

4. The great importance of public symbolic ritual to Maya kingship: Royal rites of passage (birth, accession, death) were also intensification rites for the society as a whole; other rites of intensification, such as the sacrifice of royal blood, symbolized the status of the ruler.

5. Status symbols: In representations of kings we see symbols of kingship in personal adornment.

These conclusions about Copán royalty and the chronological framework associated with them allow unusually detailed reconstruction of an ancient tradition of kingship.

Despite the extreme importance of symbolic ritual and display for the Classic Maya, because rituals are behaviorally dynamic, Maya rituals are not preserved as such in the archaeological record. Certain ritual elements do figure, however, in representational art (Fig. 9.20). Many painted vessels and stone carvings depict ritual events (Coe 1973). At the Maya center of Bonampak elaborate wall murals depict a whole set of rituals associated with the designation of a royal heir; we even know the names of some of the participants (Miller 1986).

The murals at Bonampak show rituals in action. Unfortunately, such representations are rare at Copán. However, especially at the Main Group, careful recovery of rich burials, caches, and other ritual contexts shows how important royal ritual was. For example, Rising Sun, the 16th king of Copán, commissioned a public monument showing himself as the heir to 15 generations of rulership. Recent excavations reveal that 15 jaguars—animals associated with ritual power and kingship—were sacrificed (possibly one for each of Yax Pac's predecessors) at the dedication ceremony.

The Symbolic Record Because of the richness of preserved Maya symbolic systems of all kinds, and an ever-increasing understanding of what they mean, we can reasonably know the following about the Classic Maya:

1. They were ruled by hereditary kings who had supernatural as well as political significance.

2. There were titled people other than the king who formed royal courts or royal bureaucracies, deriving their positions from the king or inheriting them in their own right. These elites were themselves internally ranked in status.

3. Elites, especially royalty, shared symbolically expressed information throughout the Maya Lowlands. This shared "Great Tradition" cross-cut political boundaries and helped form a cosmopolitan Classic Maya elite culture.

4. The ability to use and manipulate elite symbols was essential to status differentiation and political maneuvering.

5. Many autonomous Maya political systems existed, as reflected by "emblem glyphs" and other glyphic forms.

6. Despite the cultural uniformity of the Maya elite, warfare (ritual and territorial) was common, and success in war was important for Maya rulers.

These features strikingly reveal that from an anthropological perspective the Maya were like other nonindustrial hierarchical societies in terms of general social and political structure. Perhaps just as important, calendrical dates allow us to order events in the Maya past, giving us a chronological or historical framework. Most archaeologists lack such an invaluable tool for sorting out the past.

FIGURE 9.20 The Mesoamerican ball game combined athletic and ritual aspects. Here it is illustrated on a vase.

The Classic Maya: Historic or Prehistoric?

There is no doubt that in a general sense the Classic Maya had a historical cultural tradition. They wrote, we can read their writings, and we can make reasonable sense of them. Calendrical dates and other inscriptions allow us to arrange in time such events as wars, rituals, and the reigns of kings. If we lacked insights into Maya symbolic systems, our reconstructions of the elite levels of Maya society would be seriously deficient and flawed, and our sense of events and processes through time would be highly inaccurate.

On the other hand, virtually all Maya symbolism expresses the world view of the Maya elite, especially that of Maya kings. Whatever the symbols might have meant to the Maya, their greatest use for the Maya archaeologist is in determining the social and political structure and the culture history of the uppermost levels of Maya society.

It is highly probable that literacy and comprehension of the complex calendrical, mathematical, and artistic symbols with which writing was associated were confined to a very small and highly ranked segment of the Maya population—probably no more than 2 percent of the people. Although we do not know for sure that Maya rulers themselves could write, some inscriptions suggest that members of royal lineages certainly could. Scribes, whose titles sometimes appear on impressive elite structures, appear to have been important court functionaries, in some cases people of exalted rank.

Classic Maya symbolism primarily functioned to glorify and legitimize the political system and the rituals essential to it. Symbols were thus very much status markers, serving to distinguish kings and other privileged people from commoners and from one another. They did this partly through public display, openly affirming social and political dominance. Maya commoners, gazing awe-struck at the visage of a king in the plaza at Copán or watching the king carrying out a royal ritual, were reminded of their own comparative insignificance and the importance of the king to their well-being. We have no way of knowing how many of the publicly displayed symbols the commoners would have understood, but we should not forget that ignorance is sometimes as important in symbolic behavior as knowledge. The sight of incomprehensible symbols known only to the initiated elite intensified the perception of inequality, as all status symbols must.

Political symbols were used quite pragmatically by Maya rulers, as we have seen. For example, one way to assure that one had the political backing to assume and maintain royal dominance was to reward followers. In hierarchical societies such rewards include titles and offices. Many court titles may have been conferred by kings on lesser Maya nobles to guarantee their support. These thus became symbols of the trust and affection of the king, which no doubt were jealously sought after. The lesson here is that symbols are sometimes so powerful that, although intangible, people will often go to great lengths to acquire them. No doubt much of what the Maya kings express is also untrustworthy — to some extent royal propaganda that, originally intended to mislead their own people, now misleads us as well. Regardless of what we think we know about symbolic meaning, we must devise ways to test such meanings against the nonsymbolic elements of the archaeological record.

As important as what the Maya wrote is what they did not write (assuming that our present collection of written texts is representative). So far as we know, no Maya ever wrote an account of the social or political organization of his society. No Maya scribe kept track of the tax payments made in maize, cloth, or honey to his lord. Maya kings did not write down detailed information about the limits of their territories, the numbers of their subjects or the sizes of their armies. Virtually all matters relating to any concerns but those of the highest elite are utterly ignored. Given the sophistication of their script, it is surprising that Maya elites put it to such limited use, particularly ignoring the mundane administrative uses of writing which characterize much of written history elsewhere. Because the Maya recorded practically no information about the infrastructure of their society and only selective and possibly biased information about structure, they will forever be essentially a prehistoric culture.

The Classic Maya symbolic record is extremely rich, and it has been intensively studied. Despite the insights we have gained, however, it is sobering to reflect on how much still escapes us about the Maya that is of central concern to anthropology and archaeology. The larger lesson is that if our goal as archaeologists is to reconstruct all the basic behaviors and institutions of past societies, we cannot alone rely on the information derived from surviving symbolic systems but must integrate it with powerful research, using archaeological theories, methods, and techniques to investigate other aspects of culture as well.

POINTS TO REMEMBER

- All cultures have complex sets of symbols.

- Symbols are arbitrarily attached to their meanings.

- Symbols are used to store, transmit, and manipulate information.

- Symbols are rarely durable in archaeological terms, and when they are recovered, it is difficult to decipher their meanings.

- Many kinds of symbolic systems exist, including speech, art, ritual, and writing.

- Ancient societies are prehistoric if we know little about them from written records.

- Writing, if decipherable, yields detailed information about ancient cultures that is difficult to recover from other kinds of archaeological evidence.

- Different forms of writing were used in the past, but until the last 5,000 years, all cultures were prehistoric.

- Remains of status symbols, art, and ritual may tell us much about the past even if we do not know their precise meanings, provided we understand their archeological contexts.

FOR FURTHER READING*

For a general discussion of symbolic systems, Cohen's *Two Dimensional Man*, Leroi-Gourhan's *The Evolution of Paleolithic Art*, and Marshack's "Upper Paleolithic Notation and Symbol" offer perspectives on some of the earliest human symbols. Schmandt-Besserat's "The Earliest Precursor of Writing" traces the transition from three-dimensional symbols to writing. Benson's *Mesoamerican Writing Systems* reviews this field, while special studies of the Maya include Proskouriakoff's "Historical Implications of a Pattern of Dates at Piedras Negras, Guatemala," Stuart and Houston's "Maya Writing," Houston's *Maya Glyphs*, and Schele and Miller's *Blood of Kings*.

*Full citations appear in the bibliography.

CHAPTER TEN

POWER, PRESTIGE, AND WEALTH

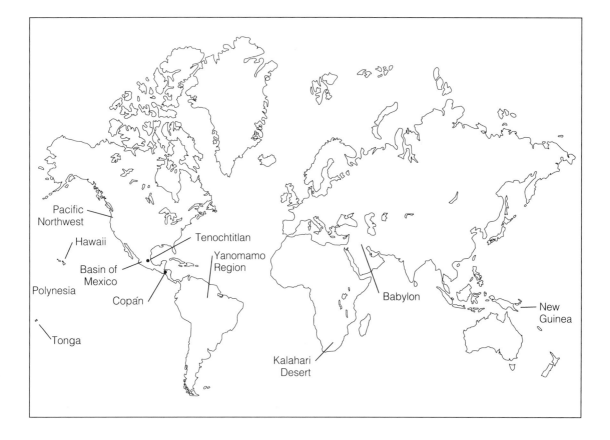

In this chapter we consider the relationship between social inequality, the ability to make and enforce decisions, and leadership—in a word, *politics*. Describing and explaining political evolution has been a central concern of archaeology for over 50 years and a particular preoccupation of the "New Archaeology" since the 1960s (Friedman and Rowlands 1979; Upham 1990).

We begin by examining in detail the model of political evolution introduced in Chapter 5. We will see how different kinds of political systems are structured and how they function, using as examples cultures known to ethnographers and historians. We will also discuss the evolution of political systems through time, the cultural subsystems of social organization and economics, and the manifestation of various kinds of political organization in the archaeological record. Finally, we review the results of Copán research for their political implications.

POLITICS, GOVERNMENT, AND POLITICAL SYSTEMS

All societies face problems of a political nature. By political problems we mean issues that are important to the survival or well-being of society as a whole, or to significant subgroups within it, but about which there is disagreement. In complex societies like our own, political issues present themselves constantly: the efficacy of existing laws or the creation of new ones, the fairness of taxation, or making policies with regard to allies and enemies. One dimension of political behavior is the creation of specialized statuses, offices, and institutions that facilitate decision making about such issues and then enforce the decisions. We call such specialized behavior **government**. Another, more familiar sort of political behavior is the maneuvering of individuals or groups to control these statuses, offices, institutions, and enforcement capabilities. This is what goes on every four years during an American presidential election. Broadly speaking, both of these kinds of behavior are the basis of political systems. The **political system** of a society includes the interest groups that maneuver to gain their ends, the means by which they do so, and the institutions, rules, laws and values that compose government. All societies have some form of government, but many have very limited formal government structure.

Even the simplest societies face political problems: how to end an internally damaging feud, how to deal with a dangerously antisocial person, whether to flee from enemies or fight, or who should assume leadership in hunting or warfare. In any society individuals or groups do not always share the same self-interests. Such differences produce tension and conflict as individuals or groups attempt to exert **power** over others to gain their ends. Power seeking lies at the root of all political behavior, and resolution of conflict is perhaps the fundamental function of all political systems. No human society can long endure unless people behave in ways appropriate

government Specialized statuses, offices, and institutions responsible for political decision making and enforcement of the decisions.

political system The interest groups that maneuver to gain their ends; the means by which they do so; and the institutions, rules, laws and values that compose government.

power The coercive capacity to ignore the interests of others while pursuing one's own and to withhold something that others want; alternatively, the capacity to oblige others to follow one's decisions even when they disagree, finding the decisions not to be in their own interests.

system-serving behavior
Actions which serve the interests of the whole group.

self-serving behavior
Actions of groups or individuals serving their own perceived interests, which may not be those of others.

for the collective good, thus minimizing the destructive effects of conflict. Such behavior is **system-serving;** that is, it serves the interests of the whole group. On the other hand, groups or individuals often act in their own perceived interests, which may not be those of others; this is **self-serving behavior** (Flannery 1972). When crises or disturbances occur, equilibrium must be restored by political decisions and actions that create consensus about how to act.

Government

The political anthropologist Peter Lloyd (1965) stated that the practice of government is:

1. an expression of interests and demands
2. the making of policies, laws, or orders
3. administration: putting decisions into effect
4. adjudication: solving disputes that arise over the implementation of these decisions
5. maintenance of public support for the governing body

Lloyd then defined the primary functions of government as (a) defending against external enemies; (b) maintaining internal order; (c) providing for the common welfare; and (d) preserving itself.

In thinking about the application of these ideas, bear in mind several questions: How are **leaders** recruited? How are political decisions made and put into effect? What happens when people do not agree with the decisions of leaders?

leader Person who has the ability or authority to initiate action and to whom other people have formed the habit of responding.

POLITICS IN EGALITARIAN SOCIETIES

Even in the smallest and simplest societies, individuals or groups of individuals suffer inequalities, both formal and informal, in opportunity, **prestige,** and **authority.**

prestige Ability to command admiration in social contexts.

When Fried (1967) called those human societies with the simplest political systems "egalitarian societies," he did not mean to imply that individuals within them were all equal in social status or opportunity. All human societies exhibit built-in differences of status and opportunity based on age, sex, and personal ability. Older people generally have more social influence than younger people, one sex sometimes has more influence than the other, and there are always individuals who are stronger, wiser, more fair or generous, more aggressive, or more dextrous than others. What Fried meant by "egalitarian" was that, within the same age-sex category, no one was denied access to positions of authority, prestige, or leadership, provided they had the necessary personal talents. In his words, "An egalitarian society is one in which there are as many positions of prestige in

authority Ability to persuade others, by argument or example, to accept one's decisions.

any age-sex grade as there are persons capable of filling them" (Fried 1967:33).

Typically very small, egalitarian societies are commonly referred to as band or tribal societies by anthropologists (see Chapter 5). Group size is maximally a few thousand people but is generally less. Most ethnographically observed hunting and gathering societies had egalitarian sociopolitical structure, as did many simple agricultural societies. In fact, until very recently, most societies have been egalitarian societies, so reconstructing their lifeways is an important archaeological concern.

We saw in Chapter 7 that the family in one form or another is the most basic human institution and that kinship provides the basic structure of egalitarian societies. Above the level of the individual, the family is the most fundamental political interest group. Apart from kinship, the most important integrative factor in egalitarian societies is face-to-face relationships. Partly because people can relate to one another so intimately, problems can often be solved or avoided in informal ways that would be impossible in larger societies, in which most people are unrelated and have little familiarity or contact with one another and where there is a wider range of interests.

Leadership

Leadership in egalitarian societies is situational, not permanent. Formal offices that confer the right to make political decisions are absent. Political leadership is primarily based on prestige, which in turn confers authority and persuasive ability. Individuals who are recognized by others as possessing unusual prestige because of their personal capabilities are those most likely to assume leadership roles when necessary (Fig. 10.1).

In many egalitarian societies there are socially recognized leadership statuses, accompanied by specific behavioral roles. Some of these statuses have names, such as "shaman." Shamans are individuals thought to have supernatural powers (we might call them magicians or sorcerers) who use these powers to benefit individuals or the group as a whole (see Chapter 12). But there is no single office or position of shaman — anyone with the proper personality may aspire to become one. Similarly, in the bison-hunting societies of the Great Plains of the United States during the 19th century, individuals recognized as war-chiefs or peace-chiefs sometimes assumed leadership. But anyone who exhibited the proper behavioral characteristics could become a war chief or a peace chief. Access to leadership roles was achieved rather than ascribed in some way, such as inheritance (see Box 10.1).

Egalitarian leaders lead by persuasion and example — they have no effective power to coerce others to follow their political decisions (no institutions such as armies or police to enforce their decisions). This is one reason so many accounts of egalitarian societies emphasize the eloquence of leaders. Public speaking and public debates were important ways to demon-

FIGURE 10.1 In the culture of the Northwest Coast, like many others, spiritual specialists have played key roles: (a) two shamans (masked figures, far left and right center); (b) item used in curing ceremonies.

(a)

(b)

strate one's ability, to compete with other potential leaders, and to build consensus for one's decisions.

Consensus of followers lies at the heart of the egalitarian political process. The Plains Indian war chief who persuaded other men to follow him on a raid had no right to compel them to carry it out if they thought it was too risky. They could simply abandon the enterprise and return home, and there was nothing he could do about it. Egalitarian leaders cannot give orders and cannot use **force** in convincing others to follow them.

force   The threat or fact of physical coercion or injury.

BOX 10.1

NEW GUINEA BIG-MEN:
EGALITARIAN LEADERS OR CHIEFS?

The "Big-Man" leadership role found among the peoples of highland New Guinea has been much studied by anthropologists (Sahlins 1970, Reader 1988). Prior to coming under Australian administration in the 1930s highland New Guinea supported hundreds of small political systems, some of them hardly larger than the local community. Hundreds of mutually unintelligible languages were spoken. Warfare was very common, especially in those regions where population densities exceeded 100 people per km².

In this segmented political environment Big-Men stood out as exceptional individuals and influential leaders. Big-Men achieved their positions by innate talent, force of character, and their own hard work and that of their wives. Their wives would grow extra food to feed pigs, which then were served at ritual feasts given for the Big-Man's prospective supporters. Initially these were close kinspeople, but eventually the Big-Man's web of political relationships incorporated many nonrelatives, including other Big-Men, some of whom were trading partners. Networks of Big-Men controlled the exchange of valued items such as shells, salt, feathers, and stone axes. By giving away some of these things, the Big-Man further enhanced his prestige and obligated others to him.

Successful Big-Men came to dominate the social relations of the highlands. Their knowledge of kin organization and history, along with their ability to threaten or persuade others, enabled them to settle disputes, create political alliances, and lead in warfare. In some ways Big-Men were typical egalitarian leaders. Their positions resulted from *achievement* (not *ascription*) and could not be inherited by their descendants. They depended heavily on authority and persuasion rather than on power and could not use essential resources (e.g.,

land or water) to manipulate others. Because they are so distinctive and well documented, Big-Man systems have often served as evolutionary models for archaeologists. Many ancient societies have had leaders rather like New Guinea Big-Men. If we could understand how these achieved leadership statuses might eventually have become inherited, it would clarify the origins of ranked political organization.

BOX 10.2

THE EMERGENCE OF PARAMOUNT CHIEFS AMONG HUNTER-GATHERERS: THE CALUSA OF SOUTHWEST FLORIDA

At the time of European contact, southwest Florida was occupied by a native people called the Calusa (Widmer 1988). According to Spanish ethnohistoric accounts, between 4,000 and 7,000 people were united under the Calusa paramount chief, who resided in a village of about 1,000 people and received tribute from about 50 subject villages, each with its own chief and each with a population ranging into the hundreds. The Spanish accounts indicate that chiefdoms like that of the Calusa were found all over southeastern North America at the time of contact.

Among the Calusa, the paramount chief was thought to have great magical powers. His position involved considerable ceremonial protocol and much sumptuary display, including the use of certain types of ornaments, some of beaten gold. At his death, some of his wives and subjects were sacrificed to accompany him into the next world, and his body was interred in a large earth mound. The center of each village would have a number of these mounds grouped around plazas, and in the paramount chief's village they were particularly large. Paramount villages established their primacy through warfare. Ritual behavior was complex, with religious and political functions, and there was highly specialized development of craft specialization related to status items of gold, shell, copper, and wood.

The Calusa case is unusual among southeastern chiefdoms in that the economy was essentially nonagricultural and based on foraging. Like the Northwest Coast peoples (see Box 6.1) the Calusa were primarily fishermen, but the size and scale of their political organization and the exalted status of the paramount chief is more elaborate than those of the Northwest Coast chiefdoms. The Calusa represent the most complex society that we know of with a foraging economy.

Southwestern Florida has a tropical climate with high rainfall (1100–1200 mm). The Calusa homeland, the coast, has numerous bays, estuaries, and offshore islands, with an extensive strip of mangrove swamps along the coast. Exhibiting high natural productivity, the product of the combination of fresh and saline water interchanges along the coastline, the area provides an extraordinarily rich microenvironment for the

RANKED SOCIETIES

When we rank things, we order them in a hierarchy of value. Ranking in this very general sense is a feature of egalitarian societies insofar as age, sex, and individual ability confer prestige. In other societies, hierarchies emerge that formalize inequalities of status, so that positions of authority are formally defined, limited in number, and confer the ability to make decisions. In his political model Fried defined societies structured this way as ranked societies (his term was *rank societies*). In such societies not everyone of the same age, sex, and personal ability has equal access to prestige

base of this ecological community, the mullet, a fish of relatively large size (0.5 to 2.5 kg). Base species are often microscopically small animals, and at the bottom of the food chain there is much more food available. Because the mullet occupies this position, the human population enjoyed a virtually limitless food supply. Humans could select either the more preferred carnivorous varieties of fish that also fed on mullet or move down the food chain to the herbivore level of the mullet during seasons of stress.

Food is not only abundant in this region but dependable from year to year and season to season, in sharp contrast with the Northwest Coast situation. The high productivity supported a dense human population. An archaeological survey of the Calusa area suggests that as many as 9,000 may have lived in the area, with a density of perhaps as many as 6 persons per km². This is not a high number for human populations as a whole, but it is exceptionally high for foraging populations and probably a maximum number for this type of economy.

A major question is: How does this subsistence strategy relate to the presence of ranked societies, and particularly to the development of paramount chiefdoms? According to Widmer, the relationships are as follows:

1. Settlement locations were centralized, most commonly on the off-shore islands or shoreline headlands, because specific fishing sites were erratic and accessible only by boat; however, the overall productivity of the region was high and dependable, year-round.

2. These island and headland settlement locations coincided with fresh water sources, which were extremely sparse and highly concentrated. Fishing populations tended to live in relatively large communities, conveniently located to these sources.

3. Because of their size, conflict resolution within the villages required the establishment of strong leadership roles.

4. Because specific marine resources were highly productive but unpredictable at any specific location, the best strategy of food procurement was to send several groups of fishermen to different areas so that at least one would be successful on any given day. The total catch would then be redistributed among the entire village population, a practice which further stimulated centralized leadership.

5. Because relatively few good residential sites existed, competition for them among local groups was intense, leading to warfare. The position of the chief as arbitrator, redistributor, and organizer of subsistence activities was critical, and competition among chiefs periodically lead, with the promotion of some and subordination of others, to political organization on a larger scale.

and leadership. Societies in which ranking dominates political structure are known as "chiefdoms" and their leaders "chiefs" (cf. Chapter 5). When, where, and why ranking first appeared are among the most important problems for the archaeologist concerned with political structure and evolution.

Although a few chiefdoms have had foraging economies (see Box 10.2), most have been based on effective food production (Drennan and Uribe 1987). Population sizes of chiefdoms have ranged from several hundred to many thousands of people. Because of their political fragility most chiefdoms probably have seldom exceeded 10,000 people, but the principle of ranking occasionally has allowed much larger chiefdoms to form, mainly through the mechanism of warfare. These large chiefdoms might be multicommunity systems with a hierarchy of chiefs ruled by a paramount chief.

Kinship remains the most important integrating force in chiefdoms despite their large size. In fact, kinship provides the basis for ranking. The principal political interest groups, families, are organized into **lineages** or theoretical descent systems, such as **clans**. In a classical chiefdom, such as the more complex societies of Polynesia, what is ranked is one's place in a system of descent (Goldman 1970). In such societies everyone is considered to be related through descent from a common ancestor, but some lines of descent are more senior than others (Fig. 10.2). Each person has a unique personal and political status, and personal relationships are channeled by nuances of relative inferiority or superiority of rank. Higher-ranked people have, in variable degrees, claims on the labor, products, and political support of lower-ranked people.

One's position in a ranking system also determines access to important offices and titles, most significantly chiefly ones, which are both limited in number and inherited. There are definite rules of succession; offices and titles could be passed on from one generation to the next within a family. Chiefly positions are thus basically ascribed, not achieved. Succession, however, is not always automatic. Sometimes a chiefly title might remain vacant if the person eligible to inherit cannot publicly demonstrate his or her suitability. Sometimes ambiguities in the succession rules make several people eligible, causing competition over titles. In both of these instances, prospective chiefs have to possess the proper personality traits as well as the requisite genealogies to acquire chiefly political status. Many ranked societies thus retain an element of achieved status in addition to that ascribed by birth.

Because only the most senior people in the highest-ranked lineages are eligible for significant political positions, the majority of people in a complex chiefdom are designated as "commoners" or "low-borns" to distinguish them from their more exalted kinspeople. This produces a set of hierarchically related social groups with a superficial resemblance to social classes as found in stratified societies, but as we shall see below it is actually quite different.

Functions of Chiefs

Chiefs have had several major functions, although the mix and importance of each would vary from one chiefdom to another (Earle 1987).

Settling Internal Disputes   Chiefs have often acted as the highest legal authorities in their political systems. They have functioned as final courts of appeal for individuals or families with serious grievances.

Religious Leadership   Chiefs have commonly been believed to have special supernatural importance because of their high rank. This was carried

lineage   Members of a group who claim common descent and can trace their genealogy back to a common ancestor.

clan   Organization in which members claim common descent but do not specify how they are related. Often the common ancestor is fictive (fictional).

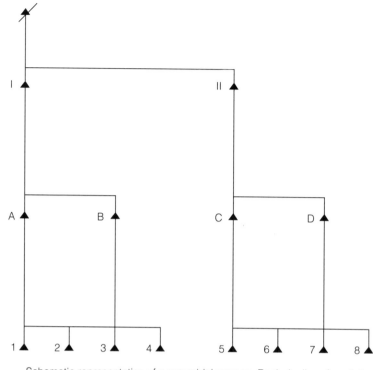

FIGURE 10.2 The ramage is a kind of descent system frequently associated with chiefdoms. The nearer the relationship to the original ancestor in terms of descent in the male line, the higher one's rank.

Schematic representation of a pyramidal ramage. Rank declines from left to right.
I: senior branch
II: junior branch
1: senior descendant of original older brother
5: senior descendant of original younger brother

to an extreme in Polynesia, where the highest chiefs were so charged with supernatural power, or **mana,** that they had to avoid contact with commoners, who could be injured by contact with them. Ancestor worship has been a feature of many chiefdoms, and deceased ancestors have been thought to have great influence over the well-being of the living. Since the chief is the closest living relative of the most highly ranked dead ancestors, he is able to intercede with them.

Chiefs accordingly carry out many rituals on behalf of their subjects, such as those related to the all-important yearly agricultural cycle. The chief's aura of sanctity serves to reinforce the political office of chief and can be used to some extent for legal or political purposes. For example, in Hawaii a chief could ritually contaminate the land of commoners who failed to obey his decisions, thus rendering it useless. The life crises of chiefs, their births, marriages, and especially deaths, were occasions for public rituals.

One reason for the importance of ritual in chiefdoms relates to the psychology of leadership. Leaders are necessary when there are social crises

mana Polynesian word referring to a supernatural force that can reside within an object or person, making that object or person more powerful or effective in its performance. For example, a canoe with much mana would be particularly seaworthy, and a mana-charged weapon would be lethal.

or disturbances, or at least when essential tasks must be done quickly and efficiently. As we have seen, egalitarian leaders emerge situationally under such circumstances, the circumstances themselves maintaining the relationship between followers and leaders. When leadership statuses are limited and (theoretically) permanent, as they are in chiefdoms, this relationship must be continually reinforced so that followers respond predictably. Since crises, disturbances, or essential tasks may be very unpredictable and intermittent, they may not provoke constant reinforcement. Rituals involving chiefly leadership, however, may be as numerous as necessary to reinforce the habitual responses of followers. Here the actual content of the ritual is less important than its occurrence, which maintains a pattern of interaction.

But rituals must be meaningful. Chiefly rituals often emphasize the role of the chief or his delegates in maintaining the proper spiritual or cosmological well-being of the whole society, or ensuring the proper outcomes of such important activities as planting or harvesting. If such rituals are perceived as ineffective, the chief may lose support. Thus, chiefs sometimes face a dilemma. Ostensibly necessary rituals may emerge to psychologically reinforce the leader-follower relationship, but if those rituals are perceived as ineffective, followers may desert the chief.

Conduct of External Political Relations and Warfare Chiefs often maintain important contacts with their counterparts elsewhere. They create alliances, settle intergroup disputes, initiate trade, and make peace. Warfare has been very common both between chiefdoms and between internal political factions within them. Chiefs mobilize their followers to defend their territories, to expand them, and to acquire and safeguard their own positions.

Trade, Exchange, and Redistribution Chiefly households often receive contributions of food and other items from their followers. These are usually not conceived of as taxes or tribute but rather as contributions given to senior kin. Part of these contributions might be returned when a chief sponsors public feasts and rituals, thus reinforcing the image of the generous, open-handed leader. Chiefs have frequently been nodes of exchange of valuable exotic items that function as status symbols. Some of these are used by the chiefs themselves to emphasize their status; others are redistributed to subchiefs as gifts to symbolize and affirm political relationships.

Mobilization of Labor Chiefs mobilize their followers to provide labor for projects of public importance (Fig. 10.3). These might include projects of economic value, such as the construction of irrigation works. Public labor has also been used to build religious precincts and the tombs of deceased chiefs, which have general religious importance.

FIGURE 10.3 Polynesian chiefs often commissioned the construction of large megalithic monuments. Such efforts required the mobilization of many followers.

Chiefly Authority and Power

Chiefdoms have more formalized government than egalitarian societies, but in many respects the exercise of chiefly authority has egalitarian dimensions. Although chiefs make public pronouncements of political decisions, very often the actual decisions are made in private consultations with other members of the chiefly lineage and with subchiefs, thus guaranteeing public acceptability.

Chiefs, like egalitarian leaders, also have very little coercive power. Although they might sometimes exert limited force in order to punish those who ignored their decisions, they can do this effectively only as long as public consensus is on their side. Chiefs have no effective armies, police, or other institutions of power at their command, but depend on their subjects at large for political support. Alienation of any significant number of supporters places the chief in a very precarious political position. For this reason, chiefly leadership involves the skilled use of persuasion and authority.

Mobilization of followers is the single most important manifestation of chiefly authority. The chief who is ineffective in such mobilization reveals his political weakness. He might be overthrown by another political faction claiming his position, or subchiefs might declare their independence. In the latter case the political system would break up. Governmental institutions could not effectively prevent fissioning.

Because of the importance of inherited positions of leadership within expanded kinship groups above the level of nuclear family, leaders other than the highest chief automatically have their own political constituencies. Thus there are always organized and potentially independent interest groups that can pursue their own ends and that can be potentially antagonistic to the chief. This segmentary structure is one of the weaknesses of chiefdom societies.

A related weakness is that many large chiefdoms are characterized by **mechanical solidarity**. This means that their component subsystems are similar to each other and are potentially independent in social, economic, and political terms—that is, there is very little interdependence to hold them together, apart from the vigor of the paramount chief and his establishment.

Wealth and Property

Chiefs and other high-ranking people have wealth of a showy, sumptuary kind. Often well-established rules restrict material status symbols such as special clothing and insignia for the use by chiefs, who often live in elaborate households that are much more impressive than those of commoners (Fig. 10.4). But chiefs generally do not monopolize essential resources such as land and water. Although some chiefs claim to "own" their territories and to "grant" others the use of land, this is essentially a fiction, since such resources are actually held in common by lineages or other corporate groups. Chiefly "wealth" thus consists of socially recognized symbols of rank, but chiefs cannot with impunity deprive others of resources essential to survival or well-being, except under unusual conditions of warfare. Wealth is thus not a completely effective instrument of political power.

STRATIFICATION AND THE STATE

A new form of ranking, stratification, characterizes the most complex hierarchical societies found in the ethnographic/historical record (Cohen and Service 1978; Service 1975). Stratification means that whole groups of people within a society are ranked as social **classes** or **castes**. Classes are large social groups that are ranked in status or prestige according to criteria such as wealth, profession, ethnicity, or sanctity. Castes are social classes that have extremely sharp social boundaries, making it difficult or impossible to move from one caste to another.

Although kinship ties may be very important within classes and castes, they do not effectively link individuals across class boundaries. Kinship is thus much less important for overall social integration than in bands, tribes, or chiefdoms. Classes are political interest groups, some with much more political authority and power than others. Chiefs derive much of their authority from the real or asserted kinship links with their lower-ranked constituents. People in high social strata often do the opposite, asserting their social distinctiveness and separateness from those they dominate.

mechanical solidarity Feature of a society in which component subsystems are similar to each other and potentially independent in social, economic, and political terms.

class Large social group ranked vis-à-vis others in terms of status, prestige, wealth, or sanctity.

caste Social class with clearly delineated boundaries; one is usually born into a caste and ascribed social and economic roles on the basis of caste affiliation. It is difficult or impossible to ascend from one caste to a higher one.

(a)   (b)

FIGURE 10.4 Labor for large tasks can be mobilized and organized by chiefs: (a) the stone foundations of the chief's dwelling on the island of Tinian; (b) reconstruction drawing of the house (note the man for scale).

The most important characteristic of stratified societies is the unequal distribution of wealth, which makes some groups much more powerful than others because they monopolize essential but limited economic resources. Such monopolization produces relatively enduring political power, and wealth becomes an effective political tool for the first time. Emergence of these new dimensions of wealth and political power creates new and unprecedented political stresses between political interest groups; stratified societies which do not quickly evolve new institutions to reinforce stratification are politically very fragile. States are stratified societies that have developed institutions that stabilize stratification. In such societies kinship is devalued as a mechanism for overall social integration, although it may be important for subgroups. In mature states the threat or application of force may serve to uphold stratification; in effect, force is recognized in all stratified societies as a legitimate means of social control.

States are typically larger than nonstate societies, with populations minimally in the thousands and often in the millions. One reason for such increased societal scale is that states are always based on effective food production rather than on foraging. Thus nonindustrial states are called "agrarian states"; they often have had very high population densities based upon very intensive forms of food production.

In states, individuals or groups in the highest strata enjoy numerous privileges, including access to political positions, freedom from manual labor, superior diet, dress and housing, special legal privileges, more access to information and specialized education, and more leisure. Social classes become political interest groups; typically people of low social class are excluded from the political process and may be dispossessed of essential resources by people of higher classes.

All states have institutions which uphold an order of stratification. These may include state religions and their associated ideologies and rituals, schools, law-making bodies, armed forces, and police.

States always have ideologies which justify and even sanctify their institutions and leaders. These ideologies may be purely social, but in ancient states they were more commonly expressed through religion. One reason ideology is so important is that no state can be integrated solely by power and secular authority over the long run. Political status quo is partly maintained because people believe that it is not only prudent to behave in certain ways but that they "ought" to behave in accordance with the "sacred" propositions of their cultures.

Highly territorial, states seek to preserve or expand their territories. States have ruling centers which may or may not be urban in character but which serve as political foci for other households or communities. States have centralized governments dominated by rulers or officials who are supported by administrative specialists, often organized into complex bureaucracies. Specialized institutions make and enforce political decisions. Governments, and the classes that dominate them, are supported by taxes, tribute, privileged ownership of capital resources, or a combination of these.

Coercive force plays a much greater role in maintaining the structure of the state than it does in nonstate societies. The threat or use of force, backed by specialized institutions, becomes an effective political tool. States are the most successful of all the political forms we have discussed in preventing fissioning, but they inevitably do disintegrate, often in violent circumstances.

segregation Evolutionary process whereby societies become more internally diverse in political, social, and economic terms. Segregation develops in close concert with centralization.

States are internally segregated (Flannery 1972), particularly in economic terms. **Segregation** produces levels of interdependence of subsystems which make fissioning much less likely than it is in rank societies, with their characteristic mechanical solidarity. In contrast, high interdependence produces **organic solidarity** (this term reflects the idea that in organisms no part is independent of the whole).

States clearly differ from chiefdoms in fundamental ways, as seen in the ability to use force as a political tool and the lack of kinship integration, but there are also important continuities between chiefdoms and states, such as ascribed access to political positions and ideologies that support political hierarchy. This is why we prefer to maintain the distinction between ranking and stratification as principles of organization, and between chiefdoms and states as societal categories.

organic solidarity In organisms, the interdependence of all parts constituting the whole, a principle which is applied analogously to certain kinds of societies in which parts are highly interdependent.

States, in summary, have political organizations conforming closely to Lloyd's ideas about government and how it functions. The institutions and structures of states are extremely different from those of egalitarian societies—the kinds of societies in which most humans have lived for most of evolutionary history. Economic stratification lies at the root of the state, but except where decipherable written records are available it is difficult to reconstruct patterns of stratification from the archaeological record. For this reason, we generally must indirectly infer the presence of stratification from the institutions that support it.

PROCESSES OF POLITICAL EVOLUTION

The political model presented above simplifies the extremely varied specific political arrangements seen in the ethnographic and archaeological records. There are many kinds of egalitarian societies, ranked societies, and states, each fascinating in terms of its specific evolutionary career. The categories are to politics what genera are to biology: They define important general political forms but ignore the actual variations in their constituent "species" — the political arrangements found in specific societies.

Some archaeologists, preferring a concept slightly different from Fried's, use the term "middle-range hierarchical societies" to refer to societies that, in organizational terms, fall between egalitarian bands or tribes and states. The labels one uses are less important than recognizing that, in any scheme of political evolution, certain societies do not fit nicely into general categories; this is not a weakness of the model but rather one of its strengths — only a poor evolutionary model lacks transitional forms. We do not see Fried's societal categories as evolutionary "stages" but rather as constellations of adaptive organizational features that proved effective under particular circumstances. There is no implication that every human society must pass through this sequence in the order discussed, or at all. Nor is there an invariable set of features that is inevitably and exclusively associated with each evolutionary category.

Fried developed his political analysis by observing how known human societies worked. On one level, he defined functional political types, using historical and ethnographic records. But he also felt that his typology revealed a convincing evolutionary process in describing how leaders were recruited and how decisions were made and enforced. Basic elements in this evolutionary model include:

1. Increasing **centralization** of political decision making in the hands of fewer individuals or subgroups.

2. Increased hierarchical structure and specialization of decision making.

3. A shift from achieved to ascribed status with an accompanying shift from authority-based political systems to those based on power and from situational to permanent leadership positions.

4. As political organization becomes more complex, wealth and coercive force are used as political tools

5. Decline of kinship institutions as the predominant political interest groups and integrative mechanisms.

centralization Evolutionary process whereby wealth, power, political decision making, and social prestige are concentrated in the hands of fewer and fewer subgroups or individuals within a society.

6. Formal institutions emerge which preserve and enhance political inequalities.

7. Greater societal size and internal segregation.

No notion of progress is implied by this evolutionary model, only directional trends. Until about 7,000 years ago all humans lived in nonstate societies. Since then egalitarian and rank societies have been assimilated, altered, or destroyed by emerging and expanding states. Virtually all of us live in state-type political systems today.

Fried's model is primarily focused on the structural aspects of different kinds of political systems. We should not forget, however, that the ways in which power and authority are exercised depend not only on structure alone but also on the personalities of leaders and on situational circumstances, such as times of crisis or opportunity. Egalitarian societies have sometimes produced very powerful leaders, while centralized states have been afflicted with weak or incompetent ones. Thus at any level in Fried's model, talented individuals may assert themselves and act in ways that subvert political structure, at least for a time. (We find it natural to think of leaders as people who manipulate others, but we should not forget that leaders themselves are often manipulated by their followers. This is especially true in egalitarian societies but also may occur in hierarchical societies.)

Archaeologists have long designed research to investigate two features of Fried's model. First, did societies that resemble those defined by Fried exist in the past (i.e., is his model useful)? We now have convincing evidence that they did. Second, and much more important than merely identifying political typology in the archaeological record, what triggered the basic evolutionary processes? Why did ranking develop, and what promotes centralization and segregation? Although we have many provisional answers to these questions (see Chapter 16), much more research on particular evolutionary sequences must be done before we can answer them with confidence.

ETHNOHISTORIC EXAMPLES AND ARCHAEOLOGICAL CORRELATES OF POLITICAL EVOLUTION

It would be very convenient if all human societies went through the same unilineal "stages" of sociopolitical evolution, with discrete and inevitable cultural correlates falling automatically into place each time a shift occurred from one stage to another. If this happened, it would be a simple matter to identify these correlates in the archaeological record and automatically assign them evolutionary labels. But precisely because there is an evolutionary continuum, this does not happen. There are few sharp, sudden transitions, so only general associations can be made between particular behavioral or institutional correlates and specific evolutionary forms. Be-

sides, we are concerned with more than just attributing labels. Our task—
a difficult but not impossible one—is to assess the operation of the processes, or trends, of political evolution in particular cultural settings. The
current archaeological record is fairly clear on when and where major
evolutionary transformations took place (see Chapters 13 and 14). Let us
turn to an examination of archaeological evidence as it relates to reconstructing the wheres and whens of the evolutionary *process,* deferring discussion of the explanations of *how* the process works until Chapter 16.

One way to begin to specify evolutionary form is by exclusion, since
certain characteristics are specific to particular kinds of societies. If we
know that people were hunter-gatherers with small, dispersed populations,
we may be sure that the institutions typical of states were absent. Conversely, the presence of huge urban centers with monumental public architecture unambiguously signals the presence of nonegalitarian sociopolitical
organization. But such gross distinctions are seldom archaeological issues;
it is the finer ones that are more important.

An alternative method is to fall back on one of the basic goals of
archaeology—to reconstruct social, economic, and political institutions of
ancient societies using archaeological correlates and then make an evolutionary evaluation. This is much more difficult for a number of reasons.
For one thing, many of the "indicators" most strongly identified with one
evolutionary form are sometimes also associated with others (Peebles and
Kus 1977). For example, impressive hierarchical ideologies and associated
rituals and facilities are found in both chiefdoms and states; how do we
handle such overlap? What kinds of clear archaeological correlates would
the presence (or absence) of organizational features such as theoretical
descent groups leave behind? How does one "dig up" unequal access to
basic resources? Even if they were originally present, would archaeological
residues of such cultural patterns survive in any recognizable forms?

One way to think about these questions is to consider some ethnographically or historically known societies that clearly relate to our scheme in
order to see what kinds of evidence their cultures would, under ideal
circumstances, leave behind for archaeologists to find. We have already
discussed two of the three societies reviewed below at some length, the
Yanomamo and the Aztecs (see especially Chapter 7). We will introduce a
new one, the large chiefdom of Tonga, to round out the proposed evolutionary continuum.

The Egalitarian Yanomamo

About 10,000 Yanomamo Indians live in the tropical forests of northern
Brazil and southern Venezuela, where they make a living both by hunting
and gathering and by shifting agriculture (Chagnon 1968). Communities
consist of widely spaced villages housing up to 250 people, though 75–
80 is a more common size. These villages are very similar to one another,
and are so scattered that overall population density is light. Inhabitants

usually share kinship relationships, but in spite of this, villages frequently fission because of internal dissension (Fig. 10.5). Except for fragile alliances, each village community is a separate political entity (though people in different villages may be kinspeople), and villages are frequently at war with each other. Although there are village leaders recognized for their personal qualities, they cannot order others about and are ineffective in resolving disputes. They must lead by persuasion and example; they possess no real power. There are no political offices. Everyone of the same age and sex undertakes the same round of economic tasks, and there is no monopolization of essential resources.

Assuming that Yanomamo material culture were well preserved and that we could carry out intensive archaeology in the region, what would reflect the quintessentially egalitarian political nature of Yanomamo society?

As in present-day Yanomamo society, communities would be small, and there would be little variation between them in size or layout—that is, there would be nothing we could reasonably identify as a distinctive, specialized political "capital" (no evidence for supracommunity political centralization). If we had enough information about Yanomamo settlements, we would probably recognize that all Yanomamo shared a common culture, but the fact that settlements were widely spaced and frequently moved would suggest that to a high degree each settlement functioned as a politically autonomous community.

Within villages, we would find great similarity of domestic facilities and no signs of economic specialization. This pattern would suggest minimal segregation in economic terms as well as a lack of ranking or stratification, since increased size and elaboration of residences are status symbols in many hierarchical societies. It would be quite clear that even the largest villages housed only a few hundred people and that many were smaller. Such community sizes would be consistent with egalitarian modes of organization.

It would be difficult to recover good evidence for Yanomamo subsistence in their humid tropical environment, but with proper analysis of recorded materials we could probably conclude that they had a mixed economy of hunting and gathering and farming. This, together with shifting and redundant settlement forms, would strongly suggest egalitarian political organization. There would be no material evidence for large, cooperative investments of labor in temples, irrigation works, or other communal facilities that would imply strong centralized leadership and labor mobilization. Also conspicuously absent would be any kind of public art celebrating social differences between people.

If we recovered a respresentative sample of Yanomamo tools, weapons, and ornaments, we would see no rare luxury items imported from great distances, or made with skilled specialized labor, that might serve as status symbols to distinguish privileged people.

Unfortunately for the archaeologist, the Yanomamo do not bury their dead but usually cremate the corpses, grind the ashes to powder, and mix

(a)

FIGURE 10.5 Because there is no strong political authority in Yanomamo society, internal feuds often get out of hand, eventually resulting in the breakup of villages, which also war on one another: (a) Yanomamo warriors dancing; (b) chart of fissioning of Yanomamo populations.

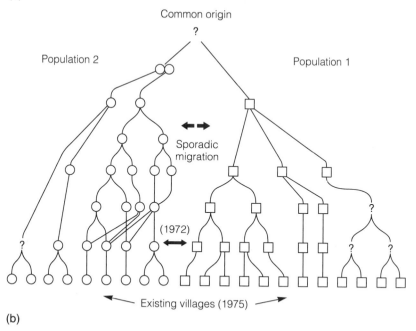

(b)

it with food at ritual feasts. Thus we would probably be unable to recover any evidence for mortuary behavior, a potentially rich source of information on sociopolitical structure, as we shall see below. Since patterns of Yanomamo warfare would probably be most easily detected in burials, we might not be able to reconstruct this politically important part of Yanomamo culture.

Reasoning as much from what was absent as from what was present in their archaeological record, we would have little doubt that the Yanomamo were basically egalitarian in evolutionary terms. We would not be able to reconstruct directly the importance of kinship in Yanomamo political organization but would probably assume it, since it is so consistent with small comunity size. Evidence for sodalities would be lacking. All things considered, we would probably be able to reconstruct the Yanomamo as a comparatively simple tribal society.

Tonga: A Polynesian Chiefdom

In the 18th century the island group of Tonga in western Polynesia boasted one of the most impressive known chiefdoms (Bellwood 1979, 1987; Gailey 1987; Goldman 1970). The main island, Tongatapu, and many smaller ones were a single political entity. We do not know how many people were involved, but 50,000 is a reasonable estimate. Although all Tongans traced kinship relationships with each other, the society was characterized by strong ranking. Three great paramount chiefly lineages, themselves ranked vis-à-vis one another, occupied the highest religious and secular positions. The oldest and greatest of these lineages produced the *Tui Tonga,* the chief who was semidivine and religiously sacrosanct; two other paramount chiefs oversaw secular affairs. Lesser district chiefs were under the authority of the paramount. The great mass of the people fell into the "low-born" category of *tua.*

Chiefs wore special symbols and clothing denoting their statuses, ate special foods, lived in distinctive houses, and were often buried in large, specially constructed tombs with accompanying impressive funeral rites, which might include human sacrifice. Gifts and presents were given to chiefs by their lesser kinspeople. In part, these gifts were used to support the households of chiefs, who apparently produced no food themselves, and some gifts were redistributed to reaffirm political ties. Long-distance voyages brought luxury objects from other islands, such as Fiji and Samoa, principally for the consumption of high-ranked people.

In the Tongan settlement system there was nothing we would recognize as an urban center, or even a rural village. Most commoners, or tua, lived in small dispersed households surrounded by gardens and fields. Lesser chiefs probably had somewhat similar, but more impressive residences. However, the establishment of the great paramount chief, the Tui Tonga, was very elaborate. Situated on the edge of the lagoon, this settlement, Mu'a, was delimited on the landward side by a substantial fortification, consisting of a ditch and bank many hundreds of yards long. Within it were the houses of the chiefs and their families and retainers. Large open spaces were provided for public ceremonies, and chiefly tombs were situated both inside and outside of the perimeter of the ditch. Although not a city or town according to our standards, the community of Mu'a was essentially the overgrown household of the greatest Tongan chiefs, with all of the ritual and civic facilities appropriate to chiefly rule.

Chiefs mobilized people for many reasons, including war, trade, and construction. Large structures of various kinds were built of earth and coral. The most impressive buildings erected with such labor are the tombs of the grandest chiefs.

Archaeological surveys would reveal the sedentary nature and scale of the Tongan population. At least a two-tiered settlement hierarchy would be apparent—the houses of dispersed farmers at one extreme, and the large establishment of Mu'a at the other. The latter would be clearly identifiable as a political and ceremonial central place. It would not be a town or city occupied by many hundreds of thousands of people, yet it would clearly be a place where a few privileged people lived. There would be striking contrasts between residences of the paramount chiefs and those of commoners. It might be possible to identify the residences of lesser district chiefs as well. At least a few chiefly status symbols would be preserved in the more elaborate houses.

Evidence would clearly indicate that there existed political authority strong enough to mobilize considerable labor to construct fortifications, tombs, and other sizable structures. The presence of elaborate tombs requiring expenditure of large amounts of public labor and situated near Mu'a would strongly suggest ranking. Excavation would reveal status objects as well as human sacrifices. Other tombs would yield large numbers of collective burials made over considerable time periods, suggesting family ossuaries of particular kin groups.

What we would not see in the archaeological record is also informative. There would be no large public works projects devoted to agricultue. There would also be little evidence for full-time occupational specialization.

Despite Tonga's large size, equivalent to that of many ancient states, archaeologists would have little difficulty in determining that the Tongan polity conformed most closely to Fried's model of ranked society.

The Imperial Aztecs

Although the Aztecs of the Basin of Mexico were conquered early in the 16th century by the Spanish, we have copious historical information about them. In fact, most of what we know about the Aztecs comes from written sources and eyewitness accounts, rather than from archaeology (Berdan 1982; Collier, Rosaldo, and Wirth 1982; Gibson 1964).

Between roughly A.D. 1430 and 1519 the Aztec empire emerged as the dominant political system of Mesoamerica. By absorbing other states through threat or outright conquest, they eventually created a loose tribute empire which may have had a population of 6,000,000 people. The core of this empire was the Basin of Mexico, a region of city-states inhabited by about 1,500,000 people, all within a few day's walk of the enormous

Aztec capital of Tenochtitlan (see Fig. 7.1). At least 100,000 people may have lived in the capital, which was the largest city in the New World. Tenochtitlan and other cities had monumental public architecture in the form of temples and other religious and civic structures, such as aqueducts. Also present were the large and elaborate palaces of rulers and the houses of powerful lords and merchants.

Aztec society was strongly stratified. There were royal lineages in major cities and towns from which hereditary rulers were recruited. Rulers themselves were ranked in importance, with the Mexica Aztec king of Tenochtitlan dominating all other rulers. A class of hereditary, nonroyal nobles also existed. Sumptuary laws reserved many status symbols for them in the form of clothing, jewelry and other insignia, and even food. Members of these privileged strata of Aztec society occupied the most important political positions. These were many and varied, since the Aztec state had well-developed civil, military, and religious bureaucracies. Privileged people derived support from their own estates, from taxes levied on commoners, and from tribute derived from military expansion. Institutions supporting stratification and the state included a state religion, with all of its associated facilities, rituals, and beliefs, a warrior class and a conscript army, an elaborate legal system, and schools for elites and commoners alike.

An effective agrarian economy supported the Aztec state (Sanders, Parsons, and Santley 1979). Most people were commoners or serfs who worked on the land. Because of the extraordinarily high population densities of the Basin of Mexico, very intensive forms of agriculture were practiced. These included elaborate terracing and irrigation, but the most important technique involved the creation of artificial fields—chinampas—by draining the swampy land around the capital (Fig. 10.6). The mature chinampa system was so huge and complicated that it could only have been designed and carried out by the Aztec state. Agricultural goods and other commodities were exchanged in local or urban markets. Aztec merchants, partly subsidized by the state, ranged over Mesoamerica, returning with valuable materials destined primarily for elite consumption. Other such materials flowed in through the tribute system (see Fig. 9.9), created by the conquests of Aztec armies (Hassig 1988). Full-time specialists produced a wide range of both utilitarian goods and status symbols, the latter mainly consumed by the elite.

Even if we lacked documentary sources on the Aztecs, archaeological research would be perfectly capable of demonstrating the scale, complexity, and major organizational features of Aztec society that allow us to classify it as a mature state. Settlement pattern studies would reveal the size and density of the Aztec population—far in excess of anything known for a ranked society. Not only would communities be very numerous, but they would be highly differentiated in form and function. At the top of the settlement hierarchy would be the immense Aztec capital, and at the bottom many small rural communities, with many other settlement types in between. At least in the Basin of Mexico, the centralization of the system on the Aztec capital would be obvious.

FIGURE 10.6 Much of the food for the Aztec capital was produced on chinampas, or drained fields. Huge areas of chinampas were constructed using public labor directed by the Aztec state.

If we investigated communities of various sorts, functional differences would be clear, indicating variation both among and within settlements. Small rural settlements would mostly have modest houses and would be associated with agricultural features, such as terraces, irrigation systems, and fields (Evans 1989b, 1990). The capital, by contrast, would have the major apparatus of the state institutions—temples, palaces, aqueducts, elite schools, and great public plazas for rituals and market exchange. Ideology (particularly that associated with religion, war, and conquest) would be reflected in carved and painted monuments, and in caches and sacrificial victims associated with public architecture.

Great variation in scale and elaboration of houses would indicate social stratification. A handful of palaces would be so large and impressive and so centrally located that we would have little trouble in identifying them as the establishments of rulers. In the capital and elsewhere we would find lesser, but still splendid residences in great numbers, which we could reasonably identify with powerful elites. Humble rural or urban residences would be most common. Such a hierarchy of architecture would demonstrate that some people had access to much more labor than others and that they could thus afford much more elaborate and impressive houses. Some of these houses would be on large rural estates. Such patterns would clearly indicate social stratification and would suggest differential control of wealth in the form of land and labor. The scale of civic structures as well as private ones would indicate the ability of centralized authorities to command and organize labor.

Both the distribution and quality of artifacts would reflect functional and social differentiation. Some kinds of occupational specialization, such as the manufacture of ceramics, stone tools or ornaments, and other durable things would be apparent, particularly since most such production seems to have been carried out in houses. It might even be possible to detect the formal marketplace where barter and exchange occurred. Particular sets of artifacts would be found in ritual places, providing a glimpse of how the state ideology operated. Collections of artifacts from elite domestic contexts would yield remains of some of the status symbols used by nobles. Many of these would be obvious imports which came from great distances—things so costly and rare that only elites could enjoy them. Some would be so finely made that we could assume that craftspeople making elite status symbols existed.

It is worthwhile to consider what lines of evidence would not be useful and what kinds of things we could not learn easily from the archaeological record. Although the Aztecs had more elaborate funeral rituals for elites than for commoners, they cremated most of their dead, so mortuary evidence for social and political structure would be impossible to recover. Details of stratification recorded in the written accounts might not be archaeologically detectable. For example, we might not be able to distinguish the house of an elite warrior from that of a wealthy merchant. Because the Aztecs usually established few or no resident soldiers or governors in the regions they conquered, we might have difficulty reconstructing the extent of their empire. But despite such shortcomings, the archaeological record would leave no doubt that Aztec society conformed to our model of statehood.

Limitations of Analysis

There is little doubt that we could sort out the general evolutionary status and relationships of the Yanomamo, Tongans, and Aztecs. We loaded the dice in our favor by using these particular societies to demonstrate the archaeological correlates of evolutionary status. They are documented by written records, so we know that they are particularly clear-cut evolutionary examples. We also treated these societies in a synchronic fashion—analyzing them as if they were static, not dynamic. We made assumptions about what we would find under ideal conditions of fieldwork and preservation. Finally, we ignored the most interesting but difficult levels of analysis. Although it was possible to discern the general outlines of the behaviors and institutions associated with egalitarian societies, chiefdoms, and states, we did not try to reconstruct such things as the details of the Aztec system of social strata or the relationships between different grades of Tongan chiefs.

ARCHAEOLOGICAL RECONSTRUCTION OF CLASSIC COPÁN MAYA POLITICS

In this final section we will consider the evolutionary status of the Classic Copán Maya. Although we will not trace this society through its whole evolutionary history, we will cite some trends over the short term that reflect evolutionary processes. We will also show that it is possible to reconstruct some fairly specific details of political organization.

The Copán polity reached its greatest size and complexity between roughly A.D. 750–800. One aim of our research since 1975 has been to reconstruct the political institutions of Copán at that time and the processes of their political maturation. Since it was clear even to the 19th-century explorers that the Copán Maya had a nonegalitarian sociopolitical system, the real issue is what kind of hierarchical society was present in Late Classic times, given the evidence summarized in Chapter 3? What would we call Copán in evolutionary terms and, more important, how does it reflect the evolutionary trends and processes we discussed earlier? In considering these questions, we will imagine that we cannot understand the meaning of the art or inscriptions at Copán in order to make the exercise more "pure" from an archaeological standpoint.

Settlement Research

The most conspicuous feature of the Copán settlement system is the dominance of the Main Group, which is vastly larger and more impressive than any other site in the valley. Although a few other sites share some of its features, such as carved monuments, ball courts, and temples, in none are they present at the same scale. All this strongly suggests that the Main Group was the permanent capital of a political system that extended over hundreds of square kilometers. We also know that many thousands of person-days of labor were necessary for the construction of the Main Group architecture and that such labor must have been provided by people living in the much smaller sites of the valley; clearly the few inhabitants of the Main Group possessed considerable prestige and authority, which were expressed by architecture and sculpture. Excavations into Main Group buildings show that carved monuments and public stone structures were built there for hundreds of years, reaching their greatest size near the end of the construction sequence. This suggests an increasing process of political centralization.

Over 1,400 smaller sites have been located in the valley, and although most of these were undoubtedly residences, they exhibit great variation in size and quality of architecture (see Fig. 3.21). Most conspicuously, Type 3 and 4 sites in some ways resemble the Main Group, especially in their large, finely cut stone buildings, which often had vaulted ceilings and elaborate sculpture (Fig. 10.7). Excavations show that many such sites had long histories, growing through time just as the Main Group did. They are also

FIGURE 10.7   An elite building recently excavated and restored at Copán. It is the central building in a larger set of buildings. All of these buildings were of high quality construction and required a total of about 18,000 person-days to construct. Over 640 pieces of sculpture, including a carved throne or bench, were associated with them, as befits their elite status. Flanked by buildings that were probably residences, this central building had religious and political functions.

like the Main Group in that labor must have been brought in from elsewhere to build them. Associated dates show that some of these elaborate residences long survived the abandonment of the capital.

In stark contrast are the much smaller Type 1 and 2 sites—by far the most numerous—that are scattered over the rural sections of the valley. These are usually simply built, and lack impressive ornamentation. Most required only the labor of their inhabitants to build, and many were occupied only for a short time.

Because we have such a good sample of sites of all kinds, both from survey and excavations, as well as an excellent sequence of dates, we can reconstruct the population with some accuracy. At its height, the Copán valley held about 27,000 people. Falling into the high end of the chiefdom range, a population of this size characterized many early states. At least 70–75 percent of the people lived in sites of low rank and presumably provided the food energy and labor to support those of high rank (Fig. 10.8).

Although there were several discernible levels to the settlement hierarchy, large centers are not as widely and evenly spaced as spatial models would predict if they had important administrative or economic functions. Rather they cluster very close to the Main Group. In fact, most sites are within a 5 km radius of the capital, and population density in this region would have been very high: 900 per km^2 at A.D. 750–800. Such densities would only have been possible if intensive (and in this setting probably destructive) forms of agriculture had been used. We know from the dating of sites that most people originally lived on the highly productive and stable soils of the valley floor but spread out onto more marginal land as population grew. Such a pattern is consistent with increasing economic

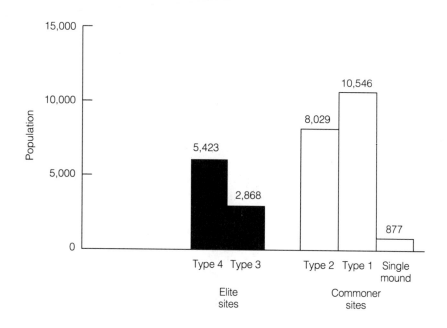

FIGURE 10.8 Copán's population in A.D. 800 was distributed among residential sites of different ranks. Type 4 sites are the highest in rank, and single mound sites are lowest. Ranking of sites was determined by scale and complexity of architecture.

stratification. Some people living in Type 4 sites do seem to specialize in making elite objects of shell, stone, and possibly cloth.

Burials

About 600 burials have been recovered from sites of all contexts at Copán, most from the mature period of political development. The most complicated tombs and grave goods that accompany these burials (Fig. 10.9) are found in and around the Main Group (Agurcia and Fash 1989). Burials elsewhere are much less impressive, but many people in complex sites are interred in well-built stone chambers with offerings of vessels and other objects. Elaborate Type 3 and 4 sites yield both fairly elaborate and very simple burials, suggesting that people of markedly different social ranks lived in the same residential compounds.

Analysis of skeletons indicates that around A.D. 800 people from all residences were short-lived and suffered from many diseases, particularly those related to poor nutrition. This occurs at the same time that both excavations and palynology show severe deterioration of the agricultural landscape.

Art

In addition to sculpture on buildings, Copán has many other monuments (such as stelae and altars) that show not only complex symbolism but also

(a)

(b)

FIGURE 10.9   (a) An elite tomb with a stone chamber at Copán; (b) a simple Copán burial with a single stone wall; (c) a simple pit burial. Such variation presumably reflects differences in wealth and social rank.

(c)

people. Such monuments are usually found in public places, particularly open plazas where large numbers of people could congregate. The portraits depict men wearing elaborate costumes and other status symbols, many of which have fairly clear religious, political, and military implications. Much of this same symbolism is seen on public buildings and tombs; small objects of stone, bone, wood, and ceramics also share it as well. Monuments and small objects are most impressive at the Main Group, but are found in other Type 3 and 4 groups as well.

Evolutionary Inferences

Given all this evidence, would we call Copán a chiefdom or a state? In terms of its territorial size and total population, the mature Copán polity could fall into either category. Population densities are very high, at levels more typical of states than chiefdoms. Population growth between A.D. 400 and 800 is very rapid, suggesting that sociopolitical evolution for that period was very dynamic as well.

By A.D. 750–850 strong political centralization is demonstrated by the dominance of a single major center, the Main Group. Not only are there major religious and civic monuments here but portraits of individuals who obviously enjoyed a mixture of high political and religious status and who could commission monuments to glorify themselves, particularly in their ritual roles. These we can be sure were rulers of some sort. Artistic representations show the elaborate status symbols indicative of high status. Emphasis on display and ritual is characteristic of well-developed chiefdoms and some early states. The scale of architecture at the Main Group indicates that leaders could mobilize large amounts of labor, but not on a scale that would have been punitive, given the size of the overall population. Rich tombs beneath temple-pyramids suggest that leaders were perhaps deified after death, if not before. But the vigor of the Main Group wanes abruptly around A.D. 800–850, an indication of the fragility of this centralized political system. This evidence offers no way to decide whether we are dealing with a rank or a stratified society.

A complex hierarchy of social and political statuses is indicated by the variation in residential scale and complexity. Particularly obvious is the existence of numerous highly ranked elite groups within Copán society with their own access to considerable labor, and ability to use and display costly status symbols, most important, carved monuments similar to those found in the Main Group. People of obviously varied rank lived in these elite sites. An implication is that there were corporate groups with their own powerful leaders in the Copán system and that these were probably kin groups. Consistent with this interpretation is the gradation of residences in the settlement system as a whole and the fact that few status objects seem to be entirely restricted to the highest-ranking people. Copán society probably had a strong segmental character, with many social and political groups that were potential competitors of the central ruler, perhaps an important factor in the political fragility mentioned above. That some major elite centers survived the collapse of the ruling line in the Main Group reinforces the idea that they had independent political resources. Typical of many chiefdoms, this situation suggests ranking rather than stratification.

Reconstructed population densities as well as studies of the skeletal population indicate that the Copán population was under great stress during its mature phase. The main cause of this stress was the deterioration of the agricultural landscape. People of all social ranks seem to suffer from nutritional diseases; no one seems to be privileged enough to be insulated from these stresses. These patterns suggest ranking, because there is no evidence for any sort of centrally controlled attempts to solve this problem, which may be another sign of the weakness of the political structure. On the other hand, elites seem to have suffered less from nutritional disease than lower-ranking individuals. The strong variations in agricultural potential of the Copán landscape would probably encourage certain forms of economic stratification, especially under conditions of high population density.

Lack of abundant evidence of well-developed economic specialization and the attachments of some specialists to the households of the elite suggest a relatively simple nonagricultural economic system, one which would neither require strong rulers to manage, nor offer opportunities for self-serving manipulative behavior. Again, this is more typical of chiefdoms than states.

For the purposes of our exercise we deliberately ignored the information tht epigraphers and iconographers have extracted from the inscriptions and art of Copán (see Chapter 9). Taking this information into account allows much finer, more detailed reconstructions of political organization, especially for the elite segment of society. For example, we can reconstruct a whole dynasty of rulers, with their names and titles. Much is known about their rituals and worldview that were central to political dominance. We are just beginning to understand the titles and political significance of the subroyal elites. But even after adding all of these insights to the larger data set, we are still left with many evolutionary questions that can only be resolved by future work.

So what final conclusions can we draw? The clearest one is that the mature Copán sociopolitical system cannot be neatly pigeonholed as either a chiefdom or a state. It exhibits characteristics of each. More important, though, it was a very dynamic system, especially in terms of population growth, with rapid, associated institutional changes in the centralization and segregation of political authority. Copán, in short, seems to be one of those revealing evolutionary cases that strongly reflects evolutionary processes inherent in our political model. It stimulates us to think about processes of change rather than simply to categorize — perhaps the most important contribution that any model can make to our larger understanding of how the world works.

POINTS TO REMEMBER

- All societies face political problems, and all societies have leaders and some form of government.

- Ethnographically observed societies provide archaeologists with models for political evolution in the past.

- Egalitarian leaders, who acquire their influence through achievement, have little or no access to power or wealth as political tools.

- Ranked societies have built-in social inequalities as well as formal offices of leadership that are inherited.

- Chiefs have many important governmental functions but relatively little access to power or wealth.

- Origins of ranking are a very important archaeological issue for those concerned with political evolution.

- States are characterized by social classes that have differential wealth, prestige, and political power.

- The process of political evolution includes increasing centralization, increasing ascription, greater segregation, and a decline of kinship as an effective mechanism of social integration.

- Political institutions have archaeological correlates that, if properly recovered, allow us to reconstruct political behavior and to arrange societies along a continuum of political evolution.

FOR FURTHER READING*

Fried's *The Evolution of Political Society* is the basic source. Upham's *The Evolution of Political Systems* presents a variety of applications of evolutionary principles. Drennan and Uribe's *Chiefdoms in the Americas,* Earle's *Chiefdoms in Archaeological Perspective,* Johnson and Earle's *The Evolution of Human Societies,* and Peebles and Kus's "Some Archaeological Correlates of Ranked Societies" look at the important transitional stage of human sociopolitical evolution, Broda, Carrasco, and Matos's *The Great Temple of Tenochtitlan* brings together economic and ideological features of Aztec society.

*Full citations appear in the bibliography.

CHAPTER ELEVEN

REALMS

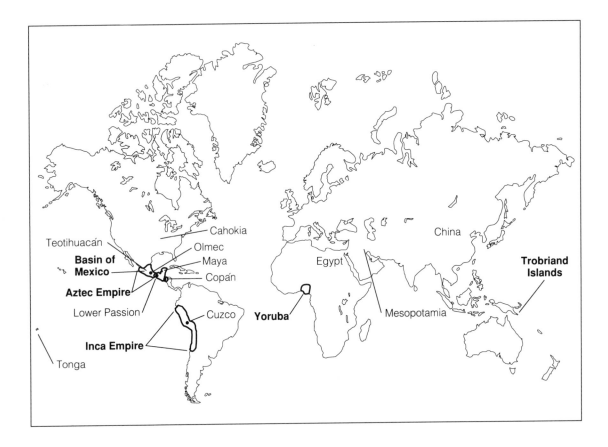

This chapter, like Chapter 10, deals with political organization, but whereas the previous chapter's focus was the evolution of political behavior and institutions, our topics here are the archaeological reconstruction of political structure at a given point in time and the interactions among political systems. Models of basic kinds of political organization (egalitarian, rank, stratified, state) given in the previous chapter provide the basis for this discussion, which will primarily focus on political organization among hierarchical societies. In analyzing political structure here we will be concerned specifically with:

1. The functions of leaders

2. The structure of government

3. How decisions are made and, if they are enforced, how they are enforced

4. The kinds of political factions and how they pursue their interests

5. The extent of the political system in terms of both population and territory

Interaction between independent political systems raises another set of issues:

1. Are the interacting political systems similar to or different from one another?

2. What kinds of interaction have taken place (e.g., warfare, royal intermarriage, diplomatic exchanges) and how are these interactions structured?

3. What are the functions of these interactions?

Later in this chapter we will consider how these questions have been addressed in two different regions, the Maya lowlands and the Central Andes. But first we will review general categories of evidence applying to political reconstruction.

APPROACHES TO RECONSTRUCTING POLITICAL STRUCTURE

Perhaps the most important thing to understand about any political system is its size. It is simple to define the limits of modern states, since these are laid out as sharp territorial lines on maps. People who live within these boundaries are citizens of the country in question or at least are subject to its laws and policies. It is much more difficult to establish the limits of past polities, particularly those for which we have no written records. Such polities frequently had no sharp territorial boundaries, and even if they did, these may be hard to detect.

In egalitarian societies there is a strong tendency for the local community to function as an autonomous political unit, so the archaeologist's task, on one level, is comparatively simple: identify such communities. On the other hand, communities may fission into antagonistic factions or situationally become allied into larger coalitions (e.g., for purposes of warfare). Egalitarian political systems are extremely dynamic in this regard, posing significant problems of reconstruction.

We are on somewhat firmer ground with hierarchical societies, which by definition have some form of institutionalized leadership and political centralization that tend to prevent fissioning. Even here, though, territory may be less important in defining the extent of a polity than the allegiance of people to a leader.

Settlement Systems and Central Places

Perhaps the single most important strategy for reconstructing the political limits and structure of an ancient society is settlement system analysis (Evans and Gould 1982; Haggett 1966; Hodder and Orton 1976; Johnson 1972). Remember that this strategy reconstructs the relationships among archaeological sites in a region; one dimension of such relationships involves politics. Perhaps the simplest insight into politics derives from the different scale, distribution, and functions of sites in complex societies.

As defined in this book, a complex society is internally differentiated and is either ranked or stratified (Fried 1967). Inevitably, in such societies, population is distributed among a number of spatially discrete settlements. Within that population, individuals and groups play different political and economic roles. Transport and communication, in energetic if not monetary terms, help determine the distribution of central places. The term *central place,* which has been introduced in previous chapters, is particularly useful for understanding the political structure of complex societies (Sanders and Webster 1988). It refers to any place, in a territory with a great number of settlements, where centralized activities occur, including political ones. Political central places administer the obligations and rights of others, usually smaller places. Central places are typically communities where people live. An advantage of the concept of central place is that it has more neutral implications than other terms we might use, such as *town, ceremonial center,* or *city.*

Egalitarian societies generally lack political central places. For example, Yanomamo villages all have the same functions and show small variations in size, as we saw in Chapter 10. In simple ranked societies involving a few thousand people and a few settlements, by contrast, the residence of the chief can be considered a central place. It is where he organizes and often leads rituals, makes political and legal decisions, and collects and redistributes economic goods. Two brief ethnographic examples help us to envision the problems of archaeological reconstruction.

The Trobriand Islands

The Trobriand Islands lie off the east end of New Guinea. In the ethnographic present the Trobrianders numbered several thousand, residing in

FIGURE 11.1
Trobriand yam storage structure. The largest and most numerous of these buildings would be associated with the households and villages of Trobriand chiefs. If they could be detected archaeologically, they would be one of the few kinds of evidence for any distinctive central place or capital in the Trobriand settlement system.

21 villages. The Trobrianders provide an interesting transitional evolutionary case because their political organization has characteristics of both egalitarian Big-Man organization (see Box 10.1) and ranked chiefdom organization. Although kinship groups were ranked in terms of their prestige, and only certain individuals had the right to assume chiefly leadership, no one automatically inherited the title of chief. Rather, like Big-Men, aspiring chiefs had to achieve their positions through personal prowess. At times, there was no effective unification under chiefs at all, because there were no individuals suited to assume the role. Particularly powerful chiefs dominated large clusters of villages.

Omarakana, the village with the residence of the most powerful chief, was the political central place, but it was not strikingly different in scale and plan from the other villages. The high chief's residence may have been larger than those of lesser chiefs but only marginally so, since he did not command labor on a scale much greater than they did. The highest-ranking chief had more wives than men of lower rank, and each wife resided in her own house. Chiefs received annual gifts in the form of foodstuffs from all villages, including his own, and these were placed in large storehouses in the capital for later redistribution at festivals. Such storehouses would perhaps be the only outstanding architectural features of the capital (Fig. 11.1).

The Trobriand political system would be difficult to reconstruct through settlement archaeology. Assuming that the sizes and locations of settlements could be determined by surface survey, it might not be possible to recognize the political capital. All villages would look much alike. Test excavations would produce basically the same range of artifacts for all of them. If we carried out large-scale excavations at several communities, we might identify the specialized storage structures and, just possibly, the somewhat larger chief's house at Omarakana. It might or might not be clear that Omarakana was a central place. All things considered, Trobriand society would probably strike us as basically egalitarian in political terms.

Tonga

In contrast, a hierarchy of settlement would be obvious in the larger chiefdoms of Polynesia (see Chapter 10). Mu'a, the Tongan central place, or capital, differed from Omarakana not so much in function but in scale, reflecting the enhanced prestige and political authority of the high chief, the Tui Tonga. He was able to mobilize much more labor than any Trobriand chief for public works, mainly expressed in the form of burial mounds (some with huge interior megaliths) and a vast walled enclosure for the large-scale public ceremonies appropriate to his exalted position.

Of particular interest is the relatively small scale of the high chief's residential platform, which is dwarfed by the great enclosure wall and tombs. In ranked societies there is little real power and coercive force at the disposal of the chief, so it is difficult for him to mobilize labor for residential construction, since this is largely a personal rather than communal concern. It is apparently much easier for chiefs to construct temples, tombs, and public places; these enhance the prestige of the chief, but are also sacred or useful places for the larger population.

What would be clear from the archaeological perspective is that Tongan settlement was differentiated into at least two levels — small dispersed rural households and the capital or central place of the chief. Careful excavation of a range of rural settlements might pick up the houses of subchiefs. In any case, there would be little doubt that there was centralized political leadership at Mu'a and that other communities or residences were politically subordinate to the capital. The hierarchical nature of Tongan society would be much more obvious than that of the Trobriands. Let us now turn to a purely archaeological example, the Olmec of ancient Mesoamerica.

The Olmec

For over 50 years archaeologists have known of large, impressive sites along the tropical rivers draining the Gulf Coast of Mexico. Collectively called "Olmec" sites, these represent a distinctive archaeological culture (Sharer and Grove 1989a, 1989b). Sites such as La Venta (Fig. 11.2) are characterized by monumental public architecture, imported stone and other exotic

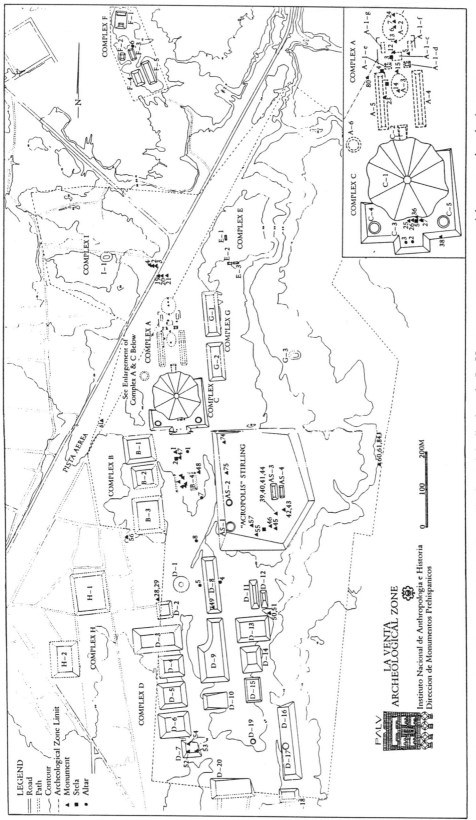

FIGURE 11.2 The core of the Olmec capital at La Venta. Having originally thought La Venta was a vacant ceremonial center, archaeologists now know that people lived there in considerable numbers and that it dominated a hierarchy of smaller settlements.

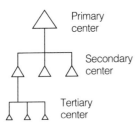

FIGURE 11.3 Recent research has shown that there were at least three distinct levels of settlement in the Olmec polity centered on La Venta. La Venta itself was the political capital. It was the largest settlement, with the most monumental public architecture as well as numerous stone sculptures. Secondary centers had earthen mounds representing civic structures; during test-pitting of them, many objects of high quality have been recovered. Tertiary settlements, which had no civic architecture in the form of earthen mounds, have yielded only basic, utilitarian artifacts. Although the outlines of the settlement hierarchy are clear, we do not know how many secondary and tertiary centers there were.

goods, some rich burials, and an impressive tradition of stone sculpture. They were originally thought to be vacant ceremonial centers, but more recently have been seen as capitals of small hierarchical societies. Unfortunately, little work was done to determine the nature of Olmec settlement outside of the large centers.

Recent surveys and associated test excavations (Rust and Sharer 1988) have produced important settlement information for the period between 800 and 500 B.C. First, the center of La Venta had a permanent resident population. Second, there were smaller communities scattered up and down the nearby rivers, and there was little or no occupation away from the rivers. Mainly located on the rich land near river channels, these smaller communities fall into two types. The larger type has earthen mounds and some high quality luxury items in the form of pottery vessels, figurines, and polished stone celts. The smaller type lacks earthen mounds, artifacts tend to be plain and utilitarian, and luxury goods are rare. Occupation debris at both kinds of sites is dense.

The picture emerges of a political system composed of three tiers of settlement, oriented along the rivers (Fig. 11.3). La Venta is clearly the central place, probably representing the political capital and the household of the ruler, though many other people lived there as well. Supporting La Venta, and politically dependent on it, were two other forms of permanent settlement associated with rich riverbank soils, but one form seems to have been ritually and politically more impressive than the other. Archaeologists commonly associate such a three-tiered settlement hierarchy with the administrative structure of chiefdoms or early states. We believe that La Venta was the capital of a chiefdom that probably had a population of at least 10,000 people. As a central place La Venta was the Olmec equivalent of Mu'a at Tonga.

Although the character of the La Venta settlement is now clearer, its territorial extent remains uncertain. Minimally, it seems to have incorporated the population along the river for a distance of 20–25 km. Future settlement survey work will eventually determine its maximal size and serve as the basis for estimates of the population of the polity.

Determining Political Boundaries

Our examples illustrate a commonsense approach to using settlement information to reconstruct the most general outlines of political structure. In the Tongan and Olmec cases, a site hierarchy is determined, and lesser places are assumed to be politically subordinate to the central place. In the case of small islands, there are natural territorial boundaries to political systems. Occasionally there are other kinds of rather obvious topographical boundaries as well. But how do we sort out territoriality and political affiliation when such natural boundaries are not clear and when there are many levels of settlement and many central places?

Archaeologists have frequently used formal spatial models, often drawn from geography, to attempt to understand the scale and organization of complex political systems. We discussed these in Chapter 7, and at that time made the point that the distribution of contemporaneous sites over the landscape has been found to conform to regularities in social and political organization. Two expressions of regularity of political organization in site distribution data are the rank-size rule (Johnson 1980) and the administrative principle of central place theory. The rank-size rule states that in a rank-ordering of settlements in a region, if the region is politically unified the size of each settlement should be a fraction of the size of the largest settlement, such that site N will be 1/Nth the size of the largest site. When the regional pattern conforms to this rule, we can assume that it is politically unified, with the capital being the largest center. If, on the other hand, the sites in order of size do not conform to the fraction rule, the pattern they show may reveal other political organization. Figure 11.4 shows the settlement pattern of the Basin of Mexico at about A.D. 1350, before political unification under the Mexica Aztecs. The ranked sizes of regional centers at that time is shown in the graph (Fig. 11.4b). By the end of the Aztec period (A.D. 1521), the basin was politically unified, centered on Tenochtitlan (see Fig. 7.1), which was six to ten times as large as the next-largest city.

If the largest centers are all roughly equal in size, but the extent of the territories they control is not known, borders may be estimated by drawing "Thiessen polygons" around the centers (Hammond 1974). At the simplest level, this involves drawing a line between these centers at the midpoint between them. The lines join to form polygons that are the territories. Note that refinements of the method are readily introduced by altering the location of these lines to account for variations in site size (and thus in the necessary area to support each center's population), in productivity of the landscape, and in the location of special features (Fig. 11.5).

We assume that in complex societies the settlement hierarchy will comprise at least two levels and that the smaller sites arrayed around higher-order centers will be politically dependent on them. *Central Place Theory* (Christaller 1966) predicts that the location of dependent sites, relative to higher-order centers, will depend on the importance of market exchange, transport facility, and political administration. The *political administration variant* shows well-defined clusters of lower-order centers around presumed capitals (Fig. 4.17). Unlike settlement distributions generated by economic forces (see Chapter 8), this distribution shows lower-order centers oriented toward only one higher-order center.

Political Structure

When written sources are lacking, functions of leaders in hierarchical societies must be inferred from other lines of archaeological evidence. One of the most direct is representational art. Images often show hierarchical scenes with rulers or other important people taking charge of particular

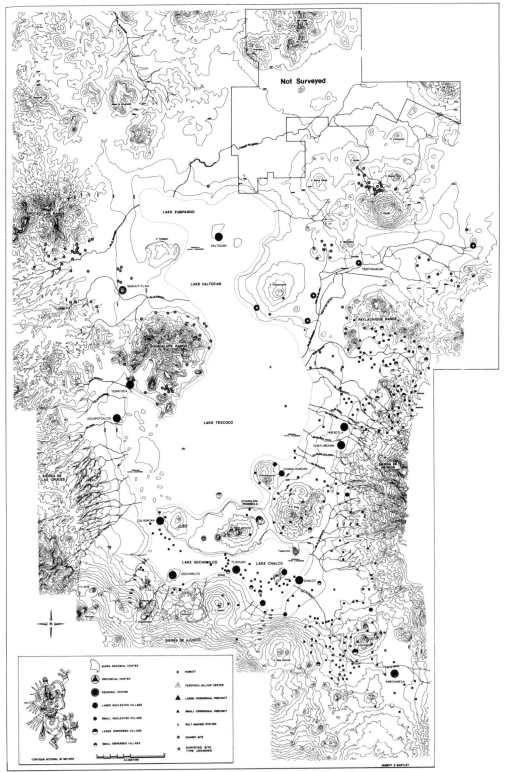

Not Surveyed

LAKE ZUMPANGO

POTZOTLAN RANGE

XALTOCAN

QUAUHTITLAN

LAKE XALTOCAN

TEOTIHUACAN

PATLACHIQUE RANGE

GUADALUPE RANGE

TENAYUCA

AZCAPOTZALCO

HUEXOTLA

COATLINCHAN

SIERRA DE
LAS CRUCES

LAKE TEXCOCO

SIERRA DE
NEVADA

CHIMALHUACAN

IXTAPALAPA
PENINSULA

CULHUACAN

LAKE XOCHIMILCO   TLAHUAC   LAKE CHALCO

CHALCO

XOCHIMILCO

SIERRA DE AJUSCO

AMECAMECA

SUPRA-REGIONAL CENTER   HAMLET

PROVINCIAL CENTER   TEZOYUCA HILLTOP CENTER

REGIONAL CENTER   LARGE CEREMONIAL PRECINCT

LARGE NUCLEATED VILLAGE   SMALL CEREMONIAL PRECINCT

SMALL NUCLEATED VILLAGE   SALT MAKING STATION

LARGE DISPERSED VILLAGE   QUARRY SITE

SMALL DISPERSED VILLAGE   SURVEYED SITE,
                               TYPE UNKNOWN

CONTOUR INTERVAL 50 METERS   KILOMETERS   ROBERT S. SANTLEY

(a)

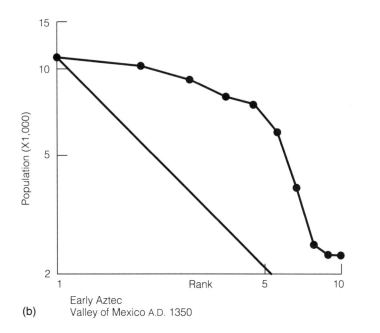

(b) Early Aztec
Valley of Mexico A.D. 1350

FIGURE 11.4 The rank-size rule identifies hierarchies in settlement systems: The greater the disparity in site sizes, the more likely that hierarchical political organization is in effect and that an area is politically unified under one political authority. On the other hand, the ranking may show little difference, as does the graph (b) of Early Aztec regional centers in the Basin of Mexico, thus indicating a lack of political unification. The map (a) shows the settlement pattern of the Basin of Mexico at the beginning of the Aztec period. Gregory Johnson's (1980) rank-size analysis shows that this ranking is consistent with regional (rather than Basin of Mexico–wide) political autonomy, substantiating accounts in native historical annals recorded in the postconquest Colonial period, which document the lack of political unification before the Aztec tribute empire. Compare this map with that of the settlement of the Basin of Mexico in 1519, Figure 7.1.

tasks. Scenes of leaders carrying out religious functions are perhaps most common, but some ancient societies have left us extremely detailed artistic representations of a wide range of other functions as well. For example, Egyptian wall paintings depict the activities of officials from the pharaoh on down (Hobson 1987). This is direct evidence of leadership functions and also shows how officials related to one another in terms of government structure and decision making.

Unfortunately most prehistoric cultural traditions were not as rich in representative art as that of the Egyptians, and even when rulers or other important people are portrayed, the scope of roles shown tends to be limited. Among the Classic Maya, rulers are usually shown carrying out ritual functions, or, more rarely, engaged in warfare (Schele and Miller 1986). Ritual was, of course, a central preoccupation of leaders in many nonindustrial societies. However, though closely related to politics, its occurrence is probably overstated in representational art.

We must usually infer the existence and function of leaders of various sorts from less direct evidence, such as the presence of a complex settlement hierarchy indicating there existed subordinate leaders or administrators in addition to the rulers. Another line of evidence is archaeological remains of organized behavior involving large numbers of people. For example, the construction of pyramids, temples or other public buildings, irrigation works, elaborate tombs, or fortifications often is assumed to indicate specialized leadership. The same is true of coordinated events such as military confrontations. When such activities are reflected in the archaeological record, we can at least make the reasonable hypothesis that managing them was part of the function of leaders.

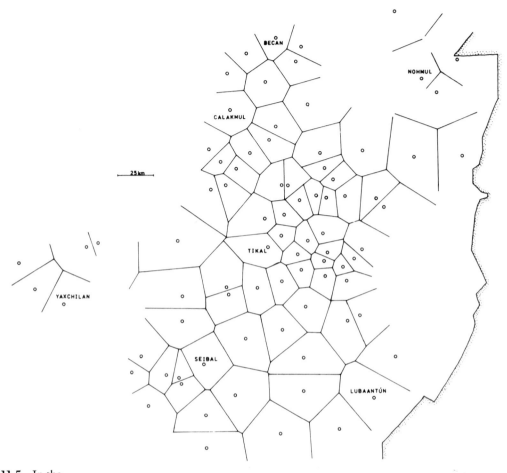

FIGURE 11.5 In the absence of any other information about the boundaries of the domains of capitals, archaeologists draw the boundaries between sites, relative to the size of each site, borrowing the use of "Thiessen polygons" from geographers. A map by Norman Hammond shows locations of Classic Maya sites in the Yucatán Peninsula and a preliminary delineation of the territory most adjacent to each site.

Burials are often quite informative about leadership functions, for two reasons. First, in hierarchical societies it is often possible to distinguish the burials of high-ranking people, who may have had some leadership roles (Binford 1971; Tainter 1978). Royal tombs are not uncommon. Second, rulers and elites often take with them into the grave status symbols that reflect their political functions. Bronze Age European chiefs were often buried with arms and armour, indicating their functions as military leaders. Similarly, the famous burial army of the Chinese emperor Shang Chi Huang Ti glorifies the military role of the leader. At Cahokia, multiple burials, undoubtedly including sacrifices, distinguish some burials as high-ranking (see Box 11.1).

Unfortunately, of the many dimensions to political status and functions, only those which are of greatest prestige or cultural significance tend to be symbolized in mortuary treatment. The Bronze Age warrior chief probably mediated legal disputes for his people as well as leading them in warfare, but this function might be less obviously, if at all, symbolized in his burial.

BOX 11.1

WAS CAHOKIA THE CAPITAL
OF A CHIEFDOM OR A STATE?

Across the Mississippi River from St. Louis stands the largest prehistoric pyramid in the United States: Monk's Mound covers 6 ha and stands 31 m high. Its construction was carried out in several stages over many years, no doubt requiring the labor of many people who lived in the surrounding community that we now call Cahokia.

Cahokia is located in the central Mississippi River valley just east of St. Louis, on a fertile floodplain. This region has been investigated by archaeologists for many years (see Smith 1978), with most attention focused on Cahokia itself, obviously the capital of the local political system. Even though the site has been heavily disturbed, archaeologists have mapped over 100 large mounds in an area of 13–15 km². Population estimates of this area during Cahokia's peak (ca. A.D. 1050–1250) range from less than 10,000 to 42,000 (Milner 1986).

Like other Mississippian centers, Cahokia's central area included mounds and a plaza (Holley et al. 1989). On the summit of Monk's Mound there was a large building that probably combined the functions of temple, ancestral shrine, and political administration for the rulers of Cahokia. Many of the other smaller mounds were also civic structures, built with the labor of the resident population, as was the defensive palisade along one edge of the site. Associated with structures, elite graves are distinguished from those of lower-ranking people by burial context, form, and grave goods. Multiple burials of both men and women, some of them undoubtedly sacrificed, were found in one of the smaller mounds. Thus, both architecture and burials suggest strong social differentiation and impressive levels of organization.

Surveys and excavations have located many other sites along the valleys north and south of Cahokia. Some of these were important centers in their own right, since they include large civic structures. Many others are tiny farmsteads situated on ridges or high land in the generally flat topography of the valley bottom, where fertile soils supported crops of maize, squash, and a variety of domesticated North American plants. Hunting, gathering, and fishing supplemented the agricultural diets of the population. Exotic items of shell and stone evidence long-distance exchange, and some archaeologists believe there is evidence of craft specialization as well.

Although there is general agreement that Cahokia was the capital of an impressive hierarchical society, archaeologists disagree as to whether that society was a chiefdom or a state. Some argue that Cahokia's political control and influence, especially its trade routes, extended for hundreds of miles up and down the river systems of midwestern and eastern North America, indicating state-level organization. Others believe that Cahokia was a ranked society whose chiefs controlled only comparatively small local populations within 15 to 20 km of the capital. The latter view seems to conform best to the evidence as we now know it, but much more work needs to be done at Cahokia and at other sites within Cahokia's hypothesized sphere of influence before archaeologists develop a consensus about its political organization.

Artifacts may provide information about political structure. Sometimes certain classes of artifacts or features reflect some of the economic functions of government. In early Mesopotamia, large quantities of crude, highly standardized bowls may indicate that an essential function of government was to issue standardized rations of grain or beer to clients of the state or temple (Redman 1978). At Teotihuacán, some of the largest concentrations of obsidian debris are in the center of the city near major temples and palaces, strongly suggesting workshops in these areas and governmental control over obsidian production. Features such as roads or government storehouses reflect the Inca empire's concern with centralized storage of taxes and with construction of roads for effective transportation and communication (see below).

By far the most difficult questions to answer about political structure are how decisions were made and enforced, and what kinds of internal political factions existed. As we shall see shortly for the Copán Maya, it is sometimes possible to make reasonable inferences about these questions when archaeological data are abundant.

POLITICAL INTERACTION

The kinds of interactions that take place between political systems depend to a large degree on the nature of those systems. Are they structured in more or less the same way? Do they have the same patterns of government and leadership? Are there significant differences in scale among them in terms of territory or population? The first step in understanding interaction is reconstructing the political organization of each of the societies involved, as we just discussed. Assuming that we can do this and define their geographical limits, then we can ask: How might they have interacted?

Warfare

Warfare is extremely common, and is reflected in the archaeological record in many ways (Ferguson 1984; Haas 1990). (See Box 11.2.) Perhaps fortification is the most obvious evidence among complex nonindustrial societies; settlements, especially politically important central places, are often fortified in some fashion (Fig. 11.6). When systems of fortification protect not only central places but also much of the larger territory, they help us to understand the extent of political systems as well as processes of interaction between them. The Great Wall of China is a good example.

Changes in settlement systems sometimes reflect warfare. In Mesopotamia shortly after 3000 B.C. many early cities were fortified and in some cases nearby rural settlements declined or disappeared as their populations sought shelter within the city walls (Adams 1966). Burning or other forms of destruction are also often signs of conflict.

BOX 11.2

WARFARE AMONG THE ONEOTA
OF THE MISSISSIPPI VALLEY

How do we recognize archaeological evidence for warfare?

Despite the fact that warfare is historically so common, archaeologists often have trouble documenting it in prehistoric contexts, particularly for egalitarian societies. But we know that warfare involves physical violence, resulting in death and injury. At least some of these injuries should show up on bones, and analysis of skeletal remains is an important line of evidence that can reveal evidence of violence, if not warfare itself.

In fact, careful study of skeletons from the upper Mississippi Valley revealed injuries from violence (Milner, Anderson, and Smith 1991). The Oneota were an egalitarian tribe who lived in small villages and practiced a mixed economy of farming, hunting, and gathering in a temperate forest environment. The photographs show human bones recovered from an Oneota cemetery dating to about A.D. 1300 in west-central Illinois. Cut marks resulting from scalping are clearly visible on the skull at the bottom. On the top is a sternum (breastbone) with the tips of two arrowheads embedded in it; both penetrated the individual from the rear.

But do such injuries indicate warfare? A feud within the community might lead to occasional lethal violence. In this case, however, there is little doubt that warfare was responsible. Of the 264 individuals found in this context, 43 individuals of both sexes (about a third of all adults) bore marks of violent death; this figure is probably conservative, since many wounds would leave no traces on bones. There are also indications that many victims were left unburied where they fell for considerable periods of time before their remains were recovered and placed in the cemetery.

This skeletal information tells us about the scale of violence, which might not be clear from other kinds of

evidence like finding weapons, or artistic representations of warriors. Conflict must have been frequent and intense to have affected so many people in this small community. Other evidence supports this interpretation. For example, in this part of Illinois, many villages dating from A.D. 1300 were fortified, or located in defensible positions, suggesting that warfare was common. The village associated with the cemetery has not been excavated, but it is in a defensible location. If excavations reveal a protective palisade, then the warfare interpretation will be further strengthened.

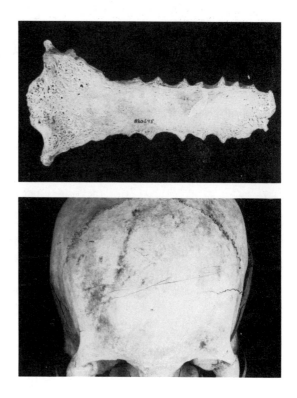

FIGURE 11.6   Maiden Castle in England. Ditches and embankments were widely used as fortifications and, fortunately for the archaeologist, are very durable.

Warfare leaves many other traces as well. Burials may show signs of war-related wounds (Milner 1991), and artifacts such as swords, shields, armor, or chariots unambiguously signal war.

Although fortifications may show that warfare occurred between polities, they rarely tell us who was fighting whom; the historical details are missing. Without such information, we cannot perceive or explain the immediate cause of the conflict or its effects. Sudden changes in the archaeological record sometimes help us here. When the ceramic styles or architectural traditions of one region abruptly replace those of another, warfare is a good bet as an explanation, and we can know in at least a general sense who the adversaries were. If art and written inscriptions are present, they may allow detailed reconstructions of historical sequences of warfare (Fig. 11.7a). In such cases it is possible to know who was fighting whom, when confrontations occurred, and what their political effects were.

Elite Interaction

Remember that the concept of civilization does not imply political unity or harmony. In many parts of the world, independent polities have coex-

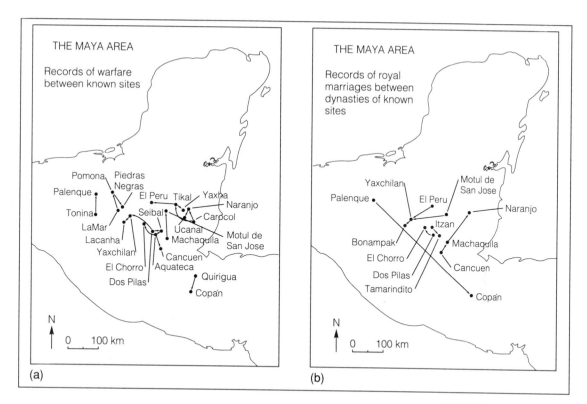

isted (and sometimes fought one another) while sharing a single Great Tradition. In such situations there may be complex interactions among rulers and elites that cross-cut political boundaries.

Diplomacy Perhaps the most obvious of these interactions (though this may involve markedly different cultures as well), diplomacy is primarily concerned with acquiring information about the condition and intentions of other leaders and with establishing or reaffirming amicable relationships with them. Diplomatic interaction usually cannot be directly inferred from the prehistoric archaeological record. Imported elite objects found at central places may reflect the elaborate gift-giving that often accompanied diplomatic missions, but without supporting evidence this remains conjecture, especially since many other kinds of relationships existed between elites.

Intermarriage and Alliance Often, elite intermarriage served to create political alliances by forming familial relationships among rulers (Culbert 1991 cites Maya instances; cf. Figs. 11.7b and 11.8). These relationships, and the shared Great Tradition, created very strong feelings of common interest among elites, even among those of warring polities. A dramatic example in Aztec history took place at the dedication of the Templo Mayor

FIGURE 11.7 (a) Inscriptions may document attacks by one center on another (direction of the arrows in the map of Maya centers indicates attack). (b) Marriages between elites at different Maya centers is documented in their inscriptions. The map shows centers linked by such arrangements; the arrows indicate the direction the bride traveled in.

FIGURE 11.8 In this illustration from the Codex Nuttall, which depicts a scene from the area around Oaxaca, a pre-Columbian royal bride is being carried by a diplomatic courier to her new husband in another city.

in Tenochtitlan in 1487. Numerous war captives were sacrificed when the great king Ahuitzotl dedicated the newly rebuilt pyramid and temple. Enemy kings, whose own warriors were being sacrificed, watched the ceremony as invited guests of Ahuitzotl, though he made sure that they were hidden from the view of the commoners:

> The reason for all of this secrecy was that they did not wish the common people — soldiers and captains — to suspect that kings and rulers made alliances, came to agreements, and framed friendships at the cost of the life of the common man, and the shedding of his blood.   *(Duran 1964:193–194)*

In many cultures elite relatives from different polities visited one another, carried out common rituals, and attended each other's funerals. Only rarely can we glimpse such interaction, important though it may have been, without the aid of written records or extremely explicit artistic images.

Trade and Commerce Elites and rulers may have controlled commercial exchanges, including those involving basic utilitarian goods, over long distances. To the extent that this was true, such exchanges had political as well as economic dimensions. There are three steps to investigating this possibility. First, identify the traded items and their sources. Second, estimate the volume of trade. Third, demonstrate that elites controlled trade. This last step is the most important and the most difficult. Sometimes archaeological contexts indicate elite patronage of commerce. The earliest Egyptian kings stocked their tombs with many foreign objects, some of which, such as timber, were imported on a large scale. Even without inscriptions, it would be obvious that kings concerned themselves with the politics of international trade. When production of materials for export is located near palaces, as at Teotihuacán, or when elite structures yield stockpiles of imported goods, the same possibility is suggested.

Let us now turn to two archaeological cases of complex societies in the New World: the Maya and the Inca. They reveal very different political traditions.

CLASSIC MAYA SITES AND POLITIES

Copán is but one of many of Classic Maya centers that reached maturity roughly between A.D. 600 and 800. As we saw in Chapter 9, a common Great Tradition, including distinctive art and architectural styles, ancestor worship, mathematical and calendrical systems, and a form of writing, was shared over an area of 250,000 km². These Great Tradition elements were most strongly expressed at sites which included huge temples and other buildings, reservoirs, and ceremonial roads as well as carved monuments. Large sites were at least 15–20 km distant from each other, and each was surrounded by smaller settlements. In some areas hierarchies of large and small centers can be discerned. Similarity in these settlement systems from one region to another, and to a somewhat lesser degree in scale, suggest parallel or duplicate functions and hence strongly imply political disunity. Large centers look very much like central places for independent political groupings.

In the early days of Maya archaeology, the largest complexes of monumental buildings were called major ceremonial centers, the smaller ones minor ceremonial centers. Centers used to be thought of as largely "vacant" places except perhaps for resident priest-rulers who worshiped at the temples and lived in monasterylike buildings (Thompson 1954). The revolution in Maya epigraphy discussed in Chapter 9, along with the discovery of royal tombs, changed this perspective; centers were obviously political central places of kings as well. Many centers are associated with **emblem glyphs** that may refer to them as places or, alternatively, to the titles or lineages of resident Maya lords. The pattern of use of such emblems may differentiate primary centers from politically dependent centers (Culbert 1991; Marcus 1976).

emblem glyphs Symbols that refer to places or alternatively to the titles or lineages of resident Maya lords.

Approximately 30–40 such emblem glyphs are known, some very old, others appearing near the end of the Classic period. These glyphs, along with what we know about the nature of the centers and their surrounding settlements, suggest two different hypotheses about Maya politics. The first is that the Maya were politically fragmented into 50–60 small, autonomous kingdoms during the Late Classic period. The second is that, at times, many kingdoms were at least temporarily united through conquest warfare. Such large Maya "superpolities" would have covered thousands of square kilometers and had populations in the hundreds of thousands. It is clear from Maya inscriptions, art, and fortifications that warfare between polities was very common, but some have argued that its purpose was mainly ritual (as opposed to political or economic) and that it was carried out on a small scale to secure elite victims for sacrifice. According to the second hypothesis, certain forms of warfare had expansionist political and territorial purposes as well.

These hypotheses bring us back to the two basic themes of this chapter: How did political systems interact? and How were they internally structured? We have many strategies for answering these questions, including:

1. Analysis of *art* and *epigraphy* (which, remember, can serve as elite propaganda, and so must be used with caution)

2. *Settlement studies*, showing politically significant concentrations or shifts in population, particularly with respect to central places

3. The presence of *artifacts*, such as weapons, and *architecture*, such as defensive fortifications (ditches, walls)

4. Analysis of the *scale of building construction* undertaken at various central places. Sharp increases or decreases in such activity, correlated with population history and epigraphic information, can indicate that conquest and political control (with attendant shifts in labor available to rulers) did in fact occur.

Copán: A Classic Maya Polity

Political Structure Information from settlement survey at Copán was summarized in Chapter 3. Such surveys, along with excavations at many house compounds of all types, provide detailed information on political structure. Recent research has also included large-scale excavation in the Main Group (the royal compound) and a concerted effort to recover and interpret the meanings of iconographic and epigraphic symbols represented in the sculpture of Copán.

Political Extent Copán is unusual among large Maya central places in that we can define the boundaries of its core political territory quite easily. There are no other centers of remotely comparable size within about 70 km, so it had no close political competitors. Insofar as there were concentrations of population within reasonable distance of Copán, they were obviously part of its political system rather than of another center. More important, Copán is in a narrow river valley surrounded by rugged upland terrain with little agricultural potential. South and east of the Copán Valley are no major Maya centers and in this mountainous zone, we find the southern culture area border of Mesoamerica as a whole. The nearest large center is Quiriguá, over 70 km to the north, over rugged terrain. The Copán River drains toward the north, into the Motagua River that connects drainage systems of the southern part of the Yucatán Peninsula (heartland of the Classic Maya), the Guatemalan highlands, and the southernmost centers, Quiriguá and Copán.

Archaeological surveys of the Copán Valley show that the population is heavily concentrated on, or near, the fertile soils near the river in the main valley, and in valleys of tributary streams. As expected, very few people lived in the rugged mountains. Of the roughly 450 km² in the drainage basin of the river, the Copán Maya probably lived on and farmed only about 20 percent.

The kingdom of Copán was thus a narrow, ribbonlike oasis of productive land 30 — 40 km long. Extensive surveys in this region indicate that its peak population at A.D. 800 was about 27,000 people. About 80 percent of these people lived within a very small area of about 40 km², within an easy day's walk of the royal center. Thus the core kingdom of Copán is both spatially and demographically quite small. No sophisticated geographical models are needed to assess its extent. During the seventh century the 12th king of Copán, Smoke Imix, erected five stelae along the length of the core territory, quite possibly to stake a claim to the most critical political real estate.

The Royal Compound As discussed in Chapter 3, the dominant central place of Copán is the Main Group, located at the heart of this small kingdom. This complex of temples, plazas, palaces, and carved monuments was essentially a royal compound, which covered an area about 460 m long and 150–300 m wide (Fash 1991). The largest buildings, some of which were originally over 30 m high, are on the southern end, forming an enormous raised platform, called the "Acropolis." Formed by 400 years of building and rebuilding, the Acropolis in its final form measured at least 160 m on a side (part of the east side has been washed away by the river). The Main Group dwarfs all other groups of elite buildings in the Copán Valley, showing that for four centuries the Copán kings were able to muster large amounts of labor for construction.

Unfortunately, when most of the buildings on the summit of the Acropolis were excavated and restored (by the Carnegie Institution between 1936 and 1946), little attention was paid to associated artifacts and features that might have indicated their functions. Ethnographic observations of royal compounds in other parts of the world provide models for understanding the Main Group.

The northern Great Court, with its many altars and statues of rulers, could easily have accommodated the whole population of the valley for the great public ceremonies that accompany royal coronations, marriages, and funerals. The more inaccessible and much smaller West Court on the Acropolis, surrounded by large temples, may have functioned as a more private ceremonial place for rulers and other elites. This is substantiated by the presence of Altar Q, showing 16 seated rulers, which was erected by Yax Pac, the 16th and last powerful king of Copán (see Chapters 3, 8, and 9). This monument asserts the legitimacy of Yax Pac's claim to royal power by showing him as descended from 15 earlier kings. Similar statements are made on statues of earlier kings in the Great Court and, on the most grandiose level, on the Hieroglyphic Staircase. These monuments would have been visible to the general public, asserting the power of kings and their right to rule.

In contrast, the East Court is probably even more restricted, the location of the residence of the ruler himself. The last four kings of Copán probably lived in buildings along the northern edge of the East Court. Along its east side were large temples, and on the south, a royal tomb (unfortunately, looted) with the associated name of Yax Pac. Recently, a building interpreted as a council house has been excavated adjacent to what we believe was the royal residence, and we will discuss its significance shortly.

Excavations into major buildings on the Acropolis suggest strongly that Altar Q records an actual dynastic sequence (Fash 1991). Architectural stratigraphy and associated buried inscriptions can be traced as far back as the third king. Judging by the sizes of the superimposed buildings there was rapid expansion of royal power peaking in the reign of 18 Jog during the early eighth century.

Kings typically have numerous relatives and retainers, and in many nonindustrial societies these people live in or immediately around the royal compound, forming the nuclei of royal courts. There is little residential architecture in the Main Group itself, though many smaller but still impressive groups are clustered around the southern and western sides of the

Acropolis. Surveys, test-pitting, and large-scale excavation indicate that these groups are residences. Given the articulation of some of the larger ones with the edges of the Acropolis, it is likely that they housed relatives, retainers, servants, and slaves of the king and the royal lineage. Excavations in one such group in 1990 turned up an inscription with the name of the brother of Yax Pac (the last powerful king of Copán).

Nonroyal Elite Residences   As mentioned in Chapters 3 and 10, surveys and excavations at Copán have identified many sites that, on the basis of scale, quality of architecture, and embellishment, were the residences of nonroyal elites (we call these Type 3 and 4 sites). Years ago, these sites would have been called minor ceremonial centers, but we now know their function was primarily residential. We already saw one such concentration near the Acropolis; another large one (Sepulturas) is to the northeast. Various research projects have excavated all or parts of four large elite residential compounds in Sepulturas. Of particular significance for reconstructing political organization is that there are elaborately sculptured, vaulted buildings in all of these compounds, sometimes with associated inscriptions (Fig. 11.9). Decorated elite residences have not been commonly found near other Maya capitals (though this may relate to research sampling rather than their actual absence).

In Chapter 9 we noted how such buildings functioned as important status symbols. But what do they imply in terms of political structure? Most elite residences were erected between about A.D. 700–800 during the reigns of the last four Copán rulers. Obviously not the only powerful people at Copán, kings apparently granted nonroyal nobles the right to use symbols and titles and to display them in their residential compounds, a tendency which may have become more pronounced as royal power eroded. The most impressive of these political symbols are carved benches or thrones. Inscriptions and associated icons on benches and building facades show that titles were associated with particular nobles; these include scribal and possibly warrior titles. Presumably such titles reflect court rank and functions, in some cases inherited in family lines. Our current hypothesis is that many of these nonroyal nobles were leaders of large kinship groups; if this turns out to be correct, they would have provided the administrative link between the general population and the king.

On the facade of the recently excavated building interpreted as a council house are symbols that may identify major nonroyal elite groups or individuals (Fash 1991). According to this interpretation, powerful nobles met together near the house of the king, and perhaps with the king himself, as a kind of ruling council. Such councils are common in nonindustrial kingdoms, for example, those in West Africa. Although this interpretation must be substantiated by further research, it is plausible and, if true, suggests that the political power of the Copán king was limited by that of other nobles. Those nobles (some of whom were probably lineage heads) enjoyed their own political and economic resources and formed political

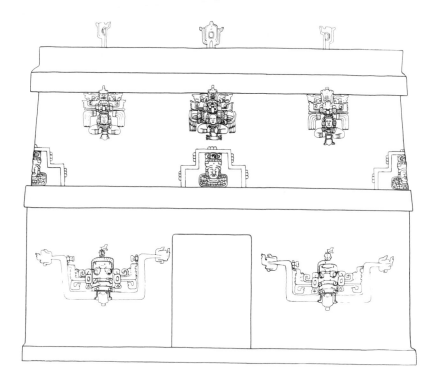

FIGURE 11.9 An elite residence from Copán, elaborately decorated with sculptured figures of humans and deities. Many such buildings were erected outside the royal compound after A.D. 750, suggesting that privileged Maya nobles had considerable economic and political resources and that they were potential competitors of the royal dynasty. Hypothetical reconstruction drawing by Barbara Fash.

factions that potentially challenged royal power. We know that some non-royal elite centers long outlasted the royal dynasty at the Main Group (see Chapter 15), a fact that strengthens this interpretation.

There are only 49 known Type 3 and 4 centers in the Copán valley. Most would have been functioning when the political system was mature, in about A.D. 800. Of these, 23 are within 700 m of the Main Group, and 19 others are within a distance of 4–5 km. This spatial pattern does not make much sense if we argue that the location of elite centers was primarily determined by the necessity to administer particular parts of the larger territory. Much more important was proximity to the rich agricultural land around the Main Group and to the court of the king.

External Relations of the Copán Polity Inscriptions provide the most detailed evidence for political interaction. Some inscriptions at Copán refer to other Maya centers, including Tikal, Palenque, and El Peru; Copán is mentioned at least twice in texts elsewhere. These references show that Copán kings took part in the wider network of elite Maya exchanges, alliances, and intermarriage, and sometimes recorded such information on their monuments. For example, Yax Pac's mother was a royal woman from the Maya center of Palenque, about 400 km away to the northwest.

By far the most interesting epigraphic example of external political relationships, however, links Copán with Quiriguá. A minor element on Altar L at Quiriguá depicts the 12th Copán ruler, Smoke Imix, apparently taking part in a ceremony there. Somewhat later, several Quiriguá monuments erected by the local ruler Cauac Sky mention the date 9.15.6.14.6 (a day in A.D. 737). This date and associated text refer to the capture, and sacrifice through beheading, of 18 Jog, then the ruler of Copán. This event is also alluded to in a glyphic inscription on the Hieroglyphic Stairway at Copán.

Prior to this event, Quiriguá was a relatively unimpressive center. Afterward, Cauac Sky was apparently buoyed by the elimination of his rival and embarked on a major program of construction. A huge plaza was laid out, in obvious emulation of the Great Court at Copán. Many stelae were erected, some of them much larger than any at Copán. Compared to his predecessors, Cauac Sky accumulated considerable power.

But what kind of political relationship between Quiriguá and Copán is evidenced? In trying to answer this we see the frustrations of relying heavily on historical records. On the one hand, the texts provide extremely detailed information on people, places, events, and dates. On the other, the meaning of this information remains uncertain. Obviously there is some sort of relationship between the rulers of the two centers. Some interpret the presence of Smoke Imix at a ceremony at Quiriguá as proof that Quiriguá was under the political control of the Copán dynasty. On the other hand, the monument may simply record one ruler visiting another and taking part in a ritual. Although 18 Jog is commonly assumed to have been captured in warfare and sacrificed, we have no direct evidence that there was a military confrontation at all. Cauac Sky may simply have captured 18 Jog during a peaceful visit to Quiriguá. This is not to imply that Copán kings were not military leaders; the iconography associated with several of them celebrates the warrior role.

The archaeological record helps clarify the situation. There is no sign of destruction or conquest at Copán. Although the ruler succeeding 18 Jog seems to have been weak, within a few years of the beheading the Copán dynasty embarks on many large construction efforts (including the Hieroglyphic Stairway) that continue until the end of the ninth century. Obviously, dynastic succession was not seriously affected by the event, and access to labor remained high. But at Quiriguá, after the death of Cauac Sky, the royal family did not sustain massive projects.

We believe that Quiriguá and Copán were two politically autonomous states, with Copán much the larger of the two. Very probably their royal families were genealogically related (though there is no direct evidence for this) and Copán rulers certainly visited Quiriguá. The incident involving 18 Jog and Cauac Sky, whether a battle or something less dramatic, clearly signals rivalry between the two leaders. Copán's history as a major Maya center is older than Quiriguá's, and the explanation we favor is that Quiriguá was founded by some junior branch of Copán's royal lineage. Thereafter, relationships were maintained between the two centers, and the rivalry between 18 Jog and Cauac Sky was essentially a dynastic squabble. Conceivably, the ruler of one of these two polities might have actually claimed the right to rule over both, and such claims might have led to open conflict or warfare.

External political relations of Copán are reflected indirectly in patterns of exchange, though these can also be hard to interpret. Many sumptuary goods were imported into Copán: jade and other minerals, fancy foreign pottery, marine shells, stingray spines, and (judging from artistic depictions) perishable items such as feathers and possibly cloth. We have no idea of the volume of imports, but they are scarce, mostly found in royal or elite contexts. Quite possibly these items wound up at Copán not because of any organized trade or commerce, but through gift exchange among politically powerful people who visited or otherwise interacted with one another.

One cheap utilitarian item, obsidian, was procured from sources far from the Copán polity (Chapter 8). It has been argued that kings and elites must have managed trade—that it was one of the functions of government. Although Copán kings may have sought to maintain amicable diplomatic relationships with distant rulers who controlled the obsidian sources, trade continued long after Copán kings and elites lost their power. This suggests that elite management of the obsidian trade was not necessary.

Whatever the political implications, Copán was certainly not an isolated Maya kingdom. In addition to the connections already mentioned, tomb offerings and foreign symbols indicate relationships with centers in highland Guatemala and even with Teotihuacán in central Mexico, between A.D. 400 and 650. Other contacts with much of northern and eastern Honduras occurred between 650 and 850.

Summary: Copán Politics Although many of our interpretations are provisional and more research is needed, our reconstruction of Copán politics is much more complete and reliable than it was 20 years ago. A dynasty of kings, ruling from their capital at the Main Group, directly controlled a small core territory with a highly concentrated population. Kings and other elites conducted rituals, organized the labor of commoners, led in warfare, and generally administered the polity. Though functions of the elites are not directly revealed by the archaeological record, the elites would have collected taxes in the form of food or labor from commoners. It is less certain whether they managed trade or commerce.

Copán kings were not all-powerful. Other great nobles with their own ambitions represented strong political factions, jockeyed for position and titles at the royal court, and advised the king. Though nobles had administrative duties, they did not constitute a bureaucracy in the modern sense. These elites, some of which were distinguished by titles, sumptuary goods, and status symbols were acquired from great distances.

The Copán elite, especially kings, participated in the wider world of

Classic Maya Great Tradition interactions, including that of royal marriage. Although they may have made claims on other centers and squabbled over them, these were too far away to control effectively and for all intents and purposes remained autonomous.

Copán's political organization probably resembled that of other Maya polities in many respects. But in the heartland of Maya civilization, the Peten region of the southern Yucatán peninsula, there were few natural boundaries, major centers were much closer to one another and populations much denser. There, interactions of all kinds, including warfare, were more intense. For short periods of time some centers seem to have forged fairly large political systems by dominating others, though in the long run these large polities fell apart. Maya civilization was characterized predominantly by political fragmentation until it was conquered by the Spanish in the 16th century.

THE INCA EMPIRE

We now turn to a political system very different from that of the Classic Maya—the Inca empire of western South America—known from both ethnohistory and archaeology (Collier, Rosaldo, and Wirth 1982; Rowe 1946; see also Chapter 14). This empire, conquered by the Spanish in 1532, was the largest political system to evolve in the New World, and one of the largest anywhere in the world. It covered roughly 1,800,000 km², a narrow band of land extending about 4,000 km along the west coast of South America from Colombia to Chile. Topographically and ecologically very complex, this huge territory supported a population of at least 6,000,000 people, all part of a single political system created by military expansion. We will first summarize what we know about Inca politics from ethnohistoric sources and then survey the archaeological remains of the empire to see whether they amend, confirm, or contradict the ethnohistoric sources.

Ethnohistory of the Inca

Political Structure At the top of the political hierarchy was the emperor himself, an absolute, hereditary monarch who enjoyed many titles: Sapa Inca (Unique Inca), Son of the Sun (an allusion to his divine descent from the Sun God), and Lover of the Poor (referring to his role as benefactor). The Sapa Inca wore special garments, carried special paraphernalia as symbols of his exalted status, sat on a special stool, lived in a massive masonry palace, and had many wives. Life crises of emperors, such as marriage and death, were the occasions of elaborate rituals. Bodies of dead emperors were mummified and displayed in their own palaces, where, still surrounded by family and servants, they were treated as gods. Although historical traditions trace the royal dynasty back through 12 generations to a godlike ancestor, the empire was largely a creation of four emperors in the 15th and 16th centuries A.D.

The term *Inca* refers to the ethnic population of Quechua (KETCH-wah) speakers that was the core of the empire, but it also became an honorific term applied to officials and close allies of the ethnic Inca. As their empire expanded, the Inca encountered an enormous diversity of culture and language. In particular, they encountered societies with many forms of political organization. On the north coast of Peru was a powerful conquest state—the Chimu Empire. Other coastal valleys were occupied by small states or chiefdoms, and on the east and south the Inca eventually met egalitarian farmers and foragers.

Administration Because of its rapid expansion, the empire faced administrative problems and developed an elaborate administrative bureaucracy to cope with them. At high administrative levels were officials holding the title of "Inca." Many of these were ethnic Incas from elite or royal families in the capital at Cuzco (KOOZkoh), but others received the title "Inca" as a reward for their services. Local chiefs were required to learn Quechua, the Inca tongue, which eventually spread over much of the empire as the most commonly spoken language. Each of the four great territorial subdivisions of the empire was presided over by a very exalted official called the "Apo," chosen from the royal family. Apos lived in Cuzco, where they formed a council of state. Smaller subdivisions, or provinces (of which there were probably more than 100) were administered by curacas, or local leaders, who inherited their positions, subject to Inca confirmation. The Inca generally allowed local political leaders to remain in control of their subjects, except in the case of very large states that could potentially threaten them.

One of the most impressive aspects of Inca administration was the taxation system. Portions of conquered territories were set aside for the Inca state and the state church, with the balance left to the people. Local commoners were mobilized to cultivate state and church land, and the products were placed in special government storehouses near each Inca provincial town. Most of these tax products were used to support the Inca populations of Cuzco and the provincial towns, as well as soldiers and laborers, but some were returned to the local population in times of need. In addition to working on the land, commoners provided the state with other labor, such as military service and work on state construction projects. A system of decimal ranking was established in many parts of the empire, primarily for tax-collecting purposes. The largest unit had 10,000 taxpayers and was further broken down into units of 5,000, 1,000, 500, and 100, each supervised by a curaca of the proper rank. Special royal inspectors monitored the conduct of local officials, and careful census records were compiled.

The Inca empire lacked a class of local aristocrats in direct control of local resources such as land. Basically the Inca state consisted of a pyramid of power linked to an administrative hierarchy, with access to labor the strategic resource (Fig. 11.10). To consolidate their control the Inca moved populations from one district to another, creating in many places a mosaic of resident ethnic groups. This technique tended to break up local loyalties and lessened the potential threat of rebellion.

The infrastructure of the empire was built by tax labor. Its chief elements included provincial capitals and a system of roads. Capitals included temples, workshops, and houses for loyal Incas. Often the surrounding hillsides were laboriously terraced to grow maize for the Inca settlers. Two great roads, one along the coast and the other in the mountains, ran the length of the empire, connected by a web of other roads. Where necessary, bridges and even tunnels were constructed. Government rest houses were built at convenient intervals for use by travelers on state business, who were fed from the associated storehouses. Smaller huts were occupied by runners, young men who transmitted messages by relay from one hut to the next. According to one source, messages could be sent over distances of 150–240 km per day, depending on terrain.

Remarkable and innovative as Inca political accomplishments were, it is important to realize that, as is the case in all evolutionary processes, many of them derived from preexisting cultural forms. The basic patterns of service to a royal lineage, acquisition of tribute through conquest, specially constructed administrative centers, and roads long predated the Inca.

Archaeology of the Incas

Suppose that we had no firsthand historical accounts of Inca society (and remember that the Inca themselves had no writing and little representative art). Would we see clear evidence of an empire and its fundamental political structure in the material remains alone?

The Capital and Its Surroundings   Cuzco was partially destroyed by the Spanish, who used materials from razed Inca structures to build their own churches, public buildings, and palatial residences. Much of what has survived lies buried under the modern city, which has over 100,000 inhabitants. Despite all this destruction, considerable Inca architecture is still visible — a tribute to the massiveness and quality of Inca masonry.

Even in its present condition, Cuzco is one of the most impressive archaeological sites in the New World, in terms of the scale and quality of its state-constructed architecture. The original core of the capital was laid out with geometric precision over an area of about 17 ha, and this plan is still visible in the modern city. Most impressive of the surviving remains are the huge walls which surrounded the palaces of individual Inca rulers (one enclosure measures 120 by 50 m) and the chief temple to the Inca pantheon of gods. These are built in distinctive royal Inca style: large blocks of very hard stone were cut into rectangular or polygonal shapes,

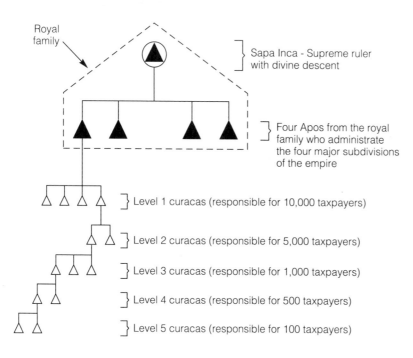

Royal family

Sapa Inca - Supreme ruler with divine descent

Four Apos from the royal family who administrate the four major subdivisions of the empire

Level 1 curacas (responsible for 10,000 taxpayers)

Level 2 curacas (responsible for 5,000 taxpayers)

Level 3 curacas (responsible for 1,000 taxpayers)

Level 4 curacas (responsible for 500 taxpayers)

Level 5 curacas (responsible for 100 taxpayers)

FIGURE 11.10 The Inca bureaucracy is documented by native and Spanish accounts in the period after Spanish conquest. At the top were the emperor and the Apos, all members of the royal family and living in Cuzco. Below them was a complex hierarchy of "curacas," lesser officials responsible for groups of taxpayers. Higher-level curacas administered provinces of the Inca empire, lower curacas administered smaller local populations, and at the lowest levels (Level 5) were probably the headmen of local kin groups or small settlements. Some curacas, especially those of high rank or in particularly sensitive parts of the empire, were ethnic Incas, but others were local leaders confirmed in their positions after absorption into the empire. Clearly, this was a very centralized and hierarchical system, but some details remain obscure. We do not know if a Level 2 curaca was subject to a Level 1 curaca, or reported directly to an Apo in Cuzco. Whatever the details, officials all had the same general responsibilities: to keep internal order, collect taxes, oversee public works, implement decisions made in Cuzco, and forward information to the capital.

perfectly fitted to one another, without mortar. Enormous amounts of labor were required to erect these structures.

If we could excavate extensively in downtown Cuzco, a number of artifacts would be preserved that would indicate the importation of materials from great distances. Although we might not know whether these were brought in as tribute or by some other form of exchange, Cuzco would clearly be an economic center of great importance.

Ringing the palatial-ceremonial civic core were the residences of native Inca families (who lived in smaller versions of the royal palaces), and still further out was a third zone, consisting of 11 different social and ethnic communities. These foreigners were brought to Cuzco from various parts of the empire and settled there as a kind of symbolic expression of the Inca state. If this area, now covered by the modern town, were available for excavation, we could probably identify these ethnic residential enclaves and identify their origins. Evidence would lie in burial customs and other non-Inca religious behavior, and might include distinctive domestic architecture, household furniture, and artifacts. The presence of these enclaves alone would suggest a great imperial state.

The size of Cuzco would be suggestive as well. The zones of occupation just described extend 800–1,000 m from the civic core, so the greater urban area covered 4–5 km². On archaeological grounds we would estimate a population in the tens of thousands. On a hill just to the north of

FIGURE 11.11 Sacsahuaman is a large fortress just outside Cuzco. Its huge stone blocks and monumental scale typify architectural projects undertaken by the Inca state.

the city the Inca state carried out one of the most ambitious single building projects in the New World—the great fortress/shrine of Sacsahuaman (SACKSahHWAHman) (Fig. 11.11), thought to have been built by Pachacuti, the first great Inca emperor. The hill was worked into a series of three huge terraces, each 600 m long, with a zigzag plan that would trap any attackers in crossfire. These terraces are constructed of huge stones, some of which weigh as much as 600 tons. Tunnels riddled the hill to allow rapid movement of defenders, and the fortress was also equipped with storerooms and a reservoir. Further out still we find great numbers of small ritual sites, primarily on hilltops, built in Inca style. These formed a system of shrines in the Valley of Cuzco.

Outlying Administrative Centers   The remains of Inca administrative towns are still visible throughout much of the empire. We would clearly identify them as Inca on the basis of architectural style alone. From the evident high degree of planning and from excavation data we would assume that these were built as major construction efforts over very short periods of time. All were much smaller than Cuzco.

An excavated center of this type is Huánaco Viejo (Morris and Thompson 1970, 1985), about 600 km north of Cuzco:

> Survey and excavations carried out at the Inca administrative center of Huánuco Viejo revealed a large city with a ceremonial and palatial section, large residential zones, and huge storage facilities. Well-cut Cuzco-style masonry was limited to the ceremonial areas which included platforms, gateways, a bath and an elaborate apartment, probably intended to house royalty or important officials.

The residential districts were Inca derived in architecture and planning and the pottery was virtually limited to Inca inspired wares, thus demonstrating a lack of influence in either architecture or ceramics of the local peasants who served at the site. The huge storage areas housed mostly highland produce which was used to sustain the city, *mita* laborers and transients, was probably not used for extensive redistribution to local villages in the surrounding area. The city, then, must be described as an artificial device imposed by the Inca for administrative and political purposes, rather than as a city which arose because of local conditions or needs.

(Morris and Thompson 1970:344)

Apart from the Inca residential facilities, **497** associated storage structures had a total volume of **37,900 m³**, testimony to the tax-collecting power of the Inca state.

Surveys around the town revealed many other settlements with architecture very different from Huánaco Viejo. Inca artifacts were very few, except at a structure identified as the house of the local curaca. Also recorded were the roads leading through the valley, with their associated rest houses and post-houses, all built in Inca style.

Agricultural Intensification Much of the steep mountain landscape around Inca administrative centers was laboriously terraced, in Inca masonry style, to form small fields. Irrigation channels were engineered to provide water to them. Even without historic sources, we would interpret such terrace systems as state-sponsored; historic documents suggest that fields were primarily used to grow maize, which in turn was made into chicha, a mildly alcoholic beverage very important in Inca rituals and high-level political meetings.

Conquest We would be able to directly detect much of the effect of Inca military expansion on settlement systems. In some cases, major non-Inca cities such as Chan Chan were abruptly abandoned. In other cases, Inca administrative facilities or shrines were set up in formerly autonomous communities. Finally, we would see that populations in many valleys were resettled, having left behind old communities and built new ones.

In conclusion, the existence of a great, highly centralized empire with an elaborate system of administration, taxation, and communication would be fairly clear from the archaeological evidence alone. We would know where the capital was and would be able to reconstruct the bureaucratic hierarchy to some degree and functions of the leaders. Although we might not detect Inca presence at the margins of their empire, we would know its rough extent in territorial terms. The very rapid appearance of Inca facilities would suggest a political system expanding by military means. Historical documents, or native traditions of writing or representative art, would not be necessary to come to these conclusions, although such sources of information add invaluable detail to our interpretations when available.

SUMMARY

Inscriptions or representative art often provide clear and detailed evidence concerning political structure and interaction. In the absence of this sort of evidence, other kinds can be brought to bear on questions about political organization. For hierarchical societies, one of the most powerful kinds of evidence derives from settlement system studies, which are particularly useful in determining the extent of polities. When elements of such systems are adequately excavated, they may show evidence for internal political factions and leadership positions, as well as warfare, exchange, or other external relationships. By far the most difficult thing to reconstruct from archaeological data alone is the nature of political decision making and political factions, but occasionally we can get a glimpse of these as well.

POINTS TO REMEMBER

- A major goal of archaeology is to reconstruct what political systems were like at particular points in time and how they interacted with one another.

- The distribution and character of central places provide clues to the nature of political systems.

- Complex, highly centralized political systems often have capitals and hierarchical arrangements of settlements of different sizes and functions. These can be detected by archaeological surveys and excavations.

- Political structure may be reflected in symbolic systems such as art or writing.

- Burials and status symbols may indicate differences in rank but may be uninformative about what the functions of leaders were.

- Clues to political functions may be reflected in the kinds of interactions that occurred between polities; these include war, diplomacy, alliance, intermarriage, and exchange.

FOR FURTHER READING*

Pfeiffer's *The Emergence of Society* is a good general introduction. Smith's *Regional Analysis* and Hodder and Orton's *Spatial Analysis in Archaeology* describe and apply important analytic principles. For the Maya, read Culbert's *Classic Maya Political History,* Culbert and Rice's *Precolumbian Population History of the Maya Lowlands,* and Schele and Freidel's *Forest of Kings.* For the Inca, consult Morris and Thompson's *Huanaco Pampa* and Collier, Rosaldo, and Wirth's *The Inca and Aztec States.*

*Full citations appear in the bibliography.

CHAPTER TWELVE

THE SPIRIT WORLD: RELIGION AND IDEOLOGY

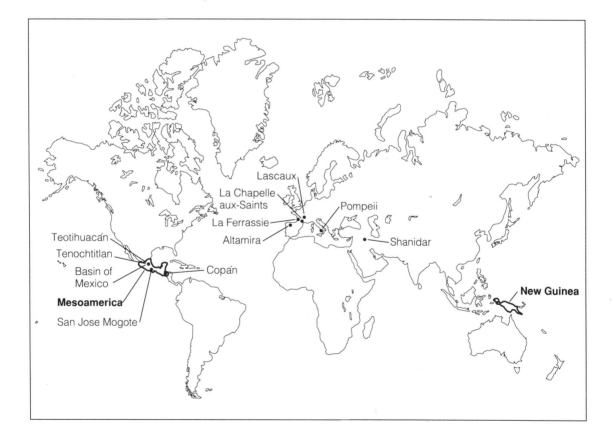

Regardless of their cultural identities, all people have many common experiences and face many common problems. These include the need to explain how the world is structured, how it originated, and how it may be manipulated; the need for psychological reassurance in the face of crises or situations they cannot control; the need to explain universal experiences such as dreams and death; the necessity of coping with the prospect of death and the ultimate fate of the human psyche; the need to create consensus about right and wrong at a societal level; the necessity to validate and symbolize important transitions in personal or communal life; and the need to legitimize and confer value on social institutions. A broad set of solutions to these essentially human issues is called an *ideology,* a topic that we have already touched on in earlier chapters (esp. Chapter 9) and that is a superstructural component of cultures. Remember that there are many kinds of ideologies, including political and economic ones. In this chapter we are concerned in particular with religious ideology and its archaeological manifestations and interpretation.

Along with the use of symbolic communication, religion in its most general sense is one of our most distinctive human characteristics (Howells 1962; Lessa and Vogt 1965; Paden 1988; Wallace 1966). Because it is a cultural universal, early anthropologists devoted much effort to studying religion using a cross-cultural perspective. Early theories sought to explain religious beliefs through universal human experiences. For example, everyone shares the experience of moving from wakeful consciousness to unconscious dreaming; Tylor (1871) held that this was the common basis for religion, since dreaming suggests a journey of the mind away from the body and thus the existence of a nonmaterial soul and the possibility of spiritual immortality. By extension, the concept of deities would have developed from this concept of souls.

To Tylor, religion was a belief in spiritual entities, and he emphasized how religion mediated between humans and the supernatural. The sociologist Emile Durkheim (1915) saw religions as social constructs, functional systems of beliefs and practices related to the sacred that served to mediate relations among people. Durkheim emphasized that religious systems united believers and that beliefs were instilled as part of the process of enculturation. In setting up a dichotomy between things *sacred* (forbidden, dangerous, unquestioned, and holy) and things *profane* (ordinary, everyday), religions set down rules as moral compulsions, and the regulation of social interactions could be accomplished by appeal to morally correct behavior (cf. Chapter 9).

In his monumental study *The Golden Bough* (1958), Sir James Frazer systematically assembled an immense array of comparative religious ideas and practices. He differentiated between magic and religion as major ways of dealing with the supernatural world and attempted to classify his cross-cultural data according to specific categories of magical or religious behavior. He also sought evolutionary trends in magic and religion.

CULTURAL EVOLUTIONISM AND BELIEF SYSTEMS

One aim of early anthropologists was to understand the relation of religion to cultural evolution in general. Nineteenth-century evolutionism suffered from an ethnocentric perspective from which non-Western cultural forms were commonly seen to represent either primitive stages of development or manifestations of cultural degradation. In fact, until the early 19th century, the Western perspective recognized four kinds of religion: Christianity, Judaism, Islam, and paganism. As more became known of the breadth of religious practice, a more sensitive, comparative approach developed, but even so, in the progressive evolutionary view of the late 19th century, religion was conceived as "evolving" from error to the "truth" of monotheistic Christianity.

By the 20th century this ethnocentrism gave way to more objective and relativistic attitudes of cultural interpretation. The amount and range of information being gathered about belief systems of the past and present stimulated generalizations about the function of religion and ideology. Christianity, as a belief system or set of institutions, could be analyzed in terms of its development and function, just as economic, political, and social ideologies and institutions could be analyzed. While anthropology offered insights into the commonality and universality of religious experience, this had the effect of subjecting established Western belief systems to the same process of scientific inquiry as that applied to other cultures.

RELIGION AND IDEOLOGY IN TRADITIONAL AND INDUSTRIAL SOCIETIES

Important contrasts distinguish the role of religion and ideology in traditional societies from their role in modern industrial societies like our own (all human societies would have been traditional ones only a few hundred years ago). First and most significantly, in traditional societies religious beliefs and practices are not strongly differentiated from other institutions or subsystems of society. For example, political leaders were also often religious leaders, a tendency most strongly expressed in the **theocratic** (from the Greek for "god-ruled") form of government (Webster 1976). Similarly, educational institutions and even military behavior and ideology were often closely interwoven with religious beliefs and rituals.

Second, in traditional societies, natural phenomena were explained in terms of religious beliefs. Modern scientific understanding of weather effects, astronomy, and the biotic and geophysical nature of the earth has drastically reduced religious interpretation of these phenomena. Equally important, modern medicine has made many diseases and disorders understandable as well as controllable, so they are no longer regarded as the mark of a god's displeasure. Archaeologists try to understand how in past times

theocracy Form of government in which authority is held by religious specialists.

the dangers and wonders of daily life in a particular place influenced the belief system, how they were featured in myths, associated with gods and spirits, and incorporated into ritual. In this way, the artifacts we find become understandable parts of a whole lifeway.

ADAPTIVE DIMENSIONS OF RELIGION

The most fundamental aspects of culture are adaptive, and this applies as much to religion as to technology or food-getting (Rappaport 1971b, 1971c). It is easy to see how in certain respects religious behavior may be inherently adaptive. For example, religious beliefs and behavior that effectively unite people and allow them to act collectively may have great survival value, allowing people to cope with situations that would otherwise exceed their organizational capabilities. Within societies, individuals and subgroups may use religious ideologies to adapt. A striking example of such behavior recently occurred in India. Although the Indian caste system was abolished in 1948, basic elements of it survived because they are so rooted in the Hindu religion, which in India structures social, political, and economic life. People of very low status (outcastes) continued to be discriminated against and enjoyed few opportunities. In the face of this mistreatment, millions of outcastes have converted to Buddhism, acquiring a new religious affiliation in which caste is irrelevant and thus escaping the traditional prejudices attached to their former Hindu statuses. These people have manipulated their religious affiliation to adapt in a situation of discrimination.

Despite religion's obvious capacity to enhance adaptation, it may be difficult to think about religion in evolutionary terms for two reasons. First (as the very word *ideology* implies), many people associate religion with mental ideas, or worldviews, regarding these as more important than the outward, behavioral aspects of religion. Yet selection acts on behavior, not on intentions or rationale. If, for example, people are mobilized to go to war because they are responding to the expressed ideological or religious exhortation of establishing peace, the archaeological record might reveal the conflict and its effects but not the justification for it. It is therefore important to distinguish between the functions that religions perform and the cognitive basis — the inspiration — for that behavior.

The second reason is the tremendous variety in religious beliefs, practices, and associated materials. Archaeologists doing fieldwork have a long-standing joke: When the function of a feature or artifact is not immediately obvious, someone will "identify" it as a "religious" or "ritual" object (Fig. 12.1). Of course such attributions are not part of the artifact accessioning process, but they do have a certain validity because, as a general category of culture, religion and its associated paraphernalia are so enormously varied and their forms so often strange and unexpected. In contrast, most people in the world consume a narrow range of basic food staples, and

FIGURE 12.1 Ceramic figurines of this style, found at Teotihuacán, are assumed to have functioned as votive figurines to whom prayers would have been offered, but there is no direct evidence substantiating this interpretation.

many basic tool types (swords, plows, or canoes) are much the same no matter where they are found. How can we possibly explain the variety of religious paraphernalia in evolutionary terms? One approach is to focus on the *function* of religious ideology and behavior, since cross-culturally many kinds of religion and ideology serve essentially the same purposes. For example, funeral rituals and their associated, shared beliefs may be important in defining social groups and enhancing group cohesion—an adaptive function that may be a human universal. But the particular set of beliefs or rituals may be largely irrelevant to this function. Presumably the Hindus who have become Buddhists still carry out funerals, but of a different kind.

RECONSTRUCTING RELIGION: RELIGION AND THE ARCHAEOLOGICAL RECORD

In the public imagination much of what archaeologists find is directly related to religion. The huge temples of the Maya were places where gods were worshiped, Egyptian pyramids protected the souls and mummified bodies of dead rulers, and King Tut-ankh-amun's tomb is the physical manifestation of a funeral ceremony. Such sites capture our imaginations because of their scale, splendor, and mystery. However, despite the preoccupation of many early archaeologists with tombs and temples, religion is a difficult aspect of culture to investigate and reconstruct from an archaeological perspective.

If we think of religion primarily in the mentalist sense (i.e., the religious

meanings in the minds of people), the difficulties are obvious. While ethnographers may have reasonably direct access to the people they study,
archaeologists must infer belief indirectly, from the physical remains of
religious behavior. It helps greatly to have inscriptions or iconography, but
even with their aid retrieval of meaning is difficult. Despite abundant
interpretations about what archaeological materials may have meant to
those who originally used them, we have no systematic, effective methods
to verify our conclusions. The ethnographic record can help a great deal,
particularly because religion is a fairly conservative cultural subsystem, the
beliefs and practices of which often endure from ancient times to the
present. But we also know that religious ideology can rapidly change, so
even this line of evidence must be used with care.

Archaeologists are generally much more successful at determining the
social behaviors and functions related to ancient religion than recovering
meaning. For example, ritual places such as temples can be identified. From
their location and form we can speculate about how these were built,
maintained, and used, and by how many people. The exact meaning of the
ritual paraphernalia exhibited by a ruler on a statue may elude us, though
we know he used these things to impress people and legitimize his rule.
Burials accompanied by personal possessions or offerings may or may not
indicate the belief in an afterlife, but they certainly show that formal funerary rituals took place as rites of passage and intensification. Fortunately,
even this level of interpretation is useful. As we shall see below, texts
sometimes allow much richer interpretations.

Ritual Behavior and Belief Systems

Ritual behavior is highly patterned. Analyzing ritual and ritual patterns is
one way that archaeologists look at belief systems. Many aspects of a belief
system, such as values or prayers may leave no material trace, but rituals
involve sacred objects, symbols, and places. Thinking about the religions
practiced today, one can easily link different rites with certain forms of
architecture (churches, temples, and mosques, for example) and artifacts,
and understand the way these material things express the belief system.

Codified dogmas document the beliefs motivating the rituals for all who
read them. In nonliterate cultures, however, ideological and religious
dogma is learned and shared through the oral traditions of prayer and
song. Sometimes graphic images (paintings, petroglyphs) and sculptural
representations (figurines, sculpted figures) symbolize proper attitudes and
expressions of belief. When the belief system changes (say, because of a
massive religious conversion like that which occurred in Mexico at the time
of the Spanish Conquest, or because of a more gradual change in values)
these undocumented traditions are quickly lost except insofar as their material remains can be accurately interpreted.

In spite of these problems, archaeologists interpret belief systems and
their relics by the same general means as we interpret the other aspects of

culture: through analysis of material remains, from available description and documentation of belief systems, analogous case examples from ethnography, and applications of general principles derived from cross-cultural research.

Social Consequences of the Concept of Sanctity

As discussed at the beginning of the chapter, religious experience draws on human emotions of an ancient and most basic kind. These emotions pre-date the ability to speak, in terms of our evolutionary history as a species. As we humans gained the ability to speak and to cognize and express abstractions, we also developed another capability unique to our kind: lying. Because it establishes an alternative to reality, lying attacks social coherence, which depends on common precepts that transcend individual choice or definition. The realm of the *sacred* establishes the most important of these precepts as inviolate. Thus human social authority bases itself on governance by sacred conventions (Rappaport 1971c). According to Durkheim, what we humans worship, in fact, beyond our gods, is social coherence.

A deliberate refusal by someone to honor society's sacred boundaries marks that individual as a threat to social harmony. Thus individual recalcitrance must be condemned as blasphemy contradicting the sacred belief system (Rappaport 1971c). The enculturation process must ensure that values are widely shared so that society can function. Clearly articulating the distinction between the sacred and the profane is a function of religious belief systems.

Religious Roots: Early Homo Sapiens At what point in the human evolutionary career did our ancestors begin to set sacred boundaries? In seeking the sources of religion, we would expect definitions of the sacred to begin with the first group thought to be capable of producing *complex* speech patterns and thus of verbalizing abstractions: *Homo sapiens neanderthalensis,* existing from about 100,000 years ago to about 50,000 years ago (Feder and Park 1989). In fact, Neanderthals give us the first material remains of rituals, including burial ceremonies, ritual cannibalism, and possible totemic rituals (see **totem**).

Neanderthals apparently pondered the meaning of life and death, and they certainly carried out the earliest known deliberate burial rituals. Humans are not alone in the animal world in feeling sadness at losing the companionship of a friend, but (to our knowledge) only humans can ponder how to incorporate death into the pattern of ongoing life, ameliorating death's conclusiveness with a belief in an afterlife and rituals to ease the transition for the deceased and the survivors. Burial of the dead is a sign of respect for the deceased and often is a mark of belief in an afterlife.

The earliest evidence of deliberate ritual burial of the dead is found at several Neanderthal sites. At a cave site in La Chapelle, France (ca. 60,000

totem Particular object (animals, natural phenomenon, place) that serves to identify a specific group such as a clan.

years ago), the skeleton of a man about 40 years old was buried with a bison leg across his chest and with many other broken animal bones and flint tools, possibly to provide the deceased with necessary goods for continued existence. From about the same period, a cemetery at La Ferrassie, France, holds the remains of two adults and four children (possibly a family), with grave goods such as flint flakes and bone fragments in the adult male's burial trench (Fig. 12.2). Even more famous Neanderthal burials are those found at Shanidar Cave (Iraq), where flowers may have been interred with deceased individuals (Solecki 1971).

Early Homo Sapiens Sapiens

Fully modern members of our species (*Homo sapiens sapiens*) have existed for at least the last 50,000 years. As we have seen, their hunting and gathering, migratory ways of life persisted widely throughout the world long after the climate shift of 10–12,000 years ago, when the most recent glacial phase of the Pleistocene ended.

The belief systems of these hunter-gatherers were artfully expressed in painting and sculpture (Leroi-Gourhan 1968a, 1968b). Although all late Pleistocene people probably had graphic expressions of religious beliefs and rituals, these are especially abundant and well preserved in western European cave sites, with their depictions of animals of the hunt (ungulates, for example). Figurines of women of ample proportions have been found at sites throughout Europe (see Box 12.1). These paintings and sculptures have been intensively studied for well over a century. Although archaeologists agree that these images had religious and ritual significance, there has been no consensus as to their religious meaning (Watson and Fotiadis 1990).

One of the oldest explanations, partly stimulated by observations of ethnographically known foragers, holds that the animal art was created as part of magical rituals that ensured success in the hunt and fecundity of the game. Famous examples of animal art are the cave paintings of southern France (e.g., Lascaux) and northern Spain (e.g., Altamira), long admired for embodying high standards of artistic expression. That they are called cave "art" acknowledges that, in overall design of layout, style, and media of execution they are masterful works, but we must remember that their functions went far beyond mere decoration. Clearly, these compositions and spatial contexts were crucial to the ritual lives of Upper Paleolithic hunters, who, through the imagery, it is thought, enacted hunting magic to make the animals healthy, the herds large, and the hunting good.

The forms of the rituals held in these painted caves are not directly evidenced, though the paintings have been analyzed to see if their composition reveals a "text" of ritual use. By means of analysis of the spatial layout of the caves, the process of entering and passing through them has been interpreted as a possible rite of passage, which initiated young men into their adult roles, including that of hunting (Pfeiffer 1969).

Representations of plump women with prominent sexual characteristics

FIGURE 12.2 This burial of several Neanderthals at La Ferrassie shows deliberate interment of the dead; grave goods accompany them.

are thought be related to fertility. This interpretation reminds us of the propositions of Darwin: Those who survive can reproduce, and the most likely to survive are those who are well fed. Today we have an abundance of food, and the Venus of Willendorf (lower left in Box 12.1 illustration) would not be a widely held ideal of feminine beauty in the United States. We do not admire her as her contemporaries would have, seeing the riches of stored fat reserves in her massive hips and pendulous breasts and belly — fat to see her through the lean months and to bring a child safely to term, then nurse it well until it is weaned.

Appealing as this set of interpretations is, we cannot independently substantiate it. Several alternative explanations have been put forward recently, including elaborate analyses by anthropologists who use structural approaches (Leroi-Gourhan 1968b). We will not discuss these here but point out instead the archaeological dilemma: We can create consensus about the general religious and ritual functions of cave art but not about its meaning. The interpretations of a century ago concerning meaning are no more obviously "true" or "false" than the more recent interpretations.

ETHNOGRAPHIC ANALOGS: RELIGION AND RITUAL IN EGALITARIAN FARMING SOCIETIES

As the challenging climate of the last glaciation warmed into our present interglacial period, conditions in some parts of the world allowed a shift from mobile hunting and gathering to settled life. In certain places, wild

BOX 12.1

RITUAL OBJECTS OR MARKERS OF SOCIAL INTERACTION? INTERPRETING THE "VENUS" FIGURINES OF THE EUROPEAN PALEOLITHIC

"Venus" figurines of the kind illustrated here were first brought to public attention at the end of the 19th century. Found at sites in north central Europe, from the Pyrenees bordering Spain and France, to Russia, they are the oldest form of representational art known from that area. The earliest figurine was made about 33,000 years ago, and the tradition continued until about 20,000 years ago (the cave painting tradition dates from about 17,000 to 10,000 years ago). The figurines are generally small, a few centimeters in length, and most are three-dimensional and made of stone, ivory, or clay. A few are bas-relief carvings. Although few have been recovered in good context, they seem to occur most frequently in habitation sites; this public setting and the time period, distinguish them from the cave painting tradition.

The circles and lines drawn onto the figurines are part of an analysis by Andre Leroi-Gourhan (1968), who noted that even though they were found hundreds of kilometers apart, their stylistic similarities are overwhelming: Breasts, abdomen, and pelvic region are enclosed within the area described by a circle. How can we account for these similarities?

Paleolithic art, like other sets of stylistic elements, serves to define the boundaries of the groups using it (Conkey 1978). Since the figurines are presumed to have been used in social settings (the habitation sites), their similarity over vast regions may signal social interaction between the groups sharing this area. Clive Gamble (1982) believes that the figurines reflect a social response to climate changes during the last European Ice Age. The greatest southern extent of the last

glacial ice sheet occurred about 18,000 years ago. Imagine the changes in ecosystems over all of Europe in the millennia preceding this. As the temperature began to drop, plants formerly able to survive perished in their old habitats, and new plant communities slowly began to establish themselves. This in turn led to changes in the composition of animal communities that lived on the plants. South of the glaciers, grazing lands for herd animals like deer, a favorite prey for human hunters, expanded, and thus the animals became more difficult to track. When hunting territories expanded, interaction among the different hunter-gatherer bands was likely to decline, reducing opportunities for alliances, such as the essential ones to establish marriages. "[O]pen social networks are a feature of poor environments and . . . the alliances necessary for the maintenance of such systems require . . . visual methods of information exchange" (Gamble 1982:103).

These figurines may have served as a visual marker for widely dispersed groups of mobile hunter-gatherers as they occasionally interacted with other groups in the course of their travels. Possibly worn as pendants, the figurines would have served as a signal of social interaction. The obvious signs of female fertility that the figurines display speak at an elemental level of the life-or-death value of mating and reproduction, functions held sacred in many societies. Quite probably, the figurines were imbued with special sacred meaning and may have been used in rituals, but with our present level of contextual information, this is impossible to know.

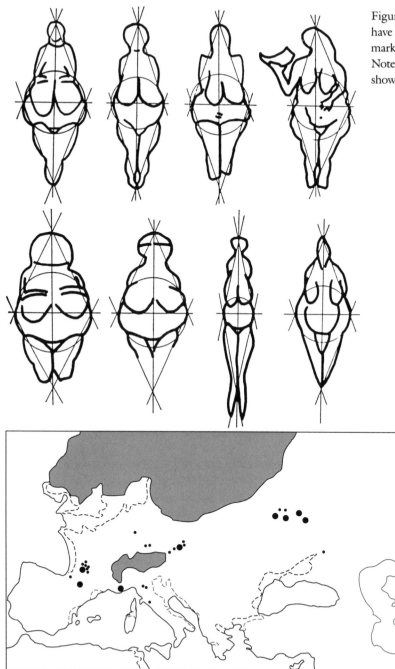

Figurines like those shown here have been found at the locations marked by dots on the map below. Note also that the shaded area shows the extent of glaciation.

food was so abundant that food needs could be locally supplied year-round. Since permanent communities demand somewhat different survival strategies, with settled lifestyle came changes in the definition of the sacred. Among mobile egalitarian hunter-gatherers, for example, personal property is minimized by the physical constraints of travel; emotional attachment to personal things is kept in check by regarding sharing and generalized reciprocity as sacred. As soon as the constraint of limited baggage is lifted by sedentism, food and goods far beyond immediate needs begin to accumulate; property and the means to protect it are now defined as sacred. Nonsedentary peoples, to be sure, identify strongly with the territory they move through on their yearly rounds. Landscape features such as mountains and springs, for example, are held sacred in many cultures, but the ideological value of land changes as land use changes. With sedentism, much more energy is invested in the landscape — in putting up buildings and eventually altering the local biotic ecosystem by favoring some food species over others or by actively taking up food production.

The end of hunting and gathering is the beginning of intensification of land use, with a concomitant increase in the value of land. The notion of the "sacred landscape" of any society focuses on the area needed to sustain it, and sometimes more. Sedentism may bring an enhanced proprietary interest in territory, with more exact territorial boundaries held as sacred. Strong territorial patterns marked the regular use by the !Kung (Chapter 7) of their productive landscape. The traveling group had a flexible composition but shared rights to resource use through a much smaller group of "waterhole owners." We assume a similar pattern for other foragers. When people settle down, they develop a closer relationship with a smaller part of the landscape, identifying with its natural features in an ideational way, as we shall see at the city of Teotihuacán shortly.

The Tsembaga

Sacred rights to territory characterize the belief systems of settled egalitarian farmers, though it is difficult to find archaeological evidence for the spatial limits of sanctity. The ethnographic record provides many examples, and one of the most famous is that of the Tsembaga (zemBAHgah) of highland New Guinea, who practice an elaborate ritual cycle related to food production and to safeguarding each community's land.

In the forested, mountainous highlands of New Guinea there live swidden farmers whose lives focus on their local villages, and each village is a politically autonomous society. The Tsembaga are the people of one such village (Rappaport 1967, 1971a). Their community of 200 people claims a territory of 8 km². Relations with other communities occasionally degenerate into warfare, but there is general stability among them. In fact, the equilibrium of relations among villages is maintained over the long term by skirmishes, through which the villages test their numbers against each other, and occasionally redistribute land when population densities become significantly imbalanced.

Warfare is part of a cycle of recurrent events, regularized in a set of elaborate rituals (Fig. 12.3), cognized as requirements for maintaining spiritual balance between two groups of local spirits: high-ground spirits (warfare-oriented) and low-ground spirits (of agriculture and vegetation). The full cycle of events may take 6–20 years, and its timing is cued by the rate at which the community's pig population increases, though the cognized reason is homicidal vengeance (or revenge for previous homicidal vengeance). The men of the community invoke the protection of the high-ground spirits in warfare against the offending community. They vow to avoid things associated with low-ground spirits (fertile earthly things like many foods, and sexual relations with women) and maintain these taboos through the warfare period, which may last weeks. Truce is marked by a big pig slaughter, at which the animals are sacrificed to honor the high-ground gods and then eaten at feasts. This begins to pay off these spirits, but more pigs are needed, so the pig population is allowed to grow while the process of observing more taboos to repay the gods more fully goes on. In time (6–20 years) there are nearly as many pigs as people, with over a third of garden crops going to feed them and the burden of extra work falling on the women.

Rappaport notes that the women's vociferous rebellion against further pig tending is the catalyst for shifting into a new phase of the ritual-and-warfare cycle. At this point, the boundaries of the community's territory are staked out, and they may be extended to include land abandoned by neighboring villages after the last bout of warfare — the enemy's guardian ancestral spirits are thought to have finally departed. Rituals mark the uprooting of the sacred *rumbim* tree, planted in peace, and feasts continue until spirits of high and low ground are regarded as in harmony. With all sacred debts paid, the Tsembaga are free to go to war again, perhaps extending their territorial boundaries in the long, cyclical process.

We do not know why the Tsembaga initially developed this cycle of activities or their cognized model of it, but the cycle's many functions are striking, particularly the fact that these conventional patterns facilitate consensus in an egalitarian group, providing direction by sanctifying a course of political action, within the limits of the group's logistical ability to support a period of warfare.

When we consider the Tsembaga as a potential archaeological case study, the limits of interpreting ideational subsystems become clear. Assuming we had no ethnographic accounts to guide our interpretations of material culture, we would have no way of detecting the ritual cycle. Key "objects" such as pigs and *rumbim* trees would leave no patterns that would provide clues to their roles in these rituals. We could detect the general territorial boundaries by locating communities and assessing the amount of land each needed to support itself, but the roles of high-ground and low-ground spirits in maintaining the balance of land among villages would be undetectable.

But if archaeologists refused to interpret material remains unless their message was absolutely clear, very little archaeology would be done. Un-

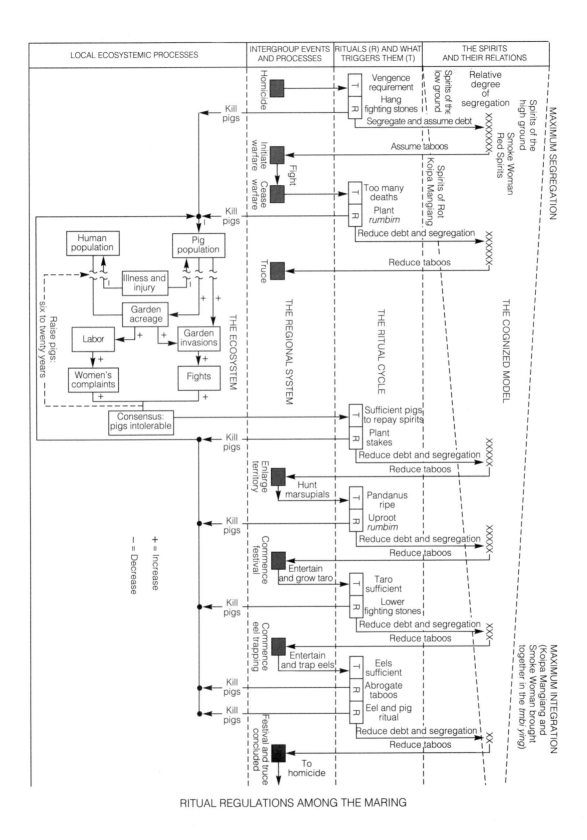

RITUAL REGULATIONS AMONG THE MARING

FIGURE 12.3 The Tsembaga ritual cycle of war and peace, diagrammed on the opposite page, served to maintain political boundaries and keep the size of pig populations in check. The photo shows a Tsembaga skirmish.

derstanding the limits of our ability to address extinct cognized models, we proceed with caution, applying ethnographically and ethnohistorically known behavior patterns where they seem appropriate.

FROM AGRARIAN VILLAGES TO CAPITAL CITIES: CULTURAL EVOLUTION AND BELIEF SYSTEMS IN MESOAMERICA

In Mesoamerica we have the fortunate conjunction of ethnohistoric documentation of belief systems at the time of European contact and an archaeological record tracing the development of cultural complexity from egalitarian hunter-gatherers to states. We can study the mythology and rituals that the Spanish documented in the 16th century in order to understand their development and expression in various regional cultural contexts and to trace their roots in the earliest settled villages of Mesoamerica.

Mesoamerican Religion

Mesoamerica as a culture area is defined by a number of shared traits, and the belief system is important among them (Carrasco 1990). Mesoamericans did not have a pantheon of deities like that of the ancient Greeks and

FIGURE 12.4 Huitzil-opochtli was the patron god of the Mexica Aztecs. As they became politically powerful, the worship of Huitzilopochtli was imposed over subject peoples.

Romans. Rather, the landscape itself, all forces of nature, and the vagaries of fortune were seen as expressions of spiritual energy and thus objects of veneration. As such, these forces sometimes took on human form, either in sculptural or artistic representations, or in the flesh as a priest or war captive or other person living as the earthly manifestation of a god for one year in Aztec Tenochtitlan, who would then be sacrificed at the yearly feast of the god. In that sense scholars talk about deities such as Quétzalcóatl (KETselKOHaht), the Feathered Serpent, who created humans and gave them maize, their most important food. The Mesoamericans would see Quétzalcóatl in statues and impersonators with his regalia but also in things that rippled and flowed (as would a feathered serpent): snakes, rivers, feather banners, roads, blood.

This belief system is based on a complex set of myths about the cyclical creation of the world and about the deities, male and female, assigned to oversee the natural world and the place of humans in it. The deities overlap and merge into each other, depending on the cultural period and area within Mesoamerica. This is clearly a dynamic system, flexible enough to encompass great variety and to show changes in godly popularity. Quétzalcóatl was one of the most enduring, dating back at least to the Late Preclassic period (1200–400 B.C.) with evidence from Olmec sites. The Rain and Thunder God is well known in the Classic and Postclassic periods; he is called Tlaloc in the central highlands and Chac by the Maya. The Aztecs are famous for their tribal god Huitzilopochtli (WEETSloh-POACHEDlee) (Fig. 12.4), whose worship they imposed on their political subjects. Subjects were not forbidden to honor their own gods, though their sacred images were taken to Tenochtitlan as holy hostages.

In our discussions of other aspects of culture we have distinguished between the Great and Little traditions. Some of the most conspicuous monuments of elite Great Traditions were dedicated to spiritual purposes, for example, pyramids built over tombs, temples for rituals honoring deities, and so forth. What are the Little Tradition roots of the belief systems these things express? In examining this problem for Mesoamerica, archaeologists trace back from the rituals and myths known from the time of contact in order to interpret evidence of religious practices.

Early Oaxacan Farmers and Their Rituals

Kent Flannery (1976a; also Drennan 1976) looked for ritual evidence in sites dating from the Early Preclassic period in the Valley of Oaxaca, focusing on contexts of ritual for the community as a whole, for the household, the sodality, and for the individual. The earliest evidence of community-wide rituals in the valley comes from the largest village. San Jose Mogote (mohGOHtay) has what Flannery calls public buildings (as opposed to residences) dating from 1400 to 1150 B.C. "Public buildings" is a deliberately vague term that encompasses buildings and open platform spaces that were the loci of communitywide activities of religious and secular kinds. These rectangular structures enclosed large areas (e.g., 5.4 by 4.4 m) that were paved and plastered, lacking the typical debris of houses (Fig. 12.5). By the period 850–600 B.C., several other villages had these structures. What was their function? Probably these large open spaces served to contain public assemblies regarding political or social matters as well as rituals,

FIGURE 12.5 The Great Tradition religious expressions we associate so strongly with Mesoamerican civic-ceremonial centers like Tenochtitlan, Teotihuacán, Monte Alban, and Copán had their roots in Folk Tradition practices, such as those that might have taken place here. This open plaza at the site of San Jose Mogote (Mexico) may have been a space for ceremonial events drawing together the people of the village, and perhaps beyond it.

though in traditional societies virtually all public activities have a strong religious component. We know from ethnohistory and from depictions of art that dance and music were important in Mesoamerica. In looking for the remains of artifacts used in these activities, Flannery found fragments of conch and turtle shells in contexts associated with public buildings. Conch-shell trumpets and turtle-shell drums were in fact widely used for these purposes. Fragments were also found in workshop contexts at sites in the Valley of Oaxaca, and since these items had to be imported from the Gulf Coast and the Isthmus of Tehuantepec (tahWAHNtahpeck), their presence evidences long-distance trade and local specialization in shell working.

Oaxaca buildings and artifacts indicate that public ceremonies were somehow first formalized in the largest village and then spread to a few other communities. The public buildings may have served as dance platforms, central to rites involving the whole community and possibly other villages as well. These patterns may indicate the formalization of a cult, which would entail the development of specialized positions of religious authority beyond that of healer, or **shaman**. Shamans are individuals who are thought to have the power to intercede in the supernatural world on behalf of other people particularly when in an ecstatic state. Often shamans enlist the aid of associated animal spirits or "alter egos". Shamanlike roles are found in many hunting-gathering societies around the world; shamans were probably the first religious practitioners. Aspects of shamanism appear to have been institutionalized in the Great Traditions of later states. For example, Maya kings seem to have possessed animal doubles.

Rituals also took place in houses, involving members of the household and perhaps also of sodalities. Flannery looked at contexts and artifacts that would be appropriate to this level. It was the practice in Mesoamerica to establish shrines in or close to the house, where images of deities were honored with incense. Some of these were wall niches and others were altars. In the courtyard of a residence at San Jose Mogote there were several possibly ritually related features, shallow (5 cm deep) wide (120 cm across) circular depressions that seem to have had no utilitarian function but were carefully finished with mud plaster and red and yellow paint.

These features were difficult to interpret, but ritual-related artifacts in residential settings were less perplexing. Ceramic figurine fragments were fairly common, many appearing to depict costumed dancers. There were also ceramic masks that may have been part of dance costumes, and other costume components such as bones of the wings of macaws, valued for their feathers.

At the individual level of ritual were items that could be used for bloodletting. Self-mutilation was practiced for penance or other dedicatory purpose, to offer flowing blood to the deities. This was best accomplished with sharp, fairly thin implements like narrow obsidian blades and stingray spines. The latter were especially popular but had to be imported into the Valley of Oaxaca, so local imitation stingray spines were made, for example,

shaman An individual who is thought to have the power to intercede in the supernatural world on other people's behalf, sometimes while in a ecstatic trance. The shaman often has a supernatural helper or alter ego in the form of a companion animal.

out of deer bone. Flannery found that in the early Preclassic, bloodletting "was probably an egalitarian ritual" but, by the middle Preclassic, bloodletting gear could be graded as to its quality and the more valued materials (imported and rare) were found in more affluent residences; genuine stingray spines were a status symbol as well as a means to piety. Bloodletting implements were found in residential and public building contexts.

Evidence from the Valley of Oaxaca reveals that formalized rituals developed during the Preclassic period on both the household and community levels. We know that Oaxaca was involved in a system of information exchange and exchange that included many other parts of Mesoamerica, including the precocious Olmec region of the Gulf Coast of Mexico (Flannery 1968b). Ritual paraphernalia from Oaxaca were used by the Olmec, and Olmec symbolic designs show up on Oaxacan ritual objects. Through such processes of exchange, and based on earlier, shared institutions such as shamanism, the distinctive religious patterns of the Mesoamerican cultural tradition emerged.

Maya Religion

The archaeologist's view of Maya religion has been radically altered by settlement pattern studies and excavations revealing the residential patterns of the Maya, and by decipherment of Maya monuments (Morley, Brainerd, and Sharer 1983; Schele and Miller 1986; Thompson 1970). Maya regal and ritual centers such as Copán and Tikal were once thought of as "vacant ceremonial centers" and now are known to have been occupied and to have served many secular functions. Pyramids are sometimes funerary monuments to kings; the themes of inscriptions are dynastic and political, portraying real people — secular rulers who have religious as well as sociopolitical functions.

These features indicate that Maya religion focused on ancestor worship, though it included higher gods. Our new model of Maya religion is that it encompassed a hierarchy of ancestral spirits linked to each level of social organization (extended family, lineage, state) with spirits of dead kings as gods of the polity. Corroboration for these patterns comes from the modern Maya, whose extended families and lineages are linked through ancestor cults (such as those at Zinacantán in Chiapas).

At Copán, evidence of ancestor rituals has been found in royal tombs and funerary temples at the Main Group, in the tombs in elite compounds at Sepulturas, wall niches and offerings at residences, and particularly in the burial of a high-status Middle Classic chief (Fig. 12.6). Another important ritual context has been revealed at Altar Q. This monument to dynastic continuity was apparently erected by the 16th ruler, who had himself depicted receiving the staff of office from the dynastic founder (Fash 1991). A remarkable offering of 15 jaguars was apparently sacrificed at the time of the erection of the monument, and since the jaguar is a

FIGURE 12.6 This individual was buried with many grave goods, some of them imported, at Copán around A.D. 450. Some of the mortuary offerings suggest that he was a *brujo,* or medicine man.

symbol of royal authority in Mesoamerica, the beasts may have represented the spiritual doubles of rulers preceding the 16th.

Teotihuacán: City of the Gods

Contemporaneous with Classic Maya culture, the great city of Teotihuacán flourished about 1,500 years ago, but by the time of the Aztecs and the Spanish conquest, its origins and purpose were cloaked in sacred mystery. To this day scholars puzzle over its political organization and the range of its political and economic ties. One thing is certain: It was one of the largest cities in the world at the time of its greatness and clearly an imposing ceremonial center (Millon 1981).

Teotihuacán was thought by the Aztecs to be the place where their world—and time—began. Although the city had dwindled to a fraction of its former size, it was still an important pilgrimage shrine. Aztec rulers and their entourages often came there from Tenochtitlan (about 40 km away) to worship, lead ceremonies, and inter the remains of important people.

The sacred zone consisted of the area around the great causeway 3 km long that we now know as the Street of the Dead (the name comes from Teotihuacán's use as a burial ground in Aztec times). Figure 12.7 shows the pyramid at the end of the Street of the Dead, with the Pyramid of the Sun along the side of the street. All along this causeway were ranged the pyramids and regal-ritual complexes that retained a strong sacred value even after they had fallen into ruin.

FIGURE 12.7 The mountain of Cerro Gordo seems to loom even larger than its actual size, because of the planning of the shape, size, and placement of the pyramids of the Sun and the Moon along the Street of the Dead at Teotihuacán.

Teotihuacán in the Landscape We can learn a great deal about the spiritual value of the landscape by studying the location and layout of the city within its larger environment (Evans and Berlo 1992). The Teotihuacán Valley is the northeastern arm of the Basin of Mexico. The city sits on the lower slope of a large conical mountain, Cerro Gordo. This mountain was called the "Mother of Waters" before the Spanish arrived, and the name is appropriate from a hydrological standpoint. Geologically, the southern slopes of Cerro Gordo cover the aquifers that fed the springs that served to irrigate the lower valley. Before the irrigation system was implemented, the Teotihuacán Valley was marginally suited to agriculture, and virtually unpopulated, but when the springs were used to irrigate the plains of the valley it became highly productive, providing enough food to support the population of the city as it developed (Sanders 1981).

Mountains. The Street of the Dead aligns the pyramids with the top of Cerro Gordo (where there was a pre-Hispanic shrine). The pyramids of the Sun and Moon mimic the general form of the hills of the Teotihuacán Valley—an architectural feature effectively highlighting the importance of Cerro Gordo. The observer standing on the Street of the Dead south of the pyramids, looking north, sees the massive Pyramid of the Sun to the right and the Pyramid of the Moon straight ahead. The two pyramids are the same shape and their summits are level with each other; the observer unconsciously expects the Pyramid of the Moon to be at least as large as the Pyramid of the Sun. This is a visual trick, pulling the observer toward the mountain by foreshortening the view, manipulating the observer's sense of the relative size of these three "mountains"; Cerro Gordo, the Mother of Waters, appears relatively larger, looming over the miniature mountains of the pyramids.

Caves.   In the Mesoamerican belief system caves were orifices of the earth's body and as such were sacred places. Many peoples of the central highlands of Mexico traced their origins to caves, such as that at Aztlán, a mythical homeland for the Aztecs. The Teotihuacán Valley has a number of caves and the Pyramid of the Sun is built over one. Archaeological excavation within it revealed stone drainage channels, evidence that ceremonies involving water were held there despite the absence of a natural water source in the cave. Some of the remains excavated out of the cave include charcoal (from fires and torches), pottery fragments, fish bones, and shell. Millon (1981) hypothesizes that ceremonies honoring things associated with water were held there.

Springs, rivers, and water.   A river ran through Teotihuacán, and as it flowed it gained water from various springs; then just downstream from Teotihuacán it was split into the several main channels of the lower-valley irrigation system to grow the food Teotihuacán needed. At the time the city was being laid out, the river's course through the sacred precinct of the city was straightened as shown on the map in Fig. 8.5 and ran perpendicular to the Street of the Dead. It flowed between the Pyramid of the Sun and the Ciudadela (the city's administrative and regal center), which is dominated by the Pyramid of the Feathered Serpent, also known as the Pyramid of Quétzalcóatl, with repeated images of a flowing feathered serpent surrounded by shells and waves (Fig. 12.8), which cover the facade. The creator of humanity and bestower of maize, the Feathered Serpent was the deity associated with things that flow. Thus roads, blood, water, and serpents are all alternative, symbolic forms of the physical embodiment of flowing. This sacred association was part of the daily life of the common people in ways we would little suspect without Colonial period sources to guide us. For example, the most auspicious day in the Mesoamerican calendar to begin a journey is that named 1-Serpent, since snakes and roads are associated in form. Rivers also flow, and the glinting scales of the serpent are like the ripples in flowing water. The juxtaposition of all these symbols in the natural and architectural environment of Teotihuacán would possess enormous significance for the believer.

Since details of an archaeological belief system are always open to questions, scholars will continue to debate the sacred value of Teotihuacán's location and layout, but one fact is certain: The city could not have grown to its immense size, density, and internal complexity without its highly productive agricultural zone, which depended on the water from the springs.

FIGURE 12.8 The facade of the Pyramid of the Feathered Serpent at Teotihuacán is covered with repeated motifs of things that flow and further decorated with carved sea shells to reinforce the water imagery.

Between Teotihuacán and the Aztec Mexica

As Teotihuacán began to decline in the 18th century, several other cities became important in the central highlands. In fact, the Basin of Mexico became something of a cultural backwater, so thinly settled that when the cities inheriting Teotihuacán's power themselves began to decline and their peoples dispersed, they found land available in the Basin. The migrant groups entering the basin the 12th and 13th centuries settled among the already established communities, and the stories of their migrations are seminal episodes in the historical annals set down in the early Spanish Colonial period. Many of these groups called themselves "Aztecs," claiming to have come from Aztlan, and among these were the Mexica, who founded Tenochtitlan.

The Mexica and the Templo Mayor

Tenochtitlan underlies present-day Mexico City, whose modern name honors the Mexica, founders of the original settlement. The Mexica capital was razed in the siege by the Spanish conquistadores in 1521. The stones forming the palaces and temple-pyramids of Tenochtitlan were assembled into the palaces and churches of the conquerors, with the center of the city remaining fixed. The National Palace of Mexico is built over the ruins of Motecuhzoma's palace, and the cathedral is built over part of the sacred precinct of Aztec times (Broda, Carrasco, and Matos 1987). Tenochtitlan's most imposing structure was the Great Temple, a pyramid probably about 25 to 30 m high with a double staircase leading up to twin temples, one to Tlaloc and one to Huitzilopochtli. The Great Temple was leveled and over the centuries its exact location was lost. Then in 1978, workers for the electric company working near the cathedral unearthed a huge (3.25 m) sculpted disk, depicting a decapitated and dismembered woman. This woman was Huitzilopochtli's traitorous sister, who had tried to kill him; the monument to her perfidy was at the bottom of the stairs leading up to his temple (Fig. 12.9).

Subsequent excavations cleared an entire city block, revealing the base of the Great Temple and adjacent shrines. Typical of buildings of the central highlands, the temple had been enlarged several times, probably to commemorate the reigns of powerful rulers. The temple had at least seven distinct construction stages, overlying an original modest structure (presumably dating from the early 14th century). Each stage enlarged the existing pyramid, and each was accompanied by dedicatory offerings. Ethnohistoric sources describe the dedication of the last construction phase, in the 1480s, as a rite involving the sacrifice of tens of thousands of people, mostly captives from military campaigns to expand the scope of the tribute empire.

Human sacrifice has long been the element of Aztec culture that captured the attention of observers (Boone 1984). The Spanish may have somewhat exaggerated its scope to justify their own actions, but there is little question that the Mexica used human sacrifice not only to feed the Sun and avert destruction of the world, according to their cognized model of the universe, but also as political terrorism to scare their allies and clients into cooperation. But what can the Great Temple tell us about the Mexica worldview?

The twin temples atop the pyramid were dedicated to an ancient deity associated with agricultural productivity (Tlaloc) and a more recent tribal deity who inspired the militaristic fervor of the Mexica (Huitzilopochtli). The locus of religious devotion here also commemorated the two mainstays of the Mexica economy: the agricultural base that sustained the capital's population, and the long-distance trade and tribute network that sustained Tenochtitlan's role as central place in a vast empire (Matos 1987). The object of Mexica devotion was not only social coherence but also their own economic lifeblood. The complexity of Mesoamerican religion at the time of the Aztecs reveals itself to be hierarchically organized, the spiritual world mirroring the strict hierarchy of Aztec sociopolitical life. The Mexica regarded themselves as the chosen people, in charge of keeping this world from destruction. This religious view was closely linked with their politics, since it provided the rationale for political expansion.

These archaeological excavations strikingly supported the accuracy of the recorded Spanish accounts of the conquest of Tenochtitlan. Although we often think of such accounts as useful in fleshing out the archaeological record, the reverse is also true. Writers of historical accounts often made

FIGURE 12.9 The Aztec world stressed military power, and Aztec society's material rewards were mostly reserved for soldiers. Since women held little political power, it is perhaps fitting that the only image of a female deity at the Templo Mayor shows her hacked into pieces for having challenged Huitzilopochtli's authority.

mistakes and had their own biases; in many cases these can be detected and corrected by the direct evidence of the archaeological record.

LIMITS OF INTERPRETATION

Even if we can reconstruct important aspects of the belief system of archaeological cultures, it is chancy to ascribe particular emotional attitudes and psychologically derived motivations in such cases. The opportunity for error is tremendous because there is little way of testing these projections. In contrast, it is relatively simple to demonstrate a region's carrying capacity (Chapter 5) and hypothesize demographic consequences of changes therein. But it is difficult to formulate testable hypotheses to guide research that would provide solid information to substantiate or challenge theories about states of mind in archaeological settings.

Yet states of mind—the emotional and attitudinal bases of belief systems—are the essence of humanity, and to ignore them in archaeological interpretation and reconstruction is to leave out highly significant motivational factors in the dynamic relation of culture and environment. These states of mind also make the archaeological culture come alive for us, and touch us emotionally. Much of the fascination people have for archaeology comes from the sense of reaching out across time and empathizing with someone long dead. Think of the poignancy of the fallen figures at Pompeii; their plight is vivid, the despair and confusion of their last thoughts seem obvious. Whether or not they were invoking the mercy of Jove in their last moments, we cannot know.

POINTS TO REMEMBER

- All people share certain basic experiences, and all societies have what can broadly be called religion.

- In traditional societies religion is not strongly differentiated from other aspects of culture.

- Religious behavior may be directly adaptive.

- Religious beliefs and behaviors exhibit more cross-cultural variation than many other aspects of culture and may thus be difficult to detect or interpret in archaeological terms.

- It is easier for archaeologists to recover the behaviors and functions related to religion than to recover meaning.

- Religious behavior is at least 50,000 years old.

- Religion is systemically linked to other aspects of culture, such as how people make a living.

- Rituals may serve to regulate cultural systems.

- The archaeological record of religion suggests that it evolves, both in terms of its meanings and its institutional forms, to reflect changes in the larger culture.

FOR FURTHER READING*

A recent general treatment of religion is Paden's *Religious Worlds;* the anthropological perspective is found in Howells's *The Heathens* and Wallace's *Religion*. Lessa and Vogt's *Reader in Comparative Religion* presents particular cases. Rappaport's *The Sacred in Human Evolution* discusses that aspect of religion. Carrasco's *Religions of Mesoamerica* is a recent treatment of a complex topic.

*Full citations appear in the bibliography.

PART FOUR

THE ARCHAEOLOGY OF ANCIENT CIVILIZATIONS

Some archaeology books focus on culture history: They provide accounts of what ancient cultures in particular parts of the world were like and how they changed. These books try to provide a comprehensive overview of the career of the human species as seen through archaeological research. This is a perfectly legitimate approach, but as it tends to focus on the uniqueness of cultures or culture sequences, it can downplay many of the evolutionary trends that evolving cultures share. Chapters 13 and 14 develop a rather different perspective on the emergence of major civilizations in the Old World and the New World, considering both general trends and specific events in cultural evolution.

The general evolutionary perspective allows us to apply, in a comparative fashion, many of the concepts we learned about in earlier parts of the book. For example, the rise of civilization, no matter where it occurred, involved the emergence of new forms of political centralization; new kinds of economic specialization and wealth; and distinctive Great Traditions of art, architecture, ritual, and sometimes writing. In other words, common processes of change are the means whereby we can evaluate different evolutionary sequences.

On the other hand, the perspective of specific evolution allows us to see how the evolutionary career of each great civilization is indeed unique and different. Put another way, we can see how the universal processes of evolution expressed themselves in the context of particular environments and historical settings.

Chapters 15 and 16 provide basic culture histories of the world's oldest civilizations. But our larger goal is to show how archaeological research has contributed not only to the reconstruction of these distinctive evolutionary sequences but to our understanding of how they are similar, how they are different, and why these similarities and differences exist.

CHAPTER THIRTEEN

THE RISE OF CIVILIZATION IN THE OLD WORLD

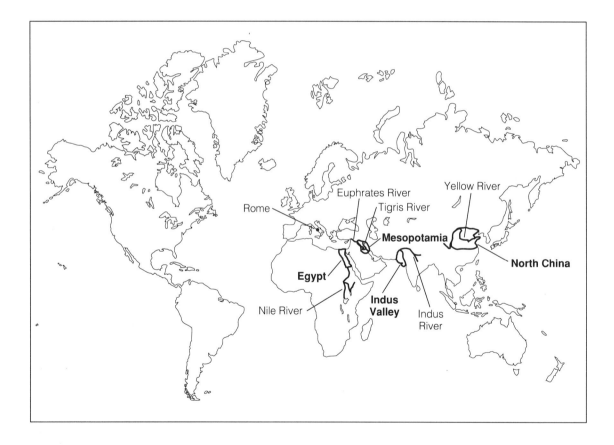

In Chapters 5 and 10, we identified several general modes of sociopolitical integration; the archaeological data suggest that these forms can be arranged in a general evolutionary sequence, with egalitarian societies at one extreme, states or civilizations at the other. In this chapter and the next, we will examine the earliest societies that seem, from our present archaeological knowledge, to have undergone the whole series of transformations — the major civilizations of both the Old World and the New World.

PRIMARY AND SECONDARY CIVILIZATIONS

Archaeologists make the distinction between **primary** and **secondary states,** or civilizations. Primary states develop independently, in the absence of influences from other societies of similar or greater complexity. Secondary states develop state-type institutions under the heavy influence of other states. Like many neat distinctions, however, this one ignores the fact that a number of the earliest civilizations, for example, those of Egypt and Mesopotamia, were in some kind of contact with one another during their early developmental phases, so evolutionary independence is a relative term. Certain complex societies have been saddled with the secondary-state label simply because they emerged later than, and in proximity to, earlier states: The idea is that because something is later, it must be derivative. The Maya were once thought of in this way.

Stylistic or organizational elements of Great Traditions may be readily transmitted from one culture to another. The Japanese elites borrowed enormously from the Chinese; their intention was to strengthen the emergent Japanese state (Sansom 1958). But the institutions of the Japanese state remained markedly different from those of China, even though the framework of Japan's socioeconomic hierarchy was cloaked in trappings of China's Great Tradition. The basic institutions of the state are much more likely to develop as a result of processes of change internal to the society, or to the set of regional societies, than because of such borrowing. Whether transformational processes are stimulated by states or cultures with other kinds of political systems is to some degree immaterial. Say, for example, that an expanding state put military pressure on a large chiefdom, causing a paramount chief to increase his political power and wealth through successful resistance. In systemic terms, political centralization and stratification, both processes associated with the emergence of the state, might be strengthened and the chiefdom would become more statelike. But why would this be different from these processes being triggered by conflict with another chiefdom? Why is one situation more "secondary" than another?

There are cases in which state formation in particular regions was heavily influenced by external factors. For example, during the 19th century the introduction of firearms allowed paramount chiefs in parts of Polynesia and Africa to increase remarkably their military and political power. This

primary state   A state that developed independently of influences from other societies of similar or greater complexity.

secondary state   A state that developed state-type institutions under the heavy influence of other states.

foreign technology stimulated political centralization and stratification, and state-type institutions rapidly emerged. Another example is the Roman Empire. Before the Roman conquest, much of western Europe and Britain probably had ranked sociopolitical organization. When, after hundreds of years, Rome withdrew from this region, it left behind a legacy of political, legal, and economic institutions, as well as Great Tradition elements, which were integrated into emergent local states. In this case, a significant transplantation of institutions occurred, and much of European state development does have a derivative character. But—and this is a very important *but*—we cannot conclude that western Europe would not have eventually developed state-type political systems if Rome had never existed.

The earliest civilizations emerged in the Old World. In this chapter we review the evolutionary careers of the civilizations of Mesopotamia, Egypt, the Indus Valley, and north China. We are particularly concerned with the early stages of their evolution—the periods during which they developed state-type institutions and laid the foundations of their accompanying Great Traditions. In all but one case (the Indus Valley) there is considerable cultural continuity through time. The terminus of each discussion will be at that point in time when historical records begin to be reasonably informative (bearing in mind that archaeology has much to say about later historical periods as well). Our emphasis here is on origins and growth. The question of the decline of civilizations is discussed in Chapter 15.

In choosing to focus on the earliest civilizations, we are in no way asserting that these are the only ones worth studying or even the only examples of primary states. They are, rather, the oldest civilizations with impressive Great Traditions, and most of their Great Tradition elements emerged as a result of independent evolutionary processes. For these reasons, they have attracted the lion's share of scholarly attention.

MESOPOTAMIA

Mesopotamia means "the land between the rivers." In the largest sense, it is the whole region drained by the Tigris and Euphrates rivers, including the arc of mountains which surrounds their alluvial plain. (Fig. 13.1) This vast region was widely settled by farming populations between 8000 and 6000 B.C., and the world's first urban centers appeared in southern Mesopotamia between 4500 and 3000 B.C. Many of these ancient cities were inhabited for thousands of years and some, such as Ur, are mentioned in the Bible. Because of Biblical references, and those of classical authors, Western society was always aware of the great Mesopotamian tradition of civilization in its later forms. But knowledge of the roots of this tradition was lost until the second half of the 19th century, when scholars began to recover direct evidence of its profound antiquity. (Basic sources for this discussion are Adams 1966, 1981; Cotterell 1980; Kramer 1963; Redman 1978; Sherrat 1980; Woolley 1934.)

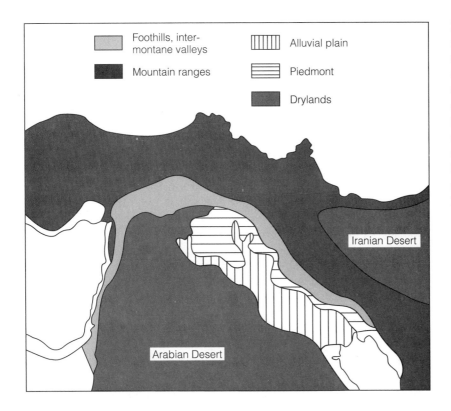

Foothills, inter-montane valleys	Alluvial plain
Mountain ranges	Piedmont
	Drylands

Iranian Desert

Arabian Desert

FIGURE 13.1 This map of the Near East shows the "Fertile Crescent" of cultivable land ringing the large interior desert zone, sites of hunting-gatherers, and early agriculturalists, and early urban centers. The heartland of ancient Sumer lies southeast of Nippur.

Environmental Setting

The core of Mesopotamia is the alluvial valley of the twin rivers of the Tigris and the Euphrates, which eventually join about 80 km north of the Persian Gulf, into which they finally flow. The southern part of this plain — the land of Sumer — is extremely flat, poorly drained, and marshy. The rivers, which have many channels, frequently shift their courses and flood over their **levees** onto the alluvial plain. The region is a desert in terms of rainfall (less than 250 mm, which falls in winter). The spring floods are extremely important because they are followed by the hot, dry summer. Just to the southwest, beyond the reach of the floods, lies the desert of northern Arabia.

levees Raised, well-drained river banks.

North of the plain is a rolling piedmont zone where rivers are entrenched and there is enough rainfall (250–500 mm) to support grassland and some marginal agriculture without irrigation. A transitional zone of foothills and low mountain valleys (elevation about 350–1,500 m) surrounds the lower plain and piedmont on three sides. Rainfall is 500–750 mm, sufficient for rainfall agriculture. Before being heavily disturbed by humans through overgrazing and deforestation, this arc of rugged country supported a savannalike parkland with numerous trees, and a diversity of animal species, many of which are now extinct. It is this attractive zone, with a climate rather like that of parts of California, that scholars call the "Fertile Crescent." Still higher, especially in southern Turkey and along the Iraq-Iran border, are the Taurus-Zagros mountains, with cool climates and rainfall in excess of 1,100 mm. In valleys where the growing season is long enough, agriculture is extremely productive. Forests are (or rather were) dense up to elevations of about 2,200 m, providing habitats for a wide variety of fauna. At the highest elevations are alpine environments useful for pasture, or rugged mountain country with no trees and little vegetation (some peaks are permanently snowcapped).

Mesopotamia was extremely varied in terms of climate, topography, flora, and fauna. Within the gross environmental zones defined above were patchworks of smaller distinctive zones of great significance for local cultural adaptation. Each zone, or microenvironment, had its own potential for human exploitation, and its own resources—including nonsubsistence raw materials such as timber and metals. Uniting the whole of Mesopotamia were the great rivers and their tributaries. Only against the background of this variation can we fully understand the emergence of Mesopotamian civilization.

Origins of Agriculture

Hunter-gatherers were widespread over the Near East and much of the mountain and foothill zones of Mesopotamia (predominantly Mediterranean/mountain biomes) at least several hundred thousand years ago. Shortly after the end of the last Ice Age (about 12,000 years ago), some of the groups of hunter-gatherers began to domesticate animals and plants, a process that laid the energy foundations for the later Mesopotamian civilization. Domesticated species included cattle; pigs; sheep; goats; various grain crops, particularly wheats; and fruit. Wild forms of all of these animals and plants were found in various Near Eastern environments. Needless to say, there was a long transition from foraging to the first agricultural communities that largely depended on domestication.

By roughly 7000–6000 B.C. agricultural settlements were widely spread over the upland zones and a few other favorable environments. A number of communities had populations of 1,000 or more, such as Jericho near the Dead Sea and Çatal Huyuk in central Turkey, but there is no compelling evidence of nonegalitarian sociopolitical structure. Trade in such things as shell and obsidian was widespread, though generally on a small scale; some objects are found hundreds of kilometers from their sources.

Between 6000 and 5000 B.C. settlements began to appear on the lower fringes of the Mesopotamian piedmont, some in areas where rainfall was insufficient to guarantee good crops each year. Irrigation works were probably used for the first time to channel water to fields. Walls and other defensive features appear at a number of sites. Networks of communities shared the same ceramic styles over very large regions. At some sites are

Table 13.1 Chronology of Mesopotamian Civilization

Early Dynastic Period III	2550–2350 B.C.	Emergence of large conquest states
Early Dynastic Period II	2650–2550 B.C.	Warring city-states
Early Dynastic Period I	2900–2650 B.C.	Warring city-states
Uruk and Jemdet Nasr Periods	3600–2900 B.C.	Population growth, political centralization
Ubaid Period	5300–3600 B.C.	Colonization of Sumer

specialized structures, perhaps especially elaborate houses, and burials with impressive grave goods. It seems very likely that chiefdoms were present in several areas by 5500–5000 B.C. But the region of Mesopotamia that was to be the most dynamic of all, the southern alluvial plain of the Tigris and Euphrates, called Sumer, was still largely unpopulated.

The Emergence of Mesopotamian Civilization

Chronology The periods, or phases, listed in Table 13.1, which mark significant transformations in settlement patterns, architecture, and various Great Tradition elements, are traced through changes in ceramics. The periods mainly apply to Sumer, which was the focus of rapid development after 5000 B.C.

Process: Settlement, Urbanization, and Agricultural Intensification Our knowledge of settlement systems, urbanization, and intensification comes from four sources: (1) excavations in the central precincts of major cities (many carried out long ago); (2) surveys carried out since the 1960s around major cities, especially Uruk; (3) recent excavations in sites of all sizes; and (4) written texts.

The *Ubaid period* is marked by the colonization of Sumer by about 5000 B.C. by people living in small agricultural communities of mud and reed structures. Settlements were few and widely spaced to take advantage of optimal agricultural locations—on the levees of rivers, and the edges of marshes, where small-scale irrigation and natural soil moisture were available for crops. There were no central places or clusters of politically integrated communities. By the end of the Ubaid period certain settlements covered as much as 10 ha, but we don't know if the largest towns had specialized functions. Unfortunately, no Ubaidian settlement has ever been adequately excavated. They are often deeply buried beneath Sumerian cities, and tiny Ubadian ritual buildings were ancestral to the great temples of later times.

During the *Uruk Period*, between 3600 and 2900 B.C., urbanization and associated agricultural intensification were remarkably rapid and the landscape of southern Sumer was socially, politically, and agriculturally transformed in fundamental ways. Cities emerged in other parts of Sumer as well. Local processes varied, but there was a general pattern of emergence of cities as regional populations grew and settlements became more clustered. Irrigation networks accompanied urban growth, becoming increasingly large and regularized. As the Early Dynastic began (2900 B.C.), many cities were fortified.

The Uruk period is named after the city of Uruk, probably Ubaid in origin, which mushroomed to an estimated 10,000 people by the end of the Jemdet Nasr period. The largest in Sumer, it reached its greatest size around 2700 B.C., covering an area of about 400 ha and enclosed by a great wall (Fig. 13.2). The core of the city consisted of two monumental temple precincts with ritual and other structures elevated on large platforms. Population was probably 40–50,000 people.

Surveys revealed how nearby rural settlement was affected by the growth of Uruk. Rural sites multiplied between 3600 and 2900 B.C., indicating rapid population growth. Uruk attained its largest size around 2700 B.C. (40–50,000 people), when farmers took up residence in the city. Only the largest rural towns remained. Depopulation of the countryside and aggregation into large towns probably reflects widespread warfare, also signaled by the fortification of the city. At roughly the same time, large-scale irrigation systems were built, so there is a general correlation between rapid urbanization and this essential form of agricultural intensification.

The basic unit of Sumerian civilization was the central city and supporting communities. Cities like Uruk dominated large rural territories with their all-essential irrigation works. We do not know in detail the extent of these territories, but by Early Dynastic times well-marked boundaries appeared. Texts and other evidence suggest that the comparatively small city of Lagash dominated a hinterland of about 1,500 km² early in this period, with 25 dependent towns and 40 villages.

Until recently archaeologists believed that this process of urbanization mainly affected Sumer and its fringes, including the important region of Elam in the adjacent Zagros mountains. New discoveries indicate that urban centers in the Sumerian tradition appeared as far away as northwestern Syria as early as late Uruk times.

Process: Political Centralization and Stratification

Ubaid period. Although a number of Ubaid towns reached respectable size, there is no convincing evidence for large, multicommunity political systems during the Ubaid period. During the Uruk period, however, there is striking evidence for political centralization. One unmistakable indication is the emergence of cities as politically dominant central places, and another is monumental construction in the central temple precincts at some

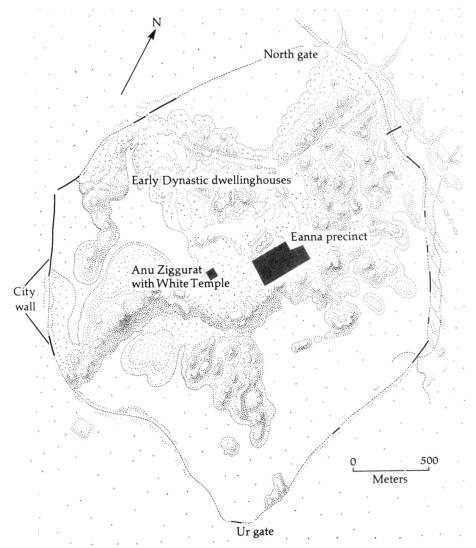

N

North gate

Early Dynastic dwellinghouses

Eanna precinct

Anu Ziggurat
with White Temple

City
wall

0   500

Meters

Ur gate

FIGURE 13.2 Map of Uruk, one of the largest of Sumerian cities.

cities. For example, the smaller of the two great temple complexes in central Uruk reached its greatest size during late Uruk times, and other projects such as irrigation works and city walls also required leaders and institutions to organize skilled and unskilled labor on a considerable scale.

Another innovation of late Uruk times is a crude, mass-produced, highly standardized ceramic form called the "bevel-rimmed bowl" (Fig. 13.3). These are so numerous that some scholars believe they reflect standardization of rations controlled by some central authority. Materials such as metals (copper and silver) and flint were long-distance imports into Sumer, possibly requiring some form of central administration of commerce. But

FIGURE 13.3 Crude bowls with this form were made in large numbers in Late Uruk times, possibly mass-produced through the use of molds. Some archaeologists believe that they were designed as standard measuring vessels issued by a central redistributive institution, such as a temple, in Sumerian society. If so, they are evidence of an economy that was to some extent centrally administered.

this is all very general and indirect evidence. What do we know in detail about political and social structure?

Titles, kingship, and art. Early written texts at the end of the Uruk period use the title *en* (which means something like "lord" or "priest-king") and another term referring to some kind of assembly of people, presumably convened to make or ratify political decisions. Unfortunately, most early texts are not very well deciphered, and the exact meaning of these terms is uncertain. Archaeologists have traditionally assumed that the early Sumerian temple complex, besides having religious functions, was the dominant political and economic institution. The *en* would thus be the priestly ruler of a theocratic society. Another idea was that the assemblies were bodies of free male citizens who met to debate and decide political issues democratically. Both of these reconstructions have been largely discarded; Sumerian society was more secular and more internally complex than was originally thought.

Was society of the Uruk period ranked or stratified? Because the connotations of the earliest titles are poorly understood and because there is a dearth of sophisticated and varied excavations at early Sumerian sites, we cannot be sure. If there were well-developed chiefdoms in Sumer, the transition to more stratified forms probably took place in Uruk times, since the succeeding developments seem much more statelike.

Texts of the Early Dynastic period are comprehensible and include historical information. A new title, *lugal,* becomes conspicuous, meaning something like "big-man" or "owner." However, the lugal seems to have originally functioned as a situational war leader, empowered to act for the duration of a military emergency. As war became endemic, the *lugal* became permanent, and the term assumed the connotation of "ruler." Political authority and economic advantage may have accrued to *lugals* through successful management of warfare, which allowed them to acquire prestige, military followings, and booty to reward personal retainers, some of whom may have been captured slaves. *En* and *lugal* became the most exalted titles used in cities with large territories during Early Dynastic times. Concomitantly, the palace emerged as a conspicuous urban feature and political institution, distinct from the temple. Centralized rule was present in all of the largest cities by the end of the Early Dynastic period.

By about 2700 B.C., the institution of kingship seems well established and individual kings can be identified (they are recorded in later king-lists). The *Epic of Gilgamesh,* about a hero-king of Uruk, seems to refer to events taking place about this time, though it was written down much later. Gilgamesh is a proud and powerful man who must, nevertheless, seek political support from constituents at Uruk for his most controversial decisions. By the end of the Early Dynastic period, the historical writing becomes coherent enough so that we may read narrative accounts of leaders and their personal accomplishments. Royal themes are expressed in art, such as found on cylinder seals and carved stone vases. Kings were seen as defenders against aggression, guardians of justice, and patrons of public works such as temples, walls, and irrigation canals. Particularly aggressive rulers carved out miniempires for themselves by conquering a few other cities and their territories, but these were unstable, rarely lasting more than a generation or two. The earliest known ruler is King (en) Men-barag-si of the city of Kish, and strong kings claimed a traditional title "King of Kish," which implied hegemony over all of Sumer, even though none really achieved such dominance.

Social stratification.   Although by Early Dynastic times certainly kingly families existed, we unfortunately do not have comparable evidence for nonroyal patterns of stratification. Striking confirmation of the degree of royal power and wealth was unearthed in the 1920s at the comparatively small city of Ur, where elite and royal shaft tombs, dating to around 2500 B.C. were interspersed with graves of commoners. The few tombs that had not been looted yielded extraordinary finds (Fig. 13.4). The richest, that of Queen Shudi-ad, contained a wealth of burial offerings, which included her most important household possessions. Approximately 70 of her retainers — ladies in waiting, guards, and charioteers — were sacrificed to accompany her. The Ur burials demonstrate the extraordinary wealth and authority concentrated in the ruling dynasty. Unfortunately, no similar tombs have been found at other cities, so we do not know how representative the Ur burials are of general political centralization and stratification.

The many nonroyal graves excavated at Ur indicate gradations of status rather than sharp social cleavages. It seems quite clear that Sumerian society included important individuals or families who in some fashion controlled agricultural resources far beyond their own needs, sometimes in the form of estates. Archaeologists have been so concerned with the central temple precincts of cities like Ur and Uruk that we have practically no information about variation in urban houses, to provide details about stratified social structure. Excavations of residential precincts at a number of small cities

FIGURE 13.4 This plan of one of the large royal graves at Ur shows the servants sacrificed in the course of funerary and burial rites.

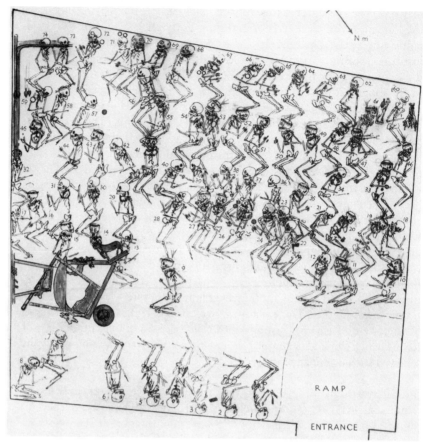

revealed congested arrangements of mud-brick houses along narrow, winding streets and alleys. The smallest houses were only about 50 m², but many were much larger, consisting of several rooms around open courtyards (Fig. 13.5). Stratified social systems certainly existed throughout much of the Early Dynastic period, if not before, and Mesopotamian cities were the focal points of city-states.

Process: Emergence of the Mesopotamian Great Tradition

Writing. Writing, the most significant Great Tradition element, probably developed at least as early as the end of Uruk times (about 3100 B.C.). The early script has considerable pictographic content and well-developed numbers. Many early texts are economic in nature (see Chapter 8). Not until the end of the Early Dynastic is the phonetic component in cuneiform writing mature, with written symbols consistent with patterns of speech.

FIGURE 13.5 Reconstructed interior of a Sumerian house at Ur. An elaborate and spacious house like this, built of mud-brick and with two stories, would probably have been the residence of a prosperous family.

For the first time texts other than economic accounts, such as historical accounts, legal documents, and literature, became common.

Architecture and Art. One of the most characteristic features of the Sumerian Great Tradition is the **ziggurat,** the high platform topped by a temple or palace. Ziggurats began to be built in Uruk times, mainly of mud-brick, though occasionally of imported stone. They have highly distinctive plans and decoration.

Artistic style is expressed through carved statues, vessels, and stone cylinder seals (probably used to denote ownership) bearing images of humans and deities, which, from the Uruk period on, fit squarely in the later tradition of Mesopotamian art. Imagery increasingly focuses on the deeds of kings, who are portrayed in highly stylized ways in hunting and battle scenes. There seems little doubt that the most important elements of the

ziggurat Mesopotamian term denoting a high platform or mound built of successively smaller terraces, one on top of another, crowned by a temple.

pantheon of Sumerian gods were present by Uruk times, if not by the end of the Ubaid period. Rituals of many kinds, particularly those associated with agricultural fertility, are recorded in representational art.

Process: Economic Specialization and Trade   Economic specialists existed as early as Uruk times — service personnel attached to temples or other institutions as administrators or accountants. Scribes are the most obvious of these, some of whom were probably full-time specialists. Carving of cylinder seals and ritual stone vases also involved specialized artisans, and the potter's wheel allowed rapid production of pottery. Certainly trade was essential from Ubaid times on, because Sumer is singularly poor in resources apart from land and water. Raw materials such as timber, metals, and stone were imported into Sumer from very early times. At least part-time specialists probably participated in such trade. By Early Dynastic times textiles (mass-produced in temples by captured slaves), finished metal items, pottery, and food were exported from Sumer in exchange for both raw and finished products. Such trade was facilitated by the location of cities on navigable rivers and canals, the use of sailing vessels, and the availability of animal transport.

There were many specialists by the end of the Early Dynastic: priests, scribes, merchants, boatmen, metal workers, stonemasons, jewelers, carpenters, potters, physicians, and weavers, as well as specialized food producers, such as shepherds and fishermen. We don't know what proportion of a city-state's population consisted of nonfood-producing specialists, but given the infrastructure of the society, it could have been very sizable. Intensive irrigation agriculture allowed high productivity (Mesopotamian crop yields astounded later Greek travelers). Individual farmers, who had metal tools, plows, and animal traction, could cultivate large areas and produce considerable surpluses. Water and animal transport efficiently moved even bulk goods like grains. Efficiency of artisans was enhanced by metal tools and the potter's wheel. Because consumers were so densely settled within the territory and particularly in the major cities, redistribution of goods was energetically cheap and demand high.

Mesopotamian Civilization in 2400 B.C.

Sumerian civilization was mature by the end of the Early Dynastic period. Great Tradition elements and the basic institutions of the state were well developed, with over a dozen city-states sharing common cultural traditions of speech, writing, technology, art, religion, and sociopolitical institutions with each other and distant city-states having (at least in part) ethnically non-Sumerian populations. Despite these commonalties, no lasting political integration united large parts of Sumer. City-states fought each other over territorial boundaries or other pretexts and also against highland marauders who saw rich pickings on the fertile Sumerian plains.

Average population of the largest class of urban communities was prob-

FIGURE 13.6 We have little evidence about early domestic architecture in Sumerian cities. They probably looked much like Erbil, shown here, except that they did not sit on high mounds, since the mounds (called "tells") result from the accumulated debris of millennia of occupation.

ably 20–25,000 people, with an occasional giant such as Uruk at twice that size and a number of significant cities as small as 5–10,000. Surrounding territories ranged from a few hundred up to several thousand square kilometers. Cities were walled, although there was some fairly dense settlement outside the defensive perimeters as well. Judging from exposures of later city levels, as well as from written texts, mud-brick houses (sometimes more than one story high) probably were densely packed along narrow, winding streets (Fig. 13.6). Apparently there were open public spaces, but we have no indications of specialized marketplaces. Cities were generally close to navigable waterways and often had port facilities.

Dynasties of rulers dominated city politics; increasingly they emphasized their religious roles, portraying themselves as principal clients of the patron deities of the city. Temples were not only religious institutions but economic corporations that owned land, exacted taxes from farmers, supported numerous specialists (including slaves), manufactured specialized products, and organized trading ventures. Stratification was well developed. Important people or families owned large estates, but the bulk of the population was composed of common food producers, along with a host of economic specialists. Some of these possessed their own lands or skills, while others were without resources and eked out a living as dependents attached to temples or estates. Trade was widespread, including regions as far away as Egypt, the Mediterranean coast, the mountains and plains of modern Turkey, Iraq, and Iran, the shores and islands of Arabia and the Persian Gulf, and even such distant and exotic places as India.

Sophisticated systems of writing, art, ritual, and mathematics expressed the Sumerian Great Tradition, and status symbols such as those unearthed earlier at Ur distinguished people of different social and political statuses. Surpluses based on intensive irrigation and agricultural technology supported all this political and economic complexity.

There is no doubt that the civilizational process had worked itself out very impressively by 2400 B.C., and here we conclude our story. Shortly after this time, all of Mesopotamia was united under the first of many successful dynasties of conquerors. Sumer itself eventually declined in population, and in political and cultural dominance, in part because agricultural land lost productivity because of salinization—the concentration of salts in the soil (see Chapter 15). Although political and cultural centers shifted to other regions, the basic institutions of Mesopotamian culture were firmly fixed, as ever-richer historical sources attest.

Summary: Mesopotamia

Mesopotamia is remarkable both because it is the earliest great Old World civilization and because of its dynamism. The processes of population growth, urbanization, political centralization, segregation, and the emergence of Great Tradition elements, were very rapid. But there is no single focal point for all of this innovation—the rise of Sumerian civilization is very much a story of different regions, populations, and political systems evolving at different rates and in different ways, all the while interacting with each other. Although these evolutionary changes are impressive, we should note the smallness of scale, even after a thousand years of development of state-type institutions. In 2400 B.C. there was no stable political unit larger than one could walk across in a few days or less. Even the largest stable city-state probably had fewer inhabitants than the number of fans who attend a major college football game today. In all probability, the administrative structure of such a city-state would have been smaller and simpler than that of a medium-sized modern university.

Also remember that our archaeological sample of early Mesopotamian culture is poor, particularly in terms of representative excavations of sites of all types. Some of the most powerful data for the processes discussed come from surface survey and collection, not from excavation. The historical record is of little help until very late; the earliest texts are difficult to read, and primarily record administrative/economic information, with little about political or social institutions or religion. Although certainly a literate civilization in one sense, early Mesopotamian civilization is still largely prehistoric; only future archaeological research will answer many questions and enlarge or amend our reconstructions.

EGYPT

Egypt has loomed larger in the historical consciousness of the West than any of the other great Old World civilizations. It figured prominently in Biblical history, and its great tombs and temples consistently aroused the wonder of travelers and scholars. As we saw in Chapter 2, scholarly and public fascination with Egyptian antiquities in the early 19th century helped stimulate the development of archaeology. (Basic sources for this discussion are Butzer 1976; Cotterell 1980; Hobson 1987; Hoffman 1991; Malek 1986; Redman 1978; Sherrat 1980.)

Environmental Setting

The Greek Herodotus (fifth century B.C.), often called "The Father of History," recorded the remark that "Egypt is the gift of the Nile"—a succinct and accurate cultural-ecological statement. The environmental setting of Egyptian civilization shares two characteristics with that of Sumer: a fertile river valley and a desert climate. But the differences between the two regions are as important as the similarities.

The Nile is an immensely long river, roughly 6,400 km. It originates in central Africa and the mountains of Ethiopia and eventually finds its way north to the Mediterranean. The last 1,100 km of its course waters a strip of land that was the heartland of ancient Egyptian civilization (Fig. 13.7). There the Nile is constricted by steep cliffs and hills, behind which lies the desert. Nowhere is the valley more than 20 km wide, and frequently it is much narrower. This narrow ribbon of green vegetation is called **Upper Egypt;** about 280 km south of the Mediterranean, the river diverges into multiple channels, forming a wide, flat, alluvial delta, known as **Lower Egypt.** Together these areas comprise only about 26,000 km² of land—much smaller than Sumer, but much more of it is cultivatable.

The Nile Valley has even less rainfall than Sumer, and the river is the source of all water (except for the very occasional rainstorms that fill the otherwise dry tributary streambeds). But unlike the meandering rivers of Sumer, the Nile flows below its plain. Only during the annual floods (now regulated by the Aswan Dam), which in late summer covered the landscape for about six weeks, was water widely available without irrigation. These floods not only brought moisture at the beginning of the agricultural season but also provided an annual deposit of thin silt that renewed soil fertility and constantly built up the level of the valley floor. Egyptian irrigation systems were designed from very early times to direct and store floodwaters and to ameliorate the worst effects of floods that were too high or too low—both of which could have disastrous consequences. Thus the Bible records the cycle of seven years of feast and seven years of famine of the ancient Egyptians, who never fully solved this problem. Floods sometimes spilled far out of the floodplain, especially to the west, creating huge oasislike environments in shallow depressions.

Upper Egypt The narrow part of the Nile Valley, about 1,100 km long, that lies north of Aswan and south of the Nile delta region. This is the southern part of the river in the modern nation of Egypt.

Lower Egypt The wide, flat, alluvial delta of the Nile River.

FIGURE 13.7 Map of Egypt showing sites named in the text.

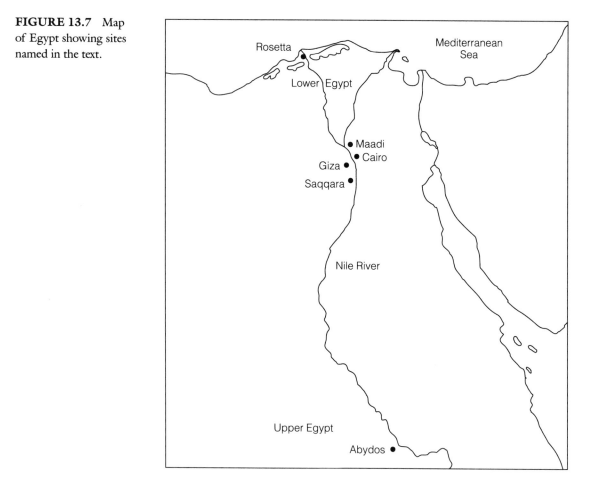

The narrow belt of irrigated land along the banks of the upper Nile varies in width, and for this reason irrigation systems tended to be fairly localized. Even with intensive irrigation, Egypt's land was not threatened by salinization, both because of the annual deposit of silt and because water could drain back off into the river. Everywhere the boundary between irrigated land and desert was extremely sharp. Towns and villages of the living were placed in the irrigated zones, while the dead were interred in the nearby desert.

Compared to southern Mesopotamia, Egypt was small and well defined by natural boundaries. All parts of it were linked by a single artery of transportation, and it was much more self-sufficient in terms of natural resources. The Nile Valley supported a richer fauna than did the alluvial plain of the Tigris-Euphrates, with fish, waterfowl, and aquatic animals such as crocodiles and hippos in the river itself, and animals such as gazelle

FIGURE 13.8 Saharan rock art painted by early cattle herders.

in the desert. Abundant mineral resources—stone of all sorts and metals such as copper and gold—could be mined from the nearby hills. Only timber was in short supply.

Origins of Agriculture

Foragers lived in the Nile Valley for many thousands of years before the introduction of agriculture; archaeological remains of them are particularly common after about 18,000 years ago along the Upper Nile. Although archaeologists once believed the Nile Valley was a region of early agricultural experimentation, it now seems probable that most domesticated species of plants and animals (with the possible exception of cattle) were introduced from the Near East.

After 6000 B.C. peoples who raised cattle, goats, and sheep utilized environments adjacent to the Nile Valley (Fig. 13.8), and settlements at least partly based on food production were present by at least 5500–4000 B.C. By 4900–4000 B.C. some of these sites were large towns, apparently occupied by thousands of people for long periods of time. Wheat was stored in special silos of basketry and clay, and well-made pottery was in use. Architecture and burials suggest egalitarian sociopolitical organization.

The Emergence of Egyptian Civilization

Chronology Egyptian civilization emerged by about 3100 B.C. and retained its identity until the Greek conquest in 332 B.C. Here we will consider the Predynastic (4900–3100 B.C.), Archaic (3100–2600 B.C.), and Old Kingdom (2600–2200 B.C.) periods. The last two of these are the most important. During the Archaic, the first rulers of a united Egypt appeared. During the Old Kingdom, a succession of stable dynasties emerged, and the basic sociopolitical institutions and Great Tradition elements became fixed.

Evidence for the evolution of early Egyptian civilization comes mainly from three sources: (1) tombs and their contents; (2) contemporaneous written inscriptions; (3) later inscriptions and archaeological materials from which we may extrapolate in reconstructing the culture history. Unfortunately, any direct evidence of the evolution of regional settlement systems or the nature of large settlements is almost entirely lacking. Not only has silt buried most early communities but archaeologists have been inordinately attracted to the impressive and well-preserved tombs in the desert areas beyond the zones of habitation.

Process: Political Centralization and Stratification   Evidence for political centralization and stratification is more abundant than for early settlement systems. By late Predynastic times (approx. 3500–3100 B.C.) many parts of Egypt were fairly densely populated, and evidence exists of hierarchical sociopolitical structure during this period, such as elaborate burial practices and status objects of extremely fine workmanship (often themselves found in tombs). The most impressive tombs are rock-cut, brick-lined chambers well provided with mortuary offerings of food and other items. Tomb paintings include scenes of battles, high-powered ships, and animals. These tombs contrast strongly with the simple pits in the sand that served as graves for common people. At least by this period well-developed local chiefdoms, if not tiny states, were distributed discontinuously up and down the Nile. Their capitals (sometimes fortified, judging from clay models) were probably located in the major pockets of good alluvial soil and had local irrigation systems. Later on, these segments of the valley, called **nomes** in Greek, became administrative subdivisions of the Egyptian state (this *nome* system may be based on much earlier traditions of local independent polities). By the end of the Predynastic, warfare seems to have been common between some of these little polities, or alliances of them, setting the stage for the later unification of all Egypt.

nome Administrative subdivision of the ancient Egyptian state.

Unification.   Between 3200 and 3000 B.C. the struggles of the petty Predynastic rulers were finally resolved, and kings emerged who claimed to rule much or all of Egypt. Evidence comes from excavations in tombs of early rulers and officials, inscriptions on status objects such as maces, palettes (stone slabs traditionally used to grind pigments), and a few royal monuments. A later king-list from about 2500 B.C. records not only the kings of the first two dynasties of united Egypt but also the names of earlier kings who seem to have ruled only parts of the country. Particularly conspicuous are rulers shown wearing the symbolic Red Crown of Lower Egypt and the White Crown of Upper Egypt (later combined into a single

(a) (b) (c)

FIGURE 13.9 The Narmer palette, made around 3100 B.C., shows images of kings wearing the crowns of Upper Egypt (a) and Lower Egypt (b). After unification, these crowns were often shown combined (c). The figure of an imposing king grasping an enemy he is about to smite is a common theme in Egyptian Great Tradition art.

piece of royal headgear symbolizing the unification of the two regions) (Fig. 13.9).

The broad outlines of the unification process are clear. There was lengthy warfare between Upper Egypt and Lower Egypt at the end of the Predynastic, a fierce and protracted struggle that probably intensified local political centralization. At first the north (Lower Egypt) had the upper hand, but by about 3100 B.C. the southern kings (whose capital was at Nekhen) eventually prevailed. Maces and palettes (Fig. 13.9a, b) found cached in a ceremonial building at Nekhen celebrate the military exploits of rulers named (or titled) Scorpion and Nar-mer, but which of these, if either, was the actual unifier of all of Egypt is unknown. The victors, whose patron deity was the hawk-god Horus, moved their capital to Abydos, whereby Egypt was embarked on its long career as a centralized state. Although the institutions of the state and the Great Tradition elements become most evident during the Old Kingdom, there is little doubt that they were in place by the end of the Archaic.

Despite the victory of Upper Egypt and the use of symbols such as the combined crowns of Upper and Lower Egypt to assert unity, the political system remained fragile during the first several dynasties. Rival political factions threatened kings, who contracted marriage alliances with women from other important families or regions to dampen conflict, and some rulers carried out military operations in Libya to the east and Nubia to the south, to stabilize Egypt's frontiers.

The First Royal Tombs.   Archaic kings of the first and second dynasties asserted their sovereignty over all of Egypt by constructing tombs of unprecedented splendor such as those near Abydos and Saqqara. Tombs were lavishly furnished with mortuary offerings; even though looters have disturbed the actual burial chambers, thousands of offerings have remained, including food, jewelry, pottery, furniture, and weapons. Most expressive of royal power are the burials of servants or retainers associated with the Abydos and Saqqara tombs. Some of these people no doubt chose to be buried near their royal masters after their own deaths, but others were clearly human sacrifices; these could number in the hundreds. Since at least one of the Saqqara tombs was that of a queen, female monarchs or consorts were obviously of very high status. The Saqqara tombs had underground pits, over which rectangular mud-brick superstructures called **mastabas** were erected. As large as 65 by 37 m, their facades decorated to resemble the facades of royal palaces, mastabas were, in essence, replicas of the residences used by living kings and nobles.

mastaba   Rectangular mud-brick superstructure covering the subterranean tomb of an early Egyptian ruler or elite person.

The Pyramids.   During the fourth dynasty of the Old Kingdom period, the mastaba pattern matured into the pyramid tradition. The first pyramids were stepped, their tiers essentially a sequence of ever-smaller mastabas stacked one on top of another. These quickly evolved into the huge, stone-built pyramids known to modern tourists, the largest of which is 150 m tall. Pyramids were really just the central features of much larger mortuary precincts that included two main temples (one by the river and one at the pyramid itself) with a covered causeway linking them, buried spirit boats, and the accompanying tombs of family members and officials. All these features, as part of the continuing cult of the king, were devoted to his well-being after death. Herodotus's estimate that 100,000 men worked daily for ten years to build the largest pyramid is probably excessive, but certainly labor was mobilized and organized on a vast scale.

Inscriptions and Statuses.   Early inscriptions record a series of obviously royal titles. Carved stone slabs (stelae) bore names and titles. By Old Kingdom times the king (portrayed wearing the symbolic dual crown) bears the title of pharaoh, and numerous other titles for lesser officials indicate a hierarchy of offices or statuses. Some officials were directly attached to the household of the king; most exalted was the vizir, a sort of chief bureaucrat, but there were also important officials in charge of the royal treasury and courts of justice. Royal governors oversaw provincial administration, and minor officials were in charge of royal estates, herds, and workshops. There were professional scribes and a hierarchy of priestly or religious statuses. These bureaucracies of the officials of Egypt (and other early states) primarily functioned to protect and enhance the well-being of the royal dynasty. Officials desired to be buried near their royal master and recorded their activities and titles in tomb paintings and inscriptions. Very early on the importance of the ruler is emphasized in art by showing him much larger than others, often engaged in heroic deeds or rituals. Battle scenes are common. One king, possibly engaged in initiating canal construction, is also shown wielding a ceremonial digging tool.

Process: Settlement, Urbanization, and Agricultural Intensification Settlement pattern data for early Egypt would probably show shifts mirroring the sociopolitical processes just discussed, but actual settlement information is practically nonexistent because of the silting of the Nile, the perishable materials used for residential architecture (including royal palaces), and archaeologists' preoccupation with tombs. One of the most serious interpretive consequences of this lack of information is that we cannot reconstruct the size, density, and distribution of the Egyptian population at any point in time or understand how it changed through time. Sumer shows clear evidence of rapid population expansion coincident with the growth of urban centers and irrigation systems, but we will probably never have comparable data from Egypt nor any showing how the evolution of local irrigation systems related to population changes. Certainly canals were present from very early times (they are shown on Predynastic works of art), but their scale and administrative centralization are unknown.

The site of Maadi, investigated in the 1930s, provides a small window into early settlement. Near modern Cairo, it was inhabited just before and during the unification of Egypt. Maadi was a prosperous farming town, covering about 18 ha and probably fortified with a timber palisade and system of ditches. Residences were partially subterranean, with perishable superstructures. Huge jars sunk into the ground or in the floors of underground chambers, stored grain, fat or oil, and meat and fish. Bones of sheep, goat, cattle, and pigs were also recovered. Children were buried in the town itself, but there were special cemeteries outside for adults. The variation in the graves of adults indicated some form of ranking.

The settlement system of unified, Old Kingdom Egypt probably included many rural agricultural villages, probably prosperous towns in the tradition of Maadi. How urbanized were they? There was clearly no long tradition of gradual urban growth on a single site, as in Sumer, because if there had been, huge mounds with many superimposed stratigraphic layers would protrude even above the Nile silt. We also know that locations of royal capitals—presumably the most impressive central places—were frequently shifted. For example, the first king of united Egypt established a new (probably fortified) capital at Memphis, on the northern edge of the delta.

These patterns suggest a fairly modest degree of urban development,

regal-ritual center A type of city which is essentially the residence of the ruler and nobles.

with cities being essentially **regal-ritual centers** (Fox 1977). The king's palace was the core of the city, with the rule of all of Egypt an extension of the administration of the royal household. Around the palace would lie the residences and facilities of officials and retainers. Urban places would have had a fairly narrow range of administrative and ritual functions, and fairly small populations. On the other hand, we know from cemeteries that huge numbers of officials seem to have been resident in capitals. The presence of large numbers of privileged administrators, as well as the royal household itself, may well have stimulated the growth of very large urban support populations of economic specialists. Efficiency of agricultural surpluses and river transport could have supplied even large urban populations with food. All things considered, it is probable that Egypt did, at least at times, develop impressive urban communities, even though the bulk of the population resided in rural settlements.

Process: Emergence of the Egyptian Great Tradition

Writing. Egyptian writing is most familiar to us in the form of picturelike hieroglyphs, although later scribes developed more convenient scripts as well (see Chapter 9). Hieroglyphic writing was present by the end of the Predynastic (about 3100 B.C.). This is slightly later than the appearance of writing in Mesopotamia, and some Egyptologists believe that contact with Sumer influenced or stimulated the emergence of Egyptian writing. The very earliest inscriptions are few and difficult to decipher; they consist mainly of labels, short inscriptions, and captions to pictorial representations. Perishable materials such as papyrus may have been used for writing, but no fragments have been found.

One of the most conspicuous uses of early Egyptian writing was political display, as rulers sought to express themselves and to impress others through public inscriptions with royal themes. In this respect the writing served a different purpose than that of early Mesopotamia, where early texts were predominantly administrative.

Art and architecture. Egyptian art and architecture are highly distinctive and instantly recognizable. They are also highly conventionalized and replete with potent political and religious symbolism. Their most impressive products relate to kings and other high personages, their families, and to religious rituals, which often had elite, political dimensions themselves. Although commoners such as farmers and craftspeople are artistically portrayed, they are usually shown in elite contexts, as subordinate to kings or officials or as participating in elite rituals. Basic elements of this artistic Great Tradition were in place at least by Archaic times. Themes include battles, hunting and fishing (elite sports), rituals, and supervision of estates or workshops.

We have already seen how tombs — the most distinctive elements of elite architecture — evolved. Although all Egyptians were probably concerned with the afterlife, it is the elite tradition of mortuary behavior that we know best. From kings to minor officials, elites tried to provide for the preservation of their corpses, which were placed in elaborate tombs stocked with the things needed both to enjoy and face the trials of the afterlife. This elite mortuary tradition undoubtedly began in Predynastic times; the later pyramids are only its most grandiose expression.

Ritual. Many Egyptian rituals centered on the king, whose well-being was essential to the state and who was the person able to intercede most directly with the gods. One of the most important was the annual *Sed* festival, present at least by Archaic times, in which the king (at least symbolically) had to publicly demonstrate his health and vigor.

The Great Tradition elements of Egyptian society were firmly in place by the end of the Old Kingdom. Although some of them changed (e.g., the replacement of pyramids by hidden, rock-cut tombs) and new variations on old themes were added, they retained a remarkable continuity for almost 3,000 years.

Process: Economic Specialization and Trade

Specialization. Objects from elite tombs are of high quality and their preservation (because of dry climate) often excellent. If we were to judge the degree of full- or part-time specialization on the basis of the quality of Egyptian objects as things in themselves (see discussion in Chapter 8), we would certainly assume impressive levels of specialization in Predynastic times. Although it is more valid to judge the degree of specialization from more general archaeological contexts, these are unfortunately very limited in Egypt.

In Old Kingdom times, when inscriptions and representative art become reasonably informative, there were numerous specialists: administrative, scribal, and religious personnel mentioned earlier, plus potters, carpenters and wood carvers, boatmen, traders, metal workers, stone workers, architects, mural painters, physicians, and a host of others (Fig. 13.10). Many were certainly full-time specialists, and most seem to have been clients directly attached to powerful patrons or institutions, including the royal and elite households, estates, and temples. No class or subgroup of independent artisans or service personnel who exchanged their products or skills in a well-developed market system is evident. Given the high productivity of Egyptian agriculture, as well as the comparative efficiency of water transport, the production and redistribution of food surpluses could have provided for a large population of nonfood producers, including those living in and servicing urban centers.

Trade. Although Egypt was well supplied with certain kinds of raw materials (such as stone), from very early on other materials were obtained from considerable distances. By late Predynastic times copper was commonly used, both for utilitarian tools and weapons and ornaments. Most

FIGURE 13.10 Carved relief panel from an Old Kingdom tomb showing metal workers forcing air into a furnace.

copper probably came from the Sinai region to the northeast of the delta, and by Old Kingdom times it seems to have been directly acquired by Egyptian expeditions sent to the mines. Other expeditions to Nubia brought back gold and ivory. Walls of Archaic tombs were lined with cedar imported from Lebanon (probably from trade per se), and precious stones such as lapis lazuli came from as far as Afghanistan. All of these raw materials were processed by artisans, and most were consumed by elites. We do not know if any traders were free entrepreneurs.

Egypt during the Old Kingdom

By about 2500 B.C. the general outlines of Egyptian society and culture are established. The entire valley was a single state ruled by the pharaoh. Ideally succession to the throne was passed from father to his eldest son by the principal royal wife, but there was no fixed, inviolate rule. Theoretically the proprietor of all the resources of Egypt, the pharaoh was expected to treat his subjects with fairness, justice, and compassion, and to protect their well-being.

Egypt lacked a hereditary aristocracy. Below the pharaoh and his family was a complicated officialdom to whom the king delegated his authority, and who effectively managed Egypt on his behalf. Officials, as clients and retainers of the pharaoh, made up a social class of a kind but were themselves ranked in status and prestige. Apparently able people from even humble backgrounds could become officials, so there was considerable social mobility, with few or no inherited administrative positions. Some artisans or professionals must also have occupied fairly enviable social positions as well.

The Old Kingdom population has been estimated at about 1,000,000 people, the vast majority of which were peasant farmers. Details of land ownership are vague, but much of the landscape, together with its farmers, was directly controlled by the state and by large institutions such as temples. There were also large estates that seem to have been attached to privileged individuals who held particular offices or statuses. Peasants cultivated the fields, built and maintained local irrigation systems, provided labor for construction projects of all sorts, and paid taxes. There were a few slaves, mainly war captives, but slaves were never very important in Egyptian society.

A state religion with a well-organized religious bureaucracy existed, and the same basic set of deities was worshiped all over Egypt, though particular regions had patron deities. Part of the state cult focused on the pharaoh and the ruling family, who had their own patron deities and around whom much royal ritual revolved. The pharaoh, who was thought to be divine or semidivine, interceded with the gods on behalf of his people. The effort expended on construction of his tomb symbolically affirmed this role. His divinity was not inherited but rather was assumed with his office. During the Old Kingdom religion became increasingly formalized, and temples appeared in many parts of Egypt. These temples were not merely places of worship but social, political, and economic institutions of considerable complexity. They were supported by grants of lands and peasants to work them, given by the king. Kings thus appeared as benefactors of religion, but in the long run such grants undermined royal political centralization and wealth.

After the end of the Old Kingdom, Egypt retained its characteristic political institutions and Great Tradition to a remarkable degree even despite periods of dynastic breakdown and civil war and incursions by foreign conquerors.

Summary: Egypt

Egyptian and Mesopotamian civilizations both largely developed in arid river valleys and depended heavily on irrigation. Both had the same basic agricultural crops and animals; both were technologically sophisticated and literate. But their specific evolutionary sequences are quite different.

Agriculture appeared in the Nile Valley fairly late (about 5500 B.C.), but it laid the foundation for rapid cultural evolution, in part because natural resources were richer and possibly because the Nile Valley is so much smaller in geographical terms (see Chapter 16 for a discussion of environmental circumscription). Population increased, and large agricultural towns appeared after 5000 B.C. Ranked societies, if not early stratified ones, were well established by 3500 B.C. The pace of evolution was much faster than that of Greater Mesopotamia, and a politically centralized state dominating the whole region emerged very early. Egypt lacked the long tradition of independent city-states so characteristic of Mesopotamia. Although a few urban centers were probably present by Old Kingdom times, Egypt also lacked the extreme urban development of Mesopotamia. The landscape retained its high productivity over the long run and did not suffer from salinization, which eventually undermined the economy of Sumer.

Egypt developed writing slightly after Sumer but used it primarily for political and religious rather than economic purposes. Both literate traditions, however, have few general historical records, and these are uninformative. Both Egypt and Sumer were essentially "prehistoric" societies during the first 1,500 years of their literate traditions.

Finally, there are striking differences in the archaeological evidence available for each. Sumer's settlement patterns are well known, but Egypt's are not, and neither are there deeply stratified Egyptian sites. Tombs and temples have attracted enormously greater attention in Egypt than in Sumer; tombs in particular are so numerous, and their contents (including representational art) so well preserved, that they are very informative. Despite more than a century of scholarly work in each region, however, much remains to be learned, and many details of our present-day reconstructions will eventually be changed.

HARAPPAN CIVILIZATION IN THE INDUS VALLEY

Egypt and Mesopotamia were never "lost" civilizations. There was reasonable continuity of culture and population in both regions, and their historical significance and Great Traditions were recognized. This is not true of Harappan civilization, which was only discovered early in this century. The most impressive Harappan sites are located in the valley of the Indus River, one of the largest rivers of Asia, which drains the western Himalayas (Fig. 13.11). Although Europeans recorded the existence of large mounds along the Indus in the mid-19th century, not until 1922 did archaeological research reveal that these belonged to a hitherto unknown early civilization. We now know that sites of Harappan civilization are spread over an area larger than that of southern Mesopotamian and Egypt combined.

In comparison with Egypt and Sumer, we know little about Harappan civilization for three reasons. First, far less archaeological research has been carried out. Second, Harappan writing has not been deciphered. Third, there is a sharp break between Harappan culture and later Indian civilization; Harappan culture and population have less obvious continuity with later societies than Egypt and Sumer. (Basic sources for this discussion are Allchin and Allchin 1982; Cotterell 1980; Possehl 1990; Redman 1978; Sherrat 1980.)

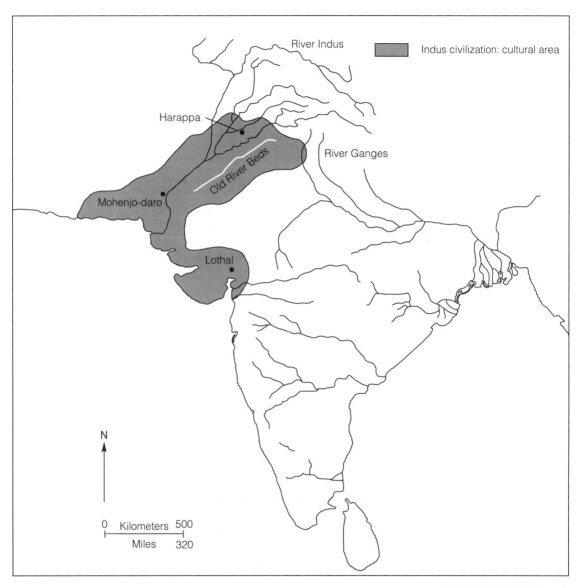

FIGURE 13.11 Map of India showing extent of Harappan civilization.

Environmental Setting

The heartland of Harappan civilization—the floodplain of the Indus River (measuring about 50,000 km²)—resembles southern Mesopotamia. It is an alluvial desert with only about 76 mm of rain per year, bordered on the east by an even drier desert and on the west and north by the mountains of Iran and Afghanistan. Summers (April through September) are reputed to be the hottest anywhere in the world. Fortunately, the Indus floods yearly, and the soil of the plain holds moisture for long periods. As in Sumer, multiple river channels frequently change course and near them in prehistoric times would have been lush forests interspersed with marshy bogs. Silting of the valley floor and movement of river channels has buried or destroyed much archaeological evidence. Fish and waterfowl would have been abundant, and other fauna would have included elephants, water buffalo, rhinoceros, and tigers.

The Emergence of Harappan Civilization

Chronology Harappan civilization is recognizable by 2500 B.C. and is in advanced decline by 1700 B.C. Obvious signs of complex social organization thus appear roughly 1,000 years later than they do in Egypt and Sumer, although there is some overlap among all three civilizations.

Origins of Agriculture Effective agriculture developed in Greater Mesopotamia over several thousand years, with many regions involved in early agricultural experiments, and food-producing communities eventually spread to the Sumerian plain. Something very much like this happened in the Harappan region as well. The highlands of eastern Iran and Afghanistan represent continuations of the same set of environments in which agriculture emerged in Greater Mesopotamia. Agricultural villages were scattered throughout these highlands at least by 7000–6000 B.C., using the same basic set of domestic plants and animals found further to the west. By 7000 B.C. the first farming communities began to establish themselves on the alluvial plain of the Indus, where a tradition of large towns eventually developed, some of them involved in widespread trade. There is no doubt that the mature Harappan civilization has its roots in such early settlements, although some components of the Harappan economy reflect eastern influences as well; water buffalo were very important, and rice was cultivated at some sites.

Process: Settlement, Urbanization, and Agricultural Intensification The first two Harappan centers found, Mohenjo-Daro and Harappa, are also the largest known. Since the 1920s, over 1,000 other sites of all sizes have been located, sixteen of which are of impressive scale. Unfortunately we have no information for regional settlement systems around the principal Harappan sites comparable to that for Uruk in Sumer. As with Egypt, patterns of change in settlement systems and population sizes and distributions are still unclear, although sophisticated surveys are now being done. Results to date suggest that it is difficult to generalize about settlement patterns. Around Mohenjo-Daro there are only faint signs of small rural settlements. Quite possibly, as at some other nonindustrial cities such as Uruk or Teotihuacán, many city dwellers there were farmers. Elsewhere

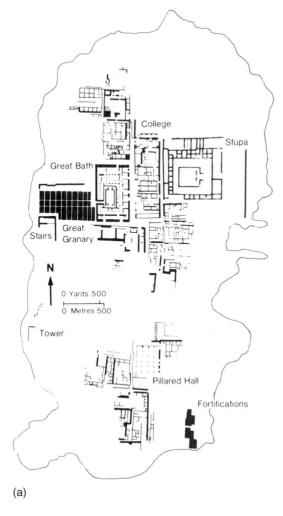

College

Stupa

Great Bath

Stairs

Great Granary

N

0 Yards 500

0 Metres 500

Tower

Pillared Hall

Fortifications

(a)

(b)

FIGURE 13.12 Plan of Mohenjo-Daro's citadel (a) with photo (b) showing regular layout of brick buildings and the Great Bath.

outside the heartland of the main valley, there are substantial towns, and then a gradation of smaller communities, right down to what appear to be individual farmsteads, but no coherent hierarchy of settlement is yet apparent in this pattern.

Cities. Since our knowledge of Harappan civilization still comes predominantly from excavations in a few major centers, our overall perspective is urban-centric. Both Harappa and Mohenjo-Daro are urban centers, fully comparable to the great early cities of Mesopotamia. Harappan architecture made heavy use of fired bricks instead of plain mud bricks, resulting in extremely good preservation of civic and residential areas.

Both Mohenjo-Daro and Harappa are somewhat over one square kilometer in area (Fig. 13.12) and at their height, each probably had

35–40,000 inhabitants. Each consists of two sections, a zone on the west raised on brick and mud foundations to a height of about 12–15 m (traditionally called the citadel), and a larger, lower town to the east. Citadels contain ritual and other civic architecture and are fortified. Lower towns are primarily residential. A conspicuous feature of each city is the regularity of its streets and structures, generally oriented to the cardinal directions and laid out on a grid pattern, with the biggest avenues running north-south. This layout suggests considerable urban planning, and is much more regular than the congested and highly irregular Mesopotamian urban arrangements.

Although access to the citadels was certainly restricted, they probably had primarily nonmilitary functions. The most impressive feature of Mohenjo-Daro's citadel is the Great Bath, a huge swimming poollike structure surrounded by smaller module rooms, probably part of a ritual complex. Other large rectilinear buildings with many rooms or pillared halls may be meeting places or elite residences (Fig. 13.13). Just to the west of the Great Bath was a building many interpret to have been a vast storehouse, or granary. Citadels were obviously planned and built with community labor; they clearly had highly specialized political, religious, and perhaps economic functions, and were utilized by the Harappan elite.

The lower towns seem to be undefended. Arranged along wide, straight streets and alleys are rectangular house compounds of fired brick and timber. The most elaborate of these contain multiple complexes of rooms, often arranged around central courtyards, and some houses were two or more stories high. The houses vary in size and quality, but most of the architecture appears well built and comfortable; there is no sign of the substandard slums found in many urban centers. Many houses were provided with elaborate drains to allow waste to flow into external cisterns. What may be specialized buildings such as neighborhood temples are also situated in the lower towns. Burials were placed in cemeteries outside the cities.

This basic pattern of separate residential and public architecture is found at other Harappan sites as well but is not, as sometimes claimed, a standard plan. Other centers are quite distinctive; Lothal, on a river near the Arabian Sea, has a brick dockyard with its own specially designed channel and nearby warehouses. Here fired bricks seem to have been reserved for civic constructions, while residences were built of mud brick.

Dense urban populations clearly depended on intensive agriculture, and irrigation must have existed to regularize agricultural production, but we have little evidence for it. Some hydraulic works may have been necessary to control destructive flooding, which eventually became a severe problem (see below).

Process: Political Centralization and Stratification   Unlike Mesopotamia and Egypt, Harappan writing does not provide titles or other

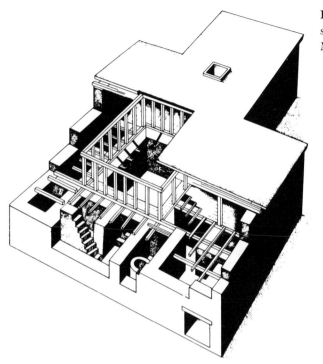

FIGURE 13.13   Reconstruction of residence at Mohenjo-Daro.

insights into political structure. Neither is there a rich tradition of well-preserved elite representational art. Our judgments about political organization must be made on the basis of archaeological materials alone.

Political Unification.   Even though they are spread over a huge area, there is no question that Harappan communities shared a common culture. The architectural tradition, elaborate systems of writing, weights and measures, and ceramics are highly uniform from one site to another. Despite such similarities, the whole Harappan culture was probably not politically unified. In Sumer, overall political unification was only achieved after 1,000 years of struggle, despite a common culture and the close spacing of Sumerian cities. Harappa and Mohenjo-Daro are about 640 km apart (we do not know how much they overlap in time), and great distances separate the Indus heartland from other regions. No single route of communication unites all communities, as in Egypt. No particular center is so large compared to others, or so specialized in its functions, that we can identify it as a political capital. Fortifications indicate at least periodic political unrest. As more surveys and excavations are carried out, regional variants on Harappan cultural themes become increasingly recognizable. All this points to political fragmentation.

Cities. The largest Harappan centers are impressive in size, well ordered, and prosperous; clearly they were centrally administered. Centralized leadership may have established their original plans, and labor was drafted on a large scale for communal projects, such as citadel construction. The elaborate systems of community streets and drains probably required effective municipal administration. Specialized facilities on the citadels indicate political as well as religious and economic functions, and we cannot rule out the possibility that some of their summit buildings were palaces. If, as seems likely, vast amounts of grain were stored in or near the citadels, effective centralization of basic economic staples existed, presumably based on the taxation of farmers; these supplies, in part, would have been redistributed by some central authority. Recent work in the lower residential areas has revealed large, elaborate structures that might also be palaces.

Stratification. Some form of stratification characterized Harappan society during its mature phase, and the institutions of the state were present. But as measured by archaeological remains, status differences are not as clearly marked as in Sumer or Egypt. Traditional Indian society in later times, however, exhibited some of the most extreme social stratification found anywhere, following what is obviously a very ancient pattern.

In Egypt and Mesopotamia burials provide some of the best evidence for stratification and political centralization, but there are only 700–800 known Harappan burials (usually interred in cemeteries). There are no known royal tombs, and not much variation is apparent from the burial sample as a whole. The scale and quality of domestic architecture tend to vary, reflecting differences in social and economic status. Similar differences could be expected to mark settlement variation where it exists.

Process: Emergence of the Harappan Great Tradition

Writing. The Harappans developed a highly distinctive script that was used throughout the mature phase, apparently uniformly over the entire region. Preserved inscriptions are short (under 20 characters) and are found on small objects such as seals and potsherds. This script is currently undeciphered; we do not know what language(s) it records, the form of the writing system, or what inscriptions mean (although seals may have included names for marking property, as in Mesopotamia). There is no known tradition of inscribed monumental public or tomb art, so writing seems not to have functioned as an element in elite display. For all practical purposes Harappan civilization is entirely prehistoric.

Art and Architecture. We have very little Harappan art, partly because of less intensive excavation, but also because art (at least in preservable form) appears to have played a lesser role in elite traditions than elsewhere. Certainly this does not imply lack of skill, because many small objects of pottery, stone, and metal are of extremely high quality, and carved seals in particular are often of breathtaking beauty. Images on seals (apart from the inscriptions) may well have elite symbolic meaning. An architectural Great Tradition is hinted at by such structures as the Great Bath and pillared halls of the citadel at Mohenjo-Daro, but until more excavations are done we cannot know how common these features were.

Process: Economic Specialization and Trade Economic specialists serving as officials, administrators, and scribes must have resided in the Indus cities, as they did in Sumer and Egypt, but we cannot identify them without titles, documents, and abundant artistic representations. Artisans are better known; there were certainly full- or part-time potters, brick makers, architects, metal workers, stone carvers, and seal cutters, judging from the abundance, quality, and contexts of their work. Workshops for producing beads and areas for smelting metal have been found at Lothal. One interesting pattern of Harappan sites is that centers of production seem to be separate from those of residence. People went to work every day, as opposed to producing things in their urban households, the pattern at Teotihuacán (Chapter 8). No marketplaces have been recognized; the apparent presence of large central granaries suggests that some basic commodities might have been redistributed by political authorities.

Boatmen and traders were important since many materials had to be imported, especially to Harappa and Mohenjo-Daro, both situated (like the southern Sumerian cities) in a landscape poor in nonagricultural resources. Metal and stone came from the mountains to the west, where there was also a thriving sea trade. Major Harappan centers are close to navigable waterways, and Lothal has special port facilities near the sea. Small objects of Harappan manufacture have been recovered from Sumerian sites and are increasingly being found on the islands and coasts of the Persian Gulf, the sea route between Sumer and India.

What Happened to the Harappans?

One reason why it is so difficult to interpret Harappan archaeological remains is the weak continuity between Harappan civilization and the later cultures of India. Many Harappan sites, including the largest ones in the Indus valley, were abandoned around 1500 B.C. in a process that lasted for generations. Archaeologists have several theories about the causes of decline, one of the earliest of which involves warfare. Literary and historical evidence documents that around 1500 B.C. northern India was invaded by people speaking Indo-European tongues, who later founded kingdoms throughout much of the region. The literary traditions of these invaders tell of the destruction of walled cities—perhaps Harappan centers. Unburied skeletons found in the streets of Mohenjo-Daro have been cited as evidence for warfare. Another idea is that high population density and overexploitation of the landscape caused severe deforestation and loss of soil fertility. This explanation best fits the big centers in the Harappan heartland, but it is hard to see how all Harappan centers would have been equally affected. A third explanation involves flooding. Geologists have detected shifts in the bedrock underlying the alluvial plain of the Indus that may have caused river channels to shift, making normal seasonal flooding more severe, disrupting both agricultural productivity and major cities themselves. At Mohenjo-Daro the most recent construction episodes, which are shoddy and makeshift, have been interpreted as attempts to cope with the effects of disastrous flooding. But this would not have directly affected sites outside the floodplain and cannot account for the general decline of Harappan culture, especially if it was not politically unified. For the moment, none of these explanations is satisfactory by itself; perhaps the Harappan decline was partly caused by multiple factors, some of which may have yet to be discovered.

Summary: Harappan Civilization

In many respects Harappan civilization resembles that of Mesopotamia, particularly in the environmental setting of its heartland. Despite the emergence of major centers almost 1,000 years later than those in Sumer, however, and despite later contacts with Mesopotamia, Harappan civilization developed largely on its own. Its urban centers are highly distinctive in plan and architectural tradition, and its Great Tradition elements are distinctive as well. We cannot reconstruct Harappan society in the same detail as for Sumer and Egypt, but the general outlines of its basic institutions are clear and are becoming more so as archaeological research continues.

CHINA

Of all the great Old World civilizations, China has by far retained the greatest continuity in population and cultural identity through time. There are families in China today that can trace unbroken descent back almost 2,500 years, modern Chinese can read characters in ancient scripts well over 3,000 years old, and China's Great Tradition survived largely intact into the 20th century. It was also the largest of the Old World civilizations in geographic and demographic scale. In many respects China today retains characteristics of the nonindustrial state.

Myths and traditions of political unification under royal dynasties refer back to a period about 5,000 years ago. Since the 1930s archaeologists have demonstrated that the beginnings of Chinese civilization extend back to at least 1700 B.C. in north China. From this core region, political, social, and Great Tradition elements spread gradually over an enormous area of eastern Asia under many dynasties of rulers. Because the Chinese were both literate and historically minded, our record of this process is very complete. In this section we will discuss only the beginnings of Chinese civilization, from about 1700 to 800 B.C. Evidence comes from archaeological surveys, excavations (particularly at royal capitals), artifacts, inscriptions, and later traditions of Chinese culture. (Principal sources for this discussion are Blunden and Elvin 1983; Chang 1980, 1986; Cotterell 1980; Reischauer and Fairbank 1960; and Sherrat 1980.)

Environmental Setting

The culture area of China as we know it today includes regions with great environmental diversity (Fig. 13.14). On the most general level, we can distinguish between north China, a midlatitude mixed woodland biome centered on the Yellow River plain, and south China, a more tropical region centered on the Yangtze River. North China's plain is extremely flat; the river flows slowly, and shifts its course, building up its bed with a heavy load of fertile yellow silt. Heavy summer flooding can be very destructive, the unpredictability of the river having been a constant problem for the Chinese. The extremely ancient irrigation works that both control the river and provide water to fields, have never been entirely effective. The growing season is short (4–6 months), and the region is semiarid, with rainfall of only 400–800 mm per year.

The Origins of Agriculture

There were probably several "hearths" of domestication in China itself, in particular, a tropical one in the south, where rice was an early staple, and one in the Yellow River Valley with millet as the staple grain. By the end of the Pleistocene, there were many well-established settlements of foragers in northeastern Asia, including Japan. Pottery, often associated with settled agricultural villages, was used by preagricultural people there by 9500–7000 B.C., the earliest pottery known anywhere in the world. Chinese legends attribute the origins of agriculture to innovations made by local foragers.

Several varieties of millet were among the first cultivated plants of north China and may have been domesticated by indigenous populations. Eventually the agricultural economy came to include wheat, and animals such as cattle, pigs, goats, and sheep, which had earlier been domesticated in the Near East. The chronology of the first appearance of these domesticates is poorly understood, and although we cannot tell if they were introduced into China or were domesticated locally, it is probably best to regard north China as an independent hearth of early agricultural development.

Sometime after 6000 B.C. in north China farmers began to live in small, apparently permanent settlements of semisubterranean houses with perishable superstructures. Pottery, storage pits, sickles, and grinding stones indicate a heavy dependence on crops, of which millet was the most

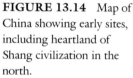

FIGURE 13.14 Map of China showing early sites, including heartland of Shang civilization in the north.

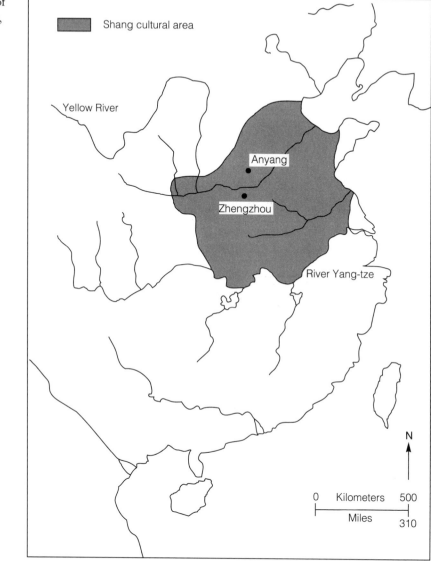

important. Regional clusters of settlements began to show distinctive cultural elements by 5500–5000 B.C. and after 3000 B.C. Neolithic populations were dense, settlements of impressive size had appeared, and some of the later hallmarks of Chinese civilization are recognizable in the archaeological record.

Emergence of Chinese Civilization

Chronology   For our discussion we will use the simple chronology in Table 13.2, which primarily refers to developments in north China.

Process: Settlement, Urbanization, and Agricultural Intensification

Settlement Patterns and Urbanization.   In the western and central portions of the Yellow River plain, a core region of about 16,000 km² emerged as the domain of the Shang kings between 1700 and 1100 B.C. Shang culture clearly has its roots in the earlier local Lungshan Neolithic culture, which itself had several regional variants in the Yellow River valley and much more widely in China as well. Although we have no clear evidence of settlement hierarchies for Lungshan times, there were large agricultural villages, sometimes surrounded by earthen or stone fortifications, which with associated weapons suggest warfare as a formative factor in the crystallization of the Shang state.

The first royal dynasty documented for China is the Shang Dynasty. Most Shang sites are on or near the Yellow River plain. Dozens of communities are mentioned in Shang inscriptions, and later Zhou dynasty records list 50 Shang city-states. Some are as far from the Shang heartland as the Yangtze Valley to the south. Each of these must have been surrounded by a network of smaller communities or farmsteads. Activity of the river and of hundreds of generations of Chinese farmers have destroyed or obscured most of the Shang settlement system, particularly small communities. Because we have no adequate overall view of any Shang regional settlement system, we cannot assess crucial ecological variables such as the growth of regional populations and the changing relationships of people to the resources on their landscapes, or to other human communities.

According to later records, Shang kings periodically moved their capitals. Of the nine known large Shang sites, at least three were probably royal capitals. Zhengzhou and Anyang (the last capital) have received most archaeological attention. Zhengzhou's fortification wall was built of rammed earth (earth pounded into wooden forms) and was about 7 km long,

Table 13.2   Chronology of Early Chinese Civilization

Early Zhou dynasty:	1100–800 B.C.
Shang dynasty:	1700–1100 B.C.
Lungshan Neolithic:	3000–1700 B.C.

enclosing an area of about 320 ha. Eighteen meters wide at the base, the wall was 9 meters high, requiring an estimated 180,000 person-years to build. This kind of construction also served for the foundation platforms and walls of Shang palaces and temples, rectangular, multiroomed wooden buildings (Fig. 13.15). No city wall has yet been found at Anyang, but it shares with Zhengzhou both palace and temple buildings, as well as a large royal cemetery.

Most of the other Shang centers would have been local capitals, ruled by subroyal elites subject to the Shang monarch at Anyang or elsewhere. Some of these sites have been excavated, and in comparison to the royal capitals, would have been very small; one had walls only 1.1 km long enclosing an area of only 0.25 km², yet it had many features of a royal capital, including a large palace and an elaborate tomb with human sacrifices.

Even the royal capitals of the Shang were only partially urban. They were essentially the households of the king, his relatives, and close retainers, and had a limited range of political and ritual functions. Population within capitals was both small in absolute terms and of low density compared to other preindustrial centers such as Teotihuacán or Rome. It was partly because of this limited scale and set of functions that Shang kings were able to shift locations of their capitals periodically. Small communities, retaining many of the house forms characteristic of Chinese Neolithic villages, were clustered closely around the margins of the capitals. Some of these were places of craft specialization for bronze workers, jade carvers, and potters. Most people subject to a ruling center must have lived in small dispersed agricultural communities.

In the Shang heartland there were probably some dozens of city-state modules of this sort, all theoretically subject to the Shang king, but many must have been independent by late Shang times. Other regions were developing their own traditions of complex sociopolitical organization and settlement, and modified forms of Shang social and cultural patterns spread widely, well beyond the limits of actual Shang political control. These regional cultures both influenced Shang society and were influenced by it.

Agricultural Intensification. Although Chinese myths credit pre-Shang culture heroes with the invention of irrigation and the taming of floods, we do not know if irrigation played an important role in the Shang agricultural economy, if any. Presumably some crops were grown on conveniently moist soils along the rivers, and if there was irrigation it was principally developed around the capitals. Fairly extensive farming seems to have been carried out for the most part on well-drained areas of the floodplain or hillsides, with fields cleared of vegetation and then cultivated until fertility declined. Although this has been described by some as swidden or slash-and-burn agriculture, it was very different from the tropical variety. Soil was deeper, leaching less of a problem, the plow may have been used, and manure was probably applied to enhance soil fertility. Production per

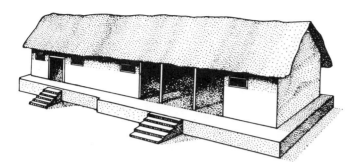

FIGURE 13.15 Elite
house, Anyang.

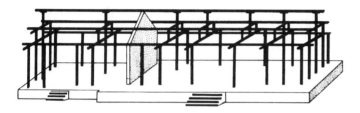

farmer would have been high, and the frequency of movement of residences or settlements low. Various forms of millet were the stable crops, but rice was also grown in some areas. Chinese farmers also had productive livestock, such as cattle, pigs, sheep, and goats.

Process: Political Centralization and Stratification Later Chinese histories retained traditional accounts of the Shang dynasty, but not until the 1930s did archaeological evidence substantiate them; kings, royal capitals, and bronze metallurgy, all hallmarks of emergent Shang civilization, are discernible in the archaeological record for the period 1700–1600 B.C.

Capitals and elite architecture. Political administration and royal ritual were centralized at royal palaces that presumably housed rulers and their retainers. Palaces, temples, and the massive walls that surrounded some capitals, were all built with public labor, which was expended on a very large scale.

Burials. Cemeteries near late Lungshan Neolithic sites indicate considerable differences in status. For example, at one such cemetery 90 percent of the burials are very plain, many entirely lacking grave goods. At the other extreme are a few rich tombs, with the dead interred in wooden coffins accompanied by many mortuary offerings, including elaborate pottery vessels, crocodile-skin drums, and polished stone musical chimes. Between

FIGURE 13.16 One of the royal tombs at the Shang capital of Anyang.

these extremes fall other tombs. Some sort of ranking is obviously present, but it is unclear whether the rich tombs represent the most highly ranked members of several large corporate families, those of a single lineage of chiefs who dominated the community, or a combination of these. The warfare indicated by the fortifications at several Lungshan towns might have been a stimulus for political centralization, promoting one family line over others.

Shang burials indicate extreme political centralization and status differentiation. Commoner burials abound, but the most celebrated tombs are those of the Shang kings and other elites, the most spectacular of which were found at the last Shang capital of Anyang (Fig. 13.16). Here eleven royal tombs presumably represent the last rulers of the dynasty. These tombs are of various sizes but share a common general plan. Deep rectangular pits (as large as 14 by 18 m) are approached by sloping ramps on two or four sides. At the bottom of the pits are cruciform or rectangular burial chambers for the royal person. Abundant grave goods include human sacrifices (as many as 165 in a single tomb), sacrifices of dogs and other animals, bronze vessels, weapons, political symbols, artifacts of bone, jade, and shell, and offerings of foodstuffs. Not only kings but also queens received such funeral treatment. The tomb of one queen contained 16 sacrificed humans, 6 dogs, 440 bronzes, 590 jades, 560 bone objects, and 7,000 cowrie shells. Such elaborate funeral offerings recall those of Archaic Egypt and the royal graves at Ur; in all these cases there was an extreme display of wealth and political symbolism, and an attempt was made to provide the deceased ruler with all necessary elements of his or her household. Outside of Anyang the largest known tomb exhibits many of these same patterns and probably represents the grave of a local ruler subordinate to the central dynasty.

Writing and titles.   Inscriptions from the Shang and subsequent Zhou dynasties provide insights into political organization and stratification. The first known writing, apart from pictographic symbols occasionally painted on Neolithic pottery, appears about 1500 B.C. as dedicatory inscriptions on bronze vessels. Shortly thereafter, oracle bone texts for royal divination become common (Fig. 13.17). Magical practitioners (shamans) regularly conducted divinatory rituals on behalf of the king, asking the royal ancestors questions about the prospects for good health, military success, hunting (a royal sport), and weather forecasting. Answers were conveyed by the pattern of cracks produced by heating pieces of bone or shell.

Shang kings bore the royal title of *wang* ("territorial chief") and another Shang word has the sense of "commoner." Other titles exist that in later Zhou times denoted subroyal nobles, but we do not know if they had the same meaning for the Shang. No system of titles clearly refers to a well-developed officialdom (as for Old Kingdom Egypt), but there were people at the royal court who had special duties, many of whom were recruited from the ranks of the large royal clan. The supreme Shang king carried out public sacrifices at his capital to Shang Ti, a deity who personified the ancestors of all Chinese of whatever status. Apparently these sacrifices were for the benefit of all the inhabitants of the Shang realm and may reflect ideas of common descent. The Shang also may have had the concept of "heaven," denoting in abstract terms the anthropomorphic first ancestor. Thus centralized around the person of the ruler, the most potent ritual observances were inextricably related to politics. Shang kingship had military and judicial as well as political and ritual dimensions.

Artifacts.   Wealth in the form of status symbols was highly concentrated in the hands of elites and royalty, as revealed in the contents of tombs. Most significant were objects of bronze, which symbolized the authority and power of rulers (Fig. 13.18). Copper was used in Lungshan times, but bronze is strongly associated with Shang technology. Bronze objects relate to elite ancestor worship, war, hunting, and political symbolism; only a few utilitarian tools are known. Sets of elaborate bronze vessels, some retaining forms earlier seen in Neolithic pottery, were used in ceremonies involving the ancestors of illustrious families. These vessels were made to order and often had inscriptions cast into them; passed down as heirlooms, they eventually found their way into tombs or caches. Perforated bronze axes served not only as royal symbols but as actual sacrificial implements. Bronze weapons were quite literal instruments of power, restricted to the elite. Along with horses and light, wheeled chariots (sometimes included in

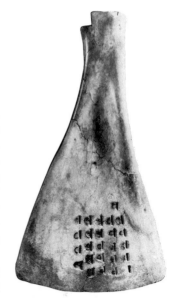

FIGURE 13.17 Text carved on a Chinese oracle bone. The practice of "scapulamancy" originated by heating the shoulder-blade bones (scapulae) of animals and then interpreting the pattern of cracks that appeared on the surface.

FIGURE 13.18   Bronze Chinese vessel used in ancestor rites. Sets of such vessels, along with the distinctive motives that decorated them, became features of the Chinese Great Tradition.

tombs), this weaponry gave armed elite warriors considerable advantages over opponents not so well equipped.

It is not clear how much the Shang kings and nobles derived their wealth from their own estates and the peasants attached to these estates as laborers, from taxation of free farmers, or from some combination of the two. Private estates were granted to members of the royal dynasty, royal consorts, and important officials; presumably these sometimes became hereditary possessions in particular families. In all likelihood no peasants were in fact free landholders but were in some fashion tied to land controlled by a royal or noble institution. Much wealth in the form of status symbols obviously relates to, and derives from, warfare. Sacrificial victims may well have been predominantly war captives.

Process: Emergence of the Chinese Great Tradition

Writing.   No other single element has so consistently defined the Chinese Great Tradition as writing (or literacy), which was a status symbol as well as a tool primarily used for ritual and royal purposes, mainly for divination. The origins of Chinese writing are traceable to painted symbols on Neolithic pottery. Early Shang writing has some highly pictographic elements, which later became conventionalized and more ideographic in content and which acquired phonetic elements as well. Around 2,000 characters were ultimately used (mainly known from inscriptions on oracle bones and bronzes), and about 20 percent of Shang pictographs still survive in some form in modern Chinese script.

Ritual and Art. Essential to Chinese thought was the centrality of the ruler, on whose relationship to heaven human well-being depended. These concepts, and the rituals associated with them, appear firmly in place by Shang times. So too does another Great Tradition component, worship of royal ancestors. Also traceable to Shang times (or even earlier) are symbols that later characterize the Chinese Great Tradition, such as the dragon. Jade, always highly venerated by the Chinese, was used extensively in late Neolithic and Shang times, as were lacquerwork and bronze vessels.

Process: Economic Specialization and Trade

Economic Specialization. Shang society had the energetic means to support numerous full- or part-time specialists, since agriculture was productive and rivers and draft animals provided effective transport. Certain products, such as elite ritual bronzes, are so sophisticated that they probably could only have been made by full-time specialists. Workshops for metal workers, jade carvers, potters, and bone workers are found in sites close to the Shang capitals, and these may have been the residences of full-time specialists who were clients of the nobility. Other full- or part-time specialists included woodworkers, lacquer workers, miners, traders, architects, shamans, and various officials. Although historical China has always had a strong tradition of local and regional markets, we do not know if these existed among the Shang.

Trade. The mountains that surround the Yellow River plain were sources of many raw materials, including timber and metal. Both copper and tin were available within reasonable distances and were obtained either by trade or expedition. Jade was imported over great distances (probably from Central Asia). Cowrie shells (used as a form of money) came from the Indian Ocean or the Pacific, and from the more tropical regions of southern China came products such as crocodile skins and turtle shell.

The Evolutionary Status of Shang Society

If we ignored written sources, the Shang archaeological record would indicate a highly stratified society. Written materials suggest another possibility—that ranking was a major principle of sociopolitical organization for the early Shang and that elements of it were retained to the end of the dynasty. This is consistent with the ancestral rituals of the Shang kings; with the possible rotation of the office of king among several royal sublineages; with the only partly urban nature of royal/elite centers; and with the traditionally strong Chinese emphasis on large, corporate kinship groups. Although the Shang had a word for "commoner," similar terms are used in large chiefdoms but without the specific implication of class structure. Certainly Shang society was very dynamic, and it changed greatly between 1700 and 1100 B.C. By the end of the dynasty stratification was probably well developed even though vestiges of simpler forms of political organization were retained. By that time, though, the Shang king may have been only the senior kinsman among many other rulers, a leader whose specific titles and traditional religious prerogatives set him symbolically apart but who had lost any politically effective authority or power over other city-states.

The Zhou Aftermath

In 1122 B.C. the Shang were displaced by the conquering dynasty of the Zhou, who may have earlier been subjects of the Shang kings. The Zhou shared, or adopted, many of the same traditions of writing, kingship, urbanism, ritual, and social organization of the Shang, and over the next 300 years spread the basic elements of Chinese civilization much more widely than the Shang ever did. Part of this process involved the founding of new cities by royal relatives, who were commissioned by the Zhou ruler with charters, titles, rituals, and elite symbols to serve both as territorial pioneers and culture-bearers of Chinese civilization. Eventually many of these rulers asserted their independence and adopted the royal title of *wang,* ushering in a long and warlike period of Chinese history that to some degree resembles the feudal period of western Europe. In 221 B.C. all of China was united by a single dynasty. After that time, new political institutions effectively eliminated a hereditary, land-holding, titled aristocracy, and substituted for it a literate officialdom and the distinctive hierarchy of social stratification — imperial family, state officials, farmers, artisans, and merchants — the basic structure of Chinese society until 1911.

OLD WORLD EARLY CIVILIZATIONS

Let us consider how these various trajectories of cultural evolution illustrate the concepts of general and specific evolution.

General Evolution

The great early civilizations of the Old World shared certain general features. All were technologically sophisticated and shared a similar set of subsistence resources that included animal husbandry as well as domestic plants. All were located in large, fertile, arid, or semiarid river valleys whose rivers allowed effective communication. Irrigation was essential for Sumer, Egypt, and Harappan civilization. In Sumer, Egypt, and China political authority and power centralized around hereditary rulers who derived much of their authority from religion. Ruling centers in Sumer, the Indus Valley, and probably Egypt assumed urban dimensions and complexity. Warfare was everywhere present, contributing to the emergence of strong rulers. Officials or other delegates of the rulers performed important managerial tasks and enjoyed access to estates, promoting both social and economic stratification. Common people, who formed the bulk of the populations in each region, provided labor and taxes for the support of elite institutions. Trade and commerce were widespread, involving elite items, in particular. Great Traditions based on writing, art, and ritual expressed the dominance of the elite and the world order of these ancient states. General evolutionary processes had produced highly recurrent patterns.

Specific Evolution

If we consider the evolutionary sequence of each Old World civilization in detail, we see much variety in specific evolutionary careers and their settings.

Environments Highly similar to one another, the regions of the Indus and the Tigris-Euphrates were most conducive to the emergence of early, large-scale irrigation, for which we have good evidence in Sumer. Unfortunately, salinization of the soil eventually became a serious problem in Sumer. Because the Nile deposited an annual layer of fertile silt, long-term productivity along the river remained high. Irrigation works to extend and control the Nile flood were more localized than those in Early Dynastic Sumer. Although China eventually became the civilization with the most complex irrigation system in the Old World, more extensive forms of agriculture were apparently relied on in Shang and even Zhou times.

The natural environment of Egypt was by far the smallest and most compartmentalized of all but was well provided with many natural resources. These had to be imported from greater distances elsewhere, one reason for which broad regional interaction was more important in Mesopotamia, Harappa, and China as these civilized traditions formed, and for which they eventually spread over much larger areas than did Egypt.

Emergence of the State The tempo with which state-type institutions emerged from simple agricultural societies was much more rapid in Egypt than it was in any of the other three regions. Egypt also achieved effective political centralization under a single ruling dynasty very early, while Sumer retained a pattern of independent city-states for over 1,000 years. In China, a single line of dynastic kings asserted dominance over a network of increasingly independent polities. Egypt was highly stratified, while the Shang Chinese retained many elements of ranking. Hereditary aristocracy disappeared in Egypt after Archaic times but became ever-stronger in China. Temples were major independent economic and political institutions in Sumer from the beginning, gradually became so in Egypt during the Old Kingdom, but were unimportant as quasi-independent institutions in early China.

Urbanism   Urban centers in Sumer and the Indus Valley developed on a similar scale but had very different settlement patterns. Shang China never developed cities comparable to those elsewhere, producing rather a pattern of capitals organized around royal or elite households. Urban or royal centers in all four regions were fortified (we have to assume this for Egypt), but walls around centers occur rather late in Sumer. Sumerian cities grew organically over many hundreds of years, while Harappan cities were highly planned. In Egypt and China royal centers were periodically moved, suggesting smaller, less complex urban forms with fewer functions than found in Sumerian cities.

Great Traditions   Writing is the most common Great Tradition element but is used in very different ways in the three cultures for which decipherable texts exist. Only very slowly does Mesopotamian writing branch out from its original administrative functions to include historical and religious information as well as literary compositions. Most important, it becomes a vehicle for kingly self-aggrandizement quite late. In Egypt the process is the reverse—from the beginning writing served primarily political ends. Early Chinese script seems to be almost entirely devoted to the magical and divinatory concerns of Shang kings. In all of these cases, however, much writing may have been done on perishable materials, so that our perception of its functions could be biased.

Other Great Tradition elements also differed. Public and funerary art played a much greater part in Egypt than elsewhere, and only in Egypt does the ruler appear to be semidivine. Although rulers in Egypt, Sumer, and China all were concerned that their funerary arrangements provide for them in the afterlife, only in Egypt did the cult of the dead king, and the dead in general, achieve Great Tradition status. Ancestor worship is most marked in China, possibly because of an emphasis on kinship and ranking.

Evolutionary Implications

In the Old World, independent processes of cultural evolution produced societies that were institutionally similar enough so that all are characterized as civilizations. Kingship, urbanization, occupational specialization, writing, and a host of other traits represent common cultural adaptations. Another implication is that in order to understand each particular variation on the civilizational theme, we must look at the specific ways in which individual cultural systems and traditions evolved through time and at the conditions that made each sequence unique.

In this chapter we have laid out the evolutionary trajectories of the major Old World civilizations in a descriptive, cultural-historical manner. What is needed in addition is a set of models that will help us to think about what factors caused complex societies to develop in a general sense and how the particular mix of such factors created diversity. We will review such models after a consideration of New World civilizations in Chapter 14.

Archaeological Implications

Despite the institutional similarities of the great Old World civilizations, the evidence is extremely varied and often inadequate. It is remarkable that the general evolutionary picture makes so much sense, given the disparate forms of evidence used to patch it together.

Although we think of early Sumer, Egypt, and China as historically documented cultures, their early written records tell us little about them. Harappa remains essentially prehistoric because its written records cannot be read. For the others, information of very different kinds is available. Much of what these records say is not only limited in scope but poorly understood, depending on extrapolations from later documents or historical information. If we had only contemporary documents for Sumer until the middle of the Early Dynastic, or Egypt until the end of the Old Kingdom, our reconstructions would be fragmentary indeed.

Another bias involves preservation and accessibility. For southern Sumer, long abandoned by dense agricultural populations, detailed settlement pattern information has been recovered. We may eventually get similar evidence for Harappa and north China, but early Egyptian settlement is largely inaccessible. This means that the most powerful single category of information for reconstructing the evolution of complex societies — the evolution of settlement systems and their associated populations — is only available for small segments of Mesopotamia. We know something about centers, but not much about their hinterlands, so our ability to build plausible models about how populations adapted to landscapes and supported centers is very limited.

Ironically, even the centers themselves are usually poorly known. In southern Sumer excavations extending over generations have exposed walls, temples, and palaces but revealed little about the general character of early urban places in terms of residences and other urban features. A similar situation exists for China. Only at the major Harappan centers do we have good exposures of urban features.

Finally, our perspective on all of these ancient civilizations is overwhelmingly an elite one. Temples, palaces, rich tombs, art, and inscriptions have captured most archaeological attention. In part, this is because early archaeologists were often humanists rather than scientists, and they failed to recognize the importance of reconstructing as many institutional aspects of ancient societies as possible. But this situation also reflects our continuing fascination with the unique, Great Tradition elements of Old World civilizations. Studies of elite art continue to outnumber studies of population changes or settlement systems. Since the 1960s this situation has begun to change, but our knowledge of the beginnings of Old World civilizations is still heavily biased by the emphasis on Great Tradition research that is now more than a century old. Until other components of these great cultural systems are better understood, we should be modest about the reliability of our interpretations.

POINTS TO REMEMBER

- Civilizations—states with distinctive Great Traditions—evolved independently in several parts of the Old World: Mesopotamia, Egypt, the Indus Valley, and China.

- The earliest civilization, distinctive for its urban development, emerged in Mesopotamia.

- Old World civilizations were all characterized by effective tool and transport technology and writing.

- All Old World civilizations shared fundamental evolutionary processes that can be contrasted and compared; these include political centralization, segregation, stratification, economic specialization, and emergence of Great Tradition elements. These are reflections of general evolution.

- Each Old World civilization had its own unique character and evolutionary history, reflecting specific evolution.

FOR FURTHER READING*

For Mesopotamia, see Adams's *The Evolution of Urban Society* and *Heartland of Cities*, Redman's *The Rise of Civilization*, and Roaf's *Cultural Atlas of Mesopotamia and the Ancient Near East*. For Egypt, see Hobson's *The World of the Pharaohs*; Hoffman's *Egypt before the Pharaohs*, and Malek's *In the Shadow of the Pyramids*. For Harappan civilization, see Allchin and Allchin's *The Rise of Civilization in India and Pakistan* and Possehl's "Revolution in the Urban Revolution: The Emergence of Indus Urbanization." For China see Reischauer and Fairbanks's *East Asia*, Blunden and Elvin's *Cultural Atlas of China*, and Chang's *Shang Civilization* and *The Archaeology of Ancient China*.

*Full citations appear in the bibliography.

CHAPTER FOURTEEN

THE RISE OF CIVILIZATION
IN THE NEW WORLD

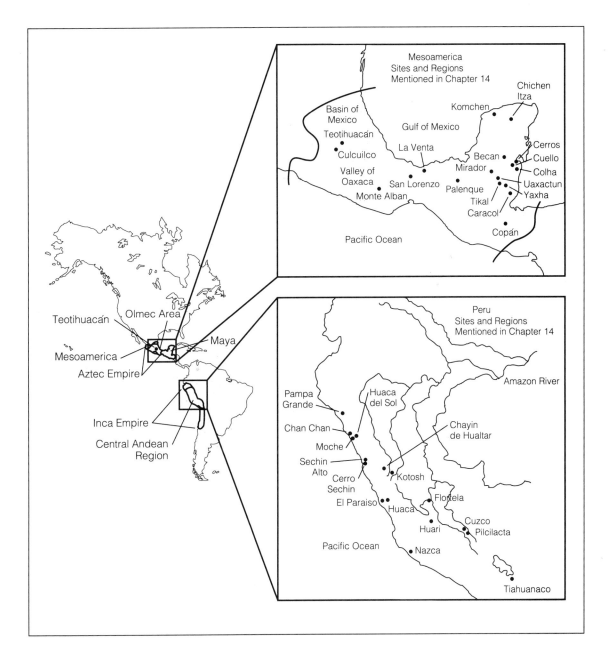

This chapter reviews the evolutionary careers of early Mesoamerican and Central Andean civilizations, looking at the same set of basic processes as did Chapter 13. The institutional similarity of New World civilizations to their Old World counterparts will be apparent, but specific evolutionary factors resulted in differences between New World civilizations and those of the Old World, and among each other. Many topics related to New World cultures have been covered already, and we will refer to these earlier discussions.

NEW WORLD CIVILIZATION: GENERAL EVOLUTION

Europeans from Bernal Diaz to Charles Darwin expressed astonishment at the variety of New World cultures: simple egalitarian foraging groups (such as those of Tierra del Fuego); tribal agriculturalists; chiefdoms of many kinds; and, in Mesoamerica and the Central Andes, impressive civilizations. Independent evolutionary processes had produced a range of societies and cultures very similar to the range found in the Old World. The first Spanish conquistadores in Mexico in the early 16th century recognized these similarities and intuitively understood the basic structure of Aztec society, because institutions and cultural attainments were comprehensible in terms of European culture (Cortés 1986; Diaz 1963). Kings and nobles dominated huge territories conquered through military expansion. Military elites competed for honors and titles and enjoyed the income from estates farmed by serfs. A class of commoners worked the land, paid taxes, provided labor for state projects, and served as conscripts for the army. Tribute, taxes, and labor poured into huge urban capitals resplendent with palaces and temples. The temples, maintained by a professional priesthood, were the foci of public religious ceremonies. Thousands of people thronged into city marketplaces taxed by the king and presided over by judges who settled disputes. All of the characteristics of what we call the state as a political form were present.

The other element defining civilization—an impressive Great Tradition—was also well established. Public art expressed political and religious themes and values (Broda, Carrasco, and Matos 1987). Public and private rituals reaffirmed the place of humans in the universe and their social relationships. Writing recorded elite history and religious information as well as lists of tribute. Mathematical and calendrical systems tracked the cycles of the cosmos.

But the Spanish were disconcerted by the combination of the familiar and the strange. It seemed natural that kings and aristocracies should dominate society, compete for power, and be supported by peasants. That politics and religion should go hand in hand made sense, and though Aztec religious practices such as human sacrifice (Fig. 14.1) seemed particularly abhorrent (Boone 1984), the Aztec religion could be placed within the

FIGURE 14.1 Human sacrifice was part of the Mesoamerican Great Tradition. This depiction of Aztec heart sacrifice is from a book made shortly after the Spanish Conquest.

16th-century European cognitive framework as paganism and devil worship—spiritual practices well known to and successfully combatted by the Spanish proselytizing clergy. Tribute and market exchange were familiar, but the Spanish found it difficult to understand how this complex economic system could lack some of the familiar standardized measures (for example, of weight) and all-purpose metal coinage (though the Aztecs had measures and forms of money of their own). And how could a society so sophisticated in its basic institutions lack large domestic animals, effective metal tools, wheeled vehicles, sailing vessels, and a host of other technological essentials of European life?

This combination of familiar and foreign elements continues to fascinate, primarily because of its evolutionary implications. Research over the last 150 years has confirmed the accuracy of the first impressions of the Spanish: that in general organizational terms the great New World civilizations were very similar to those of the Old World. That the Great Tradition elements were so distinctive points to the independence of the evolutionary processes in each part of the world. For at least 15,000 years, since the time when all the earth's peoples were foragers, cultures of the New World and Old World had evolved independently of one another, but they wound up looking much alike in certain fundamental ways.

There were also important differences. Perhaps most significant was the technological simplicity of New World societies (see Chapter 8). We do not know the reason for this, though it was certainly not due to a deficiency of ingenuity or intelligence. Some kinds of technology, such as irrigation works, were certainly refined and utilized on a larger scale in later New World societies than they had been earlier. Some minor innovations such as molds for producing batches of uniform pottery vessels did appear. Obsidian cutting tools were the sharpest the world has even known. Innovative techniques were used to produce items in gold, silver, copper, and bronze in the Andes. But there were no major technological innovations of the kind that had rapidly transformed many Old World societies, for example, the development of a cheap, tough metal like iron. It is fair to say that the Aztecs in 1519 had the same basic technological system as their predecessors in the Basin of Mexico 1,500 years earlier. But in that time enormous changes occurred in social and political institutions. Consider the evolutionary implication: The evolution of social and political structure is not *necessarily* linked to associated changes in technology. This contrasts strongly with the linkage between complex sociopolitical organization and technological innovation apparent to us today from the processes ongoing in the Western cultural tradition for at least the last 500 years.

Ancient New World societies were low-energy societies. Technology was simple, and effective domestic animals largely absent. Primary reliance on human muscles powered by food energy in the New World placed serious constraints on the course of development of food production, transportation, trade, specialization, and urbanization. Writing systems were present in Mesoamerica but absent in the Central Andes of South America. Other devices, such as the quipus used by the Incas, recorded complex forms of information but cannot be read today. Calendars existed in the Andes; however, dates were not recorded in the form of inscriptions. That Andean peoples had such an impressive cultural tradition despite the lack of these things shows how varied Great Tradition elements can be. Unfortunately, their absence does make cultural reconstruction more difficult.

ARCHAEOLOGICAL APPROACHES

Part of the distinctiveness of the New World archaeological record results from a particular tradition of research. We saw in Chapter 2 that in the Americas archaeology and anthropology had a close relationship, much closer than in Europe. Especially after World War II, American archaeologists increasingly adopted overtly scientific, behavioral perspectives and designed research to reconstruct the social and cultural institutions of ancient cultures. The enormously powerful tool of settlement survey was one such innovation (Sanders, Parsons, and Santley 1979; Willey 1953). As we will see, information on settlement, population, and use of the landscape is often very complete, providing unusually detailed perspectives on the evolutionary processes that gave rise to New World civilizations. Another difference is that the great New World civilizations were not nearly so remote in time as those of the Old World — in fact, European eyewitness accounts are available for their final stages — and there is considerable continuity with the ethnographic present. Finally, New World civilizations evolved in spatially more constricted regions, making adequate archaeological coverage easier. Information about the rise of New World civilization is accordingly very rich, especially for Mesoamerica.

MESOAMERICA

The region called Mesoamerica includes much of the area covered by modern Mexico, Guatemala, Belize, Honduras, and El Salvador. At the time of contact (particularly the early 16th century), this region was densely settled by agricultural populations ruled by native elites. There was a great deal of ethnic diversity (we know of approximately 260 Mesoamerican languages) and no overall political unification, though the Aztecs drew trade and tribute from much of the northern and central areas. Crosscutting this diversity was a Great Tradition with various forms of writing, mathematical systems and calendars, a set of religious concepts, rituals, and deities, a ball game played both for sport and ritual purposes, and shared architectural and artistic conventions.

The northern boundary of Mesoamerica lies just north of Mexico City, beyond it conditions were too dry to support dense agricultural populations using native technology and crops. The southern boundary of Mesoamerica runs through the mountainous zone spanning Honduras and El Salvador, marking a continental linguistic boundary. Most languages to the south were closely related to those of South America, and many of the Great Tradition elements of Mesoamerican civilization failed to penetrate further south, for poorly understood reasons.

Environmental Setting

Mesoamerica lies entirely in the tropics, but environmental variation is as much determined by altitude as by latitude. Most of it is dominated by rugged mountain systems (highest peaks over 5,900 m), and some of these systems are very young, with frequent earthquakes and active volcanoes, particularly in southern Mexico and Guatemala. Volcanoes produce obsidian (an important material in the basic culture technology) and construction stone (e.g., basalt), and volcanic debris eventually weathers into unusually fertile soil.

Altitude strongly influences climate and vegetation. Lowland zones along the Pacific and Gulf coasts are hot, with vegetation varying from scrub forest to dense tropical forest, depending on the rainfall. At elevations of 1–2,000 m are temperate mountain valleys and basins. With sufficient rainfall they support a luxurious vegetation of grasses, deciduous trees, evergreen oaks, and pine. Some are arid and have xerophytic vegetation. Between 2,000 and 2,400 m are a few high cool valleys. Pre-Columbian agriculturalists did not plant crops above about 2,400 m because the frost-free growing season was too short. High mountain vegetation was alpine or cloud forest type, with permanent snowfields at the highest elevations.

Mesoamerica's pronounced annual weather pattern of summer wet seasons and winter dry seasons varies regionally, certain zones receiving rain in each month of the year. Total rainfall, which ranges between 500 and 4,000 mm annually in different parts of Mesoamerica, can be locally quite unpredictable, especially in arid or semiarid regions.

Large rivers drain into the Gulf of Mexico and the Pacific, but none is remotely comparable to the Tigris-Euphrates, the Nile, the Indus, or the Yellow River. Mesoamerican civilizations for the most part were not riverine-oriented, unlike their Old World counterparts. Classic Maya civilization, in fact, flourished in the Yucatán Peninsula, where there was little surface drainage.

The striking environmental diversity of Mesoamerica means that a short journey leads through remarkably different environments. This pattern, plus the compartmentalization produced by the often rugged topography, presented a variety of adaptive problems and opportunities for separate populations and fostered the ethnic diversity reflected in the large number of Mesoamerican languages. More so than in the Old World, the rise of Mesoamerican civilizations is a story of distinctive regional evolutionary sequences. In this section we will examine two of these in detail: Teotihuacán in the Basin of Mexico and the Classic Maya. Other impressive regional variants of Mesoamerican civilization appeared on the Gulf Coast, the Valley of Oaxaca, and the highlands of Guatemala.

The Emergence of Mesoamerican Civilization

Chronology Archaeologists long ago developed a general chronological scheme for Mesoamerica as a whole and still conventionally refer to the time periods listed in Table 14.1.

Table 14.1   Chronology of Mesoamerican Civilization

Postclassic	A.D. 900–1519
Classic	A.D. 300–900
Preclassic	2500 B.C.–A.D. 300
Archaic	7200–2500 B.C.
PaleoIndian	Before 7200 B.C.

FIGURE 14.2 Although archaeologists and botanists are still seeking the wild ancestor of maize, we know how the plant was transformed during the domestication process. On the left is a very primitive form of maize from about 5000 B.C. in the Tehuacán Valley. By A.D. 1500, maize had been transformed into the form shown on the right (all cobs are actual size). Maize was the most important single plant food in Mesoamerica, and was grown widely in the Andes as well.

Here we will mainly be concerned with the Preclassic and Classic periods. Regional variants of these schemes will be introduced where appropriate.

Origins of Agriculture Early hunting-gathering societies were in Mesoamerica by at least 12,000 B.C., and there is circumstantial evidence for even earlier human occupation of this region. This was the end of the Pleistocene, with changes in climate and vegetation, accompanied by a wave of faunal extinctions. Thereafter, wild plant and animal resources were notably less diverse than those of Old World civilization habitats; large herd animals were particularly scarce, so Mesoamerican foragers depended more on a wide range of wild plants and small game (Flannery 1968b).

Early experiments in plant domestication probably took place in many regions, but our best evidence comes from dry highland valleys where preservation of plant and animal remains is good (Byers 1967). By about 7000 B.C. the bottle gourd had been domesticated, primarily for use as a container. Maize, the most important staple crop of Mesoamerica, already was modified from the wild form (probably a plant called teocintle) by 5000 B.C. (Fig. 14.2). During the next 3,000 years other plants were domesticated and moved into new areas, with the result that complexes of energetically and nutritionally effective plants (along with a few animals such as the dog and turkey) became widely available. Between 2000 and 1000 B.C. sedentary communities were established; they were based in part on agriculture, and wild resources remained important. After about 800 B.C. a spurt in population growth occurred and agricultural settlements spread; these phenomena were possibly the result of new maize hybrids more productive than earlier forms. Also at this time were some of the first indications of large-scale irrigation.

Mesoamerica and the Near East differed strikingly in the rate of the evolution of food production. Settled agricultural communities were established in the Near East 2,000 years after the first signs of domestication. The same process in Mesoamerica required 5–6,000 years, partly because of the lack of domesticable animals, and partly because wild maize required far more genetic manipulation than wild wheat to make it a productive domestic staple. One effect of this extended process is that Mesoamerican civilization emerged later than that of Mesopotamia.

The Preclassic: Emergence of Hierarchical Societies

In the first half of the Preclassic period, sedentary food-producing populations spread, and after about 1200 B.C. hierarchical societies (with ranked sociopolitical organization) appeared in several parts of Mesoamerica.

The Preclassic Olmec   Between 1200 and 400 B.C. new forms of settlement emerged in the humid tropical forests of the Mexican Gulf Coast (Sharer and Grove 1989a, 1989b). At centers such as La Venta and San Lorenzo large ceremonial precincts were constructed using mass labor. Some buildings, such as the 33-m-high pyramid at La Venta, are as large as later, Classic architecture. Associated with these constructions were monumental sculptures (some pieces weigh as much as 50 tons): altars, stelae, and huge boulders sculpted into depictions of human heads (Fig. 14.3). Distinctive carved stylistic motifs also appeared on portable objects such as pottery and carved jades, and the whole artistic repertoire was labeled "Olmec," a term now used for the culture as a whole.

More is known about Olmec art than other aspects of their culture. Although highly distinctive, Olmec sculpture includes many motifs, symbols, and themes found in later Classic art: status symbols such as ear plugs, ball-game costumes, depictions of animals such as serpents and jaguars, hybrid human/animal figures, and—possibly—early glyphs or calendrical symbols. The whole tradition of large, public, stone monuments (especially stelae and altars) is also characteristic of certain Classic societies.

Archaeologists once thought that the largest Olmec sites were vacant ceremonial centers where a few priests lived and conducted communal rituals bringing together a larger population living in outlying agricultural communities. In fact, Olmec centers did have resident populations (though even the largest had probably less than 1,000) and a three-tiered settle-

FIGURE 14.3 An Olmec basalt sculpture from San Lorenzo Tenochtitlan. This huge sculpture is 2.58 m high and is one of the most characteristic products of Olmec art. Made to be displayed in a public space, such monuments are thought to be portraits of rulers.

ment system, with large centers such as La Venta functioning as capitals for smaller communities (located along rivers), the largest of which had earthen temple mounds in addition to houses, while the smallest lacked public buildings (Rust and Sharer 1988). Art and luxury objects are mainly found in capitals and in outlying sites with temple mounds.

Archaeologists agree that Olmec society was nonegalitarian. Some believe the Olmec represent a pristine Mesoamerican civilization, while others think that, while they had a distinctive Great Tradition, the Olmec lacked stratification and the institutions of the state. According to this book's perspective, Olmec polities represent complex chiefdoms, of which there were probably several at any given time, each supported by populations in the thousands. Although they shared a common culture, these chiefdoms were politically independent and possibly even at war with one another. According to this model, centers such as La Venta were chief's capitals with political as well as religious functions. The great stone heads found in them may be portraits of rulers.

Olmec (or Olmec-style) objects, including monumental sculpture, are found all over Mesoamerica, from the highlands of central Mexico to Honduras and El Salvador (e.g., Grove 1987). Jade, obsidian, and mirrors made of iron minerals traveled from the highlands to the Gulf Coast. Other Preclassic hierarchical societies evolved in several parts of Mesoamerica in addition to the Gulf Coast during the Preclassic. In the Valley of Oaxaca they emerged slightly later than in the Olmec zone, and by 400–500 B.C. rank societies occurred over much of Mesoamerica, including the central highlands of Mexico, the highlands and Pacific coast of Guatemala, and the Maya lowlands. Rapid population growth is associated with these changes, particularly in the Maya lowlands. Various elements of Classic Mesoamerican civilization become evident (though we cannot be sure where they originated), including the use of writing and mathematics, elite status symbols, calendars, deities, and many artistic and architectural conventions.

The Olmec were only one regional culture undergoing rapid change as a result of local evolutionary processes (Flannery 1968b). Emergent chiefs in different parts of Mesoamerica interacted with each other, exchanging both objects and information. Various elements of the Mesoamerican Great Tradition were developed in a variety of places and eventually widely adopted, and then adapted to specific regions and cultures.

Teotihuacán: Mesoamerica's First Urban State

Two things hinder understanding the origins of urban civilization in much of the Old World: a general lack of good regional settlement system data through time and inadequate knowledge of specific urban patterns. Fortunately we have both kinds of data for Teotihuacán, the greatest early urban state in Mesoamerica (Millon 1981; Millon, Drewitt, and Cowgill 1973). Its regional setting, the Basin of Mexico, has been intensively surveyed by William Sanders and his colleagues (Sanders 1981; Sanders, Parsons, and Santley 1979). The city, which is still largely intact, its well-preserved remains visible on the surface, has been extensively studied by Rene Millon and his colleagues. These research efforts have permitted a detailed reconstruction of the adaptation of a population to its natural and social environments. Spanning the late Preclassic and the Classic periods, the growth of Teotihuacán demonstrates cultural adaptation to a distinctive natural and social environment.

Setting   The Teotihuacán Valley is an arm of a larger mountain valley system, the Basin of Mexico (7,000 km²), with a set of shallow lakes in its center (elevation ca. 2,240 m). Rainfall is heaviest (1,000 mm) in the southern part of the valley and dwindles to 400–500 mm in the northeast. Because of the high altitude, growing seasons are short and frosts between October and March threaten crops, especially along the lakeshore and at higher elevations in the surrounding mountains. The Teotihuacán Valley is a northeastern offshoot of the main basin. It is about 35 km long and has an area of about 500 km². Although rainfall there is low and erratic, springs provide a permanent source of water.

As a whole, the Basin of Mexico offered farmers advantages and disadvantages. Fertile soils, easy transportation and aquatic resources on the lakes, and an abundance of timber, construction stone, and obsidian and flint for tools, were the plusses, countered by risks such as the short grow-ing season with its possibility of frosts, low and unpredictable rainfall, and tendency toward soil erosion. Greater in some parts of the valley than others, the risks affected patterns of settlement and land use.

Process: Settlement, Urbanization, and Agricultural Intensification in the Basin of Mexico

Foragers lived in the Basin of Mexico by at least 12,000 B.C. (probably much earlier), but the first agricultural settlements date later than 1600 B.C.

1500–1150 B.C. Only a few sites ($n = 19$) are known from the period of 1500–1150 B.C., and all are located in the southern and western parts of the basin, most within reasonable distance of the lakeshore. Most were very small rural hamlets, perhaps not even permanently occupied. The largest had several hundred people. There is no sign of community cluster-ing indicating supracommunity political systems, nor is there clear evidence of public architecture. Settlements were situated in the most attractive zones of the valley both for early agriculture and for exploiting the wild plants and animals of the freshwater lakes. Domesticated plants, including maize, were in use, although they were probably less important to the diet than wild foods in this mixed economy. The total population of the basin at this time was probably only 4–5,000 people.

1150–650 B.C. Many more sites ($n = 75$) are known from the period of 1150–650 B.C. (Fig. 14.4), and more large villages appeared. Most of the population still clustered in the southwestern part of the valley, but small pioneer settlements pushed further north along both shores of the lake, and the first small hamlets appeared in the Teotihuacán Valley. Distances between communities were still substantial, and no clustering is obvious, nor is there public architecture. There seems to have been an overall in-crease in population (estimated at 20,000 by 650 B.C.), probably related to a much heavier reliance on food production. Crops were probably grown along the lakeshore or streambeds where moisture was high, and also on clearings on the hillsides where there was sufficient rainfall. In a few places there are signs of floodwater irrigation (runoff caught in small streams after rains and channeled into fields by small canals).

650–300 B.C. 650–300 B.C. was a period of great change in the Basin of Mexico. Population increased rapidly, to about 80,000 people, and more settlements filled in zones already occupied, particularly along the eastern side of the lake and the Teotihuacán Valley (Fig. 14.5). Excavations in a large village on the western side of the lake revealed substantial houses, the presence of maize and beans (along with other probable domesticates) and many food storage facilities. Despite the continued use of some wild foods, farming was obviously well established.

474

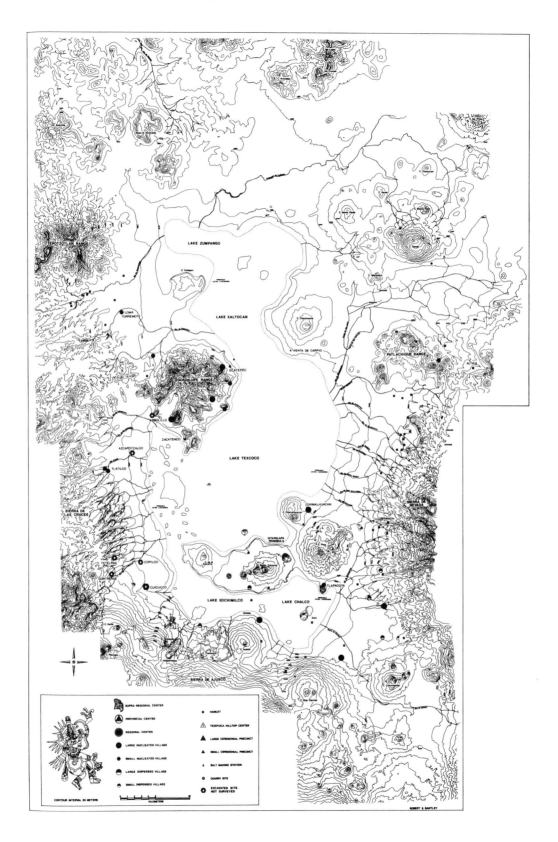

LAKE ZUMPANGO

LAKE XALTOCAN

LAKE TEXCOCO

LAKE XOCHIMILCO   LAKE CHALCO

TEPOTZOTLAN RANGE

GUADALUPE RANGE

PATLACHIQUE RANGE

SIERRA DE LAS CRUCES

SIERRA DE AJUSCO

ECATEPEC

LOMA TORREMOTE

EL TEBOLILLO

ZACATENCO

AZCAPOTZALCO

TLATILCO

TETELPAN

COPILCO

CONTRERAS

CUICUILCO

CHIMALHUACAN

IXTAPALAPA PENINSULA

TLAPACOYA

C. Tultepec

C. Chiconautla

VENTA DE CARPIO

CONTOUR INTERVAL 50 METERS

KILOMETERS

SUPRA-REGIONAL CENTER

PROVINCIAL CENTER

REGIONAL CENTER

LARGE NUCLEATED VILLAGE

SMALL NUCLEATED VILLAGE

LARGE DISPERSED VILLAGE

SMALL DISPERSED VILLAGE

HAMLET

TEZOYUCA HILLTOP CENTER

LARGE CEREMONIAL PRECINCT

SMALL CEREMONIAL PRECINCT

SALT MAKING STATION

QUARRY SITE

EXCAVATED SITE, NOT SURVEYED

ROBERT S. SANTLEY

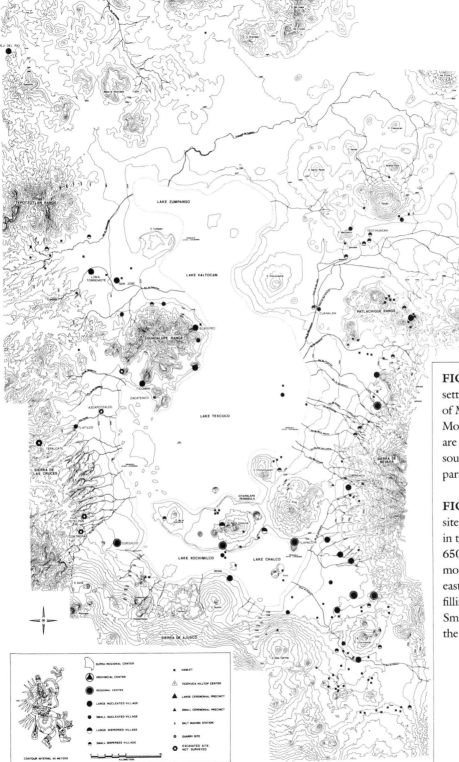

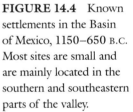

FIGURE 14.4 Known settlements in the Basin of Mexico, 1150–650 B.C. Most sites are small and are mainly located in the southern and southeastern parts of the valley.

FIGURE 14.5 (opposite) Known settlements in the Basin of Mexico, 650–300 B.C. There are more large sites and the eastern part of the valley is filling in with population. Small villages appear in the Teotihuacán Valley.

Where settlements were widely spaced, extensive forms of agriculture were still feasible, but there are also traces of early irrigation. New kinds of settlements appeared, most notably large regional centers in the southern part of the basin. The largest have pyramid mounds (presumably temple platforms) and one of them, Cuicuilco, may have had a population of 5–10,000. There is some tendency for sites to form regional clusters, and centers such as Cuicuilco must have served as an administrative central place, dominating many smaller villages and hamlets. Interestingly, no such center is yet found in the Teotihuacán Valley.

300–100 B.C.   300–100 B.C. is one of the most dynamic periods in the basin's whole history (Fig. 14.6). The overall population doubles, reaching about 150,000. Changes in settlement patterns reflect adjustments to both the natural and social environments. The 200 known sites from this period show that new settlements are particularly common along the eastern side of the lake and in the Teotihuacán Valley. Some zones along the western edge of the basin decline in population. There are twice as many large regional centers (12) as before, and two of these — Cuicuilco and Teotihuacán — are much larger than the others, and presumably dominate complex hierarchies of smaller communities, though much of the growth of the large centers resulted from the depopulation of smaller rural settlements.

Cuicuilco covered an area of about 400 ha, with perhaps 20,000 people. At Cuicuilco's center was a massive circular pyramid–temple 80 m across and 20 m high.

Teotihuacán covered 600–800 ha, with between 20,000 and 40,000 people; only 10 percent of the Teotihuacán Valley population lived outside this center. Unfortunately its public architecture from this period is obscured by later construction. Concentration of population into these two emergent cities almost certainly reflects political antagonism and warfare, a process that we saw earlier at Uruk and other centers in Mesopotamia, and also among polities in Predynastic Egypt.

Extensive systems of agriculture were used where population remained light, but various forms of sophisticated irrigation must have supported Teotihuacán, situated as it is in an area of low rainfall and high agricultural risk. Terracing to hold moisture and retard erosion is also known from some sites in this period.

Around 100 B.C. a series of volcanic lava flows covered the countryside around Cuicuilco, drastically reducing its agricultural productivity. Cuicuilco ceased to be a serious political rival of Teotihuacán and dwindled to the status of a small regional center (a later flow around 200 A.D. entirely destroyed the community).

100 B.C.–A.D. 100   The demise of Cuicuilco left Teotihuacán free to dominate the whole Basin of Mexico and ushered in the most revolutionary changes in the whole archaeological sequence (Fig. 14.7). Teotihuacán expanded rapidly to an area of about 20 km², with a population of around 60,000 people (some of them, possibly, Cuicuilco refugees). This extraor-

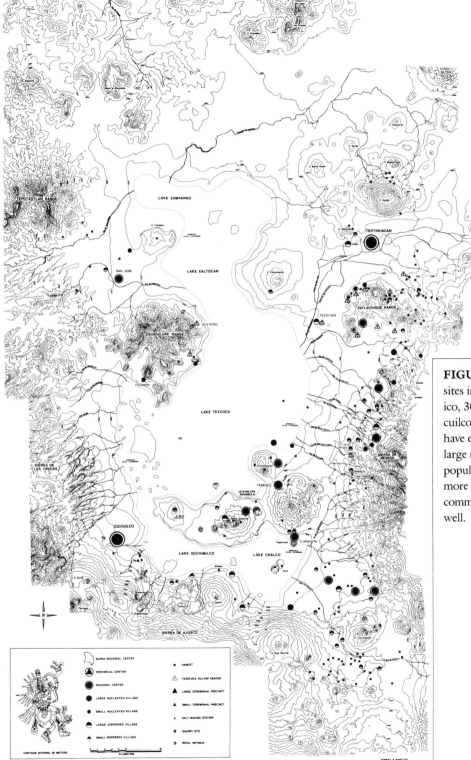

FIGURE 14.6 Known sites in the Basin of Mexico, 300–100 B.C. Cuicuilco and Teotihuacán have emerged as two rival large regional centers, and population is becoming more nucleated into larger communities elsewhere as well.

dinary urban growth drew from the other large settlements in the basin, resulting in the disappearance of most other sizable communities. The southern section of the valley, where the oldest, densest populations were located, was virtually abandoned. Only about 15,000 people remained anywhere in the basin outside the city. Much of this resettlement must have been carried out as a political policy of the Teotihuacán elite, and reflects the subordination of the entire basin to Teotihuacán. That such reorganization was stressful and possibly coerced is suggested by the stabilization, or even decline, of the overall population of the basin as a whole after a millenium of uninterrupted growth. Although this process may have begun under conditions of competition, it was finished as a purely internal political effort.

To feed Teotihuacán's population would have required a food supply produced reasonably close to the city. Because of the dry climate, crops were only secure if they were irrigated, accomplished by intensification (here, channeling water from the permanent springs), possibly managed by the Teotihuacán elite.

Other changes affected the city itself (see Chapter 8). The basic grid of streets was established, including the main north-south ceremonial axis, the Street of the Dead. Apartment compounds proliferated, and the city's people built the pyramids of the Moon and Sun. The latter has a mass of about 1,000,000 m³ and is the second largest structure in the New World. Many other Mesoamerican temples grew by accretion in distinct building phases over many years, but the Pyramid of the Sun was built in a sustained effort lasting only a generation or so.

Summary Settlement surveys indicate six interrelated processes in the Basin of Mexico and the Teotihuacán Valley:

1. Early colonists settled in the areas with least risk for crops and where wild resources were most abundant. Only gradually were riskier, more marginal zones colonized.

2. As settlements multiplied and spread, population tended to concentrate in the largest settlements.

3. Population growth characterized most of the sequence; as more productive areas became fully settled, the more marginal regions were colonized as well. Rates of population growth were high, at times doubling every 200 years, which is unusually high for a preindustrial population.

4. As population increased, hierarchies of related settlements emerged, land use became more intensive, and competition developed between two large political systems.

5. Urban growth fed on, and severely reduced, the rural population of the basin.

6. Expansion of large-scale irrigation facilities on the high quality land near Teotihuacán overcame the problem of transport costs in a low-energy society, allowing the buildup of a dense urban population.

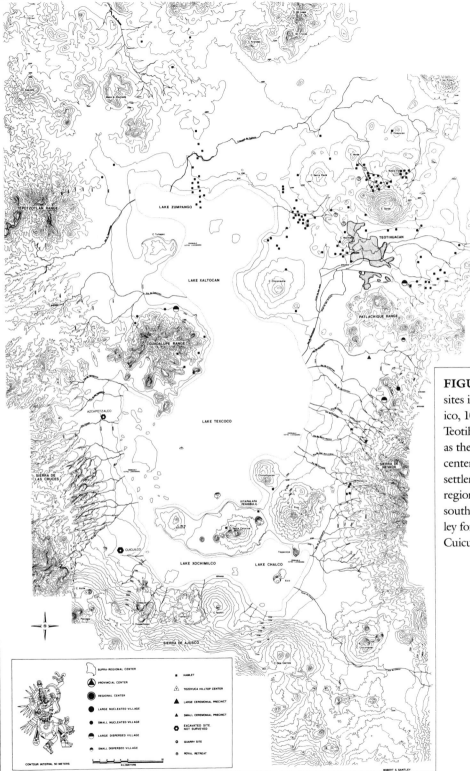

FIGURE 14.7 Known sites in the Basin of Mexico, 100 B.C.–A.D. 100. Teotihuacán has emerged as the dominant urban center, pulling in much settlement from outlying regions, including the southern parts of the valley formerly dominated by Cuicuilco.

Process: Political Centralization and Stratification at Teotihuacán

Art and Writing   Inhabitants of Teotihuacán may have had some sort of writing system, but it was apparently so limited in use that we lack titles, dynastic geneaologies, or references to elite events that would help us understand political structure. Teotihuacán had an elaborate tradition of both residential and public mural art (unlike the Maya and the Olmec, who emphasized monumental sculpture). Mural paintings are more perishable than stone carving, so our corpus of Teotihuacán art is limited. More important, the themes and symbols of the artistic tradition are not easily interpreted. Many of them seem to be primarily religious in content, but the figures wear earrings, fancy headdresses, and elaborate costumes that elsewhere in Mesoamerica are associated with elite status. Depictions of animals include jaguars or pumas, also generally associated with Meso-american royalty or elites. Warfare is a minor but conspicuous element in Teotihuacán art, and it is difficult to decode Teotihuacán iconography into overt political messages.

Architecture   Architecture provides much more evidence, particularly of the organization necessary to establish the plan of the Classic city and its civic core and to complete its construction (Millon 1981; Millon, Drewitt, and Cowgill 1973). The Pyramid of the Sun was built on a huge scale and at impressive speed, indicating tremendous centralization of political power and authority. Just as impressive was the centralization of population at Teotihuacán, which drastically disrupted older traditions of settlement.

Variation among the city's houses reflects political centralization and stratification. No single building can be identified as a royal palace or administrative center, but recent excavations suggest that a huge complex of buildings straddling the Street of the Dead may have served both purposes. Large and elaborate palaces form an upper stratum of residences, most located near the center of the city. Dwellings were apartment compounds built around patios, with blank walls facing the gridded streets. They could have held up to 100 people, presumably in extended family households. These compounds vary greatly in quality of construction, from mansions near the civic-ceremonial district to slums on the edge of the city. Clearly there were great differences in access to labor consistent with social stratification.

Many burials have been recovered from beneath the city's room floors and patios of apartment complexes. Most are quite simple, though even in the poorest compounds elaborate burials are occasionally found, probably representing family heads. No royal burials have been found comparable to those from Sumer, Egypt, or China, but there are hints that they exist. Recent excavations in and around the pyramid inside the Ciudadela enclosure have revealed approximately 200 apparent sacrificial victims (Cabrera,

Sugiyama, and Cowgill 1991). Adult males, many with weapons and other indicators of warrior status, were buried, hands tied behind backs, in shallow trenches surrounding and underlying the pyramid. A large cavity in the interior of the building, unfortunately disturbed, may be the remains of a royal tomb.

Some archaeologists believe that Teotihuacán's concentrated population and huge labor force for construction projects reflects religious devotion more than coercive, elite political policy. In traditional societies the values of the belief system are more tightly integrated into an individual's social and economic roles, and Teotihuacán was itself a potent sacred landscape of hills (the pyramids) and sacred caves (such as that beneath the Pyramid of the Sun), crosscut by the flowing waters of the river fed by the springs, an earthly representation of the rippling undulation of the Feathered Serpent god, Quétzalcóatl. Construction of Teotihuacán's extensive public architecture may have been an act of religious devotion for the workers, but we know of no similar ethnographic or historical situation that was not strongly initiated and controlled by powerful elites for economic and political purposes as well.

Religious authority appears to have been highly centralized. The city's temples were its most impressive buildings, but residencelike rooms were often associated with them, sometimes with evidence of craft specialization, particularly obsidian processing. Probably a number of Teotihuacán temples served political and economic functions as well, operating as corporations with resident priests supported by the temple's own resources. The city was a major Mesoamerican pilgrimage center, immensely impressing visitors with its splendor as they made their way along the Street of the Dead toward the great pyramids towering against the mountain called Mother of Waters.

Given the Mesoamerican belief in the vital power of the landscape itself (discussed at length in Chapter 12), it would not be surprising if Teotihuacán won significant ideological dominance over Cuicuilco after the disasters in the southern basin. Not only were people moved, but innovations in agricultural strategy were devised to support them. Although there is no direct proof, the Teotihuacán elite may have managed the surrounding irrigation systems. The apparent struggle between Cuicuilco and Teotihuacán at the end of the Preclassic and the increasingly obvious militarism apparent in Teotihuacán art and burials toward its end suggest that warfare stimulated political centralization in important ways.

Teotihuacán as a Political Capital Teotihuacán quickly became the basin's political capital after the collapse of Cuicuilco. As the city matured between A.D. 100 and 700, the settlement system normalized somewhat; outlying settlements were reestablished and the population of the basin grew again, to a maximum of about 250,000 people. Teotihuacán remained the dominant center, however, in political, economic, and cultural terms. Millon, who directed the project to map the city, believes that by

A.D. 500–600 Teotihuacán also dominated a region of about 25,000 km² in the surrounding highlands of central Mexico, with a population between 300,000 and 500,000 people.

Although Teotihuacán probably exercised no direct political control over more distant regions, the city had wide influence. Teotihuacanos are depicted in the art of contemporaneous Classic states: Monte Alban in the Valley of Oaxaca and Tikal in the Maya lowlands. Tikal's architecture shows Teotihuacán influence, and Teotihuacán symbols form elements of Maya elite regalia. Teotihuacanos settled in distant centers such as Kaminaljuyu in the Guatemala highlands. At Teotihuacán were enclaves of foreigners, most obviously from Oaxaca but perhaps also from the Maya lowlands and elsewhere. The significance of these contacts is obscure, but they demonstrate Teotihuacán's preeminence as a political and cultural center for all of Mesoamerica.

Process: Emergence of the Teotihuacán Great Tradition

Teotihuacán's signature Great Tradition elements emerged and developed rapidly after 100 B.C. The architecture was imitated in the Maya highlands and lowlands. Art — sculpture and painting — portrays Mesoamerican spiritual entities such as the Mesoamerican Water Goddess, the Feathered Serpent, and many others. Gods or priests garbed in typical Mesoamerican style, jaguars or pumas, and a host of other widely shared themes and images are common. But several distinctive elements of the Mesoamerican cultural tradition — writing, calendars, and ball courts — seem to be lacking at Teotihuacán, while in use elsewhere. This shows how Great Tradition elements vary more than basic sociopolitical institutions in early civilizations.

Process: Economic Specialization and Trade at Teotihuacán

Economic Specialization Although most households at Teotihuacán must have included at least part-time farmers, they also specialized in a wide variety of craft activities. Over 800 of the city's 2,000 apartment compounds evidence specialized economic activity such as obsidian processing, a pattern detectable as early as 100 B.C.–A.D. 100, which became more common as the city matured (A.D. 500–700). The state may have played an active role in both production and distribution.

Trade Teotihuacán objects (particularly obsidian and ceramics) are found over most of Mesoamerica; obsidian was probably distributed through trade. The colony at Kaminaljuyu may have been trying to control Guatemalan obsidian sources. Other forms of exchange, such as gifts between elites, may account for the distribution of other items.

What Happened to Teotihuacán?

As its maturity between A.D. 600 and 700, Teotihuacán was the greatest Classic Mesoamerican civilization, with marked stratification upheld by a well-organized state religion. Evidence suggests bureaucratic management of irrigation resources, elite warrior groups and militarism. As a political system, Teotihuacán surpassed all others in scale and influence in the emergence of a broad Classic Mesoamerican civilization. As a capital, Teotihuacán meets all of the requirements of a well-developed urban center: large population (at least 125,000), high density (6–7,000 per km²), evidence for stratification, internal diversity, and multiplicity of functions, accompanied by a distinctive Great Tradition.

Before archaeological surveys were made in the basin and at Teotihuacán, the city was thought to have been destroyed and abandoned at about A.D. 700–750. In fact, its population shrank to between 30,000 and 40,000 as migrants left for other centers in the basin and elsewhere that were assuming greater political and economic importance. There was burning and destruction in the ceremonial precincts, but Teotihuacán never was abandoned and has never ceased to function as an urbanized center. Perhaps Teotihuacán's decline was precipitated by competition with other centers, but its causes remain ambiguous.

This is an important archaeological lesson. Teotihuacán's fall seemed abrupt and inexplicable as long as there was only little information available. But evidence from the city itself and about the settlement and population history of the Basin of Mexico as a whole showed that this decline was intelligible in the context of the larger political process.

Classic Maya Civilization

The Postclassic Maya states in Yucatán were conquered by the Spanish in the 16th century (see Chapter 15), but traces of Classic Maya civilization remained largely unrecognized until the mid-19th century. Early explorers such as Stephens and Catherwood publicized the abandoned Maya cities overgrown by tropical forest, and by the turn of the century the Classic Maya had been intensely studied. To date, more archaeology has probably been done in the Maya lowlands than in any other region of comparable size in the New World.

Classic Maya culture is reconstructed from a rich set of sources: archaeological remains, Maya inscriptions, accounts by the Spanish describing the Maya in the 16th century (Tozzer 1941), and studies of modern Maya populations. The environment the Maya lived in has been reconstructed, based on present-day environment, estimates of changes over the last thousand years and their effects, and archaeological information about cultigens and farming practices. Since the 1950s many large-scale settlement studies have been carried out, so we have reliable information about how Maya

FIGURE 14.8 The tops of the great temples at Tikal, Guatemala, rise above the tropical forest that has engulfed them since the site was abandoned.

populations adapted to their tropical environment. (Principal sources for this discussion are Adams 1977; Coe, Snow, and Benson 1986; Culbert 1973, 1991; Culbert and Rice 1990; Morley, Brainerd, and Sharer 1983; and Schele and Freidel 1990.)

Environmental Setting Classic Maya civilization developed over about 250,000 km^2 of lowlands in southern Mexico, northern Guatemala, Belize, and parts of Honduras and El Salvador. All of this land is under 1,000 m; its climate is hot, with a pronounced wet season/dry season cycle. Rainfall is abundant, as much as 2,000 mm measured in the central and southern tropical forest zones (Fig. 14.8), grading down to 700 mm in the scrub forest of the northwestern tip of the Yucatán Peninsula. Most of the rainfall sinks into the limestone bedrock. Surface streams, rivers, and lakes are rare, but natural sinkholes occur, called **cenotes**.

cenote Naturally occurring limestone sinkhole, often used as a reservoir by the Maya.

The Emergence of Maya Civilization

Chronology We will use the traditional chronological framework presented in Table 14.2, noting that time periods were originally defined on the basis of features that we now know to have been timed somewhat differently and that varied from area to area. Note how all terms refer to the Classic period, when the major elements of Maya civilization were thought to have appeared (Adams 1977). Many of these elements actually appeared in the Preclassic, but our major concern is the Classic period, particularly the last two centuries, when Maya civilization reached its peak. Postclassic developments are discussed in Chapter 15.

FIGURE 14.9 Reconstruction drawing of early Maya buildings found at Cuello, Belize.

Early Preclassic and the Origins of Agriculture: 2500–1250 B.C.

Although hunter-gatherers may have been thinly scattered over much of the Maya lowlands for many thousands of years, effective food production appeared rather late. Early Maya farmers used and domesticated plants native to their lowland tropical forests, but important staple foods like maize and beans were originally derived from the highlands of Mesoamerica. Effective food production required that early forms of these cultigens be diffused into the lowlands by trade or immigration of people using them, or both.

The age of the first farming villages in the lowlands is debated by archaeologists. Cuello (Belize) is a small hamlet of pottery-using maize farmers; such communities may date back to 1500–1000 B.C. (Hammond 1977). Even if these dates are too early, farming communities like Cuello (Fig. 14.9) were no doubt scattered over much of the lowlands by 800 B.C., but few sites are known since they are difficult to find. They tend to be located in riverine areas with their rich alluvial soils and associated wild resources. Although we call the inhabitants of these communities farmers, they may actually have had very mixed subsistence economies in which wild foods were extremely important. Settlements and associated populations were small and scattered, and probably basically egalitarian in sociopolitical structure.

Table 14.2 Chronology of Maya Civilization

Postclassic	A.D. 900–1520
Classic	A.D. 300–900
Late Preclassic	450 B.C.–A.D. 300
Middle Preclassic	1250–450 B.C.
Early Preclassic	2500–1250 B.C.

The Middle Preclassic: 1250–450 B.C.   Settlements became more numerous and widespread, but are similar to earlier ones. Although public spaces and possible small civic structures are found at sites such as Cuello, egalitarian organization persists. Products originating both within the lowlands (elg., chert for tools from northern Belize) and beyond (e.g., obsidian from highland Guatemala) were traded in.

Emergence of Complexity: The Late Preclassic, 450 B.C.–A.D. 300

Population growth   Population growth was rapid in the Late Preclassic, as was the spatial spread of Maya populations, marked by the highly uniform ceramic types used throughout the region. Traces of Late Preclassic settlements underlie virtually all large Classic centers. The cause of this spurt remains uncertain, but perhaps new, more productive forms of maize and other cultigens became available, increasing food production and permitting a boost in birth rates.

Extensive slash-and-burn cultivation was probably the dominant subsistence system, with more intensive systems around a few centers. Some archaeologists assume more intensive forms of agriculture such as **drained fields** (Pohl 1990) at some centers, but if such forms existed, they were probably small in scale and localized. In any case, the agrarian foundations of Maya civilization were in place.

drained fields   Intensive form of agriculture in which fields are created by draining plots of swampy land.

Political evolution   By far the most striking development in the Late Preclassic was the emergence of hierarchical political systems out of the older, egalitarian societies. Between 450 and 300 B.C., large-scale public architecture appeared, usually in the form of temples, and by the end of the period enormous structures over 30 m high were being constructed.

Such projects required much more labor and organization than egalitarian societies normally muster. Some centers (Cerros [northern Belize], Komchen [Yucatán], Mirador [northern Guatemala]) reached sizes comparable to many later Classic Maya centers. Mirador may in fact be one of the largest Maya centers ever built. Tikal, which later became the greatest of all Classic Maya centers, had several huge civic-ceremonial complexes at this time.

Public structures were often ornamented with plaster sculpture and paint. The motifs on Late Preclassic architecture and on artifacts recovered from caches and burials often prefigure iconographic conventions of the Classic period. The symbols so strongly expressed in Classic Maya religion and rulership have their roots in the Late Preclassic. For example, the mat symbol indicated Maya royal authority just as the throne did for European monarchs. Maya calendrics and writing undoubtedly first appeared in the Late Preclassic, although direct evidence is sparse.

Essentially the expanded households of emerging Maya elites, impressive Late Preclassic centers presumably dominated sizeable territories, including smaller centers with hundreds or even thousands of people. Early

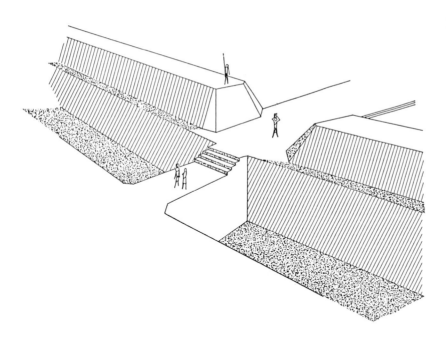

FIGURE 14.10 Becan: reconstruction of a section of the fortifications.

historical texts are lacking and archaeological information on early settlements is difficult to retrieve, so Late Preclassic territorial organization or political structure is obscure. In the lowlands there were probably many political arrangements (just as there were among the Maya of the 16th century), some of which were very complex in degree of centralization.

Were the most complex Late Preclassic polities ranked or stratified? Many archaeologists believe that class-structured societies with extremely powerful kings — states — had emerged at polities such as Mirador. While the most impressive Late Preclassic political structures were probably characterized by complex ranking, one of the problems of interpretation here is the comparatively loose "fit" between the Great Tradition elements and their associated sociopolitical arrangements.

Large-scale warfare was present by the end of the Preclassic, but only recently have we perceived the Maya as warlike. Until the 1960s, the Classic Maya were thought unique among world civilizations in lacking warfare except on a small scale for religious ritual (sacrificial) purposes. Now we know that the "peaceful Maya" had complex patterns of warfare in the Preclassic as well as the Classic period. Evidence includes artistic depictions, burials of mass sacrifices of young captives, and, by the end of the Preclassic, one of the largest defensive systems ever discovered in Mesoamerica was constructed at Becan (Fig. 14.10).

Trade or exchange More goods circulated more widely than before, especially elite and ritual items of jade, shell, and stingray spines. The high quality of many objects, from whole buildings down to small ornaments, indicates skilled artisans who were (at least) part-time economic specialists.

Summary: The Preclassic Maya Until 30 years ago archaeologists saw a sharp boundary between the Preclassic and Classic periods, with the latter beginning when known dated monuments began to be raised, about A.D. 300. This chronological boundary has almost entirely broken down as more and more continuities between the two periods are discovered. Virtually all of the elements defining Classic Maya civilization emerged in some form before A.D. 300, indicating a longer and more gradual evolutionary process.

Calendrics and writing were in use elsewhere in Mesoamerica long before they appear in the Maya lowlands. These Great Tradition elements were imported into the Maya area, reworked by the Maya, and integrated with a set of political forms and institutions which evolved in the lowlands themselves. Whether the Late Preclassic Maya were "civilized" in our specific sense of the word remains debatable, but the distinctive Maya civilizational package was almost mature.

Classic Period Maya

In this section Classic Maya society at its most complex during the Late Classic (A.D. 650–900), is evaluated according to our basic set of evolutionary processes.

Time and Definition The Classic period was originally defined on the basis of Great Tradition elements, particularly the Maya Long Count dating system, which has been correlated with our own (Chapter 9), providing the most accurate historical framework we have for any part of Mesoamerica. Many of the other Maya Great Tradition elements—elaborate art, architecture, and writing—seemed contemporaneous with Long Count dates, so the Classic period (as its name implies) was seen as a cultural peak for the Maya and for Mesoamerican cultures in general.

For many years the Classic Maya were thought to be not only the most innovative and sophisticated of all Mesoamerican civilizations, but also the "Mother Culture" of the Mesoamerican cultural tradition. As we just noted, many innovations ascribed to the Classic Maya appear much earlier than A.D. 300, in the Maya lowlands and elsewhere, so this pattern of diffusion is no longer plausible. Cultural developments in the Maya region are now known to be contemporaneous with the establishment and growth of Teotihuacán and Monte Alban in the highlands of Mexico.

Maya Long Count dates still provide the most detailed and accurate historical record we have for Mesoamerica, however. The earliest known decipherable date on an intact lowland Maya monument is from Tikal, A.D. 292. Thereafter, dated monuments such as stelae and altars proliferated over much of the lowlands, marking the spread of what has come to be known as the **stela cult,** one of the most prominent and unique Maya Great Tradition markers (see Figs. 1.1 and 3.22).

Imagine a darkened map of the Maya lowlands in the third century. In A.D. 292 a light appears at Tikal—the first appearance of a dated monument. In 327 another light blinks on at the nearby center of Uaxactun. Still another appears at Yaxha in 357. Radiating out from the Petén region of northern Guatemala would be an ever-larger constellation of lights from centers of all sizes. During the fifth century the lights would extend sporadically to the limits of the lowlands: In 435 at Copán on the southeastern frontier, then to the far north at Chichen Itza and east at Caracol (Belize) by 485. After 600 the pace quickens and the map fills with lights, until between 700 and 800, the height of Classic civilization, the whole map is lit. Thus the spread of dated monuments defines the Classic period.

Process: Settlement, Urbanization, and Agricultural Intensification

Centers and Urbanization Hundreds of Maya centers are known; some consist of a few elite buildings around a single courtyard, and others have huge architectural complexes extending over several square kilometers. Tikal, the largest Classic center, has a civic-ceremonial core extending over approximately 4 km². Far more representative is the Main Group at Copán, which covers only about 0.15 km². Common features at these centers are temples, palaces, ball courts, causeways, and reservoirs.

Because Maya religious architecture is impressive, and Maya art and inscriptions were commonly interpreted as religious in content, centers were once thought to be uninhabited "vacant ceremonial centers," another way the Maya were unique among human cultures. We now know that the centers served many of the same residential, political, and economic functions as urban places in other societies. Although Maya centers are often called cities, they had smaller, less dense populations, less economic complexity, and a narrower range of functions than major cities in some other civilizations, both in Mesoamerica and elsewhere. Major palace complexes at the cores of sites were probably occupied by royal families and their retainers, but overall densities were light, though significantly higher than in the surrounding rural areas. Sometimes the site cores were surrounded by clusters of other residences; at Copán, the population density of the residential zones of Sepulturas and El Bosque (see Chapters 3 and 15) was 9–10,000 people per km², but only over very small areas. More commonly, site cores are surrounded by lighter settlement. At Tikal the central zone had perhaps 800 people per km², but these densities markedly decreased with distance from the central zone.

Smaller centers are often distributed around larger ones, and the rural population typically resided in small, dispersed clusters of houses scattered across the agricultural landscape. There is often a continuous gradient of settlement density extending from centers themselves to outlying rural

stela cult The widespread use of inscribed monoliths, one of the most prominent and unique Maya Great Tradition markers.

zones, with no sharp boundary between center and countryside. Most Maya centers were not as strongly differentiated from rural settlements as were centers in other ancient civilizations.

Agricultural Intensification   The historically and ethnographically known Maya practice of slash-and-burn agriculture involves cutting down and burning natural vegetation, then using the field thus created for a few seasons before moving to a new one (see Chapter 6). This system is nicely adjusted to tropical ecosystems as long as there is sufficient land to permit the regrowth of the forest and replenishment of soil fertility. Large harvests of maize, beans, and other crops can be produced with low labor input, as long as mature vegetation can be cleared. Slash-and-burn agriculture encourages dispersed settlement patterns.

As population grows and becomes denser, fields must be cultivated longer and fallowed for shorter periods; mature forest does not become reestablished. This process of agricultural intensification usually results in more work for less return, and may ultimately destroy soil fertility since it accelerates leaching (washing away nutrients by rain) and erosion in hilly terrain, where often the most fertile soils are found.

Slash-and-burn agriculture works best when population densities are low, as when an area is first colonized, such as the Maya lowlands during much of the Preclassic. Before regional settlement studies were done, it was thought to be the style of Classic period cultivation as well. But population densities up to 800 people per km^2 are too high to be supported by even more intensive varieties of slash-and-burn agriculture. Other Classic Maya agricultural practices include hillside terracing, new and more productive cultigens, and draining swamps to reclaim the land. These all use the landscape more intensively and to some degree are more stable. Archaeological evidence indicates that these and other innovations were tried, but scholars disagree about their timing and contributions to subsistence.

We believe that by the end of the Classic period, the Maya used a variety of agricultural strategies, from extensive to highly intensive, depending on local environmental conditions and population history. This mix resulted from local processes of intensification as land quality declined and population rose. Long-distance transport of large amounts of food was lacking, so centers were mainly supported by local production, and Maya farmers exercised different options, with the long-term result of increased intensification. Some Mayanists believe that the Classic Maya were able to intensify agricultural production while avoiding environmental degradation, but others think that intensification eventually caused severe declines in soil fertility, contributing to the decline of Classic society (see Chapter 15).

Process: Political Centralization and Stratification

Polities and Capitals   The concept of civilization does not necessarily imply centralization under a single ruler or capital. Sometimes this occurred (Egypt), but often the same Great Tradition was shared by many independent polities (early Sumer). Although scores of impressive Late Classic Maya centers are known, they were never integrated into a single political system. The largest Maya centers functioned as political capitals. They were the seats of royal households, with all of their associated administrative and religious apparatus—places from which political authority emanated. As noted in Chapter 13, we call them "regal-ritual" cities (Fox 1977; Sanders and Webster 1988). Large centers sometimes dominated smaller ones, each with its own supporting population, but no capital succeeded in forging a lasting political system that incorporated all, or even a majority, of the others.

Among the many politically independent Maya political systems there was great variation at any given time in their number, size, complexity, and relation with each other. Some were tiny—single small centers with perhaps a few thousand farmers living within a few kilometers of the palace. Other polities, like that of Copán, covered hundreds of square kilometers. A few giants, such as Tikal, probably controlled thousands of square kilometers for extended periods of time. Unfortunately, inscriptions offer no clear direct evidence of the territorial extent of polities.

Rulers, Titles, and Inscriptions The institution of kingship supported and promoted political centralization and stratification. Maya inscriptions give us detailed insights into their political structure. Maya rulers had special titles, signaled by the *ahaw* symbol, which seems to have the general meaning "lord" and was used to denote nobility in general, not just kingship. Dynastic continuity is indicated by royal inscriptions listing dynastic succession, and royal titles are associated with historical events in the lives of rulers, including rites of passage (births, marriages, deaths), rites of intensification (especially public sacrificial ceremonies), and military expeditions. Other titles (lesser political statuses, priestly and scribal statuses or offices) are also sometimes associated with succession. Thus the central ruling apparatus of a Maya polity focused on a ruler, presumably hereditary, who was surrounded by a retinue of titled individuals who may have lived at his capital. Some centers have associated emblem glyphs, perhaps personal symbols of independent rulers (Culbert 1991; Houston 1989; Marcus 1976).

Maya rulers probably thought of their polities as loose aggregates of lesser elites and commoners over whom they had varying levels of political influence depending on distance and mutual interests. Population size of these polities varies. Copán at its height had about 27,000 people. Most polities were smaller, but a few were much larger. The core of the Tikal system may have had 50–60,000 people, and when its influence over nearby centers was strong, it may have had limited political control over several hundred thousand people.

By the Late Classic period titles such as *sahal* ("feared man") were borne by governors of centers subject to more powerful capitals. The successful domination of secondary centers (extracting allegiance, labor, and goods from them) was highly situational, reflected archaeologically in the discontinuous episodes of architectural activity and monument erection at individual royal centers. Reigns of strong rulers (indicated by such activity) are interspersed by periods of royal weakness and stagnation lasting as long as a century even at huge centers like Tikal. Although the king was the central political personage, his power was far from absolute (see Chapter 10).

Art and Architecture Public portrayal of kings and their status symbols and activities was essential to Maya politics and iconography, particularly as expressed in stone sculpture and painting on stelae, altars, and facades of buildings (Fig. 14.11). Royal ritual is one of the most conspicuous themes of Maya art, which emphasizes the political, ritual, and military roles of rulers, and their central roles in society and cosmos. The Maya clearly believed that proper royal rituals were necessary for the well-being of the universe as a whole and the social order. In good Mesoamerican style, many rituals were sacrificial, featuring personal bloodletting by the king or other high nobles. There also seems to have been a strong emphasis on ancestor worship in Maya society. Elite ancestors were important supernatural figures, and powerful Maya rulers may have been deified when they died. Certain temples, such as the Temple of the Inscriptions at Palenque, served as mortuary structures dedicated to the ruler buried beneath them and presumably to his personal cult. Rich elite graves occur throughout the Classic period, some of the earliest of which include human sacrifices.

Rulers sponsored ambitious building projects, laying out and adding to great plazas with temples for public worship and royal palaces. At some centers, these projects were also carried out by nonroyal elites. Economic institutions existed which could mobilize and organize human labor on a large scale for elite purposes.

Warfare The lack of overall political integration is reflected in widespread warfare, which was often noted in inscriptions and art. Warfare was a royal preoccupation, closely linked to royal rituals; rulers used warfare to unite their polities, to defend them, and occasionally to expand them, especially toward the end of the Late Classic. Although there are many examples of short-lived expansion, long-term successful integration of large kingdoms was apparently impossible. Intense warfare is reflected in formal fortifications but also involved unfortified centers. Military institutions were strongly controlled by and identified with the elite, according to their art and inscriptions.

Stratification The structure of Maya societies has been debated because (1) details of social organization are not found in the inscriptions, (2) Maya polities showed so much variation, and (3) archaeological research has only recently focused on all levels of Maya society. No one denies that most Maya were farmers and of fairly humble rank. Everyone would also

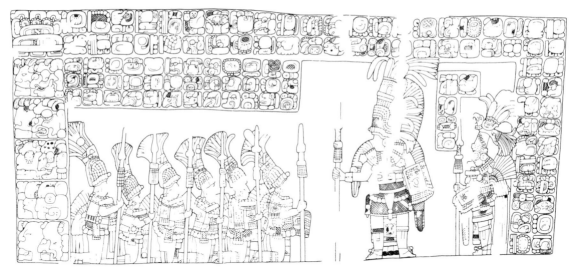

agree that the Maya had complex hierarchical sociopolitical organization. Not only were there kings, but many other lesser elites also bore the title of *ahaw*. But agreement ends when we debate whether Maya society was ranked or stratified.

There are two perspectives on this issue. One view is that Maya society was internally well stratified with state-type institutions. Another view (that we share) is that the Maya were less characterized by class structure than by principles of complex ranking, with kinship still very important as an integrating mechanism, crosscutting hierarchical differences between individuals and subgroups.

Maya sociopolitical organization was "segmental," holding socially, politically, and economically powerful elite groups which could compete with the royal dynasty. Thus some nobles of high rank below the king had their own supporters (particularly kin), resources, and social titles and ranks not derived from royal affiliations. Maya kings probably spent much of their careers trying to keep such erstwhile competitors in line, hardly in keeping with the powers of autocratic kings. We would agree, though, that many Maya societies, especially the largest, probably exhibited features of stratification — especially in the separation of the royal lineages from other subgroups. The Classic Maya seem to be a transitional case in evolutionary terms, moving toward greater political centralization and segregation.

The broad base of the Maya social pyramid was its commoners (Fig. 14.12), perhaps 80–90 percent of the population of a particular polity. They were principally farmers, and their surplus labor and products supported elites. The community arrangements varied from isolated family groups in rural areas to clustered houses nearer the centers. Their household organization would resemble that of Cerén (Sheets 1979, 1983a,

FIGURE 14.11 Scene from a carved limestone wall panel from the Classic Maya center of Piedras Negras. The large figure is identified by the inscription as Ruler 2. He is presiding over what seems to be an initiation ceremony for young elite men, who are possibly acquiring warrior status. Scenes such as this in Maya art not only help us to appreciate the elements of the Maya Great Tradition but provide detailed glimpses of behavior — in this case an elite ritual preserved in stone. This monument, and others like it, are replete with hierarchical images, reflecting the complex nature of Maya social organization.

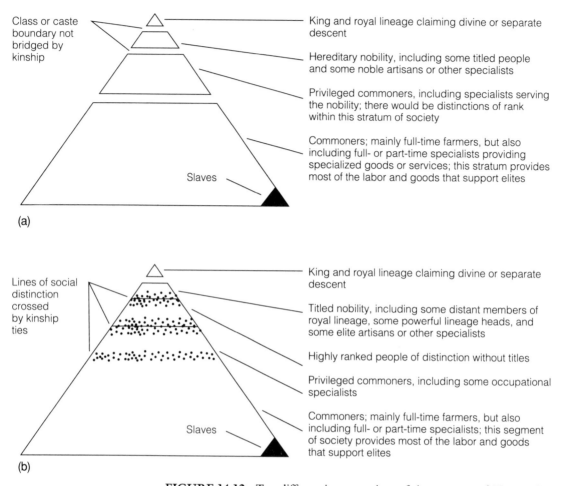

Class or caste boundary not bridged by kinship

King and royal lineage claiming divine or separate descent

Hereditary nobility, including some titled people and some noble artisans or other specialists

Privileged commoners, including specialists serving the nobility; there would be distinctions of rank within this stratum of society

Commoners; mainly full-time farmers, but also including full- or part-time specialists providing specialized goods or services; this stratum provides most of the labor and goods that support elites

Slaves

(a)

Lines of social distinction crossed by kinship ties

King and royal lineage claiming divine or separate descent

Titled nobility, including some distant members of royal lineage, some powerful lineage heads, and some elite artisans or other specialists

Highly ranked people of distinction without titles

Privileged commoners, including some occupational specialists

Commoners; mainly full-time farmers, but also including full- or part-time specialists; this segment of society provides most of the labor and goods that support elites

Slaves

(b)

FIGURE 14.12   Two different interpretations of the structure of Maya society at the end of the Classic period. Social stratification is a feature of both, since royal lineages and slaves are highly differentiated segments. In (a) there is more stratification, because there are sharp social boundaries not effectively bridged by kin ties. In (b) there are social distinctions, but kinship ranking integrates social groups and lines of separation are not sharp. Although these models are different in important ways, archaeologists might find it difficult to substantiate one versus the other, based on material remains.

1983b; Zier 1983), or the rural Aztecs (Chapter 7), with a range of productive activities including farming and off-season artisan work, making utilitarian products like simple pottery or baskets on a part-time basis. Although there is no direct evidence for slaves in Classic society, very likely they were present but probably not common. Among the 16th-century

Maya there were a few slaves — often war captives — attached to the house-holds of men of high rank (Tozzer 1941).

Between the commoners and the top-ranking titled elites (the royal family and nonroyal noble families) there was another group, privileged above the commoners but not having the birthright, sufficient social posi-tion, or means to live as nobles. These people were special artisans retained by elites to provide prestigious goods and services. Some, such as scribes, architects, and sculptors, may have been full-time professionals in the ser-vice of elites, and some may themselves have been nobles. Recently deci-phered inscriptions on stelae, altars, and pottery vessels include the names of individual artisans, sometimes coupled with the title *ahaw,* indicative of elite status.

Process: Emergence of the Maya Great Tradition

Iconography associated with kingship is among the many elements of the Maya Great Tradition that can be traced back to the Preclassic. The Early Classic spread of the stela cult, with all of its associated royal and ritual imagery and inscriptions, is the most dramatic Great Tradition process of the Classic period. Eventually a well-defined set of epigraphic, icono-graphic, calendrical, architectural, and ritual conventions united Maya cen-ters throughout the lowlands. Local expressions of the Great Tradition vary, but it is recognizably Maya wherever it occurs.

Broadly shared Great Tradition elite elements express the close social ties among Maya elites that crosscut local political boundaries. Elite fami-lies throughout the lowlands were related through bloodlines and mar-riage. They visited one another for funerals and other rituals, and made political and military alliances with each other. These ties tended to set elites apart as a dominant subgroup with common values, symbols, and behaviors, strongly portrayed in the art of major centers such as Copán and Tikal.

Process: Economic Specialization and Trade

There is considerable evidence for economic specialization in the abun-dance and quality of elite items (including architecture) at Maya sites (Fig. 14.13). There is no question that skilled artisans existed, though some reconstructions of Maya society overestimate the amount of labor and skill required to produce buildings, stelae, and other objects.

We saw in Chapter 8 that a number of commoners were at least part-time specialists, producing utilitarian goods such as manos, metates, and obsidian blades. Where raw materials are particularly abundant, whole communities may have been engaged in at least part-time specialization. At Colha (Belize) chert was mined and finished into products that were distributed over a considerable portion of the eastern lowlands for hundreds of years.

FIGURE 14.13 A sec-tion of a Classic Maya polychrome vessel. Often used as funerary offerings, such finely made vessels constitute a distinctive fea-ture of the Maya Great Tradition. Representa-tional scenes such as this one provide detailed infor-mation on status symbols, rituals, and political behavior.

Some archaeologists think that the Classic Maya had an economic system comparable to that of the Aztecs, with professional traders, large formal marketplaces, well-developed craft specialization, and long-distance exchange of all kinds of commodities, under elite control and thus serving to enhance elite dominance. But there is little evidence of this level of economic complexity among the Maya. Bulk commodities such as food were consumed very close to where they were produced, and full-time specialization involved very small numbers of people. Certainly there was exchange among centers, even distant ones elsewhere in Mesoamerica. But most of the widely traded raw or finished products tended to be light-weight (easy to carry) and intended for a small, generally elite set of consumers—for example, the highly valued feathers of tropical birds, sought by highland and lowland nobles for their crowns of office, insignia, and costumes. Remember that anything carried a long distance had to share the load with food for the load's bearer, a human porter. Thus heavy goods like manos and metates were less likely candidates for long-distance trade than were lighter, more valuable materials. Chert and obsidian tools were sometimes traded far from their places of origin and used by people of all statuses, but even these were generally not consumed on a massive scale far from where they were produced.

The Pinnacle of Classic Maya Society

The Classic Maya peaked between A.D. 700 and 800. Great Tradition elements were highly developed and there was (to some extent) political centralization and social stratification, supported by institutions firmly in place. Foremost among these was kingship itself, closely associated with (and supported by) religious institutions and symbols. Other institutions included the military (also strongly identified with kings) and organized trade in elite items and status symbols promoting stratification. The Classic Maya civilizational package was mature and splendid but short-lived and about to lose its integration in a spectacular manner—the subject of Chapter 15.

CENTRAL ANDEAN CIVILIZATION

In 1532, 40 years after Columbus first arrived in the New World, a small band of Spaniards penetrated into the heartland of the Inca empire, the largest and most complex political system in the Americas (see Chapter 11). Centered on the mountain valleys of the Central Andes (Peru) and its adjacent Pacific coasts, this empire extended along the western margin of South America, from Colombia in the north to central Chile in the south (see map in Chapter 11). Despite its size, the Inca empire was less than a century old, itself heir to a tradition of complex cultural evolution extending back 4,000 years. It is the emergence of this tradition that we review below (Jennings 1983; Rowe 1946; Willey 1971).

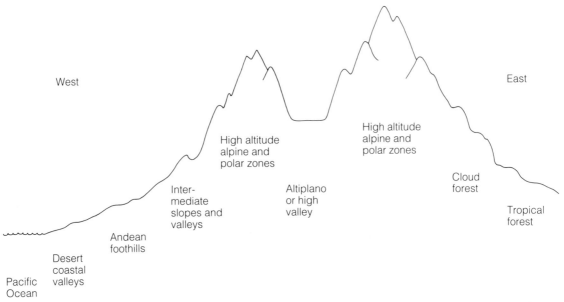

West

East

High altitude
alpine and
polar zones

High altitude
alpine and
polar zones

Cloud
forest

Inter-
mediate
slopes and
valleys

Altiplano
or high
valley

Tropical
forest

Andean
foothills

Desert
coastal
valleys

Pacific
Ocean

FIGURE 14.14 Schematic cross-section of the Central Andes, showing major topographical and biotic features. This kind of complex zonation is typical of mountain biomes, especially in the tropics.

Environmental Setting

The Andean region and adjacent lowland zones to the east and the west exhibit even more environmental diversity than Mesoamerica (Fig. 14.14). Beginning at the west side, the Pacific coastal zone of Peru (10–30 km wide) is one of the driest deserts on earth, supporting patches of seasonal vegetation nourished by fog rather than rain. Flora and fauna are not abundant in the desert itself, but the sea offers a wealth of marine mammals, birds, fish, and shellfish. Numerous small rivers, rising in the mountains, cross this desert to the Pacific, creating oases of permanent vegetation in an otherwise bleak environment. Upstream, to the east, these rivers flow through deep, narrow gorges in the foothills of the Andes, which at higher elevations become larger valleys with somewhat higher rainfall.

Higher up (3–4,000 m) are wide mountain basins called **altiplanos** (high plains), with cool, moist climates. Most of the human population is found in the altiplanos, the intermediate mountain basins, and the Pacific coastal valleys. The altiplanos have rich, deep soils suitable for potatoes and other specialized highland crops. Natural grassy vegetation provides pasture for **llamas** and **alpacas** (domesticated New World camels). There are virtually no permanent human communities above 4,000 m; conditions there are too cold for agriculture, though animals are pastured in some areas. At the highest elevations (some peaks are over 6,000 m high) are permanent snowfields and glaciers. East of the mountain crest are similar cold zones, but at lower elevations cloud forest grades into the hot, dense tropical forest of the upper Amazon River drainage.

altiplanos Wide mountain basins that are found at high elevations in the Central Andes (3–4,000 m) and that have cool, moist climates.

llama Domesticated South American camelid used as a beast of burden and for wool and food.

alpaca Domesticated South American camelid noted for its soft wool.

The whole region of the central Andes (centered on modern Peru and Bolivia) was a distinctive culture area in the early 16th century. As in Mesoamerica, there were many distinct ethnic groups, with dozens of mutually distinct languages and local populations scattered over diverse environments. Through conquests the Inca empire had, by 1532, expanded the Central Andean cultural tradition far beyond its earlier limits.

The Emergence of Andean Civilization

Chronology The very general time periods listed in Table 14.3 provide a framework for culture history. Emphasis here will be the evolution of Andean cultures through the Middle Horizon, by which time many basic patterns had emerged.

From the end of Preceramic times to European contact, Andean prehistory alternated between periods of regionalism and unification. The latter are "horizons," periods with some sort of archaeologically perceptible marker of common culture unifying much of the Central Andes. During Inca times unification was clearly political, but other earlier horizons may mark processes such as the spread of religious institutions or ideas. Because Andean peoples lacked writing and did not record dates, chronological placement of sites is often difficult, and Andean archaeology lacks a historical dimension comparable to that of the Maya. Another problem stems from the sheer abundance of archaeological sites. Many of the largest and most important centers are known only from surface remains or small-scale testing, providing only a general view of Central Andean culture prior to the Inca Empire.

Origins of Agriculture Foraging cultures spread through the Andes by at least 10–14,000 years ago, and possibly even earlier. After the end of the Pleistocene, experiments in food production began, and early cultigens include two forms of bean (as early as 8500–5500 B.C.). As in Mesoamerica, mixed economies persist for a long time; not until the second millenium B.C. are there signs of an effective complex of domesticated plants and animals: maize, beans, squash, and possibly several other plants, as well as the herding of camelids. By about 2000 B.C. root crops such as **manioc** may have been grown along rivers in the eastern tropical forest zone.

The extreme dryness of the coast of Peru preserves organic materials well, so archaeologists have been able to reconstruct the subsistence base. By about 6000 B.C. coastal populations were quite dense, subsisting on foraged food, particularly fish. Anchovies were apparently netted by the millions, dried, and ground into a paste. Two of the earliest domesticated coastal plants were not edible: gourds and cotton were used to make nets and net-floats. Domesticated food plants such as manioc, potatoes, and sweet potatoes were present by 2000–1800 B.C., as was maize.

manioc Tropical, domesticated root crop especially used in tropical forest regions.

Table 14.3   **Chronology of Andean Civilization**

Late (Inca) Horizon	A.D. 1476–1532
Late Intermediate Period	A.D. 1000–1476
Middle Horizon	A.D. 600–1000
Early Intermediate Period	A.D. 1–600
Early Horizon	800 B.C.–A.D. 1
Initial Period	1800–800 B.C.
Preceramic Period	3000–1800 B.C.

The Preceramic Period

Well-established and substantial foraging and fishing communities inhab-ited the Peruvian coast by 3000 B.C. Thereafter, population appears to rise. Some settlements have large complexes of buildings, clusters of rooms and courts raised on terraced platforms. At El Paraiso in the Chillon Valley six large mounds supporting masonry buildings are scattered over about 6 ha. These buildings are probably residential and grew by accretion. Middens of shoreline sites yield abundant marine resources and some cultivated plants. Perhaps the large, sedentary, coastal communities farmed the natu-rally moist soils near the rivers, but if they subsisted almost entirely on marine resources, as some archaeologists believe, then they represent one of the few dense, sedentary, foraging societies known to anthropologists.

Agriculture was probably much more important in the highlands of Peru, as populations built up during the Preceramic. By 1800 B.C. ritual buildings appear at several sites, most notably Kotosh in the Huallaga Valley. Since highland products are often found in coastal sites, there seems to have been some kind of exchange between the two zones.

The Initial Period

This period begins with the spread of ceramics throughout the Central Andes. Coastal region sites are well inland and have more plentiful remains of domestic plants. These patterns probably reflect greater dependence on agriculture and irrigation. Huge constructions appear, the largest being Huaca Florida, a platform 250 m long, 50 m wide, and 30 m high, built around 1700 B.C. near the modern capital of Lima. In this period linear arrangements of platforms and courts typical of later civic architecture are established, for example, Cerro Sechin, with carved stone slabs depicting some figures gorgeously attired with weapons or scepters, and others partly dismembered. Although many residential sites surround these coastal cen-ters, too few have been excavated to understand the complete settlement

FIGURE 14.15 Large stone image from inside the main temple at Chavin de Huantar, Peru, an Early Horizon center.

system for an Initial period polity. Highland developments are not as well known as those on the coast, although some Preceramic centers such as Kotosh continued to function. The earliest traces of metalwork in gold come from this period.

The Early Horizon

Between 800 B.C. and 1 A.D., much of Peru shared a distinctive art style with iconographic themes such as jaguars, eagles, serpents, and humans; humans were often portrayed with highly stylized attributes of felines and serpents, such as fangs. This may reflect a much older shamanistic tradition of identification with supernatural animal helper spirits. The art style uses complex, flowing, curvilinear representations (Fig. 14.15) carved on stone, modeled in clay on the facades of buildings, hammered onto gold objects, portrayed on ceramic vessels, and woven into textiles. A deity known as the Staff God becomes important and is a later theme in Andean art.

It was once believed that this complex artistic tradition spread over Peru from a particular place of origin, Chavin de Huantar, a center located high in the mountains of northern Peru; hence the art style was labeled "Chavin" (shahVEEN). Chavin de Huantar is a massive set of platforms and courts built of stone (some blocks weigh over a ton), honeycombed with interior passageways and chambers. Although about 40 ha of residential remains lie nearby, many archaeologists believe that the site, located in a small valley, was also a cult center drawing people from a large area.

We now know of considerable artistic variation in Early Horizon Peru, so origin of the Chavin style at a single dominant highland center no longer seems plausible. Many different centers were emerging in Peru, contributing to the Chavin tradition, modifying and expressing it in their own ways (a process similar to that of Preclassic Mesoamerica during the spread of the "Olmec" style). Some centers of the period are much larger than Chavin. The biggest, Sechin Alto, has a single, monumental, stone-faced platform (300 by 250 m, 35 m high) surrounded by many other structures, but their functions remain unknown.

There isn't enough archaeological information to understand the significance of widespread "Chavin" imagery. Many parts of the Central Andes do not evidence it, and there is no sign of large-scale political unification. Chavin art, religious in content, has long been assumed to mark the spread of a cult. Although diffusion hypotheses no longer seem plausible, the art is still perceived as religious. The close linkage of religion and politics in pre-Columbian America indicates that the extent of Chavin style may owe as much to political transformations of the Early Horizon as it does to religion.

The Early Intermediate Period

Chavin style gradually disappeared, sufficiently transformed so that it lost its distinct identity. Between about A.D. 1 and 600 throughout the central Andes there emerged a series of striking regional cultures, and of these, Nazca on the south coast and Moche on the north coast are the best known. Most Nazca materials have come from elaborate graves, the dry desert sands having preserved textiles, wood, and other organic materials. Nazca's settlement system is less well known despite large temples and associated residential structures. The Nazca are famous for the huge patterns (lines, geometric motifs, and animal effigies hundreds of meters long) they created in the desert by sweeping coarse gravels away to expose underlying smoother soil.

We know more about the Moche, who flourished along a 400 km strip of coast between about A.D. 100–700. The Moche (MOHchay) exploited abundant sea resources, and their irrigation systems extended as much as 50 km inland, watering an estimated 40,000 ha of agricultural fields in eight coastal valleys. The total population of these valleys was probably well in excess of 50,000 people. Individual communities like Pampa

Grande may have housed as many as 10,000 people, and each valley also boasted major civic constructions in the form of huge adobe pyramids. The largest of these, the Huaca del Sol, was 340 by 160 m (nearly 6 ha) and stood 40 m high; made of an estimated 140,000,000 mud bricks, it is one of the largest buildings in the New World. Like other Moche pyramids, it probably served ritual and administrative purposes. Rich burials containing lavish offerings of pottery, cloth, shell, copper, silver, and gold, as well as human and animal sacrifices, are often associated with these civic structures. What seem to be royal burials are found in several valleys, and it is not clear if the Moche were politically unified or (like the Maya) had multiple contemporary political systems.

Moche culture declined about A.D. 600–700, possibly because of increased warfare and competition from other expanding Andean political systems. It is also possible that earthquakes caused uplift of parts of the coast (as occurs today), disrupting the irrigation canals essential to agriculture. Decline of the Moche political system did not bring population decline, and the former Moche realm was still heavily populated in 1532.

The Middle Horizon

Between A.D. 600–900 the Central Andes experienced a second period of unification, marked by shared art styles and burial practices, particularly in the central and southern regions. One hypothesis holds that this horizon spread from the impressive urban center of Tiahuanaco (TEEahwah-NAHkoh), high in the altiplano of Bolivia. Another hypothesis favors a similar expansion from the city of Huari (itself influenced by Tiahuanaco), in the central highlands of Peru. It has long been argued that military conquest caused this unification and that it resulted in a Peruvian empire similar to the later Inca empire. Evidence for militarism is seen in the sudden establishment of highly regimented centers laid out according to a preconceived plan. The most impressive of these, Pikillacta (PICKee-YACKtah), had a wall ca 600 m on a side, enclosing an area of about 45 ha (Fig. 14.16). Inside were multistory buildings (aligned in regular rows) and large open courts but no obvious monumental religious structures. Pikillacta also had 502 storage structures. As an administrative center, Pikillacta is a prototype of those later established by the Inca. As a settlement, Pikillacta most closely resembles Huari in its construction, but its layout is much more regimented. Its political relationships with either Huari or Tiahuanaco, however, remain obscure.

As yet there is no way to substantiate hypotheses about the unifying forces of the Middle Horizon. In fact, more research into particular regional cultures has made it evident that not all parts of the Central Andes region were involved in Middle Horizon political expansion. For example, a variant of Moche society survived on the north coast, unincorporated into any larger political system. Whatever empire building Huari and Tiahuanaco (or other centers) may have done ebbs midway through the

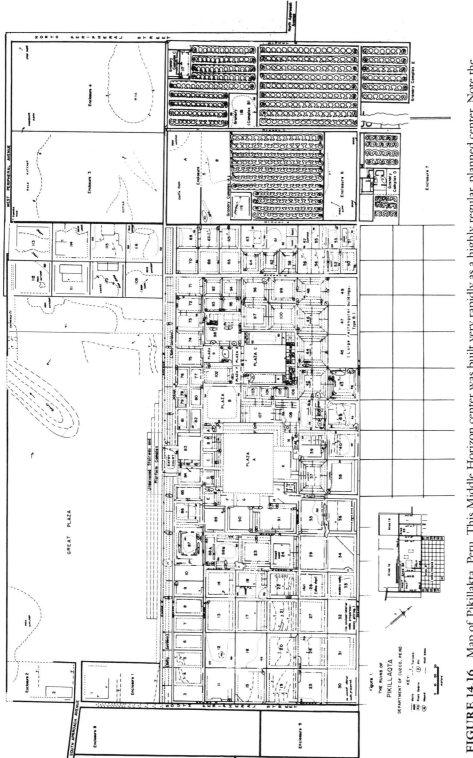

FIGURE 14.16   Map of Pikillakta, Peru. This Middle Horizon center was built very rapidly as a highly regular, planned center. Note the many standardized storage facilities on the eastern edge (right). The Incas later built centers that functioned like Pikillakta throughout the regions they conquered. Pikillakta may represent a similar Middle Horizon process of conquest and political consolidation.

Middle Horizon. It was not until much later in the 15th century that the final episode of Andean unification began, under the Inca (see Chapter 11).

Process: Settlement, Urbanization, and Agricultural Intensification

The culture history of emergent Andean civilization provides information for evaluating basic evolutionary processes.

Settlement Patterns and Urbanization From at least about 3000 B.C. there were large sedentary settlements, especially in the coastal valleys, living on marine resources and, later, irrigation agriculture. Population increased steadily from the end of the Preceramic period, and the coastal areas may have reached their maximum in Early Intermediate times. Highland trends are less well known. As populations grew so did community size, up to 10,000 people.

A few Preceramic sites had large, special-purpose civic buildings, but in the Initial period large communally built structures began to appear widely, both in the coast and highlands. They vary in plan, but all consist of combinations of courts, terraces, and platforms. Some of these structures clearly grew over long periods of time but still attest to the efficient organization of large labor crews. Although these structures undoubtedly had ritual functions, some may have had associated residential and administrative facilities as well. Some are near residential sites, while others are more isolated; all served as political and religious foci for populations in small coastal and highland valleys.

Urbanization Settlements large and complex enough to be called "urban" were in some of the coastal valleys at least by the Early Intermediate period. None has been adequately excavated but population estimates suggest sizes up to 10,000 at Pampa Grande. By the Middle Horizon, centers such as Tiahuanaco and Huari were urban in scale and density, with populations estimated at 10–35,000 people. The form of these cities varies: Tiahuanaco is dominated by a large ceremonial enclosure, whereas Huari lacks religious buildings on a similar scale (though a Tiahuanaco-like open civic space has recently been detected at Huari). Another variant is the planned center (e.g., Pikillacta).

Agricultural Intensification Agriculture in the coastal valleys in Preceramic times involved planting in naturally humid zones along the rivers. Population growth quickly outstripped the productive potential of this strategy, and canal irrigation became necessary. These irrigation systems may date as early as late Preceramic times and were very modest; because such systems have been constantly used and revamped right up to the present, direct evidence is difficult to get. Irrigation expanded greatly with the population increases of the Initial period and the Early Horizon. They seem to have reached maximal size in the northern coastal valleys occupied by the Moche people, who tapped the upper reaches of rivers with major canals many kilometers long, and in at least one place ran a canal between two adjacent valleys.

Most highland cultivation depended on rainfall. Intensive agriculture there often involved terracing, sometimes associated with small irrigation canals, and was certainly present by Middle Horizon times. Another, contemporaneous form of intensive agriculture is the system of drained fields found around the margins of Lake Titicaca, at an elevation of about 3,800 m. These new fields were highly fertile, could be cropped heavily, and were important to the economy of nearby Tiahuanaco and the dense rural population of the altiplano. Maize, which usually does not grow at such high altitudes, can be grown in the drained field microenvironments, and so can potatoes.

Process: Political Centralization and Stratification

Political Centralization   During the Preceramic there is no convincing evidence for nonegalitarian political structure apart from the impressive size of some coastal structures, which may indicate some sort of ranking. As populations rose and agriculture replaced wild resources in the coastal valleys, political centralization was stimulated. Some of the large constructions of the Initial period strongly suggest centralized political authority in coastal societies, and a few of these are found in the highlands as well. Presumably such constructions were foci of political systems embracing much or all of the population of a valley, whether or not they were capitals in the sense of dominant administrative settlements. Managing large canal systems also probably necessitated some sort of central political structure. Until the end of the Early Horizon there is no clear indication of the political unification of many coastal or highland valleys into larger political systems, and only in the Early Intermediate period do multivalley capitals appear. By Middle Horizon times some centers (Tiahuanaco, and perhaps Huari), are clearly capitals for large regions of the highlands, if not mini-empires. Some sort of rank societies emerged on the coast of Peru during the Initial period and Early Horizon. States were present at least by Early Intermediate times.

Stratification   In the absence of inscriptions, the best evidence for stratification comes from burials and art. Despite the abundance of well-preserved burials recovered from coastal cemeteries, marked differences in status do not become obvious until Moche times, when enormous social differentiation is evident. Most Moche burials are quite simple, but several apparently royal burials have been found, two since 1987 (Alva 1990). These were in a large mud-brick pyramid at the site of Sipan. The uppermost, placed in a log-covered pit dug into the pyramid, included the body of a ruler in a wood coffin accompanied by five human sacrificial victims of both sexes as well as a dog. Rich offerings included imported shells, feather ornaments, rich fabrics, and a wealth of metal objects made of copper, silver, and gold. Also found were war clubs, shields, and atlatl darts.

Lower down, in an earlier phase of the same building, an even richer tomb was encountered. Although this tomb lacked sacrificial victims, other mortuary offerings make it the richest burial ever found in the New World. These include fabric and shell items, but most impressive are the ornaments and larger metal sculptures made of copper, gold, and silver, many with iconographic motifs that may have been potent political symbols. For example, the sculpture of a crab deity is associated in Moche art with warfare and ritual sacrifice, and another deity is shown with a knife and a severed human head, a common Peruvian theme laden with political significance. Both burials included elaborate weapons.

Because Moche art is highly representational, it provides information on stratification (Benson 1972; Donnan 1990). Many subjects pertain to elites and the supernatural; gorgeously attired figures, including warriors, are prominent in Moche art, and portrait heads on ceramic vessels may represent individual rulers. Moche artists created objects of great elegance; those made of metal are mainly found in elite contexts such as the graves discussed above.

Although differences in residential architecture exist, no Moche community has been sufficiently studied that residence type can be used to analyze social status, as it can for Teotihuacán or the Classic Maya. The summit of one of the largest Moche constructions, the Huaca de la Luna, contains numerous rooms and may have served as an immense royal palace. Moche ceramic vessels depict extremely elaborate dwellings which, if they actually existed, would have housed elites.

Settlement patterns, irrigation projects, burials, and art indicate that Moche society was hierarchically structured. Conceivably, Moche rulers were paramount chiefs who dominated rank societies, but we believe that Moche society was stratified and that the political institutions of the state were present. If all of the north coast valleys were unified into a single Moche polity, this state would have incorporated well over 50,000 people, possibly as many as 150,000.

The political status of polities elsewhere in the Central Andes during the Early Intermediate period is less certain. Nazca culture on the south coast appears less hierarchical than the Moche and may have been far less stratified. Because the Central Andes is so varied and compartmentalized, there was undoubtedly great local variation in political evolution. It does seem safe to say that stratification emerged at least by about A.D. 100. The large urban centers of Huari and Tiahuanaco were almost certainly the capitals of very large Andean states, if not expansive military empires, during the Middle Horizon, and a series of elite tombs has been discovered at Huari.

Warfare was fundamental to increasing political centralization and stratification, especially in the coastal valleys. Initial Period sculptures at Cerro Sechin depict dismembered bodies and what may be elite warriors. Fortifications appear at various centers in late Early Horizon times, and become common during the Early Intermediate period. Moche art and burials provide abundant evidence for warfare and associated rituals of torture, sacrifice, and decapitation. The presence of weapons in royal tombs indicates that rulers had important military functions.

Process: Emergence of the Central Andean Great Tradition

In the absence of writing, the Andean Great Tradition must be traced in architecture, art, and artifacts. As in Mesoamerica, the Great Tradition was marked by the construction of monumental public buildings. This architectural tradition underwent many modifications, but its basic elements were in place by the Initial period. About the same time there emerged the first large-scale public art, which almost certainly had political as well as religious functions. At centers such as Cerro Sechin leaders portrayed themselves garbed in elaborate costumes and in threatening postures, surrounded by dismembered and decapitated figures. Such depictions ushered in a long tradition of military and sacrificial themes strongly identified with Andean elites. During the Early Horizon artistic conventions and themes were established that, though modified, remained characteristic of the Andean tradition until the Spanish conquest. These included complex animal symbolism and the worship of the Staff God. Elite status artifacts begin to appear at about the same time, and by the Early Intermediate period they appear abundantly in tombs, as we saw at Sipan.

Process: Economic Specialization and Trade

Trade Because the Central Andes is so environmentally varied, many products moved far from their places of origin as early as Preceramic times. Andean economic systems encompassed the movement of goods from one altitudinal zone to another, sometimes by exchange, sometimes by the movement of people exploiting more than one zone.

The Andeans had a transportation resource unknown to Mesoamerica—the llama was used as a pack animal. From Middle Horizon times, extensive road systems also facilitated exchange. Although these features made the transport of cheap, bulky commodities over long distances somewhat easier than in Mesoamerica, food supplies for most Andean populations were locally produced. Beginning in Initial period times there is a detectable exchange of elite or ritual materials and objects. By Moche times this exchange is extremely impressive. Materials from as far away as Ecuador (shells) and Chile (lapis lazuli) are found in Moche graves, and judging from the frequent and sophisticated portrayals of boa constrictors, jaguars, parrots, and monkeys, contacts with the tropical forest to the east were frequent, probably involving the exchange of perishable materials. The

FIGURE 14.17 Design on an embroidered and woven garment from the coast of Peru. Andean peoples carried weaving technology to aesthetic levels unparalleled elsewhere in the New World. Often placed in graves, such textiles have been preserved in pristine condition by the hot, dry conditions of the Peruvian coast. Motifs include many identified with the Andean Great Tradition.

Andes are rich in minerals; gold, silver, and copper were widely traded and used to make status symbols, weapons, and religious objects.

Specialization Ethnohistoric sources in the Contact period document highly developed occupational specialization in Inca and immediately pre-Inca times. Although we lack economic texts, archaeological evidence indicates that specialization emerged very early. The most obviously specialized craft was metal working. Andean peoples made gold objects by Initial period times, and Moche metal workers created objects of extraordinary beauty and technical sophistication. Special knowledge and technology were necessary to create such elite objects, and at least some metal workers must have been full-time artisans in the service of Moche lords. By the 16th century, Andean metal work was by far the most sophisticated in the New World, including some processes then unknown in Europe. Much of this expertise was expended on ritual objects and status symbols, and thus did not result in any important utilitarian technological breakthroughs of energetic significance. Bronze objects, including weapons and tools, did become reasonably common by the 16th century. Unfortunately, few workshops or other places of specialized economic activity have been excavated in Andean sites, so although we see the products of specialization, the ways in which it was organized remain problematical.

Textiles and ceramics also may have been products of specialization. Textiles, especially those preserved in the graves of the south Peruvian coast, were extremely fine (Fig. 14.17). That they were produced in large quantities is obvious, since individual burials are sometimes accompanied by many meters of cloth wrappings. Weaving was probably a skill all women mastered, and even the finest cloth may have been produced as a domestic household task. In Cuzco, the Inca capital, groups of women who were attached to the emperor's household wove special fabrics for royal use and were thus specialists of a sort, though not in the usual economic sense. The finest ceramic objects, such as Moche effigy vessels, were elaborately sculpted and painted; it is tempting to assume that specialists produced them. Many were mass-produced using molds, a form of technology highly suggestive of full-time specialization. Ceramic effigies themselves suggest the presence of other specialists, such as curers, musicians, and fishermen.

The Andes on the Eve of the Spanish Conquest

During the Late Intermediate period the Central Andes again experienced vigorous regionalism, with political fragmentation into many local states and chiefdoms. By the 14th–15th centuries some of these states had expanded into miniempires through conquest. The most successful of these was the Chimu empire on the north coast of Peru. By 1450, Chan Chan, its capital (Moseley 1975), was one of the most impressive urban centers in the New World (Fig. 14.18). Supported by taxes and tribute drawn from

rich, irrigated coastal valleys, the city had a population of 25–30,000 in an area of about 6 km².

The most impressive features at Chan Chan were nine huge walled compounds that were the fortified palaces of Chimu kings, who claimed a divine descent, separate from that of their lowly subjects. Each king built a new palace upon succession to the throne, and his descendents and retainers continued to occupy it after his death. Residences for the household of the ruler, palaces also had facilities for administration and the storage of taxes and tribute. Each contained a large funerary structure as well, where the king was eventually buried with accompanying sacrificial victims—mostly young women. Outside the royal compounds were houses of lesser elites and commoners, many of whom were occupational specialists.

Even as Chan Chan thrived, the seeds of a greater empire were growing. Beginning in the early 15th century, the Inca of the central highlands of Peru began a spectacular career of military expansion, built on conquest and intimidation. Perhaps their biggest victory was the defeat of the Chimu; about A.D. 1470 they sacked Chan Chan and carried off its artisans to enrich their own capital, Cuzco.

By 1532 the Inca had created the largest empire ever known in the New World (Rowe 1946). For the first time the entire Central Andes, as well as regions to the north and south, were united under one political system incorporating approximately 6,000,000 people. A complex administrative system linked all parts of the empire with Cuzco. Officials of the empire, some of whom were former rulers of independent polities, and other Inca governors, represented the Inca emperor. They communicated with the capital, using a road network (incorporating earlier roads) that was well over 20,000 km in length. Along these roads the Inca built rest facilities for those traveling on imperial business, as well as local administrative centers, often inhabited by Inca colonists. Taxes and tribute flowed into Cuzco and into state storehouses in the provinces. One well-known administrative center had 480 such storehouses, with storage capacity (mainly for food) of nearly 40,000 m³. Quipus were used to record and transmit information, helping the whole complex system to run smoothly.

CONTACT WITH THE OLD WORLD

In Mesoamerica the Spanish effectively subdued the Aztec empire between 1519 and 1524 and during the next 25 years extended their control over the Valley of Oaxaca and the Maya highlands and lowlands. Galvanized by the initial successes of Cortes and his followers, other Spanish adventurers ranged over much of the rest of the New World, hoping for similar opportunities. Weakened by epidemic diseases and a devastating civil war, the Inca empire fell to a handful of Spanish soldiers under Francisco Pizarro in 1532, though native resistance to Spanish rule continued much longer. With its fall, the last great independent New World civilization came to an end. Contrary to popular belief, however, many elements of New World civilization survived the conquest, albeit in altered form. Both in Mesoamerica and the Central Andes, complex states with new Great Traditions emerged from the chaos of conquest, states which thrive today.

POINTS TO REMEMBER

- New World civilizations had many of the same characteristics as those of the Old World, despite the fact that they evolved independently. This indicates regularity in the general processes of evolution.

- New World civilizations emerged later in time than those of the Old World, partly because they were lower-energy societies in terms of energy and technology.

- In Mesoamerica, distinct regional civilizations shared many Great Tradition elements but differed in many other ways, such as urbanization, scale, and political structure.

- In northern South America an independent evolutionary sequence lead to the emergence of civilization. Andean civilization lacked writing.

- The same processes of change that we used to understand the evolution of Old World civilizations are useful for understanding New World civilizations as well.

FOR FURTHER READING*

For a general perspective, Coe, Snow, and Benson's *Atlas of Ancient America*. For Mesoamerica, see Sharer and Grove's *Regional Perspectives on the Olmec;* Sanders, Parsons, and Santley's *The Basin of Mexico;* Millon, Drewitt, and Cowgill's *The Teotihuacán Map;* Sanders and Webster's "The Mesoamerican Urban Tradition"; Berdan's *The Aztecs of Central Mexico;* Diehl's *Tula;* and Adam's *The Origins of Maya Civilization*.

For South America, see Jennings's *Ancient South Americans;* Morris and Thompson's *Huanaco Pampa: An Inca City and Its Hinterland;* and Rowe's "Inca Culture at the Time of the Spanish Conquest."

*Full citations appear in the bibliography.

PART FIVE

EXPLAINING THE PAST

Developing explanations of why things happened in the past is the most difficult and most important task facing scientific archaeology. Science ultimately entails explanation, even though no scientific explanation is ever really "true" or "final" in any strict sense of the word. Although we touched on the problem of explanation in earlier parts of this book, we were mostly concerned with how we use archaeological methods and techniques to reconstruct past behaviors and institutions and to show how they evolved.

In the final two chapters we turn to a more formal examination of explanation in archaeology. We do this by first taking an issue that has long intrigued archaeologists: the collapse of civilizations. In Chapter 15 we use the decline of Classic Maya civilization as documented at Copán because it deals with changes of sweeping evolutionary significance and involves, directly or indirectly, all of the concepts, institutions, and processes fundamental to this book. Especially prominent is the theme of adaptation. After centuries of vigorous development, the institutions of the Classic Maya proved to be evolutionary failures, and we want to know why. Furthermore, having already reviewed much Copán research, we can now apply it to a specific explanatory problem.

In reviewing the demise of the Copán kingdom, we will also see that part of the research battle is framing the questions we want to ask in the proper ways. Considerable research in recent years has focused on the issue of the collapse, and we have learned some surprising things. Although we have no final answers, we can now offer more plausible and useful descriptions of, and explanations for, the collapse of Copán society than ever before. What we have learned at Copán has implications for the collapse of Classic Maya society as a whole.

The final chapter takes a broader view. Here we investigate some of the major explanations that archaeologists and other scholars have advanced to account for the processes of change we see in the archaeological record, especially those marking the evolution of civilizations reviewed in Part 4. Although there is no consensus that any one explanation, or any combination of them, holds the key to understanding the past, our models of cultural evolution are much more sophisticated and plausible than they were a century or even a generation ago.

CHAPTER FIFTEEN

THE FALL OF
CIVILIZATIONS: ANOTHER
LESSON FROM COPÁN

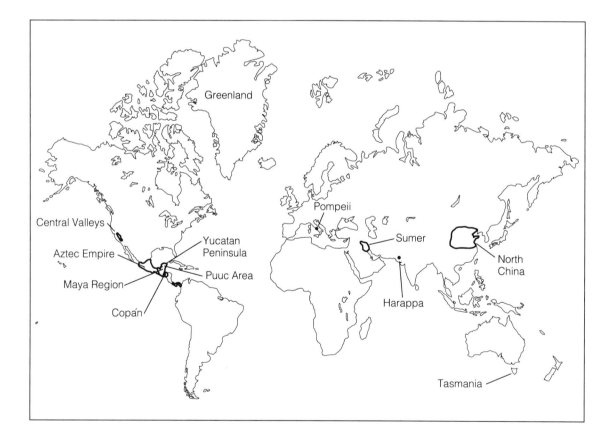

The main concern of archaeology is, by definition, the study of cultures that are extinct, or have been radically transformed. Labels such as "Roman," "Aztec," or "Classic Maya" refer to societies whose technology, customs, institutions, beliefs, and values, if they have survived at all, no longer function as integrated cultural systems associated with living populations. Extinction is part of any evolutionary process, and from an evolutionary perspective archaeologists study failed cultures: particular systems of learned behavior that may have been extremely successful at one time but that eventually did not survive the selection process.

This sort of study is not as grim as it sounds, because failure can mean many things. Cultures sometimes fail in the ultimate sense — the human populations that manifest them become extinct. After several centuries of colonization, Norse settlers in Greenland utterly disappeared (around 1500), their culture apparently unable to cope with environmental changes. The indigenous foraging people of Tasmania (a large island off the southern tip of Australia) disappeared as well. They were able to adapt to their natural environment but were hunted to extinction by European colonists in the 18th and 19th centuries. They were unable to survive in a highly competitive social environment.

But these are extreme and unusual cases. Because cultural behavior is so rapidly learned and so flexible, most systems fail in a much more positive sense — their technology, customs, institutions, beliefs, and values change to accommodate new stresses and opportunities. One might object that transformation is not really failure, but it is. Elements of the original cultural systems become obsolete; they fail to perform their cultural tasks effectively. On the other hand, the transformations enabling a population to survive in the face of the failure of traditional practices are the essence of the evolutionary process.

COLLAPSING CIVILIZATIONS

Sometimes changes are so abrupt and so radical that we talk about the "fall" or "collapse" of cultures, and nowhere is this theme more pronounced than in the literature on ancient civilizations. Countless books emphasize it. One of the first was Edward Gibbon's *Decline and Fall of the Roman Empire* (1776–1778), and for many years the standard, popular work on the ancient Maya was J. E. S. Thompson's book *The Rise and Fall of Maya Civilization* (1954). Such titles capture our imaginations with their drama, promising to explain failures of complex cultures that, for good or bad reasons, are impressive because of their unusual scale, significance, or splendor in human history (or prehistory).

Think back over the civilizations we reviewed in Chapters 13 and 14. At one extreme there is China, where a continuous set of transformations links past to present and where cultural identity was not seriously disrupted until the 20th century. At the other extreme is Harappan civilization, which from our perspective ends abruptly with no comparable link with later cultures. Although in one sense Aztec civilization was abruptly transformed by the Spanish conquest, which eliminated much of its Great Tradition and political structure, important elements survived to become fused with the culture of the conquerors (Fig. 15.1). The concept of the "fall" of civilization thus has many meanings in specific evolutionary terms. It is a metaphor for the processes by which a set of highly integrated organizational/ideological cultural components loses integration, however suddenly or gradually this may happen and however many such components survive in some way.

Such processes fascinate archaeologists and historians, and much research has been designed to investigate them (Tainter 1988; Yoffee and Cowgill 1988). Perhaps the most intensive and sustained efforts have focused on the demise of Classic Maya civilization. In this chapter we will use the Maya, and in particular the Copán Maya, as a case study to show how such research is designed and carried out and what we have learned from it.

THE COLLAPSE OF CLASSIC MAYA SOCIETY

In Chapter 14 we used the image of lights appearing on a map of the Maya lowlands as dated elite monuments spread, marking the expansion of the Classic Maya Great Tradition. But eventually this process reverses itself, and the lights begin to blink out; the last date at Pusilha is A.D. 731, at Palenque 786, at Yaxha 803. Some old centers hang on a while longer. Tikal blinks out at A.D. 869, Uaxactun at 889. At only a handful of centers are there fitful glimmers extending beyond 900, and these soon disappear as well, until the whole map is in darkness. This cessation of Long Count dates has long been the benchmark of the so-called Classic Maya collapse, just as their spread marked the crystalization of the Classic pattern. Of course, long before we could read Maya dates, the effects of the collapse were evident to travelers such as Stephens and Catherwood. One only had to stand amid the forested ruins to know that something dramatic and puzzling had happened to a vigorous civilization (Culbert 1973).

What the dates provided was a sense of the timing of the process. Archaeologists found that at some centers royal construction projects were begun about the time of the latest dates but were never finished. The abrupt cessation of Long Count dates at particular centers and their disappearance over virtually the entire Classic Maya heartland perpetuated the "mystery" of the Maya collapse so powerfully evoked by the words and images of Stephens and Catherwood. Granted, the terminal dates are scattered over a period of roughly 150 years (about the same amount of time that separates us from Stephens and Catherwood's 1839 visit) and a lot can happen in 150 years. But Maya civilization, which took so long to form and to grow, from our perspective, still lost its integration very suddenly.

FIGURE 15.1 Artist's conception of the conquest of the Aztecs by the Spanish. One way the Great Tradition of a civilization can end is through conquest, but when this occurs, the new tradition is often an amalgam of the Great Tradition of the conquered and that of the conquerors.

Not only did kings and elites disappear, construction projects ended, and basic social and political institutions withered away. Eventually the whole southern part of the Maya lowlands, where millions of people had lived, was virtually abandoned. This is a mystery of the highest order, and probably more research and ink have been devoted to solving it than any other issue in Mesoamerican archaeology.

The Postclassic Maya

What caused Maya civilization to collapse? It will help to step back for a moment and consider what the Spanish found when they began to explore the Yucatán Peninsula early in the 16th century (Farriss 1984; Roys 1965; Sabloff and Andrews V 1986; Tozzer 1941).

The Peninsula as a whole was far from deserted. In northern Yucatán and along the eastern and western margins of the peninsula, they encountered dense Maya-speaking populations—probably 600–800,000 people in all. The Maya were organized into 17 autonomous political systems, or "provinces." These ranged from large, politically centralized domains containing as many as 60,000 people to loose confederations of small independent towns allied for mutual defense. Powerful rulers (*halach uinics*) presided over the larger polities, supported by lesser lords (*batabs*), and professional priests, warriors, and scribes. Smaller independent polities or individual towns were ruled by *batabs* themselves. Social systems were stratified, though kinship was still an important integrating mechanism. In addition to these provinces, Maya speakers were also found on the southeastern and southwestern margins of the peninsula, although their political arrangements are unclear.

In the northern provinces rulers and other elites occupied impressive houses filled with relatives, retainers, and slaves. These were located in the centers of prosperous towns, generally near temple-pyramids, built with public labor, where deities, possibly including ancestral spirits, were worshiped. Palaces and temples were built for Maya rulers by commoners, who also paid taxes and cultivated elite fields as well as their own. Slaves owned by high-ranked Maya cultivated especially valuable fields, where commercial crops such as **cacao** (the source of chocolate) were grown, and acted as porters for elite trading enterprises. Trading parties went by water as well as overland, carrying commodities such as honey, cotton mantles, salt, and cacao. Columbus encountered a large Maya trading canoe on one of his earliest voyages.

cacao The seed or bean of a tropical plant, used to make chocolate.

Most people were commoners who lived in dispersed farming settlements. Maize and beans were staple crops, and slash-and-burn cultivation was the dominant agricultural system. Although there were individuals and even whole towns that specialized in activities such as salt making, economic specialization was quite simple compared to that, say, of contemporaneous Aztec society in the highlands of Mexico.

Warfare was common and occurred for many reasons. It had definite ritual overtones but was also fought for basic resources such as salt beds, land, and slaves, as well as to extend or defend political territories. The first Spanish who set foot in Yucatán found themselves opposed by effective Maya armies numbering in the thousands.

Scribes continued the tradition of Maya writing, although hieroglyphs were confined to books and apparently not used on carved monuments or buildings. Time was reckoned using complex calendars and an arithmetical system which had both been used earlier by the Classic Maya, although Long Count calendrical calculations were no longer made.

All of this should sound quite familiar, given our previous discussion of the Classic Maya. Clearly, in northern Yucatán and on the peripheries of the peninsula, a variant of what we call Maya civilization was doing quite well in the 16th century. Nor was this a recent revival. Between 900 and 1450 a succession of Maya centers thrived in the region. One of these, Chichén Itzá, was founded in Classic times—it has a Long Count date of A.D. 485—but by 1250 was one of the largest centers in the Maya lowlands, distinctive for its combination of Maya architectural techniques and Mexican-influenced sculpture. Still further back in time, vigorous regional centers flourished in Yucatán during the Classic period, and one of the largest Preclassic sites—Komchen—is found there as well. In short, there was a strong and lengthy tradition of Maya civilization in Yucatán that began early and never "collapsed" at all.

In the western part of Yucatán — the Puuc region — there occurred an enormous buildup of population and an explosion of monumental construction beginning about 900, even as the old Classic centers to the south declined. Some of the largest and most famous Maya centers, such as Uxmal, Labna, and Sayil, thrived there for several hundred years. A number of archaeologists think that the entire Puuc culture was in large part stimulated by migrants or refugees from the older Classic centers, who established new centers with somewhat different, but still recognizably Maya, Great Tradition elements.

By now the reader is probably somewhat confused about the Maya collapse. It seems that Maya civilization didn't disappear at all but rather went through a series of transformations and relocations. In a sense this is correct, and this conclusion is a useful antidote to the overly facile and romantic generalizations about the "collapse of Maya civilization" so strongly entrenched in the popular imagination. But there is nevertheless a dramatic story here, something important to explain. Let us approach it in another way.

An Empty Landscape

In 1524, three years after he led the conquest of the Aztecs of Central Mexico, Hernan Cortés set off with a small army to march overland to Honduras (Cortés 1986). Their route took them through the central and southern parts of the Yucatán Peninsula — the very region where the oldest and largest Classic centers had emerged and flourished. We cannot reconstruct Cortés's route exactly, because he became lost in trackless tropical forest. His army, accustomed to living off the land, almost starved because there were so few Maya settlements in their path from which maize or other supplies could be obtained. Eventually Cortés reached Honduras after great hardships. The old heartland of the Classic Maya, where the stela cult had originated and which had been one of the most populous regions on earth in A.D. 800, was practically abandoned in 1524. Only an estimated 50–100,000 Maya lived in the interior of the peninsula, where about three million Classic Maya had lived 700 years earlier, a reduction of at least 95 percent.

Cortés left no records suggesting that he had visited abandoned Classic centers such as Tikal, even though he must have passed within a few kilometers of many of them. By 1524, these centers were as overgrown and forgotten as they were in Stephens's and Catherwood's time, and forest had reclaimed thousands of square kilometers of what had once been cleared farmland. This pattern extended over almost half of the Maya lowlands — about 100,000 km². Most strongly affected were precisely the areas where Classic civilization had been earliest and most vigorous.

Cortés's experience enables us to revise our views about the Maya "collapse." Even though in some parts of the lowlands one or another form of Maya civilization endured, something very puzzling happened in the oldest, most populous areas, and it happened on a tremendous scale.

The Classic civilizational pattern utterly disappeared over a huge area, and at least 95 percent of the population that supported it eventually did so as well.

Until recently, archaeologists envisioned this decline as an extremely rapid process, involving no more than a century or a century and a half for the affected region as a whole. Most archaeologists assume that it was even faster at individual centers, thus justifying the use of dramatic terms such as "collapse" and "catastrophe," even if some Maya polities survived elsewhere. To use an analogy, let us imagine that in the middle of the 19th century in the United States, all of the great cities to the east of the Mississippi, with their associated urban and rural populations, disappeared within a few generations. Even if western cities such as Denver, St. Louis, and San Francisco survived and prospered, maintaining their particular regional variants of U.S. civilization, we would still have something dramatic to explain. The problem archaeologists face with the Classic Maya is very much like this.

The Problem

We must explain

1. What happened to royal dynasties and their associated elites over an area of 100,000 km² and why populations as a whole eventually disappeared almost completely in the same region.

2. Why this vast region has remained virtually empty almost up to the present, despite the existence of Maya and other populations on its peripheries that could have recolonized it.

Our method must be to examine the careers of individual Maya polities, such as Copán, to see how they relate to this general picture. The Maya collapse is really a series of specific collapses, each with its own special properties. We must construct our larger explanations by extrapolating from these individual cases.

EXPLANATIONS OF THE CLASSIC MAYA COLLAPSE

Many hypothetical explanations of the Classic collapse have been proposed (Culbert 1973), which can be divided into two general classes. First, *elite collapse explanations* focus only on the royal and elite levels of Maya society, primarily trying to account for the rapid disappearance of the Classic Maya Great Tradition and its supporting political institutions. Second, *total system explanations* try to account for the loss of population as well. These classes of explanations, along with their postulated mechanisms, are summarized in Table 15.1.

Let us briefly examine these various explanations, in the order we have listed them, to assess their plausibility.

Elite-Collapse Explanations

Peasant Revolts   The influential Mayanist J. E. S. Thompson (1954) was the chief proponent of the peasant revolt hypothesis. He believed Maya society was essentially divided into two classes — the rulers and the ruled — the thought that the excessive demands of rulers for labor and other support so antagonized commoners that they rebelled and overthrew their oppressors. This was an attractive idea because it accounted for the apparent suddenness of the disappearance of elite Great Tradition and institutions and the broken, toppled stelae at Maya sites; also, we have many historical examples of such revolts — successful or otherwise. Although he did not emphasize it, Thompson's hypothesis envisioned the survival of the Maya peasantry, who in his view made up 90 percent of the society.

The peasant revolt hypothesis has two main problems. First, where successful revolts have happened elsewhere historically, they have resulted in the emergence of new elites and in new patterns of centralized rule and state-type political institutions. This did not happen in the case of the Maya. Second, the hypothesis does not explain what happened to the bulk of the population, which should have not only endured but thrived after the stress of oppression was removed.

Table 15.1   Explanations of the Maya Collapse

I. Elite-Collapse Explanations

   A. Peasant revolts
   B. Foreign (non-Maya) invasion
   C. Disruption of trade networks
   D. Internal warfare

II. Total System Collapse Explanations

   A. Nonecological causes

     1. Collapse of trade networks
     2. Ideological fatigue

   B. Ecological causes

     1. Catastrophic ecological events

       a. Earthquakes
       b. Volcanic eruptions
       c. Climatic change (drought)
       d. Epidemic diseases of humans
       e. Epidemic diseases of plants essential to the Maya economy

     2. Long-term ecological processes

       a. Grass invasion of agricultural fields
       b. Degradation of the agricultural landscape through overuse

Foreign (Non-Maya) Invasions   Foreign invasions can also destroy local elites, as history amply demonstrates. But such invasions do not totally destroy populations in the millions. They also typically result in new, albeit foreign, sets of elites replacing the old native ones, with continuing socio-political complexity and new Great Traditions.

Disruption of Trade Networks   Another argument asserts that elite power was based on the display or distribution of imported goods. No one has ever constructed a convincing model of how this would work, and what we know about Maya society makes the opposite assumption more likely—trade was mainly in nonessential status symbols and luxury items, which could easily be replaced with functionally equivalent local counter-parts. Disruption of trade networks is only a viable explanation if it can be shown that elite dominance was dependent on commerce. Again, what happened to all the people?

Internal Warfare   Internal warfare can seriously disrupt complex societ-ies and often destroys elites in particular polities. Recent research in the eastern part of the Maya lowlands by Arthur Demarest indicates very destructive levels of warfare as well as possible local depopulation, by the eighth to ninth centuries. But there are always winners in the long run, and new patterns of stability and complex organization eventually emerge. Populations may be disrupted by warfare, but they rapidly recover. Since winners would have been themselves Maya, rather than foreign intruders, this explanation does not even account for the loss of the Great Tradition elements.

In thus criticizing the elite collapse hypotheses we do not suggest that there is no evidence for them or that they could not have contributed in some way to what happened to the Classic Maya—a point we will return to later. The chief objection to all of them is that they do not account for the total collapse of Classic Maya systems, including disastrous and sus-tained population losses.

Total-System-Collapse Explanations

However quickly the debacle that overtook the Maya occurred, it unques-tionably resulted in total system collapse over 100,000 km², so this class of explanation looks more promising.

Nonecological Causes   Two hypotheses present themselves. The first maintains that the Maya in general (not just the lords) were so heavily involved in pan-Mesoamerican commerce that when trade networks were heavily disrupted, the Maya simply moved away. Another explanation fo-cuses on the Maya obsession with cycles of time and prophecies related to these cycles, positing that the Maya succumbed to their own prophecies of doom—to a kind of cultural fatigue. There is no convincing evidence for either of these ideas, and they are not widely favored by archaeologists.

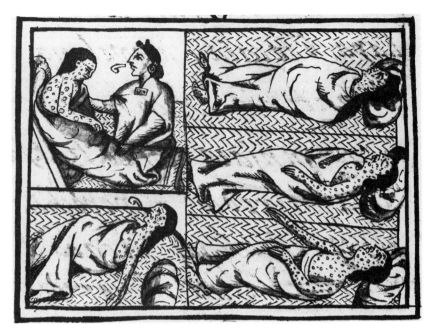

FIGURE 15.2 Disease can have disastrous effects on human populations. Diseases introduced by the Europeans reduced the Aztec population greatly during the 16th century. This drawing by an Aztec artist shortly after the conquest shows Aztec victims of a smallpox epidemic.

Catastrophic Ecological Causes   Events that are not controllable often disrupt human societies. Earthquakes have periodically wreaked havoc in China for thousands of years, and volcanic activity, as we all know, destroyed Pompeii. We know of no cases, however, where such destruction has been on a scale large enough permanently to disrupt state-type systems with large populations over many thousands of square miles. Both earthquakes and volcanoes are common in Mesoamerica, but when they occur they have few lasting effects except in strictly local terms. There is no sign of remarkable destruction in lowland Maya centers, so we may confidently dismiss these sorts of geological catastrophes as important causes of the disruption of Classic society. The same may be said for sudden, drastic climatic change, particularly drought. Not only does climate remain reasonably stable throughout Maya prehistory, but the areas that would be least affected by widespread drought — for instance, the southern lowlands where rainfall is most abundant — are those which suffered most.

Epidemic Disease   Diseases sometimes affect human populations severely, consequently disrupting complex sociopolitical systems. One such disease, bubonic plague, killed half or more of the population of some parts of Europe during the 14th century. New World populations seem to have been quite free of epidemic diseases such as smallpox, influenza, and measles before European contact began in the late 15th century (Fig. 15.2), and there are no convincing signs of epidemic diseases that would have had comparable effects either in pre-Columbian native histories or archae-ological remains. Even if epidemic diseases existed in pre-Columbian times, they probably would not have caused the effects postulated for the Classic Maya. No epidemics affect everyone; human fertility is sufficiently high so that populations recover in a few generations, as happened in the case of the bubonic plague in Europe. If epidemic disease caused the Maya collapse, why did it fail to spread to adjacent, heavily populated regions? Epidemic diseases thus seem poor candidates for explanations of the col-lapse. Many of the same objections apply to epidemic diseases affecting staple crops.

Long-Term Ecological Processes   Another set of hypotheses refers to processes of deterioration, caused by humans themselves, that degrade essential environmental resources such as air, water, or agricultural land. Examples include deforestation, erosion, and loss of soil fertility. For non-industrial civilizations, agricultural land is the prime resource likely to be damaged in this manner; when the productive capacity of the landscape is undermined, such populations may suffer severely as carrying capacity declines.

One of the earliest hypotheses of this kind posits that if tropical forest were extensively cleared for cultivation, grasses would quickly invade fields and form turf layers difficult or impossible to cultivate using only stone and wooden tools. Modern studies of tropical vegetation in the Maya lowlands, as well as studies of ancient vegetation changes, indicate that the grass hypothesis alone is not a likely explanation.

Another persistent explanation is degradation of soils through human overuse. As we discussed in Chapter 6, in tropical forest ecosystems organic components of soils tend to decay rapidly because high year-round tem-peratures and abundant rain promote intensive microbacterial activity. Heavy rain also leaches nutrients from soils more quickly than in temperate zones. Rather than being heavily concentrated in soils, nutrients in tropical forests are concentrated in the living plants. Any human activity that seri-ously disturbs the natural vegetation cover results in rapid loss of soil fertility and also, in hilly areas, in erosion of soil during heavy rains. Many modern attempts to clear tropical forest for commercial agriculture have failed because the fragile nature of tropical ecosystems has not been recognized.

Extensive slash-and-burn agriculture was one option open to the Maya. As long as population densities are low, such a system is unlikely to cause any long-term deleterious effects on the landscape. As land is used more intensively (reduction of rest periods), soil degradation threatens. In some environments, and with modern crops, technology, and fertilizers, high levels of intensification are possible. However, in the tropical environment of the ancient Maya, with their limited crops and technology, intensifica-tion could have been disastrous.

The agricultural degradation hypothesis, simply stated, is that Maya

BOX 15.1

SOIL DEGRADATION IN ANCIENT SUMER AND MODERN CALIFORNIA

The Copán Maya severely damaged their fragile tropical environment, with drastic political and demographic effects. Other environments have experienced similar human-induced degradation.

Salinization is a process that draws dissolved mineral salts to the uppermost soil layers. In hot, dry climates, the rate of water evaporation is so high that soil moisture is constantly being drawn up to the soil surface, bringing the mineral salts with it. These salts concentrate in the upper soil, rendering it poisonous for plants. This process can occur naturally but is often induced by humans trying to farm in desert habitats.

We saw in Chapter 13 that irrigation was essential to the economy of Sumerian civilization. The river channels in southern Sumer are higher than the surrounding plains, so irrigation water flowed by gravity onto the fields. Unfortunately, the elevation of the channels meant that excess water could not drain away from the fields. As water evaporated in this desert environment, it drew the salts upward, eventually rendering much of the soil toxic. By late Sumerian times agricultural productivity had declined enormously, and thousands of square kilometers were abandoned. A map of Iraq shows how salinization correlates with the old heartland of Sumer (Szabolcs 1989).

Could the Sumerians have solved their problem with modern technology? Do we have the means today to farm the deserts and avoid salinization? The answer to both questions is *no*.

The Central Valley of California is the richest agricultural landscape in the world, yet parts of it are desert (with less than 100 mm of rainfall yearly) and are irrigated by water pumped in from distant sources. Irrigation makes this desert bloom, but salinization is rapidly undermining the fertility of the region. If the process continues, much of the valley will be desertified within a few decades.

A short-term solution to salinization is to flush out the salts with massive amounts of irrigation water. Not only is this costly and difficult, but, ironically, it accelerates salinization. As was the case in ancient Sumer, in modern California, too many people are using the land too intensively and according to short-term concepts of benefit; in doing so, they have severely damaged the land on which they depend.

---

population densities eventually became so high that the productive landscape was severely damaged. As we saw in Chapter 6, all societies must effectively provide energy for themselves, and in the case of the agrarian Maya most energy was in the form of food. If food energy became limited, the whole foundation of Classic Maya civilization would have been threatened with total system collapse. Certainly we see disastrous effects of environmental degradation in other ecosystems. Agricultural intensification in ancient Sumer resulted in toxic concentrations of natural mineral salts in the topsoil, a problem now being felt in modern California (see Box 15.1).

Interaction of Causes

People like nice, neat, simple solutions to problems such as the Maya collapse. Unfortunately, complex processes such as the decline of a large cultural-ecological system are rarely simple and often involve several interacting causes (Fig. 15.3). When confronted with such a set of causes, we must try to determine which is most fundamental. The agricultural degradation hypothesis can subsume many of the others. For example, declining agricultural productivity might have stimulated revolts in the face of elite demands for food and labor, even if these demands were not otherwise excessive. Warfare among Maya polities might have been aggravated by attempts at territorial expansion to acquire new land. Warfare may also have depleted resources or disrupted agricultural cycles. Internal weaknesses among certain Maya polities may have attracted foreign invaders. An influx of invaders could upset a fragile balance between agricultural productivity and population size. While poor nutrition might not have caused epidemic diseases, many endemic diseases are linked to it, as are lowered fertility and increased mortality. The link between poor nutrition and disease is particularly strong in tropical climates.

Not only are these causal interactions complex, but the collapse process would have been gradual, requiring a considerable amount of time at any particular center. Archaeologists often emphasize the rapidity of the Maya collapse process, making it seem a sudden catastrophe; reconstructions of the declines of particular Maya polities reflect this suddenness. To understand the causes of the collapse, better chronology was needed. Recent research at Copán was designed to clarify the sequence of events and its timing.

COPÁN RESEARCH: NEW PERSPECTIVES ON THE MAYA COLLAPSE

Explaining the collapse process at Copán has been one of the fundamental goals of the research carried out since 1975. This goal is related to the larger topic of the adaptation of the Copán population to its environment (see Chapter 3). Remember that another goal has been the reconstruction of the Copán polity at its peak, just before the presumed collapse, since its structure could yield valuable clues about what happened.

Copán Collapse: The Traditional View

Until recently, the reconstruction of events at Copán was as follows. No dated monuments were completed and erected after about A.D. 800. The career of the last effective ruler, Yax Pac, obviously came to an abrupt end, despite the apparent vigor of his polity. Yax Pac might even have had to flee Copán, because we last hear of him carrying out a ceremony at the

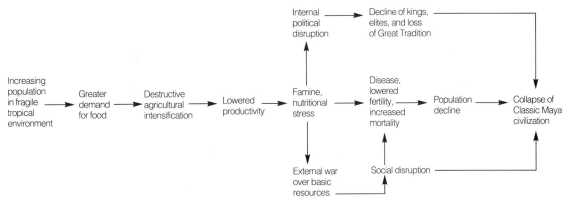

FIGURE 15.3   One model, or hypothesis, of how long-term, human-induced ecological damage might have stimulated the collapse, however quickly it occurred, of Classic Maya civilization in the southern Maya lowlands. Note that this model emphasizes a process that would take considerable time and that it subsumes several more limited explanations, such as disease, external warfare, and internal political upheaval.

center of Quiriguá in A.D. 810. It was assumed that the subroyal elites disappeared rapidly at about the same time, followed by a rapid population decline that left the valley almost completely empty by A.D. 850 or by A.D. 900 at the latest (Baudez 1983). In this reconstruction the political collapse of the Copán Maya happened in only one or two generations, and the whole system, including population, withered away in 50–100 years. Two questions arose when intensive work resumed at Copán in 1975: Was this picture correct, and if so, what were the most likely causes of decline?

New Perspectives on the Copán Collapse

In this section we will briefly return to the research design and findings summarized in Chapter 3 to review their implications for the Copán collapse.

Studies of Art, Writing, and Architecture   Although many new carved monuments have been recovered at Copán since 1975, in one respect they reinforce the traditional view—there was virtually no construction of royal monuments after about A.D. 800, when Yax Pac's reign ended. A single unfinished altar, with a date that may fall into the year 822 has been discovered (Fash 1991), possibly indicating a last feeble attempt by a Copán king to assert royal authority.

That the dynasty of Copán kings did abruptly lose its power is also suggested by architectural studies in the Main Group and elsewhere. Stratigraphic excavations in royal buildings by William Fash and his colleagues show that many formerly attributed to Yax Pac were really built earlier, suggesting that royal power was waning at the end. No known large structures were built in the Main Group after his time, so the tradition of royal building comes to an abrupt end just as the dated monuments disappear.

We also know that Yax Pac adopted new symbols, including those glorifying himself as a powerful warrior. Judging from associated evidence, this seems to be part of an unsuccessful attempt to buoy up his image as king.

From large-scale excavations outside the Main Group come two more new, revealing pieces of information. First, there were many powerful nobles in addition to the kings. Especially after A.D. 750, these nobles lived in increasingly large and splendid palace groups of their own. Second, many of them were able to decorate their houses and other buildings with elaborate sculpture, and some had carved benches and altars on which they asserted their importance. We usually find such monuments only in royal compounds. The conclusion is that powerful nobles constrained the power of the king and perhaps competed with him—that is, Copán's political centralization was comparatively weak (see Chapter 10).

Such weakness may be reflected by a building recently discovered in the Main Group. The structure is interpreted, on the basis of its location and iconography, as a council house where major nonroyal nobles met with the king to make decisions. If this interpretation is correct, it means that the king had to share power with these nobles, which supports the idea of a weak royal institution.

Settlement, Population, and Carrying Capacity

Reconstruction of settlement trends through time reveal many important insights related to the problem of the collapse. Before A.D. 600 the population of the valley was low, but in the next 200 years it expanded at a rate unusual for nonindustrial societies, eventually reaching a peak of about 27,000 people. Most were concentrated in the Copán pocket, the most fertile part of the valley.

Our ethnographic studies of modern Maya farming, together with specialized studies of soils, show that most upland zones are fragile when cultivated too frequently; they not only rapidly decline in productivity but erode quickly. These processes would have operated in the past as well, particularly without soil conservation techniques or other forms of intensive agriculture, for which we have found little evidence in the archaeological record.

Because we have studies of modern farmers and are now quite sure that the standard Maya crops of maize and beans were staples at Copán, we can reconstruct the carrying capacity of the valley reasonably well. This reconstruction indicates that carrying capacity of the Copán Valley (about 22,000) was reached and exceeded late in the eighth century (Fig. 15.4). Test excavations reveal pronounced erosion about that time, indicating severe damage to the environment (Fig. 15.5). It is also just about this time that the population begins to decline and spread out to utilize more distant parts of the valley in a pronounced fashion.

Palynology Our single analyzed pollen core (Rue 1987) does not go back far enough to capture a complete record of Maya exploitation of the valley, but it does show that at A.D. 900 natural vegetation had been altered to a

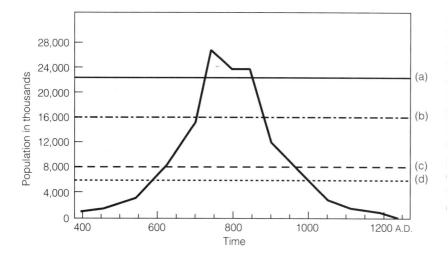

FIGURE 15.4 Population of the Copán polity through time. The horizontal lines represent our calculations of the carrying capacity of the valley for agricultural systems of increasing intensity. The most intensive system, permanent cropping, is indicated by line (a). Note the maximum population exceeds even this value.

remarkable degree as farmers cleared more and more land. Surprisingly, regrowth of the natural forest is first detectable later than we expected — around A.D. 1200.

Another pollen core taken from a lake about 150 km east of Copán produced a lengthy sequence of deposits, dating back 3,000 years. Although some human-induced changes are obvious in this core, there is no obvious indication of drastic climate change. This suggests that climate in the region as a whole, including Copán, has been quite stable for many centuries. In turn this suggests that drastic climate change (such as extended drought) did not play a role in the collapse at Copán.

Dating Even more surprising was the range of dates we obtained from analysis of excavated artifacts and features, particularly using the obsidian hydration method (Webster and Freter 1990a, 1990b). Rather than disappearing abruptly in A.D. 850–900, population declined slowly for 400 years (Fig. 15.6, p. 531). This is consistent with the palynological evidence, which indicates the continued presence of swidden farmers much later than previously believed. In addition, there was activity in elite compounds long after the royal collapse, at least one of which was not even founded until A.D. 1000. Neither the demographic or political collapse at Copán happened as quickly or catastrophically as we formerly believed.

Burials Early burial populations at Copán appear to have been healthier than later ones. As population rose during the eighth century all segments of Copán society appear to have experienced physiological stress, consistent with poor nutrition (Storey 1992a). Reproductive fertility also declined (Fig. 15.7, p. 532).

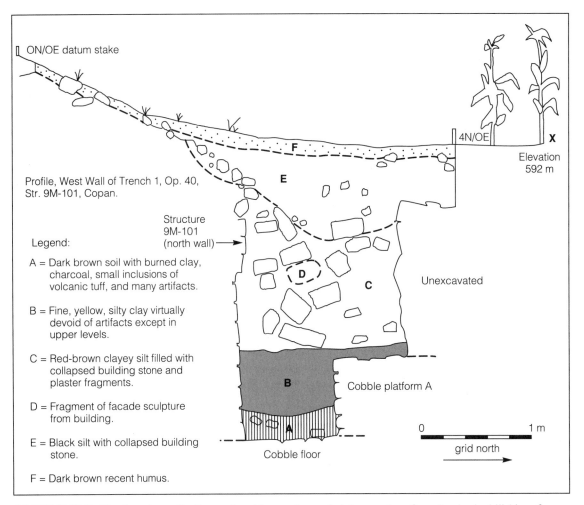

ON/OE datum stake

4N/OE

X

Elevation
592 m

F

E

Profile, West Wall of Trench 1, Op. 40,
Str. 9M-101, Copan.

Structure
9M-101
(north wall)

Legend:

D

C

Unexcavated

A = Dark brown soil with burned clay,
charcoal, small inclusions of
volcanic tuff, and many artifacts.

B = Fine, yellow, silty clay virtually
devoid of artifacts except in
upper levels.

C = Red-brown clayey silt filled with
collapsed building stone and
plaster fragments.

B

Cobble platform A

D = Fragment of facade sculpture
from building.

A

0   1 m

E = Black silt with collapsed building
stone.

Cobble floor

grid north

F = Dark brown recent humus.

FIGURE 15.5   Erosion pit profile. Excavating this trench revealed the severity of erosion in the hillsides of the Copán region. The Maya built the cobble floor, which overlies the original land surface, and a structure and a platform on top of the floor. Subsequently the narrow corridor between the two accumulated about 20–30 cm of trashy, middenlike deposits, including sherds and obsidian tools. Next, while Structure 9M-101 was still intact, about 70 cm of silt washed into the corridor, apparently in one rapid episode, since there were few artifacts in this deposit (B). The Maya were still using this area; a large flat stone (not shown) was found on top of the silt. Then Structure 9M-101 collapsed, forming deposit C. More soil eroded, forming deposit E, and finally the recent humus layer F developed. Structure 9M-101, a Classic Maya building dating from about A.D. 750 to 800, was largely buried. It was originally at least 4 m high, but now its remaining 2.3 m are covered by soil, most of which came from nearby hills to the north. This erosion was occurring even while the Maya still lived in or near this building and continued after the building collapsed. This massive erosion process, undoubtedly reflecting intensive land use of hillsides as Copán's population peaked in about A.D. 800, is excellent evidence for environmental degradation.

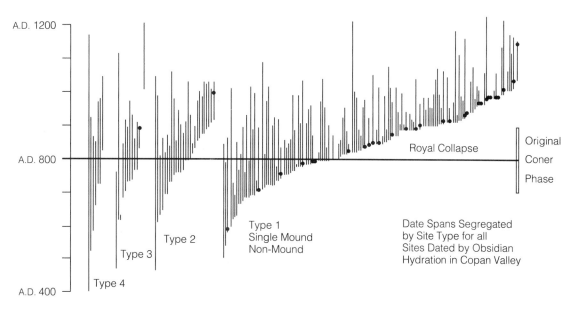

FIGURE 15.6 Obsidian dates from 200 Copán sites broken down by site types. Each vertical connects earliest and latest dates at each site. According to standard interpretations of the Copán collapse, few sites of any kind should have dates after A.D. 850–900. Our sample indicates that sites of all kinds, including elite ones, were occupied and even founded long after this time.

Experimental Archaeology Our studies of building construction (Abrams 1989) indicate that even the largest construction projects of the Copán kings required less time and energy than previously thought. Since the proportion of nonfood producers to food producers at Copán was also very low, farmers would only have had to produce small surpluses to support them. Elite demands for the time and labor of commoners, in the absence of other stresses, probably would not have been unusually taxing for the population at large. Only in the context of population pressure on resources and declining nutrition and disease would elite demands become significant factors in the collapse.

Studies of the Nonagricultural Economy Although many items were imported into the Copán Valley, and others undoubtedly exported as well, specialization and trade seem to have been organized on a fairly small scale (cf. Chapter 8). Most of what was imported consisted of elite goods; an exception was obsidian, which was widely used, although at low rates of consumption. Flow of obsidian into Copán seems to be remarkably constant despite the vicissitudes of the political system.

The Collapse at Copán

If conclusions based on our recent research are correct, any comprehensive explanation of the demise of the Classic Copán polity must take into account all of the foregoing pieces of evidence. Let us see how they square with the hypothetical explanations reviewed earlier.

FIGURE 15.7 Skull (from Teotihuacán) showing lesions, nutritionally related markers of disease, similar to those seen on Copán skulls.

Elite Collapse: Partial System Failure Simple elite-collapse explanations do not work on their own. There is no sign of internal warfare or invasion, and the basis of the Copán economy was local, not heavily dependent on trade. Internal revolts of subroyal elites and/or commoners may have driven out the royal dynasty, but elite groups survived. Although the royal part of the system failed abruptly, there was no associated abrupt collapse of overall hierarchical structure.

Total System Collapse There was an eventual total system collapse at Copán, in the sense that both elites and commoners ultimately disappeared from the valley in the 400 years following the collapse of the royal line. But this process was so gradual that *collapse* is too dramatic a word for it.

Nonecological Causes There is no evidence for collapse of essential trade networks or ideological fatigue. In fact, the one useful commodity that was widely traded, obsidian, continues to be commonly available in the absence of kings or elites.

Catastrophic Ecological Causes Earthquakes were a recurrent problem at Copán in ancient times as they are today, but no evidence suggests serious disruption of the Copán system by them. Pollen evidence suggests no widespread abrupt climatic change. There is no evidence for volcanic eruptions, climatic change, or plant diseases. Human disease is present but appears endemic rather than epidemic. There is no abrupt population loss on a massive scale consistent with plague or extreme famine.

Long-Term Ecological Processes   While grass invasion of agricultural fields cannot be demonstrated as a specifically serious problem, there did occur long-term replacement of the natural arboreal vegetation by grasses and shrubs, consistent with massive land clearance. There is direct evidence of degradation of the agricultural landscape in the form of deforestation and erosion, and indirect evidence in the form of extremely high population densities. Modern agricultural practices are producing similar effects (Fig. 15.8). The initial settlement and subsequent expansion of the population are consistent with use of increasingly marginal and fragile parts of the agricultural landscape. The poor health of the population after about A.D. 750 suggests declines both in the quality and quantity of food. The timing of overall population loss is consistent with a long-term ecological process (Fig. 15.9).

A Synthetic Explanation   The explanation on our list which is the most satisfactory of all is the agricultural degradation process. This explanation incorporates as subsidiary causes overpopulation; disease; the obvious fragility of the Copán political system; and the possibility of abrupt, and possibly violent, overthrow of the last kings, who were convenient scapegoats for the difficulties of the system. To the extent that rulers were regarded as responsible for their peoples' well-being, an ideological basis for the Copán collapse can also be posited. Within the context of the explanation as a whole, both revolts and ideological fatigue are symptoms of infrastructural stresses.

Aftermath

By A.D. 1200 the valley was virtually empty. What happened to the last few thousand inhabitants we cannot tell. Certainly the alluvial floodplain of the valley floor would still have provided food for a population of this size, so we cannot explain their absence by lack of agricultural potential. In all likelihood families gradually trickled away to join more vigorous political systems elsewhere, just as some of their ancestors probably had migrated into the valley, attracted by strong Copán kings. Gone were the elite Great Tradition, the complex political institutions, and eventually the people themselves. The Copán Maya, who seemed to have made such a spectacular adaptation to their tropical environment, sowed the seeds of their own demise, and the forest reclaimed its own.

LESSONS FOR SCIENTIFIC ARCHAEOLOGY

We started out in this chapter to investigate a mysterious and dramatic process: the collapse of civilizations. One lesson is that such processes are only mysteries in the sense that we have not thought about them correctly or gathered the proper information to understand them. The broad out-

FIGURE 15.8 Burning off hillside fields at Copán. If long fallow periods were still possible, vegetation in the form of shrubs and trees would be cut and burned. In this field cultivation occurs so regularly that only grasses have time to reappear. Yields are correspondingly low.

lines of what happened at Copán are much clearer now than they were in 1975—and much less mysterious, dramatic, and abrupt than we thought. Certain kinds of evidence (e.g., the dates of the erection of the last royal monuments) have held up well. Much new and unexpected evidence has been acquired (e.g., the dating of the collapse process), and our current explanations combine both old and new data.

Copán's fate is only one piece of the larger jigsaw puzzle of what happened to Classic Maya civilization in general. It remains to be seen to what extent we can generalize for the Maya as a whole from what we know about Copán. But many other pieces of the puzzle are falling into place as archaeologists work elsewhere, making our comprehensive view of the emergence and decline of Maya civilization much more trustworthy today than it was a generation ago. Most Maya archaeologists would now probably agree that, by the end of the Classic, population densities around most major centers for which we have adequate settlement information reached destructive levels and that overpopulation is related to the Classic collapse.

This is not to say that no major problems remain. For example, one primary element of the Maya collapse puzzle—the failure of people until recently to recolonize regions abandoned in Classic times—rests unexplained. It is still mysterious to us why this should be so. However, the important point is that this is not an inherently mysterious issue but one that can be resolved with time and work.

Archaeology, unlike many other forms of science, produces little that is of immediate practical value. The primary satisfaction in doing it is that it

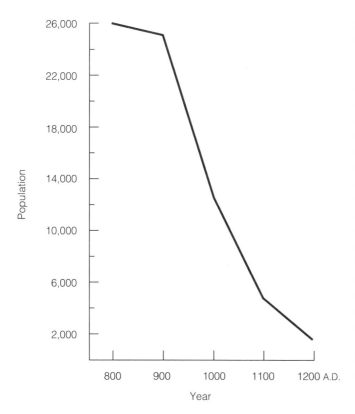

FIGURE 15.9 Copán's population peaked at just over 27,000 people between about A.D. 750 and 800. It then went into a small decline for over a century, then into a more rapid decline between 900 and 1200, with an annual rate of decrease of about 1 percent. Such a serious rate of demographic loss could be caused by an excess of deaths over births or by people leaving the region. From the point of view of the individual, the loss would be perceptible but not catastrophic. If you were born into a Copán community of 100 people and this rate of decrease continued throughout your lifetime, there would be only 56 people left by the time you were 60 years old.

helps make sense out of human cultural and social experience and elucidates the role humans play in the larger natural world. But sometimes more important results are gained than intellectual satisfaction. In the case of the Classic Copán Maya overpopulation and overexploitation of resources led, however gradually, to complete collapse of their civilizational package and the population that supported it. We commonly think of human societies as primarily threatened by natural disasters we can't control, but the Maya and the Sumerians teach us a more fundamental lesson: We are most threatened by the things we do to ourselves (Fig. 15.10).

At the beginning of World War II the world's population was just over two billion people. In 1988 it reached five billion. Populations in many parts of the world are doubling every 20–25 years—three times faster than the fastest rates of increase we can measure for the Copán Maya. The traditions, political institutions, and economies of modern civilizations are being undermined by too many people consuming too much too quickly. More important, the ecosystem is being damaged on a global scale. And unlike the last Copán Maya, we have nowhere else to go.

FIGURE 15.10 Map of southeastern Mexico (a) and NASA satellite photo of northwest Guatemala (b). The abrupt angle is the border between the two countries. On the left, tropical forest has been largely eliminated by clearing. To the right, in Guatemala, the forest is largely intact. Thirty years ago the whole region would have been heavily forested.

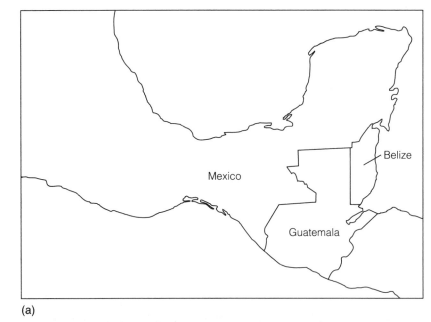

(a)

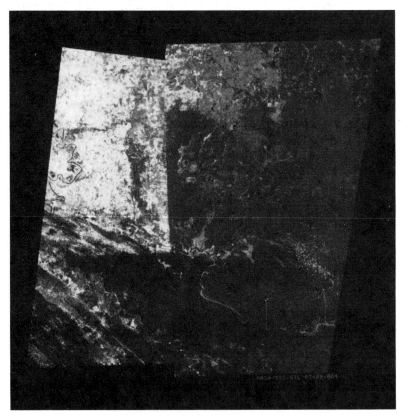

(b)

POINTS TO REMEMBER

- Essential to all evolutionary processes is decline and extinction; these affect societies as well as organisms.

- Cultural systems usually fail in the sense that new cultural behaviors are substituted for old ones.

- Tracing the decline of cultural systems is as important a task for archaeologists as is charting their growth.

- The Classic Maya provide a case example of one of the most mysterious and complete cultural declines.

- Examining a complex archaeological problem necessitates reviewing what is known and asking the proper questions.

- Many explanations may be advanced for any complex archaeological problem, but some are more plausible and likely than others.

- The best way to sort out any complex archaeological problem is to seek multiple kinds of independent evidence.

- The most convincing and fundamental explanation is that the decline of Maya civilization at Copán was due to overpopulation and environmental degradation, which in turn had political, social, and economic effects.

- Like all explanations of complex archaeological processes, this explanation is not exhaustive.

- Degradation of environments, which is reflected in the archaeological records of ancient societies besides that of the Maya, remains a problem in the present.

FOR FURTHER READING*

Tainter's *The Collapse of Complex Societies* and Yoffee and Cowgill's *The Collapse of Ancient States and Civilizations* are general treatments. The Maya are the focus of Abrams and Rue's "The Causes and Consequences of Deforestation Among the Prehistoric Maya," Sabloff and Andrews's *Late Lowland Maya Civilization,* and Culbert's *The Classic Maya Collapse*.

*Full citations appear in the bibliography.

CHAPTER SIXTEEN

EXPLANATION AND ARCHAEOLOGY

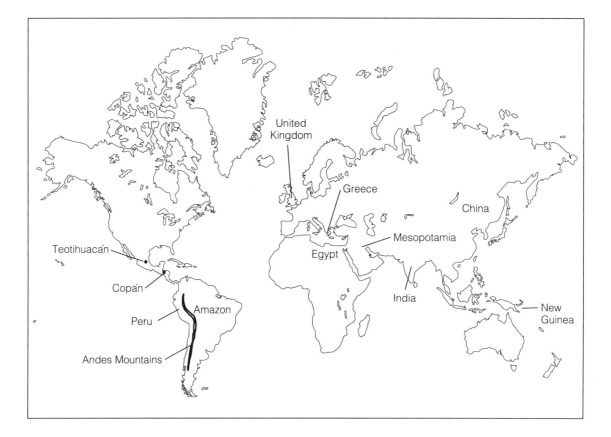

This chapter reviews the basic explanatory process of scientific archaeology and examines a set of hypothetical models often used as provisional explanations for the evolution of states and civilizations. The chapter concludes with a short overview of prospects for the future.

As we saw in Chapters 3 and 4, archaeologists must answer several basic questions from the material (and occasionally historical) residues of the past:

1. What kinds of patterns are there in the archaeological record, and how can these be linked to patterns of behavior?

2. Where and when did these patterns occur?

3. Why did the cultural behavior occur?

The ability to apply increasingly sophisticated methods, techniques, and research designs on a large scale enables us to answer the first two questions with some certainty and agreement. The last question is by far the most difficult but also the most important from a scientific perspective (Fritz and Plog 1970; Salmon 1975, 1976, 1978), because it involves explanation. Remember that explanation in archaeology occurs on two levels: *what* behavior was responsible for patterns in the archaeological record and *why* such behavior took place.

"Why" questions may focus on relatively small problems (such as why different kinds of artifacts are consistently associated with one another) or on more ambitious ones, such as why Maya civilization collapsed or why stratification independently developed in many cultures. "Why" is also the most controversial level of interpretation, because the same data may call forth different interpretations. In any science, and particularly in archaeology, there are usually competing explanations. Most archaeologists are likely to agree about the basic descriptive outlines of the early culture history of Old World and New World civilizations presented in Chapters 13 and 14. They do not necessarily agree about why political centralization occurred, why cities appeared, or why Classic Maya society collapsed.

Scientific explanation links specific observations about the world with general propositions about how the world works. The theoretical framework used in this book is that of evolution and, more specifically, cultural evolution. In Chapter 15 we saw how a particular research project generated an explanation of a significant evolutionary problem—the collapse of a regional Maya polity. Now we will take these issues further and review a number of basic explanations that have been proposed for the evolution of the early civilizations reviewed in Chapters 13 and 14.

Evolutionary explanations must function on two levels. On the level of specific evolution we must try to explain why particular changes occurred in particular cultural sequences—for example, why did kings appear in Egypt? On the level of general evolution we must try to explain why there are recurrent, independent, patterns of change—for example, why did powerful rulers appear in both Egyptian and Aztec society? Put another way, how do basic processes such as political centralization, agricultural intensification, or social stratification operate to produce both the unique characteristics of particular cultures and the general similarities revealed by a comparative view?

Many archaeologists prefer not to generalize, believing that the unique aspects of each cultural sequence should be analyzed and explained in their own terms; they confine themselves to issues of specific evolution or culture change, often identifying themselves as culture historians. One might object that Egyptian rulers, after all, were different in so many respects from Aztec rulers that comparisons between the two would be misleading. This is a legitimate concern, and the culture-historical approach has long been part of archaeology, yielding many insights about the past. But cross-cultural comparisons, carefully made, are essential to scientific, anthropological archaeology, which ultimately must concern itself with explanation. Enough regular patterns have been found on the level of general evolution to warrant attempts at general explanation. For example, in a classic comparative study of Mesoamerican and Mesopotamian civilizations, Robert M. Adams concluded that

> the parallels in the Mesopotamian and Mesoamerican "careers to statehood", in the forms that institutions ultimately assumed as well as the processes leading to them, suggest that both instances are most significantly characterized by a common core of regularly occurring features.
>
> *(Adams 1966:174–175)*

Most of what passes for high-level explanations in archaeology consists in fact of provisional explanatory models that have not been sufficiently tested so they have not produced consensus. But many archaeologists agree with the basic components of the explanations presented below, and much current work is being done, as we shall see, to test and refine them.

EXPLANATORY MODELS FOR THE EVOLUTION OF COMPLEX SCIENCE

The major classes of explanation reviewed below emphasize population, warfare, exchange and trade, technology, information and ideology, and systemic interactions with the environment.

Population Explanations

Population change is often cited as a causal factor in cultural evolution. Population growth, for example, has been noted as a feature of the origins of early states, and demographic shifts have been related to other major evolutionary trends as well, including the origins and spread of agriculture (Coale 1971; Cohen 1977; Dumond 1965; Hassan 1974, 1981). How do such changes stimulate the emergence of new cultural patterns?

Malthus   Modern interest in the relationship between cultural patterns and population size and density goes back at least to Thomas Malthus, who in 1798 published an influential analysis of the issue. As we saw in Chapter 2, Malthus's ideas significantly influenced Darwin's evolutionary thought.

Malthus began with the observation that humans, like other organisms, can increase their numbers very rapidly under optimal conditions. He further observed that the capacity to increase the food supply cannot keep up with this reproductive potential (except in unusual circumstances and for short periods of time). Various cultural or natural checks (e.g., famine, disease, war, infanticide, contraception, celibacy, and late marriage) curb population growth either by increasing mortality and/or lowering birth rates (Fig. 16.1). Technological innovations or new crops periodically increase agricultural production and carrying capacity, allowing more population growth up to a new, higher threshold. In Malthus's model, technological innovation (or, less often, the introduction of new crops, or opportunities to colonize vacant landscape) is what allows population growth.

Malthus concluded that because reproductive potential will generally outstrip expansion of the food supply, the various cultural and natural checks on population growth will strongly determine many cultural patterns, including social and political stratification, economic institutions, and social mobility. His theory is often called the "dismal theory" because he asserted a basic biological flaw in the perfectability of human society, an issue very much on the minds of his contemporaries.

Since Malthus's time the world's population has exploded, but so far food supplies have been generally sufficient to support the increase. These two facts are the core of the current debate among archaeologists about the role of population in cultural evolution. One group argues that the relationship of population to resources (including nonfood resources) strongly determines the nature and evolution of cultural systems, because human fertility is only weakly constrained and many essential resources are limited. An opposite view holds that humans have effective control over their own reproduction, that populations are nicely adjusted to their natural and cultural environments, or that they adapt quickly and successfully to resource shortages. We can try to sort out these cause-and-effect relationships by looking at an ethnographic study of population growth and agricultural intensification.

Boserup   The economist Ester Boserup (1965) studied changes in Asian agricultural systems. Boserup maintains that increasing population density itself stimulates innovations, which then allow further population increases. She also believes that agricultural intensification or innovation results in a greater output than Malthus envisioned and that sociocultural systems are more dynamic than Malthus believed.

As long as the challenge of increasing numbers can be readily met with

FIGURE 16.1 Malthus realized that there was a connection between rates of population growth and social institutions. These population pyramids show the percentage of the total population represented by each age cohort. In the United States (middle) and United Kingdom (bottom) there are high proportions of adults to children, indicating that the population is growing comparatively slowly. Contrast this with India (top), whose pyramid has a very wide base, indicating that there are many children and young people and that rapid population growth will continue.

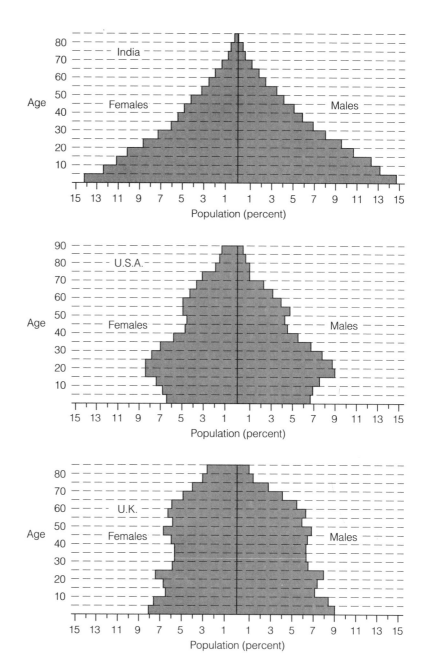

the response of increased productivity, there is little reason for fundamental cultural change. "Population pressure" occurs when it becomes difficult to maintain an adequate food supply, and it is often cited as an important source of evolution, since imbalances (stresses) in the relationships between people and their resources stimulate selection for new cultural behaviors that reduce stress. For example, the naturally humid soils on the floor of a Peruvian coastal valley, which contrast with the surrounding desert environment, would have attracted early agriculturalists. With little effort these soils produced ample crops, but their extent was limited. If local population rose so that naturally humid land was insufficient to support people, these areas could be extended by irrigation, thus creating more fields. As irrigation systems increased in size, they would need to be properly managed, whereupon some individuals would assume managerial roles, giving them greater access to resources and the power to decide who gets access to them. Such a process would be heavily determined by population pressure, in this case caused by population growth.

Closely related to population pressure is the concept of carrying capacity. Some archaeologists argue that since humans innovate to increase productivity and hence population size, carrying capacity is not a useful concept. Obviously population pressure and carrying capacity are not absolute values where humans are concerned but are dynamic. Carrying capacity increases because of innovation. Innovation is often inspired by population pressure, as Boserup maintains, and we can recover archaeological indications of it (e.g., the colonization of the inhospitable land of Sumer by people from the better-watered Mesopotamian uplands reviewed in Chapter 13). Population pressure is often assumed to require population growth, but this is not necessarily the case. A population may be stable, or even declining, and still be under stress (the latter was probably the case with the Copán Maya after A.D. 800 — see Chapter 14). What matters is whether the perception or fact of resource limitation affects people and their cultural behavior.

Population Growth Arguments Some demographic models focus on effects of population growth and are only indirectly related to population pressure. Many anthropologists, for example, Robert Netting (1972), have noted that there is a general direct relationship between the size and density of social groups and the complexity of their institutions. As numbers of people in a social system increase, individuals tend to be more distantly related to one another and their interactions become more impersonal. At the same time, the possibility of disputes rises because there are more people. To resolve disputes, new statuses may emerge, or old statuses of leadership may take on new dispute-resolving functions, thus reducing the stress of intragroup conflict. Such explanations constitute one class of what are sometimes called **conflict theories**.

Management: The Hydraulic Theory of Karl Wittfogel Agricultural intensification often takes place on a small scale, instituted by individual farmers. But in some cases the innovations require management at a higher organizational level, and this in itself promotes greater sociopolitical complexity. One of the earliest general managerial explanations of cultural

conflict theories Theories that trace the origin of the state to warfare or intragroup conflicts.

oriental despotism
Kind of government in which autocratic power was monopolized by a centralized ruler and bureaucracy. No other institutions existed that could politically challenge the central apparatus of the state.

evolution was the hydraulic theory of the historian Karl Wittfogel, summarized in his book *Oriental Despotism* (1957; see also Downing and Gibson 1974; Millon 1962; Steward 1949). By **oriental despotism,** Wittfogel meant a kind of government in which autocratic power was monopolized by a centralized ruler and bureaucracy. No other institutions existed that could politically challenge the central apparatus of the state. Such despotism was thought to be particularly characteristic of traditional states in regions such as China, India, and Egypt. The explanation for this recurring political type, Wittfogel believed, lay in one form of intensive agriculture: canal irrigation. In arid or semiarid regions, only irrigation agriculture could support large, dense populations. The one essential agricultural resource that could be effectively manipulated by humans was water.

Wittfogel hypothesized that large canal irrigation systems required a managerial elite to plan them, organize their construction, provide for their maintenance, and resolve conflicts over water use. In systemic terms, there was a positive feedback relationship between the emergence of rulers and bureaucracies (political centralization) and the growth of irrigation systems (Fig. 16.2). Control of water rendered governments extremely powerful and despotic. Although Wittfogel's scheme depends on a particular kind of agricultural technology (irrigation), its primary implications are organizational. Its does not logically apply to all types of agricultural intensification systems. For example, in some parts of the New Guinea highlands, drained fields separated by water-filled ditches are constructed. These are small in scale, simple to build, require only household labor, and do not move water as a scarce resource from one place to another (rainfall is high). That such fields are built by egalitarian people is not at all inconsistent with the hydraulic hypothesis.

As originally expressed, Wittfogel's hydraulic hypothesis strongly favored cultural materialism and evolutionism. It posited an explanatory link between environment, an essential technoeconomic feature (irrigation), and various cultural institutions, most notably centralized government. Stressing adaptation, the hypothesis offered an explanation for why similar forms (strongly centralized political systems) could independently develop in specific evolutionary sequences. Julian Steward, among others, used the idea of irrigation society to show how specific evolutionary sequences could develop in very similar ways, thus demonstrating that there were cross-culturally valid regularities in cultural evolution.

But Wittfogel's hypothesis has not fared well for a number of reasons. As originally conceived, the hydraulic argument had mainly multilinear evolutionary implications. It was useful for showing how certain kinds of states (despotic) emerged as opposed to others (nondespotic states), and why there could even be variation among irrigation-based states. Unfortunately, Wittfogel (and to some extent Steward) made the mistake of twisting a former multilinear argument into a unilinear one. The argument

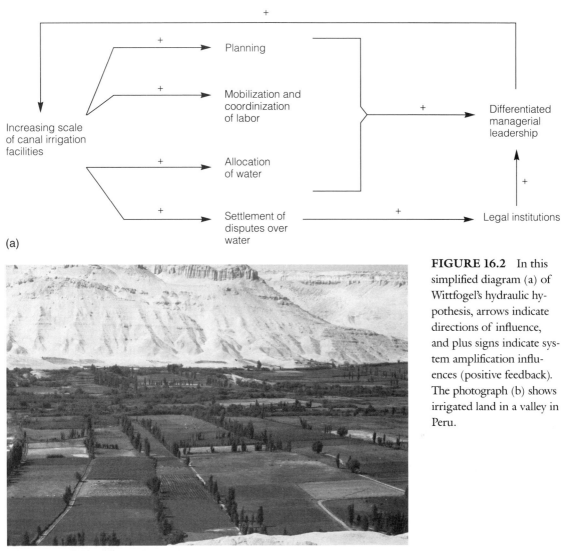

FIGURE 16.2 In this simplified diagram (a) of Wittfogel's hydraulic hypothesis, arrows indicate directions of influence, and plus signs indicate system amplification influences (positive feedback). The photograph (b) shows irrigated land in a valley in Peru.

implied that all states derived from irrigation-based despotic states through a process of influence or diffusion.

Furthermore, much evidence seemed to contradict the hydraulic hypothesis. Many early states developed in regions where irrigation, or at least large-scale canal irrigation, was unknown, so Wittfogel's hypothesis did not have the general application he envisioned. Also, archaeological evidence on the emergence of early states was very poor in 1958, so it was difficult to evaluate the hydraulic hypothesis. Since then, archaeologists such as

Robert M. Adams have asserted, on the basis of field research, that the relationship between political centralization and irrigation is not as direct as Wittfogel claimed.

Finally, Wittfogel emphasized managerial roles at the expense of other aspects of irrigation systems that could have promoted stratification or political centralization. For example, differential access to irrigated versus nonirrigated land (a possible pattern in the Teotihuacán Valley) might have strongly stimulated stratification, an important feature of states. Managerial roles that emerged in conjunction with irrigation may have had their greatest evolutionary effects in other ways, such as organization for warfare.

Despite all these criticisms, the central idea raised by Wittfogel remains a valid hypothetical explanation for the evolution of social complexity if we restate it as follows: *Some systems of agricultural intensification (including irrigation) select for specialized managerial features that, in turn, intensify the process of stratification or political centralization.* To the extent that agricultural intensification is caused by population pressure, the larger model is related to those of Malthus and Boserup and is a hypothesis that stresses population pressure.

Warfare

Warfare is unfortunately an all-too-common form of cultural behavior, which appears to be frequently, or even universally, associated with the emergence of early civilizations, as we saw in Chapters 13 and 14. It has long been emphasized by historians and social philosophers as an important factor in cultural evolution, especially because centralized control of coercive force is often seen as a defining characteristic of the state (Ferguson 1984; Haas 1990).

The anthropologist Robert Carneiro (1970) proposed a strong relationship between warfare, as a form of human competition, and the origin of the state. This is another kind of conflict theory. Carneiro believes that the emergence of states involves the welding together of previously autonomous political groups and that this process never takes place voluntarily but only coercively. Warfare provides the basic coercive mechanism of his model. Warfare (no matter what the cause) between politically autonomous groups produces winners and losers once it escalates to a certain point. Because losers wish to avoid destruction or political domination, one response (often noted by ethnographers studying warfare) is to flee. As long as this option is open, warfare has few evolutionary effects. In some geographical circumstances, however, flight may be impossible (e.g., a small island). Carneiro calls this situation **environmental circumscription**. Even when the landscape is not physically limited, limitations on movement may be imposed by other populations. Carneiro calls this **social circumscription**.

Where warfare occurs under conditions of either kind of circumscription, victorious groups subordinate losers, creating political and economic

environmental circumscription Geographical restrictions on the movement of groups.

social circumscription Social restrictions (e.g., the presence of other societies) on the movement of groups.

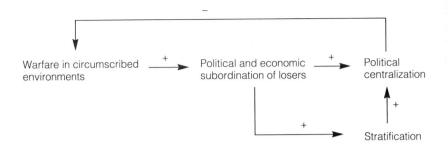

FIGURE 16.3 Simplified diagram of Carneiro's warfare hypothesis. Plus signs indicate system amplification influences (positive feedback).

stratification and new forms of political centralization (Fig. 16.3). Presumably such a process serves to reduce the incidence of warfare, at least locally, although Carneiro's theory does not emphasize this point.

One of the useful things about Carneiro's theory is that it suggests why the tempo of evolution might vary. This is ultimately a more important insight than his rather typological approach of defining circumscribed versus uncircumscribed environments. Any environment, regardless of its scale, will eventually become circumscribed in some sense if population growth continues long enough. State-type institutions should emerge faster (i.e., the mechanism of warfare should work faster) in small-scale Peruvian coastal valleys than in the extensive Amazon Basin, because the Peruvian valleys are much smaller, and more circumscribed. In fact, states formed early on the coast of Peru but never appeared in the Amazon Basin.

Another implication relates to agricultural intensification. If warfare is caused by population pressure, victors may use the labor of subordinated groups to create new, or more extensive, systems of intensive agriculture. The great expansion of the chinampa zone south of the Aztec capital was a state project, made possible in large part by the labor of people recently absorbed into the Aztec empire.

Warfare may stimulate political complexity in other ways not emphasized by Carneiro. Successful war leaders, for example, are in a position to build up their own wealth and to reward followers, thus augmenting personal political support (Webster 1975). Such a process can create new institutions based more on patronage than kinship, one of the trends associated with the origin of the state.

Exchange and Trade

Elaboration of exchange and trade is, as we saw in Chapters 12 and 13, characteristic of emergent civilizations (Polanyi 1957). Some, such as ancient Sumer, developed in regions that lacked necessary or desirable resources of many kinds. Archaeological explanations often single out exchange and trade as causal factors in the origins of hierarchical societies.

In one early model, Service (1971) postulated that emergent chiefs functioned as centralized nodes of redistribution. People living in different local environments produced different kinds of staple products. These flowed into the chief's household, from which they were redistributed to provide everyone with products of all zones. More recent examinations of ethnographically observed chiefdoms suggest that redistribution of staple products was not as important as Service thought, although gifts of luxury items helped cement relationships between powerful leaders.

economic symbiosis
Economic interdependence of population units in a region for the good of all.

A more elaborate version of the exchange explanation argument stresses regional **economic symbiosis** as an important factor in the growth of the state. By symbiosis is meant the economic interdependence of population units in a region for the good of all. Increasing interdependence eventually selects for new managerial roles and institutions and stimulates political centralization and specialization.

William Rathje (1971) constructed a specific exchange model for the emergence of Maya civilization. The earliest centers manifesting the Classic Great Tradition elements appeared in the southern Maya lowlands. This region lacked certain commodities that Rathje identified as essential, or at least highly desirable: salt, obsidian, and hard stone for manufacturing grinding implements. He reasoned that the core zone acquired these commodities from peripheral Maya populations in exchange for various finished products or elite/ceremonial items. Maya rulers promoted themselves by managing such exchange.

Although Rathje's model has not held up well in the face of archaeological evidence, it does serve to remind us that exchange explanations must be tailored to specific evolutionary sequences and that they must be testable. Similar models of economic interaction have been developed for Mesoamerica (Sanders and Price 1968) and Mesopotamia (Wright 1972; Wright and Johnson 1975).

Technological Explanations

Technological innovation may or may not be closely associated with the emergence of early civilizations (see Chapter 13). Where such innovations do occur, they have frequently been singled out as explanations. Gordon Childe (1950, 1951a) emphasized the role of irrigation, as a particular form of technology, in the production of agricultural surpluses. Focusing on urban civilization in Mesopotamia, he postulated that such surpluses enabled growing numbers of economic specialists to congregate in towns and cities. These, in turn, were supplied with food and other raw materials by wheeled vehicles and by ships plying irrigation canals as transport routes. Of particular technological importance was metallurgy, a highly developed craft that stimulated trade and commerce, since the raw materials had to be acquired from considerable distances.

Although we mainly associate changes in technology with transformations of the material subsystems of culture, there may be other effects as well. For example, throughout much of the Old World bronze became a strategic military material. Because of its expense, only wealthy people could own arms and armor. In some societies, such as Bronze Age Greece, a warrior elite armed with superior bronze weaponry was politically dominant.

Information Systems Explanations

All of the foregoing explanations for the evolution of complex societies focus on particular aspects of culture, such as irrigation, warfare, or population growth. A number of archaeologists, stimulated by the concepts developed to characterize living systems of all kinds, have taken a more abstract approach. The basic idea is that living systems require exchanges of matter, energy, and information between their parts. Exchanges of matter and energy have long been fundamental to an ecological understanding of culture. Information flow and decision making have been accorded less study. Some evolutionary transformations in complex cultural systems may be best understood by the informational demands of the system rather than those related directly to energy and matter.

Kent Flannery argues that "in an ecosystem approach to the analysis of human societies, everything which transmits information is within the province of ecology" (1972:400). Such an expanded ecosystem approach incorporates superstructural elements of culture such as art, religion, ritual, and writing, since these may be essential in encoding, transmitting, and regulating information, and legitimizing new hierarchical institutions.

Flannery distinguishes three levels of systemic phenomena:

1. Level 1: *Socio-environmental conditions*. The first level includes population growth, warfare, circumscription, irrigation, economic symbiosis, and trade. Few, if any, of these conditions are found universally, and when they are present, they exhibit a great local variation.

2. Level 2: *Mechanisms*. Unlike socioenvironmental conditions, the mechanisms of **promotion** and **linearization** are universal, in the sense that they are properties of all evolving sociocultural systems. By promotion, Flannery means that an institution can rise to a higher level in the hierarchy of information control systems, often taking on more general functions in the process. For example, a person who formerly had a purely religious function might take on the more general responsibility of arbitrating disputes for the community or society as a whole.

By linearization, Flannery means that a high-level part of a system steps in to control the system when lower-level parts have failed to do so, thus bypassing them. Suppose that local community leaders have traditionally settled disputes over irrigation rights but that conflicts became so intense that they can no longer be resolved on the community level. A solution is for the central government to permanently intervene as a higher-level decision maker. This is linearization. When modern

promotion Elevation of an office or institution to higher levels in the hierarchy of information control systems, where it can regulate more of the system and have more general functions than it did previously.

linearization Simplification of hierarchy of regulation in a system, permitting a high-level part of a system to bypass controls at lower levels.

pathology Condition in which one part of a system inefficiently usurps, or meddles with, another part, thus creating stress or disequilibrium.

governments declare martial law, they bypass local police or legal institutions, an example of the same mechanism that is familiar to all of us.

Both promotion and linearization are adaptations to stress. Flannery also identifies **pathologies** that affect systems, such as when one part of a system inefficiently usurps, or meddles with, another part. Such pathologies create stress; thus they may themselves stimulate promotion and linearization.

3. Level 3: *Processes*. We already introduced Flannery's processes, segregation and centralization (cf. Chapter 10). Segregation refers to the degree of differentiation or specialization of parts of a system. An example would be the creation of new, diverse, highly specialized bureaucratic offices as government grows in complexity. Centralization is the degree to which the highest-order parts of a hierarchical system are linked to the lower-level parts. In the case of the irrigation system discussed above, the government appropriates decision-making functions formerly in the hands of lower-level community leaders. Thus decision making becomes more centralized.

Flannery combines these three levels into an explanatory model whereby socioenvironmental stresses select for mechanisms, which then affect the evolutionary processes. Flannery's model is characterized by feedback relationships between its parts, particularly those which receive and evaluate messages and make decisions (regulators). Feedback may be negative, in the sense that centralization and segregation buffer stress, as shown in Figure 16.4. In some situations feedback might be positive as well. Increasing political centralization allows the mobilization of greater amounts of labor. This labor can be used to further enlarge irrigation systems, which in turn selects for more effective management mechanisms and hence more political centralization.

Although he emphasizes the ways in which parts of systems act for the well-being of the whole (by keeping the system operating within tolerable limits), Flannery notes that self-serving behavior becomes increasingly frequent as evolution occurs. This happens because with more segregation, the interests of particular, high-status individuals or subgroups diverge more and more from those of the population as a whole. Such individuals or subgroups use their control over regulatory statuses and information to advantage themselves at the expense of others, thus producing new stresses.

Flannery's explanatory model reminds us that there are many causes for a complex process such as the origin of the state and for the feedback relationships among these causes. It forces us to think of causation on different levels and provides well-defined concepts for doing so, particularly concepts that describe the workings of living systems in general. Granted that there is feedback, is new information more likely to be generated on the level of socioenvironmental stresses or on the levels of mechanisms or processes? From our materialistic perspective, we lend more weight to socioenvironmental conditions. These are what vary and what must be

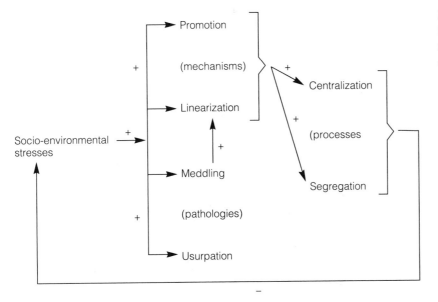

FIGURE 16.4 Simplified diagram of Flannery's evolutionary model based on information flow.

investigated to see how they affect the universal mechanisms and processes (Sanders and Webster 1978).

Superstructural Explanations

Few questions provoke as much controversy as the relationship between the evolution of complex societies and the superstructural elements of culture (ideology and its manifestations in art, religion, ritual, and writing). This is especially true today as mentalist and idealist perspectives become more popular. Much of the traditional anthropological literature addresses this issue in a general sense (e.g., Kroeber 1957; Willey 1962). More recently, Flannery's information system model was an attempt to show how superstructural elements could be integrated into a larger causal framework. He is perfectly correct in stating that "the critical contribution of state religions and state art styles is to legitimize that hierarchy, to confirm the divine affiliation of those at the top by inducing religious experiences" (1972:407). Put another way, a major function of ideology, religion, ritual, and art, is to create a consensus about what is sacred and hence unquestioned (or, more cynically, what leaders would like to be sacred and unquestioned). By legitimizing the control hierarchy of systems, these aspects of culture thus play essential roles in regulation. The Great Traditions characteristic of civilizations that have matured over long periods of time are, seen in this way, manifestations of hierarchical control.

Many anthropologists have included superstructural elements in their analyses of how cultural systems function and change. Rappaport (1971a,

1971b, 1971c) has explored the role of ideological factors, most important, those reflected in ritual, in regulating human systems. Although he correlates various changes in ritual and ideology with evolutionary change, Rappaport's main emphasis is on the conservative, system-maintaining role of ritual regulation rather than its system-changing implications. Robert Netting (1972) has argued that the stresses for political centralization often promote individuals with sacred authority to new positions of leadership. He sees such promotion, however, as driven by the stress of population pressure, so this is not basically a superstructural argument. Mary Helms (1979) shows that an important factor in promotion and legitimization of Panamanian chiefs is privileged access to esoteric information and associated status items.

That ideology, art, or ritual contribute to cultural evolution is not disputable. What is disputable is whether they explain as much as the socio-environmental conditions and whether their influences can be detected and measured. The challenge to those who favor ideological or mentalist explanations of cultural evolution is to develop testable models in which superstructural factors can be shown to promote change more powerfully than infrastructural or structural factors.

Prime Movers versus Multiple Factors

Archaeologists frequently break up explanations focusing on irrigation, warfare, and exchange into the categories of *managerial theories* (Wittfogel, Rathje) and *conflict theories* (Carneiro). Unfortunately, this classification implies a spurious simplicity. Although each of the theories outlined above emphasizes a particular aspect of cultural behavior, each also depends on a complex interplay of many factors. For example, irrigation may stimulate the development of new managerial roles, but it also produces a subgroup of people with inordinate access to wealth, new pretexts for warfare (appropriation of the irrigation systems of others), and thus greater potential for self-serving behavior. Warfare may indeed produce stratification, but it also produces new economic relationships and new managerial roles.

prime mover The causal variable in a simple, direct, and inevitable relationship, resulting in a particular effect.

Explanations such as those of Wittfogel or Carneiro are sometimes characterized as **prime mover** approaches to cultural evolution. Unfortunately, this term implies a simple, direct, and invariable relationship between two things or that a particular cause has a universal effect. In a prime mover perspective, Carneiro, for example, would seem to postulate that there is always warfare and that whenever it occurs in a circumscribed environment, the institutions of the state appear. A similar perspective would be that wherever certain thresholds of population size and density are reached by agriculturalists, the institutions of the state inevitably emerge. We know of no archaeologist who takes such an oversimplified position. Many of the proposed causes (e.g., irrigation) are not found everywhere. More important, ethnographic studies show that no simple set of relationships exists between evolutionary causes and effects. For example, warfare was intense in many parts of the highlands of New Guinea until a few decades ago, particularly in regions where population densities were high (100–200 people per km²). While these concentrations of people stimulated many small-scale evolutionary effects (e.g., particularly intensive forms of agriculture, warfare, and complex relationships among big-men), political organization remained essentially egalitarian.

Clearly our explanations operate only under certain sets of conditions, and our job as archaeologists is to specify what those conditions are. From the ecological perspective, the most fruitful source of explanations is the relationship of particular cultures to their environments, since these vary greatly. Population growth in New Guinea took place within environmental settings with little variation in agricultural productivity and plenty of rainfall. The Teotihuacán Valley, by contrast, is a highly varied agricultural environment where low rainfall creates considerable agricultural risk and differential productivity. Population growth in two such contrasting regions may have very different evolutionary consequences. This is a plausible hypothesis about why New Guinea retained egalitarian organization, whereas economic stratification and political centralization were stimulated at Teotihuacán.

While it would be unfair and incorrect to attribute a prime mover perspective to any of the theorists cited above, each has tried to single out one or two factors of particular explanatory importance. Any explanation of a process as complex as state formation must include many interacting factors, but it does not follow that each has the same significance. The idea that, because many causes contribute to a particular effect, they all operate at the same intensity is fallacious. Neither Wittfogel nor Carneiro would deny that exchange can contribute to the emergence of stratification, but would only assert that it does not act as powerfully to stimulate centralization and stratification as does irrigation or warfare.

Systems-Ecological Explanatory Models

The explanatory models diagramed above are general evolutionary explanations in that they should operate universally (Malthus, Boserup, Flannery) or very broadly (Wittfogel, Carneiro). Elements of all these explanations may be assembled into larger, multivariant models that refer to specific evolutionary situations. Redman (1978) calls these "systems-ecological models." Such models can be expressed as flow charts. Helping us to envision larger sets of relationships between many factors, these models force us to think about what factors must be included in the first place, how they work as systems, and the relative importance of each. Most important, they provide clues about how to design research and test various explanatory components. Figure 16.5 shows a model constructed by Redman for the emergence of civilization in Mesopotamia. This model emphasizes change, or positive feedback relationships, and is mainly intended to show how rapid transformations could take place in a system until new constraints produced new conditions of stability. Note that it has many components such as irrigation and warfare but also that it closely

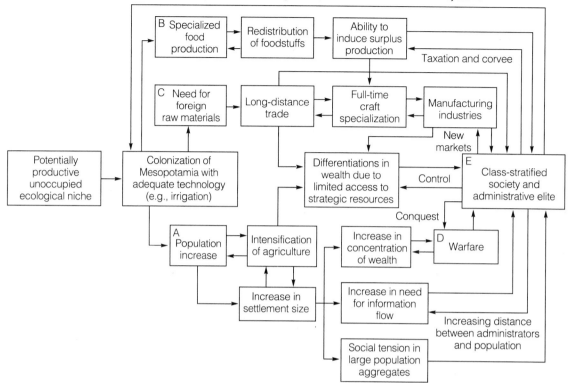

Expansion in new regions and extension of water control systems

FIGURE 16.5 Systems-ecological explanatory model for the evolution of civilization in Mesopotamia.

follows the logic of Flannery's information model. Certain components, such as irrigation, are particularly crucial to the evolving Mesopotamian system. Note also how richly interconnected the parts of the model are. Connections are not merely linear but mutually reinforcing. For example, population growth causes increases in settlement size, which in turn causes intensification of agriculture, which stimulates more population increase and still larger settlements. Similarly, concentrations of wealth stimulate warfare, which in turn stimulates more concentrations of wealth.

This model could be made more complex in many ways. We could add more feedback loops — increase in the size of settlements was undoubtedly stimulated by warfare. We could go further and add more components to it. Another way of altering the model would be to make parts of it more detailed or specific. For example, some specific technological developments singled out by Childe, such as bronze metallurgy or wheeled vehicles, are subsumed in such components as "full-time craft specialization" and "manufacturing industries." These could be added in more explicit fashion, thus revealing their own particular relationships with other variables, such as warfare or increases in wealth.

A Systems-Ecological Model for the Maya Figure 16.6 shows a model for the evolution of Maya civilization. Although there are many similarities

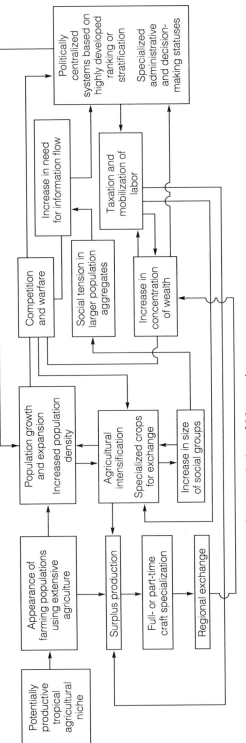

FIGURE 16.6 Systems-ecological model for the evolution of Maya society.

between it and Redman's, there are important dissimilarities as well. For one thing, the original environmental settings are different. Agricultural intensification in the form of a particular technology—canal irrigation—is necessary very early in arid Mesopotamia. By contrast, canal irrigation is absent in the Maya lowlands. Various forms of intensification do occur but do not involve great technological change. Need for foreign raw materials is absent or minimal in the Maya case. The outcome of the Maya model is also different, in that the presence of well-developed stratification is not as clear.

Another difference lies in the explanatory weight of the variables included in the model. Although intensive agriculture is found in both, it undoubtedly played a far greater role in Mesopotamia than in the Maya lowlands. Similarly, warfare appears to have had larger systemic effects in the evolution of Mesopotamian civilization than it did for the Maya. Similar models could be presented for the origins of other early civilizations in China, India, Egypt, or the Central Andes, but these two suffice to demonstrate how they are structured.

Using Systems-Ecological Models   The way in which one devises a model explanation depends on the issues one wishes to investigate. Redman's model is qualitative rather than quantitative, in the sense that no measures are used to determine the intensities of the various influences or to try to show which have the most effect. His main purpose is to make us think about how systems work and to present, in a descriptive sense, ideas about what might explain the evolution of Mesopotamian civilization. In order to be even more useful, model explanations must involve at least partial quantification, so their components must be chosen with the possibility of measurement in mind. Most of the variables Redman has chosen are at least theoretically quantifiable, assuming that we had enough information. Some, such as "social tension in large population aggregates" could probably never be quantified.

It is currently very difficult to quantify a process as complex and poorly understood as the rise of civilization in Mesopotamia or the Maya lowlands. A more workable research approach is to single out restricted sets of variables, such as the relationship between population increase and agricultural intensification, and try to adequately measure these. With enough research, we can eventually build up quantitative measures of many variables (Box 16.1). We saw that for the Copán Maya it is possible to quantify population trends through time, the rough carrying capacity of the valley, occupation spans of sites, rates of decline of crop yields due to agricultural intensification, and many other variables.

Discussion

All of the foregoing explanations are evolutionary in the sense that they identify stresses in cultural systems that select for specific kinds of innova-

BOX 16.1

WHAT DO QUANTITATIVE MODELS REVEAL ABOUT THE PAST? MODELING NEW WORLD ANIMAL EXTINCTIONS

When Europeans brought the horse to the New World in the 16th century they were actually reintroducing this animal to the Americas. The horse and other large animals such as mammoths and mastodons became extinct in the Americas at the end of the Pleistocene, the last Ice Age, about 10,000 to 12,000 years ago, but we still do not know why these extinctions happened. Did environments change so rapidly that species were unable to adapt? Or did New World peoples hunt these species to extinction, an idea called the "overkill hypothesis," inspired by the discovery that these extinctions roughly coincided with the first occurrence of abundant evidence of hunting peoples in North America.

However, this evidence has not been sufficient to test the overkill hypothesis directly. Mosimann and Martin (1975) proposed an alternative means of assessing the hypothesis's strength. They devised a complex simulation of the interaction between hunting peoples and the animals they hunted. This model assumed that hunting peoples colonized North America as a front (not unlike a weather front) or wave, radiating out from a point in what is now southern Canada and rapidly exterminating the animals in their path, many of them never before preyed upon by humans.

Further assumptions included a point of departure, rapid human population growth, heavy reliance on meat in the diet, ability to kill animals effectively, and the availability of large populations of animals. Mosimann and Martin made their model operative by assigning hypothetical numerical values to these components—thereby quantifying them. For example, the original population numbered 100 hunters of both sexes, beginning 11,500 years ago and doubling in population size every 30 years. The model called for 75 million "animal units" (individuals of various prey species), each 450 or 1,000 kg in weight, and consumed by humans at a rate of 7–13 animal units per person per year.

These and other quantified variables were the raw data for a computer simulation that plotted changes in the size of human and animal populations over time and over the geographical space of North America. Mosimann and Martin plugged in different values to see their effects, but most of the simulations resulted in rapid extinction of animals, within a few hundred years. They concluded that the overkill hypothesis is plausible but pointed out that such simulations do not prove anything about the past. Rather, simulations are experiments in model building that can lead to more effective, testable hypotheses, which in turn can test the model. For example, if we recovered evidence that large numbers of people inhabited North America far earlier than Mosimann and Martin had assumed, then the model of extinction would be seriously undermined. Although many archaeologists disagree with Mosimann and Martin's conclusions, their simulation was an excellent scientific exercise notable for its use of quantification.

tion and change. Although there is no overall agreement about any particular explanation or set of explanations concerning the evolution of complex societies, much progress has been made. Archaeological thinking about alternative explanations is much more sophisticated than it was 30 years ago. Arguments tend to focus less on whether a particular factor—warfare or irrigation—should be included in an model explanation, and more on how a factor stimulated evolutionary change. Much of this refinement derives from fieldwork, which has provided a wealth of new data.

A pertinent example is the research of Robert M. Adams in Mesopotamia, where the first urban civilizations appeared. In his original comparative work on Mesopotamian and Mesoamerican civilization, Adams asserted that in both regions (based on admittedly poor information), "appreciable population increases generally followed, rather than preceded, the core processes of the Urban Revolution. Particularly in Mesopotamia. . . . there is simply no evidence for gradual population increases that might have helped to precipitate the Urban Revolution after reaching some undefined threshold (1966:44–45). During the next few years, Adams carried out extensive settlement surveys in several regions of Mesopotamia. Principal goals of his research were to test both population and irrigation hypotheses concerning the evolution of the earliest Sumerian urban states. As we saw in Chapter 12, there turns out to be convincing evidence for considerable growth of population in southern Mesopotamia. One of Adams's main conclusions was that "reconnaissance findings in the Warka [Uruk] region and elsewhere prompt a reconsideration of the role of 'population pressure' as an important historical variable" (Adams and Nissen 1972:91). By the same time, other research showed that there were population increases associated with the emergence of states in Mesoamerica as well (Chapter 13). That Adams changed his perspective on this issue demonstrates one of the strengths of the scientific approach, rather than a weakness.

Many similar examples can be given. Few argue today that warfare was infrequent or insignificant among the Maya, that the statuses of powerful chiefs were heavily derived from the redistribution of essential foodstuffs, that diffusion explains the emergence of early states, or that surpluses automatically appear with agriculture, thus stimulating specialization and stratification. Such changes in our archaeological perceptions are not merely reflections of explanatory fashion. They represent, rather, things that we have found out about the world, and our views of the Sumerians or the Maya will never be the same again. However accurate our perspectives are now, they are demonstrably more accurate than they were before. The lesson is that our explanatory models about the origins of civilization and the state have proved testable. That they are insufficiently tested to provide all the answers, or to produce consensus, is less important than the fact that we have made notable progress in understanding the evolution of complex societies.

LESSONS FROM THE PAST,
PROSPECTS FOR THE FUTURE

We have come a long way since Stephens and Catherwood stood in the ruins of Copán. During its short lifespan, archaeology has made encouraging progress in reconstructing what happened in the past. It has also provided us with sets of explanations about what happened that are far more plausible and useful than those available in Stephens and Catherwood's time, or even a generation ago. Although we argue about specific interpretations and explanations, these arguments have become more focused and resolvable. All these things are measures of the steady maturation of the field as a whole. Symptomatic of archaeology's immaturity, as well as its diverse origins, are the hotly debated and highly diversified opinions about the value and usefulness of what we have accomplished to this point and what the goals of archaeology should be in the future.

What lies ahead for archaeology? Changes, certainly. Archaeology is a dynamic enterprise — it evolves, as did the ancient cultures it studies. Good ideas and data endure, and bad ideas and information eventually are discarded. As we saw in Chapter 2, the last major transformation in the field occurred with the emergence of processual archaeology in the 1960s. New technological innovations (e.g., chronometric dating), new methods (e.g., settlement system studies), and the adoption of new scientific/materialistic/ecological theoretical perspectives combined to reinvigorate a field formerly preoccupied by description, classification, and particularism. What fuels much of the current debate about the future of archaeology is the issue of how successful processual archaeology has been since the 1960s. On the one hand, there is no doubt that our general picture of the past is enormously more detailed and accurate than it used to be. On the other hand, some of our most important questions remain unanswered, many of our explanations are still highly provisional, and many important aspects of ancient cultures remain inadequately studied.

It is fitting, at the end of this book, to return to the theme of science. The mathemetician Jacob Bronowski (1978) draws a parallel between common sense and science as ways of knowing. Both, he observes, are based on observations of the world, and both are primarily concerned with helping us to order our empirical experiences in productive ways. Most important, both common sense propositions and scientific propositions are continually tested against the real world, and are accordingly changed and revised. In evolutionary terms, both are subject to selection. Neither deals with ultimate truth but rather with ideas and behaviors that work well enough to be useful in the short run. Commonsense explanations are those which we find effective in our ordinary, day-to-day lives. Similarly, "scientists are satisfied to consider as true either that which appears most probable on the basis of the available evidence, or that which is consistent with more, or more compelling, facts than competing hypotheses" (Mayr 1988:26).

As a way of knowing, science has several basic objectives: (1) Science seeks to organize knowledge in a systematic way, endeavoring to discover patterns of relationship among phenomena and processes. (2) Science strives to provide explanations for the occurrence of events. (3) Science proposes explanatory hypotheses that must be testable, that is, accessible to the possibility of rejection. More broadly, science attempts to subsume the vast diversity of the phenomena and processes of nature under a much smaller number of explanatory principles.

(Mayr 1988:23)

Many nonscientific fields share some of these objectives—for example, the observation and description of data, the organization of knowledge in systematic ways, and the quest for explanations. What distinguishes science is the search for generalizations and, perhaps most important, its insistence on gathering and describing data in rigorous ways, communicating information objectively, routinely detecting error, and awarding innovation.

Archaeologists frequently err in their interpretations. At Copán we were wrong about how large the population was and how it was distributed on the landscape. We were wrong about the labor investment necessary to build impressive monuments. We were wrong about how abruptly the collapse of the Copán polity occurred and how it affected kings, nobles, and commoners. But we would not know we had been wrong if we had not found out something new. Being wrong is part of the process of science. Beware the scientist who claims to be always right; this betrays either the lack of testable ideas or of active, productive research.

There is no hard-and-fast recipe for science, especially the kind practiced by archaeologists, but there are some commonsense rules. Start with a strong theoretical perspective. Decide which problems are most important and focus your research on them. Develop ideas (hypotheses) about the ways things would work in the real world if your theory is sound, and find ways to test them. Operate on as large a scale as possible, using as many different lines of research as you can. Look for independent lines of evidence that lead to the same conclusions; these are likely to be correct. Be skeptical. Criticize your own work as well as that of your colleagues, and expect criticism in return. Remember that the people you have to convince are the skeptics, not those who already share your views. Don't worry about being wrong, only about being wrong-headed. And never aspire to find the truth. The best you can do is eliminate old, false ideas and replace them with new ones that explain observations in more useful or convincing ways.

Because of their overt self-criticism, all scientific fields are dynamic. Thomas Kuhn (1970) proposed that scientific "revolutions" are characterized by sudden shifts in basic paradigms, an idea we explored in Chapter 2. This may be more true for some sciences than others. For example, it has been argued that modern biology, despite its many recent surprising discoveries, progresses more by the constant refinement of its basic concepts than by sudden, revolutionary paradigm shifts (Mayr 1988).

Whether there will be another shift in our archaeological perspectives comparable to that of the 1960s remains to be seen. Our own opinion is that continued progress in archaeological understanding is more likely to involve, as in biology, the slow accumulation of new information and gradual refinement of ideas. This process is what Kuhn calls "normal science" to distinguish it from the dramatic conceptual breakthroughs that introduce new paradigms.

Many kinds of archaeological research require years of normal science before there is any kind of payoff. One of the most powerful and informative methodological innovations, settlement system research, is a case in point. Wherever regional settlement studies have been completed, they have vastly improved our understanding of evolutionary processes (e.g., the work of R. M. Adams cited above). Despite the fact that this method has been available for a long time, its large-scale application is so slow and cumbersome that many regions have never been adequately surveyed, and modern development is rapidly altering what remains of the archaeological record. The point is that reconstructing and explaining something as complex as past cultural behavior requires much time and patience, even given the best of theories and methods. The lesson of the last 30 years is that patience is rewarded.

Postprocessual archaeologists have expressed disillusionment with processual archaeology, particularly with cultural materialism, because it does not explain everything. Of course, no one ever said it did. No single paradigm in any science can possibly explain all of our observations or render the world predictable in any ultimate sense. Those who seek alternatives to cultural materialism within a scientific framework have the obligation to provide competing paradigms that explain more about more important things. As Marvin Harris has observed, "We do not demean a theory by its failure to explain everything, but rather by its failure to explain as much as its nearest rivals" (1968:662).

An often-voiced criticism of scientific archaeology is that it (and science in general) is culture-bound, as are other worldviews. On one level this is perfectly correct. Individual scientists, whether physicists, biologists, or archaeologists, are conditioned by their cultural experiences, and inevitably their conduct of science is biased by such experiences. But on another level, science provides a worldview of a unique and revolutionary kind, precisely because it encourages empiricism, skepticism, self-correction, objective communication, and generalization. As a result, the scientific worldview is not bias-free, but it is much less so than competing worldviews. Scientific perspectives have consequently spread and been accepted much more widely than other worldviews, such as major religions. The laws of thermodynamics demonstrably work in any cultural context, and those who do not recognize their existence or their utility are at a competitive disadvantage in real, material terms. Because science concerns itself most fundamentally with those things that are least culture-bound, there cannot be, as some critics have suggested, "multiple sciences" tailored to specific cultural traditions. As a cross-culturally useful way of knowing science is not by any means perfect, but it is by far the best alternative we have.

For some postprocessual archaeologists, the recovery of the minds or worldviews of ancient peoples, as opposed to their behavior, is the ultimate goal, and such reconstruction is only possible by focusing the unique aspects of particular cultures:

> Cultures. . . . are arbitrary in the sense that their forms and content are not determined by anything outside of themselves. . . . culture then is not reducible, it just is.
> *(Hodder, 1986b:2)*

The opposite view brings us back to the most fundamental assumption of processual archaeology: Humans are parts of nature, and human cultures are the products of interaction with the natural world, and adaptations to it. Interesting though specific cultures are, their greatest significance lies in their linkage with the evolutionary process:

> Nature is seen by men through a screen composed of beliefs, knowledge, and purposes, and it is in terms of their cultural images of nature, rather than in terms of the actual structure of nature, that men act. Therefore, some anthropologists . . . have called our attention to the necessity, if we are to understand the environmental relations of men, to take into account their knowledge and beliefs concerning the world around them, and their culturally defined motives for acting as they do. But it should be kept in mind that although it is in terms of their conceptions and wishes that men act in nature it is upon nature herself that they do act, and it is nature herself that acts upon men, nurturing or destroying them.
> *(Rappaport 1971a:246–247)*

Archaeology today stands at a crossroads. Whether most archaeologists will continue down the scientific/materialistic/ecological road, or turn onto another characterized by cultural particularism remains to be seen. What is certain is that we should welcome diversity of opinion, because it is essential to the growth of archaeology, as to any evolutionary process. In the long run selection will eliminate weaker perspectives and favor stronger ones. Today, more so than at any previous time, it is necessary to understand the relationship between human culture and the larger process of nature. Scientific, anthropological archaeology, often pursued as an exercise in intellectual curiosity, has a larger, useful role in informing us about the career of the human species and its consequences, with which we all must live. We are confident that scientific, anthropological archaeology will survive.

POINTS TO REMEMBER

- Explanation is the most difficult but most essential task of scientific archaeology.
- Explanations for the evolution of complex societies focus on the relationship of

population to resources, management of irrigation, warfare, exchange and trade, technology, regulation of information, and changes in ideology.

- No single explanation can explain a complex process, though some explanations are more effective than others.

- Combining many variables into systems of cause and effect helps archaeologists to formulate explanations in complex ways.

- Although archaeologists may never all agree that a particular explanation is the correct one, and since no explanation is final in any case, we can reject bad ideas and generate more useful and plausible accounts of what happened in the past.

FOR FURTHER READING*

For a solid introduction to evolutionary theory and explanation, see Mayr's *The Growth of Biological Thought*. Watson, LeBlanc, and Redman's *Explanation in Archaeology* presents scientific principles for archaeological interpretation. Sources for some of the ideas discussed in this chapter are Malthus's *An Essay on the Principle of Population*, Spooner's *Population Growth*, Boserup's *Conditions of Agricultural Growth*, Carneiro's "A Theory of the Origin of the State," and Hodder's "Postprocessual Archaeology."

*Full citations appear in the bibliography.

APPENDIX
CRITICAL THINKING SKILLS

Scholarship is demanding work. It requires organization, concentration, and, even more important, sharp thinking. To study effectively, you must absorb information and perspectives so that you can evaluate and interpret facts and ideas, ultimately developing your own synthesis, your own original viewpoint. Too often in the course of our education we are never explicitly taught the skills we need to study and to express our ideas. This appendix provides guidelines for reading and critiquing articles and books and for writing a paper.

GUIDELINES FOR CRITIQUING

A basic skill of scholarship is the ability to read articles and books so that

1. information is derived and retained,
2. the value of each work is assessed, and
3. ideas in the work and generated by the work are noted so that they may be used to develop a synthetic overview of a body of material relating to a particular topic.

To achieve these goals efficiently, a systematic method of note taking is necessary. This ensures careful reading, promotes retention, permits a rapid review of material, and facilitates creative thinking. Proper note taking simplifies the process of organizing and writing a paper as well.

An adequate set of notes on an article or a book should include a summary of the following points:

1. *Purpose.* Why was the book or article written? What kind of information is being presented? Examples include

    overall description of a research project,
    focus on a description of the data gathered by a project,
    focus on the analysis of data,
    presentation of the development or use of a particular method of research or analysis,
    critical review of pertinent literature on a topic,
    synthesis or overview of a topic, such as the presentation of a new theoretical perspective.

    Many scholarly works combine two or more purposes, but in most cases (especially articles) the purpose is fairly simple.

2. *Subject matter.* An archaeological site? A collection of sherds? Ideas of the New Archaeologists? Briefly describe what the writer is analyzing.

3. *Method.* What analytical technique was used to draw generalizations and conclusions? Simple description and comparison? Statistical methods? Geophysical or chemical analytic techniques?

4. *Observations.* Here the subject matter becomes "data" as the author organizes observations into categories and describes general patterns or trends. Describe these observations. For example: What kinds of remains were unearthed at the site? What types of potsherds, and how many, make up the sample under study? What kinds of innovative perspectives did the New Archaeologists introduce?

5. *Results.* Describe what the author concludes on the basis of the observations.

6. *Interpretation.* Evaluate the work, citing the *contributions* made by it and the *problems* it presents. How might further research exploit the contributions and address the problems?

Format   Whether your notes must be submitted as part of assigned coursework or are strictly for your personal scholarly use, certain procedures tend to save time in the long run. First, if possible use a computer; if writing longhand, use ink. Try to use decent-quality paper (newsprint deteriorates rapidly); size 8.5 by 11 inches is most versatile.

Second, head the page on the top right with the full citation in a standard format. Copying the full citation saves time when compiling bibliographies, and upper-right placement enables you to locate notes easily. Here is a standard citation format for *American Antiquity*.

article:
Allen, W. L., and J. B. Richardson
    1971. "Reconstruction of Kinship." *American Antiquity* 36:41–53.

book:
Bohannon, Paul, and George Dalton (eds.)
    1962. *Markets in Africa.* Evanston: Northwestern University Press.

Third, paraphrase carefully. Avoid taking notes in such an automatic manner that you barely change the author's phrasing. In the first place, this indicates that you are avoiding the intellectual internalization of the material; a good self-test of understanding is the ability to summarize concisely and originally. In the second place, you may unwittingly come close to plagiarism. If the author phrased the concept so well that you wish to save the quote, do so exactly (using quotation marks) and note the appropriate page(s), so you need not return to the book for the page numbers if you use it in a paper. *Exercise caution* when quoting, however, since copying extensive quotes is time-consuming.

Fourth, be sure to include your own ideas and questions as they occur to you as you take notes, but devise a way of marking them as separate from notes from the work itself—put them in [[double brackets]], for example. The thoughts that are provoked in the course of reading can provide the basis for your own original approach to a topic, particularly if you are doing research in preparing to write a paper or take an exam.

This leads us to the fifth point: *Use your notes.* Skim through them often. As the term progresses and you begin to accumulate a set of notes on a particular topic, review them. This is much easier than reviewing all the books and articles themselves and has the great advantage of filling your mind with a large body of information in a short space of time. New ideas will occur to you, and the information you've taken so much trouble to extract will be retained much more easily and will have far greater value to you as a scholar.

Studies of how the brain works show that beneficial physiological changes are induced by concentrated thinking. Like physical exercise, however, there are few benefits to intellectual concentration three times a semester; keeping to a regular schedule of frequent sessions results in greater intellectual capability. As the mind becomes stronger and more accustomed to mastering knowledge and formulating interesting questions and conclusions about that knowledge, clear, critical thinking is easier.

Critiquing and the Cycle of Science   Note that when you critique, you are looking for the steps in the scientific process (diagrammed as the cycle of science in Chapter 2). We use a deductivist perspective here in the sense that the circumstances of a particular case are deduced from a larger general perspective. Begin with generalization (the theoretical perspective that spells out the larger purpose the work serves), then move to the observation (experiment) stage and the summary of the units of observation (the data). Next, interpret the meaning of this summary according to the basic principles set out at the beginning. Finally, make a value judgment: What's the value of this work? Does it expand our knowledge? Sidetrack our thinking in a profitless direction? Call forth a revision of the theory?

GUIDELINES FOR WRITING

A major distinction between science and art is how creativity is channeled—or, one might say, how creativity is rewarded. Both the artist and the scientist are rewarded for demonstrating mastery over a medium and for using the medium in a creative way that expands our understanding. Whereas artists are rewarded for creating works that are unmistakably unique, scientists can only gain stature for works that can be replicated by other scientists.

Because science places a high value on shared knowledge and on the theoretical potential ability of all scientists to reproduce one scientist's results, given the same experimental conditions, it is not surprising that scientific writing is highly structured. An artistic prose work such as a piece of fiction may be treasured for innovative style, but scientific writing is systematically presented and gets its power from the strength of its purpose and conclusions, originality of observations and interpretations, and the clarity of conciseness of its expression. Scientific reports need not be dull — they can be riveting. The structure that helps ensure the writer gets to the point fast should not be seen as shackling but as liberating. That is, you don't need to invent a new approach to the writing of reports; you can save your energy and expressive talent for making each part of the work as comprehensive, accurate, and succinct as possible.

The component parts of a report are much like those of a critique, because you are looking for the same set of elements that compose the steps of the scientific cycle. This structure can be used for any type of nonfiction prose. Use these parts as the basic headings of your outline. Briefly, they are:

1. *Purpose.* What problem are you trying to solve? What question are you answering? What is your goal in writing and in doing the research preparatory to writing? You may be writing a straightforward description of an archaeological site or a comparison between two sites to elucidate similarities and differences. Or you may be hypothesizing about the conditions of a particular case from the general terms of a broad theory.

2. *Subject matter.* To fulfill the purpose, what kind of things must you investigate? For a report on an archaeological site, you would need to know what architecture and artifacts were found at the site and how these were related to material culture resources at other similar sites. For a report on settlement pattern studies, you would need to determine which settlement pattern research projects you wished to include in your study out of the many such projects that have been done. NOTE: It is important to set limits on the purpose of your work, depending on the range and availability of subject matter. Do not become overwhelmed by an ungovernable avalanche of materials to study; redefine the purpose of your report if necessary so that you can focus on a manageable subset of these materials.

3. *Method.* Method may encompass two levels: You will always describe your own method of observing the cases under study (e.g., comparing various settlement pattern research projects in regions of emerging civilizations with regard to sampling design, mapping strategies, types of settlements found, etc.), and you may also need to describe the methods used in the projects you are studying.

4. *Observations.* Next you must organize your case studies into categories that are meaningful to your purpose and describe the similarities and differences among them. For example, settlement patterns of Mesopotamia and Mesoamerica both show differentiation of communities as civilization began to emerge, but each area had a different set of community types and a different range of cultivation systems the communities depended on. Site hierarchy, kinds of communities, and kinds of farming systems would be categories of observation by which we could

organize our case studies. In summarizing your observations, use existing categories (with appropriate citation) or, if they do not suit your purposes, formulate new categories. Here it is important to remember the principle of replicability. The basis for your observations and observation categories should be clear so that if any other researcher followed the procedure you set out, the results would be the same.

5. *Results.* The results section of a report consists of an overview of the observations from the perspective of the purpose of the work. Here you state how the observations, summarized in the preceding section, fulfill the purpose of the work, how they support your hypothesis, or, alternatively, how they fail to substantiate it.

6. *Interpretation.* In the final "critical evaluation" section, you can present your own opinions about the observations and results and consider how existing knowledge might be enhanced and the interpretive model improved by future research. Note that the sections on observations, results, and interpretation represent successive stages on a continuum between greater objectivity and greater subjectivity. It is common in scientific research that another researcher will be more interested in the observations you are reporting and less concerned with your summary of results and interpretations. In fact, as you look back over old articles and reports, you may find that the "observations" sections remain useful decades later, whereas the "interpretations" may seem like quaint vignettes of long-forgotten fashions in theory—a good example of the effect of paradigm change, as discussed in *Out of the Past*, Chapter 2.

Getting the Work Done   "Writing a paper" is a general expression used to signify the whole process of planning, researching, documenting, constructing and refining the narrative of the report, and submitting the hard copy. The "writing" part—constructing and refining the narrative—accounts for only part of the process. If the rest of the steps have been well planned and completed according to a workable schedule, the writing is almost automatic. Planning and organization are crucial to success and can spell the difference between a satisfying intellectual exercise and an unpleasant obligation.

To plan a research and writing project, consider the span of time that will lapse before the due date, and think about your other obligations—midterms, other projects, finals. Block out on a calendar those periods when you'll need to focus on other things, and then schedule your research and writing for the remaining time. Make a few photocopies of the "guidelines template" at the end of the appendix for note taking.

The work might be scheduled in the following stages:

1. *Draft 1.* The first draft should be an outline that includes preliminary statements of purpose and subject matter (including a preliminary list of sources—articles and books—to be researched), a brief statement of method, and a brief projection of what the observations and results will

be. (Interpretations will not be addressed at this point). One of the most important things to do at this point is to begin assembling the list of sources for your subject matter. Look for appropriate books and articles in the textbook reading lists and bibliography and in the bibliographies of recent, comprehensive review articles related to your topic.

If possible, get feedback from your instructor about your outline. Ask whether the purpose statement is too broad or narrow, and ask for suggestions about materials and method. Do this *after* having done the preliminary research noted above. Be able to give your instructor the list of sources you have compiled, and ask how many and what kinds of references are appropriate for the paper assigned and for the topic you have chosen. This will give you an idea of how much time you need to master them.

2. *Subject matter research*. The reading list you compile has to be mastered in a finite time period. If you are working through it too slowly to complete it, then focus on the most important sections in each source, and keep working through the list. Get the information you need, and if necessary revise your reading list, dropping materials that aren't useful, going after other, more pertinent sources if necessary. Your materials research involves noting the observations that are relevant to your purpose; you should be drawing observations out of your references and keeping track of them as they accumulate.

3. *Draft 2*. The second draft is a more fully annotated outline. Revise your statement of purpose, if necessary. Assume that your subject matter section is in semifinal shape (from now on you will continue to research the sources you've already chosen, with only a few changes). As you develop your research method, make notes to revise this section. Make preliminary observations based on initial research, and revise your projected results. If you need advice, take the draft to your instructor.

4. *Observations* and *Results*. Next, focus on observations and results. This is when you come to grips with the purpose of your project. What are you finding out, and what does it mean? What trends are becoming obvious in the materials you've read and the observations you've made? What are the similarities and differences among the case examples, and why do you think they occur?

By this stage of your work, the subject matter section should be near completion, the methods section should be in semifinal form, and your observations and results outlines should be approaching their final form. At this point, it would be useful to note a few preliminary opinions in the interpretations section.

Now complete your observations and results sections and extend your outline of interpretations. Read through the entire draft of the paper, which will include some outlined parts and some narrative, and prepare to write the final draft. Retain at least some of the general headings of the outline in your final paper to help orient the reader.

5. *Draft 3*. The third draft is the paper in its completed, narrative form. After you have written all the sections, read the paper through for continuity and comprehension (the best way to perceive problems in these respects is to read aloud) and make necessary changes. Produce the final draft, including compiling the bibliography and producing any necessary figures or tables. Make a copy for yourself. Turn in the paper.

TEMPLATE FOR RESEARCH AND WRITING

Purpose:

Subject Matter:

Method:

Observations:

Results:

Interpretation:

GLOSSARY

absolute age The amount of time elapsed, with reference to a specific time scale, since an object was made or used.

absolute dating The use of methods developed to establish the number of years elapsed since an object was made or used.

achieved leadership Leadership gained through one's own abilities rather than inheritance of a position.

action archaeology See **experimental archaeology**.

activation analysis Method to determine the elements of a material by inducing radioactive reactions to produce radiation characteristic of material composition.

activity area Localized zone of intensive, generally repeated use, as evidenced by artifacts, assemblages, and special-purpose features. Sometimes the activity area coincides with a particular room in a building, as it does in the kitchen (the food-preparation activity area) of a modern house, but often this is simply an area, indoors or out, exhibiting a particlar kind of use. There may be several features associated with a single activity area.

adobe Building material comprised of earth and other materials such as straw or gravel to enhance structural solidity; commonly in the form of sun-dried bricks.

Age of Discovery A time of European exploration, discovery, and enlightenment about the world which occurred from about the 15th through the 18th centuries.

alpaca A domesticated South American camelid noted for its soft wool.

altiplanos Wide mountain basins found at high elevations in the Central Andes (3–4,000 m), and which have cool, moist climates.

amino acid racemization Dating method based on the natural clock in bone which traces the shift in the form of amino acid molecules after an organism's death. The change from left- to right-orientation takes place at a regular rate and can be measured. This technique has a long dating range from 1,000 to 1,000,000 years.

anthropological archaeology The tradition of archaeology that is derived from, and most strongly oriented toward, the larger field of anthropology. Classical archaeology is another, distinctive tradition.

anthropology The study of human physical and cultural diversity and similarity, throughout the world, for the whole history of our species.

antiquarianism The study of antiquity (the ancient past and its customs) and antiquities (the relics of the ancient past).

archaeological culture Culture identified by a set of recurring material remains of features, house types, pottery forms, and burial styles.

archaeology The study of past cultures, based on their material remains.

archaeomagnetism A method of absolute dating that analyzes remnant patterns of magnetic orientations toward previous locations of magnetic north, which moves in an irregular path around the north pole.

artifact Anything that has been made, modified, or transported by humans and that can provide information about human behavior in the past.

ascribed leadership Leadership assigned by birthright, sex, or some other fixed criterion.

assemblage The whole set of artifacts representing the material culture inventory or repertoire used in a given cultural setting over a limited period of time. For example, the range of things in a modern Sears or Spiegel catalogue is a fairly complete assemblage of durable household goods for middle-class Americans.

attribute A minor characteristic or recognizable quality of an artifact that is useful for describing, analyzing, or categorizing it. For example, among the attributes of a potsherd are those related to its "surface treatment," such as whether it is painted or unpainted.

authority Ability to persuade others, by argument or example, to accept one's decisions.

bands Small, highly mobile egalitarian societies based on hunting and gathering and characterized by a lack of formal government institutions and economic specialization. Political dominance is gained through achieved leadership rather than ascribed leadership; as many leadership positions exist as circumstances require and there are qualified people to fill them.

barter A type of direct exchange of different goods, not using any sort of currency, in which each party tries to get an advantage, however slight.

baulk The intentionally unexcavated portion of a trench, preserved to retain a stratigraphic profile for future reference and control. Also called **witness column**.

biased sample Sampling technique in which certain units have more chance of inclusion than others.

biomes Communities of plants and animals.

bride-price Compensation offered to the bride's family, usually by the groom's family, for the loss of her companionship and labor to another group upon marriage.

Bronze Age Period of time marked by the mastery of metallurgy and the predominance of tools of bronze, preceded by the Stone Age.

cacao The seed or bean of a tropical plant, used to make chocolate.

Calendar Round The meshing of the two Maya calendars, the Tzolkin and the Haab, in a 52 year cycle.

calendrics The decipherment and study of calendars.

calpulli Corporate group in Aztec society which functioned above the level of the household. Calpullis had social, political, and economic functions. They occupied whole villages or neighborhoods of towns and cities; members corporately held rights to farm plots as long as they continued to use them.

carrying capacity The theoretical limit to which a population may grow and maintain itself without deleterious effects on its environment.

caste Social class with clearly delineated boundaries; one is usually born into a caste and ascribed social and economic roles on the basis of caste affiliation. It is difficult or impossible to ascend from one caste to a higher one.

catastrophism Theory that explains change through a succession of sudden catastrophes.

cenote Naturally occurring limestone sinkhole, often used as a reservoir by the Maya.

central place theory Theory of community location and arrangement that posits regular patterns of settlement distribution over the landscape, influenced by the constraints of the environment and the opportunities provided by economic and political interaction.

centralization Evolutionary process whereby wealth, power, political decision making, and social prestige are concentrated in the hands of fewer and fewer subgroups or individuals within a society.

chiefdom The kind of political system characteristic of most ranked societies, politically dominated by chiefs.

chinampas Extremely productive and fertile rectangular plots of land created in swampy lakes by piling up mud from the lake bottom. This agricultural technique was employed by the Aztecs and is in use today in Mexico.

chipped stone tools Tools produced by flaking or chipping of pieces from a stone core to produce an implement.

chronometric date A date indicating that a measured value of time (years, centuries) has elapsed since a past event occurred.

civilization Complex sociopolitical form defined by the institutions of the state and the existence of a distinctive Great Tradition.

clan Organization in which members claim common descent but do not specify how they are related. Often the common ancestor is fictive (fictional).

class Large social groups ranked vis-à-vis others in terms of status, prestige, wealth, or sanctity.

Classic period A.D. 300–900 in Mesoamerica, when Maya culture reached its highest level of sociopolitical complexity.

closed system Type of system which does not exchange matter, energy, or information with other systems.

cognized model A representation of reality which is based in part on idealized expectations about the real situation.

component Materials representing activities during a particular period of occupation at an archaeological site.

community A general term for different kinds of settlements, from clusters of a few households to huge urban aggregates.

conflict theories Theories that trace the origin of the state to warfare or intragroup conflicts.

conjunctive approach The integrated use of evidence from archaeology, ethnohistory, and ethnography to solve problems of reconstruction and interpretation.

context An object's setting in time and place, its affinity to other things of similar form, and its general relationship to other objects in the archaeological record.

Copán pocket In the Copán Valley (Honduras), a region of about 24 km² immediately surrounding the Main Group; contains dense alluvial soils that are excellent for agriculture.

corbel vaulting Building technique which forms a false arch; corbel vaults do not effectively transfer the weight of the roof to the walls (as do true arches), and thus are weak.

cross-dating Establishing the age of one find by its similarity to or association with a find of known age.

cross-sectional trenches A type of excavation in which a set of superimposed strata are cut across by deep trenches that expose the history of deposition. Also called **slot trenches**.

cultural chronology Cultural things, events, or processes arranged in chronological order.

cultural ecology The theoretical perspective that culture and environment interact so that each sets limits and possibilities on the other in a dynamic relationship; a methodological program for analyzing cultures, based on understanding adaptation to the environment as well as technoeconomic, sociopolitical, and ideological organization.

cultural materialism Approach which seeks to understand the structure and evolution of cultures through scientific investigation of the material conditions of life and which emphasizes culture as basically adaptive in function.

cultural processes Sets of interrelated changes occurring through time, operating very broadly in geographical, social, and temporal terms over the course of a culture's history.

cultural relativism The belief that all cultures are unique and thus can only be evaluated in their own terms, and that cross-cultural comparisons and generalizations are invalid or inappropriate.

cultural resource management (CRM) The managing of the archaeological record through salvage operations and protective legislation.

culture Patterned, learned, shared behavior based on symbolic communication.

culture area The area inhabited by societies sharing cultural traits such as language, belief systems, sociopolitical organization, food-getting practices, and basic technology. Culture areas are most usefully defined on the basis of broadly shared stylistic or ideological features.

culture core Technological, organizational, and ideological features most directly related to meeting the most important material needs of a society.

culture history The chronological arrangement of the time phases and events of a particular culture.

cuneiform Earliest writing system, with wedge-shaped symbols inscribed on a wet clay tablet with a stylus.

cutting tools Tools used for cutting, gouging, shaving, piercing, scraping, and sawing.

datum point The reference point in an archaeological excavation used as the basis for all measurements on a site.

daub Mud packed around the wattles, or framework, of a structure.

deconstructionism School of literary criticism asserting that the meaning of texts is revealed by identifying the hidden or unconscious biases affecting the authors. This viewpoint assumes that essential meaning is based on subjective attitudes.

deductive reasoning Logical process of deducing the circumstances of particular cases from the conditions specified by general theories.

demography The statistical study of human populations, particularly in terms of age-sex structure.

dendrochronology Establishing dates through tree-ring patterns (also known as tree-ring dating).

descent reckoning The rules by which people in a particular culture determine membership in defined kin groups.

diagnostics Artifacts that can be used as index fossils in a cultural context.

differential access to key resources Situation in which different individuals or groups within a society do not share equal access to necessary resources.

differential reproduction The measure of fitness calculated by the relative rates at which different individuals produce live offspring.

diffusion Spread of a trait from one culture to another.

diffusionism Explanatory model of culture change that focuses on the spread of traits from one culture to another rather than on independent development of traits.

direct historical approach A research method which assumes that if there is continuity in culture through time in a given region, it is possible to interpret prehistoric archaeological remains by direct comparison with the historically known part of the culture sequence.

distribution The means by which things are transferred from producers to consumers.

division of labor by age and sex Task allocation based on the ages and sex of individuals.

domestication Selection of particular plants and animals for breeding, which makes them more useful and productive for human purposes.

drained fields Intensive form of agriculture in which fields are created by draining plots of swampy land.

earth sciences Sciences concerned with the study of formation processes that affect the earth's surface.

ecofact Floral, faunal, or geophysical material not necessarily used, altered, or transported by humans but of value in interpreting archaeological cultures—for example, a pollen sample that provides valuable information about past climates.

ecological community The different biotic species of a specific region and the network of interrelationships that exists among them.

ecology Study of the relationships of plants and animals within their habitats.

economic specialization Situation in which necessary or useful economic tasks are not equally shared by all members of society, making individuals or groups economically interdependent.

economic symbiosis Economic interdependence of population units in a region for the good of all.

ecosystem Ecological community of plants and animals together with the physical environment.

egalitarian societies Collective term for bands and tribes, societies in which all members have equal access to basic resources. Leadership is situational and attainable by achievement within the confines of age and sex.

electron spin resonance See **thermoluminescence**.

emblem glyphs Symbols that refer to places, or alternatively to the titles or lineages of resident Maya lords.

enculturation The process of learning whereby an individual acquires the beliefs, customs, values, and behaviors appropriate to a specific culture.

endogamy Choosing a marriage partner from within one's own group.

energy The ability to do work.

environmental circumscription Geographical restrictions on the movement of groups.

environmental setting The physical and biotic surroundings—plants, animals, climate, inorganic resources—that influence social groups and their associated cultures, including other human groups.

epigraphy The study and interpretation of ancient inscriptions.

equilibrium State of relative stability within a system.

error factor The measurement error inherent in every chronometric dating technique, indicating the range of accuracy of the estimated date; usually expressed as plus or minus a certain number of years.

ethnoarchaeology The study of the observable, dynamic behavior of living people in order to develop models to interpret archaeological remains.

ethnographic analogy Use of both material and nonmaterial aspects of a living culture to form models to test interpretations of archaeological remains.

ethnographic present That point in time when a traditional culture came into contact with individuals from literate cultures, and was documented by them.

ethnographic study The study of cultural characteristics of a particular ethnic or social group.

ethnography The careful and accurate description of a particular group of living people based on direct observation, sometimes supplemented by written or other records.

ethnohistory The study of original documents describing the past, such as those written by travelers, explorers, and missionaries.

ethnology The proper term for the systematic and comparative study of culture, including both modern and past cultures.

evolution Modification through a process of natural selection, resulting in adaptive change.

excavation Systematic exploration of subsurface remains in the archaeological record by means of removing soil or other matrix and sometimes removing cultural materials as well.

exchange The transfer of goods or services from one party to another.

experimental archaeology The controlled testing of hypotheses about what happened in the past by observing and manipulating processes or behavior in the present. Also known as **action archaeology**.

extended family Family type consisting of relatives by descent and marriage belonging to several generations: for example, grandparents, their offspring and spouses, and grandchildren.

extensive excavations See **lateral excavations**.

facilities Nonportable artifacts, such as the remains of an ancient structure.

fallow period The time allowed for a field to rest, when no crops are grown on it.

fallowing Practice of letting agricultural fields lie unused through one or more planting seasons in order to restore their fertility.

fauna Animals.

feature Any highly localized area of human use or modification, sometimes part of a work area (e.g., a hearth that is part of a cooking area) or the location of activities (e.g., a built-in bench that serves as work area and sleep area).

feedback The mutual effect of the interaction of two parts of a larger system.

field notes A daily record and careful description of excavation activities.

field operations journal A running record of activities and finds during an archaeological excavation.

fission track dating See **thermoluminesence**.

flora Plants or vegetation.

flotation Type of water screening which recovers small plant, animal, and artifactual remains from a soil sample.

Folk Traditions Local traditions and beliefs associated with small-scale egalitarian societies or the nonelite antecedents of complex societies, usually expressed in media other than writing.

food chain The set of relationships among plant and animal species in an ecosystem through which energy is channeled. Also called **food web**.

food production The use of domestic plants and animals to supply food energy.

food web See **food chain**.

force The threat or fact of physical coercion or injury.

formal context The affinity of an object to a general class of objects sharing general characteristics of form.

forms Standardized information sheets designed to record data in a programmatic way—that is, lot forms, trench forms, feature forms, and burial forms.

full-time specialist A nonfood producer who earns a living by an occupation other than farming and who must exchange goods or services for food.

F-U-N method Relative dating technique which compares concentrations of fluorine, uranium, or nitrogen in various samples from the same matrix to determine contemporaneity.

gene flow Sharing traits by mating between otherwise distinct populations of the same species.

general evolution Broad trends of human cultural change observed on a worldwide, comparative basis.

genetic drift The branching off of a separate population that bears some but not all of the traits of the parent population; sometimes called "founder's effect."

government Specialized statuses, offices, and institutions responsible for political decision making and enforcement of the decisions.

gradualism The view that changes occur slowly and cumulatively rather than rapidly and disjunctively.

grave goods Items and offerings interred with the deceased.

Great Tradition Sets of elite values and behaviors that emerge from Folk Traditions during the evolution of complex societies and that are expressed in distinctive rituals, art, writing, or other symbolic forms.

grid A rectilinear system of X, Y coordinates which is established over the area to be excavated so that spatial control can be maintained.

ground stone tools See **polished stone tools**.

habitation sites Archaeological sites where people lived in the past.

hierarchy Ranked, multiple levels of complexity and scale within a system.

high-energy societies Societies characterized by high per-capita consumption of energy, mostly through non-food sources. Industrial societies, with their reliance on fossil fuels, are high-energy societies.

higher-order central place A large and functionally diverse community in a regional hierarchy of communities differentiated by number, size, and function.

historical archaeology The study of the material remains of those cultures for which historic documents are available.

horizon Period of time during which a distinctive set of archaeological remains (e.g., religious symbols, ritual objects, and art styles) spreads over a very large region. When these distinctive remains are found at different sites, the sites may be assumed to be roughly contemporaneous.

household Group of co-residing individuals who share a set of facilities and act cooperatively on a day-to-day basis.

hunter-gatherers People or societies dependent on wild food resources. Such societies are usually technologically simple, small in size, and highly mobile. Hunter-gathers are also sometimes called "foragers."

hypothesis Tentative and testable premise that accounts for relationships between empirical observations.

Ice Ages The successive periods of glaciation that occurred during the Pleistocene.

iconography Illustrations based on stylized symbolic forms, or icons; also the study and interpretation of such images.

ideograph Symbol conveying an idea without resembling what it conveys.

ideology The belief system of a particular society, including values and ethics, the place of humans in the natural world and their relationship with the supernatural, and the justification for the existing social and political order.

in situ Latin for "in its original place." Refers to the location of archaeological finds that have been preserved in the same place in which they were originally used. Alternatively, something still in the position where it was originally found.

index fossil An organism whose presence in various strata over a great distance links them to the same time period.

inductive reasoning The logical process of inducing the general conditions of a whole set of cases from the particular circumstances of one or a few.

industry The set of artifacts made out of the same material, using the same kind of techniques of production.

infrastructure Materialist term for "the interface between nature in the form of unalterable physical, chemical and biological constraints, and culture which is *Homo sapiens'* primary means of optimizing health and well-being" (Harris 1991:73).

innovations New ideas, practices, or inventions which may lead to change.

institution Organization with socially recognized functions, established by custom or charter whose life span extends beyond that of any of its individual constituent members.

institutionalized specialization Situation in which people specialize to make all or part of their living; work on a permanent or at least frequently recurring basis; and are dependent on exchanges with others in social groups beyond the family for their survival and well-being.

integration Mutual cause-and-effect relationships of a system's interrelated parts.

intensification The use of a piece of agricultural land more frequently or with the input of increased labor or other resources.

intersubjectivity The validated correspondence of the subjective perceptions of different scientific observers.

Iron Age Era during which humans mastered the complicated process of making tools and goods out of iron; preceded by the Stone and Bronze ages.

itinerant trader A person who travels from place to place selling services or wares rather than being stationed in one place, as in a market.

joint family household Household type that consists of two or more families, not necessarily related.

K-Ar dating Absolute dating technique that traces the transformation of one isotope into another (potassium [K] into argon [Ar]). Its range is 100,000 years to 1.3 billion years.

kcal The kilocalorie is a measure of food energy, popularly known as the calorie. It is the amount of energy needed to raise the temperature of a kilogram of water one degree centigrade.

kiva Underground room in a pueblo, used for ceremonial purposes.

lateral excavations The excavation or opening up of large areas so that subsurface features and architecture are broadly exposed. Also called **extensive excavations**.

law of biotic potential Rule stating that most organisms have the potential to produce far more offspring than can possibly be supported by their environments.

law of least effort Rule stating that organisms will generally accomplish necessary tasks with a minimal expenditure of time and effort.

law of superposition The principle that the order of deposition in stratified material under normal circumstances is from bottom to top so that the older material is on the bottom.

leader Person who has the ability or authority to initiate action and to whom other people have formed the habit of responding.

Leibig's law Rule stating that the numbers of a population are regulated by the essential resource in shortest supply.

levees Raised, well-drained river banks.

lifeways Everyday cultural customs and practices, that is, ways of living.

lineage Members of a group who claim common descent and can trace their genealogy back to a common ancestor.

linearization Simplification of hierarchy of regulation in a system, permitting a high-level part of a system to bypass controls at lower levels.

Little Tradition Folk elements which survive alongside the Great Tradition.

llama Domesticated South American camelid used as a beast of burden and for wool and food.

loci (*sing.* **locus**) Small concentrated areas.

logograph Abstract written symbol that corresponds to actual spoken words.

Long Count Term for the Maya calendar that counts the number of elapsed days from an initial day in 3114 B.C.

lot Any unit of collection in which artifacts are presumed to share the same particular context, typically, a level of a trench.

low-energy societies Societies in which most energy comes from food and there is little dependence on non-human forms of energy.

Lower Egypt The wide, flat, alluvial delta of the Nile River.

lower-order central place A small and functionally simple community in a regional hierarchy of communities differentiated by number, size, and function.

Main Group At the Maya site of Copán (Honduras), the central core of monumental remains, including temples, palaces, and ballcourts, which served as the political, social, and economic center and the royal household during the Classic Period; it covers an area of approximately 0.15 sq. km.

maize The domesticated corn plant, *Zea mays*, native to the New World.

mana Polynesian word referring to a supernatural force that can reside within an object or person, making that object or person more powerful or effective in its performance. For example, a canoe with much mana would be particularly seaworthy, and a mana-charged weapon would be lethal.

manioc Tropical, domesticated root crop especially used in tropical forest regions.

mano Cylindrical stone held in the hands, usually used in combination with a metate for grinding.

manufacturing process See **technology**.

market Variable meanings: (1) a process of buyer-seller exchange (as in "doing the marketing"), (2) the demand (market) for something, or (3) a kind of economy (market economy).

marketplace A designated place where goods and services are exchanged.

Marxist archaeologists Archaeologists who interpret and reconstruct cultural relations as expressions of class struggles, as did Karl Marx.

mass spectrometry Method to determine the elements of a material by converting it to a gas and dispersing its components according to mass to identify the composition.

mastaba A rectangular mud-brick superstructure covering the subterranean tomb of an early Egyptian ruler or elite person.

material Substance of which an artifact is made, such as bone, obsidian, jade, and so forth.

material remains The physical remnants of a past society, including ecofacts, artifacts, features, architecture, and the ways these are distributed and patterned.

matrilocal postmarital residence Residential situation in which a newly married couple lives with or near the bride's mother's family.

matrix The material within which the archaeological evidence is embedded, such as soil, lava, and water.

Maya Term referring to people who speak a set of related languages (Mayan) in southern Mesoamerica. It also refers to the general culture of Mayan speakers, especially those of the Classic and Postclassic periods of Mesoamerican culture history.

mechanical solidarity Feature of society in which component subsystems are similar to each other and potentially independent in social, economic, and political terms.

mentalist approach Any approach to archaeology (including postprocessualism) which stresses the importance of symbolism, ideology, and meaning.

mercantile city Urban center whose primary function is the control of trade.

Mesoamerica The archaeological culture area that includes present-day Mexico, Guatemala, Belize, Honduras, and parts of El Salvador.

metallurgy The knowledge of metals and their components, and its application in metal working.

metate Slablike stone used as a grinding surface in combination with the mano.

midden Trash heap at an archaeological site, accumulated during the occupation of the site.

middle-range theory The ideas and concepts archaeologists use to reconstruct the behaviors that have resulted in the material culture record.

mode of production "A specific, historically occurring set of social relations through which labor is deployed to wrest energy from nature by means of tools, skills, organization, and knowledge" (Wolf 1982:75).

model A representation of reality, often devised for the purpose of testing hypotheses.

modes of sociopolitical integration Distinctive, recurring sets of political, social, economic, and religious behaviors and institutions that define societies in general adaptive or evolutionary terms (e.g., tribes, chiefdoms, states).

monumental architecture Large buildings such as temples, palaces, and pyramids, readily identifiable in the archaeological record and assumed to have been built by means of the collective labor of many people.

morphology The shape, size, and superficial characteristics of artifacts, features, structures, sites, and so forth, provided by measurements (including weight) that permit comparative statistical analysis of attributes and frequencies.

Mossbauer spectroscopy Method of determining the elemental composition of an artifact by measuring gamma ray absorption.

mutation Random shifts of the genetic code.

natural selection The effect of the constraints and possibilities presented by the natural environment on the patterns of survival and reproduction by individuals within species, and species competing against each other.

nearest-neighbor statistic Measure of the relationship between a cluster of points in a pattern based on the expected value (d_e) and the observed value (d_o). The statistic (R) equals d_o/d_e.

negative feedback Feedback that dampens or reduces impulses toward change and thus helps keep systems in equilibrium or within tolerable limits.

negative reciprocity A type of exchange in which one person gains at the expense of another.

Neolithic Latter part of the Stone Age commonly known as the "New Stone Age," characterized by refined polished stone tools and modern flora and fauna; term now generally synonomous with the period during which food production originated in the Old World.

neutron activation analysis Method of determining the composition of an artifact by bombarding the sample with neutrons in a nuclear reactor. The radiation released reveals the constituent elements.

New World The continents of North and South America, and associated smaller land masses.

niche The particular position of a species within the environmental network.

nomes Administrative subdivisions of the ancient Egyptian state.

norms Common behavioral patterns of particular social groups.

nuclear family Two-generation family unit, consisting of one or both parents and unmarried children.

obsidian hydration dating A dating technique that measures the depth of moisture absorbed by obsidian, that is, the hydration rim of the obsidian. Depending on whether the rate of hydration for a particular kind of obsidian has been established, the technique may establish relative or absolute dates.

Old World The continents of Europe, Asia, Africa, and Australia and all associated smaller land masses.

open system Type of system that exchanges matter, energy, or information with other systems.

operational model A representation of reality that is based on observation of how the component parts of the real situation operate.

optical emission spectroscopy Method of determining the composition of an artifact by vaporizing the sample to release energy measurable as wavelengths of light distinctive of particular elements.

organic solidarity In organisms, the interdependence of all parts constituting the whole, a principle which is applied analogously to certain kinds of societies in which parts are highly interdependent.

oriental despotism Kind of government in which autocratic power was monopolized by a centralized ruler and bureaucracy. No other institutions existed that could politically challenge the central apparatus of the state.

Paleolithic Earliest part of the Stone Age, commonly known as the "Old Stone Age" in Europe, defined by flaked tools and many now-extinct mammals, such as mammoths, before the end of the last Ice Age.

palynology The study of ancient pollen with the objective of reconstructing the flora of a certain time period and the changes in flora through time. Such changes may reflect human activity or climatic change, for example.

paradigm A general set of ideas and observations accepted by most of the trained practitioners of a particular field of science at any point in time.

part-time specialist A food producer who also specializes in nonfood goods or services.

particularism An interpretative framework that characterized American archaeology in the early 1900s, whereby individual cultures were documented without comparative reference to others.

pastoralism Mode of subsistence based primarily on herd animals.

pathology A condition in which one part of a system inefficiently usurps, or meddles with, another part, thus creating stress or disequilibrium.

patrilineal descent Descent traced through the male line.

patrilocal Residential situation in which a newly married couple lives with or near the groom's father's family.

period Particular time interval, or **phase,** within a sequence; characterized by similar behavior patterns, resulting in similar patterns of distribution of material remains.

periodic market Locus of exchange that convenes on a regular but not a daily basis.

phase See **period.**

pictograph Element of a type of writing in which symbols depict directly and in reasonably realistic form what they are meant to convey.

plant opal phytoliths Fossils of plant cellular structures, distinctive of particular species or genera.

Pleistocene Geological period lasting from 1.8 million years ago to about 12,000 years ago.

polished tools Tools produced by the pecking or grinding of hard stones. Also called **ground stone tools.**

political organization The way in which a society is organized to make and enforce political decisions and to resolve conflict within the social setting and between societies.

political system The interest groups that maneuver to gain their ends; the means by which they do so; and the institutions, rules, laws and values that compose government.

polyandry The practice of multiple husbands sharing a single wife.

polygamous families One individual and several spouses and their children.

polygamy Feneral term for the practice of marrying more than one spouse at the same time.

polygyny The practice of multiple wives sharing a single husband.

population The whole set of things to be analyzed or on which observations are to be made.

positive feedback Feedback that causes a system to change from a former state.

postprocessual archaeology A school of archaeology that emerged in the 1980s, partly in reaction to processual archaeology. A commonly shared assumption of postprocessual archaeologists is that it is impossible to study and write objective accounts of past cultures because archaeologists are always consciously or unconsciously biased.

potlatch Festive event characteristic of the Northwest Coast Indians of North America. Guests were laden with gifts, whereby the host enhanced his own prestige.

potsherd A piece of a broken pottery vessel.

power The coercive capacity to ignore the interests of others while pursuing one's own and to withhold something that others want; alternatively, the capacity to oblige others to follow one's decisions even when they disagree, finding the decisions not to be in their own interests.

prehistoric Generally refers to societies that lacked writing but also can refer to societies about which the written record is largely uninformative.

prestige Ability to command admiration in social contexts.

primary state A state that developed independently of influences from other societies of similar or greater complexity.

primate Order of mammals that includes monkeys, apes, and humans.

prime mover The causal variable in a simple, direct, and inevitable relationship, resulting in a particular effect.

problem orientation The question or issue that a particular research effort is designed to address.

processual archaeology School of scientific archaeology that emphasizes concern with the broad processes of change revealed in the evolutionary record, as opposed, for example, to description or classification of material remains.

profane Pertaining to everyday matters.

promotion Elevation of an office or institution to higher levels in the hierarchy of information control systems, where it can regulate more of the system and have more general functions than it did previously.

provenience The exact location in three-dimensional space of any material in its archaeological context.

quipu Record keeping device of the Incas, consisting of patterns of knots on a set of strings.

radiocarbon dating Absolute dating method developed by physicist Willard Libby which determines the absolute age of an organic object (wood, charcoal, bone) by measuring the amount of decay of radioactive carbon (^{14}C).

random sample Sampling technique in which each unit or sample has an equal chance of being selected.

rank-size rule Principle stating that in a politically integrated area, for sites ranked according to size, each site's size is a fraction of that of the largest site in the region, the denominator of the fraction being equal to the smaller site's rank; thus the third-largest site is one-third the size of the largest, and so on.

ranked societies Societies in which individuals are ranked vis-à-vis one another in terms of kinship status and social prestige, which are largely ascribed. Fewer positions of authority or leadership exist than there are individuals capable of filling them, and access to these positions is generally ascribed.

rebus writing Drawings of objects which may indicate another part of speech than what is visually suggested.

reciprocity Roughly equivalent exchanges of goods or services between two parties.

redistribution Acquisitions of goods by one individual or institution, often politically dominant, who then redistributes them to others.

regal-ritual center A type of city which is essentially the residence of the ruler and nobles.

region Geographically defined area containing a series of interrelated communities that usually share similar cultural patterns.

regulation The force needed to maintain stability in a system.

relative age The chronological relationships among relatively younger and older things, even though no actual dates are available.

relative dating The use of methods developed to establish the age of sites or artifacts, relative to other sites and artifacts.

Renaissance The rebirth of European intellectual curiosity about the natural world and the role of humans in it, originating in the 14th century in Italy and spreading throughout Europe. Changing social, political, and economic conditions, as well as rediscovery of Classical texts, were fundamental to this rebirth.

replicability The ability of different scientists using the same methods of observation or experimentation to achieve the same results.

research design The strategy of investigating a particular problem which combines appropriate methods and techniques.

research proposal A formally presented research strategy describing an intended project and its predicted results.

residue analysis Identification of the traces or residues of materials left on tools or in vessels.

rite of intensification Ritual that symbolizes group concerns and solidarity, especially at critical times.

rite of passage Ritual symbolizing a transition in the life of an individual and his or her altered relationships to others.

Romer's Rule Rule stating that successful biological or cultural innovations are initially conservative in the sense that they function to maintain traditional ways of life.

sacred Pertaining to beliefs or propositions so valued that they are unquestioned.

salinization Buildup of chemical salts in soil.

sample Any subset of a population.

science The systematic study of the physical or material world, seeking to discover and formalize general laws through testing hypotheses and careful observation of results.

secondary state A state that developed state-type institutions under the heavy influence of other states.

sedentism Practice of settling in one place for an extended period of time.

segregation Evolutionary process whereby societies become more internally diverse in political, social, and economic terms. Segregation develops in close concert with centralization.

self-serving behavior Actions of groups or individuals serving their own perceived interests, which may not be those of others.

sequence A series of periods of time in the history of a particular culture, each characterized by recognizably different material remains. Also, the arrangement of material culture into a time framework.

seriation Placement of items in their proper order in a series.

settlement pattern The distribution of archaeological sites over the landscape of a defined region.

settlement system The sites in a particular region during a particular period of time, and their social, economic, and political relationships.

shaman An individual who is thought to have the power to intercede in the supernatural world on other people's behalf, sometimes while in a ecstatic trance. The shaman often has a supernatural helper or alter ego in the form of a companion animal.

sign Innately understood signal to which meaning is attached in a nonarbitrary way.

site A spatially isolated area of concentrated archaeological remains, ranging from a scatter of stone fragments where someone sharpened a stone tool to cities inhabited for centuries.

site types Kinds of sites, as distinguished by size and function. Examples would include habitation sites, quarrying sites, burial sites, and so forth.

site formation process The natural and cultural processes or transformations that have, in combination with each other, produced archaeological sites.

site layout The locations and spatial interrelations of artifacts, features, activity areas, and remains of structures at a site.

slash-and-burn agriculture See **swidden farming**.

slot trenches See **cross-sectional trenches**.

social circumscription Social restrictions (e.g., the presence of other societies) on the movement of groups.

social organization The way relationships among members of a culture are structured, and how much differentiation (in terms of status or wealth, for example) exists.

social philosophers Scholars interested in explaining human social conditions and their moral implications, who were especially prominent in Europe in the 18th century.

societies Groups of people who share the same culture, usually reside in the same locality, and are politically autonomous.

sodality Social group organized around specific interests or goals, whose members are not necessarily kin.

spatial analysis General statistical approach used to recover geographical patterns inherent in the data on any level (i.e., within one site or within an entire region).

spatial context The location of an object and its spatial relation to other objects as found in the archaeological record.

specific evolution Changes in particular societies and cultures whose specific evolutionary sequences may vary greatly.

speculative period The period in the history of archaeology in the New World between 1400–1840, characterized by unsystematic and speculative interpretations about the past.

spindle whorls Weights for the staffs used to spin yarn or other fibers.

stable isotope analysis Method used to distinguish between the different kinds of plant foods consumed; based on the fact that plants have several distinct pathways for fixing carbon dioxide and nitrogen, elements which become characteristic of the bones of the plant-eating organisms.

staple Important or principle crop or product.

state Stratified society that has developed the institutions that effectively uphold an order of stratification. States are strongly territorial, with complex, well-defined political leadership, hierarchies of settlement, and often elaborate and highly specialized bureaucracies. Populations can range from the thousands to the millions.

stela cult The widespread use of inscribed monoliths, one of the most prominent and unique Maya Great Tradition markers.

stelae (*sing.* **stela**) Standing monumental stone slabs, sometimes elaborately carved.

Stone Age Term often used to characterize cultures that used stone for cutting and other primary tools, thus designating a stage of technological development.

stratification The process of development of social strata (layers) or subdivisions within a society; the differential ranking of social groups with regard to prestige, power, and wealth.

stratified sample A selection of cases which includes representatives from each of several important subgroups of the whole population.

stratified society Large society in which whole groups of people are ranked vis-à-vis one another, with high-ranking groups having more access to political office, authority, and wealth than lower-ranking ones.

stratigraphic profiles Drawings of natural and/or cultural deposits of strata of a trench which can be correlated with the collections recovered from that trench.

stratigraphy The deposition, distribution, and age of strata, or layers. Stratigraphy is used as a relative dating technique.

structure Materialist term for the social and political organizational components of human cultures.

structuralism Viewpoint which assumes that much of the content of culture can only be understood by recognizing the constraints on variability that are built into the human brain.

subassemblage Set of artifacts representing the tools used for a particular task (such as food-preparation vessels and tools).

subsistence Means of supporting life, in particular by obtaining food.

subsistence strategy Decisions and actions that affect the raw material procurement of a society.

subsystems Parts of a system that have distinctive functions and that are arranged in hierarchical levels.

superstructure Materialist term for "the realm of values, beliefs, aesthetics, rules, symbols, rituals, religions, philosophies, and other forms of knowledge, including science itself" (Harris 1991:74).

surface survey and mapping The systematic location and recording of surface remains in the archaeological record; subsurface remains are also often mapped.

swidden farming Type of agriculture based on cutting and burning natural vegetation to provide nutrients to the crops. In this method, it is necessary to change fields every few years. Also known as **slash-and-burn agriculture**.

symbol Expression which is arbitrarily associated with what it conveys.

symbolic systems Sets of symbols that mutually reinforce each other and that are used in combination to convey meaning.

system Group of interrelated and interdependent parts forming a whole.

system-serving behavior Actions which serve the interests of the whole group.

systematic sample Sample that incorporates randomness and determinacy by specifying that the random selection of a case example has to occur within a certain group of cases.

systematic settlement survey Reconnaissance of a region based on a sampling design ensuring that all types of areas within the region will be surveyed.

taiga Coniferous forest in the northern latitudes.

taphonomy The study of natural and cultural processes affecting organic remains after death, and their depositional characteristics.

technoeconomic organization The way energy and materials (including food and other necessities) are produced, distributed, and consumed, the way labor is organized, and how technology is used.

technology The steps taken, or **manufacturing process** used, to produce an artifact.

temporal context The age or date of an object and its temporal relation to other objects in the archaeological record.

theocracy Form of government in which authority is held by religious specialists.

theory A scientific explanation of the world as we perceive it that has been widely tested and accepted as more useful than competing explanations.

thermoluminescence Relative dating technique which examines the natural radiation occurring in ceramics, minerals, glass, and bone and which measures changes that have occurred in the physiochemical structure of the various materials. Other such techniques are **fission track dating,** and **electron spin resonance**.

three-age sequence A classification system developed by C. J. Thomsen which orders the cultural remains of the Old World into three major phases based on the raw material of such remains and technology—that is, the Stone Age, the Bronze Age, and the Iron Age. Inherent in this system is the idea that a chronological order could be achieved by placing things in this sequence.

total system approach Research based on the assumption that in order to reconstruct an ancient culture, all parts of it must be examined.

totem Particular object (animals, natural phenomenon, place) that serves to identify a specific group, such as a clan.

trade A special kind of exchange whereby raw resources or finished goods not locally available are obtained somewhere else, often from distant sources, in exchange for other goods.

traditional Adjective applied to societies and economies strongly shaped by conservative adherence to long-established customs.

trait list A list of characteristics describing an archaeological culture.

tribal societies Egalitarian societies larger and more complex than bands, often sedentary; practice either hunting and gathering or food production, with politically autonomous communities. Political dominance is gained through achieved leadership rather than ascribed leadership, and sodalities are important in intergrating the social system.

trophic levels Levels within the food chain characterized by similar energy consumption.

tundra Plant community comprised of grasses, lichens, sedges, mosses, and scattered dwarf trees.

typology Process of establishing and selecting categories for data and for the systems of categories themselves.

uniformitarianism The geological principle that the configuration of the earth's surface is the product of processes that may be observed to operate in the present; more generally, the principle that observations in the present are the key to understanding the past.

unilinear evolution The idea, especially associated with 19th-century evolutionists such as L. H. Morgan, that all cultures pass through the same sequence of evolutionary changes, or stages.

Upper Egypt The narrow part of the Nile Valley, about 1,100 km long, that lies north of Aswan and south of the Nile delta region. This is the southern part of the river in the modern nation of Egypt.

urban core At the Maya center of Copán (Honduras), an area of dense archaeological settlement, one square kilometer in size, located around the Main Group; consists of the Main Group and the ancient residential neighborhoods known as Sepulturas and El Bosque.

use-wear analysis Technique for determining the use of an artifact which is based on the assumption that different activities leave characteristic microscars, polishes, edge-wear, rounding, and striations on tools and vessels.

wattle Framework of poles and other thin pieces of wood for the construction of a wall.

witness column See **baulk**.

xerophytic Adapted to grow in arid environments.

X-ray emission Method to determine the elements of a bone by bombarding it with electrons to produce a signature pattern of X-rays.

X-ray fluorescence analysis Method of material-composition analysis in which X-ray irradiation reveals characteristic wavelengths of elements.

ziggurat Mesopotamian term denoting a high platform or mound built of successively smaller terraces, one on top of another, crowned by a temple.

BIBLIOGRAPHY

Numbers in brackets [ ] at the end of each entry refer to chapters in which the topic is discussed.

Abler, R., J. S. Adams, and P. Gould. 1971. *Spatial Organization*. Englewood Cliffs, N.J.: Prentice-Hall. [7, 10]

Abrams, E. 1987. Economic specialization and construction personnel in Classic period Copán, Honduras. *American Antiquity* 52:485–499. [3]

———. 1989. Architecture and energy: An evolutionary approach. In *Archaeological Method and Theory,* vol. 1, ed. M. B. Schiffer, pp. 47–87. Tucson: University of Arizona Press. [3]

Abrams, E., and D. Rue. 1989. The causes and consequences of deforestation among the prehistoric Maya. *Human Ecology* 16:377–395. [3, 15]

Adams, R. E. W., ed. 1977. *The Origins of Maya Civilization*. Albuquerque: University of New Mexico Press. [14]

Adams, R. E. W., W. E. Brown, Jr., and T. P. Culbert. 1981. Radar mapping, archaeology, and ancient Maya land use. *Science* 213(4515):1457–1463. [3, 4, 14]

Adams, R. M. 1966. *The Evolution of Urban Society*. Chicago: Aldine. [13]

———. 1981. *Heartland of Cities*. Chicago: University of Chicago Press. [2, 13]

Adams, R. M., and M. J. Nissen. 1972. *The Uruk Countryside*. Chicago: University of Chicago Press.

Adams, R. N. 1981. Natural selection, energetics, and "cultural materialism." *Current Anthropology* 22(6): 603–624. [2, 5]

Adovasio, J. M., J. Donahue, and R. Stuckenrath. 1990. The Meadowcroft Rockshelter radiocarbon chronology 1975–1990. *American Antiquity* 55:348–54. [4]

Agurcia, R. F., and W. Fash. 1989. A royal Maya tomb discovered. *National Geographic Magazine,* 176(4): 480–487.

Aitken, M. J. 1974. *Physics and Archaeology*, 2nd ed. Oxford: Clarendon Press. [4]

———. 1985. *Thermoluminescence Dating*. Orlando, Fla.: Academic Press. [4]

Allan, W. 1965. *The African Husbandman*. New York: Barnes and Noble. [6]

Allchin, B., and R. Allchin. 1982. *The Rise of Civilization in India and Pakistan*. Cambridge: Cambridge University Press. [13]

Allen, K. M. S., S. W. Green, and E. B. W. Zubrow. 1990. *Interpreting Space: GIS and Archaeology*. London: Taylor and Francis. [4]

Allen, W. L., and J. B. Richardson, III. 1971. The reconstruction of kinship from archaeological data: The concepts, the methods, and the feasibility. *American Antiquity* 36(1):41–53. [7]

Alva, W. 1990. New tomb of royal splendor. *National Geographic Magazine* 177(6):2–16. [14]

Ambrose, W. 1976. Intrinsic hydration rate dating of obsidian. In Taylor, ed., pp. 81–105. [4]

Ammerman, A. J. 1981. Surveys and archaeological research. *Annual Review of Anthropology* 10:63–88. [4]

Ammerman, A. J., L. L. Cavalli-Sforza, and D. K. Wagener. 1976. Toward the estimation of population growth in Old World prehistory. In Zubrow, ed., pp. 27–61. [7, 13]

Anderson, A., and C. Dibble, trans. 1978 [1555]. *The War of Conquest*. Salt Lake City: University of Utah Press. [1]

Anderson, D. D. 1968. A stone age campsite at the gateway to America. *Scientific American* 218:24–33. [2]

Anderson, P. C. 1980. A testimony of prehistoric tasks: Diagnostic residues on stone tool working edges. *World Archaeology* 12:181–194. [4]

Andresen, J. M., B. F. Byrd, M. D. Elson, R. H. McGuire, R. G. Mendoza, E. Staski, and J. P. White. 1981. The deer hunters: Star Carr reconsidered. *World Archaeology* 13:31–46. [6]

Andrews, A. 1980. The salt trade of the ancient Maya. *Archaeology* 33:24–33. [8]

Andrews, A., F. Asaro, F. Stross, and P. C. Rivero. 1989. The obsidian trade at Isla Cerritos, Yucatán, Mexico. *Journal of Field Archaeology* 16:355–362. [8]

Angel, J. L. 1969. The bases of paleodemography. *American Journal of Physical Anthropology* 30:427–437. [4]

Anonymous Conqueror. 1917. *Narrative of Some Things of New Spain and of the Great City of Temestitán, Mexico*. Translated and annotated by M. H. Saville. New York: Cortés Society. [1]

Armillas, P. 1971. Gardens on swamps. *Science* 174:653–661. [6]

Arnold, D. E. 1985. *Ceramic Theory and Cultural Process*. New York: Cambridge University Press. [4]

Arnold, J. R., and W. F. Libby. 1949. Age determinations by radiocarbon content: Checks with samples of known age. *Science* 110:678–680. [4]

Artamonov, M. I. 1965. Frozen tombs of the Scythians. *Scientific American* 212:100–109. [4]

Ascher, R. 1968. Time's arrow and the archaeology of a contemporary community. In *Settlement Archaeology*, ed., K. C. Chang, pp. 43–52. Palo Alto, Calif.: National Press Books. [7]

Ashmore, W. 1991. Site-planning principles and concepts of directionality among the ancient Maya. *Latin American Antiquity* 2:199–226. [3, 12]

Ashmore, W., and R. R. Wilk. 1988. Household and community in the Mesoamerican past. In Wilk and Ashmore, eds., pp. 1–27. [7]

Atkinson, R. J. C. 1966. Moonshine on Stonehenge. *Antiquity* 40(159):212–216. [12]

Aveni, A. F. 1981. Archaeoastronomy. *Advances in Archaeological Method and Theory*, vol. 4, ed., M. B. Schiffer, pp. 1–77. New York: Academic Press. [12]

———. 1989. *Empires of Time*. New York: Basic Books. [9, 12]

Aveni, A., and S. L. Gibbs. 1976. On the orientation of Precolumbian buildings in central Mexico. *American Antiquity* 41:510–517. [12]

Bada, J. L., and P. M. Helfman. 1975. Amino acid racemization dating of fossil bones. *World Archaeology* 7:160–173. [4]

Baillie, M. G. L. 1982. *Tree-Ring Dating and Archaeology*. Chicago: University of Chicago Press. [4]

Ball, J. W. 1974. A Teotihuacán-style cache from the Maya lowlands. *Archaeology* 27:2–9. [11]

Bamforth, D. B., and A. C. Spaulding. 1982. Human behavior, explanation, archaeology, history, and science. *Journal of Anthropological Archaeology* 1(2):179–195. [2, 5, 16]

Bannister, B., and W. J. Robinson. 1975. Tree-ring dating in archaeology. *World Archaeology* 7(2);210–225. [4]

Barth, F. 1956. Ecologic relationships of ethnic groups in Swat, North Pakistan. *American Anthropologist* 58:1079–1089. [6]

Bascom, W. 1955. Urbanization among the Yoruba. *American Journal of Sociology* 60:446–454. [7]

Baudez, C., ed. 1983. *Introduccion a la arqueología de Copán, Honduras*, vols. 1–3. Tegucigalpa: Secreteria del Estado en el Despacho de Cultura y Turismo. [3]

Baumhoff, M. A. 1963. Ecological determinants of aboriginal California populations. University of California Publications in American Archaeology and Ethnology 49(2):155–236. [6]

Bayard, D. T. 1969. Science, theory, and reality in the "new archaeology." *American Antiquity* 34(4):376–384. [2, 16]

Beadle, G. W. 1977. The origin of Zea mays. In *Origins of Agriculture*, ed., C. A. Reed, pp. 615–635. The Hague: Mouton. [5, 14]

Behrensmeyer, A. K., and A. P. Hill, eds. 1980. *Fossils in the Making: Vertebrate Taphonomy and Paleoecology*. Chicago: University of Chicago Press. [4]

Bellwood, P. 1979. *Man's Conquest of the Pacific*. New York: Oxford University Press.

———. 1987. *The Polynesians: Prehistory of an Island People*. New York: Thames and Hudson. [8, 10]

Benedict, R. 1934. *Patterns of Culture*. Boston: Houghton Mifflin. [2, 5]

Bennett, J. W. 1976. *The Ecological Transition: Cultural Anthropology and Human Adaptation*. New York: Pergamon. [6]

Benson, E., ed. 1971. *Mesoamerican Writing Systems*. Washington, D.C.: Dumbarton Oaks. [9]

Benson, E. 1972. *The Mochica*. New York: Praeger.

Berdan, F. F. 1982. *The Aztecs of Central Mexico: An Imperial Society*. New York: Holt, Rinehart and Winston. [7, 10, 14]

Bernal, I. 1980. *A History of Mexican Archaeology*. London, New York: Thames and Hudson. [1]

Berry, B. J. L. 1967. *Geography of Market Centers and Retail Distribution*. Englewood Cliffs, N.J.: Prentice-Hall. [4, 8]

Bettinger, R. L. 1977. Aboriginal human ecology in Owens Valley: Prehistoric change in the Great Basin. *American Antiquity* 42(1):3–17. [5]

———. 1980. Explanatory/predictive models of hunter-gatherer adaptation. In *Advances in Archaeological Method and Theory*, vol. 3, ed., M. B. Schiffer, pp. 189–255. New York: Academic Press. [5, 6]

———. 1987. Archaeological approaches to hunter-gatherers. *Annual Review of Anthropology* 16:121–142. [5, 6]

Binford, L. R. 1962. Archaeology as anthropology. *American Antiquity* 28:217–225. [1, 2]

————. 1964. A consideration of archaeological research design. *American Antiquity* 29(4):425–441. [4]

————. 1965. Archaeological systematics and the study of cultural process. *American Antiquity* 31(2):203–210. [5, 16]

————. 1967. Smudge pits and hide smoking: The use of analogy in archaeological reasoning. *American Antiquity* 32(1):1–12. [1]

————. 1968a. Archaeological Perspectives. In *New Perspectives in Archaeology*, eds., S. R. Binford and L. R. Binford, pp. 5–32. Chicago: Aldine. [1, 2]

————. 1968b. Post-Pleistocene adaptations. In *New Perspectives in Archaeology*, eds., S. R. Binford and L. R. Binford, pp. 313–341. Chicago: Aldine. [5]

————. 1968c. Some comments on historical versus processual archaeology. *Southwestern Journal of Anthropology* 24(3):267–275. [2]

————. 1971. Mortuary practices: Their study and their potential. In *Approaches to the Social Dimensions of Mortuary Practices*, ed., J. Brown. *Memoirs of the Society for American Archaeology* 25:6–29. [4, 10, 11]

————. 1972. *An Archaeological Perspective.* New York: Seminar Press. [5]

————. 1978. *Nunamiut Ethnoarchaeology.* New York: Academic Press.

————. 1983a. *In Pursuit of the Past: Decoding the Archaeological Record.* London: Thames and Hudson. [5, 16]

————. 1983b. *Working at Archaeology.* New York: Academic Press. [5, 16]

Binford, S. R., and L. R. Binford, eds. 1968. *New Perspectives in Archaeology.* Chicago: Aldine. [2]

Birdsell, J. B. 1953. Some environmental and cultural factors influencing the structure of Australian aboriginal populations. *American Naturalist* 87(834):171–207. [6]

Bishop, R. L., R. L. Rands, and G. R. Holley. 1982. Ceramic compositional analysis in archaeological perspective. In *Advances in Archaeological Method and Theory*, vol. 5, ed., M. B. Schiffer, pp. 275–330. New York: Academic Press. [4]

Blake, M., S. LeBlanc, and P. Minnis. 1986. Changing settlement and population in the Mimbres valley, Southwestern New Mexico. *Journal of Field Archaeology* 13:439–464. [6]

Blanton, R. E. 1978. *Monte Alban: Settlement Patterns at the Ancient Zapotec Capital.* New York: Academic Press. [14]

Blanton, R. E., S. A. Kowalewski, G. Feinman, and J. Appel. 1981. *Ancient Mesoamerica: A Comparison of Change in Three Regions.* Cambridge: Cambridge University Press. [14]

Blunden, C., and M. Elvin. 1983. *Cultural Atlas of China.* New York: Facts on File. [13]

Bobrowsky, P. T., and B. F. Ball. 1989. The theory and mechanics of ecological diversity in archaeology. In Leonard and Jones, eds., pp. 4–12. [5]

Boone, E. H., ed. 1984. *Ritual Human Sacrifice in Mesoamerica.* Washington, D.C.: Dumbarton Oaks. [12]

Boone, J. L. 1987. Defining and measuring midden catchment. *American Antiquity* 52:336–345. [4]

Boorstin, D. J. 1983. *The Discoverers.* New York: Random House. [1]

Boyd, C. C., and D. C. Boyd. 1991. A multidimensional investigation of biocultural relationships among three late prehistoric societies in Tennessee. *American Antiquity* 56:75–88. [4]

Boserup, E. 1965. *Conditions of Agricultural Growth: The Economics of Agrarian Change under Population Pressure.* Chicago: Aldine. [5, 16]

Bourdier, J.-P., and T. T. Minh-ha. 1985. *African Spaces.* New York: Africana Publishing. [7]

Braidwood, R. J. 1960. The Agricultural Revolution. *Scientific American* 203:130–148. [5, 13]

Brainerd, G. W. 1951. The place of chronological ordering in archaeological analysis. *American Antiquity* 16:301–313. [4]

Braun, D. P., and S. Plog. 1982. Evolution of "tribal" social networks: Theory and prehistoric North American evidence. *American Antiquity* 47(3):504–525. [10]

Broda, J., D. Carrasco, and E. Matos Moctezume. 1987. *The Great Temple of Tenochtitlan: Center and Periphery in the Aztec World.* Berkeley: University of California Press. [12, 14]

Bronowski, J. 1978. *The Common Sense of Science.* Cambridge: Harvard University Press. [1, 2, 16]

————. 1956. *Science and Human Values.* New York: Harper and Row. [1, 2]

Brose, D. S. 1985. The Woodland Period. In Brose, Brown, and Penney, eds., pp. 47–92. [7, 8, 10]

Brose, D. S., J. A. Brown, and D. W. Penney, eds. 1985. *Ancient Art of the American Woodland Indians.* Detroit: Detroit Institute of the Arts.

Brothwell, D. R. 1963. *Digging Up Bones: The Excavation, Treatment and Study of Human Skeletal Remains.* London: The British Museum. [4]

————. 1986. *The Bog Man and the Archaeology of People.* Cambridge: Harvard University Press. [4]

Brothwell, D., and E. Higgs, eds. 1970. *Science in Archaeology: A Survey of Progress and Research,* 2nd ed. New York: Praeger. [4]

Browman, D. L. 1981. Isotopic discrimination and correction factors in radiocarbon dating. In *Advances in Archaeological Method and Theory,* vol. 6, ed., M. B. Schiffer, pp. 241–295. New York: Academic Press. [4]

Brown, J. A., ed. 1971. *Approaches to the Social Dimensions of Mortuary Practices.* Memoirs of the Society for American Archaeology, no. 25. [4, 10]

Brown, J. A. 1975. Spiro art and its mortuary contexts. In *Death and the Afterlife in Pre-Columbian America,* ed., E. P. Benson, pp. 1–32, Washington D.C.: Dumbarton Oaks.

Bruhns, K. O., J. H. Burton, and G. R. Miller. 1990. Excavations at Pirincay in the Paute Valley of southern Ecuador, 1985–1988. *Antiquity* 64:221–233. [14]

Brumfiel, E. 1987. Consumption and Politics at Aztec Huexotla. *American Anthropologist* 89:676–686. [8, 10]

Bryant, V. M., Jr., and R. G. Holloway. 1983. The role of palynology in archaeology. In *Advances in Archaeological Method and Theory,* vol. 6, ed., M. B. Schiffer, pp. 191–224. New York: Academic Press. [3, 4, 15]

Bryant, V. M., Jr., and G. Williams-Dean. 1975. The coprolites of man. *Scientific American* 232:100–109. [4]

Buchler, I. R., and H. A. Selby. 1968. *Kinship and Social Organization.* New York: Macmillan. [7]

Buikstra, J. E. 1976. *Hopewell in the Lower Illinois Valley: A Regional Study of Human Biological Variability and Prehistoric Mortuary Behavior.* Northwestern Archaeological Program Scientific Papers, no. 2. [4, 8]

Buikstra, J. E., and D. C. Cook. 1980. Paleopathology: An American account. *Annual Review of Anthropology* 9:433–470. [4]

Buikstra, J. E., and L. Konigsberg. 1985. Paleodemography: Critiques and controversies. *American Anthropologist* 87:316–333. [4]

Bullard, W. R. 1960. Maya settlement pattern in northeastern Petén, Guatemala. *American Antiquity* 25:355–372. [2]

Butzer, K. W. 1971. *Environment and Archaeology,* 2nd ed. Chicago: Aldine. [6]

————. 1976. *Early Hydraulic Civilization in Egypt: A Study in Cultural Ecology.* Chicago: University of Chicago Press.

————. 1980. Civilizations: Organisms or systems? *American Scientist* 68:517–523. [5]

————. 1982. *Archaeology as Human Ecology.* Cambridge: Cambridge University Press. [6]

Byers, D. S., ed. 1967. *The Prehistory of the Tehuacán Valley: Environment and Subsistence,* vol. 1. Austin: University of Texas Press. [5, 6, 14]

Byland, B., and J. Pohl. 1992. *In the Realm of 8 Deer: Archaeology and Ethnohistory of the Mixtec Codices.* Norman: University of Oklahoma Press. [10]

Cabrera, R., S. Sugiyama, and G. Cowgill. 1991. The Templo de Quétzalcóatl Project at Teotihuacán: A Preliminary Report. *Ancient Mesoamerica* 2:77–92. [12, 14]

Calnek, E. E. 1973. The localization of the sixteenth century map called the Maguey Plan. *American Antiquity* 38:190–195. [7, 14]

————. 1976. The Internal Structure of Tenochtitlan. In *The Valley of Mexico,* ed., E. Wolf, pp. 287–302. Albuquerque: University of New Mexico Press. [7]

————. 1982. Patterns of empire formation in the Valley of Mexico, Late Postclassic Period, 1200–1521. In Collier, Rosaldo, and Wirth, eds., pp. 43–62. [14]

Cambel, H., and R. J. Braidwood. 1970. An early farming village in Turkey. *Scientific American* 222:50–56. [5, 13]

Campbell, B. 1979. *Humankind Emerging,* 2nd ed. Boston: Little, Brown. [6]

————. 1985. *Human Ecology.* New York: Aldine. [6]

Carbone, V. A., and B. C. Keel. 1985. Preservation of plant and animal remains. In *The Analysis of Prehistoric Diets,* eds., R. I. Gilbert and J. H. Mielke. New York: Academic Press. [4]

Carneiro, R. L. 1967. On the relationship between size of population and complexity of social organization. *Southwestern Journal of Anthropology* 23:234–243. [10]

————. 1970. A theory of the origin of the state. *Science* 169:733–738. [10, 16]

Carr, C., ed. 1985. *For Concordance in Archaeological Analysis: Bridging Data Structure, Quantitative Technique, and Theory.* Kansas City, Mo.: Westport. [4]

Carrasco, D. 1990. *Religions of Mesoamerica.* San Francisco: Harper and Row. [12]

Carrasco, P. 1964. Family Structure of Sixteenth Century Tepoztlán. In *Process and Pattern in Culture: Essays in Honor of Julian H. Steward,* ed., R. A. Manners, pp. 185–210. Chicago: Aldine. [7]

————. 1971a. The peoples of central Mexico and their historical traditions. In *Handbook of Middle American Indians,* vol. 11, ed., R. Wauchope, pp. 459–473. Austin: University of Texas Press. [14]

———. 1971b. Social Organization of Ancient Mexico. In *Handbook of Middle American Indians,* vol. 10, ed., R. Wauchope, pp. 349–375. [7, 14]

———. 1982. The Political Economy of the Aztec and Inca States. In Collier, Rosaldo, and Wirth, eds., pp. 23–40. [8, 10, 11, 14]

Carter, H. 1954. *The Tomb of Tutankhamen.* London: Excalibur. [2]

Chagnon, N. 1983. *Yanomamo: The Fierce People.* New York: Holt, Rinehart and Winston. [7, 8, 14]

Champion, T. C., ed. 1989. *Centre and Periphery.* London: Unwin Hyman. [7, 10, 11]

Chandler, T., and G. Fox. 1974. *3000 Years of Urban Growth.* New York: Academic Press. [8]

Chang, Kwang-chih. 1980. *Shang Civilization.* New Haven: Yale University Press. [13]

———. 1986. *The Archaeology of Ancient China.* New Haven: Yale University Press. [13]

Chaplin, R. E. 1971. *The Study of Animal Bones from Archaeological Sites.* London and New York: Seminar Press. [4]

Chapple, E., and C. Coon. 1942. *Principles of Anthropology.* New York: Henry Holt. [1, 6]

Charlton, T. H. 1978. Teotihuacán, Tepeapulco, and obsidian exploitation. *Science* 200:1227–1236. [8, 14]

Charnay, D. 1888. *The Ancient Cities of the New World Being Voyages and Explorations in Mexico and Central America from 1857–1882.* New York: Harper. [2, 14]

Chartkoff, J. L., and K. K. Chartkoff. 1984. *The Archaeology of California.* Stanford, Calif.: Stanford University Press. [5, 14]

Chase, A. F., D. Z. Chase, and H. W. Topsey. 1988. Archaeology and the ethics of collecting. *Archaeology* 41:56. [1, 2]

Childe, V. G. 1925. *The Dawn of European Civilization.* London: Kegan Paul. [2, 13]

———. 1950. The urban revolution. *Town Planning Review* 44:3–17.

———. 1951a. *Man Makes Himself.* New York: New American Library. [2, 13]

———1951b. *Social Evolution.* New York: Henry Schuman. [5]

Chippendale, C., N. Hammond, and J. A. Sabloff. 1988. The archaeology of Maya decipherment. *Antiquity* 62:119–122. [9]

Chisolm, B. S., D. E. Nelson, and H. P. Schwarz. 1982. Stable-carbon isotope ratios as a measure of marine versus terrestrial protein in ancient diets. *Science* 216: 1131–1132. [4]

Christaller, W. 1966. *Central Places in Southern Germany.* Englewood Cliffs, N.J.: Prentice-Hall. [4, 7, 11]

Claassen, C. 1986. Shellfishing seasons in the prehistoric southeastern United States. *American Antiquity* 51: 21–37. [5]

Clark, J. D. G. 1972. *Star Carr: A Case Study in Bioarchaeology.* McCaleb Module in Anthropology, no. 10. Reading, Mass.: Addison-Wesley. [6]

———. 1954. *Excavations at Star Carr, an Early Mesolithic Site at Seamer, near Scarborough, Yorkshire.* Cambridge, Cambridge University Press. [5, 6]

Clark, J. E. 1989. Obsidian tool manufacture. In Voorhies, ed., pp. 215–228. [6, 8]

Clark, P. and F. Evans. 1954. Distance to nearest neighbor as a measure of spatial relationships in populations. *Ecology* 35:445–453. [4, 10, 11]

Clarke, D., ed. 1977. *Spatial Archaeology.* New York: Academic Press. [4, 7, 10, 11]

Clarke, D. L., and B. Chapman. 1978. *Analytical Archaeology,* 2nd ed. New York: Columbia University Press. [2, 4, 5]

Coale, A. 1971. The history of the human population. *Scientific American* 231(3):40–51. [6]

Codex Magliabechiano. 1983 [1903]. *The Book of the Life of the Ancient Mexicans.* Reproduced in facsimile with introduction, translation, and commentary by Z. Nuttall. Part I: *Introduction and Facsimile.* Berkeley: University of California Press. [2, 14]

Codex Nuttall. 1975. *A Picture Manuscript from Ancient Mexico.* Peabody Museum Facsimile, edited by Z. Nuttall [1902]. With a new introductory text by A. G. Miller. New York: Dover. [11, 14]

Coe, M. 1961. Social typology and the tropical forest civilizations. *Comparative Studies in Society and History* 4(1):65–85. [5]

———. 1973. *The Maya Scribe and His World.* New York: Grolier Club. [9]

———. 1991 A Triumph of spirit (How Yuri Knorosov cracked the Maya hieroglyphic code). *Archaeology* 44: 39–44. [2, 14]

Coe, M., and K. Flannery. 1964. Microenvironments and Mesoamerican prehistory. *Science* 143:650–654. [5, 6, 14]

Coe, M., D. Snow, and E. Benson. 1986. *Atlas of Ancient America.* New York: Facts on File. [6, 14]

Cohen, A. 1974. *Two-Dimensional Man.* Berkeley: University of California Press. [9]

Cohen, M. N. 1977. *The Food Crisis in Prehistory: Overpopulation and the Origins of Agriculture*. New Haven: Yale University Press. [6, 16]

Cohen, M. N., and G. J. Armelagos, eds. 1984. *Paleopathology at the Origins of Agriculture*. Orlando, Fla.: Academic Press. [5, 6, 16]

Cohen, R., and E. Service, eds. 1978. *Origins of the State: The Anthropology of Political Evolution*. Philadelphia: ISHI. [5, 10, 16]

Coles, J. M. 1979. *Experimental Archaeology*. New York: Academic Press. [4]

Colinvaux, P. 1973. *Introduction to Ecology*. New York: J. Wiley. [5, 6]

Collier, G. A., R. I. Rosaldo, and J. D. Wirth, eds. 1982. *The Inca and Aztec States 1400–1800*. New York: Academic Press. [14]

Conkey, M. W. 1978. Style and information in cultural evolution: Toward a predictive model for the paleolithic. In Redman et al., eds., pp. 61–85. [12]

————. 1980. The identification of prehistoric hunter-gatherer aggregation sites: The case of Altamira. *Current Anthropology* 21:609–630. [7]

————. 1991. Contexts of action, contexts for power: Material culture and gender in the Magdalenian. In Gero and Conkey, eds., pp. 57–92. [2, 7]

Conkey, M. W., and J. Spector. 1984. Archaeology and the study of gender. In *Advances in Archaeological Method and Theory,* vol. 7, ed., M. B. Schiffer, pp. 1–38. Orlando, Fla.: Academic Press. [2]

Connolly, B., and R. Anderson. 1987. *First Contact*. New York: Viking Penguin. [6]

Conticello, B. 1990. Rediscovering Pompeii. In *Rediscovering Pompeii*, pp. 2–25. Rome: L'Erma di Bretschneider. [1, 13]

Coon, C. 1958. *Caravan*. New York: Holt, Rinehart and Winston. [8, 13]

Cordell, L. S. 1984. *Prehistory of the Southwest*. San Diego, Calif.: Academic Press. [6, 7, 14]

Cornfeld, G. 1976. *Archaeology of the Bible*. New York: Harper and Row. [12, 13]

Cortés, Hernan. 1986. *Letters from Mexico*. Edited and translated by Anthony Pagden. New Haven: Yale University Press. [1, 14]

Costin, C. L., and T. Earle. 1989. Status distinction and legitimation of power as reflected in changing patterns of consumption in late prehispanic Peru. *American Antiquity* 54:691–714. [14]

Cotterell, A., ed. 1980. *The Encyclopedia of Ancient Civilizations*. New York: Mayflower. [13, 14]

Cowgill, G. L. 1975. On the causes and consequences of ancient and modern population changes. *American Anthropologist* 77:505–525. [5, 16]

————. 1983. Rulership and the Ciudadela: Political inferences from Teotihuacán Architecture. In *Civilization in the Ancient Americas, Essays in Honor of Gordon R. Willey*, eds., R. Leventhal and A. Kolata, pp. 313–343. Cambridge, Mass.: University of New Mexico and Harvard University [10, 12, 14]

Crabtree, D. E. 1968. Mesoamerican polyhedral cores and prismatic blades. *American Antiquity* 33:446–478. [6, 8, 14]

Crawford, G. W., and H. Takamiya. 1990. The origins and implications of late prehistoric plant husbandry in northern Japan. *Antiquity* 64:889–911. [5, 6, 13]

Creamer, W., and J. Haas. 1985. Tribe versus chiefdom in lower Central America. *American Antiquity* 50:738–754. [5, 14]

Crumley, C. 1976. Toward a locational definition of state systems of settlement. *American Anthropologist* 78(1):59–73. [10, 11]

Culbert, T. P., ed. 1973. *The Classic Maya Collapse*. Albuquerque: University of New Mexico Press. [14, 15]

————. 1991. *Classic Maya Political History*. New York: Cambridge University Press. [10, 11]

Culbert, T. P., and D. S. Rice, eds. 1990. *Precolumbian Population History in the Maya Lowlands*. Albuquerque: University of New Mexico Press. [10, 11, 14, 15]

Custer, J., S. Watson, and C. De Santis. 1987. An early Woodland Household cluster at the Clyde Farm Site, Delaware. *Journal of Field Archaeology* 14:229–235. [7]

D'Altroy, T. N., and R. L. Bishop. 1990. The provincial organization of Inka Ceramic Production. *American Antiquity* 55:120–138. [8, 14]

Daniel, G. 1975. *One Hundred and Fifty Years of Archaeology*. London: Duckworth. [2]

————. 1981. *A Short History of Archaeology*. London: Thames and Hudson. [2]

Daniel, G., and C. Renfrew. 1988. *The Idea of Prehistory*. Edinburgh: University of Edinburgh Press. [1, 2]

Darwin, C. 1958 [1859]. *The Origin of Species, by Means of Natural Selection or the Preservation of Favoured Races in the Struggle for Life*. Introduction by Sir Julian Huxley. New York: New American Library. [2, 5]

————. 1980. *Metaphysics, Materialism, and the Evolution of Mind*. Transcribed by P. H. Barrett. Chicago: University of Chicago Press.

David, N. 1971. The Fulani compound and the archaeologist. *World Archaeology* 3:111–131. [4]

———. 1972. On the life span of pottery, type frequencies, and archaeological inference. *American Antiquity* 37:141–142. [4]

Davis, G. R. 1990. Energy for Planet Earth. *Scientific American* 263:3. [6]

Davis, H. A. 1972. The crisis in American archaeology. *Science* 175:267–272. [2, 16]

Dawkins, R. 1986. *The Blind Watchmaker*. New York: Norton. [5]

Dean, J. S. 1978. Tree-Ring Dating in Archaeology. *University of Utah Miscellaneous Anthropological Papers,* no. 24, pp. 129–163. [4]

———. 1978. Independent dating in archaeological analysis. In *Advances in Archaeological Method and Theory,* vol. 1, ed., M. B. Schiffer, pp. 223–255. New York: Academic Press. [4]

Deetz, J. 1965. *The Dynamics of Stylistic Change in Arikara Ceramics.* Urbana: University of Illinois Press. [2]

———. 1967. *Invitation to Archaeology.* Garden City, N.Y.: Natural History Press. [1]

———. 1968. The inference of residence and descent rules from archaeological data. In *New Perspectives in Archaeology,* eds., S. R. Binford and L. R. Binford, pp. 41–48. Chicago: Aldine. [7]

———. 1977. *In Small Things Forgotten: The Archaeology of Early American Life.* Garden City, N.Y.: Anchor Books. [1, 2, 4]

———. 1982. Households: A structural key to archaeological explanation. *American Behavioral Scientist* 25:717–724. [7]

———. 1988. Material culture and worldview in colonial Anglo-America. In *The Recovery of Meaning: Historical Archaeology in the Eastern United States,* eds., M. Leone and P. Potter, pp. 219–233. Washington, D.C.: Smithsonian Institution Press. [2, 9]

Deetz, J., and E. Dethlefsen. 1967. Death's head, cherub, urn and willow. *Natural History* 76:28–37. [2]

Deiss, J. J. 1985. *Herculaneum.* Cambridge: Harper and Row. [1]

deLumley, H. 1969. A Paleolithic camp at Nice. *Scientific American* 220:42–50. [7]

Denham, W. W. 1979. Research design and research proposal checklists. In *Anthropology Newsletter* of the American Anthropological Association, vol. 20, no. 4, pp. 9–11.

DeNiro, M. J. 1987. Stable isotopy and archaeology. *American Scientist* 75(2):182–191. [4]

DeNiro, M. J., and M. J. Schoeniger. 1983. Stable carbon and nitrogen isotope ratios of bone collagen: Variations within individuals, between sexes, and within populations raised on monotonous diets. *Journal of Archaeological Science* 10(3):199–203. [3, 4, 15]

Diaz del Castillo, B. 1963. *The Conquest of New Spain.* Baltimore, Md.: Penguin Books. [1, 7, 10, 11, 14]

Diehl, R. A. 1983. *Tula: The Toltec Capital of Ancient Mexico.* London: Thames and Hudson. [14]

Dillehay, T. D. 1988. How new is the New World? *Antiquity* 62:94–97. [2, 6, 14]

———. 1989. *Monte Verde: A Late Pleistocene Settlement in Chile.* Washington, D.C.: Smithsonian Institution Press. [2, 6, 14]

Dillehay, T. D., and D. J. Meltzer, eds. 1991. *The First Americans, Search and Research.* Boca Raton, Fla.: CRC Press. [2, 14]

Dillon, B. D., ed. 1989. *Practical archaeology: Field and laboratory techniques and archaeological logistics.* Archaeological Research Tools 2. Los Angeles: Institute of Archaeology, University of California. [4]

Dimbleby, G. 1967. *Plants and Archaeology.* New York: Humanities Press. [4, 6]

Diskin, M. 1976. The structure of a peasant market system in Oaxaca. In *Markets in Oaxaca,* eds., S. Cook and M. Diskin, pp. 49–65. Austin: University of Texas Press. [8]

Dixon, J. E., J. R. Cann, and C. Renfrew. 1968. Obsidian and the origins of trade. *Scientific American* 218:38–46. [6, 8]

Donnan, C. B. 1990. Masterworks of art reveal a remarkable pre-Inca world. *National Geographic Magazine* 177(6):17–34.

Doran, J. 1970. Systems theory, computer simulations and archaeology. *World Archaeology* 1(3):289–298. [2, 5, 16]

Douglass, A. E. 1929. The secret of the Southwest solved by talkative tree rings. *National Geographic* 56(6):736–770. [2, 4]

Dow, J. W. 1967. Astronomical orientations at Teotihuacán. *American Antiquity* 32:326–334. [12]

Dowman, E. A. 1970. *Conservation in Field Archaeology.* London: Methuen. [4]

Downing, T. E., and M. Gibson, eds. 1974. *Irrigation's Impact on Society.* University of Arizona Anthropological Papers, no. 25. [6]

Drennan, R. D. 1976. Religion and social evolution in formative Mesoamerica. In Flannery, ed., pp. 345–363. [12]

Drennan, R. D., and C. A. Uribe, eds. 1987. *Chiefdoms in the Americas*. Lanham, Md.: University Press of America. [5]

Drucker, P. 1972. *Stratigraphy in Archaeology: An Introduction*. Addison-Wesley Modular Publications in Anthropology, no. 30. [4]

Dumond, D. E. 1965. Population growth and cultural change. *Southwestern Journal of Anthropology* 21(4): 302–324. [5, 16]

Dunn, M. E. 1983. Phytolith analysis in archaeology. *Mid-Continental Journal of Archaeology* 8(2):287–301. [4]

Dunnell, R. C. 1970. Seriation method and its evaluation. *American Antiquity* 35(3):305–319. [4]

———. 1971. *Systematics in Prehistory*. New York: Free Press. [2]

Duran, F. D. 1964. *Histories of the Indies of New Spain*. New York: Orion Press.

———. 1971. *Book of the Gods and Rites and The Ancient Calendar*. Translated and edited by F. Horcasitas and D. Heyden. Norman: University of Oklahoma Press. [12, 14]

Durkheim, E. 1915. *Elementary Forms of the Religious Life*. London: Allen and Unwin. [12]

———. 1933. *The Division of Labor in Society*. New York: Free Press. [6, 8]

Earle, T. 1978. *Economic and social organization of a complex chiefdom: The Halelea District, Kauái, Hawaii*. Museum of Anthropology Anthropological Papers, no. 63. Ann Arbor: University of Michigan. [5, 10]

———. 1987. Chiefdoms in archaeological perspective. *Annual Review of Anthropology* 16:279–308.

Ebert, J. I. 1984. Remote sensing applications in archaeology. In *Advances in Archaeological Method and Theory*, vol. 7, ed., M. B. Schiffer, pp. 293–362. New York: Academic Press. [4]

Ebert, J. I., and T. R. Lyons. 1980. Prehistoric irrigation canals identified from Skylab III and Landsat imagery in Phoenix, Arizona. In *Cultural Resources Remote Sensing*, eds., T. R. Lyons and F. J. Mathien, pp. 209–228. Washington, D.C.: Cultural Resources Management Division, National Park Service. [4]

Ehrenberg, R. E. 1987. *Scholars' Guide to Washington, D.C. for Cartography and Remote Sensing Imagery*. Washington, D.C.: Smithsonian Institution Press. [4]

Eighmy, J. L., and D. E. Doyel. 1987. A reanalysis of first reported archaeomagnetic dates from the Hohokam area, southern Arizona. *Journal of Field Archaeology* 14(3):331–342. [4]

Eisenstadt, S. N., and A. Shachar. 1987. *Society, Culture, and Urbanization*. Newbury Park, Calif.: Sage.

Eldredge, N., and S. J. Gould. 1972. Punctuated equilibria: An alternative to phyletic gradualism. In *Models in Paleobiology*, ed., T. S. M. Schopf, pp. 82–115. San Francisco: Freeman, Cooper. [2]

Englebrecht, W. 1987. Factors maintaining low population density among the prehistoric New York Iroquois. *American Antiquity* 52:13–27. [5, 6]

Erasmus, C. J. 1965. Monument building: Some field experiments. *Southwestern Journal of Anthropology* 21: 277–301. [3]

Erickson, C. 1988. Raised field agriculture in the Lake Titicaca basin (Putting ancient agriculture back to work). *Expedition* 30(3):8–16. [6, 14]

Evans, S. T., ed. 1989a. *Excavations at Cihuatecpan*. Vanderbilt University Publications in Anthropology, no. 36. [7, 10, 14]

———. 1989b. House and household in the Aztec world: The village of Cihuatecpan. In MacEachern, Archer, and Garvin, eds., pp. 430–440. [7]

———. 1990. The productivity of Maguey terrace agriculture in Central Mexico During the Aztec Period. *Latin American Antiquity* 1:117–132. [10]

———. 1991. Architecture and authority in an Aztec village: Form and function of the Tecpan. In *Land and Politics in the Valley of Mexico*, ed., H. R. Harvey, pp. 63–92. Albuquerque: University of New Mexico Press. [7]

Evans, S. T., and J. C. Berlo. 1992. Teotihuacán: An Introduction. In *Art, Polity, and the City of Teotihuacán*, ed., J. Berlo. Washington, D.C.: Dumbarton Oaks. [12]

Evans, S. T., and P. Gould. 1982. Settlement models in archaeology. *Journal of Anthropological Archaeology* 1:275–304. [7, 10]

Fagan, B. M. 1975. *The Rape of the Nile: Tomb Robbers, Tourists and Archaeologists*. New York: Scribners. [1, 2]

———. 1985. *The Adventure of Archaeology*. Washington, DC.: National Geographic Society. [1, 2]

———. 1988. *In the Beginning: An Introduction to Archaeology*, 6th ed. Glenview, Ill.: Scott, Foresman. [1]

Fairbank, J. K., E. O. Reischauer, and A. H. Craig. 1973. *East Asia: Tradition and Transformation*. Boston: Houghton Mifflin. [13]

Fairservis, W. 1975. *The Roots of Ancient India*. New York: Macmillan. [13]

Farriss, N. M. 1984. *Maya Society under Colonial Rule*. Princeton, N.J.: Princeton University Press. [14]

Fash, W. L. 1991. *Scribes, Warriors and Kings: The City of Copán and the Ancient Maya*. New York: Thames and Hudson. [3, 14]

Fash, W. L., and B. W. Fash. 1990. Scribes, warriors, and kings (The lives of the Copán Maya). *Archaeology* 53:26–35. [3, 14]

Feder, K. L. 1990. *Frauds, Myths, and Mysteries: Science and Pseudoscience in Archaeology*. Toronto: Mayfield. [1]

Feder, K. L., and M. A. Park. 1989. *Human Antiquity*. Mountain View, Calif.: Mayfield. [1, 12]

Feinman, G., and J. Neitzel. 1984. Too many types: An overview of sedentary prestate societies in the Americas. In *Advances in Archaeological Method and Theory*, vol. 7, ed. M. B. Schiffer, pp. 39–102. New York: Academic Press. [5, 10]

Ferguson, B., ed. 1984. *Warfare, Culture, and Environment*. New York: Academic Press. [11, 16]

Ferguson, W. M., and J. Q. Royce. 1984. *Maya Ruins in Color*. Albuquerque: University of New Mexico Press. [1, 2, 3, 14]

Fish, S. K., and S. A. Kowalewski, eds. 1990. *The Archaeology of Regions: A Case for Full-Coverage Survey*. Washington, D.C.: Smithsonian Institution Press. [4]

Flanagan, D. 1989. *Flanagan's Version*. New York: Vintage. [1]

Flannery, K. V. 1967. Culture history vs. cultural process: A debate in American archaeology. *Scientific American* 217(2):119–121. [1, 2]

———. 1968a. Archaeological systems theory and early Mesoamerica. In Meggers, ed., pp. 67–87. [5, 6]

———. 1968b. The Olmec and the Valley of Oaxaca. In *Dumbarton Oaks Conference on the Olmec*, ed., E. Benson, pp. 79–110. Washington, D.C.: Dumbarton Oaks. [11, 12]

———. 1972. The cultural evolution of civilizations. *Annual Review of Ecology and Systematics* 3:399–426. [5, 10, 14, 15, 16]

———. 1973a. Archaeology with a capital *S*. In *Research and Theory in Current Archaeology*, ed., C. L. Redman, pp. 47–53. New York: Wiley. [2]

———. 1973b. The origins of agriculture. *Annual Review of Anthropology* 2:271–310. [5]

———. 1976a. Contextual analysis of ritual paraphernalia from Formative Oaxaca. In Flannery, ed., pp. 333–345. New York: Academic Press. [12]

———, ed. 1976b. *The Early Mesoamerican Village*. New York: Academic Press. (7, 8, 12, 14)

———. 1982. The golden Marshalltown: A parable for the archaeology of the 1980s. *American Anthropologist* 84(2):265–278. [2, 4]

Flannery, K. V., and Winter, M. C. 1976. Analyzing household activities. In *The Early Mesoamerican Village*, ed., K. V. Flannery, pp. 34–44. New York: Academic Press. [7]

Fleischer, R. L. 1975. Advances in fission track dating. *World Archaeology*, 7:136–150. [4]

Fleming, S. 1979. *Thermoluminescence Techniques in Archaeology*. New York: Oxford University Press. [4]

Flenniken, J. J. 1984. The past, present, and future of flint-knapping: An anthropological perspective. *Annual Review of Anthropology* 13:187–203. [4, 5]

Ford, J. A. 1954. The type concept revisited. *American Anthropologist* 56:42–54. [4]

Ford, R. I. 1979. Paleoethnobotany in American archaeology. In *Advances in Archaeological Method and Theory*, vol. 2, ed., M. B. Schiffer, pp. 285–336. New York: Academic Press. [4]

Forde, C. D. 1963. *Habitat, Economy, and Society*. New York: Dutton. [5, 6]

Fowler, B. 1991. Scientists enthralled by Bronze Age body. *New York Times*, 1 October 1991, p. C1. [6]

———. 1991b. Mummified man in ice is tied to Neolithic Age. *New York Times*, 17 December 1991, p. C2. [6]

Fowler, D. D. 1982. Cultural resources management. In *Advances in Archaeological Method and Theory*, vol. 5, ed., M. B. Schiffer, pp. 1–50. New York: Academic Press. [2]

———. 1986. Conserving American archaeological resources. In Meltzer, Fowler, and Sabloff, eds., pp. 135–162. [2, 4]

Fox, R. G. 1977. *Urban Anthropology*. Englewood Cliffs, N.J.: Prentice-Hall. [8, 10]

Frake, C. O. 1962. Cultural ecology and ethnography. *American Anthropologist* 64:53–59. [2, 5, 6]

Frazer, J. 1958. *The Golden Bough*. New York: Macmillan. [12]

Freter, A. 1992. Chronological research at Copán: methods and implications in ancient Mesoamerica. 3:114–134. [3, 15]

Fried, M. H. 1967. *The Evolution of Political Society*. New York: Random House. [2, 5, 10]

Friedman, J. 1974. Marxism, structuralism and vulgar materialism. *Man* 9:444–469. [2, 16]

Friedman, J., and M. Rowlands, eds. 1979. *The Evolution of Social Systems*. Pittsburgh: University of Pittsburgh Press. [5, 10]

Fritts, H. C. 1978. *Tree Rings and Climate*. New York: Academic Press. [4]

Fritz, J. and F. J. Plog. 1970. The nature of archaeological explanation. *American Antiquity* 35:405–412. [16]

Gailey, C. W. 1987. *Kinship to Kingship: Gender Hierarchy and State Formation in the Tongan Islands*. Austin: University of Texas Press. [10]

Gamble, C. 1982. Interaction and alliance in Palaeolithic society. *Man* 17:92–107. [7, 12]

Gamio, M. 1922. *La Población del Valle de Teotihuacán*. Facsimile Edition, Clásicos de la Antropología Mexicana, no. 8. 5 vols. Mexico: Instituto Nacional Indigenista. [2, 14]

———. 1928. Las Excavationes del Pedregal de San Angel y la cultura arcaica del Valle de Mexico. *Annals of the XX International Congress of Americanists, II,* Rio de Janeiro, pp. 127–143. [2]

Gardner, W. M. 1986. The Paleoindians of the Shenandoah Valley, Virginia (Thunderbird Museum and Archaeological Park). *Archaeology* 39:28–34. [14, 16]

Gasser, R. E. and E. C. Adams. 1981. Aspects of deterioration of plant remains in archaeological sites: The Walpi Archaeological Project. *Journal of Ethnobiology* 1:182–192. [4]

Gellner, E. 1982. What is Structuralisme? In Renfrew, Rowlands, and Segraves, eds., pp. 97–123. [2]

Gennep, A. van. 1960. *The Rites of Passage*. Chicago: University of Chicago Press. [9, 12]

Gero, J. M., and M. W. Conkey, eds. 1991. *Engendering archaeology*. Oxford: Blackwell. [2, 7]

Gibbon, E. 1963. *Decline and Fall of the Roman empire*. New York: Washington Square Press. [15]

Gibbon, G. 1984. *Anthropological Archaeology*. New York: Columbia University Press. [1, 2]

Gibson, C. 1964. *The Aztecs under Spanish rule*. Stanford, Calif.: Stanford University Press. [10, 14]

Gifford, D. P. 1978. Ethnoarchaeological observations of natural processes affecting cultural materials. In Gould, ed., pp. 77–102. [4]

———. 1981 Taphonomy and paleoecology: A critical review of archaeology's sister disciplines. In *Advances in Archaeological Method and Theory,* vol. 4, ed., M. B. Schiffer, pp. 365–438. New York: Academic Press. [4]

Gifford, J. C. 1960. The type-variety method of ceramic classification as an indicator of cultural phenomena. *American Antiquity* 25:341–347. [2, 4]

Gilbert, R. I., Jr. 1985. Stress, paleonutrition, and trace elements. In Gilbert and Mielke, eds., pp. 339–360. [4, 15]

Gilbert, R. I., and J. H. Mielke, eds. 1985. *The Analysis of Prehistoric Diets*. Orlando, Fla.: Academic Press. [4]

Gilman, P. 1990. Social organization and classic Mimbres period burials in the Southwest United States. *Journal of Field Archaeology* 17:457–469. [4]

Glassow, M. A., and L. R. Wilcoxon. 1988. Coastal adaptations near Point Conception, California, with particular regard to shellfish exploitation. *American Antiquity* 53:36–51. [6]

Glob, P. V. 1969. *The Bog People*. London: Faber and Faber. [4]

Gnivecki, P. L. 1987. On the Quantitative Derivation of Household Spatial Organization from Archaeological Residues in Ancient Mesopotamia. In Kent, ed., pp. 176–235. [7, 13]

Goldman, I. 1970. *Ancient Polynesian Society*. Chicago: University of Chicago Press. [10]

Goldstein, L., and K. Kintigh. 1990. Ethics and the reburial controversy. *American Antiquity* 55:585–591. [2]

Gordon, G. B. 1896. *Prehistoric Ruins of Copán, Honduras*. Memoirs of the Peabody Museum, Harvard University, vol. 1, no. 1. Cambridge, Mass.: Harvard University Press. [2, 3]

Gould, R. A., ed. 1978. *Explorations in Ethnoarchaeology*. Albuquerque: University of New Mexico Press. [4]

———. 1980. *Living Archaeology*. Cambridge: Cambridge University Press. [4]

Gould, R. A., and M. B. Schiffer, eds. 1981. *Modern Material Culture: The Archaeology of Us*. New York: Academic Press. [4]

Gould, R. A., and P. J. Watson. 1982. A dialogue on the meaning and use of analogy in ethnoarchaeological reasoning. *Journal of Anthropological Archaeology* 1(4): 355–381. [4]

Gould, S. J. 1991. Fall in the House of Ussher. *Natural History* 11:12–21. [2]

Gowlett, J. 1984. *Ascent to Civilization*. New York: Knopf. [2, 4, 13, 14]

Grayson, D. K. 1973. On the methodology of faunal analysis. *American Antiquity* 38(4):432–439. [4]

———. 1984. *Quantitative Zooarchaeology: Topics in the Analysis of Archaeological Faunas*. Orlando, Fla.: Academic Press. [4]

Graves, M. 1986. Organization and differentiation within Late Prehistoric ranked social units, Mariana Islands, Western Pacific. *Journal of Field Archaeology* 13: 139–154. [10]

Greenfield, H. J. 1991. Fauna from the Late Neolithic of the Central Balkans: Issues in subsistence and land use. *Journal of Field Archaeology* 18:161–186. [4, 5, 13]

Gregg, S. A., ed. 1991. *Between Bands and States*. Occasional Paper No. 9, Center for Archaeological Investigations. Carbondale: Southern Illinois University. [5]

Grigg, D. 1975. *The Agricultural Systems of the World*. London: Cambridge University Press. [5, 6]

Grootes, P. M. 1978. Carbon-14 time scale extended: Comparison of chronologies. *Science* 200(4337):11–15. [4]

Grove, D. C., ed. 1987. *Ancient Chalcatzingo*. Austin: University of Texas Press. [14]

Guderjan, T. H., J. F. Garber, H. A. Smith, F. Stross, H. V. Michel, and F. Asaro. 1989. Maya maritime trade and sources of obsidian at San Juan, Ambergris Cay, Belize. *Journal of Field Archaeology* 16: 363–369. [8]

Guidoni, E. 1978. *Primitive Architecture*. New York: Abrams. [7]

Gumerman, G., and B. S. Umemoto. 1987. The Siphon Technique—An Addition to the Flotation Process. *American Antiquity* 52:330–335. [4]

———. 1973. The reconciliation of theory and method in archaeology. In *Research and Theory in Current Archaeology,* eds., C. L. Redman et al., pp. 287–299. New York: Wiley. [5, 16]

Haas, J., ed. 1990. *The Anthropology of War*. New York: Cambridge University Press. [11, 16]

Haggett, P. 1966. *Locational Analysis in Human Geography*. New York: St. Martin's Press. [4, 7, 11]

Hall, G. D., S. M. Tarka, W. J. Hurst, D. Stuart, and R. E. W. Adams. 1990. Cacao residues in ancient Maya vessels from Rio Azul, Guatemala. *American Antiquity* 55:138–143. [4, 14]

Hally, D. 1986. The identification of vessel function: A case study from Northwest Georgia. *American Antiquity* 51:267–295. [4]

Hammond, N. 1974. The distribution of Late Classic Maya major ceremonial centres in the central area. In *Mesoamerican Archaeology,* ed., N. Hammond, pp. 313–334. Austin: University of Texas Press. [7, 11, 14]

———. 1977. The earliest Maya. *Scientific American* 236:116–133.

Hammond, N., K. A. Pyburn, and J. Rose. 1988. Excavation and survey at Nohmul, Belize, 1986. *Journal of Field Archaeology* 15:1–15. [14]

Hardesty, D. L. 1977. *Ecological Anthropology*. New York: Wiley. [6]

Harner, M. J. 1970. Population pressure and the social evolution of agriculturalists. *Southwestern Journal of Anthropology* 26(1):67–86. [5, 6, 16]

Harpending, H., and H. Davis. 1977. Some implications for hunter-gatherer ecology derived from the spatial structure of resources. *World Archaeology* 8:275–286. [5, 6]

Harris, E. C. 1979. *Principles of Archaeological Stratigraphy*. London: Academic Press. [4]

Harris, M. 1968. *The Rise of Anthropological Theory*. New York: Crowell. [2, 16]

———. 1974. *Cows, Pigs, Wars and Witches: The Riddles of Culture*. New York: Random House. [1]

———. 1979. *Cultural Materialism: The Struggle for a Science of Culture*. New York: Random House. [2, 5]

———. 1988. *Culture, People, Nature: An Introduction to General Anthropology*. New York: Harper and Row. [1]

———. 1991. Anthropology: Ships that crash in the night. In *Perspectives on Social Science: The Colorado Lectures,* ed., R. Jessor, pp. 70–114. Boulder, Colo: Westview Press. [5, 16]

Harris, M., and E. B. Ross. 1987. *Food and Evolution: Toward a Theory of Human Food Habits*. Philadelphia: Temple University Press. [6]

Harris, J. E., and K. R. Weeks. 1972. X-raying the pharaohs. *Natural History* 81:54–63. [4]

Harrison, P. D., and B. L. Turner II. 1978. *Pre-Hispanic Maya Agriculture*. Albuquerque: University of New Mexico Press. [3, 6, 14]

Harvey, H. R. 1985. Household and Family Structure in Early Colonial Tepetlaoztoc: An Analysis of the Códice Santa María Asunción. *Estudios de Cultura Nahuatl* 18:275–294. [7, 14]

Hassan, F. A. 1973. On the mechanisms of population growth during the Neolithic. *Current Anthropology* 14:535–542. [5, 6, 16]

———. 1974. Population growth and cultural evolution. *Reviews in Anthropology* 1:205–212. [5, 6, 16]

———. 1981. *Demographic Archaeology*. New York: Academic Press. [5, 16]

Hassig, R. 1985. *Trade, Tribute, and Transportation*. Norman: University of Oklahoma Press. [8, 14]

———. 1988. *Aztec Warfare*. Norman: University of Oklahoma Press. [11, 14]

Hastorf, C. 1990. The effect of the Inka state on Sausa agricultural production and crop consumption. *American Antiquity* 55:262–290. [5, 14]

Hatch, J. W., J. W. Michels, C. Stevenson, B. Sheetz, and R. Geidel. 1990. Hopewell obsidian studies: Behavioral implications of recent sourcing and dating research. *American Antiquity* 55:461–479. [8, 11]

Haviland, W. A. 1985. *Anthropology,* 4th ed. New York: Holt, Rinehart and Winston. [1]

———. 1988. Musical Hammocks at Tikal. In Wilk and Ashmore, eds., pp. 121–134. [7]

Hayden, B., ed. 1979. *Lithic Use-Wear Analysis.* New York: Academic Press. [4]

Hayden, B., and A. Cannon. 1984. *The Structure of Material Systems: Ethnoarchaeology in the Maya Highlands.* Society of American Archaeology Papers, no. 3. [4]

Healan, D. M. 1977. Architectural implications of daily life in ancient Tollan, Hidalgo, Mexico. *World Archaeology* 9:140–156. [7, 14]

Healy, P. F. 1988. Music of the Maya. *Archaeology* 41: 24–31. [9, 14]

Hedges, R. E. M., and J. A. J. Gowlett. 1986. Radiocarbon dating by accelerator mass spectrometry. *Scientific American* 254(1):100–107. [4]

Heilbroner, R. L. 1985. *The Making of Economic Society.* Englewood Cliffs, N.J.: Prentice-Hall. [8]

Heizer, R. F., and M. A. Baumhoff. 1962. *Prehistoric Rock Art of Nevada and Eastern California.* Berkeley: University of California Press. [9, 12, 14]

Helms, Mary. 1979. *Ancient Panama.* Austin: University of Texas Press. [9, 10, 14]

Hempel, C. G. 1965. *Aspects of Scientific Explanation: Other Essays in the Philosophy of Science.* New York: Free Press. [2, 4]

Hendon, J. 1989. Elite household organization at Copán, Honduras: Analysis of activity distribution in the Sepulturas Zone. In MacEachern, Archer, and Garvin, eds., pp. 371–380. [3, 7]

———. 1991. Status and power in Classic Maya society: An archaeological study. *American Anthropologist* 93:894–918. [3]

Henry, D. O. 1990. From foraging to agriculture: The Levant at the end of the Ice Age. *American Journal of Archaeology* 94: 489–490. [5, 13]

Hester, T. R., R. F. Heizer, and J. A. Graham. 1975. *Field Methods in Archaeology,* 6th ed. Palo Alto, Calif.: Mayfield. [4]

Heyerdahl, T. 1950. *The Kon-Tiki Expedition.* London: Allen and Unwin. [5]

Hietala, H. 1984. *Intrasite Spatial Analysis in Archaeology.* Cambridge: Cambridge University Press. [4, 7, 11]

Hill, A. 1985. Natural disarticulation and bison butchery. *American Antiquity* 50:141–145. [4]

Hill, J. N. 1968. Broken K Pueblo: Patterns of form and function. In Binford and Binford, eds., pp. 103–142.

———. 1970. *Broken K Pueblo: Prehistoric Social Organization in the American Southwest.* Anthropological Papers of the University of Arizona, no. 18 [7]

———. 1978. Individuals and their artifacts: An experimental study in archaeology. *American Antiquity* 43:245–257. [4, 7]

Hill, J. N., and J. Gunn. 1977. *The Individual in Prehistory: Studies of Variability in Style in Prehistoric Technologies.* New York: Academic Press. [9]

Hill, J. N., and R. H. Hevly. 1968. Pollen at Broken K Pueblo: Some new interpretations. *American Antiquity* 33:200–210. [4]

Hirth, K. G. 1978. Problems in data recovery and measurement in settlement archaeology. *Journal of Field Archaeology* 5:125–131. [4, 7]

———, ed. 1984. *Trade and Exchange in Early Mesoamerica.* Albuquerque: University of New Mexico Press. [8]

Hirth, K., and J. A. Villasenor. 1981. Early state expansion in central Mexico: Teotihuacán in Morelos. *Journal of Field Archaeology* 8:135–150. [11, 14]

Hirth, K., and A. C. Guillen. 1988. *Tiempo y Asentamiento en Xochicalco.* Mexico City: Universidad Nacional Autonoma de Mexico.

Hobson, C. 1987. *The World of the Pharoahs.* London: Thames and Hudson. [13]

Hochschild, A. 1989. *The Second Shift.* New York: Avon [2]

Hodder, I., ed. 1978. *The Spatial Organisation of Culture.* London: Duckworth. [4, 7, 11]

———. 1982a. *Symbols in Action: Ethnoarchaeological Studies of Material Culture.* Cambridge: Cambridge University Press. [2, 9]

———. 1982b. *Symbolic and Structural Archaeology.* Cambridge: Cambridge University Press. [2, 9]

———. 1985. Postprocessual archaeology. In *Advances in Archaeological Method and Theory,* vol. 8, ed., M. B. Schiffer, pp. 1–26. Orlando, Fla.: Academic Press. [2, 16]

———. 1986a. *Reading the Past: Current Approaches to Interpretation in Archaeology.* New York: Cambridge University Press. [16]

———. 1986b. *Archaeology as Long Term History.* Cambridge: Cambridge University Press. [2, 16]

Hodder, I., and C. Orton. 1976. *Spatial Analysis in Archaeology.* Cambridge: Cambridge University Press. [7, 11]

Hodge, M., and L. Minc. 1990. The spatial patterning of Aztec ceramics: Implications for prehispanic exchange systems in the Valley of Mexico. *Journal of Field Archaeology* 17:415–437. [8]

Hodges, H. 1964. *Artifacts: An Introduction to Primitive Technology*. New York: Praeger. [6]

Hodson, F. R., D. G. Kendall, and P. Tautu, eds. 1971. *Mathematics in the Archaeological and Historical Sciences*. Edinburgh: Edinburgh University Press. [2, 4]

Hoffman, M. A. 1991. *Egypt Before the Pharoahs*. New York: Knopf. [13]

Hole, F., and R. F. Heizer. 1973. *An Introduction to Prehistoric Archaeology*, 3rd ed. New York: Holt, Rinehart and Winston. [1]

Hole, F., K. V. Flannery, and J. A. Neely. 1969. *Prehistory and Human Ecology of the Deh Luran Plain: An Early Village Sequence from Khuzistan, Iran*. Memoirs of the Museum of Anthropology, no. 1. Ann Arbor: University of Michigan. [5, 13]

Holley, G. R., N. H. Lopinot, W. I. Woods, and J. E. Kelly. 1989. Dynamics of community organization at prehistoric Cahokia. In MacEachern, Archer, and Garvin, eds., pp. 339–349. [7, 11]

Hosler, D. 1988. Ancient West Mexican metallurgy: A technological chronology. *Journal of Field Archaeology* 15:191–217. [6, 14]

Houston, S. D. 1988. The phonetic decipherment of Mayan glyphs. *Antiquity* 62:126–135. [9, 13]

———. 1989. *Maya Glyphs*. Berkeley: University of California Press/British Museum [9, 10, 13]

Howells, W. W. 1962. *The Heathens: Primitive Man and His Religions*. New York: Doubleday. [12]

Humboldt, A. von. 1810. *Vues des cordillères er monuments des peuples indigènes de l'Amérique [Views of the Mountains and Monuments of the Indigenous People of America]*. Paris.

Huss-Ashmore, R., A. H. Goodman, and G. J. Armelagos. 1982. Nutritional inference from paleopathology. In *Advances in Archaeological Method and Theory*, vol. 5, ed., M. B. Schiffer, pp. 395–474. New York: Academic Press. [2, 4, 5]

Huxley, J., ed. 1940. *The New Systematics*. Oxford: Oxford University Press. [2]

Hyland, D. C., J. M. Tersak, J. M. Adovasio, and M. I. Siegel. 1990. Identification of the species of origin of residual blood on lithic material. *American Antiquity* 55:104–112. [4]

Ingersoll, D., J. E. Yellen, and W. MacDonald, eds. 1977. *Experimental Archaeology*. New York: Columbia University Press. [4]

Jacobsen, T., and R. M. Adams. 1958. Salt and silt in ancient Mesopotamian agriculture. *Science* 128:1251–1258. [13, 15]

Jelliffe, D. B., and E. F. P. Jelliffe. 1989. *Community Nutritional Assessment*. Oxford: Oxford University Press.

Jennings, J. D. 1957. *Danger Cave*. University of Utah Anthropological Papers, no. 27. [5, 6]

———. 1983. *Ancient South Americans*. San Francisco: Freeman. [14]

Jochim, M. A. 1989. After the Ice Age: From hunters to farmers. *Archaeology* 42:42–45. [5]

Johnson, G. A. 1972. A test of the utility of central place theory in archaeology. In Ucko, Tringham, and Dimbleby, eds., pp. 769–785. London: Duckworth. [7, 11, 13]

———. 1980. Rank-size convexity and system integration: A view from archaeology. *Economic Geography* 56:234–247. [4, 10]

Johnson, A. W., and T. Earle. 1987. *The Evolution of Human Societies: From Foraging Group to Agrarian State*. Stanford, Calif.: Stanford University Press. [5, 10]

Jones, G. D., R. R. Kautz, and E. Graham. 1986. Tipu: A Maya town on the Spanish colonial frontier (Belize). *Archaeology* 39:40–47. [14]

Jones, P. R. 1980. Experimental butchery with modern stone tools and its relevance for Paleolithic archaeology. *World Archaeology* 12:153–165. [4]

Joukowsky, M. 1980. *A Complete Manual of Field Archaeology: Tools and Techniques of Field Work for Archaeologists*. Englewood Cliffs, N.J.: Prentice-Hall. [4]

Joyce, R. 1986. Terminal Classic interaction on the southeastern periphery. *American Antiquity* 51:313–329. [14, 15]

Judge, W. J., J. I. Ebert, and R. K. Hitchcock. 1975. Sampling in regional archaeological survey. In *Sampling in Archaeology*, ed., J. W. Mueller, pp. 82–123. Tucson: University of Arizona Press. [4, 7, 11]

Kamp, K. A. 1987. Affluence and image: Ethnoarchaeology in a Syrian village. *Journal of Field Archaeology* 14:283–296. [4]

Keeley, L. H. 1980. *Experimental Determination of Stone Tool Uses: A Microwear Analysis*. Chicago: University of Chicago Press. [4]

Keene, A. S. 1981. *Prehistoric Foraging in a Temperate Forest: A Linear Programming Model*. New York: Academic Press. [5, 6]

Keesing, R. M. 1974. Theories of culture. *Annual Review of Anthropology* 3:73–97. [7]

———. 1975. *Kin Groups and Social Structure*. New York: Holt, Rinehart and Winston. [7]

Kehoe, A. 1991. No Possible, Probably Shadow of a Doubt: Fertility Symbols of Paleolithic Europe. *Antiquity* 65:129–131. [9]

Kehoe, A. B., and T. F. Kehoe. 1973. Cognitive models for archaeological interpretation. *American Antiquity* 38:150–154. [16]

Kent, S., ed. 1984. *Analyzing Activity Areas: an Ethnoarchaeological Study of the Use of Space*. Albuquerque: University of New Mexico Press. [4, 7]

———, ed. 1987. *Method and Theory for Activity Area Research: An Ethnoarchaeological Approach*. New York: Columbia University Press. [4, 7]

———, ed. 1990. *Domestic Architecture and the Use of Space*. New York: Cambridge University Press.

Kenyon, J. L., and B. Bevan. 1977. Ground-penetrating radar and its application to a historical archaeological site. *Historical Archaeology* 11:48–55. [4]

Kidder, A. V. 1924. *An Introduction to the Study of Southwestern Archaeology*. New Haven: Yale University Press. [2, 14]

Killion, T., J. Sabloff, G. Tourtellot, and N. Dunning. 1989. Intensive surface collection of residential clusters at Terminal Classic Sayil, Yucatán, Mexico. *Journal of Field Archaeology* 16:273–294. [4, 14]

King, T. F. 1977. Issues in contract archaeology. *Archaeology* 30:352–353. [2]

King, T. F., P. P. Hickman, and G. Berg. 1977. *Anthropology in Historic Preservation: Caring for Culture's Clutter*. New York: Academic Press. [2]

Kirchhoff, P. 1943. Mesoamerica. *Acta Americana* 1:92–107. [14]

Kirkbride, D. 1966. Beidha: An early neolithic village in Jordan. *Archaeology* 19:199–207. [5, 13]

Kirkby, A. 1973. *The Use of Land and Water Resources in the Past and Present, Valley of Oaxaca, Mexico*. Memoirs of the Museum of Anthropology, no. 5. Ann Arbor: University of Michigan. [6, 14, 16]

Kish, L. 1965. *Survey Sampling*. New York: Wiley. [4]

Klein, J., J. C. Lerman, P. E. Damon, and E. K. Ralph. 1982. Calibration of radiocarbon dates: Tables based on the consensus data of the workshop on calibrating the radiocarbon time scale. *Radiocarbon* 24(2):103–150. [4]

Klepinger, L. L. 1984. Nutritional assessment from bone. *Annual Review of Anthropology* 13:75–96. [3, 4]

Klippel, W. E., and D. F. Morey. 1986. Contextual and nutritional analysis of freshwater gastropods from Middle Archaic deposits at the Hayes site, middle Tennessee. *American Antiquity* 51:799–813. [4]

Knight, V. 1986. The institutional organization of Mississippian religion. *American Antiquity* 51:675–687. [12]

Kolata, A. 1986. The agricultural foundations of the Tiwanaku state: A view from the Heartland. *American Antiquity* 51:748–762. [14]

Kolata, G. B. 1974. !Kung hunter-gatherers: Feminism, diet, and birth control. *Science* 185:932–934. [5]

Kramer, C., and B. Stark. 1988. The status of women in archaeology. *Anthropology Newsletter* of the American Anthropological Association, vol. 29, no. 1, pp. 11–12. [2]

Kramer, S. N. 1966. *The Sumerians*. Chicago: University of Chicago Press.

Kroeber, A. L. 1957. *Style and Civilization*. Ithaca N.Y.: Cornell University Press. [5]

Kroeber, A. L., and C. Kluckhohn. 1952. *Culture: A Critical Review of Concepts and Definitions*. Papers of the Peabody Museum, Harvard University, no. 47(1), Cambridge, Mass. [2, 5]

Kuhn, T. 1970. *The Structure of Scientific Revolutions,* 2nd ed. Chicago: University of Chicago Press. [2]

Lange, F. W., and C. R. Rydberg. 1972. Abandonment and post-abandonment behavior at a rural Central American house-site. *American Antiquity* 37:419–432. [4, 7]

Larsen, C. S. 1987. Bioarchaeological interpretations of subsistence economy and behavior from human skeletal remains. In *Advances in Archaeological Method and Theory*, vol. 10, ed., M. B. Schiffer, pp. 339–445. Orlando, Fla.: Academic Press. [4]

Latta, M. A. 1990. Iroquoian stemware. *American Antiquity* 52:717–724. [4]

Leakey, M. 1971. *Olduvai Gorge*. Vol. 3: *Excavations in Beds I and II*. Cambridge: Cambridge University Press. [2, 4]

Leakey, R., and R. Lewin. 1977. *Origins*. New York: Dutton. [1]

LeBlanc, S. A. 1976. Archaeological recording systems. *Journal of Field Archaeology* 3:159–168. [4]

Lee, R. B. 1968. What hunters do for a living, or, How to make out on scarce resources. In Lee and DeVore, eds., pp. 30–48. [5, 6]

———. 1979. *The !Kung San: Men, Women, and Work in a Foraging Society*. Cambridge: Cambridge University Press. [5, 6, 7]

Lee, R. B., and I. DeVore, eds. 1968. *Man the Hunter*. Chicago: Aldine. [5, 6, 7, 8]

Lekson, S. H. 1987. *Great Pueblo Architecture in Chaco Canyon, New Mexico*. Albuquerque: University of New Mexico Press.

Lekson, S. H. 1987. *Great Pueblo Architecture in Chaco Canyon, New Mexico*. Albuquerque: University of New Mexico Press.

Lentz, D. L. 1991. Maya Diets of the Rich and Poor: Paleoethnobotanical evidence from Copán. *Latin American Antiquity* 2:269–287. [3]

Leonard, R. D. 1989. Resource specialization, population growth, and agricultural production in the American Southwest. *American Antiquity* 54:491–503. [5]

Leonard, R. D., and G. T. Jones, eds. 1989. *Quantifying Diversity in Archaeology*. Cambridge: Cambridge University Press. [5, 6]

Leone, M. P. 1982. Some opinions about recovering mind. *American Antiquity* 47(4):742–760. [5]

———. 1986. Symbolic, structural, and critical archaeology. In Meltzer, Fowler, and Sabloff, eds., pp. 415–438.

Leroi-Gourhan, A. 1968a. *The Art of Prehistoric Man in Western Europe*. London: Thames and Hudson. [12]

———. 1968b. The evolution of Paleolithic art. *Scientific American* 218:58–68,70. [12]

Lessa, W. A., and E. Z. Vogt, eds. 1965. *Reader in Comparative Religion: An Anthropological Approach*. New York: Harper and Row. [12]

Levi-Strauss, Claude. 1963. *Structural Anthropology*. New York: Basic Books. [2, 16]

———. 1970. *Tristes Tropiques: An Anthropological Study of Primitive Societies in Brazil*. New York: Atheneum. [2]

Lewarch, D. E., and M. J. O'Brien. 1981. The expanding role of surface assemblages in archaeological research. In *Advances in Archaeological Method and Theory*, ed., M. B. Schiffer, pp. 297–342. New York: Academic Press. [4]

Libby, W. F. 1955. *Radiocarbon Dating*, 2nd ed. Chicago: University of Chicago Press. [2, 4]

Lightfoot, K., and R. M. Cerrato. 1988. Prehistoric shellfish exploitation in Coastal New York. *Journal of Field Archaeology* 15:141–149. [6]

Limbrey, S. 1975. *Soil Science and Archaeology*. London: Academic Press. [4]

Lippi, R. D. 1988. Paleotopography and phosphate analysis of a buried jungle site in Ecuador. *Journal of Field Archaeology* 15:85–97. [4]

Little, M. A., and G. Morren. 1976. *Ecology, Energetics, and Human Variability*. Dubuque, Iowa: Brown. [5, 6]

Lloyd, P. 1965. The political structure of African kingdoms. In *Political Systems and the Division of Power*, ed., M. Banton, pp. 62–112. London: Tavistock. [10, 11]

Loendorf, L. 1991. Cation-ratio varnish dating and petroglyph chronology in southeastern Colorado. *Antiquity* 65:246–255. [4]

Loker, W. M. 1983. Recent geophysical explorations at Cerén. In *Archaeology and Volcanism in Central America*, ed., P. Sheets, pp. 254–274. Austin: University of Texas Press. [4]

Longacre, W. A. 1964. Archaeology as anthropology: A case study. *Science* 144: 1454–1455. [2]

———. 1976. Population dynamics at the Grasshopper Pueblo, Arizona. In Zubrow, ed., pp. 169–184. [7, 14]

———. 1981. Kalinga pottery: An ethnoarchaeological study. In *Pattern of the Past: Studies in Honour of David Clarke*, eds., Hodder, Isaac, and Hammond, pp. 49–66. Cambridge: Cambridge University Press. [4]

———, ed. 1991. *Ceramic Ethnoarchaeology*. Tucson: University of Arizona Press. [5, 6]

Longacre, W. A., and J. E. Ayres. 1968. Archaeological lessons from an Apache wickiup. In Binford and Binford, eds., pp. 151–160. [4, 7]

Longyear, J. M. 1952. *Copán Ceramics*. Carnegie Institution of Washington. [3]

Loy, T. H. 1983. Prehistoric blood residues: Detection on tool surfaces and identification of species of origin. *Science* 220:1269–1271. [4]

Lyell, C. 1850. *Principles of Geology*, 8th ed. London: Murray. [2]

Lyman, R. L., and M. O'Brien. 1987. Plow-zone zooarchaeology: Fragmentation and identifiability. *Journal of Field Archaeology* 14:493–498. [4]

Lyons, T. R., and T. E. Avery. 1984. *Remote Sensing: A Handbook for Archaeologists and Cultural Resource Managers*. Washington, D.C.: National Park Service, U.S. Department of the Interior. [4]

MacEachern, S., D. Archer, and R. Garvin, eds. 1989. *Households and Communities*. Calgary: University of Calgary Archaeological Association.

MacNeish, R., M. Fowler, A. Garcia, C. F. Peterson, A. Nelken-Terner, and J. A. Neely, eds. 1972. *The Prehistory of the Tehuacán Valley*. Vol. 5: *Excavations and Reconnaissance*. Austin: University of Texas Press. [5, 14]

MacNeish, R., F. Peterson, and J. Neel. 1972. The archaeological reconnaissance. In MacNeish et al., eds., pp. 341–495. [4, 14]

Malek, J. 1986. *In the Shadow of the Pyramids: Egypt during the Old Kingdom*. Norman: University of Oklahoma Press. [13]

Mallory, J. K., III. 1984. *Late Classic Maya Economic Specialization: Evidence from the Copán Obsidian Assemblage*. Ph.D. dissertation, Pennsylvania State University, University Park.

Malthus, T. 1970 [1798]. *An Essay on the Principle of Population*. New York: Penguin. [2, 5, 16]

Marcus, J. 1976. *Emblem and state in the Classic Maya Lowlands*. Washington D.C.: Dumbarton Oaks. [3, 9, 10, 11]

Margain, C. R. 1974. Pre-Columbian Architecture of Central Mexico. In *Handbook of Middle American Indians*, ed., R. Wauchope, pp. 45–91. Austin: University of Texas Press. [7]

Marquardt, W. H. 1978. Advances in archaeological seriation. In *Advances in Archaeological Method and Theory*, vol. 1, ed., M. B. Schiffer, pp. 257–314. New York: Academic Press. [4]

Marshack, A. 1972a *The Roots of Civilization*. New York: McGraw-Hill. [9]

———. 1972b. Upper Paleolithic notation and symbol. *Science* 178:817–828. [9]

Maruyama, M. 1963. The second cybernetic: Deviation—Amplifying mutual causal processes. *American Scientist* 51:164–179. [5]

Matos Moctezuma, E. 1987. The Templo Mayor of Tenochtitlan: History and interpretation. In Broda, Carrasco and Matos Moctezuma, eds., pp. 15–60. [12]

Matson, R. G. 1991. *The Origins of Southwestern Agriculture*. Tucson: University of Arizona Press. [5, 6]

Maudslay, A. P. 1889–1902. *Biologia Centrali-Americana: Archaeology*, vols. 1-5. London: Dulau. [3, 14]

Mayr, E. 1988. *The Growth of Biological Thought*. Cambridge: University of Chicago Press. [1, 5, 16]

Mazess, R. B., and D. W. Zimmermann. 1966. Pottery dating from thermoluminescence. *Science* 152:347–348. [4]

McAnany, P. A. 1990. Water storage in the Puuc region of the northern Maya lowlands: A key to population estimates and architectural variability. In Culbert and Rice, eds., pp. 263–284. [14]

McGimsey, C. R., III. 1972. *Public Archaeology*. New York: Seminar Press. [2]

———. 1973. *Archaeology and Archaeological Resources*. Washington, D.C.: Society for American Archaeology. [2, 4]

McGuire, R. 1989. The greater Southwest as a periphery of Mesoamerica. In Champion, ed., pp. 40–66. [14]

McHargue, G., and M. Roberts. 1977. *A Field Guide to conservation Archaeology in North America*. Philadelphia: Lippincott. [4]

McKern, W. C. 1939. The Midwestern Taxonomic Method as an aid to archaeological culture study. *American Antiquity* 4:301–313. [2]

McNett, C. A. 1985. *Shawnee Minisink: A stratified Paleoindian-Archaic site in the Upper Delaware Valley of Pennsylvania*. New York: Academic Press.

Meggers, B. J. 1954. Environmental limitation on the development of culture. *American Anthropologist* 56:801–824. [5]

———, ed. 1968. *Anthropological Archaeology in the Americas*. Anthropological Society of Washington, D.C. [14]

———. 1986. Prehistoric environments. In *Handbook of North American Indians*, vol. 11, ed., W. D'Azevedo, pp. 31–50. Washington, D.C.: Smithsonian Institution. [6, 14]

Meighan, C. W. 1976. Empirical determination of obsidian hydration rates from archaeological evidence. In Taylor, ed., pp. 106–119. [4]

Meltzer, D. J. 1979. Paradigms and the nature of change in American archaeology. *American Antiquity* 44:644–657. [2]

———. 1989. Why don't we know when the first people came to North America. *American Antiquity* 54:471–490. [6, 16]

Meltzer, D. J., D. D. Fowler, and J. A. Sabloff, eds. 1986. *American Archaeology Past and Future: A Celebration of the Society for American Archaeology 1935–1985*. Washington, D.C.: Smithsonian Institution Press. [2, 16]

Mendoza, R. 1986. Plant and animal domestication: Direct versus indirect evidence. *Antiquity* 60:7–14. [5]

Metcalfe, D., and K. Heath. 1990. Microrefuse and site structure: The hearths and floors of the Heartbreak Hotel. *American Antiquity* 55:781–796. [4]

Metcalfe, D., and K. T. Jones. 1988. A Reconsideration of animal body-part utility indices. *American Antiquity* 53:486–504. [4]

Meyer, K. E. 1973. *The Plundered Past: The Story of the Illegal International Traffic in Works of Art*. New York: Atheneum. [2]

Michael, H. N., and E. K. Ralph, eds. 1971. *Dating Techniques for the Archaeologist*. Cambridge Mass.: MIT Press. [4]

Michels, J. W. 1973. *Dating Methods in Archaeology*. New York: Seminar Press. [4]

Michels, J. W., and I. S. T. Tsong. 1980. Obsidian hydration dating: A coming of age. In *Advances in Archaeological Method and Theory*, vol. 3, ed., M. B. Schiffer, pp. 405–444. New York: Academic Press. [4]

Miksicek, C. H. 1987. Formation processes of the archaeobotanical record. In *Advances in Archaeological Method and Theory*, vol. 10, ed., M. B. Schiffer, pp. 211–247. New York: Academic Press. [4]

Miller, J. A. 1969. Dating by the potassium-argon method—Some advances in technique. In Brothwell and Higgs, eds., pp. 101–105. [4]

Miller, D., and C. Tilley. 1984. *Ideology, Power and Prehistory*. Cambridge: Cambridge University Press. [9, 12, 16]

Miller, M. E. 1986. *The Murals of Bonampak*. Princeton, N.J.: Princeton University Press. [9]

Millon, R. 1962. Variations in social responses to the practice of irrigation agriculture. In *Civilization in Desert Lands*. University of Utah Anthropological Papers., no. 62, pp. 56–88. [5, 6]

———. 1967. Teotihuacán. *Scientific American* 216:38–49. [8, 12, 14]

———. 1973. *the Teotihuacán Map*, vol. 1, pt. 1. Austin: University of Texas Press. [8, 12, 14]

———. 1981. Teotihuacán: City, State, and Civilization. In *Supplement to the Handbook of Middle American Indians*, vol. 1, ed., J. Sabloff, pp. 198–243. Austin: University of Texas Press. [8, 12, 14]

Millon, R., B. Drewitt, and G. Cowgill. 1973. The Teotihuacán map, vol. 1, pt. 2. Austin: University of Texas Press. [8, 12, 14]

Milner, G. R. 1986. Mississippian period population density in a segment of the central Mississippi river valley. *American Antiquity* 51:227–238. [14]

Milner, G. R., E. Anderson, and V. G. Smith. 1991. Warfare in Late Prehistoric west-central Illinois. *American Antiquity* 56:581–603. [10, 14]

Minnis, P. E. 1989. Prehistoric diet in the northern Southwest: Macroplant remains from Four Corners feces. *American Antiquity* 54:543–563. [4, 5]

Monaghan, J. 1990. Sacrifice, death, and the origins of agriculture in the Codex Vienna. *American Antiquity* 55:559–569. [5, 14]

Monks, G. G. 1981. Seasonality studies. In *Advances in Archaeological Method and Theory*, vol. 4, ed., M. B. Schiffer, pp. 177–240. New York: Academic Press. [5]

Montgomery, B. K., and J. J. Reid. 1990. An instance of rapid ceramic change in the American Southwest. *American Antiquity* 55:88–97. [4]

Montmollin, O. de. 1988. Tenam Rosario—A political microcosm. *American Antiquity* 53:351–370. [14]

Moore, C. B. 1907. Moundville revisited. *Journal of the Academy of Natural Sciences of Philadelphia* (2nd series) 13:337–405. [2]

Moore, J. A., and A. S. Keene, eds. 1983. *Archaeological Hammers and Theories*. New York: Academic Press. [5]

Moore, J. D. 1988. Prehistoric raised field agriculture in the Casma Valley, Peru. *Journal of Field Archaeology* 15: 265–276. [6, 14]

Moorehead, A. 1978. *Darwin and the* Beagle. New York: Penguin. [1]

Morgan, L. H. 1877. *Ancient Society*. New York: World. [2]

Morison, S. E. 1974. *The European Discovery of America: The Southern Voyages* A.D. *1492–1616*. New York: Oxford University Press. [1, 2]

Morley, S. G. 1920. *The Inscriptions of Copán*. Carnegie Institution of Washington, Publication, no. 219. [3, 9]

Morley, S. G., G. W. Brainerd, and R. Sharer. 1983. *The Ancient Maya*. Stanford, Calif.: Stanford University Press. [3, 14]

Morris, C., and D. E. Thompson. 1970. Huanuco Viejo. *American Antiquity* 35(3):344–366. [14]

———. 1985. *Huanuco Pampa: An Inca City and Its Hinterland*. New York: Thames and Hudson. [14]

Moseley, M. E. 1975. Chan Chan: Andean alternative to the preindustrial city. *Science* 187:219–225. [14]

Mosimann, J., and P. S. Martin. 1975. Simulating overkill by Paleoindians. *American Scientist* 63:304–313.

Mueller, J. W. 1975. *Sampling in Archaeology*. Tucson: University of Arizona Press. [4]

Munsell Soil Color Charts. 1954. Baltimore, Md.: Munsell Color, Macbeth Division of Kollmorgen Corp. [4]

Murdock, G. P. 1965. *Social Structure*. New York: Free Press. [7]

Murra, J. V., and C. Morris. 1976. Dynastic oral tradition, administrative records and archaeology in the Andes. *World Archaeology* 7:269–279. [9, 14]

Nabokov, P. 1989. *Native American Architecture*. New York: Oxford University Press. [7]

Nance, J. D. 1983. Regional sampling in archaeological survey: The statistical perspective. In *Advances in Archaeological Method and Theory*, vol. 6, ed., M. B. Schiffer, pp. 289–356. New York: Academic Press. [4]

Naroll, R. 1962. Floor area and settlement population. *American Antiquity* 27:587–589. [7]

Nelson, S. M. 1990. The Neolithic of Northeastern China and Korea. *Antiquity* 64:234–248. [13]

Netting, R. M. 1972. Sacred Power and Centralization. In *Population Growth: Anthropological Implications,* ed., B. Spooner, pp. 219–244. Cambridge, Mass.: MIT Press. [10, 12, 16]

———. 1977. *Cultural Ecology.* Menlo Park, Calif.: Cummings. [5]

Netting, R. M., R. R. Wilk, and E. J. Arnould, eds. 1984. *Households, Comparative and Historical Studies of the Domestic Group.* Berkeley: University of California Press. [7]

Newcomer, M. H., and L. H. Keeley. 1979. Testing a method of microwear analysis with experimental flint tools. In Hayden, ed., pp. 195–205. [4]

Nichols, D. L. 1982. A Middle Formative irrigation system near Santa Clara Coatitlán in the Basin of Mexico. *American Antiquity* 47:133–144. [14]

———. 1988. Infrared aerial photography and prehispanic irrigation at Teotihuacán: The Tlajinga Canals. *Journal of Field Archaeology* 15:17–27. [8, 14]

Nicholson, H. B. 1971. Religion in pre-Hispanic Central Mexico. In *Handbook of Middle American Indians,* ed., R. Wauchope. Vol. 10: *Archaeology of Northern Mesoamerica, Part One,* pp. 395–446. Austin: University of Texas Press. [12]

Noel Hume, I. 1969. *Historical Archaeology.* New York: Knopf. [2]

O'Brien, M. J. 1987. Sedentism, population growth, and resource selection in the Woodland Midwest: A review of coevolutionary developments. *Current Anthropology* 28(2):177–197. [5, 6, 14]

O'Brien, P., and H. Christiansen. 1986. An Ancient Maya Measurement System. *American Antiquity* 51:136–151. [9, 14]

O'Shea, J. M. 1984. *Mortuary Variability: An Archaeological Investigation.* Orlando, Fla.: Academic Press. [10, 14]

Odum, E. P. 1971. *Fundamentals of Ecology,* 3rd ed. Philadelphia: Saunders. [5]

Offner, J. A. 1983. *Law and Politics in Aztec Texcoco.* Cambridge: Cambridge University Press. [11, 14]

Olin, J. S., and A. D. Franklin, eds. 1982. *Archaeological Ceramics.* Washington, D.C.: Smithsonian Institution Press. [4]

Oliver, P. 1987. *Dwellings: The House across the World.* Austin: University of Texas Press. [7]

Olsen, S. J. 1968. *Fish, Amphibian, and Reptile Remains from Archaeological Sites. Part. 1: Southeastern and Southwestern United States.* Papers of the Peabody Museum of American Archaeology and Ethnology, vol. 61, no. 2. 61(2). [5, 6, 14]

———. 1973. *Mammal Remains from Archaeological Sites. Part. 1: Southeastern and Southwestern United States.* Papers of the Peabody Museum, Harvard University, vol. 56, no. 1, Cambridge, Mass. [5, 6, 14]

Orser, C. E. 1988. The archaeological analysis of plantation society: Replacing status and caste with economics and power. *American Antiquity* 53:735–751. [4]

Ortner, D. J., and W. G. J. Putschar. 1985. *Identification of Pathological Conditions in Human Skeletal Remains.* Washington:, D.C. Smithsonian Institution Press. [4]

Orton, C. 1980. *Mathematics in Archaeology.* New York: Cambridge University Press. [4]

Paden, W. E. 1988. *Religious Worlds.* Boston: Beacon Press. [12]

Palerm, A., and E. R. Wolf. 1957. Ecological potential and cultural development in Mesoamerica. In *Studies in Human Ecology.* Pan American Union Social Sciences Monograph, no. 3, pp. 1–35. [5, 6]

Parkes, P. A. 1986. *Current Scientific Techniques in Archaeology.* New York: St. Martin's Press. [4]

Parrington, M. 1983. Remote sensing. *Annual Review of Anthropology* 12:105–124. [4]

Parry, W. 1987. *Chipped Stone Tools in Formative Oaxaca, Mexico, Their Procurement, Production and Use.* Ann Arbor: University of Michigan, Museum of Anthropology. [8, 14]

Parsons, J. R. 1972. Archaeological settlement patterns. *Annual Review of Anthropology* 1:127–150. [4]

———. 1974. The development of a prehistoric complex society: A regional perspective from the Valley of Mexico. *Journal of Field Archaeology* 1:81–108. [5, 14]

———. 1976. The Role of Chinampa Agriculture in the Food Supply of Aztec Tenochtitlan. In *Cultural Change and Continuity,* ed., C. Cleland, pp. 233–257. New York: Academic Press. [5, 14]

———. 1990. Critical Reflections on a Decade of Full-Coverage, Regional Survey in the Valley of Mexico. In Fish and Kowalewski, eds., pp. 7–31. [4, 14]

Pasztory, E. 1983. *Aztec Art.* New York: Abrams. [12]

Patterson, T. C. 1971. The emergence of food production in central Peru. In Struever, ed., pp. 181–207. [5, 14]

Paynter, R. W. 1983. Expanding the scope of settlement analysis. In Moore and Keene, eds., pp. 233–275. [4]

Pearsall, D. M. 1978. Phytolith analysis: Applications of a new paleoethnobotanical technique in archaeology. *American Anthropologist* 84(4):862–870. [4]

Pearsall, D. M., and D. Piperno. 1990. Antiquity of maize cultivation in Ecuador: Summary and reevaluation of the evidence. *American Antiquity* 55:324–337. [5, 14]

Peebles, C. S. 1971. Moundville and surrounding sites: some structural considerations of mortuary practices II. In Brown, ed., pp. 68–91. [4]

———. 1987. Moundville from 1000 to 1500 AD as seen from 1840 to 1985 AD. In *Chiefdoms in the Americas,* eds., R. Drennan and C. Uribe, pp. 21–41. Lanham, Md.: University Press of America. [2, 10]

Peebles, C. S., and S. M. Kus. 1977. Some archaeological correlates of ranked societies. *American Antiquity* 42:421–448. [5, 10]

Pfeiffer, J. E. 1969. *The Emergence of Man.* New York: Harper and Row. [5, 12]

———. 1977. *The Emergence of Society: A Prehistory of the Establishment.* New York: McGraw-Hill. [10]

Piddocke, S. 1965. The potlatch system of the South Kwakiutl: A new perspective. *Southwestern Journal of Anthropology* 21:244–264. [6]

Piperno, D. R. 1988. *Phytolith Analysis: An Archaeological and Geological Perspective.* San Diego, Calif.: Academic Press. [4]

Pitts, M. 1979. Hides and antlers: A new look at the gatherer-hunter site at Star Carr, North Yorkshire, England. *World Archaeology* 11:32–42. [5, 6, 13]

Plattner, S., ed. 1989. *Economic Anthropology.* Stanford, Calif.: Stanford University Press. [8]

Plew, M. G., J. C. Woods, and M. G. Pavesic, eds. 1985. *Stone Tool Analysis: Essays in Honor of Don E. Crabtree.* Albuquerque: University of New Mexico Press. [4, 6]

Plog, F. T. 1974. *The Study of Prehistoric Change.* New York: Academic Press. [5]

———. 1982. Is a little philosophy (science?) a dangerous thing? In Renfrew, Rowlands, and Seagraves, eds., pp. 25–33. [2, 5, 16]

Plog, S. 1980. *Stylistic Variation in Prehistoric Ceramics.* Cambridge: Cambridge University Press. [4]

Plog, S., and J. L. Hantman. 1990. Chronology construction and the study of prehistoric culture change. *Journal of Field Archaeology* 17:439–456. [4]

Plog, S., F. Plog, and W. Wait. 1978. Decision making in modern surveys. In *Advances in Archaeological Method and Theory,* vol. 1, ed., M. B. Schiffer, pp. 383–421. New York: Academic Press. [4, 7, 11]

Pohl, M. D., ed. 1990. *Ancient Maya Wetland Agriculture.* Boulder, Col.: Westview. [5, 6]

Polanyi, K., C. M. Arensberg, and H. W. Pearson, eds. 1957. *Trade and Market in the Early Empires.* Glencoe, Calif.: Free Press. [5, 8]

Pope, K., and B. Dahlin. 1989. Ancient Maya Wetland Agriculture: New Insights from Ecological and Remote Sensing Research. *Journal of Field Archaeology* 16: 87–106. [14, 15]

Possehl, G. L. 1990. Revolution in the Urban Revolution: The Emergence of Indus Urbanization. *Annual Review of Anthropology* 19:261–282. [13]

Powers, W., and J. R. Hoffecker. 1989. Late Pleistocene Settlement in the Nenana Valley, Central Alaska. *American Antiquity* 54:263–287. [14]

Pozorski, S. G., and T. G. Pozorski. 1987. *Early Settlement and Subsistence in the Casma Valley, Peru.* Iowa City: University of Iowa Press. [14]

Price, B. J. 1982. Cultural materialism: A theoretical review. *American Antiquity* 47:709–741. [5, 16]

Proskouriakoff, T. 1946. *An Album of Maya Architecture.* Carnegie Institution of Washington, Publication 558. [3, 9, 12, 14]

———. 1960. Historical implications of a pattern of dates at Piedras Negras, Guatemala. *American Antiquity* 25:454–475. [9]

———. 1961. The lords of the Maya realm. *Expedition* 4:14–21. [10, 11]

Pyddoke, E. 1961. *Stratification for the Archaeologist.* London: Phoenix House. [4]

Raab, L. M., and A. C. Goodyear. 1984. Middle-range theory in archaeology: A critical review of origins and applications. *American Antiquity* 49(2):255–268. [2, 5]

Rahtz, P. A. 1974. *Rescue Archaeology.* London: Penguin. [2]

Ralph, E. K. 1974. Carbon-14 dating. In Michael and Ralph, eds., pp. 1–48. [4]

Ralph, E. K., and M. C. Han. 1966. Dating of pottery by thermoluminescence. *Nature* 210:245–247. [4]

Rapaport, A. 1969. *House Form and Culture.* Englewood Cliffs, N.J.: Prentice-Hall. [7]

Rapp, G., and J. A. Gifford, eds. 1985. *Archaeological Geology.* New Haven: Yale University Press. [4]

Rappaport, R. A. 1967. *Pigs for the Ancestors: Ritual in the Ecology of a New Guinea People.* New Haven: Yale University Press. [12]

———. 1971a. Nature, culture, and ecological anthropology. In *Man, Culture and Society,* ed., H. L. Shapiro, pp. 237–267. New York: Oxford University Press. [5, 6]

———. 1971b. Ritual, sanctity and cybernetics. *American Anthropologist* 73(1):59–76. [12]

———. 1971c. The sacred in human evolution. *Annual Review of Ecology and Systematics* 2:23–43. [12]

Rathje, W. L. 1970. Socio-political implications of lowland Maya burials: Methodology and tentative hypotheses. *World Archaeology* 1:359–374. [3, 10]

———. 1971. The origin and development of Classic Maya civilization. *American Antiquity* 36:275–285. [8, 14]

———. 1974. The garbage project: A new way of looking at the problems of archaeology. *Archaeology* 27: 236–241. [2, 5]

Rathje, W. L., and C. Ritenbaugh, eds. 1984. *Household Refuse Analysis.* ABS, vol. 28, no. 1. Newbury Park, Ill.: Sage. [7]

Rathje, W. L., and M. B. Schiffer. 1982. *Archaeology.* New York: Harcourt Brace Jovanovich. [1]

Read, D. W. 1986. Sampling procedures for regional surveys: A problem of Representativeness and Effectiveness. *Journal of Field Archaeology* 13:477–491. [4]

Reader, J. 1988. *Man on Earth.* Austin: University of Texas Press. [6]

Redfield, R. 1953. *The Primitive World and its Transformations.* Ithaca, N.Y.: Cornell University Press.

Redman, C. L. 1973. Multistage fieldwork and analytical techniques. *American Antiquity* 38(1):61–79. [4]

———. 1974. *Archaeological Sampling Strategies.* Addison-Wesley Modular Publications in Anthropology, no. 55. [4]

———. 1978. *The Rise of Civilization: From Early Farmers to Urban Society in the Ancient Near East.* San Francisco: Freeman. [5, 13]

———. 1987. Surface Collection. Sampling, and Research Design. *American Antiquity* 52:249–265. [4]

———1991. In defense of the seventies—The adolescence of New Archaeology. *American Anthropologist* 93(2):295–307. [2]

Redman, C., M. J. Berman, E. V. Curtin, W. T. Langehorne Jr., N. M. Versaggi, and J. C. Wanser, eds. 1978. *Social Archaeology.* New York: Academic Press. [4, 5]

Reischauer, E. O., and J. K. Fairbank. 1960. *East Asia: The Great Tradition.* New York: Houghton Mifflin. [13]

Reitz, E., I. Quitmyer, and H. S. Hale. 1987. Application of Allometry to Zooarchaeology. *American Antiquity* 52:304–317. [4]

Renfrew, C. 1971. Carbon 14 and the prehistory of Europe. *Scientific American* 225:63–72. [2, 4, 5, 13]

———. 1972. *The Emergence of Civilization: The Cyclades and the Aegean in the Third Millennium B.C.* London: Methuen. [14]

———. 1973. *Before Civilization: The Radiocarbon Revolution and Prehistoric Europe.* New York: Knopf. [2]

———. 1979. *Problems in European Prehistory.* Edinburgh: Edinburgh University Press. [13]

———. 1988. *Archaeology and Language: The Puzzle of Indo-European Origins.* New York: Cambridge University Press. [13]

Renfrew, C., and R. M. Clark. 1974. Problems of the radiocarbon calendar and its calibration. *Archaeometry* 16:5–18. [4]

Renfrew, C., and K. L. Cooke. 1979. *Transformations: Mathematical Approaches to Culture Change.* New York: Academic Press. [4, 5]

Renfrew, C., J. E. Dixon, and J. R. Cann. 1966. Further analyses of Near Eastern obsidian. *Proceedings of the Prehistoric Society* 34:319–331. [8, 13]

Renfrew, C., M. J. Rowlands, and B. A. Segraves, eds. 1982. *Theory and Explanation in Archaeology.* New York: Academic Press. [2, 5, 16]

Renfrew, J. 1973. *Paleoethnobotany: The Prehistoric Food Plants of the Near East and Europe.* New York: Columbia University Press. [4, 5, 13]

Rice, P. 1987. *Pottery Analysis.* Chicago: University of Chicago Press. [4, 7]

Riddell, H. S. 1951. *The Archaeology of a Paiute Village Site in Owens Valley.* University of California Archaeological Survey Reports, no. 12, pp. 14–28. [5, 6]

Rindos, D. 1984. *The Origins of Agriculture: An Evolutionary Perspective.* Orlando, Fla.: Academic Press. [5, 6, 16]

———. 1989. Diversity, variation and selection. In Leonard and Jones, eds., pp. 13–23.

Roaf, M. 1990. *Cultural Atlas of Mesopotamia and the Ancient Near East.* New York: Facts on File. [5, 13]

Robicsek, F. 1972. *Copán: Home of the Maya Gods.* New York: Museum of the American Indian. [3, 13]

Robinson, W. S. 1951. A method for chronologically ordering archaeological deposits. *American Antiquity* 16:293–301. [4]

Rocek, T. R. 1988. The behavioral and material correlates of site seasonality: Lessons from Navajo ethnoarchaeology. *American Antiquity* 53:523–536. [4]

Roosevelt, A. C. 1980. *Parmana: Prehistoric Maize and Manioc Subsistence Along the Amazon and Orinoco.* New York: Academic Press. [5, 6, 14]

Rose, J. C., K. W. Condon, and A. H. Goodman. 1985. Diet and dentition: Developmental disturbances. In *The Analysis of Prehistoric Diets,* eds., R. I. Gilbert and J. H. Mielke, pp. 281–305. Orlando, Fla.: Academic Press. [5, 15]

Ross, K. 1978. *Codex Mendoza: Aztec Manuscript*. Fribourg, Switz.: Miller Graphics.

Rounds, J. 1982. Dynastic succession and the centralization of power in Tenochtitlan. In Collier, Rosaldo, and Wirth, eds., pp. 63–89. [10, 11, 14]

Rouse, I. 1960. The classification of artifacts in archaeology. *American Antiquity* 25(3):313–323. [2, 4]

Rovner, I. 1983. Plant opal phytolith analysis: Major advances in archaeobotanical research. In *Advances in Archaeological Method and Theory,* vol. 6, ed., M. B. Schiffer, pp. 225–266. New York: Academic Press. [4]

Rowe, J. 1946. Inca Culture at the Time of the Spanish Conquest. In *Handbook of South American Indians* vol. 2, ed., J. Steward, pp. 183–330. Washington: Bureau of American Ethnology. [11, 14]

Roys, R. 1965. Late Maya Native Society at Spanish Contact. In *Handbook of Mesoamerican Indians,* vol. 3, edited by R. Wauchope. Austin, Tex.: University of Texas Press, pp. 659–678.

Rudofsky, B. 1977. *The Prodigious Builders*. New York: Harcourt Brace Jovanovich. [7]

Rue, D. 1987. Early agriculture and early Postclassic Maya occupation in western Honduras. *Nature* 326: 285–286. [3, 15]

Rust, W., and R. Sharer. 1988. Olmec settlement data from La Venta, Tabasco, Mexico. *Science* 242:102–104. [11]

Ryder, M. L. 1969. *Animal Bones in Archaeology*. Oxford: Blackwell Scientific. [4]

Sabloff, J., and E. W. Andrews V, eds. 1986. *Late Lowland Maya Civilization*. Albuquerque: University of New Mexico Press. [14, 15]

Sackett, J. R. 1977. The meaning of style in archaeology: A general model. *American Antiquity* 42:369–380. [4]

Sahagun, F. B. de. 1950–1963. *General History of the Things of New Spain (Florentine Codex)*. Translated by A. Anderson and C. Dibble. 12 vols. Santa Fe, N.M.: The School of American Research and the University of Utah. [1, 7, 10, 14]

Sahlins, M. D. 1970. Poor Man, Rich Man, Big-Man, Chief: Political Types in Melanesia and Polynesia, in *Cultures of the Pacific,* eds., T. G. Harding and B. J. Johnson, pp. 203–215, New York: Free Press.

———. 1972. *Stone Age Economics*. Chicago: Aldine-Atherton. [5, 8]

Sahlins, M. D., and E. R. Service. 1960. *Evolution and Culture*. Ann Arbor: University of Michigan Press. [5]

Salmon, M. H. 1975. Confirmation and explanation in archaeology. *American Antiquity* 40:459–464. [5, 16]

———. 1976. "Deductive" versus "inductive" archaeology. *American Antiquity* 41:376–381. [2, 5, 16]

———. 1978. What can systems theory do for archaeology? *American Anthropologist* 43:174–183.

Salmon, M. H., and W. C. Salmon. 1982. Alternative models of scientific explanation. *American Anthropologist* 81(1):61–74. [2, 5, 16]

Sanders, W. T. 1972. Population, agriculture, history, and societal evolution in Mesoamerica. In Spooner, ed., pp. 101–153. [5, 14]

———. 1981. Ecological adaptation in the Basin of Mexico: 23,000 B.C. to the present. In *Supplement to the Handbook of Middle American Indians,* vol. 1, ed., J. A. Sabloff, pp. 147–197. Austin: University of Texas Press. [5, 6, 14]

———, ed. 1986. *Excavaciones* en el *Area Urbana* de Copán. Tegucigalpa: Secreteria del Estado en el Despacho de Cultura y Turismo. [3]

Sanders, W. T., and J. Marino. 1970. *New World Prehistory: Archaeology of the American Indian*. Englewood Cliffs, N.J.: Prentice-Hall. [14]

Sanders, W. T., J. R. Parsons, and R. Santley. 1979. *The Basin of Mexico: The Cultural Ecology of a Civilization*. New York: Academic Press. [5, 6, 7, 14]

Sanders, W. T., and B. Price. 1968. *Mesoamerica: The Evolution of a Civilization*. New York: Random House.

Sanders, W. T., and D. Webster. 1978. Unilinealism, multilinealism, and the evolution of complex societies. In Redman et al., eds., pp. 249–301. [5]

———. 1988. The Mesoamerican Urban Tradition. *American Anthropologist* 90(3):521–546. [7, 8, 14]

Sansom, G. 1958. *A History of Japan to 1334*. Palo Alto, Calif.: Stanford University Press. [13]

Santley, R. S. 1980. Teotihuacán, in *The Encyclopedia of Ancient Civilizations,* ed., Arthur Cotterell, pp. 325–332. New York: Mayflower.

Santley, R. S., P. Arnold, and C. Pool. 1989. The ceramics production system at Matacapán, Veracruz, Mexico. *Journal of Field Archaeology* 16:107–132. [8]

Saraydar, S., and I. Shimada. 1971. A quantitative comparison of efficiency between a stone axe and a steel axe. *American Antiquity* 36:216–217. [6]

Scarborough, V. L. 1986. Civic and residential settlement at a Late Preclassic Maya Center. *Journal of Field Archaeology* 16:405–425. [7, 14]

Schele, L., and M. E. Miller. 1986. *Blood of Kings*. New York: G. Braziller, in association with the Kimbell Art Museum, Fort Worth, Texas. [3, 9, 12, 14]

Schele, L., and D. Freidel. 1990. *Forest of Kings.* New York: Morrow. [3, 9, 12, 14]

Schiffer, M. B. 1972. Archaeological context and systemic context. *American Antiquity* 37:156–165. [1, 2, 4]

———. 1976. *Behavioral Archaeology.* New York: Academic Press. [4]

———. 1987 *Formation Processes of the Archaeological Record.* Albuquerque: University of New Mexico Press. [1, 4]

Schiffer, M. B., and G. J. Gumerman, eds. 1977. *Conservation Archaeology: A Guide for Cultural Resource Management Studies.* New York: Academic Press. [2]

Schmandt-Besserat, D. 1978. The earliest precursor of writing. *Scientific American* 238(6):50–59.

Schoeninger, M. J., M. J. DeNiro, and H. Tauber. 1983. Stable nitrogen isotope ratios of bone collagen reflect marine and terrestrial components of prehistoric human diet. *Science* 220:1381–1383. [3, 4, 15]

Schortman, E., P. Urban, and W. Ashmore. 1986. Interregional interaction in the southeast Maya periphery. *Journal of Field Archaeology* 13:259–272. [11, 14]

Schreiber, K. A. 1987. Conquest and consolidation: A comparison of the Wari and Inka occupations of a Highland Peruvian valley. *American Antiquity:* 52: 266–284. [11, 14]

Schuyler, R. 1978. *Historical Archaeology: A Guide to Substantive and Theoretical Contributions.* Farmingdale, N.Y.: Baywood. [2, 4]

Schwerdtfeger, F. W. 1982. *Traditional Housing in African Cities.* New York: Wiley. [7]

Scientific American. 1979. *Energy.* San Francisco: Freeman. [5]

———. *Evolution.* 1978. San Francisco: Freeman. [5]

Sease, C. 1987. *Archaeological Research Tools,* vol. 4: *A Conservation Manual for the Field Archaeologist.* Los Angeles: Institute of Archaeology, University of California. [4]

Seltzer, G., and C. Hastorf. 1990. Climatic change and its effect on prehispanic agriculture in the Central Peruvian Andes. *Journal of Field Archaeology* 17:397–414. [6, 14, 15]

Semenov, S. A. 1964. *Prehistoric Technology.* London: Cory, Adams and Mackay. [6, 8]

Service, E. R. 1971. *Primitive Social Organization: An Evolutionary Perspective,* 2nd ed. New York: Random House. [2, 5, 10]

———. 1971. *Cultural Evolutionism: Theory in Practice.* New York: Holt, Rinehart and Winston. [5]

———. 1975. *Origins of the State and Civilization: The Process of Cultural Evolution.* New York: Norton. [5, 10]

Shanks, M., and C. Tilley, 1987. *Reconstructing Archaeology: Theory and Practice.* Cambridge: Cambridge University Press. [2, 16]

Sharer, R., and D. Grove, eds. 1989a. *The Olmec and the Development of Formative Mesoamerican Civilization.* New York: Cambridge University Press. [14]

———. 1989b. *Regional Perspectives on the Olmec.* Cambridge: Cambridge University Press. [14]

Sharer, R. J., and W. Ashmore. 1987. *Archaeology: Discovering Our Past.* Mountain View, Calif.: Mayfield. [1]

Sheehy, J. 1991. Structure and change in a Late Classic Maya domestic group at Copán, Honduras. *Ancient Mesoamerica* 2:1–19. [3]

Sheets, P. D. 1979. Maya recovery from volcanic disasters: Ilopango and Cerén. *Archaeology* 32:32–42. [4, 8, 14]

———, ed. 1983a. *Archaeology and Volcanism in Central America.* Austin: University of Texas Press. [1, 7]

———. 1983b. Introduction. In Sheets, ed., pp. 1–13. [1, 4, 7]

Sheets, P., K. Hirth, F. Lange, F. Stross, F. Asaro, and H. Michel. 1990. Obsidian sources and elemental analyses of artifacts in southern Mesoamerica and the northern intermediate area. *American Antiquity* 55:144–158. [4, 8, 14]

Sheets, P., and T. Sever. 1988. High-tech wizardry: Aerial photography and scanning in archaeological research. *Archaeology* 41:28–35. [4]

Shennan, S. 1988. *Quantifying Archaeology.* Edinburgh: Edinburgh University Press. [4]

Shepard, A. O. 1956. *Ceramics for the Archaeologist.* Washington, D.C.: Carnegie Institution of Washington Publication, no. 609. [4]

Shelton, J. 1966. *Geology Illustrated.* San Francisco: Freeman. [2]

Sherrat, A., ed. 1980. *The Cambridge Encyclopedia of Archaeology.* New York: Cambridge University Press. [13, 14]

Shetrone, H. C. 1936. *The Mound-Builders.* New York: Appleton-Century. [2]

Shott, M. 1987. Feature discovery and the sampling requirements of archaeological evaluations. *Journal of Field Archaeology* 14:359–371. [1, 4]

Simon, A. W., and W. A. Coghlan. 1989. The use of indentation testing to obtain precise hardness measurements from prehistoric pottery. *American Antiquity* 54: 107–122. [4]

Simek, J. F. 1987. Spatial order and behavioural change in the French Palaeolithic. *Antiquity* 61:25–40. [2, 7]

Simms, S. R. 1987. *Behavioral Ecology and Hunter-Gatherer Foraging: An example from the Great Basin*. Oxford: B.A.R. [5, 6]

Sinopoli, C. 1988. The organization of craft production at Vijayanagara, South India. *American Anthropologist* 90:580–597. [8, 13]

Smith, B. D., ed. 1978. *Mississippian Settlement Patterns*. New York: Academic Press. [7, 10, 14]

———. 1982. Explanation in archaeology. In Renfrew, Rowlands, and Segrave, eds., pp. 73–82. [16]

Smith, C. 1976. *Regional Analysis*. 2 vols. New York: Academic Press. [7, 11]

Smith, M. E. 1984. The Aztlan migrations of the Nahuatl Chronicles: Myth or history? *Ethnohistory* 31: 153–186. [14]

Smith, M. E., P. Aquirre, C. Heath-Smith, K. Hirst, S. O'Mack, and J. Price. 1989. Architectural patterns at three Aztec-Period sites in Morelos, Mexico. *Journal of Field Archaeology* 6:185–203.

Smith, P. E. L. 1976. *Food Production and Its Consequences*. Menlo Park, Calif.: Cummings. [5, 6]

Smith, P. E. L., and T. C. Young, Jr. 1972. The evolution of early agriculture and culture in greater Mesopotamia: A trial model. In Spooner, ed., pp. 1–59. [5, 14]

Solecki, R. S. 1971. *Shanidar: The First Flower People*. New York: Knopf. [12]

South, S. A. 1977. *Method and Theory in Historical Archaeology*. New York: Academic Press. [2]

———, ed. 1977. *Research Strategies in Historical Archaeology*. New York: Academic Press. [2, 4]

South, S. A., and R. Widmer. 1977. A subsurface sampling strategy of archaeological reconnaissance. In South, ed., pp. 119–150.

Spaulding, A. C. 1953. Statistical techniques for the discovery of artifact types. *American Antiquity* 18:305–313. [2, 4]

———. 1960. The dimensions of archaeology. In *Essays in the Science of Culture in Honor of Leslie A White*, eds., G. E. Dole and R. L. Carneiro, pp. 437–456. New York: Crowell. [2]

———. 1968. Explanation in archaeology. In Binford and Binford, eds., pp. 33–39. [2, 16]

———. 1973. The concept of artifact type in archaeology. *Plateau* 45:149–164. [4]

———. 1977. On growth and form in archaeology: Multivariate analysis. *Journal of Anthropological Research* 33:1–15. [4]

Spector, J. D. 1983. Male/female task-differentiation among the Hidatsa: Toward the development of an archaeological approach to the study of gender. In *The Hidden Half: Studies of Plains Indian Women*, eds., P. Albers and B. Medicine, pp. 77–99. Lanham, Md.: University Press of America. [2, 7]

Spence, M. W. 1986. Locational analysis of craft specialization areas in Teotihuacán. *Research in Economic Anthropology*, Supplement 2, pp. 75–100. Greenwich, Conn.: JAI Press. [8]

———, ed. n.d. Tlailotlacán, a Zapotec enclave in Teotihuacán. In *Art, Ideology, and the City of Teotihuacán*. Washington, D.C.: Dumbarton Oaks.

Sperlich, N., and E. K. Sperlich. 1980. *Guatemalan Backstrap Weaving*. Norman: University of Oklahoma Press. [8]

Spielmann, K. A., M. Schoeninger, and K. Moore. 1990. Plains-Pueblo interdependence and human diet at Pecos Pueblo, New Mexico. *American Antiquity* 55:745–765. [5, 6]

Spinden, H. 1913. *A Study of Maya Art*. Memoirs of the Peabody Museum, Cambridge, Mass. [2]

Spink, M. 1983. *Metates as Socio-Economic Indicators During the Late Classic Period at Copán, Honduras*. Ph.D. dissertation, Pennsylvania State University, University Park.

Spooner, B., ed. 1972. *Population Growth: Anthropological Implications*. Cambridge, Mass.: MIT Press. [5, 6, 16]

Spores, R. 1984. *The Mixtecs in Ancient and Colonial Times*. Norman: University of Oklahoma Press. [14]

Spriggs, M. 1984. *Marxist Perspectives in Archaeology*. Cambridge: Cambridge University Press. [2]

Stahle, D. W., and D. Wolfman. 1985. The potential for archaeological tree-ring dating in eastern north America. In *Advances in Archaeological Method and Theory*, vol. 8, ed., M. B. Schiffer, pp. 279–302. New York: Academic Press. [4]

Stallings, W. S., Jr. 1939. *Dating Prehistoric Ruins by Tree-Rings*. Santa Fe, N.M.: Laboratory of Anthropology, Bulletin No. 8. [2]

Stark, B., and D. Young. 1981. Linear nearest neighbor analysis. *American Antiquity* 46:284–300. [4]

Stein, J. K. 1986. Coring archaeological sites. *American Antiquity* 51:505–527. [4]

Stephens, J. L. 1969 [1841]. *Incidents of Travel in Central America, Chiapas and Yucatán*. 2 vols. New York: Dover. [1, 3, 15]

Steponaitis, V. P. 1978. Locational theory and complex chiefdoms: A Mississippian example. In B. Smith, ed. pp. 417–453. [7, 10, 14]

————. 1983. *Ceramics, Chronology, and Community Patterns: An Archaeological Study at Moundville*. New York: Academic Press. [4, 14]

Steponaitis, V. P., and J. P. Brain. 1976. A portable differential proton magnetometer. *Journal of Field Archaeology* 3:455–463. [4]

Steward, J. H. 1939. *Basin-Plateau Aboriginal Sociopolitical Groups*. Bureau of American Ethnology Bulletin, no. 120, Washington, D.C. [2, 5, 6]

————. 1949. Cultural causality and law: A trial formulation of early civilization. *American Anthropologist* 51: 1–27. [2, 5]

————. 1951. Levels of sociocultural integration: An operational concept. *Southwestern Journal of Anthropology* 7:374–390. [2, 5, 10]

————. 1955. *Theory of Culture Change*. Urbana: University of Illinois Press. [1, 5]

Stini, W. A. 1985. Growth rates and sexual dimorphism in evolutionary perspective. In Gilbert and Mielke, eds., pp. 191–226. [4]

Stone, T., D. Dickel, and G. Doran. 1990. The preservation and conservation of waterlogged bone from the Windover Site, Florida: A Comparison of Methods. *Journal of Field Archaeology* 17:177–186. [4]

Storey, R. 1992a. People of Copán: Issues in paleodemography and paleopathology, in *Ancient Mesoamerica*, vol. 2, pp. 107–118. [3, 15]

————. 1992b. *Life and Death in the Ancient City of Teotihuacán*. Tuscaloosa: University of Alabama Press. [8, 10, 14]

Storey, R., and R. J. Widmer. 1989. Household and Community Structure of a Teotihuacán Apartment Compound: S3W1:33 of the Tlajinga Barrio. In MacEachern, Archer, and Garvin, eds., pp. 407–415.

Stover, L. 1974. *The Cultural Ecology of Chinese Civilization*. New York: Pica Press. [13]

Strong, W. D. and C. Evans, Jr. 1952. *Cultural Stratigraphy in the Virú Valley, northern Peru*. Columbia University Studies in Archaeology and Ethnology, no. 4. [2]

Struever, S. 1968a. Flotation techniques for the recovery of small-scale archaeological remains. *American Antiquity* 33(3):353–362. [4]

————. 1968b. Woodland subsistence settlement systems in the lower Illinois valley. In Binford and Binford, eds., pp. 285–312. [6, 14]

————, ed. 1971. *Prehistoric Agriculture*. Garden City, N.Y.: American Museum of Natural History. [5, 6]

Struever, S., and J. Carlson. 1977. Koster site: The new archaeology in action. *Archaeology* 30:93–101. [2]

Struever, S., and F. A. Holton. 1979. *Koster: Americans in Search of their Prehistoric Past*. Garden City, N.Y.: Anchor Press/Doubleday. [2]

Stuart, D., and S. Houston. 1989. Maya writing. *Scientific American* 261: 82–89. [3, 9, 14]

Stuart, G. E. 1989. Copán: City of kings and commoners. *National Geographic Magazine* 176(4):488–505.

Sullivan, T. D. 1982. Tlazolteotl-Ixcuina: The great spinner and weaver. In *The Art and Iconography of Late Post-Classic Central Mexico*, ed., E. Boone, pp. 7–35. Washington, D.C.: Dumbarton Oaks. [7, 12]

Szabolcs, I. 1989. *Salt Affected Soils*. Boca Raton: CRC Press.

Tainter, J. 1978. Mortuary practices and the study of prehistoric social systems. In *Advances in Archaeological Method and Theory*, vol. 1, ed., M. B. Schiffer pp. 105–141. [4, 10]

————. 1988. *The Collapse of Complex Societies*. New York: Cambridge University Press. [15]

Tarling, D. H. 1975. *Paleomagnetism: Principles and Applications in Geology, Geophysics and Archaeology*. London: Chapman and Hall. [4]

Taube, K. 1989. The maize tamale in Classic Maya diet, epigraphy, and art. *American Antiquity* 54:31–51. [5, 9]

Taylor, W. W. 1967. [1948] *A Study of Archeology*. Carbondale: Southern Illinois University Press. [1, 2]

Taylor R. E., ed. 1976. *Advances in Obsidian Glass Studies*. Park Ridge, Ill.: Noyes Press. [4]

————. 1987. *Radiocarbon Dating: An Archaeological Perspective*. New York: Academic Press. [4]

Taylor, R. E., and C. W. Meighan, eds. 1978. *Chronologies in New World Archaeology*. New York: Academic Press. [4]

Teltser, P. A. 1991. Generalized core technology and tool use: A Mississippian example. *Journal of Field Archaeology* 18:363–375. [6]

Theler, J. L. 1987. *Woodland Traditional Economic Strategies; Animal Resource Utilization in Southwestern Wisconsin and Northeastern Iowa*. Iowa City: Office of the State Archaeologist, University of Iowa. [8, 14]

Thomas, C. 1885. "Who Were the Mound Builders?" *American Antiquarian and Oriental Journal* 2:65–74.

Thomas, D. H. 1986. *Refiguring Anthropology: First Principles of Probability and Statistics*. Prospect Heights: Waveland Press.

Thompson, J. E. S. 1954. *The Rise and Fall of Maya Civilization*. Norman: University of Oklahoma Press. [15]

————. 1970. *Maya History and Religion*. Norman: University of Oklahoma Press. [12]

Thompson, H. S. 1986. *The Great White Shark Hunt*. New York: Warner Books.

Thompson, M. W. 1977. *General Pitt-Rivers: Evolution and Archaeology in the Nineteenth Century*. Wiltshire, England: Moonraker Press. [2]

Todd, L., J. Hoffman, and C. B. Schultz. 1990. Seasonality of the Scottsbluff and Lipscomb bison bonebeds: Implications for modeling Paleoindian subsistence. *American Antiquity* 55:813–827. [4, 16]

Topic, T. L., T. H. McGreevy, and J. R. Topic. 1987. A comment on the breeding and herding of llamas and alpacas on the north coast of Peru. *American Antiquity* 52:832–839. [6, 14]

Tozzer, A. M. 1941. *Landa's Relación de las Cosas de Yucatán*. Papers of the Peabody Museum, Harvard University, no. 18, Cambridge, Mass. [15]

Tuohy, D. R., and L. K. Napton. 1986. Duck decoys from Lovelock Cave, Nevada, dated by C_{14} accelerator mass spectrometry. *American Antiquity* 51:813–816. [4, 5]

Trigger, B. G. 1971. Archaeology and ecology. *World Archaeology* 2:321–336. [5, 6, 16]

————. 1981. Archaeology and the ethnographic present. *Anthropologica* 23:3–17. [6]

————. 1989. *A History of Archaeological Thought*. New York: Cambridge University Press. [2]

Tylor, E. B. 1871. *Primitive Culture*, vols. 1 and 2. London: Murray. [1, 5]

Ucko, P. J., and G. W. Dimbleby, eds. 1969. *The Domestication of Exploitation of Plants and Animals*. Chicago: Aldine. [5, 6]

Ucko, P. J., R. Tringham, and G. W. Dimbleby, eds. 1972. *Man, Settlement and Urbanism*. London: Duckworth. [7, 11, 13]

Upham, S. 1990. *The Evolution of Political Systems: Sociopolitics in Small-Scale Sedentary Societies*. Cambridge: Cambridge University Press. [5, 10]

Vaillant, G. C. 1966. *Aztecs of Mexico*. Revised by S. B. Vaillant. Baltimore, Md.: Penguin. [7]

van der Merwe, N. 1982. Carbon isotopes, photosynthesis, and archaeology. *American Scientist* 70:596–606. [4]

Vaughn, P. C. 1985. *Use-Wear Analysis of Flaked Stone Tools*. Tucson: University of Arizona Press. [4, 6]

Veblen, T. 1953. *The Theory of the Leisure Class*. New York: New American Library. [9]

Vita-Finzi, C. 1978. *Archaeological Sites in their Settings*. London: Thames and Hudson. [6]

Vita-Finzi, C., and E. S. Higgs. 1970. Prehistoric economy in the Mount Carmel area of Palestine: Site catchment analysis. *Proceedings of the Prehistoric Society* 36: 1–37. [5]

Voorhies, B., ed. 1989. *Ancient Trade and Tribute: Economies of the Soconusco Region of Mesoamerica*. Salt Lake City: University of Utah Press. [8, 14]

Wagner, G. E. 1990. Charcoal, isotopes, and shell hoes: Reconstructing a 12th century native American garden. *Expedition* 32(2):34–43. [6, 14]

Wainwright, G. 1989. *The Henge Monuments*. London: Thames and Hudson. [4]

Wallace, A. F. C. 1966. *Religion: An Anthropological View*. New York: Random House. [12]

Watson, P. J. 1974. Flotation procedures used on Salts Cave sediments. In *Archaeology of the Mammoth Cave Area*, ed., P. Watson, pp. 107–108. New York: Academic Press. [4]

————. 1979. *Archaeological Ethnography in Western Iran*. Viking Fund Publications in Anthropology, no. 57. [4, 13]

Watson, P. J., and M. Fotiadis. 1990. The razor's edge: Symbolic-structuralist archeology and the expansion of Archeological Inference. *American Anthropologist* 92:613–629. [4]

Watson, P. J., S. A. LeBlanc, and C. L. Redman. 1971. *Explanation in Archaeology: An Explicitly Scientific Approach*. New York: Academic Press. [2, 5, 16]

Watson, R. A., and P. J. Watson. 1969. *Man and Nature: An Anthropological Essay in Human Ecology*. New York: Harcourt, Brace and World. [6]

Wauchope, R. 1962. *Lost Tribes and Sunken Continents*. Chicago: University of Chicago Press. [2]

Weaver, M. P. 1981. *The Aztecs, Maya, and their Predecessors*, 2nd ed. New York: Academic Press. [14]

Webster, D. 1975. Warfare and the origin of the state. *American Antiquity* 40:464–471. [11]

————. 1976. On theocracies. *American Anthropologist* 78:812–828. [10, 12]

————. 1977. Warfare and the evolution of Maya civilization. In Adams, ed., pp. 335–372. Albuquerque: University of New Mexico Press. [10, 11]

————. 1985. Recent settlement survey in the Copán Valley, Honduras. *Journal of New World Archaeology* 5(4):39–51. [3, 15]

————, ed. 1989. *The House of the Bacabs*. Studies in Precolumbian Art and Architecture, no. 29. Washington, D.C.: Dumbarton Oaks. [3, 10, 15]

Webster, D., and A. Freter. 1990a. The Demography of Late Classic Copán. In Culbert and Rice, eds., pp. 37–61. [3, 15]

———. 1990b. Settlement history and the Classic collapse at Copán. *Latin American Antiquity* 1:66–85. [3, 15]

Webster, D., and N. Gonlin. 1988. Household remains of the humblest Maya. *Journal of Field Archaeology* 15: 169–190. [3, 7]

Webster, D., W. T. Sanders, and P. van Rossum. 1992. A Simulation of Copán Population History and its Implications, in *Ancient Mesoamerica*. 3:185–197.

Wenke, R. J. 1980. *Patterns in Prehistory: Mankind's First Three Million Years*. New York: Oxford University Press. [1]

Whalen, M. E. 1988. Small community organization during the Late Formative Period in Oaxaca, Mexico. *Journal of Field Archaeology* 15:291–306. [7, 14]

Whallon, R. E., Jr. 1973. Spatial analysis of occupation floors I: Application of dimensional analysis of variance. *American Antiquity* 38:266–278. [4, 7]

Wheat, J. B. 1967. A Paleo-Indian bison kill. *Scientific American* 216:44–52. [4, 5, 16]

———. 1972. *The Olsen-Chubbuck Site: A Paleo-Indian Bison Kill*. Society for American Archaeology Memoir, no. 26. [4, 5, 16]

Wheatley, P. 1970. Archaeology and the Chinese city. *World Archaeology* 2:159–185. [13]

Wheeler, M. 1943. *Maiden Castle, Dorset*. London: Society of Antiquaries. [2, 11]

———. 1954. *Archaeology from the Earth*. Oxford: Oxford University Press. [2, 4]

White, L. A. 1949. *The Science of Culture*. New York: Grove Press. [2, 5]

———. 1959. *The Evolution of Culture*. New York: McGraw-Hill. [2, 5]

Whitehead, A. N. 1967. *Science and the Modern World*. New York: Free Press. [1, 2]

Whitehouse, D., and R. Whitehouse. 1975. *Archaeological Atlas of the World*. San Francisco: Freeman Press. [13, 14]

Whittaker, J. C. 1987. Individual variation as an approach to economic organization: Projectile points at Grasshopper Pueblo, Arizona. *Journal of Field Archaeology* 14:465–479. [4]

Widmer, R. 1988. *The Evolution of the Calusa*. Tuscaloosa: University of Alabama Press. [10]

Wildesen, L. E. 1982. The study of impacts on archaeological sites. In *Advances in Archaeological Method and Theory*, vol. 5, ed., M. B. Schiffer, pp. 51–96. [2]

Wilk, R. R. 1989a. Decision making and resource flows within the household: Beyond the black box. In Wilk, ed., pp. 23–52. [7]

———, ed. 1989b. *The Household Economy: Reconsidering the Domestic Mode of Production*. Boulder: Westview Press. [7, 8]

Wilk, R. R., and W. Ashmore, eds. 1988. *Household and Community in the Mesoamerican Past*. Albuquerque: University of New Mexico Press. [7, 14]

Wilk, R. R., and W. L. Rathje, eds. 1982a. *Archaeology of the Household*. ABS, vol. 25, no. 6. Newbury Park, Ill.: Sage. [7]

———. 1982b. Household archaeology. In Wilk and Rathje, eds., pp. 617–639. [7]

Willey, G. R. 1953. *Prehistoric Settlement Patterns in the Virú Valley, Peru*. Bureau of American Ethnology, Bulletin 155. [2, 14]

———, ed. 1956. *Prehistoric Settlement Patterns in the New World*. Viking Fund Publications in Anthropology, no. 23. [4, 7]

———. 1962. The early great styles and the rise of the Precolumbian civilizations. *American Anthropologist* 64:1–14. [5, 14]

———. 1966. *An Introduction to American Archaeology*. Vol. 1: *North and Middle America*. Englewood Cliffs, N.J.: Prentice-Hall. [2, 14]

———. 1971. *An Introduction to American Archaeology*. Vol. 2: *South America*. Englewood Cliffs, N.J.: Prentice-Hall. [2, 14]

———. 1977. The rise of Maya civilization: A summary view. In Adams, ed., pp. 383–423. [3, 14]

Willey, G. R., W. R. Bullard, J. B. Glass, and J. C. Gifford. 1965. *Prehistoric Maya Settlements in the Belize Valley*. Papers of the Peabody Museum, Harvard University, no. 54, Cambridge, Mass. [2]

Willey, G. R., R. Leventhal, and W. Fash. 1978. Maya settlement in the Copán Valley. *Archaeology* 31:32–43. [3]

Willey, G. R., and P. Phillips. 1958. *Method and Theory in American Archaeology*. Chicago: University of Chicago Press. [2, 4]

Willey, G. R., and J. A. Sabloff. 1980. *A History of American Archaeology*. San Francisco: Freeman. [1, 2]

Williams-Dean, G., and V. M. Bryant. 1975. Pollen analysis of human coprolites from Antelope House. *The Kiva* 41:97–111. [4]

Wills, W. H. 1988. *Early Prehistoric Agriculture in the American Southwest*. Santa Fe, N.M.: School of American Research Press. Distributed by University of Washington Press, Seattle. [5, 6]

Wilmsen, E. N. 1974. *Lindenmeier: A Pleistocene Hunting Society*. New York: Harper and Row. [5]

Wilson, D. J. 1988. Desert ground drawings in the lower Santa Valley, north of Peru. *American Antiquity* 53:794–804. [14]

Wing, E. S., and A. B. Brown. 1979. *Paleonutrition: Method and Theory in Prehistoric Foodways*. New York: Academic Press. [4, 5, 6]

Winterhalder, B., and E. A. Smith. 1981. *Hunter-Gatherer Foraging Strategies: Ethnographic and Archaeological Analyses*. Chicago: University of Chicago Press. [5]

Wirth, L. 1938. Urbanism as a way of life. *American Journal of Sociology* 44: 3–24.

Wittfogel, K. A. 1957. *Oriental Despotism: A Comparative Study of Total Power*. New Haven: Yale University Press. [16]

Wobst, H. M. 1977. Stylistic behavior and information exchange. In C. E. Cleland, ed., *Papers for the Director: Research Essays in Honor of James B. Griffin*, pp. 317–334. Museum of Anthropology, Anthropological Papers, no. 61. Ann Arbor: University of Michigan. [9]

Wolf, E. R. 1962. *Sons of the Shaking Earth*. Chicago: University of Chicago Press. [14]

———. 1966. *Peasants*. Foundation for Modern Anthropology Series. Englewood Cliffs, N.J.: Prentice-Hall. [5, 9, 10]

———, ed. 1976. *The Valley of Mexico: Studies in Pre-Hispanic Ecology and Society*. Albuquerque: University of New Mexico Press. [5, 6, 14]

———. 1982. *Europe and the People Without History*. Berkeley: University of California Press. [5, 6, 13]

Wolfman, D. 1984. Geomagnetic dating methods in archaeology. In *Advances in Archaeological Method and Theory*, vol. 7, ed., M. B. Schiffer, pp. 363–458. [4]

Woolley, C. L. 1934. *Ur Excavations*. 2 vols. Vol. 2: *The Royal Cemetery*. The British Museum and The University Museum, Philadelphia. [2, 13]

Woot-Tsuen Wu Leng with Marina Flores. 1961. *Food Composition Table for Use in Latin America*. The Institute of Nutrition of Central America and Panama, Guatemala City, and the Interdepartmental Committee in Nutrition for National Defense, National Institutes of Health, Bethesda, Maryland.

World Almanac and Book of Facts: 1990. 1990. New York: World Almanac.

Wright, H. 1972. A Consideration of interregional exchange in Greater Mesopotamia: 4000–3000 B.C. In *Social Exchange and Interaction*, ed., E. Wilmsen, pp. 95–105. Museum of Anthropology Anthropological Papers, no. 46. Ann Arbor: University of Michigan. [8, 13]

Wright, H. T., and G. A. Johnson. 1975. Population, exchange, and early state formation in southwestern Iran. *American Anthropologist* 77:267–289. [8, 13]

Yellen, J. E. 1976. Settlement patterns of the !Kung: An archaeological perspective. In Lee and DeVore, eds., pp. 47–72. Cambridge, Mass.: Harvard University Press. [6, 7]

———. 1977. *Archaeological Approaches to the Present: Models for Reconstructing the Past*. New York: Academic Press. [2, 4]

———. 1979. The decline and rise of Mesopotamian civilization: An ethnoarchaeological perspective on the evolution of social complexity. *American Antiquity* 44: 5–35. [13, 15]

Yerkes, R. W. 1987. *Prehistoric Life on the Mississippi Floodplain: Stone Tool Use, Settlement Organization, and Subsistence Practices at the Labras Lake Site, Illinois*. Chicago: University of Chicago Press. [7, 8, 14]

Yoffee, N., and G. Cowgill. 1988. *The Collapse of Ancient States and Civilizations*. Tucson: University of Arizona Press. [15]

Zantwijk, R. van. 1985. *The Aztec Arrangement*. Norman: University of Oklahoma Press. [12]

Zarins, J. 1990. *Early Pastoral Nomadism and the Settlement of Lower Mesopotamia*. Bulletin of the American Schools of Oriental Research, vol. 280, pp. 31–65. [5, 13]

Zeitlin, R. N. 1990. The Isthmus and the Valley of Oaxaca: Questions about Zapotec Imperialism in Formative Period Mesoamerica. *American Antiquity* 55:250–261. [14]

Zier, C. 1983. The Cerén Site: A Classic Period Maya residence and agricultural field in the Zapotitán Valley. In Sheets, ed., pp. 119–143. [1, 7]

Zubrow, E. B. W. 1971. Carrying capacity and dynamic equilibrium in the prehistoric Southwest. *American Antiquity* 36(2):127–138. [5, 6]

———. 1976. Demographic anthropology: An introductory analysis. In Zubrow, ed., pp. 1–25. [4, 5]

———, ed. 1976. *Demographic Anthropology: Quantitative Approaches*. Albuquerque: University of New Mexico Press. [4, 5]

ACKNOWLEDGMENTS

Chapter 1

Page 3 Fig. 1.1: From "Incidents of Travel in Central America, Chiapas, and Yucatan," by John L. Stephens, edited by Richard Lionel Predmore. Copyright © 1949 by The Trustees of Rutgers College in New Jersey.

Page 5 Fig. 1.2: Lienzo de Tlaxcala, © 1979 by Editorial Cosmos

Page 6 Fig. 1.3: Conrad Martens, A Fuegian family. Courtesy Mark Smyth, Cottesloe, Western Australia

Page 8 Fig. 1.4: Courtesy of the Institute for Intercultural Studies, Inc., New York

Page 9 Fig. 1.5: Robert F. Sisson, © 1961 National Geographic Society. Courtesy Mary Leakey

Pages 12–13 Fig. 1.6a & Fig. 1.6b: Reproduced from *Herculaneum — Italy's Buried Treasure* by Joseph Jay Deiss (Revised edition, 1989, J. Paul Getty Museum, Malibu, Calif.)

Page 14 Fig. 1.7: Courtesy Payson Sheets, University of Colorado

Page 15 Fig. 1.8: Courtesy Hester Davis, University of Arkansas

Page 19 Box 1.1: After *Invitation to Archaeology* by James Deetz, illustrated by Eric Engstrom, copyright © 1967 by James Deetz. Used by permission of Doubleday & Co., Inc.

Chapter 2

Page 29 Fig. 2.1: Peter Apian, geocentric diagram of the universe, from the *Cosmographia,* 1539. The Bancroft Library, University of California, Berkeley.

Page 31 Fig. 2.2: Courtesy of the Trustees of the British Museum

Page 33 Fig. 2.3: From *The Mound Builders* by H. C. Shetrone, © 1930

by D. Appleton & Co. Used by permission of the publisher, Dutton, as an imprint of New American Library, a division of Penguin Books USA, Inc.; Fig. 2.4: John J. Egan, *Panorama of the Monumental Grandeur of the Mississippi Valley,* 1850 (detail). The Saint Louis Art Museum. Purchase: Eliza McMillan Fund

Page 35 Fig. 2.5: The Society of Antiquaries of London

Page 37 Fig. 2.6: (a) Courtesy of the Trustees of the British Museum; (b) and (c) Photography by the Egyptian Expedition, The Metropolitan Museum of Art

Page 42 Fig. 2.7: From William A. Haviland, *Anthropology,* 5th ed., © 1989, Holt, Rinehart and Winston, Inc. By permission of William A. Haviland.

Page 43 Fig. 2.8: Reprinted from Edward Bacon, *The Great Archaeologists,* © 1976 by The Illustrated London News and Martin Secker & Warburg Ltd.

Page 44 (top) Fig. 2.9a: Courtesy of the Committee of the Egyptian Exploration Society; (bottom) Fig. 2.9b: Courtesy of the Petrie Museum, University College, London

Page 45 Fig. 2.10: Hirmer Fotoarchiv, Munich

Page 46 Fig. 2.11: From *Frauds, Myths, and Mysteries: Science and Pseudoscience in Archaeology,* by Kenneth L. Feder. © 1990 by Mayfield Publishing Co. Courtesy of the author.

Page 48 Fig. 2.12: Courtesy of the National Geographic Society

Page 50 Fig. 2.13: National Museum of Anthropology, Mexico City

Page 52 Fig. 2.14: Courtesy of the Trustees of the British Museum

Page 53 Fig. 2.15: Roger-Viollet, Paris

Page 56 Fig. 2.16: The Oriental Institute Museum, University of Chicago

Page 57 Fig. 2.17: #N77839, Peabody Museum of Archaeology and Ethnology, Harvard University

Chapter 3

Page 70 Fig. 3.1: Tatiana Proskouriakoff, #N28094, Peabody Museum of Archaeology and Ethnology, Harvard University.

Page 71 Fig. 3.2: Courtesy of Hasso Hohmann & Annegrete Vogrin, in *Die Architektur von Copán,* © 1982 Akademische Druck– u. Verlaganstalt, Graz, Austria.

Page 77 Fig. 3.3: Courtesy of David Lentz, photos by Barbara Arroyo

Page 78 Fig. 3.4: Courtesy of David Rue

Page 79 Fig. 3.5: Courtesy of David Rue

Page 80 Fig. 3.6: Copán Project Phase II

Page 82 Fig. 3.7: Copán Project Phase II

Page 83 Fig. 3.8: Peabody Museum Sustaining Area Project; Fig. 3.9: Courtesy of David Webster

Page 85 Fig. 3.10: Ceramic illustrations reprinted from John M. Longyear III, *Copán Ceramics, A Study of Southeastern Maya Pottery,* Figs. 3–7, by Carnegie Institution of Washington; and from George Byron Gordon, *Caverns of Copán,* Honduras, plate 1. © 1898 The Peabody Museum of American Archaeology and Ethnology.

Page 86 Fig. 3.11: Courtesy of David Webster

Page 87 Fig. 3.12: Courtesy of David Webster

Page 89 Fig. 3.13: Courtesy of David Webster

Page 90 Fig. 3.14: Courtesy of Barbara and William Fash

Page 92 Fig. 3.15: Copán Project Phase II

Page 93 Fig. 3.16: Courtesy of Barbara Fash

Page 94 Fig. 3.17: Courtesy of Randolph Widmer

Page 95 Fig. 3.18: Courtesy of David Reed

Page 97 Fig. 3.19a: The University Museum, University of Pennsylvania; Fig. 3.19b: Courtesy of Wendy Ashmore

Page 99 Fig. 3.20: Courtesy of Elliot Abrams

Page 100 Fig. 3.21: Courtesy of Elliot Abrams

Page 101 Fig. 3.22a: Courtesy of David Webster; Fig. 3.22b: photo by J. P. Cowan, courtesy of Claude Baudez

Page 103 Fig. 3.23: Courtesy of Instituto Hondureño de Antropología e Historia, Tegucigalpa

Page 105 Fig. 3.24: Photo by Kathe Trujillo, courtesy of Will Andrews

Page 106 Fig. 3.25: Courtesy of David Webster

Chapter 4

Page 114 Fig. 4.1: Courtesy Michael Brian Schiffer, University of Arizona

Page 116 Fig. 4.2: © NASA

Page 117 Fig. 4.3: Neg. #329206. Courtesy Department of Library Services, American Museum of Natural History

Page 118 Fig. 4.4: Courtesy of Susan Evans

Page 119 Fig. 4.5: After Redman and Watson, reproduced by permission of the Society for American Archaeology, adapted from *American Antiquity* 35:281–282, 1970

Page 120 Fig. 4.6: Courtesy of the British Tourist Authority

Page 122 Fig. 4.7: Courtesy of Susan Evans

Page 123 Fig. 4.8: Courtesy Patty Jo Watson, Stanford University

Page 125 Fig. 4.9: Courtesy of David Webster

Page 126 Fig. 4.10: Courtesy of Susan Evans

Page 130 Fig. 4.11: After Ford, Pan American Union, General Secretariat, Organization of American States, 1962. From *Archaeology: Discovering Our Past*, 2nd ed., © 1993, 1987 by Mayfield Publishing Co. Courtesy of Wendy Ashmore.

Page 132 Fig. 4.12: Courtesy Sächsische Landesbibliothek, Dresden

Page 133 Fig. 4.13: From *Prehistory of North America*, 3rd ed., by Jesse D. Jennings, © 1989 by Mayfield Publishing Co. Courtesy Jesse Jennings

Page 138 Fig. 4.14a–c: Reprinted from Joe Ben Wheat, *The Olsen Chubbock Site, A Paleoindian Bison Kill.* © 1972 by the Society for American Archaeology. Fig. 4.14d: Neg. #318898. Courtesy Department of Library Services, American Museum of Natural History

Page 139 Fig. 4.15: Courtesy Nationalmuseet, Copenhagen. Photo: Kit Weiss

Page 142 Fig. 4.16: Courtesy of Nan Gonlin & David Reed

Page 144 Fig. 4.17: Courtesy of Susan Evans

Chapter 5

Page 149 Fig. 5.1: Jim Moore/ Anthro-Photo

Page 155 Fig. 5.3: Redrawn after Fred Plog

Page 162 Fig. 5.4: BS 751 Aranda family, Alice Springs, 1896. Baldwin Spencer Collection. Reproduced with the permission of the Museum of Victoria Council

Page 167 Fig. 5.5: Robert Harding Picture Library, London

Page 168 Fig. 5.6: J. E. S. Thompson, *Maya History & Religion,* Fig. 3, © University of Oklahoma Press.

Page 178 Fig. 5.9: After Maruyama 1963

Chapter 6

Page 190 Fig. 6.1: Courtesy of David Webster

Page 191 Fig. 6.2: Courtesy of David Webster; Fig. 6.3: after *Energy* 1971

Page 199 Fig. 6.4: Based in part on Campbell, *Human Ecology*

Page 200 Fig. 6.5: Photo by David Webster

Page 202 Fig. 6.6: Cotton Coulson/ Woodfin Camp & Associates

Page 203 Fig. 6.7: Richard Lee/ Anthro-Photo

Page 204 Fig. 6.8: Photo by David Webster

Page 206 Fig. 6.9: Gary Braasch/ Woodfin Camp & Associates

Page 212 Fig. 6.10: Borys Malkin/ Anthro-Photo

Chapter 7

Page 220 Fig. 7.1a: Reprinted from *The Basin of Mexico: Ecological Processes in the Evolution of a Civilization.* © 1979, by Academic Press, Inc.; Fig. 7.1b & Fig. 7.1c: Courtesy of Susan Evans

Page 223 Fig. 7.2: F. W. Schwerdtfeger, *Traditional Housing in African Cities,* plan 19.7, © 1982, David Fulton Publishers.

Page 226 Fig. 7.3: from *Archaeology and Volcanism in Central America: The Zapotitan Valley of El Salvador*, edited by Payson D. Sheets. © 1983. Reprinted by permission of the author and the University of Texas Press. Drawing by Christian Zier.

Page 227 Fig. 7.4: Reprinted from *Dwellings, The House Across the World*, by Paul Oliver. © 1987. By permission of the University of Texas Press

Page 229 Fig. 7.5a & b: © Wilfred Thesiger. Reproduced by permission of Curtis Brown Agency Ltd.

Page 231 Box 7.1: Courtesy of James Hatch

Page 237 Fig. 7.6: William Strode/ Woodfin Camp & Associates

Page 239 Fig. 7.7: J. Yellen. Reprinted by permission of the publishers from *Kalahari Hunter-Gatherers* by R. B. Lee and I. DeVore, Cambridge, Mass: Harvard University Press, © 1976 by the President & Fellows of Harvard College.

Page 241 Fig. 7.8: (top) Courtesy Raymond Hames, University of Nebraska; (bottom) Reprinted from Enrico Guidoni, Primitive Architecture, page 55. © Electra Editrice, 1975

Page 244 Fig. 7.9: © Paul Logsdon

Page 245 Fig. 7.10: After Carlson, 1970

Page 248 Fig. 7.11: Mapa Quinatzin, reprinted from D. Robertson, *Mexican Manuscript Painting of the Early Colonial Period*, 1959, Yale University Press

Page 249 Fig. 7.12: Courtesy of Susan Evans

Chapter 8

Page 259 Fig. 8.1: The National Library of Australia. Courtesy George Leahy

Page 260 Box 8.2: The Detroit Institute of Arts. Photo: Dirk Bakker

Page 263 Fig. 8.2: Courtesy of David Webster

Page 265 Box 8.3: Map, courtesy of Kenneth Hirth. Photo: Compania Mexicana Aerofoto, S.A. Both reprinted from *Tiempo y Asenta-*

miento en Xochicalco, by Kenneth Hirth and Anne C. Guillen. © 1988, Universidad Nacional Autónoma de Mexico.

Page 267 Fig. 8.3: The National Archives of New Zealand, #AAQT, Acc. 3537

Page 268 Fig. 8.4: Photos by David Webster

Page 271 Fig. 8.5: Reproduced from *Past Worlds: The Times Atlas of Archaeology* by kind permission of Times Books

Page 273 Fig. 8.6: Compania Mexicana Aerofoto, S.A.

Page 275 Fig. 8.7: Courtesy of Randolph Widmer and Rebecca Storey

Page 276 Fig. 8.8: Courtesy of James Sheehy

Page 279 Fig. 8.9: After Oakley, 1956

Page 284 Fig. 8.10: Courtesy of Randolph Widmer

Page 285 Fig. 8.11: Courtesy of Randolph Widmer

Page 286 Fig. 8.12: Drawings by David Webster and Anne Dowd

Chapter 9

Page 291 Fig. 9.1a: Hirmer Fotoarchiv, Munich; Fig. 9.1b: Archiv für Kunst und Geschichte, Berlin; Fig. 9.1c and Fig. 9.1d: Robert Harding Picture Library, London; Fig. 9.1e: The Art Institute of Chicago, Eduard Gaffron Collection, Buckingham Fund Purchase; Fig. 9.1f: Photo by David Webster

Page 293 Fig. 9.3: Courtesy Alexander Marshack

Page 295 Fig. 9.4: Alan D. Iselin, from "The Earliest Precursor of Writing," by Denise Schmandt-Besserat. Copyright © 1978 by Scientific American, Inc. All rights reserved.

Page 297 Fig. 9.5: Alinari/Art Resource

Page 299 (Box 9.1): Reprinted from *Images of the Past*, by T. Doug-

las Price and Gary M. Feinman, Mayfield Publishing Co. © 1993, T. Douglas Price and Gary M. Feinman.

Page 301 Fig. 9.6: National Museum of the American Indian

Page 304 Fig. 9.9b: Courtesy of the Bodleian Library, University of Oxford

Page 305 Fig. 9.10: © 1989 by Scientific American, Inc. All rights reserved.

Page 306 Fig. 9.11: p. 157, C. Hobson, *The World of Pharaohs*. © 1987 Toppan Printing Co.

Page 307 Fig. 9.12a: © Trustees of the British Museum; Fig. 9.12b: Dilip Chakrabarti

Page 308 Fig. 9.13: Victor R. Boswell, Jr., © National Geographic Society

Page 309 Fig. 9.14: Museo Nacional de Antropologia, Mexico City. Photo: The Bettman Archive

Page 310 Fig. 9.15: John Running

Page 314 Fig. 9.17: Reprinted from *Archaeology: Theories, Methods and Practice*, by Colin Renfrew and Paul Bahn, © 1991, Thames and Hudson Co. By permission

Page 315 Fig. 9.18: Drawing by A. P. Maudslay, 1889–1902, *Biologia Centrali-Americana*, Vol. 1, Illustration 26; iconography interpreted by Linda Schele, in W. M. Ferguson & J. Q. Royce, *Maya Ruins in Central America in Color*, © 1984, University of New Mexico Press.

Page 318 Fig. 9.19: Courtesy of David Webster and Randolph Widmer; reconstruction by Barbara Fash.

Page 321 Fig. 9.20: Courtesy Dallas Museum of Art. Photo: Justin Kerr

Chapter 10

Page 328 Fig. 10.1a: Neg. #42314. Courtesy Department of Library Services, American Museum of Natural History; Fig. 10.1b: P. A.

Hearst Museum of Anthropology, the University of California at Berkeley

Page 329 Box 10.1: Courtesy Leopold Pospisil, Yale University

Page 333 Fig. 10.2: Diagram, p. 51, from *Kinship to Kingship* by Christine Galley. Copyright © 1987 by the University of Texas Press. Used by permission of the publisher

Page 335 Fig. 10.3: From *Le Monde des Megaliths* by J.-P. Mohen. © Casterman, Tournai, Belgium

Page 337 Fig. 10.4a: The Bishop Museum, Honolulu, #CA10.644; Fig. 10.4b: Drawing, p. 147, by William N. Morgan, from *Prehistoric Architecture of Micronesia* by William N. Morgan. Copyright © 1988 by the University of Texas Press. Used by permission of the publisher

Page 343 Fig. 10.5: (top) Napoleon Chagnon/Anthro-Photo

Page 347 Fig. 10.6: Photo by Susan Evans

Page 350 Fig. 10.7: Photo by David Webster

Page 351 Fig. 10.8: Courtesy of David Webster

Page 352 Fig. 10.9: Courtesy of David Webster and Randolph Widmer

Chapter 11

Page 359 Fig. 11.1: Courtesy Annette B. Weiner, New York University

Page 361 Fig. 11.2: National Institute of Anthropology and History, Mexico

Page 364 Fig. 11.4a: Reprinted from *The Basin of Mexico: Ecological Processes in the Evolution of a Civilization.* © 1979 by Academic Press, Inc.

Page 365 Fig. 11.4b: Courtesy of Gregory Johnson

Page 366 Fig. 11.5: Reprinted from *Mesoamerican Archaeology: New Approaches*, edited by Norman Ham-

mond. © 1974 by Gerald Duckworth and Co. Ltd. Courtesy of Norman Hammond

Page 369 Box 11.2: Courtesy of George Milner and the Illinois State Museum

Page 370 Fig. 11.6: Ashmolean Museum, Oxford University

Page 371 Fig. 11.7: (both) From "Royal Visits and Other Intersite Relationships Among the Classic Maya" by Linda Schele and Peter Matthews, in *Classic Maya Political History,* T. Patrick Culbert, ed. © 1991 Cambridge University Press

Page 372 Fig. 11.8: Courtesy of the Trustees of the British Museum

Page 377 Fig. 11.9: Courtesy of Barbara Fash

Page 383 Fig. 11.10: Courtesy of David Webster

Page 384 Fig. 11.11: Courtesy Jennifer Blitz, University of Wisconsin

Chapter 12

Page 391 Fig. 12.1: National Museum of the American Indian

Page 395 Fig. 12.2: Courtesy Musée de l'Homme, Paris. Photo: C. Lassalle

Page 397 Box 12.1: Drawings by Andre Leroi-Gourhan and Clive Gamble

Page 400 Fig. 12.3: (drawing) Drawn by R. Rappaport

Page 401 Fig. 12.3: (photo) Courtesy Roy A. Rappaport, University of Michigan

Page 403 Fig. 12.5: Courtesy Kent Flannery, University of Michigan

Page 406 Fig. 12.6: Photo by Melissa Diamanti

Page 407 Fig. 12.7: Photo by Susan Evans

Page 409 Fig. 12.8: Barry Kass/ Anthro-Photo

Page 411 Fig. 12.9: Museo Nacional de Antropología, Mexico City

Chapter 13

Page 417 Fig. 13.1: After C. Redman, *The Rise of Civilization*, Fig. 2.4. © 1978 W. H. Freeman & Co.

Page 421 Fig. 13.2: Fig. 8.10 in C. Redman, *The Rise of Civilization*.

Page 422 Fig. 13.3: Courtesy Gregory A. Johnson

Page 424 Fig. 13.4: The University Museum, University of Pennsylvania, neg. #1237

Page 425 Fig. 13.5: Fig. 17.3 in A. Sherratt, *The Cambridge Encyclopedia of Archaeology*. © Trewin Copplestone Publishing Ltd., 1980

Page 427 Fig. 13.6: Aerofilms Ltd.

Page 430 Fig. 13.7: Courtesy of David Webster

Page 431 Fig. 13.8: Robert Harding Picture Library, London

Page 433 Fig. 13.9a & b: Hirmer Fotoarchiv, Munich

Page 438 Fig. 13.10: Werner Forman Archive, London

Page 441 Fig. 13.11: Courtesy of David Webster

Page 443 Fig. 13.12a: p. 178, A. Cotterell, *The Encyclopedia of Ancient Civilizations*. Mayflower Books, New York; Fig. 13.12b: Werner Forman Archive, London

Page 445 Fig. 13.13: p. 179 in A. Cotterell, *The Encyclopedia of Ancient Civilizations*

Page 453 Fig. 13.15: p. 290 in A. Cotterell, *The Encyclopedia of Ancient Civilizations*

Page 454 Fig. 13.16: Courtesy Institute of History & Philology, Academia Sinica, Taipei

Page 455 Fig. 13.17: Robert Harding Picture Library, London

Page 456 Fig. 13.18: Ceremonial vessel of the type *huo*. Chinese bronze, late An-yang period. Courtesy of the Freer Gallery of Art, Smithsonian Institution, Washington, D.C.

Chapter 15

Chapter 16

INDEX

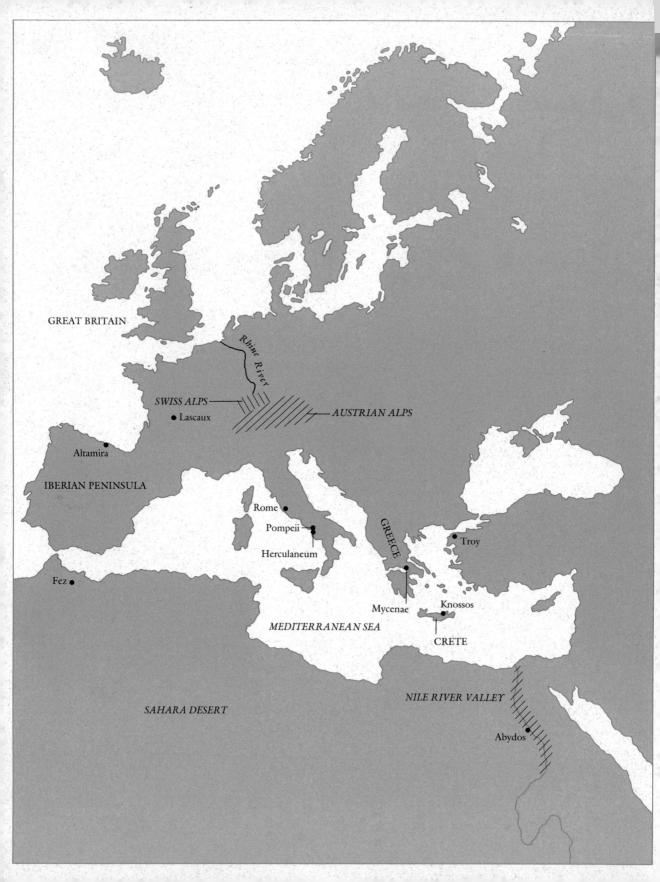

GREAT BRITAIN

Rhine River

SWISS ALPS

AUSTRIAN ALPS

● Lascaux

Altamira ●

IBERIAN PENINSULA

Rome ●

Pompeii ●

Herculaneum

GREECE

● Troy

Fez ●

Mycenae

Knossos ●

MEDITERRANEAN SEA

CRETE

NILE RIVER VALLEY

SAHARA DESERT

Abydos ●